CLASSROOM-BASED ASSESSMENT

Evaluating Instructional Outcomes

Gerald A. Tindal
University of Oregon

Douglas B. Marston
Minneapolis Public Schools

MERRILL PUBLISHING COMPANY
Columbus   Toronto   London   Melbourne

Published by
Merrill Publishing Company
Columbus, Ohio 43216

This book was set in Italia.

Administrative Editor: Ann Castel
Production Coordinator: JoEllen Gohr
Cover Designer: Russ Maselli

Library of Congress Catalog Card Number: 89-63855
International Standard Book Number: 0-675-20913-7
Printed in the United States of America
1 2 3 4 5 6 7 8—94 93 92 91 90

PREFACE

Assessment and testing have become an integral part of the educational lives of both students and teachers. By the time students graduate from high school, they have taken nearly every kind of test on general achievement, specific skills, and content knowledge. If they have postsecondary plans to attend either a technical trade school or a college or university, their involvement with testing will continue. Teachers in turn are heavily invested in the same activities. They administer many tests that are mandated by states and districts and many that arise from their own need to structure instruction.

Even though our educational system devotes numerous hours to testing, little organization or systematicity occurs in the administration and use of tests. Test information is used to sort students into groups within and across general and special education, ascertain what students know and how they should be taught, certify students as having mastered certain materials, and report individual, group, grade level, building, and district accomplishments to others. Student performance data on any one test are often considered in isolation and rarely are considered in conjunction with other test data.

Ironically, while teachers are heavily involved in testing, and while tests form a core information base to make many educational decisions, the entire process of developing and interpreting test information is virtually accidental. Tests are adopted with little regard to their technical adequacy; performance is interpreted with little focus on the goal of schooling; in the end, data are generated that are both unused and unusable.

The purpose of this book is to integrate the areas of testing and decision making. The only caveat is that all testing and decision making must be focused on one issue: improvement of instruction and student learning. Teachers must become more central in the decision-making process: What tests should they use to make what types of decisions? How should tests be constructed to reflect important classroom behaviors that reflect the goal of instruction? How should performance be quantified so it is both reliable and valid? What interpretations can teachers make, and which guidelines do they need to make statements about change?

This book began with the research conducted at the University of Minnesota Institute for Research on Learning Disabilities. Working with Dr. Stanley Deno, we conducted a number of studies to develop empirically a measurement system that would be useful for structuring instruction for very low-achieving students. As a result of our research, which has continued over the past 15 years, curriculum-based measurement was developed and investigated. Eventually, many studies were done in which student performance was used not just to evaluate instruction, but also to make a host of other decisions, such as screening and placement in specialized settings and evaluating overall program outcomes. Since 1979, scores of studies have been completed supporting curriculum-based measurement.

The book also was shaped by the need to consider special and general education as different settings on the same continuum, rather than two unique environments with no commonalities. An era of collaboration and coordination of services across settings has begun. Teachers must be cognizant of student learning problems before they become too serious and programs must be developed on the basis of student need rather than classroom schedules.

In summary, these themes of integrated testing across decisions and educational settings are brought to focus in the academic skill domains. Rather than cover all assessment activities, including the use of interviews, behavioral ratings, classroom observations, and personality or interest inventories, we have limited the material to testing in academic areas only. This focus reflects our intention of developing an integrated testing and assessment program across a range of educational decisions. And, although we have not addressed instructional interventions, it is assumed that, once a teacher defines the goal of instruction, he or she can shape a measurement system for ascertaining progress toward that goal, using the information provided in this book. The procedures we describe in the various content area chapters are broadly conceived to allow a focus on a wide range of instructional purposes.

Focus

Assessment of both content area knowledge and basic skills (in reading, spelling, written expression, math, pre-school skills, and language) is addressed with a range of options from which teachers can select behaviors they deem important in their classrooms. This information is relevant to elementary or secondary and general or special education teachers who work with either high- or low-performing students. We provide many assessment options that allow teachers to be active decision makers. We also offer formats that allow adaptation of specific testing to be tailored to instructional intent. In summary, teachers can use the assessment strategies described in this book with any type of instructional goal or tactic.

The material in the basic skills chapters incorporates the latest research-based practices on curriculum-based measurement, the fastest growing assessment innovation in the past 20 years. Each skill chapter begins with a review of pertinent literature, then focuses on specific strategies that have been thoroughly researched and supported, and finally presents exemplary procedures. Therefore, teachers can be aware of measurement issues and become proficient in developing, adopting, or adapting a wide array of measures.

A decision-making framework is used for developing specific assessment practices for screening students, placing them in specialized settings, plan-

ning instruction, formatively evaluating its impact, and summarizing its outcomes. It is assumed that decision making is more efficient and effective when it is integrated, increasing the likelihood of its being adopted in practice when teachers leave preservice training. Throughout the book, we provide many classroom examples for these decision areas. Each academic content area includes an integrated assessment example that applies information from the chapter through the entire range of educational decisions. In addition, interpretations of student performance are anchored from three decision guides or references, allowing maximum flexibility in communicating test results.

This book provides a complete analysis of and design for assessing student learning that is relevant for a wide range of audiences: students, parents, teachers, psychologists, principals, directors of special education, or other related personnel (speech therapists, social workers, etc.). The information is pertinent for general and special education teachers. The full range of skills is covered, so that teachers of both elementary and secondary students will find the information useful. This book also is appropriate for school psychologists who view their role in schools as that of consultants on measurement and evaluation issues.

Organization

The book is divided into three sections. The first section, chapters 1–6, presents general measurement concepts, principles, and test construction strategies. It deals first with measurement planning, emphasizing the purpose and design of testing programs. Second, it reviews practices in test construction for knowledge tests. Third, there is a review of basic measurement concepts. Fourth, a discussion of reliability is presented, with an emphasis on using it to establish parameters of error and estimation of performance. Fifth, we consider validity, with particular attention to decision making.

In chapters 7 through 10, we provide specific assessment strategies in the basic skill areas (reading, spelling, writing, math, preschool, and language areas). Each chapter presents a decision-making model that allows teachers to decide *what* student academic performance they want to assess and *how* they want to assess it.

In the third section, chapters 11–15, we present three evaluation strategies that refer student performance to appropriate peers (norms), standards on specific skills or content (criterion), or previous performance (individual). These three references allow performance to be meaningfully summarized and reported to guide educational decision making.

Features

Each chapter follows a similar format. At the beginning of the chapter, objectives offer a succinct focus for the reader. Then key vocabulary words are paired with colloquial synonyms to help anchor their meanings. The material presented in the body of the chapter is summarized in a flowchart, which corresponds to the headings in the text and emphasizes the role of the reader and teacher as an active decision maker in the assessment-testing process. Finally, each chapter ends with a summary and overview.

An instructor's manual accompanies the book, presenting a summary of the important ideas and study questions to help readers focus their attention on applications and implications. The study questions rarely are limited to summarizing information; rather, they are configured to force the reader to process the information and apply it to everyday decision-making practices in the classroom.

In conclusion, the book provides a cogent, empirical, and innovative approach to assessment and testing; it represents the culmination of more than 15 years of research and training. Instructors and teachers using it in their training programs have the necessary information from these 15 chapters to begin changing current practices and making educational decision in more systematic ways.

ACKNOWLEDGMENTS

The amount of work needed to put all of this material together does not come from the authors alone. Two key people who have been instrumental in the completion of the book are Katie Essick and Clarice Skeen from the University of Oregon. They have provided critical editing and important feedback on both content and format. And although the task may have appeared thankless when trying to complete their work around a hectic schedule and incredible cross-pressures, they performed faultlessly and with style. Thank you.

We would also like to acknowledge the helpful suggestions of the following reviewers of the manuscript: Elizabeth Reis, Baruch College, CUNY; Jim Burns, College of St. Rose; Diane Woodrum, West Virginia University; Bertina Hildreth, Texas Tech University; Nancy Klein, Cleveland State University; David Lillie, University of North Carolina; Mary Ann Parter, Southern Illinois University; Barry McNamara, Lehman College; Mary P. Hoy, Iowa State University; Kay Stevens, University of Tennessee; Deborah L. Speece, University of Maryland; Mary Beirne-Smith, University of Alabama.

The book would not be possible without the keen organizational work done by Vicki Knight, Amy Macionis, and Ann Castel from Merrill. They provided the right blend of prompting, monitoring, and supporting to allow us accomplishment of our goal. We also would like to express our gratitude to the students at the University of Oregon who read through draft versions of this manuscript and provided feedback that was invaluable in helping us structure and sequence the content. Finally and most importantly, this book would not have been possible without the support of our families and their patience in accommodating the long hours we spent in front of our computers.

This book is dedicated to our wives,

Linda and Debbie; and to

our children, Sevrina, Nicky, and Jessica

CONTENTS

CHAPTER 1

Perspectives

"There's an old Army saying, 'If it moves, salute it.' Today some [education] reformers seem to be saying, 'If it moves, test it' " (Fiske, 1988, pg. 2E). This statement was made by Gregory Anrig, president of the Educational Testing Service, in an interview with the Associated Press and is appropriate in addressing the vast amount of testing taking place today in schools nationwide. In fact, in that newspaper report, it was further stated that over 100 million standardized tests are administered each year to elementary and high school students. About 56 million of these tests are state or locally mandated standardized achievement, minimum competency, or basic skills tests.

Is all of this testing justified? What educational decisions are being made on the basis of test data? The purpose of this book is to train educators in the testing process, a broad-ranging activity that often is the center of assessment.

CHAPTER OBJECTIVES

By the end of this chapter, you should have the necessary knowledge and skills to

- Understand testing's enormous impact in schools.
- Critique current assessment and testing programs.
- Comprehend various dimensions of testing and decision making.
- Employ an evaluative model of assessment.
- Operationalize the evaluative model using three distinct phases.

KEY VOCABULARY

In this chapter, a distinction is made between *testing,* a more limited activity that quantifies student performance and *assessment,* which encompasses a wide range of information collection. The chapter focuses on *decision making,* which includes screening of students, deeming them eligible for specialized programs, teaching them in a specific manner, and evaluating their learning in both general and specialized classroom *settings* (i.e., Chapter I, resource room, etc.). We describe two levels of data: *survey,* in which test items are broadly sampled and many skills are represented, and *specific,* wherein test items are arranged narrowly around a few skills (Howell & Morehead, 1987). We emphasize classroom-based testing and assessment rather than *pull-out* testing and assessment, which students complete outside the classroom context under the guidance of professionals other than teachers. One reason for this focus is that we are interested in *typical performance,* in which learning is displayed through relevant classroom tasks. This focus contrasts with the emphasis on *optimal performance* levels, for which the tasks are not comparable to those required for successful classroom functioning. We interpret performance through three *evaluation references,* which anchor interpretation to (a) other peers (normative), (b) established standards (criterion), or (c) previous performance (individualized).

Litigation and *legislation* play important roles in structuring the necessary reforms in assessment. We briefly describe P.L. 94–142, the Education for All Handicapped Children Act, because it significantly impacts the organization of special education programs. We take an *empirical* approach, which stresses practices that have been investigated and proven useful, rather than an approach calling for *classification,* which creates serious problems by labeling students. The empirical approach is *evaluative,* meaning that data are collected throughout the delivery of programs and used to assay their effectiveness. We prefer the evaluative approach because we believe that teachers should view their profession scientifically. Thus, in establishing *hypotheses*, or plausible explanations of phenomena, we develop and evaluate them systematically. Assessment and testing occur in three distinct phases: (a) *construction*, in which we create instruments for measuring student performance; (b) *analysis*, in which we scrutinize these instruments for possible flaws; and (c) *interpretation*, in which we summarize and interpret performance outcomes.

The structure of this book is based on the premise that a cogent set of assumptions is necessary to formulate a model and guide its translation into practice. Figure 1.1 presents chapter organization.

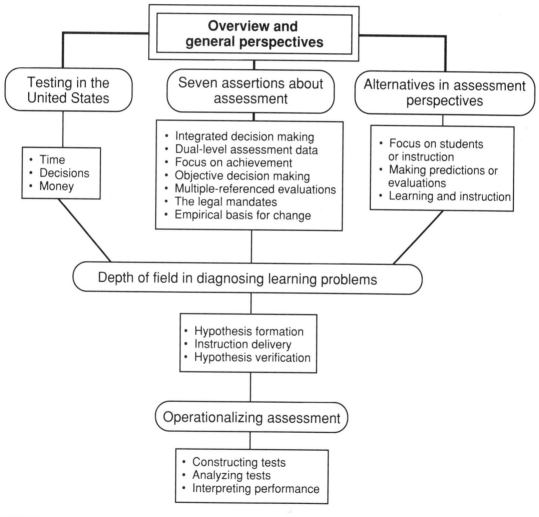

FIGURE 1.1
Overview and general perspectives of assessment

TESTING IN THE UNITED STATES

How Much Testing Occurs?

In the early 1980s, researchers at the Center for the Study of Evaluation at the University of California, Los Angeles (UCLA), began a series of studies entitled the Test Use Project to examine achievement testing in the nation's schools. Using complex sampling procedures, they gathered information throughout the country from districts that contained schools of differing sizes, socioeconomic makeups, and geographic regions. The researchers concentrated on testing in the 4th, 6th, 10th, and 12th grades and addressed four questions:

1. How much testing was occurring?
2. What kinds of tests were being given?
3. What purpose was being accomplished by testing?
4. How much did testing cost?

The UCLA researchers found a considerable amount of testing going on in U.S. classrooms. For example, in 4th and 6th grades, 5% of the total annual instructional time was devoted to testing, including 10 hours for reading tests and 12 ½ hours for math tests. In high schools, about 10% of the instructional time was given to testing. In 10th-grade English, 26 ½ hours were spent in testing, and in 10th-grade math, a little more than 24 hours were consumed by testing activities. More than half of the time was devoted to tests embedded in curricula (end-of-unit or chapter tests) or to school/teacher-developed tests, and teacher-made tests took three-fourths of the time (Burry, Catterall, Choppin, & Dorr-Bremme, 1982). Yet, they also found that teachers value their own observations and students' work as the most important and useful information collected in the classroom although they are often unable to quantify such information effectively or efficiently.

Next, they value the tests they create and those embedded in their curricula (Lazar-Morrison, Polin, Moy, & Burry, 1980).

Teachers devote a considerable amount of time to testing, but they receive little assistance from school districts in constructing tests, assessing achievement by alternative procedures, helping students take tests, interpreting different types of tests, integrating the content of tests in the curriculum, or using tests to improve instruction. Given the substantial investment in testing, it is only fair to question the use of tests and the data they generate.

How Are Tests and Test Results Used?

Tests are used to plan teaching, group students, change groups, decide on grades, and motivate pupils. They also provide feedback for teachers and students about recent learning. Generally, both elementary and secondary teachers agree with the following statements about tests:

1. Tests motivate students to work hard.
2. Commercial tests are high-quality products.
3. Skills on required tests are similar to those taught in classrooms.
4. The pressure of testing has a beneficial effect.
5. Teachers now spend more time preparing students for tests than they did in the past.
6. District-developed tests are very good.
7. Curricula are more complex today than they were in the past.
8. Teachers shouldn't be held accountable for students' scores on published achievement tests.
9. Students are often rigidly tracked into skill/ability groups.
10. Minimum competency or functional literacy should be required for promotions at certain grade levels.

11. Some students are unfairly treated by minimum competency tests.
12. Basic skills instruction and assessment account for a much larger proportion of the time and effort than content skills (Burry et al., 1982).

In summary, teachers accept testing as an integral part of their professional lives and devote a considerable amount of time to it.

How Much Money and Time Are Spent on Testing?

Dorr-Bremme, Burry, Catterall, Cabello, and Daniels, (1983) studied the cost of testing in American Public School, and found that the cost of the testing program for basic skills averaged $11 per elementary student, $21 per junior high student, and $2.50 per high school student in a suburban district. The cost of testing basic skills in an exemplary urban school district averaged $26 per elementary student.

In both settings, the single largest item in each school's budget was teachers' time for assessments. In a small school in the suburban district, about 100 hours were needed per year, representing ½-hour per pupil per year. In a large school in the urban district, 375 hours per year were needed, which also averaged ½-hour per pupil per year. Administration of commercial curriculum tests took 45% of teacher testing time in the suburban school and 35% in the urban school. Time spent on teacher-constructed tests consumed 22% of the time in the suburban school and 48% of the time in the urban school.

Testing time obviously does not affect only teachers; students also spend significant amounts of time taking tests. In the suburban school, they averaged 88 hours in a year, and in the urban school, 76 hours. These amounts represent approximately 10% and 8.5% of the time spent in the classroom for the suburban and urban districts, respectively.

In summary, great sums of money and time are spent administering tests. A reexamination of the role of testing in our schools may be needed that addresses critical issues and questions current practices. Only with a clear and strong focus can we integrate testing sensibly into curricula, instruction, and decision making.

To redefine the role of testing, we first must answer the questions, "What comprises good testing programs, and how do they fit within an overall assessment system?" To this end, seven assertions can serve as structural guides about what is important and what can be accomplished in the testing and assessment process. These assertions form the basis for the answers to questions such as the following:

- What types of tests are or should be used?
- How should tests and testing programs be adopted and/or implemented?
- What types of tests and results should be available and to whom?
- How should test results be used?
- What decisions need to be made with the help of test data?
- What are the implications of addressing or failing to address these issues?

Although testing forms the mainstay of any assessment system, the issues quickly expand beyond testing alone and become a part of a wide range of decision-making practices.

SEVEN ASSESSMENT ASSERTIONS

The following assertions reflect preferred practice; they are also posed in reaction to many current practices. Therefore, for each assertion, a critique sets the stage for an alternative perspective. This critique of prevailing practices is generally based on an empirical analysis of re search in assessment. The assertion them- selves represent a logical alternative for over- coming the problems of current practices.

Assertion 1: Data for Decision Making Should be Integrated Across Settings

Currently, disparate data are collected for dif- ferent educational decisions. Little relationship exists among the data sources, and the rec- ommendations that result from them are not always consistent. For example, in response to referrals from teachers, psychologists give in- telligence, perception, reasoning, and achieve- ment tests, most of which have little relationship to relevant classroom behaviors. Although these psychologists often think that the tests they ad- minister are useful for planning instruction, few teachers agree (Thurlow & Ysseldyke, 1982). Special education teachers therefore must ad- minister single-skill, classroom-focused and multiskill, generalized achievement tests in reading, spelling, math, and writing to obtain relevant information for planning instruction.

Individuals use many tests to make diag- nostic decisions about instruction, but few tests have been validated for such purposes. During and/or following instruction, teachers give other tests, most of which are embedded in curricula, to determine if materials are properly mas- tered. Yet often these tests have poor technical adequacy—low reliability and validity (Tindal, Fuchs, Fuchs, Shinn, Deno & Germann, 1985). Finally, as part of assessment programs in gen- eral education, schools give a wide range of published achievement tests once each year that are quite unrelated to actual school curri- cula. In summary, many tests are being given, and most of them are unrelated to each other and each decision is based on different test information, making it difficult to compare per-

formance across decisions or to validate either the data or the decisions.

A more organized approach is to coordinate the administration of these different tests. Psy- chologists and both general and special edu- cation teachers would give only those tests that allowed them to improve student performance. Furthermore, all parties would be communi- cating, so that test results would be both in- terpretable and useful for each person. Certainly, as the need for pre-referral interventions in- creases (Graden, Casey, & Christenson, 1985), data from general education could be linked to data from special education.

Assertion 2: Both Survey and Specific-Level Assessment Data Are Needed

Two general classes of tests are administered to students: published, norm-referenced (sur- vey level) and curriculum, criterion-referenced tests (specific level). Presently, these two types of tests are unrelated to each other. Planning instruction from the norm-referenced tests is not possible because of the lack of curriculum overlap (Good & Salvia, 1988; Jenkins & Pany, 1978a; Leinhardt, 1983; Shapiro & Derr, 1987). Overall evaluation of general achievement is not possible with the criterion-referenced tests because of their limited focus on instructional domains. Thus, in most schools there is little or no overlap in the types of behavior sampled by these tests or the formats of the test items. Therefore, planning instruction from a survey assessment is precarious, and program eval- uation based on specific assessments is limited.

A more sensible approach is to join these two testing systems using survey- and specific- level testing, both of which are curriculum- based. Survey-level assessment determines student status and guides further instructional assessment. Once completed, specific-level assessment addresses the extent of skills within students' repertoires and helps teachers to plan instruction (Howell & Morehead, 1987). To integrate different decisions, assessment should be related systematically across these two levels. At the survey level, test items provide a broad view of performance and allow comparisons to be made over a wide range of skill levels, time frames, and instructional program orientations; specific-level assessments define and individualize skills more precisely. Performance on a survey-level task should precede and direct specific-level instruction and assessment, so that measures of achievement can then provide a gauge of general functioning over time and specific functioning at any one time. However, to accomplish this objective, we must consider Assertion 3.

Assertion 3: A Classroom Focus on Achievement Is Imperative

Most assessment practices are wasteful, expensive, and ineffectual in helping to make instructional decisions. Currently, many tests lack technical adequacy (Salvia & Ysseldyke, 1988; Hall, 1985). Teacher-made tests and those embedded in curricula do not have documented technical adequacy (Tindal, et al., 1985). Intelligence and personality tests are used to plan or evaluate instruction, yet have no foundation for supporting those types of decisions (Salvia & Ysseldyke, 1988). Furthermore, multidisciplinary teams make decisions, rarely integrating the data from assessments in any systematic fashion (Ysseldyke, Algozzine, & Mitchell, 1982).

Frequently, test data have little relationship to relevant classroom behavior. That is, tasks unrelated to those presented in the classroom are administered regularly to students outside of the classroom by unfamiliar professionals who then predict how these students will per-

form in the classroom. For example, psychologists take children out of classrooms and test them on any of several specialized batteries of intelligence and achievement measures; speech clinicians and language specialists pull children from classrooms to administer a wide range of language or speech tests; and reading specialists administer a diverse range of reading tests to children they have removed from the classroom.

Such "pull-out" assessment is tenuous at best and utterly wrong at worst. Fuchs and Fuchs (1986) found that student performance may be differentially influenced by examiner familiarity, with lower performance occuring in the presence of familiar examiners for students of low socio-economic status, taking comparatively difficult tests. Often, low-achieving students appear to be more affected than those whose achievement is adequate. Above all, these assessments do not provide the necessary information to structure teaching (Reynolds, 1982; Will, 1986). Because they are designed to document optimal performance, specialized, pull-out assessments may not provide data that are representative of typical performance levels in the classroom.

This book uses classroom-based assessments to generalize assessment data. That is, teachers take tasks from curricula *and* their instruction to determine students' level of performance. To determine the effects of teaching, it is imperative to look at learning *when* and *where* it is occurring (Fuchs, Deno, & Mirkin, 1984). The most important part of the assessment process is to document what is working in the classroom.

To systematize this process, schools must take inventory of what tests are administered. Then, they must ascertain which tests can be used to make functional decisions. Finally, they should modify those practices that are not helpful. Schools cannot operate without testing and measuring learning. If we begin structuring tasks for all educational decisions from the classroom focus, Assertions 1 and 2 can be addressed: Decisions can be integrated (Assertion 1), using both survey- and specific-level assessments (Assertion 2). However, we must systematically and sensitively document student performance to guide decision making.

Assertion 4: Objective Performance Data Provide the Basis for Decision Making

Teachers have a wealth of qualitative information and a dearth of quantitative information on student performance. When asked about student progress, teachers' common answers include the following generalizations: "Matthew just isn't doing that well," "Jenny doesn't seem to get it; she seems stuck," or "Sam has been failing miserably for a long time." (Kurlinski, 1986). These statements represent a serious problem in current classroom decision making. Although they may be perceptive, their validity need to be ascertained and eventually quantified. There is no way of knowing what *not doing that well, failing,* or *not getting it* mean.

Not only should qualitative estimates be made meaningful through quantitative data, but a distinction must be made between *documenting* student achievement and *interpreting* that achievement. For example, Gerber and Semmel (1984) hypothesize that teachers often sort their students subjectively into groups they expect to succeed and not to succeed. But such decisions can be more objective (Shinn, Tindal, & Spira, 1987) if objective information is collected *and* strategies are developed for using data systematically to make decisions about students. Tests should be accurate and mean-

ingful reflections of performance and they should be used appropriately.

Assertion 5: Multiple-Reference Evaluation Strategies Are Needed

Students' performance is rarely summarized from several perspectives, often because of the disjointed data collection that occurs in most schools. When they are compared to their peers, it is on tasks not presented in the classroom; when they are measured for mastery, growth over time and comparability in performance are not considered. Consequently, multiple perspectives are not possible, and interpretations are inherently confounded by different tasks, standards, and time frames.

Ideally, three types of decision-making evaluations are needed: norm-referenced, criterion-referenced, and individual-referenced. The differences between these strategies relate to the standards employed in making interpretations. We should match tests to the types of decisions that need to be made. For example, norm-referenced evaluations compare students to each other and are therefore often useful in making screening or placement decisions, but they are probably less useful in evaluating instructional outcomes. Criterion-referenced evaluations focus on mastery of specific skills and are appropriate for diagnostics and program planning. They are less useful for program evaluation and certification. Individual-referenced evaluations, which present student progress over time, are the best devices for instructional evaluation and program certification, since they compare students' performances to each other, not to those of other students. They are also useful in support of other decisions involving screening and diagnostics. Table 1.1 illustrates the types of deci-

TABLE 1.1
Types of decisions, assessment procedures, and tests available to educators

Types of Decisions Confronting Educators	Type of Assessment Necessary	Type of Test to Be Used
Screening/placement	Survey level	Norm-referenced Individual-referenced
Diagnostic/program planning	Specific level	Criterion-referenced Individual-referenced
Program evaluation/ program certification	Survey level Specific level	Norm-referenced Criterion-referenced Individual-referenced

sions, assessment procedures, and tests available to educators.

Assertion 6: The Legal Mandate for Change Is Present

Litigation and the resulting court rulings have had a significant impact on school assessment. Many cases have established limits and constraints upon the use of educational assessment data; most cases bring into question test bias in relation to the placement of minority students in specialized programs for the retarded. Of primary concern is the overrepresentation of black and Hispanic children in special education. Table 1.2 lists cases that involve black or Hispanic plaintiffs who argued that diagnostic and placement decisions discriminated against students of a specific race or ethnicity. The most well known is *Larry P. v. Riles* (1979), in which the court deemed that wrongful placement in special education based in large part on IQ performance, produced irreparable harm. As a result, the use of standardized intelligence tests for the purpose of placing black students in educable mentally retarded (EMR) classes has been suspended in California. Additionally, the defendants were ordered to correct the imbalance in the proportion of black students placed in special education. The decision stated that it was extremely un-

likely "that a color-blind system of placement would have resulted in the overenrollment of black children and underenrollment of non-black children in the classes for EMR that actually had occurred in 1976–77" (p. 24).

Cultural background is at the heart of the problem. For example, many tests are given to children whose primary language is not English. In *Diana v. State Board of Education* (1970), the court ruled that such children must be assessed in both their primary language and in English.

Also, the protection of parents' and children's rights in placement proceedings is a significant issue. In general, these cases address violations of the equal protection clause of the 14th Amendment to the U. S. Constitution. *Mills v. D. C. Board of Education* (1972) established the need for informed parent involvement during placement and the right to a hearing in the event of disagreement with a school's placement decision.

Because of the turmoil over making placement decisions and the concern over equal educational opportunities and violations of the 14th Amendment to the Constitution, increasing legislation—rather than litigation—began to take shape in the 1970s. P.L. 94–142, the Education of All Handicapped Children Act (EHA), which was passed in 1975, mandated minimum procedures for schools to follow in their

TABLE 1.2
Summary of court cases involving assessment and decision making

Case	Date	Class Status	Test Type	Type of Decision/Issue
Hobson v. Hanson	1967	Black	Achievement Intelligence	• Placement into low ability groups • Inappropriate standardization sample
Arreola v. Santa Ana Board of Education	1968	Hispanic	Intelligence	• Identification of educable mental retardation • Placement into special classes • Failure to provide due process • Cultural bias
Spangler v. Pasadena Board of Education	1970	Black	Intelligence	• Placement within classes and schools
Diana v. California Board of Education	1970	Hispanic	Intelligence	• Placement into classes for mentally retarded • Testing in non-native language • Culturally biased items and tests • Inappropriate standardization sample
Steward v. Phillips	1970	Poor Black	Intelligence	• Inappropriate use of IQ as measure of ability • Placement into classes for mentally retarded
Covarrubias v. San Diego Unified District	1971	Hispanic	Intelligence	• Placement into classes for mentally retarded • Failure to provide due process
Guadalupe v. Tempe Elementary District	1971	Hispanic	Intelligence	• Placement into classes for mentally retarded • Testing in non-native language • Failure to provide due process

placement practices. Although it related only to children with special needs, the law has had tremendous impact on education and society. All assessment procedures used for decision making must be technically adequate and culturally fair and they must help guide instruction within an Individual Educational Program (IEP). Thus, while P.L. 94–142's influence can be seen in special education, there are increasing implications for those in general education (Heller, Holtzman, & Messick, 1982).

The EHA mandates a free and appropriate education for all children and guarantees due process in educational placement decision making. The law prescribes six steps to ensure appropriate placement of students into programs for the educable mentally retarded:

1. Intellectual functioning, adaptive behavior, and school performance must all be considered in making any definition or identification of mental retardation.

TABLE 1.2, *continued*

Case	Date	Class Status	Test or Type	Type of Decision/Issue
Larry P. v. Riles	1971	Black	Intelligence	• Placement into classes for mentally retarded • Professional training of test administrator • Culturally biased items and tests
PARC v. Pennsylvania	1971	Retarded		• Exclusion of handicapped from public schools • Failure to provide due process
Mills v. Board of *Education*	1972	Handicapped		• Exclusion of handicapped children from a free and appropriate education
PASA[a] *v. Hannon*	1980	Black	Intelligence	• Classification as mentally retarded
Marshall v. Georgia	1985	Black	Achievement	• Overrepresentation in low educational groups • Classification as Educable Mentally Retarded (EMR) and Learning Disabled (LD) • Violations of procedural regulations
S1 v. Turlington	1986	Black	Intelligence	• Over-representation of blacks in EMR programs • Test bias • Interpretation of socio-cultural background as specified in Education of All Handicapped Children Act (EHA) regulations

[a]PASE: Parents in Action on Special Education
PARC: Pennsylvania Association for Retarded Children

2. States must have procedures to identify all children who are handicapped and in need of special education.
3. Procedural safeguards and due process must be present to ensure a free and appropriate education and fully involve parents in the decision-making process.
4. A full evaluation of the child's educational needs must be conducted prior to placement, with many specific requirements of the testing procedures outlined below.
5. Before placement into any specialized programs, an Individual Educational Plan must be developed; furthermore, it must be updated annually.
6. A range of alternative placements must be available to allow children to be placed in the least restrictive environment in accord with their handicapping condition (Swanson & Watson, 1982).

The law requires that tests be (a) given in the child's native language, (b) validated for the type of decision for which they are being used, (c) administered in a standardized manner by trained personnel, (d) related to specific educational needs rather than simply global estimates of ability, (e) not reflective of sensory, manual, or speaking impairments, (f) considered as only one piece of information, and (g) interpreted within a multidisciplinary team (Swanson & Watson, 1982).

Reschly, Kicklighter, and McKee (1988a) report the following:

> Perhaps the clearest and most important implication of Marshall is that assessment procedures and grouping practices which have a manifest relationship to instruction, are based upon a widely agreed upon criteria (i.e., the regular curriculum), and which lead to beneficial outcomes can survive legal challenge despite disparate impact on minority students. . . . Meeting an outcomes criterion requires appropriate assessment related to instruction or interventions which are, in turn, beneficial to students. . . . The kind of assessment clearly fostered by the Marshall Court is what has been called curriculum-based assessment (CBA) in the current literature (Deno, 1985; Galagan, 1985; Gickling & Thompson, 1985; Germann & Tindal, 1985; Marston & Magnusson, 1985; Shapiro & Lentz, 1985; and Tucker, 1985). (pp. 19–20)

Assertion 7: Empirical Basis for Assessment Practices Is Required

It is possible to read about preferred practices in books on assessment that include no supporting data base. Even though there have been years of research on assessment and testing, common practices do not always reflect empirical findings. In tests of both content area knowledge and basic skills, assessment practices result less from the basis of systematic investigations than from a concern with pragmatics and tradition.

However, assessment technology must be empirically and experimentally derived. Research has produced a considerable amount of literature in the last 30–50 years on the tech-

nical adequacy of different assessment systems. A wealth of information is available on such issues as how to: (a) sample and format items, (b) administer and score performance in basic skills and content area knowledge, (c) determine which decisions can be made using what kinds of data, and (d) summarize performance in a maximally sensitive manner. All of these issues must guide the kind of data collected in classrooms and their use in making decisions. We can no longer collect information simply because it seems appropriate: Reliable and valid data for making educational decisions must be established empirically.

ALTERNATIVES IN ASSESSMENT PERSPECTIVES

The preceding assertions address measurement and decision making in general, the type of data collected and how they are used in particular. They represent reactions to the current state of the art in assessment. Yet the problems of current practice should also direct alternative strategies. To move from these assertions to changes in assessment practices, it is important to understand two perspectives that implicitly guide current practice and are key in developing alternatives: (a) focus on instruction instead of the student, and (b) emphasize assessment concurrent with and following instruction, rather than prior to it.

Situation-Centered versus Child-Centered Assessment

As Englemann, Granzin, and Severson (1979) note, a dilemma in all assessment is sorting out the degree to which performance is a function of innate capacity (child characteristics and predisposition) versus natural environment (classroom characteristics and manipulation).

In a situation-centered approach, the focus turns to a functional analysis of the environment and its interaction with the child to explain performance. In a child-centered approach, the focus is on identifying characteristics that help explain performance. (See chapter 15 for a paradigm describing the situation-centered approach.)

Most assessment focuses on children: Instruction is rarely evaluated for purposes of modification. Tests are given to define etiology (causes of certain problems), diagnose children for planning instruction, place students in different instructional programs, and ensure mastery of content. They usually do not concentrate on evaluating the impact of the curriculum or instruction. Probably the most significant child-based categorization scheme has been classification. Most tests, such as those for intelligence, personality, diagnosis, and perceptual/processing, center on predisposition. They are predicated on documenting student performance levels for making inferences about children's potential or capabilities.

Such an approach has been problematic, as Ysseldyke and Christenson (1988) point out: "For each of the traits, abilities, or characteristics, psychologists and educators develop tests. This enables practitioners to profile students on lists of variables of presumed importance but of little relevance to instructional intervention" (p. 93).

This concern with child-based assessment and categorization systems is not new. Over 15 years ago, Elliot L. Richardson, Secretary of Health, Education, and Welfare under President Lyndon Johnson, called for a systematic review of how children are classified. His concern resulted in the formation of the Project on the Classification of Exceptional Children, which published its recommendations in a landmark book in 1975 by Hobbs (1975a, 1975b).

Similarly, Goldstein, Arkell, Ashcroft, Hurley, and Lilly (1975) have noted four serious limi-

tations for using a classification system to organize educational programs for students with handicapping conditions. First, classification systems ignore what a child can do. The result is that when educators perceive children as certain types, based on numerical values and test scores, they tend to operate on biases formed from having previously taught children who had the same labels. Classification systems have been successful in other sciences, but they do not work well in education. Lovitt (1976) compares problems with them to those of

> a grocer who chose to classify his stock according to color. In the white section he placed together the eggs, milk, flour, salt, bread, onions, paper towels, oysters, toothpaste, white wine and vanilla ice cream. In the yellow, red, and blue sections the items were equally divergent. The purchaser could not shop for items according to any useful dimension. Furthermore, the grocer would have to design unusual shelves and storage spaces for each section— he would, for example, have to provide refrigeration units for all of the sections.

A second disadvantage of classification systems is that they are self-sustaining: They contribute to the reification of labels that were devised originally to describe children, not to explain them. But the labels eventually are used to explain causes of behavior rather than describe them, and the circuitous reasoning leads educators to

> insert speculations about learning potential from the associations [they] have built up around the score. To say, on the basis of the test score, that the child has not achieved well because he or she is mentally retarded is tantamount to saying, "He/She has not achieved well on the test because he/she has not achieved well on the test." (E. Deno, 1978, p. 25)

Thus, labels that initially were meant to be descriptive constructs become explanatory concepts (Lilly, 1979).

Third, assessment and classification systems ignore the interplay of the student and teacher in instruction and, as noted earlier, assume that instructional problems are embedded within the child. Child-based labels fail to acknowledge the significance of environmental effects. Classifying the learner does not provide the teacher with instructional clues that can lead to improved performance. Frequently, school personnel cannot do anything with a diagnosis, and although it may sound impressive to use a medical term such as *dyslexia,* the label says nothing new and is not relevant to developing instruction for the child (Graden, Zins, Curtis, & Cobb, 1988). Learning difficulties are not the sole property of the child, to a large degree they are characteristic of the classroom situation (Ysseldyke & Christenson, 1988). As Howell (1986) noted,

> Additionally, if the ultimate goal of evaluation is to alter current instructional practice, not merely to describe or make predictions about it, the greatest amount of attention should be directed toward variables that have the most impact on the interaction and are easiest to alter. (p. 325)

The fourth problem is that classification systems eliminate the burden of proof for ensuring that children learn, and they allow for the justification for repeated failure. A teacher who becomes frustrated by his or her ability to teach a particular child can rationalize his or her failures by pointing to the child's diagnosis as the reason for the child's slow progress. As Lovitt (1967) noted more than 20 years ago:

> when the child does not adequately perform, the teacher need only draw out her file and read the diagnosis to reassure herself that the student's poor performance is unalterably de-

termined by some medical or psychological malady. Then no teaching obligation follows for altering the stimulus or consequence conditions of the program, nor is there any necessity for an assessment of possible errors within the teacher's management techniques. (p. 234)

To move an assessment system away from a child-centered toward a situation-centered perspective, the timing of assessment activities must shift. Rather than taking data prior to instruction and making predictions about students and programs, data need to to be taken during and after instruction. This perspective is reflected in an evaluative approach to assessment, which is labeled *back-loaded* and is covered in Chapter 15.

Back-loaded versus Front-loaded Assessment

Probably the most fundamental call for restructuring a child-centered approach in favor of a situation-centered approach arose from litigation during the 1970s and from problems in test bias and minority overrepresentation in special education. The Panel on Selection and Placement of Students in Programs for the Mentally Retarded was established in 1979 to (a) identify factors that could account for the disproportionate placement of minority students in programs for the educable mentally retarded and (b) to identify placement practices that would result in such disproportionality. Although commissioned to address the causes of disproportionality, the panel attended to a larger, more difficult question: Why is disproportionality a problem? Members tackled the thorny dilemma of disproportionality when invalid assessments are used and when low-quality instruction is delivered as a consequence. The panel made the following recommendations:

1. It is the responsibility of teachers in the regular classroom to engage in multiple educational interventions and to note the effects of such interventions on a child experiencing academic failure before referring the child for special education assessment. It is the responsibility of school boards and administrators to ensure that needed alternative instructional resources are available.

2. It is the responsibility of assessment specialists to demonstrate that the measures employed validly assess the functional needs of the individual child for which there are potentially effective interventions.

3. It is the responsibility of the placement team that labels and places a child in a special program to demonstrate that any differential label used is related to a distinctive prescription for educational practices and that these practices are likely to lead to improved outcomes not achievable in the regular classroom.

4. It is the responsibility of special education and evaluation staff to demonstrate systematically that high-quality, effective special instruction is being provided and that the goals of the special education program could not be achieved as effectively within the regular classroom.

5. It is the responsibility of the special education staff to demonstrate on at least an annual basis that a child should remain in the special education class. A child should be retained in the special education class only after it has been demonstrated that he or she cannot meet specified educational objectives and that all efforts have been made to achieve these objectives.

6. It is the responsibility of administrators at the district, state, and national levels to monitor on a regular basis the patterns of special education placements, the rates for particular groups of children or particular schools and districts, and the types of instructional services offered to affirm that appropriate procedures are being followed or to redress inequities found in the system.

(Heller, Holtzman & Messick, 1982, pp. 94–95)

In summary, the panelists said: "Our message is a strikingly simple one. The purpose of the entire process from referral for assessment to eventual placement in special education is to improve instruction for children" (p. x).

The premises of this text are based on the panel's findings, which are essentially evaluative rather than prescriptive. Although most evaluators make assessment decisions prior to instruction (front-loaded) rather than evaluating the effects of instruction (back-loaded), teaching should occur first under varied conditions, followed by a valid assessment of performance to determine whether instructional programs are effective.

To achieve the recommendations of the panel, therefore, all assessment questions are subsumed within two questions: How can student performance be improved? and What specific teaching behaviors are responsible for improved student performance? To address these questions, student performance outcomes must be monitored systematically while the best instructional programs are being implemented. All educational decisions should be made with reference to these outcomes so that, rather than having screening and placement decisions predicated on diagnostic tests, they are predicated on program effectiveness. When programs aren't effective, that is, when students' learning is not improving, more structured environments are invoked. Instead of using tests to diagnose students and predict placement, evaluators use them to monitor changes in progress systematically.

Of the court cases listed in Table 1.2, *Marshall* provides the essential logic for this approach (Reschly, Kicklighter, & McKee, 1988a, 1988b, 1988c). This case was considerably different than many of the others listed in the table. Probably the most important distinction was the emphasis on achievement testing rather than ability testing. All cases, except *Hobson* and *Marshall*, revolved around the measurement of ability and intelligence. And although *Hobson v. Hansen* also involved potential discriminatory grouping decisions, the two cases had radically different outcomes. Both involved statistically significant overrepresentation of blacks in low achievement groups. In *Hobson*, biased decision-making was found to be occurring in the district, while in *Marshall*, the district was exonerated from any wrongful practice. These two cases exemplify an important concept; Table 1.3 provides an abbreviated review.

Reschly summarized the issues surrounding *Hobson* and *Marshall* by writing the following:

> If assessment activities result in needed services, effective interventions, or expanded opportunities for individuals, then assessment is useful and by the definition proposed here, unbiased. If the assessment activities do not lead to appropriate services and are not related to effective interventions, then the assessment activities must be regarded as useless for the individual, and biased or unfair if members of minority groups are differentially exposed to inappropriate programs or ineffective interventions. (1979, pp. 215–216)

DEPTH OF FIELD IN DIAGNOSING LEARNING PROBLEMS

The remainder of this chapter presents a more specific focus on the assessment process as it applies to educational decision making. Figure 1.2 depicts a concrete example of assessment divided into three stages: (a) hypothesis formation, (b) instruction, and (c) hypothesis verification. It is similar to depth of field in photography. If the object is too far away or too close, the image is not clear. To attain an accurate focus, the lens needs to be adjusted so that the image is properly focused.

TABLE 1.3

Summary of major differences between *Hobson* and *Marshall*

Hobson	Marshall
Focused on ability to learn.	Focused on achievement, skills, age grouping, and performance in the basal curriculum.
IQ formed the basis for grouping.	Daily achievement and classroom tests were used to make grouping decisions.
Grouping was not linked to practices.	Grouping was based on instructional skills in the curriculum and was highly related to instruction.
Grouping was relatively permanent.	Grouping was flexible and subject to changes based upon student need.
Effect of grouping was a reduction of opportunity, resources, and assistance.	Grouping resulted in greater opportunities, resources, and quality instructional programs.
No direct beneficial outcomes.	Clear and convincing evidence of positive impact on achievement and improved learning.
Etiology of problem more rooted in learning ability, with schools viewed as more passive in responding to problems.	Etiology of problem rooted in poor background experiences in tasks demanded in schools, which were viewed as actively structuring instruction.

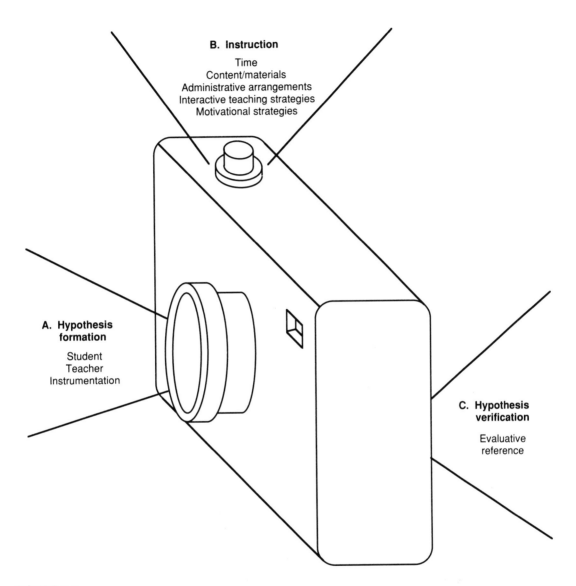

FIGURE 1.2
Focus of assessment: Hypothesis formation, instruction, and hypothesis verification

During the *hypothesis formation* phase, which occurs early in the assessment process, three facets are relevant: student characteristics, teacher/test administrator characteristics, and instrumentation. During *instruction,* the focus is on at least five issues: (a) time, (b) content or materials, (c) administrative arrangements, (d) interactive teaching strategies, and (e) motivational strategies. Concurrent with and immediately following instruction, *hypothesis verification* occurs based on one of three evaluative references (norm, criterion, and individual) in which evaluators interpret performance and make decisions.

Hypothesis Formation: Initial Assessment Phase

In the early stages of hypothesis formation, the necessary information comes from a variety of sources. Often the focus is broad and the depth of field is easy to establish, as with a wide-angle photographic lens. The depth of field can be increased or decreased somewhat, but generally, wide-angle lenses are insensitive to any fine adjustments. The goal is to obtain as much relevant information as possible before integrating it. During this phase, the focus often is not sharp, and it isn't until instruction actually begins that feedback on assessment data is available.

Student Characteristics. All educators have predetermined expectations about student characteristics, most of which arise from previous experience and professional training. For example, first-graders are not expected to be proficient readers, and third-graders are not expected to be competent in cursive writing. The process of schooling is one of acculturating students—acquainting them with teacher expectations—and eventually providing instruction in the basic skill areas.

Many of these expectations are not just developmental notions about all children but specific expectations of individual students. For example, research has demonstrated that a child's natural characteristics can affect the outcome of the assessment process. Ross and Salvia (1975) investigated the extent to which students' attractiveness influenced teachers' decisions. Using pictures of educationally competent children who varied in attractiveness, they found that personal attractiveness was a biasing factor in the teachers' diagnosis of cog-

nitive functioning. Salvia, Algozzine, and Sheare (1977) replicated the study in an examination of teacher grades and student attractiveness. Ysseldyke, Algozzine, Regan, and McGue (1979) found that other factors such as student sex, socioeconomic status, physical appearance, and behavior to be influential in the decision-making process; although test data reflected average performance, decision-makers frequently classified students as emotionally disturbed.

Student characteristics play an important role in establishing certain assessment procedures and set the occasion for the collection of certain types of data. Sometimes these expectations apply to students in general; at other times, they apply to specific students.

Teacher and Test-Administrator Characteristics. Educators also have expectations of classrooms (Witt & Elliott, 1985). Teachers often base their classroom management on ideas of what they should be like, how instruction should be delivered, and what kinds of materials and teaching behaviors should be applied or implemented. Support personnel often judge teachers by these same considerations. An informal assessment of classrooms may include a focus on materials, routines, expectations, and strategies.

Although this book concentrates on the assessment of student performance in academic achievement areas, classroom and instructional expectations are also important. Teacher expectations and tolerances also play important roles in the development of hypotheses about student performance. An increasing amount of research indicates that expectations and tolerances are important discriminative cues that control how students behave.

Instrumentation. Hypotheses are often influenced by the context and format of the instrumentation used in the assessment process.

Tests can vary in many dimensions, such as the material or content that is being tested, the manner in which questions are framed and responses are structured, and how performance is scored. Some questions on tests are more difficult than others, and some responses are more difficult to score than others. Evaluators must consider instrumentation issues when interpreting student performance. For example, an assessment of students on a phonics-based test (e.g., Woodcock Word Attack subtest) in a classroom using a whole-language approach to reading, may yield some contradictory results.

Even before instruction occurs, a considerable amount of information is available from student assessment data and from the expectations of students, teachers, and teaching. Teachers use all of this information to help students and plan instruction, which is the fulcrum of the assessment process.

Delivery of Instruction

Instruction is a complex package of materials and procedures. It consists of five major components that can be manipulated individually or in concert. First, *time* is an important dimension of any instructional program. Over the past decade, researchers have gathered a large amount of information on time in all of its forms. For example, although the elementary school day is approximately 350 minutes long, the instructional day includes only 183 minutes; reading takes up 120 minutes, active engagement in reading activities takes up about 25 minutes, and actual oral reading occurs for only about 10 minutes per day (Thurlow, Graden, Greener & Ysseldyke, 1982).

Second, students are always taught with certain *materials,* with content delivered in different areas and from different sources. Teachers most often use published curriculum materials although teacher-prepared materials are im-

portant supplements. This material may have an adequate arrangement and a systematic sequence, and include sufficient examples and review to provide enough structure for learning to occur. On the other hand, it may be poorly organized and inadequately sequenced, with few examples and haphazard review.

The third component of instruction is the *administrative arrangement.* Students can be taught in one large group, in small groups, or independently; they can gather with peers or aides in certain rooms of their building with specific individuals, and so forth. Changing any part of an arrangement can affect student performance.

Fourth, *interactive teaching strategies* occur in instruction, such as modeling, explaining, describing, and illustrating. Such interactions precede and follow student responses, providing a range of feedback and correction procedures that can reinforce and/or correct students' performance.

The last component of instruction involves the use of *motivational strategies.* For many students, learning is a difficult task. Learning environments should provide some payoff for performing tasks and completing work, in the expectation that as students become more fluent in their skills, naturally occurring reinforcers will support the relevant behaviors.

We may also identify four different phases of instruction. They include training in initial acquisition of skills, in which the focus is on attaining accuracy and correct performance, and in fluency, with an emphasis on smooth and effortless performance. Later, maintenance becomes the focus of learning. Following that comes the adaptation phase, which encourages students to export their learning to new realms, different contexts, or unique settings. During instruction, teachers use much of the information collected initially to adjust program content (Wolery, Bailey, & Sugai, 1988).

Hypothesis Verification: Evaluation of Instruction

The focal point of assessment is the hypothesis-verification phase. That is, a determination of an instructional program's success is not possible until instructors collect data on program effects and use them to make evaluative decisions. Once assessments are conducted and instruction is delivered, the real job of evaluation begins. Three types of evaluative reference are available, all of which involve anchoring a student's performance to an interpretive guide. A student's performance can be compared (a) to that of others (providing a norm-referenced evaluation), (b) to established standards on specific skills (providing a criterion-referenced evaluation), or (c) to previous levels of performance (providing an individual-referenced evaluation).

In this book, the focus is on the hypothesis-verification stage; data taken from this stage are fed back into the hypothesis-formation phase, in which instructors adjust programs to meet the needs of students. Thus, the instructors use data to ensure success, as defined in a multireferenced manner. To ensure that the focus is clear, testing and assessment must be analyzed in depth.

OPERATIONALIZING ASSESSMENT

This book presents a measurement model that contains three main factors: (a) test construction, (b) test analysis, and (c) test interpretation. Test construction involves structuring tasks for students and obtaining responses from them. In test analysis, the teacher analyzes performance to ascertain the adequacy of instrumentation. Finally, test interpretation involves evaluating performance and making decisions. To provide an adequate interpretation of performance, teachers should consider not only content but also format. In addition, they should scrutinize the tests to determine if they are technically adequate for making specific educational decisions.

Test Construction

The first factor to consider in any assessment is the *stimulus-response* attributes of the test, including test items and their adequacy as indicators of performance. Instructors should consider the focus of content, type of response, and scoring of the response when constructing tests. Figure 1.3 shows the three dimensions of test construction.

Focus of Content. All tests can assay proficiency in domains of either basic skills or content knowledge, which should be considered as two extremes on the same continuum of achievement. However, tests usually emphasize one dimension over the other. Examples of basic skills include oral reading fluency, spelling correct letter sequences, and concatenating words in correct sequence. Examples of content knowledge include verbal information in content areas, rules for sequencing information, and oral or written expressions of material.

Basic skills, which are motoric behaviors representing automatic responding in the application of knowledge, have been identified for reading, written expression, spelling, math, preschool skills, and language. Research and development in curriculum-based measurement over the past decade have significantly influenced the coverage of basic skills (Deno, 1985).

Knowledge, representing the expression of information, has been organized around six intellectual operations: (a) reiteration, (b) summarization, (c) illustration, (d) prediction, (e) evaluation, and (f) application. Knowledge also comprises three content formats: (a) facts, (b) concepts, and (c) principles. Test items are developed by linking intellectual operations and

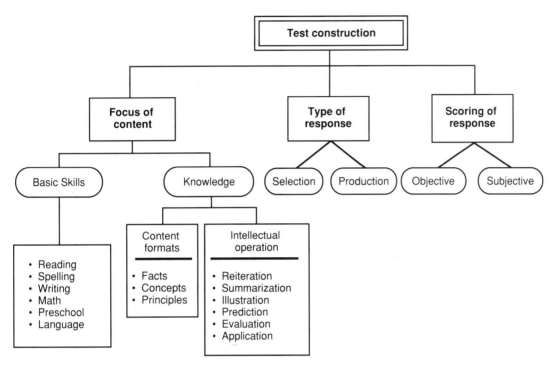

FIGURE 1.3
Three dimensions of test construction

content formats. We have adopted this item configuration, which represents a modern version of the learning taxonomy proposed by B. S. Bloom and associates in 1956, from Roid and Haladyna (1982).

Type of Response. We can think of test items as opportunities for students to respond, which in turn requires analysis of the responses themselves. Two types of responses are possible: selection and production (Hopkins & Antes, 1978). For a selection response, in which all information for answering the item is within the item itself, students select correct answers; they do not produce them. Multiple-choice tests, for example, require selection responses. A production response requires students to pro-

duce the answer, which is not embedded within the item itself, either orally or in writing. Short-answer and essay questions are examples of items that require production responses.

Scoring of Response. The third component of test construction deals with scoring procedures, with two options available: subjective and objective. These options often are closely aligned with the type of response: Selection responses are usually scored objectively, and production responses are usually scored subjectively. However, it is possible to create test items requiring selection responses that are scored subjectively or production responses that are scored objectively. Therefore, scoring (subjective and objective) is actually independent of the response format (i.e., whether the test item demands a selection or production response).

We may create tests using any combination of these attributes. For example, a test might focus on content area knowledge, reflect a lower-order intellectual operation and content format (i.e., reiteration or summarization of a fact), and require selection responses, that are objectively scored. Such a test would be similar to most of those that schools use. In contrast, a test can focus on basic skills, require production responses, and be scored objectively. This test would be similar to the curriculum-based measures developed by the Institute for Research on Learning Disabilities at the University of Minnesota.

Test Analysis: Technical Considerations

The second major factor in operationalizing assessment involves analyzing the test to ascertain whether it is an appropriate instrument. Test analysis addresses three major issues: (a) item characteristics, or the distribution of students within any one of the items, (b) test-distribution characteristics, or the distribution of students across all test items, and (c) technical adequacy, which is the test's reliability and validity. The three dimensions of test analysis appear in Figure 1.4. Don't worry about the specific definitions of the new vocabulary; you will be reading about this material in later chapters.

Item Characteristics.   Test analysis should begin with an investigation of individual items to determine their difficulty and discrimination. The focus is on how difficult the item is (how many students pass or fail it) and how discriminating the item is in predicting overall performance (the relationship between the individual item

and the total test score). Difficulty and discrimination can be analyzed logically or empirically (Roid & Haladyna, 1982). A logical analysis is based on an educated scrutiny without reference to specific quantitative summaries to determine whether an item is easy or difficult or whether it can discriminate between students who know and don't know the material. The empirical approach takes data on student performance and uses it to determine whether that item was difficult and/or discriminating.

Test Distribution Characteristics.   Given the arrangement of many items that differ in difficulty, and discrimination, responses to a test fall along a continuum, or distribution, that can be described according to *kurtosis,* the spread of the responses, or *skewness,* the bunching of scores at a low or high end. For example, with a very narrow kurtosis, often referred to as *leptokurtic,* responses are within a limited range of scores. In a *platykurtic* distribution, responses fall across a wide range of scores. The two types of skewness are positive and negative. If the distribution is positive, most scores are at the low end, and the skewness (the tail of the distribution) is at the high end (hence the name *positively skewed*). With a *negatively skewed* distribution, most scores are at the high end, and the tail is at the low end.

Technical Adequacy.   The last dimension of test analysis involves technical adequacy, which deals with reliability and validity. Reliability focuses on the consistency and repeatability of scores and validity focuses on the truthfulness of scores (does the test really measure the behavior of interest). Those who administer tests are usually interested in obtaining scores, but if test scores are to be useful in making decisions, they should be repeatable and meaningful reflections of behavior.

Evaluating Performance and Making Decisions

Evaluation of performance may be norm-, criterion-, or individual-referenced. Each approach utilizes a different comparative standard for interpreting performance and providing meaning to any test scores. Figure 1.5 presents these three approaches.

Norm-Referenced Evaluation. A norm-referenced interpretation compares student performance to that of comparable students, who usually are referred to as the *standardization* or *normative sample.* Different summary outcomes are available with this approach.

Criterion-Referenced Evaluation. Absolute criteria can be used to ascertain outcomes on

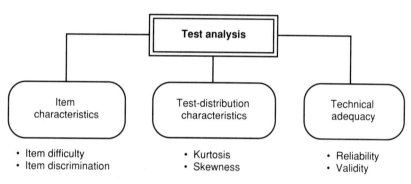

FIGURE 1.4
Three dimensions of test analysis

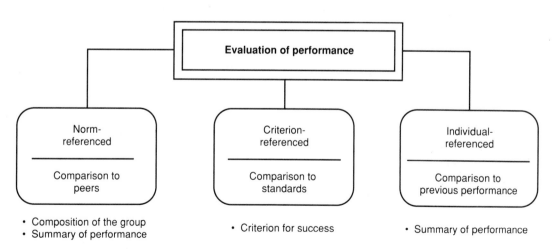

FIGURE 1.5
Three dimensions for evaluating performance

a specific set of skills. Frequently, the evaluator uses performance to divide students into two groups: those who are *at and above* or those who are *below* a certain minimal performance level, which can be established using several different sources.

Individual-Referenced Evaluation. This approach uses time-series, or repeated, measurement data to determine student improvement over time. The purpose of this approach is to track changes in student performance over time, employing several specific measures: *average performance,* changes in *step* (immediate changes occurring when programs are introduced), *slope* (the rate of change), *variability* (inconsistency of performance), and *overlap* (data values that are in common across different programs). This evaluation strategy is similar to that used in the Dow Jones Charts, which track the stock market on a daily basis and display average changes (slope) and fluctuations (variability).

CHAPTER SUMMARY

Testing is big business in our nation's schools, but the assessments are of such low quality that change is needed. However, to effect change we must give careful consideration to the purposes of testing and the types of decisions that need to be made.

This chapter identifies two issues that are central to the model presented in this book: (a) whether assessment is child-centered or situation-centered, and (b) whether it is conducted before instruction to diagnose students or during and after instruction to document specific learning outcomes as the criteria for decision making; we prefer an evaluation-oriented model of assessment.

Although most assessments are predicated upon predictions of performance, the optimal focal point occurs *during* and *after* instructional delivery. Any initial assessments are, therefore, placeholders to help us initiate the process and provide some tentative hypotheses from which to begin the job of teaching. Only data that are collected concurrent with and following instruction can verify these hypotheses. Throughout this process, we must address issues relating to students, teachers, instrumentation, instructional programs, and evaluation strategies in order to execute appropriate decisions. Finally, the assessment process consists of three phases, in which we construct tests, analyze them, and use them to make decisions.

These measurement characteristics are covered within the problem-solving model (hypothesis formation, instruction, hypothesis verification) and test application model (test construction—analysis—evaluation). We should use student performance data not just to evaluate whether programs are effective but also to evaluate the appropriateness of tests being used to make decisions. Therefore, the various components in the test application model must be referenced continually. For example, item configuration, a focus on skills or knowledge, and the types of questions and scoring systems are important components of test-construction dimensions. They have an important influence on the test-analysis dimensions, such as item difficulty, the distributions of students, and the technical adequacy of the instrument. All of these factors inherently limit any interpretations of performance that can be made and must be considered to evaluate student performance, the tests themselves, and instructional programs.

CHAPTER 2

Establishing Measurement Plans

wo friends were planning their annual vacation when one suggested that for a change of pace, they should just get in their car and start driving. The other, somewhat confused, replied, "Well, if we don't know where we're going, how will we know when we get there?"

The same problem exists for teachers with ill-defined goals for assessment. Without a game plan, a purpose, and specific strategies for accomplishing that purpose, assessment is bound to result in confusion. Measurement cannot dictate policy and planning. Rather, policy and planning must be established first. An important concept underlying this book is that assessment must follow instruction, not dictate it. Assuming that such instruction has been defined, this chapter reviews general planning considerations for any assessment program.

CHAPTER OBJECTIVES

When you have finished this chapter, you should have the skills and knowledge to

- Differentiate between assessment and testing and know how and when to apply each.
- Delineate three major sources of assessment information to collect on students and provide a description of their interrelationships.
- Distinguish between formal and informal assessment procedures and standardize any data-collection system.
- Describe the major purposes of testing, particularly as they relate to decision making.
- Operationalize a test that reflects either a skills or knowledge focus.
- Plan the format and content of a skills test.

- Plan the format and content of a knowledge test, considering three types of content formats and six basic intellectual operations.
- Take into account the content and focus of a test (skills and/or knowledge) to define domains for sampling items on it.
- Select a domain to reflect the types of items to be included within the test.

KEY VOCABULARY

The vocabulary in this chapter is test-specific. *Assessment* centers on the collection of information. Three sources of information in this process differ greatly in the type of data and methods employed. *Observations* are noninteractive, *interviews* are interpersonal, and *testing* focuses on quantifying performance. All three sources vary on a dimension of *standardization*, which relates to the degree of controlled and structured implementation (formal to informal). Three decisions are considered: (a) *screening*, in which the search is for deviance, and *eligibility*, with a focus on grouping, categorizing, and/or labeling; (b) *instructional planning*, including diagnostics, and *formative evaluation*, where changes in instruction are made in response to student outcomes; and (c) *program certification*, which emphasizes *summative program evaluation*. These three decisions are closely aligned with the three types of tests: *norm-referenced*, using the performance of other students; *criterion-referenced*, using absolute standards on specific skills and content; and *individual-referenced*, using previous performance and rate of change.

A major part of this chapter concerns the content of tests. Items are either *skills*-oriented, emphasizing tool movements (White & Haring, 1980) and motoric responses, or *knowledge*-based, focusing on manipulation of information. We defer most discussion of skills to the content chapters because they are specific to the material being tested. However, tests of knowledge employ common formats that are derived from the technology of item writing; therefore we review them in one chapter (chapter 3). The knowledge strand is divided into a two-dimensional matrix, including tasks or intellectual operations (*reiteration, summarization, illustration, prediction, evaluation,* and *application*) and content (*facts, concepts,* and *principles*). The intellectual operations, which were developed by Roid and Haladyna (1982), are an alternative to B. S. Bloom and associates' (1956) taxonomy and improve upon the idea of levels of knowledge; they range in complexity from the simplest, reiteration, to the most complex, application. These levels cannot be displayed without a specific content that reflects the type of knowledge in problem-solving. Together, intellectual operations and tasks must be defined further in terms of specific informational content. We review two types of domains, *ordered* (specified apriori, with constant definition, and sequenced into a continuum of achievement) and *unordered* (test-defined, idiosyncratic across and within individuals and over time, and not confined to a continuum of achievement). Finally, we present an example of a test objective. Figure 2.1 presents a road map of decision making that reflects these issues.

FUNDAMENTALS OF ASSESSMENT

Before planning specific assessment strategies we must consider three issues representing a mix of assumptions and/or perspectives. First, we must establish a definition of assessment; second, we must translate this definition into specific strategies; and third, the purpose for conducting an assessment must be clear. Consideration of these issues avoids confusion later when interpreting test results.

Defining Assessment

Testing, appraisal, diagnosis, measurement, performance review, and *evaluation* are some of the labels used in education to refer to assessment, the process that helps determine children's skills and knowledge. This wide array of descriptors, however, has often served to confuse rather than clarify what occurs in the assessment process. Following is the definition that we have used as the foundation for this book.

Assessment is the systematic process we use to gather data that allow us to instruct students more effectively. At first glance, such a definition might seem too simplistic and narrow to serve the purposes of educators. But it encompasses a wide array of information sources.

First, concentrate on three key words from the definition and their significance. *Systematic* signifies the importance of a purposeful, step-by-step plan in which one gathers information about a student. When assessment proceeds in a haphazard manner, the information collected probably is not useful.

Data imparts the need for information that is factual and can be communicated with accuracy for use in decision making. Often, the information provided after assessment is not reliable or valid. Using inaccurate student data to make decisions creates educational problems for both child and teacher.

Third, if educators are to *instruct* students effectively, they must link good assessment practice to effective instruction. Too often, assessment is conducted only to place students in programs or to label them. When assess-

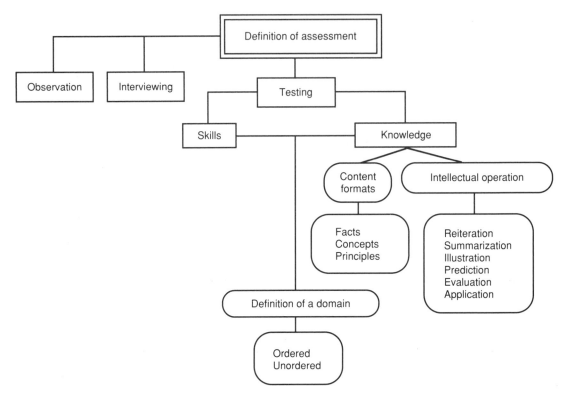

FIGURE 2.1
Decision-making flowchart for testing

ment data are instructionally relevant, we can determine successful interventions or evaluate teaching strategies.

Strategies for Operationalizing Assessment

How do we gather and evaluate assessment data? Educators have three possible sources of information: observations, interviews, and tests. The level of inference or interpretation is defined by these sources of information, providing a direct, indirect, or analog interpretation, respectively. The other dimension, standardization procedures, can be either *formal* (completed in a very replicable manner) or *informal*

(completed in a manner that is difficult to duplicate). Figure 2.2 shows the interrelationships of these two dimensions.

Observations, interviews, and tests vary in their degree of intrusiveness, standardization, and the level of inference they possess. **Observations** are noninteractive reports of the environment; **interviews** are interactive with others in the environment, and **tests** are structured interactions with correct and incorrect answers. These components provide different levels of interpretation for making statements about student performance in the classroom. Observations are the most direct, with behavior assessed and coded as it actually occurs. Interviews are indirect or secondary, as they consist of behavioral descriptions that report-edly occur. Tests structure the data collection process in a specific manner, providing a direct view of behavior outside of the classroom tasks and functions. The **standardization** dimension reflects the degree of explicit structure and di-rection that is embedded in the data collection system. When formal and standardized, any-one can complete a procedure repeatedly in the same manner. When informal and unstan-dardized, each data-collection procedure has a different format.

Many people mistakenly think that *stan-dardized* means *published* or *norm-referenced.* Neither term is inherently a component of standardization. A teacher-made test can be standardized (see the discussions of curric-ulum-based measurement in the content area chapters), while published tests can be admin-istered informally, which violates the standard-ization procedures. One reason for the confusion may occur because of the often-used phrase *standardization sample,* which typically refers to the group upon which a norm-refer-enced test is based. However, any type of test (norm- , criterion- , or individual-referenced)

can be administered with either formal or in-formal standardization procedures.

Observations. Classroom observations are a rich source of assessment information. Recent advances in this area have made available many valid systems (Evertson & Green, 1984) with which to examine student behaviors (Dancer et al., 1978; Kerr & Nelson, 1989) and teacher behaviors (Greenwood, et al. 1984).

Depending upon the level of standardiza-tion, observation systems can be administered repeatedly or limited to single administrations. When conducted formally, we may classify ob-servation systems as category- , sign- , or mul-tiple-coding systems (Medley, Coker, & Soar, 1984). Category observations supply broad de-scriptions of behavior that include specific sam-ples or instances of the behavior. For example, teachers may be described as *supportive* in their questioning of students. The specific be-havior samples that reflect the term *supportive* may include smiling, making positive state-ments, and using the student's name. Sign ob-servation systems use only very specific, discrete behaviors that have been precisely de-

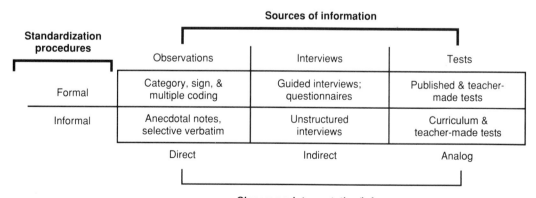

FIGURE 2.2
Two dimensions of assessment: Sources of information and standardization procedures

fined. For example, *talk-outs* may be confined to only loud, verbal behavior that occurs without the student raising a hand and receiving permission to speak. Multiple observation systems include both category and sign systems. For example, a category labeled *compliance* may include a range of specific behaviors, such as task completion within a specific time limit, no verbal behavior, and enthusiasm in the task completion.

All observation systems have an inherent validity because the behaviors of interest are assessed directly. When conducted informally, observation systems are idiosyncratic, providing an unstructured or unsystematic glimpse of classroom behavior. Typically, data from such observations are nonquantified, written descriptions of verbal and/or nonverbal behavior, referred to as *narrative* recording by Evertson and Green (1984). Often, ethnographic depictions of classrooms utilize this system, providing a complex view of classrooms. These systems are considered informal because they provide few guidelines for defining what and/ or how behavior is to be coded.

Interviews. Assessments often must include information about individuals to help understand test and performance data. An interviewer asks questions and obtains reactions, but the correctness of answers is not an issue. If conducted properly, interviews can be an important source of information to help guide further assessment (Kaufmann, 1989).

Interviews can vary widely in standardization format or formality. They can range from a very structured set of questions to a general discussion (Gordon, 1969). Formal and systematic interviews are considered planned; often, they include a questionnaire that contains a list of specific questions and statements designed to obtain limited responses. A guided interview is less structured, containing specific

questions that can elicit a range of possible answers. An unguided interview may contain preestablished questions and/or follow-up questions and be accompanied by a range of open-ended queries to which interviewees structure their own responses. A completely unstructured interview contains no apriori questions and may be a conversation or discussion. Such interviews are very difficult to replicate and are considered informal. Any of these standardization formats may be useful, since the success of the interview is dependent only upon the interviewers' ability to attain relevant information during the session.

Tests. Because tests have such broad applications in so many different areas, they are difficult to define succinctly. Tests can focus on achievement, intelligence, or perceptual/motor skills, and they can be used to scale accomplishments, determine eligibility, confer certification, or evaluate outcomes. Test content is virtually unlimited.

For our purposes, a test is a structured presentation of items in which a respondent's answer is scored in terms of correctness. Testing has a far more limited definition than assessment. The two important dimensions of testing are structure and correctness.

Structure can be identified with two characteristics: domain representation and decision making. To qualify as a test, the set of items must be systematically sampled from a larger domain, and there must be a formal evaluation system for making decisions (norm-, criterion-, or individual-referenced). Correctness, although seemingly simple, is no longer black and white; a new era of testing may be forthcoming with the introduction of multiple-choice tests using rating scales for testing comprehension (see the Illinois Initiative in chapter 7). We will define correctness as a judgment of quality/accuracy based on an a priori standard. Such a definition is broad enough to include a range of rating scales as well as the correct/incorrect scoring of traditional multiple-choice tests.

This definition of a test is quite specific. It excludes worksheets because they are often constructed from ill-defined domains, incorporate little structure into their administration and/or scoring, and do not provide an interpretive application. The medium is not important in the definition: Tests can be presented or completed in writing, orally, or through sign language. Furthermore, the actual layout of the test is not important in the general definition.

Purposes of Testing

Armed with definitions of assessment and testing and strategies for operationalizing them, we may now consider the purpose of testing. The topic is critical because, as already stressed, measurement must follow policy.

More than 10 years ago, the Secretary of Health, Education and Welfare, Joseph A. Califano Jr., convened a National Conference on Achievement Testing and Basic Skills. The conference members concluded that testing in America had four major purposes (Tyler & White, 1979).

First, tests hold teachers, schools, and school systems accountable. Most school administrators, as well as the public, use educational tests as an index of how well their schools, programs, and teachers are doing. When test scores show improvement, people are satisfied; when test scores reflect poor performance, educational changes usually are considered.

A second purpose of testing is to make decisions about individual students. A student may be assigned to a slower-paced program if both ability and achievement scores are low, or to a program for the gifted if both are high; a low achievement score coupled with a high ability score raises the possibility of a learning disability.

The third reason for testing is to evaluate the effectiveness of educational innovations and experimental projects. During the past three decades, there has been a tremendous increase in new approaches to teaching children. To be accountable for the financial resources allotted to research and training projects that create these innovations, universities, private foundations, government agencies, and school systems must use testing to evaluate their projects' effectiveness.

The fourth purpose of testing, according to the conference, is to provide direction for teachers in the classroom. When tests are administered for specific decision making, the impact is directly present, if not always immediate; when teachers tailor instruction to test content, the impact may be indirect, but nevertheless influential in providing direction for classroom practices.

In this book, we focus on the second and third purposes outlined above, expanding upon them to include three major outcomes that occur prior to, during, and following instruction (Gronlund, 1988).

The first outcome relates to the allocation of resources. The corresponding decision at this level is screening and identification. The emphasis is on measuring the continuum of skills and determining deviance (**screening**), which then is translated into placement into specialized programs (**eligibility**). These decisions typically occur prior to instruction.

The second major outcome centers on the delivery of instruction, with two important functions: diagnostics/planning and **formative evaluation**. Once students are placed into an appropriate level of service, teachers must make decisions about what and how to teach them. Obviously, teachers make these decisions concurrently with instruction.

Third, programs must be evaluated for many reasons, including documenting outcomes, securing funding, and providing accountability. The important function at this level is the collection and analysis of performance data across students, but within programs. These decisions follow instruction.

Because screening and eligibility are based on notions of deviance, there is a need to know normality. But **instructional planning** is individually defined, so the need is to document student responses in specific instructional materials. The evaluation of instruction is relevant only in relation to individuals and their previous levels of performance, whether the interpretation is improved rates of progress or mastery of specific objectives.

Finally, we may evaluate a program by using any of the three types of tests. With a norm-referenced test, the interpretation is usually a score on a distribution; a student's performance is compared to that of other students. In a **criterion-referenced** approach, the outcomes are formatted as percentages of students mastering specific materials or objectives; student's performance is compared to some absolute standards. With an **individual-referenced** strategy, the outcome metric is the average rate of progress for a number of students; comparing current performance to previous levels of performance achieved by the same student.

These interpretations relate closely to the purposes of testing. Norm-referenced tests usually support screening and eligibility decisions, although individual-referenced tests may also serve this function. Instructional planning is best completed with either criterion-referenced or individual-referenced tests. Formative evaluation also can be accomplished on the basis of both criterion- and individual-referenced evaluations, though the latter are probably preferable. Finally, **program certification** can employ any or all of the tests though norm-referenced tests are most frequently used for this purpose. Figure 2.3 provides a breakdown of these relationships.

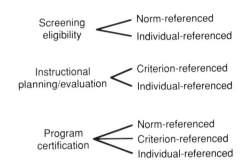

FIGURE 2.3
Relationship between purpose and type of test

With these outcomes of testing in mind and references for interpreting performance, the final decisions in measurement planning are to decide whether the test focuses on skills or knowledge and to provide some definition for the domain universe—the types of items (the range of examplars) to be included within the test.

Defining the Domain

The development of domains involves two considerations: content (the range of item diversity) and breadth (the number of similar items). Both are needed for a sharp focus on which items to include within the domain and which items to exclude. At this point, the concern is with content (we cover breadth in the next chapter under the topic of sampling plans), which can be based on skills or knowledge.

Skills or Knowledge Focus. To understand the difference between skills and knowledge, pretend you have just completed your degree in teacher education and are now certified to teach. You earned straight *A*'s in your education courses, but failed all of the practica and student teaching experiences. In other words, you have very adequate knowledge about teaching but little skill in actually teaching. In contrast, assume you miserably failed all of your coursework on campus, but received rave reviews from your supervisor, principal, and mentor teacher for your student teaching. Thus, you have great skills but poor knowledge.

As these examples highlight, the difference between skills and knowledge is that one involves *knowing,* and the other involves *doing.* It means having immediate access to information versus being fluent in conducting oneself. It is an emphasis on verbal skills versus verbal and motor skills.

Skills. When the focus is on skills, we view the behavior sampled on the test as a tool movement (White & Haring, 1980), which is a requisite behavior for producing other behavior that is being assessed. For example, handprinting is a requisite skill (tool movement) for written expression; number formation is critical in solving math computation problems; and articulation is a tool movement for orally answering questions on a test.

Determining a domain is less of a problem with skill tests than it is with those that assess knowledge. Skills typically can be sorted into a hierarchy that ranges from most restrictive to most encompassing. For example, in a test of math facts, the domain could include the following hierarchy:

1. Single-digit numbers from 1 to 9 added to each other.
2. Single-digit and double-digit numbers added to each other, *without* carrying.
3. Single-digit and double-digit numbers added to each other, *with* carrying.
4. Double-digit numbers added to double-digit numbers, *without* carrying.
5. Double-digit numbers added to double-digit numbers, *with* carrying.

We can format tests to include only problem types at one of the numbered steps or problem types encompassing several steps. Also, we may establish in advance the percentage of problems that sample a particular type. Be-

cause skills tests are behavior-specific, it is not possible to discuss their format without reference to specific behaviors. Therefore, we cover skills tests in more detail within each of the content area chapters.

Knowledge. In contrast, knowledge represents information that may be the end product itself (such as knowing material in content areas) or have bearing in producing a skill. We can consider skills as motoric, in part, with an element of fluency, while content knowledge is more inferential and limited to verbalizing information at varying degrees of abstraction. "Knowledge originates in information which can be received directly from observations or indirectly from reports of observations. These observations may be external (objects or events) or internal (thoughts and feelings)" (Ebel, 1982, p. 267).

Knowledge is subject-specific, needing a content area to serve as a medium. One cannot simply *know.* Rather, one knows something *about* a topic: social studies, the Civil War, football at the turn of the century, the Vietnam war, and so forth.

Any academic area can include a focus on skills and/or knowledge. For example, assessment of reading could focus on oral reading fluency or on knowledge of structural characteristics of words and syllabication. In written expression, assessment could focus on words written in correct sequence, or knowledge of syntactical and grammatical generalizations about the English language. In summary, knowledge is "a system of articulated relations among concepts and ideas" (Ebel, 1982; p. 268); it, however, can be expressed only in reference to some content.

As you see, assessment can focus on one or both of these areas. In a **skills** test, problems are presented that engage students in an active response; they must read, write, spell, compute, verbalize, etc. A **knowledge** test seeks an active or passive response from students; they may be asked to respond by writing or reading, or by filling in a bubble to signify understanding of a problem.

Therefore, the distinction made in chapter 1 between selection and production responses is only partly valid. It is not possible to create a skills test using a selection response. One problem with selection responses is that the signified behavior is inferred rather than overtly demonstrated. For example, with a multiple-choice test using four responses following a short passage, any response can be implied as indicating knowledge; however, it may also represent other artifacts (prior knowledge, guessing, contextual clues within the distractors). Therefore, it is difficult to understand selection-type knowledge tests definitively without these confounding influences.

Although skills and knowledge are different, it is important to consider them as two extremes of the same dimension; in fact, they are probably highly interrelated. Generally, if people know a lot about something, they can also engage in practical behavior that reflects such knowledge. As you will see in the content area chapters, the research on curriculum-based measurement supports this argument. When students know a lot about decoding rules and comprehension strategies, they are more fluent readers (or vice versa).

Domain boundaries for knowledge tests are often ambiguous, particularly regarding level of inference or evaluation. In other words, domains are difficult to establish without some guidelines about level of inference or abstraction. Items for a test on the Civil War could include names of battles, dates, events, individuals, causes, outcomes, implications, and so forth. It is difficult to forge a domain adequately unless we use some taxonomy of knowledge to sort the degree of emphasis on not only content, but also format of that content. Following is a taxonomy for categorizing knowledge.

This book adheres to a taxonomy for intellectual operations proposed by Williams and Haladyna (1982), which they call *Logical Operations for Generating Information Questions (LOGIQ)*. In adopting their scheme for classifying question types, we agree that the taxonomy originally proposed by B. S. Bloom in 1956 encompassing (a) knowledge, (b) comprehension, (c) application, (d) analysis, (e) synthesis, and (f) evaluation has been useful only heuristically. The order of these operations follows approximate complexity, although difficulty does vary within the different categories. The biggest problem with Bloom's taxonomy is that it addresses the internal intellectual processing required of students rather than describing situations presented to students and the skills they need to solve those situations. Another problem is that it is easier to classify a question after its construction than to use the taxonomy in actually constructing it. As Williams and Haladyna note, their system represents a refinement of work reported earlier (H. G. Miller & Williams, 1973; H. G. Miller, Williams, & Haladyna, 1978; Williams, 1977) and is actually an expansion on those works.

The premise of this typology is that we can classify any instructional objective, test item, or other environmental demand on an individual according to: (a) the content format of information, and (b) the task or intellectual operation to be performed. A third dimension (covered in depth in chapter 3) is added for test formating purposes: (c) response mode.

Content format can be divided into three types: facts, concepts, and principles. **Facts** are associations between names, symbols, objects, locations, and so forth. They represent one-to-one correspondences between words and singular exemplars. **Concepts** are classes of objects or events that share some common attribute and can be grouped together based on this attribute. They reflect multiple correspondences between words and a range of possible exemplars. **Principles** represent statements of relationship among objects or events and are often communicated as if-then statements or cause-effect propositions. They generally reflect a dimension of time and/or space.

Tasks incorporate six intellectual operations that refer to the manner in which content is used. Following is a description of each operation, with examples for each of the three types of content.

The lowest intellectual operation is **reiteration,** which requires examinees to recognize or produce information in basically the same form in which it was received. The response is expected to be an exact wording, as taught in the book or lecture. Reiteration can include all three of the content areas. Examples are

- Reiterate a fact: *Who was the first president of the United States?*
- Reiterate a concept: *Define the four types of reliability.*
- Reiterate a principle: *Describe the relationship between air and moisture when the temperature cools.*

The second intellectual operation is **summarization.** This task requires individuals to paraphrase or summarize the general content of information accurately, but not verbatim; irrelevant information that originally was embedded in the presentation of material can be excluded as long as the essential information is present. Again, it is possible to summarize all three content types. Examples are

- Summarize a fact: *Relate the events leading up to the Bay of Pigs invasion.*
- Summarize a concept: *Describe the characteristics of children with learning disabilities* (a concept representing a constellation of attributes).

- Summarize a principle: *Describe the law of gravity* (reflecting an if-then or cause-effect relationship).

The third task dimension is **illustration,** in which examinees are required to recognize or provide a previously unseen or unused example of either a concept or principle. It is not possible to illustrate a fact.

- Illustrate a concept: *Give an example of a haiku poem.*
- Illustrate a principle: *Describe the effects from a particular schedule of reinforcement, given a definition of all four major types.*

Prediction is the fourth type of task. It requires individuals to employ a rule when given a previously unencountered situation and predict either (a) changes in the same situation that will occur later, or (b) changes that will occur in similar situations. Prediction can be used only with concepts and principles, as exemplified below.

- Predict a concept: *Describe the impact of any changes in the definition of learning disabilities from an ability-process deficit to an achievement-only deficit.*
- Predict a principle: *Predict the environmental outcomes resulting from a ban on fluorocarbons in health-care products.*

The fifth type of intellectual operation involves **evaluation,** which utilizes criteria for making a judgment, decision, or selection. It consists of analyzing a problem or situation to determine factors that one should consider in making a judgment or decision and weighing each of these factors. Evaluation is generally employed only with principles because it involves anticipating the consequences of an act and then judging whether those consequences are acceptable, according to some criteria. Evaluation items require four steps. First, we must select the criteria. Second, we must operationalize the criteria. Third, we must make a judgment based on these criteria. Fourth, we must support the judgment with the criteria. An example follows:

- Evaluate a principle: *If we are to upgrade the quality of teachers in the profession, what criteria should we invoke for both training programs and hiring practices within our public schools and institutions?*

Application is the sixth intellectual operation identified by Williams and Haladyna. It is the reverse of prediction; examinees who are given a desired outcome and a description of the initial stage or situation must arrange the conditions necessary to achieve that desired outcome. It involves several of the previous types described earlier: summarization, prediction, and evaluation. Again, only principles can be employed with this application. An example follows:

- Apply a principle: *Given the laws of human behavior as defined by Skinner, create social contingencies that would alleviate or preclude antisocial behaviors from occurring.*

Mid-Chapter Summary

At this point, you have learned four major points about assessment. First, it is a broad concept with specific applications. Second, testing, although limited in definition, is probably the most important component of assessment. Third, although used for many purposes, tests have three major outcomes based on three references. Fourth, we can create either skills or knowledge tests, the latter of which may reflect any of several content foci and intellectual operations. So how can we configure a test to reflect a domain? Eventually, a test must consist of specific content, which we then interpret. This information is less pertinent for norm- and individual-referenced tests; however, any test reflects a domain of content. The remainder of this chapter, defines criterion-referenced testing further.

CRITERION-REFERENCING: DELIMITING THE DOMAIN

Domain definition is a complex process. Should we include only certain problem or item types? Should we use specific chapters or pages in a book? Can we focus on all dimensions of an item, or are some features more relevant than others?

We approach the testing process with two fundamental premises. First, all tests reflect some type of domain sampling, which may be accidental or planned. Second, all testing eventually must be useful for instruction. Given this foundation, we begin the testing process by examining domains, an area most closely linked with criterion-referenced testing. The term *criterion-referenced testing* often is used as a synonym for cut-off scores or passing scores, but it does not require these types of scores (Nitko, 1984). Criterion-referenced testing implies only that a uniformity has been achieved in defining the skill or behavior being sampled. A problem does arise, however, in interpreting mastery decisions that are not based on a criterion-referenced domain: What is being mastered? Thus, you can have a criterion-referenced test without a mastery score, but you cannot have a mastery score without a criterion-referenced test.

Definitions of Domains

Many authors have wrestled with a precise definition of domain. Nitko (1984) interprets it as a score that describes a student's repertoire of specific skills rather than performance relative to peers. Glaser (1963) gives a similar definition that focuses on providing explicit information as to what an individual can or cannot do on a continuum of competence, specifying the content of the behavioral repertoire. Popham (1984) delimits criterion-referenced domains with two qualifications: (a) the items represent a relatively homogeneous collection of instances of a single skill, and (b) the nature of the item has been described sufficiently for us to know precisely what it measures. Glaser and Nitko (1971) define a domain within the context of a criterion-referenced test as follows:

> [It is] deliberately constructed to yield measurements that are directly interpretable into terms of specified performance standards. Performance standards are generally specified by defining a class or a domain of tasks that should be performed by the individual. Measurements are taken on representative samples of tasks drawn from this domain, and such measures are referenced directly to this domain for each individual measure. (p. 653)

All of these definitions emphasize a continuum of competence, and confine interpretation of student performance to a limited criterion for defining the content area tested. The most important concept is that specifying a well-developed domain of tasks, behaviors or knowledge helps to determine which items belong or don't belong to that domain. Importantly, the items included within a domain then allow us to make statements about specific skills and knowledge that students have or lack.

Because all items from a domain do not appear on the test, we infer student performance on the domain. Therefore, we must be careful in specifying a domain: we must know what it means and how to generate it. Two general types of domains are appropriate for criterion-referenced testing; in one, the domain is well-defined and ordered a priori; in the other,

the domain is unordered, with definitions of item inclusion defined broadly and conceptually.

Ordered Domains. When we establish a domain with uniform a priori guidelines that determine what item-types are included and excluded, we consider it **ordered**. Ordering refers to a commonality among the different items that places them along a continuum of achievement. Nitko (1984) describes five types of ordered domains.

The first type of ordering is based on quality or social acceptance; it defines all judgments of performance in terms of social validity. As you will see later, such a focus is an important part of domain definition in the areas of written expression and reading assessment. For example, many tests of handwriting order skills within the domain by the quality of the writing, using specific guidelines for making judgments.

The second ordering can be according to the subject matter, difficulty, or complexity. Bloom and associates' (1956) and Roid and Haladyna's (1982) taxonomies of objectives are examples of this kind of ordering. For example, we can develop a test domain that includes only reiteration of facts, or we can define one more broadly and include all three content formats (facts, concepts, and principals) and all six tasks or intellectual operations (reiteration, summarization, illustration, prediction, evaluation, and application). This domain may be ordered with respect to different information in many different subject areas (i.e. history, geography, etc.).

The third type of ordered domain is based on the degree of proficiency. The tests in this type of domain are referenced along a scale from *low* or *novice proficiency* to *high* or *expert proficiency*. Many tests used in vocational classes, such as typing and computer data entry are based on this definition. The domain is not defined so much in terms of quality or comprehension of information, but in terms of fluency on specific skills. Many curriculum-based measures utilize fluency to define a domain. Using reading fluency or proficiency to place students into instructional groups is one example of this domain definition.

The fourth kind of ordering is based on developmental sequences. The tasks in this domain type are hierarchically ordered, so that mastery of earlier items is a prerequisite for subsequent mastery of later items. Many curricula are founded upon a developmental sequence. Mathematics is an example of a hierarchically arranged domain, in which mastery of addition and subtraction is necessary before instruction in multiplication can proceed; likewise, students must master subtraction and multiplication before they can learn division.

The fifth ordering is founded upon latent traits. This domain contains a wide range of behavioral responses used as indicators of a larger dimension or factor that is considered an inferred trait. Very little achievement testing is premised on this type of domain. The variety of tests used to identify talented and gifted students represents this domain. Tests given to these students often present an amalgam of specific tasks, requiring a wide range of behaviors that are unrelated except for their hypothesized connection to the construct of talent and giftedness.

Unordered Domains. Not all domains and learning outcomes can be ordered a priori on a continuum of achievement; a domain may have well-defined content and still be unordered. In **unordered** domains; problem-types of varying content and difficulty/discrimination are included within the same test, but they are criterion-referenced: Learning is not sequentially ordered. Following are four examples of well-defined but unordered domains.

The first type makes use of the stimulus properties of items to specify a codified and well-developed domain, using the surface features of the items that are thought to influence performance. An example is a spelling test in which words are selected according to phoneme-grapheme correspondences or structural characteristics. Such features become particularly important if the test represents but a small sample of items from the entire domain. To make generalizations about performance based on a limited sample requires that the items be representative.

The second type of unordered domain focuses on both the stimulus and responses required within the test; behavioral objectives that focus on form, content, and level of difficulty can be examples of such a domain specification. The following situation is a specific example of such criterion-referencing: After reading a series of short fictional stories, students respond to questions that involve a sequence of events by selecting the correct answer from an array of five alternatives. In this domain, the content may be different from story to story, but the essential characteristic of the test remains the same (i.e., making judgments about sequences of events).

The third type focuses on diagnostic categories; we define the domain relative to student performance. This system assumes that prior information has been collected regarding students' performance, either through a survey-level assessment or through observations of work samples. For example, students may take a survey-level spelling or math test comprising many different item types. A spelling test may include a wide array of words, representing many different phoneme-grapheme relationships. In math, a survey test may include several different operations or problem-types within operations. We then analyze students' performance on these tests to identify consistent error patterns, reflecting entry-level behaviors or algorithmic misrules. These error types are then sampled more thoroughly to establish follow-up, specific-level assessments based on a domain. This system is at the heart of the curriculum-based evaluation described by Howell and Morehead (1987).

The fourth type of unordered domain focuses on behavior that delimits an abstraction, trait, or construct used to determine whether items are within or outside of the domain. Reading comprehension is a good example of such a domain because several asymmetrical demarcations define which items are included and which are excluded. Terms such as *literal, inferential, evaluative,* and *analytical comprehension* are used to define whether an item is within a reading comprehension domain. Since the abstraction has wide meaning, it is possible to sample a very unordered group of items with this system.

In summary, what started out as a simple idea has become quite complex through close analysis. But it is also the center of all testing.

Without reference to the content that comprises the domain from which items are sampled, all interpretations of performance are without substance. Yes, we can state that Johnnie has improved on the norm-referenced test and is now just below the middle of the group, or say with certainty that Sally has mastered the major units. Statements about improvement relative to previous levels can be made for Jim, and we can feel assured that the program is effective. But lacking in all of these interpretive statements is any notion about the content within which students have improved. Eventually, we must always consider this content in the statements we make. Table 2.1 presents a summary of ordered and unordered domains.

The central problem in defining domains is to find a point at which specification is detailed sufficiently. For example, one could demarcate a math computation domain as comprising math subtraction facts, which may be too im-

TABLE 2.1
A scheme for classifying and distinguishing criterion-referenced tests

Well-Defined and Ordered Domains	Well-Defined But Unordered Domains	Ill-Defined Domains	Undefined Domains
Ordering based on judgments of the social or aesthetic quality of an examinee's product or performance.	Specifying the stimulus properties of the items to be included in the domain.	Poorly articulated behavioral objectives.	No attempt to define the domain to which test performance is referenced.
Ordering based on the level of difficulty or complexity at which a topic or subject is learned.	Specifying the stimuli and the responses in the domain.	Defining the domain only in terms of the particular items on the test.	Using a cut-off score, but not defining a performance domain.
Ordering based on degree of proficiency with which a complex skill is performed.	Specifying the diagnostic categories of the domain.		
Ordering based on prerequisite sequences for acquiring an intellectual or psychomotor skill.	Specifying the abstractions, traits, or constructs that define the domain.		

Source: Reprinted with permission from Nitko, Anthony J., "Distinguishing the many varieties of criterion-referenced tests" *Review of Educational Research*, 1980, *50*, 461–85, Table 1 (p. 466). Copyright 1980, by the American Educational Research Association, Washington, D.C.

precise; as comprising math subtraction problems with all combinations of one- and two-digit numbers subtracted from each other, which is more precise; or as a list of very specifically defined problem types:

- One digit minus one digit.
- Two digits minus two digits, no borrowing.
- Two digits minus two digits with borrowing.
- Three digits minus two digits, no borrowing.
- Three digits minus two digits, with borrowing.

The problem is compounded when the test involves knowledge rather than skills. Reviewing a series of specification strategies, Popham (1984) notes that behavioral objectives are typically too broad to provide adequate direction in constructing tests; however, the item forms developed by Hively, Maxwell, Rabehl, Sension, and Lundin (1973) are far too specific and generate too many item forms. Popham's original compromise was to develop an *amplified objective,* which was more elaborate than the behavioral objectives, but broader than the forms of Hively et al. Eventually, Popham (1978) employed a *limited focus* strategy to create a number of test descriptions small enough so that item writers would attend to them but still containing enough detail to foster precise communication.

Example of a Domain-Defined Test Item

Four steps are embedded in the item-planning process. First, the evaluator provides a one- or two-sentence general description of what the test measures. Occasionally, we refer to this as the *objective,* but *general description* is more defensible. It is not meant to serve as a specific map of the domain or behavior sampled on the test, but as an overview of what will be described later in the full specifications. The second step in planning test specifications is to generate a sample item, including directions to the student, that test reviewers can use to get a very clear description of what the test measures. It also provides format cues for those who generate the test. The third step is to describe the stimulus materials from which items are to be sampled. Finally, as a fourth step, a complete test specification provides a description of the response attributes, specifying either a selection or a production response discussed in the next chapter). With a selection response, rules must be included not only for determining the nature of the correct response but also the nature of the incorrect options. For example, the specifications should include guidelines for determining the correct answer and what the various classes of wrong answers represent. Even more problematic are definitions of response attributes for production responses. Here, the specifications must provide criteria that allow the person scoring the response to make reliable judgments.

General Description.   The following item focuses on one element within reading comprehension: establishing a sequence of events based on information presented in the story.

Sample Item.   The following is an example of a sample item.

After reading the story on nuclear winters, describe the sequence of events. Place the following items in the correct order by numbering each statement as it would occur after a nuclear holocaust:

_____ **A.** The food supply will quickly be depleted and not replenished.

_____ **B.** Humans will have to establish new forms of communication.

_____ **C.** Scientists will have to reestablish new strains of crops.

_____ **D.** The darkness covering the earth will force temperatures down.

Description of Stimulus Materials. Fifteen sequence-of-events questions will be asked following the 1000-word expository passage on "Problems Confronting the World Today."

The questions will vary in the response they require, with half requiring selection responses, and the other half requiring production responses. All items will be developed with events sampled directly from the text, but listed in a different order. Correctness will be determined by matching the events outlined in the passage to those identified by the student.

CHAPTER SUMMARY

This chapter began with a broad definition of assessment, but quickly focused on one aspect, testing. In the process, we considered two issues: the standardization of procedures and the level of interpretation or inference. We considered four purposes of testing and focused on three specific outcomes: screening/placing, planning instruction, and evaluating outcomes. Each has a specific reference. The chapter covered specific testing of skills or knowledge, with primary consideration given to the latter. It presented three types of content formats and six types of intellectual operation using selection or production responses. Finally, we considered ordered and unordered domains.

For too long, assessment and instruction have been conducted independently, with the result that the test information collected has not been useful to the instructional activities of the teacher. Such information is superfluous (Thurlow & Ysseldyke, 1982). The approach to measurement planning that this chapter presents defines the process through a series of deliberate steps. Whether a decision is related to adoption or construction of a test, the issues remain the same. First, assessment must be carefully planned and must therefore involve the systematic collection of data. In addition to observations and judgments, assessments will include some measures of student performance, a quantified index of performance. However, this information must be consistent with the purpose for testing and the type of decision to be made. Any test, for any purpose, must sample from either a skills or a knowledge domain. While the academic area defines content and format of the former test type, knowledge tests can employ a framework that cuts across academic areas, by considering content formats or intellectual operations to sample behavior. In viewing tests, whether norm-, criterion-, or individual-referenced, we must consider the concept of a domain. All tests represent a limited sample of behavior, from which we make inferences to (a) larger contexts, (b) generalized situations, or (c) another time, following instruction. Just as the introduction of the Macintosh transformed the computer industry with the notion of WYSIWYG (What You See Is What You Get), test planners should transform the practice of assessment and demand no less.

CHAPTER 3

Constructing Tests of Knowledge

F orget about education for a minute and pretend you work in the construction industry. You own a company that builds houses. Two clients, Mr. and Mrs. Richbags have contacted you about building their dream home. They know exactly what kind of house they want and how it should look. It is a Victorian house, with four bedrooms, two baths, a living room, family room, dining room, and walkout basement. They even know how big the rooms should be, what the windows should look like, and what kind of flooring should be laid in each room. Yet more specific information is needed to actually construct the house. How much concrete should be prepared? Where should it be poured? How much lumber needs to be ordered? Of what dimensions? How should the house be framed to accommodate windows and doors? A host of very specific planning tasks must be completed before and throughout the actual construction process in order for their home to be completed. Obviously, you can't just start laying foundations, cutting boards, and putting up walls. Instead, you must ask for the blueprints, which have been developed by an architect. In the construction industry, the roles of design and construction are separate. In the testing industry, they are usually the same: The person who designs a test also constructs it. However, the procedures and tactics for each role are different.

Just as contractors work from blueprints, you must have a blueprint to guide the development of tests and provide specific directions on (a) what items to include, (b) how to format them, and (c) how to arrange them within the test. Your task in this chapter is to move from planning tests to their actual construction. Using a blueprint to frame your ideas into a useful test helps you to make decisions.

This chapter describes strategies for moving from a measurement plan to a test. As mentioned in the previous chapter, tests can focus on skills or knowledge. Because skills are con- tent-specific, we have not included them here; they appear in the chapters on basic content areas (chapters 7–12). But knowledge tests can employ the same formats regardless of content, so we have organized this chapter around the process of test construction.

CHAPTER OBJECTIVES

After you have read and studied this material, and practiced making tests using some of the strategies described in the chapter, you should have the skills and knowledge to

- Adopt or construct a test to reflect a domain.
- Create or adopt a test that maps items according to the intellectual operations outlined previously.
- Create or adopt a test with a variety of response types, including three production responses and three selection responses.
- Format and structure items within tests.
- Develop or modify a scoring system for each type of response.

KEY VOCABULARY

This chapter presents many terms that may be unfamiliar to you. Test construction is a *decision-making system,* which specifies the decisions to make and the choices available. One of the first steps in actually constructing tests within this system, assuming you have specified a domain, is to transform instructional content into test items. Central to this step is the idea of a *thought unit,* another term for a concept that has been presented in either the material or instruction and for which you want to develop a test item. Thought units are first identified, then condensed, and finally related to specific intellectual operations (reiteration, summarization, illustration, prediction, evaluation, and applications) using one of three content formats (facts, concepts, and principals). Almost concurrent with the development of an item is consideration of the *response type,* which reflects the test-taker's behavior. Only two response-types are available: (a) Examinees they can *select* the answer from an array of alternatives, or (b) they can *produce* it. Although knowledge tests can utilize either response, all skills tests must employ production responses. The more specific varieties of each response probably will be obvious because you most likely have taken many tests that use them

(e.g., one word fill-in-the-blank, multiple-choice, matching). The next topic in this chapter is a discussion of strategies and options for structuring both items and tests. Finally, two types of scoring systems are presented using *objective* criteria, in which correctness can be externally verified, or *subjective* criteria, in which correctness cannot be verified externally. Study the flowchart in Figure 3.1, which depicts these steps.

After preparing for knowledge tests, framing and constructing of the test items must occur.

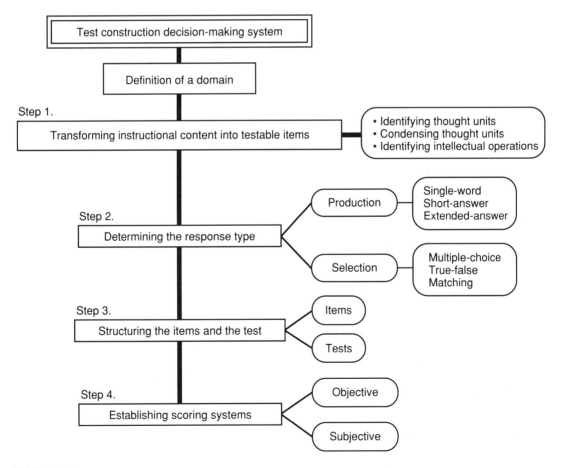

FIGURE 3.1
Steps in the construction of knowledge tests

At this point, we must determine the **response type** and structure the test items, as well as establish a scoring system. Each item should reflect a specific response needed to answer it correctly, employing either (a) production responses, for which examinees **produce** answers or (b) selection responses, for which examinees **select** answers from among several alternatives. The type of response should match the content of assessment and the type of decision to be made. Determining the correct response type will then format the test item or stimulus automatically. Following is a description of each of the major steps.

STEP 1: TRANSFORMING INSTRUCTIONAL CONTENT INTO TESTABLE ITEMS

To make the measurement plan operational as a test, guidelines are necessary for transforming instructional content into appropriate test items for either of the two response types. Unless we follow systematic procedures for constructing test items, it is likely that recall of factual information will result. Only through a very deliberate strategy will higher order intellectual operations or cognitive categories be represented on a test. By providing an algorithm for item writing, it is possible to make test developers more aware of both the various types of content formats and alternative intellectual operations and enable them to create precise and diverse items on tests (Williams & Haladyna, 1982). The following steps, although described in sequence, most often occur simultaneously in translating instructional content into test items. These steps are adapted from Williams and Haladyna, who originally employed them in the construction of multiple-choice tests. The same procedures are important, however, in the development of production responses and other types of selection responses.

We can accomplish the process of translating instructional content into testable items by: (a) identifying instructional content and thought units that are to be tested, (b) condensing these thought units into test items, and (c) identifying which intellectual operation should be addressed.

Identifying Thought Units

The first step involves selecting the information to be tested through the identification of **thought units,** which can be defined as segments of material to be learned that are organized around singular themes, concepts, or focal ideas (Williams & Haladyna, 1982). We usually employ this step whether or not we use a systematic procedure. Information, including the materials, organization, and content, must be reviewed with attention to subheadings and topic sentences, as well as any diagrams or supplemental materials, and we must also consider key facts, concepts, and principles.

Thought units are not limited to one or two sentences; they may be expressed in several sentences or even a paragraph. Furthermore, within a paragraph, sentences may be more or less important in expressing the essential thought unit. The important point is to identify information as vital because of its application in some relevant environment (classroom, natural world, social context, etc.). Following is an example of a thought unit.

> The noted limitations notwithstanding, the results of this study indicate that there is a statistically significant difference in student achievement when comparing the placement of handicapped pupils in regular education to service within special education. Pupils who had been instructed approximately 10 weeks in regular education almost doubled their reading progress when taught in resource rooms for an approximately equal period. The time series analysis of these data indicates that special education, in the form of daily reading instruction

in the resource room, was indeed a more effective intervention for 10 of 11 mildly handicapped children than service in regular education. (Marston, 1987b, p. 22)

This paragraph can be considered a thought unit that contains one major theme: Reading improvement was significantly greater in special education than in regular education with students who had been referred and eventually placed in special education.

In considering which information to test, teachers should address content formats. As described in chapter 2, all material can be classified as fact, concept, or principle. As you will see in Step 3, not all content can be formatted into all six intellectual operations. Therefore, when we have identified relevant information, we should preview the available intellectual operations. Content based on principles can utilize any of the six tasks or intellectual operations; concepts can also be based on these six content formats. Facts can employ only reiteration and summarization, the two lowest levels of

the hierarchy (Williams & Haladyna, 1982). Figure 3.2 charts the interactions between intellectual operations and content formats.

Condensing Thought Units

The second step involves translating the thought unit into a focal idea by summarizing or condensing it. The focal idea should be a brief statement that summarizes the important information in the thought unit (Williams & Haladyna, 1982). Occasionally, the focal idea and the thought unit may be very similar; however, the focal idea may be drastically different from any explicit statement within the text. This kernel idea may be elaborated upon, but it represents a core or simplified idea that has been expressed in a variety of ways. For example, a statement of fact may include a range of associated information, a concept may include a host of defining attributes, and principles may include conditional issues that must be present for something to happen. Nevertheless, we

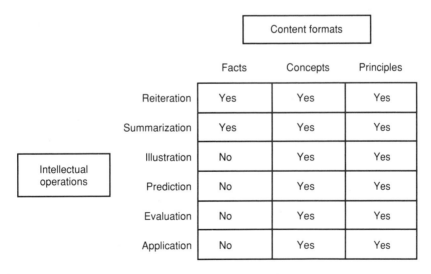

| | Content formats | | |
	Facts	Concepts	Principles
Reiteration	Yes	Yes	Yes
Summarization	Yes	Yes	Yes
Illustration	No	Yes	Yes
Prediction	No	Yes	Yes
Evaluation	No	Yes	Yes
Application	No	Yes	Yes

Intellectual operations

FIGURE 3.2
Applicable interactions between intellectual operations and content

must sort all of the embedded information and identify just the key facts, concepts, or principles.

There is no firm rule for condensing information; it may come from one paragraph or from several pages. The choice is likely a function of subject matter or the manner in which material is written and/or taught. Because most units of instruction contain a wide variety of key ideas, it is important for the item writer to focus on those that are critical in either the instructional environment or inherently important in the natural environment.

The following is an example of a focal idea taken from the thought unit previously given as an example: For students eventually served in special education, program effectiveness can be ascertained by comparing their prior performance in regular education to their current performance in special education.

Identifying Intellectual Operations

The third step is to determine the intellectual operation to be measured. Depending upon the particular thought unit and/or focal idea, some tasks or operations may be more or less amenable to assessment than others. For example, summarization may be the important intellectual operation for material involving facts. However, in assessing learning of principles, application or prediction may be more relevant.

It is possible to translate a thought unit or a focal idea into more than one level of operation. For example, examinees may be required to reiterate or summarize a principle. In contrast, they could be required to illustrate a previously unused example or predict an outcome, given certain situations. Finally, the two highest levels of intellectual operation may require examinees to actually evaluate both the criteria and the outcome, given a certain situation, or to apply certain criteria in solving a problem. All of these tasks may focus on the same content material. The important issue in identifying an

appropriate task or intellectual operation is that the content be well fitted to its use (Gronlund, 1988). For example, if a measurement course emphasizes validity, summarizing the concept may be less important than applying it when judging a test's worth. The important distinction in these different content categories comes from this third step, which is to identify the intellectual process for organizing the content.

As you will see, each task or operation comes with its own wording for conveying the category: To ensure that the test item focuses on reiteration, examinees should be directed to "restate exactly," "repeat the statement," and so forth. In contrast, when the test item requires summarization that is not verbatim from the text or material, the directive may be to "summarize the results," "review the categories," "present the positions," or "describe or explain the material." Illustration uses such phrases as "give an example," or "illustrate the point." Prediction items employ directives like "predict the outcome," "anticipate the results," or "forecast the consequences." Evaluation items include phrasing such as "consider the criteria," "evaluate the positions," and "interpret the criteria needed." Finally, application items may be written with phrases like "establish the conditions," "vindicate the perspective," or "justify the outcome."

To provide the range of options for all three types of content (facts, concepts, and principles) and all six intellectual operations, the next section includes specific definitions and examples. Remember that a fact is basic; it cannot be further reduced to a simpler form; and it is an association between a word and a single exemplar. A concept reflects attributes with something in common with each other; multiple exemplars are therefore associated with concepts. A principle presents an if-then or cause-effect relationship and includes a dimension of time or space. Although we cover the two response types later in this chapter, you should note at this time that both production- and a selection-response items are presented for each content task below.

Reiteration. The task of reiteration is limited to verbatim accounts of material that was taught or read. In reiteration items, examinees should receive sufficient information and then be told to specifically name the date, name, person, place, and so forth. Following are examples of reiteration items for facts, concepts, and principles.

The first test to be employed in making massive policy decisions was the _____(reiterating a fact).

List each type of interpretive test reference and describe their essential features (reiterating a concept).

It is necessary but not sufficient for a test to be _____(reiterating a principle).

Following is an example of a selection response for reiteration of a fact.

The term *standardized* means that the test has been
a. normed on a standard group of students.
b. published in a standard language.
c. administered and scored in a standard fashion.
d. released at standard intervals.

Following is an example of a selection-response for reiteration of a concept. The information is not a basic fact because some disagreement exists about the actual number of producible sounds and therefore the definition of a sound. Assuming that the information was taught exactly as it was presented in the test item, it should be considered as reiteration.

How many sounds can be produced in the English language?
a. 31
b. 44
c. 17
d. 71

Following is an example of reiteration of a principle. Reiteration assumes that the information in the test item is exactly as presented during instruction; an if-then condition with a focus on a principle.

When air temperature decreases, airborne water molecules
a. multiply.
b. evaporate.
c. breakdown.
d. condense.

Summarization. In contrast to reiteration, summarization requires examinees to paraphrase or summarize the information, not to report the original information. They include only relevant material. Following are examples of summarization of a concept.

List the major findings on effective teaching as reported by Brophy and Good's (1986) review in the *Third Handbook of Research on Teaching* (summarizing facts).

Summarize the major components of the University of Oregon variety of Direct Instruction (summarizing a concept).

What is meant by the following phrase: Reliability is a function of the number of items in the test? (summarizing a principle).

While the above items require examinees to produce answers, the items below require them only to select the correct answer from an array of alternatives. In the first item, a fact is summarized. As a basic unit of information with a single exemplar, it cannot be further reduced. As summarization, it is assumed that the information in the item does not represent verbatim repetition as presented during instruction. Following is an example of summarization, using a selection response.

> In chapter 2, assessment and testing are synonymous terms and comprise essentially the same types of activities.
> T F (summarizing a fact)

The item below also reflects summarization of a concept. Notice that the concept is criterion-referenced testing and its essential features. Assuming that the information is not exactly as presented during instruction, the item asks for summarization, not reiteration.

> What are the essential feature(s) of criterion-referenced tests?
> a. A universe of items is established.
> b. Rules for selecting items are present.
> c. Criteria exist for determining success.
> d. All of the above.

Assuming the information presented during instruction was not as it appears in the test item, it represents summarization. Also the presentation of an if-then format indicates that a principle is involved. Below is an item reflecting summarization of a principle.

> Airplanes can fly because of the differential air pressure over the wings versus under the wings, creating a vacuum on top and allowing the plane to become airborne.
> T   F (summarizing a principle)

Illustration.   An illustration item provides examinees with an unused example of a concept or a principle and requires them to name it; or, given a certain name, they are asked to construct a new example. There are two content formats for which illustration applies: One focuses on concepts and the other on principles. Following are examples of illustration.

> List the major descriptors of learning disabilities and give examples of their operationalization (illustrating a concept).

> Illustrate the Premack Principle, by giving an example of its implementation in an elementary school (illustrating a principle).

Selection responses also are available for illustration items, although they may not be the best for this intellectual operation. Educational decision making of various types is considered a concept because of its concern with definitional boundaries and multiple exemplars; the item below exemplifies illustration because it asks for a previously unused example. Following is an example of an illustrated concept.

> Giving the Raven's Progressive Matrix to determine the presence/absence of learning disabilities is an example of what type of educational decision?
> a. Screening.
> b. Placement.
> c. Program planning.
> d. Program evaluation.

The item below is an illustration of a principle that underlies behavioral theory. As a previously unused example, it is assumed that the specific information during instruction was not like that presented in the item. Because it is a principle, a cause-effect statement is present.

> When a behavior is reinforced in the presence of a given stimulus, the probability of that behavior occurring in the presence of that stimulus will be increased. Which of the

following is an illustration of this principle (establishment of a discriminative stimulus)?
a. Stopping for red lights.
b. Praising for work completion.
c. Scolding for noncompliance.
d. Getting paid tokens.

Prediction. Prediction items present examinees with a new situation that contains some antecedent conditions that normally lead to a consequence or outcome and requires them to employ a rule or principle to anticipate this outcome. Examinees are given a situation and asked to describe the likely outcome, or if they are to choose among different outcomes, they are asked to identify the appropriate rule or generalization. As mentioned earlier, prediction items focus on if-then kinds of relationships or antecedent-consequence conditions. Often, information based on predictions can be stated in the form of rules, with statements of relationship between or among objects, properties, or events. The stem in a prediction item describes a situation by indicating the presence or absence of an antecedent condition and directs the student to actually select the correct consequence. In writing a prediction item, it is critical that the focal idea or content base for the item describe a relationship between events, but it need not be bound by time or cast only in the future: We could predict across various dimensions, including space, distance, and the past. The item stem may include a fair amount of information, some of which is more or less relevant for solving or predicting the consequence. In writing the *foils* (those items that serve as distractors) and the answer, the important issue is to ensure that the student can answer the multiple-choice item correctly only through the cognitive process of prediction, not simply by recall. Like illustration, prediction can be completed only for information that is represented as a concept or a principle.

What would happen to special education training/certification programs if PL 94–142 were revoked? (predicting a concept).

If a study on effective teaching utilizes an inadequate outcome measure of student performance, what are the implications? (predicting a principle).

Again, selection responses could be employed, but they become increasingly less appropriate for higher intellectual operations. The following item represents prediction of a principle using a selection response. Given certain information, examinees must predict the consequences (in this case an if-then relationship).

If my test is not reliable, what will happen to estimates of performance? Scores will be
a. inflated.
b. deflated.
c. variable.
d. rounded.

Another example of an if-then relationship is displayed below. Again, examinees are required to predict the consequences.

If I use a norm-referenced test but do not attend to the composition of the norm group, my interpretation of relative performance is
a. wrong.
b. suspect.
c. correct.
d. unstable.

Answers and/or foils for multiple-choice prediction items can be of two types: They can require a prediction, or they can require a prediction plus recognition of the grounds for that prediction. Obviously, the first type is slightly simpler. If the item employs a selection response, scoring issues are related to generation of the foils. With both systems, it is important that the answer be *clearly* correct.

Evaluation.   An evaluation item requires examinees to analyze a situation, choose an appropriate criterion, and make a decision; essentially, we are concerned with employing a criterion or criteria to make a judgment, decision, or selection. There are five specific issues to be considered in writing effective evaluation items. First, we must determine whether the evaluation is to be based on an absolute standard or on a normative standard. Second, evaluation need not be bound to the present, but can include historical eras, both past and future. Third, evaluation may require examinees to select the most appropriate criterion or to employ a criterion that is given, with three possible strategies: (a) to select the correct evaluation, when given a criterion, (b) to select the most appropriate criterion, given a certain evaluation, or (c) to select the criterion and make the evaluation. Fourth, the criterion can include many dimensions of quality, performance, quantity, efficiency, and so forth. In a related manner, the criterion can be expressed with more or less clarity. Finally, in writing the item stem, the focal idea need not be rewritten. Rather, it should provide instruction on the use of some criterion or describe a situation to be evaluated. The only important issue in writing the item stem is to determine whether you want the student to provide the criterion or to select the criterion and make the evaluation (Williams & Haladyna, 1982). Generally, selection responses for evaluation items, though possible to construct, are not frequently used. Following is an example of an evaluation item.

> If you could develop an optimal educational delivery system for high school students, evaluate the components of this system, the empirical support for their selection, and the likely outcomes (evaluating a principle).

Application.   In an application item, examinees receive a description and a desired outcome and are told to describe or demonstrate what would have to be present to produce that desired outcome. Application items incorporate four important steps, including the ability to (a) sense the problem, (b) define the problem in such a way as to solve it, (c) select some method suitable for solving it, and (d) evaluate alternative solutions and implement the most appropriate one. In this sense, application is the reverse of prediction. As in evaluation, selection responses generally are not appropriate for application levels of knowledge. Following is an example of an application item.

> To create an effective classificatory label, the descriptors of the classification system must be exhaustive and exclusive. Given the current definitions of learning disabilities, summarize what is necessary to make it a legitimate label (applying a principle).

Mid-Chapter Summary

The preceding examples match three content formats with six intellectual operations. In some cases, this match was inappropriate: Facts were appropriate only for the two lowest intellectual operations; concepts and principles were appropriate for all six tasks or operations. Furthermore, the last two types of operations, evaluation and application, typically employ production responses rather than selection responses.

STEP 2: DETERMINING THE RESPONSE TYPE

The item stem must be written once the instructional content has been translated into a testable item in which: (a) important content information or thought units were identified, (b) this information was condensed and

(c) intellectual operations and content formats were selected for assessing student's knowledge. At this time, we must choose whether to employ a production or selection response. Actually, this step is often part of the decision that identifies the intellectual operation, since the two issues are so interrelated.

Items can utilize either production or selection responses. The previous examples employed both production and selection responses. As the summary of that section states, production or selection responses may be more appropriate for specific intellectual operations.

Production Responses

Production responses require students to produce their own answers. They have complete freedom to produce their answers and organize their thoughts and ideas with their own words. Three types of production responses are available: (a) simple, one-word completion of a statement, (b) short-answer completion (one to several sentences), or (c) extended-answer or essay responses.

Although production tasks allow for a great deal of flexibility in generating items, some guidelines are necessary. The most important consideration is to match the content with the level of intellectual operation in order to employ an appropriate response. The distinctions among the three types of responses listed below are important only in relation to the level of intellectual operation deemed appropriate. A single-word, completion-type item generally is probably not appropriate for higher levels of knowledge, whereas short- or extended-answer items could be used for higher order intellectual operations.

Single-word Items. Single-word items employ a fill-in-the-blank format referred to as *cloze* in chapter 7. One word in a sentence is presented with a standard-length blank, and the student is directed to provide the word that most accurately completes the sentence. In the construction of such test items, the missing word should be located near the end of the sentence and should be a significant word or concept. Furthermore, word-completion items should not contain so many blank spaces or deleted words that the meaning of the sentence is lost.

The advantages of such test formats are ease of construction, objectivity in scoring, and increase in the number of items presented. Because students can respond quickly and easily, more items can be included on a test.

One disadvantage of such a test format is the limited focus on factual and verbatim knowledge; assessment of higher intellectual operations is not likely with this item type. Also, some problems may develop from lack of interpretability of the statement given the deletion of specific words.

Short-answer Items. Short-answer items employ answers that range from a phrase or sentence to a short paragraph. The stem is divided into two parts: The first establishes the content area and knowledge to be addressed, and the second directs the format and structure of the response. Strategies for constructing short-answer items are a bit more difficult to follow than for single-word items. The overriding guidelines for structuring short-answer items are to use statements that set the occasion for only one clear, correct answer and to identify the degree of precision needed to answer them.

Short-answer test items have four advantages: (a) They can assess higher levels of knowledge or intellectual operations than single-word items, (b) scoring of responses is easier and likely to be completed with more consistency than for extended answers, (c) they can be completed in enough time to include several items of this type, and (d) their production format allows a range of variation that probably provides a more accurate reflection of student differences in learning.

The disadvantages of this item type arise mainly from two major difficulties in scoring them. It is difficult to write good, short-answer items that delimit the question enough to avoid confusing the student. It also is difficult to create clear and objective scoring systems. As you will see in the later chapters on technical adequacy, the former problem is a validity issue and the latter problem is related to reliability. Both call into question the results of the test.

Extended-answer Items. Such item types are frequently used in content areas to assess higher levels of knowledge or intellectual operations. Like short-answer items, they contain two parts: (a) a brief description of an issue, position, problem, or event, and (b) a directive for the student to respond in some manner. Occasionally, items using an extended answer include supplementary information about its value on the total test. Such information is helpful, and probably essential, in furthering test-taking strategies, particularly in structuring examinees' attention to individual items.

With extended-answer items, *enough* information must be embedded in the question to inform examinees of the specific area of knowledge or content being tested and to show them how to frame their answer. The first part of the item should provide both background context and specific information that is being addressed. The second part, should tell students how to structure their responses; it should contain a specific, active verb. For example, *discuss, review, highlight, present,* and *address* are weak, nonspecific, and nondirective. *Compare, contrast, place in chronology,* and *criticize* are more specific; they both specify the information that should be presented and say how it should be formatted.

Extended-answer responses have several advantages. First, they require students to produce their own answers, rather then recognize a correct answer. This eliminates blind guessing, and it prevents students from taking advantage of other clues embedded in the test. Often, teachers think this format provides a more valid assessment of student's knowledge; however, as explained in chapter 6, this is a weak argument. A second advantage to extended-answer responses is that they are most appropriate for assessing complex intellectual operations, synthesizing, organizing, and sequencing large amounts of diverse information. Such items, however, are much less useful for reiterating or summarizing factual information. The third advantage is that they take very little time to construct and often require much less paper, making them easier to produce.

These advantages, however, must be considered in light of several limitations, because essay tests allow students to produce their own answers and usually include only a few items. First, scoring can be difficult and unreliable. This is probably the most serious disadvantage: Without reliability, there can be no validity. Unreliability results from comparing one judge's score with another's or comparing one scorer's judgments at one time with that scorer's judgments at another time. Second, a great deal of scoring time may be needed to get the job done correctly. Although preparation time is minimal, the time required to score performance adequately may outweigh the time saved in preparing the test. Sometimes this disadvantage can be avoided by limiting or directing the type of responses required or by providing a clear and objective scoring key for grading the papers. Finally, essay tests assess only a relatively small range of behavior to determine a student's knowledge. For example, the amount of time expended in writing may be less than that spent thinking about or formulating answers. Potential problems with reliability appear because there are fewer items to score. Generally, reliability can be improved by increasing the number of items on a test.

Selection Responses

Selection responses require students to select the correct answer; therefore, they provide complete information about the question, directives, and all options for answering. Three types of selection responses are available: (a) multiple-choice, (b) true-false, and (c) matching. The second and third types can be considered specific varieties of the first. Descriptions of each type follow, with consideration given to construction and formatting.

Multiple-choice. The most popular item type to appear in modern testing is the multiple-choice format. It predominates in nearly all forms of testing, from published norm-referenced to curriculum-embedded achievement tests. It is relatively easy to construct, flexible, adaptable to all types and levels of knowledge, capable of generating many items, easy to score, and it has the potential of generating reliable results. With multiple-choice, the difficulty of test items is easy to manipulate, and because many items can be constructed, they provide complete coverage of information.

H. G. Miller, Williams, and Haladyna (1978) define a multiple-choice test as

> an objective device for obtaining information about how much knowledge students have acquired. The term *objective* in this context means that the correctness of any possible answer is determined before the test is given and its scoring error is minimized. By *knowledge,* we are saying that most school achievement is essentially intellectual (cognitive) in nature. The multiple-choice item generally consists of two

parts: The item stem and several options (possible answers), one of which is the answer and the rest of which are foils (sometimes called *distractors*) (p. 4).

An example of such an item appears in the previous material.

The more broadly used form of the multiple-choice item provides a stem with a range of four or five options listed beneath, only one of which is correct. This item type has been used for measuring knowledge domains, ranging from factual recall to most higher-order levels of knowledge or intellectual operations. The most difficult problem in writing multiple-choice items is creating effective options among which to include the correct answer. The task is to write foils that attract examinees who don't understand the content or who don't know how to use the material appropriately; however, the foils must not fool those students who know the content or who can use the material appropriately. Foils should be plausible responses for students whose mastery of the content is incomplete, but they should not trick knowledgeable students into incorrect responses.

A number of strategies are useful in creating effective foils. One of the best tactics is to anticipate the kinds of misunderstandings or errors that examinees will make. Then, each foil can serve as an example of that error type. Another strategy for creating foils is to create a production-response, short-answer test first, administer it to a group of students, and use their answers to develop foils. Foils may also come from the material that is discarded within the condensation step. Finally, we can create foils by using key nouns or phrases that appear in the text.

In all of these strategies, not only must we identify certain information to include in the foils, but we must also format it to be either correct or incorrect in the form of foils. Again, several strategies are available. One technique is to use technical language in an incorrect manner. A sensible but trivial answer can also be included as a foil. Alternatively, a foil can be a correct answer to a different question or a response that doesn't answer truly or completely, but is straight from the text. An effective foil may be partially correct but exclude some components that make a different response more correct.

Many strategies are available for writing effective multiple-choice questions that measure knowledge beyond the factual level. Each of the different intellectual operations beyond factual content may require separate techniques, but certain strategies apply to all multiple-choice items regardless of the intellectual level (Gronlund, 1988).

1. Use a direct question or an incomplete statement as the item stem; however, no fast rule dictates which format is more appropriate. The direct question usually is easier to write. Nevertheless, an incomplete statement can offer a clearer and more concise description of the problem.

2. State the problem clearly and completely in a succinct manner. Provide only essential information in the problem.

3. Make the answer clearly correct and the foils clearly incorrect. If necessary, content experts should review the items for clarity and correctness.

4. Most of the wording should appear in the stem. Any word or phrase that otherwise would be repeated should appear within the stem, thereby precluding its repetitious inclusion in the different foils and alternative responses.

5. Avoid negatively stated items, particularly in the true-false format. If a negative statement is included, the negating word or phrase should be *underlined* so that it is very clear to the examinee.

6. Words used in a stem should not provide clues to any of the alternative responses; therefore, the foils should be independent of each other.

7. Avoid grammatical clues in which the use of articles, *the, a,* or *an,* indicate that one of the alternate responses is correct or incorrect (i.e., the answer is a noun or a word beginning with a vowel sound).

8. Avoid responses that overlap. If more than one answer is correct or incorrect, provide clues to the correctness of one of them over the other.

9. Limit the use of *none of the above* as an alternative to those items in which the correct answer is *absolutely* not included. If included, use it early in a test to alert students of its existence, and avoid it thereafter. *None of the above* should never be considered an all-purpose answer.

10. Use *All of the above* very sparingly. Use it only when no differences exist between the various foils in their correctness. *Any of the above* should *not* be used as an alternative response.

11. All responses should be plausible, so that the person who lacks the information will be equally inclined to select any one of the distractors.

12. The serial position of the correct response should vary across the items (spread out over the first, second, third and fourth positions), to avoid differential frequency with any one option (e.g., always the first position).

13. Write the items clearly and concisely with the following general grammatical and syntactical considerations: (a) Use letters rather than numbers to denote alternative responses; (b) place letters for the alternate responses directly beneath the beginning of the item stem; and (c) capitalize each word in the alternative responses; if the responses complete a statement in the

stem, however, the words should not be capitalized. If the stem is an incomplete statement, use a period after each response; otherwise, no period should appear after each response. Numbers used in the alternate responses should be right-justified, increase from lowest to highest, employ the same number of decimal points, and/or contain the unit of measurement (dollars, inches, centimeters).

14. Write the options with parallel construction, following symmetrical/grammatical structure. Use parallel wording to avoid providing examinees with accidental clues for answering the item. If an incomplete sentence is used for the item stem, the options should provide a grammatically complete and correct statement.

15. In addition to the positively stated prescriptions listed above, a few negatively stated proscriptions also should be considered. Avoid the following:

- Foils that are clearly out of line.
- Foils with differential amounts of context clues.
- Determiners like *absolute, always,* and *never.*
- Foils using responses of unequal length.

In summary, multiple-choice items are very popular, primarily because of their great flexibility for assessing very diverse content and intellectual operations. When properly constructed, they can be very helpful in distinguishing what students know about a subject. They can also reflect differences that are useful in any of the three interpretations: Norm- , criterion- , or individual-referenced. Important advantages of this response mode are that an established technology exists for creating multiple-choice items, with considerable empirical support. In contrast to production responses, for which the steps for application (creation, administration, and scoring) are not definitive, multiple-choice items can be established in a cookbook fashion, which enhances reliability. In many of the content areas, validity data have been collected: A considerable amount of research supports the use of multiple-choice items for assessing many basic skills. Even an individual teacher or tester can complete item analyses to ascertain the functional effect of an item or a foil.

These advantages are accompanied by several problems, however. The biggest problem is the labor (time, effort, and money) required to construct multiple-choice items. An evaluator must consider many issues if the items are to be correctly formatted. Related to their construction is the issue of correctness. Although seemingly objective in its assessment of knowledge, any multiple-choice item must have a defensible rationale accompanying the foils. Seldom is this information included with tests. The second major disadvantage results from the use of a selection response. When students answer an item incorrectly, it is not possible to know why: They may not have known the information, or they may have been tripped by a foil that represented a trick option. It is also possible that they didn't try and guessed incorrectly. Furthermore, it only shows what they don't know. They may be operating from totally faulty algorithms or only partially incorrect ones; that is, they might not have been close to the correct answer, or they might have just missed choosing the correct answer, but we cannot tell the difference.

True-False. The true-false format, which has been very popular for many achievement tests, is actually a specific form of a multiple-choice item that contains only one distractor. True-false items are particularly appropriate for factual recall of information, which is a high priority among most achievement testers. However, this format is probably less useful for assessing more complex intellectual operations and may suffer from the lack of validity because students can guess correct answers.

True-false items contain a stem and two options: True/False or Yes/No. As we discuss later, the construction of the item stem is the same as for multiple-choice items. True-false items require only the presence of statements that are phrased in unequivocal terms, with which examinees must agree or disagree. Because they usually require little reading, many items can be included, allowing broad coverage of the material. Finally, objective scoring is possible, assuming statements are absolutely true or false. Most of the preparation work is completed in constructing the test, but even that effort is quite focused since only single statements are developed. Examples appear in the preceding material on intellectual operations.

As with multiple-choice items, we can use specific guidelines for constructing true-false items to ensure a valid outcome (Gronlund, 1988):

1. Use only statements that are true or false without qualifications. If there is any doubt about the statement, do not use it. The statement should contain only one central idea; if several ideas are included, it is difficult to judge their truth in concert. However, if the statement expresses an opinion or belief, it must provide enough context to make a judgment (i.e., source, time, place of the statement).
2. Avoid long and complex statements with many qualifying clauses. Such statements increase reading time and present many irrelevant distractors, some of which may influence student response. Furthermore, tacking on conditional clauses may qualify the truth or falseness of the statement and thereby create confusion.
3. Avoid statements that contain the words *all, always, never, none,* and *only.* Many times, the inclusion of such absolute qualifiers pro-

vides a clue that the item is not true, since there are very few absolutes in this world. Words such as *sometimes, often, generally, typically,* and *considerably* should be avoided also, since they also provide clues to the truth or falseness of the answer.

4. Avoid negative statements, in particular double negatives, because they often require a (re)thinking of whether the statements are true or false, and double negatives require great care in determination of an answer, either true or false. If used, they should be emphasized (underlined or italicized).
5. Avoid trick items, in which the truth or falseness of the statement revolves around some very small and irrelevant feature.
6. Avoid ambiguity in terms of degree or amount. Because the issue is the absolute truth or falseness of a statement, any introduction of degrees of truth is likely to be misleading.

True-false items have a few advantages and disadvantages in addition to those listed in the more general form of a multiple-choice format. They are short and concise, and give an obvious directive to the student; they are particularly useful for factual information that is central to understanding; and they can be constructed quickly, with less attention to the creation of distractors that have an equivalent plausibility as correct answers (the foil is simply the opposite of the answer, however it is phrased). Nevertheless, the disadvantages include the limitation to factual information and the high probability of student guessing, given only one foil.

Matching. Like the true-false format, matching is a variant of the multiple-choice item. In this format, a list of *premises* and alternate or synonomous *responses* common to the premises are listed side by side. Students must match items from one list (the responses) to the earlier list (the premises). The premises are based on only one of the responses, which are considered a subset, synonym, or exemplar of these premises. Typically, one list has numbers (reflecting test items) preceded by a blank, and the other list contains letters (reflecting response options). Students are directed to place the letter in front of the matching item that is related to it. There are two ways to ensure that students are not using the process of elimination to get items correct: (a) The number of items on the two lists can be unequal, and (b) more than one item can be matched for one concept on the other list. This format is particularly pertinent for repetitious use of responses across a number of different items (premises). Since no examples for matching were given in the preceding material on intellectual operations, we have included the following example of a matching format.

In the table below, several educational decisions are listed on the left, with a blank appearing before the item *number*. Three types of tests are listed on the right, each preceded by a *letter*. Place the letter next to the type of test that best fits the educational decision on the blank.

Educational Decision	Type of Test
___ 1. Screening	A. Norm-referenced
___ 2. Instructional grouping	B. Criterion-referenced
___ 3. Special education placement	C. Individual-referenced
___ 4. Instructional diagnostics	
___ 5. Formative evaluation	

As this example illustrates, the matching format is easy to create if done correctly. The following strategies are important in writing good matching items (Gronlund, 1988):

1. Directions should clearly explain the basis for matching. Rather than stating that Column B (responses) should be matched with Column A (premises), the items in Column B should be described as examples of the content for Column A.
2. The units reflected in the premises and responses should be clearly related so that, within one column (the premises), all items are of the same type (e.g., only dates, years, length of measurement, or time is present). Within the other column, all items should be similarly parallel to each other.
3. The list of premises and responses should be short, ranging from 5 or 6 premises and/or responses and rarely exceeding 10 or 12 of either or both.
4. Write the premises and responses so they are clear and easy to read. For example, place longer statements on the left as premises and the shorter responses in logical order on the right.
5. The number of premises and responses should not be equal: Either the number of premises or the number of responses should be greater.

Matching items have several advantages. They are easy to produce and can be employed with a wide range of tasks. They also allow for generation of a large number of items since they involve little reading and require few concepts to generate multiple answers. With the proper instructional content, it is possible to generate a great number of items, potentially increasing the amount of behavior sampled on the test. Since all the effort in construction is test development, scoring is easy and efficient. The matching format is particularly useful for concepts in which characteristics are listed in taxonomical groupings, with members of the set presented alongside both members and nonmembers. Their biggest disadvantage is that tasks may be limited to reiteration and summarization of content, thereby reflecting an emphasis on lower rather than higher levels of intellectual operations. Of course, the format itself is sufficiently limiting, in that not all content or information is suitable for testing by matching.

STEP 3: STRUCTURING THE ITEMS AND THE TEST

Regardless of whether the choice is a production response, utilizing a one-word, short-answer, or extended-answer, or whether it is a selection response, utilizing a multiple-choice, true-false, or matching/classification format, knowledge tests must be formatted to yield valid assessments of what students know. The assessment can be manipulated at two levels: the individual item or across items on the entire test.

Items

For both response types, two important elements are present. First, the stem must set the scene or describe the situation to provide information about people, places, events, and so forth. If concepts or principles are used, considerable information must be given, including both relevant and irrelevant features. When the item is more than simple reiteration or summarization, the information and format should be presented so that answering correctly is not possible through memory alone. Therefore, use paraphrases rather than exact words or phrases from the text or classroom. Second, the item must show examinees how they are to demonstrate their knowledge. This directive can be in the form of a question to be answered or in the form of a statement that requests them to perform a task. The important issue is the action that is required to answer the item.

This stimulus, both in depicting information and directing examinees to respond, must be clear and relevant. The task should be appropriate to classroom, school, or natural social environments. However, compromises are often necessary. For example, the test may be unnatural because alternatives are specified that ordinarily would not appear within the environment outside of schools. In the natural world, how often are people required to spell a list of words? How often are they asked to calculate the answers to computation problems on sheets of paper? The test may not allow the use of aids in answering the question, when actually the natural environment would allow such aids (i.e. calculators, reference books). Nevertheless, it is important that the item clearly state the information in a way that students can respond in a way that is consistent with both the content and some relevant environment (Williams & Haladyna, 1982).

To *develop* an effective and efficient measure of achievement, one should follow certain strategies. In constructing objective tests that generate appropriate responses, it is important to limit the nature of the correct response to generate agreement on the answer. The two strategies that accomplish this objective are (a) narrowing the information being analyzed and (b) focusing the response to reiterations and/or summarizations of facts, concepts, or principles. General strategies for writing objective test items, regardless of their specific format, are available and have been reviewed by many authors (Carey, 1988; Ebel & Frisbie, 1986; Gronlund, 1988; and Lindeman & Merenda, 1979):

1. Phrase the item in a clear and understandable manner, with simple and direct wording. If an item references an expert or authority, that person should be duly noted.
2. Items should be clearly independent of each other to avoid interitem clues.

3. Reading difficulty should be appropriate and below the reading ability of the group of students taking the test; the test item should assess students' knowledge, not their reading skill.
4. Questions and answers should be closely related to objectives from instruction and/or material used during instruction.
5. Avoid using statements and phrases from the text verbatim in the test item. They should be paraphrased or summarized, following three steps: (a) identification of the important information, (b) translation of the information into a thought unit, and (c) establishment of a task or an intellectual operation for assaying understanding.
6. Phrase items so that students know what information to include and how to format their answers. The item should clearly direct them to compare and contrast, present supportive findings, review what is known, explain different views, etc.
7. Construct the test so students have enough time to answer the questions. Speed should not be a factor if extended answers are used, because they are often difficult to complete. One way teachers can ensure that students have enough time to take the test is for them to take it first. In this way, teachers can judge how long students will take to complete the same test. Of course, time adjustments need to be made for those students who are not as knowledgeable as the teacher.
8. Require examinees to respond to all items. The test should not offer a range of items from which students can pick one or two questions, because the questions are probably not equivalent in difficulty or importance and will therefore provide noncomparable results.
9. Examine the test for item difficulty/discrimination and test reliability and validity fol-

lowing its administration. This tactic is useful for eliminating poor items and providing suggestions for constructing better tests later.

10. Provide examinees with clues regarding scoring criteria at the time they take the test. For instance, if the test focuses on organization, clarity, and logical and empirical support for arguments, tell them in advance that these considerations are important. Include time estimates in the directions for the test or state them at the time the test is administered. For example, examinees may be told that the first item is worth 10 points, and they should spend approximately 15 minutes on it and that the next 10 questions are each worth 2 points each, and they should spend 20 minutes on them altogether.

Tests

Once individual test items are generated, they should be arranged on the test in a systematic manner that is conducive to generating optimal scores from examinees. Following are suggestions from psychometric experts (Carey, 1988; Ebel & Frisbee, 1986; Gronlund, 1988; and Lindeman & Merenda, 1979):

1. Group items with the same *format* in one place on the test. Ideally, all multiple choice questions should be grouped together, as with the true-false, matching, and so forth. This strategy allows examinees to focus quickly on the knowledge of the task required by the test item rather than having to struggle with the format of the test item.
2. Within each section, group items of similar *content,* thereby allowing students to focus on one area of knowledge before moving to another. This strategy provides smoother transitions to different content areas and reduces examinee frustration.

3. The intellectual *operations* and *response types* depend on the *content* and objectives being tested. For example, matching items are useful for testing relationships between two sets, dates, names and problem types, all of which may focus on facts or particular concepts. Production responses are suitable for evaluation and application operations.

4. Generally, the test should proceed from easy to more difficult items. Provide a couple of items that most students will get correct at the beginning of the test. Place the most difficult items near the end, so students who would not get them correct do not waste their time trying to solve them.

5. A very important issue is the provision of direction to examinees. It is absolutely critical that students know *how* to answer each item. The directions should be both written at the beginning of the test and within each major section. Students should be prepared for transitions across different test formats. For example, the first 20 items may be true-false, in which case examinees are given a brief statement that says: "The next 20 items require true-false answers; you are to respond by either circling the T or the F." Following these 20 items, examinees may be given 20 multiple-choice items, for which they are told: "The next 20 items are statements or incomplete sentences that have five alternate choices. You are to read the statement and, for each item, select the response that is correct by circling the letter A, B, C, D or E."

Not only must the directions tell students how to respond, they also should contain explicit information regarding scoring procedures and the amount of credit for different item types. For production responses in particular, students should be alerted to the important dimensions of their response. Selection responses warrant much less consideration of response format because few alternative responses are available. The only consideration for selection responses is whether a correction-for-guessing strategy (where students are penalized more for incorrect responses than for leaving items blank) will be used. However, since this procedure is generally not endorsed in the measurement world, we do not cover it here.

STEP 4: ESTABLISHING SCORING SYSTEMS

Until this point, we have focused on creating appropriate stimulus conditions for ascertaining students' knowledge. Although the last step in generating test items is to define a scoring system for marking the correctness of the response, many decisions made in the previous steps delimit the range of options. Thus this step, although it appears last, should be considered part of the initial construction phase, because the stimulus format is strongly influenced by this issue.

Basically, two options are available: objective or subjective scoring systems. It is important not to confuse these two scoring systems with the terms *selection* and *production,* which describe the nature of the student response. **Objective** refers to the use of external criteria to judge correctness or quality, while **subjective** refers to the use of internal criteria to judge correctness or quality. Objective scoring systems utilize consistently correct answers that are obviously true or false with no ambiguity in scoring. Subjective scoring systems possess a sliding scale for determining the correctness of the response. They utilize judgments, often in the form of a rating scale with a model or key to score examinees' answers.

It is possible for a selection response to employ a subjective criterion. For example, in an English class on critique writing, the test can focus on assessing students' judgments of creative written expression, in which they are directed to select a value from 1 (low quality) to 5 (high quality) that reflects the writing quality of several compositions. These answers may be judged by the teacher in terms of their correctness to determine if students are becoming better writing critics. In this test, students select a response (judgment of 1 to 5), which is in turn judged subjectively in terms of its appropriateness (match with the teacher's judgment). Nor does a production response need to be scored only objectively. The same English class may include a test to assess students' writing skill directly (rather than their skill in critiquing writing), with each composition judged by the teacher on creativity. In this latter example, students produce (construct) answers on the test, which the teacher subsequently scores subjectively. In summary, it is possible to use either scoring system with either response mode, as shown in Figure 3.3.

With production responses, the answers are composed of a word (single-word completion), phrase, sentence (short-answer), or a paragraph (extended-answer).

Single-word Items. Two types of scoring systems can be used with a single word. If an objective scoring system is employed, only exact matches are considered correct; if subjective scoring systems are used, synonyms may be used instead of exact words. If the latter system is used, the evaluator should define criteria for crediting certain responses and rejecting others.

Short and Extended Answers. Prior to or following the administration of the test, the instructor must develop a key for scoring examinee responses when students write short answers or extended answers. Ideally, this key provides both model responses and the criteria reflecting their status. Often, a system for weighting points, a sliding scale from full credit to no credit, is embedded in this key. Regardless of the intellectual operation, the following guidelines are important for making keys for production-response items:

1. Prior to the review and grading of papers, every item should have a clear key that contains important scoring criteria and a range of responses. For example, if organization is important, it should be highlighted. If clarity, conciseness of an argument, and/or composition are important, they should be clearly noted. It is important to judge each answer on only those factors that are crucial to the question, dis-

FIGURE 3.3
Matrix depicting two types of responses and two types of scoring systems

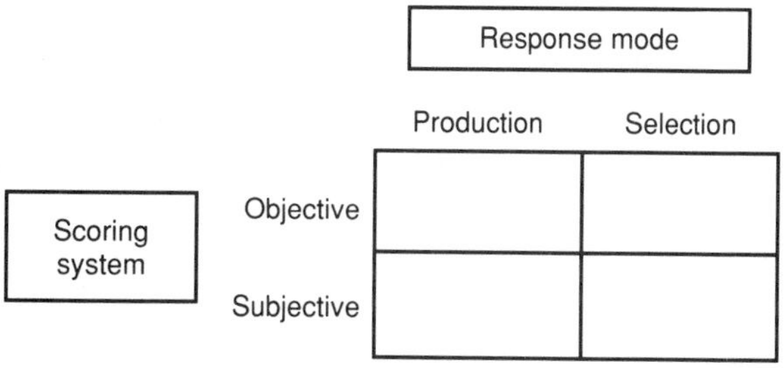

carding other issues and irrelevant features. It is helpful to prepare a model answer for each point value.

2. To ensure that the response is reviewed only on the basis of information on the test, maintain student anonymity during scoring. Teachers can assign student numbers or have students put their names on backs of their papers. After the papers have been scored, students' identities can be made known and their scores tallied.

3. Score all papers one item at a time; that is, rather than scoring one entire paper and then another, reviewers should score all papers item-by-item. This strategy allows examiners to see quickly the range of responses for any item, thus helping to (a) determine the adequacy of the item and (b) judge responses individually, not in relation to other items. Each item should be scored for all students without interruption to establish a judgment set that is not disrupted or that does not contain drift. Strike a balance between judging the items during one time period and avoiding fatigue and judgmental drift. Finally, handwriting quality should not influence scorer judgment; neither should the amount of information present be critical in determining the adequacy of the response. However, as explained in the chapter on written expression, the relationship between the amount written and the legibility of the response is often very high.

Selection

Scoring selection responses typically revolve around three issues: (a) identification of appropriate distractors for multiple choice items, (b) truthfulness and its counterpart for true-false items, and (c) taxonomic rules for matching items.

If the item type is reiteration or summarization, we can develop the correct answer from the condensation of the thought into a key phrase or idea. In distinguishing between reiteration and summarization tasks, it is important that the answer be verbatim in reiteration and paraphrased in summarization. For illustration or prediction items, two responses are possible: (a) An example or selected outcome, or (b) an example or outcome along with the criteria for making that selection. For illustration items, the criteria focus on critical attributes that make an object or event a member of a class. For prediction items, the criteria focus on characteristics needed for a rule to apply, or they focus on naming the rule plus the most likely outcome. In both tasks, test items should be new to examinees, thereby ensuring that they know how to use the rule. Finally, for both evaluation and application items, selection responses are probably less appropriate.

CHAPTER SUMMARY

This chapter has explained how to construct knowledge tests. The content area chapters will describe how to construct skills tests. As the building industry has specified roles for architects and construction people, so too must test-builders delineate these roles. In the previous chapter on measurement planning, we focused more on the role of the architect; in this chapter, we have become the builders, or test constructors. We presented a model for transforming instructional content into test items that defines three basic content formats—facts, concepts, and principles—and the six basic tasks or intellectual operations. Test items were configured to reflect one of two response modes: production or selection, each of which has three specific types. We have argued that these response modes were highly related to the type of content and the intellectual operations considered in the test. Finally, although we cover scoring procedures in great detail in later chapters, we addressed some basic issues in scoring responses particularly as they influence the format of the test stimulus. To provide an enriched format that encapsulates many test-construction issues, we present the chart in Table 3.1 to assist in test reviews, whether the tests are adopted or teacher-developed.

TABLE 3.1
A technical review form for items (sample)

Technical Review Form for Items (Sample)

---

1. Is the readability of the test item stem and answer choices suitable for the examinees being tested?
2. Does the item stem describe a single problem for an examinee?
3. Is the item stem free of ambiguities and/or irrelevant material?
4. Is the content of the test item matched closely to the goal statement, objective, or task?
5. Are all negatives underlined?
6. Do the item stem and answer choices follow standard rules of punctuation, capitalization, and grammar?
7. Are the answer choices arranged logically (if such an arrangement exists)?
8. Is there *one* correct or *clearly best* answer?
9. Is the placement of the correct answer made on a random basis?
10. Are the answer choices free of irrelevant material?
11. Are numbers or letters used to label the answer choices?
12. Is any material provided in another test item that will provide a clue to the correct answer?
13. When pictoials, tables, or figures are used, are they printed clearly and labeled correctly?
14. Can the test items be answered by simple logic or common sense?
15. a. Have words that give verbal clues to the correct answer, such as: *always, may, none, never, all, sometimes, usually, generally, typically,* and so forth been avoided?
    b. Have repetitious words or expressions been removed from the answer choices?
    c. Will the distractors be plausible and appealing to examinees who do not know the correct answer?
    d. Are the answer choices of approximately the same length?
    e. Has the use of *all of the above* or *none of the above* as answer choices been avoided?
    f. Are four or five answer choices used?
    g. Have double negatives been avoided?
    h. Have "clang" associations with the stem been avoided for the correct answer?
    i. Have distractors that mean the same thing or are opposites been avoided?
    j. Are the answer choices for an item similar in type, concept, and focus so that they are as homogeneous as possible?
    k. Is the correct answer stated at the same level of detail as the other answer choices?
16. Disregarding any technical flaws which may exist in the test item (addressed by the first 25 questions), how well do you think the content of the test item matches with some part of the content defined by the objective? (Remember the possible ratings: 1 = poor, 2 = fair, 3 = good, 4 = very good, 5 = excellent.)

Source: Reprinted with permission from Hambleton, R. K. (1984). Validating the test scores. In R. A. Berk (Ed.) *A guide to criterion-referenced test construction* (pp. 199–230). Baltimore, MD: John Hopkins University Press.

Measurement Concepts

I kke for alt i verden, kanne forstå jeg hvorfor du arbeide så megen. Du skal dø svart. Og da, hva gjøre du når staselig huske, ikke, endog familien din?

Did you understand any of the previous paragraph? Unless you know some Norwegian, you have no idea whether you are reading sage advice, a funny story, or senseless babble. To know what was said, you must know how to speak the language; to find the English translation of the previous paragraph, you must read to the end of this chapter. The first three chapters introduced new material, some of which was probably somewhat familiar. The first chapter was a challenge to try something new and break with the poor practices of the past. The second chapter provided specific strategies for planning measurement. Chapter 3, introduced tactics for test construction. This chapter and the remainder of the book are more technical; the content might be called "testing as a second language." Knowledge of this language distinguishes those who know testing well enough to be critical and innovative from those who are led and must rely on current practices. To be a legitimate player in this game, you need to know specific terms, so you can decide which route to take.

CHAPTER OBJECTIVES

When you have finished reading this chapter, you should have the knowledge and skills to

- Create a test with a distribution that fits the purpose of testing by manipulating the sampling plan and item difficulty/discrimination.
- Know the types of scales that are available and their influence on calibrating achievement.
- Know how to plot a distribution using histograms or frequency polygons.

- Understand two parameters of distributions based on central tendency or dispersion.
- Utilize the concept of correlation for understanding relationships between and among tests and other important measures of student performance.

KEY VOCABULARY

As you can see from the objectives, this chapter contains new vocabulary. We will consider what a test looks like by plotting its *distribution,* which is a pictoral description of the scores obtained from a group of students. Generally, distributions can be *open-ended,* in which performance ranges from low to high across a broad scale, or *mastery,* in which performance is more restricted to one end of the scale (the low end prior to instruction and the high end after instruction). Depending upon the type of educational decision, we create these distributions by considering three issues. First, *sampling plans,* tactics used to select test items must be identified. Four types of sampling plans are presented: (a) exhaustive sampling, which includes all items in a domain, (b) random sampling which specifies some unknown set of items be included, (c) random stratified, with clear criteria being used to select an unknown set of items of some type, and (d) stratified content, which specifies a well-defined subset of items. Second, *item difficulty and discrimination* need to be addressed; these words describe how many students pass an item and which types of students (mastered or non-mastered students) pass. Third, as we create or adopt tests with known distributions, we must be aware of the *measurement scales* upon which they are based; these are the units used to measure pupil performance. In the end, we need to consider *measures of central tendency,* how much students are group(ed) together and where; *measures of variation or dispersion,* how students differ from each other; and *correlation,* how tests relate to other tests and measurement standards. Along with the new vocabulary, this chapter introduces you to a fictional fourth-grade classroom of 10 students, whom we follow throughout the rest of the book to illustrate various principles. To help you understand the terms and concepts in this chapter and the remainder of the book, we will be reporting data from this regular education classroom. Here are the names of these pupils, in alphabetical order, and a brief description of their backgrounds.

Andy: One of the better students in class, Andy loves to read adventure stories and typically brings books from home to school to show other kids.

Bonnie: Academically, Bonnie is average, although at times she seems unmotivated and performs below average. Bonnie also has problems making friends.

Jennifer: Probably the top student, Jennifer excels academically and socially.

Johnny: Johnny is an active fourth-grade boy who loves sports but doesn't carry the same enthusiasm into the classroom. He is usually below average compared to peers. He may need help outside the regular classroom.

Linda: Linda's academic performance is very typical when compared to fourth-grade peers. She occasionally is a behavior problem in class.

Megan: A popular student among classmates, Megan's above-average performance is sometimes affected by her socializing.

Michael: Quiet and reserved, Michael's performance is typical of fourth-graders. He seems shy and at times is inattentive.

Nicky: Another active student, Nicky performs in the average to above-average range. He seems bored at times with academic tasks.

Shawn: Shawn has difficulty in reading because of poor decoding skills. Shawn appears to be normal verbally, but his academic work falls below that of peers. He doesn't seem to be working up to his potential and probably needs extra help.

Sue: Her performance in reading has been average, although she seems to really like math. Her math scores tend to be much higher than her reading and language skills.

This chapter has two sections: (a) an overview of distributions, their sources of influence, and their relationship to decision making and (b) a technical analysis of distributions and their characteristics, specifically indices of central tendency, variation or dispersion, and alignment (correlation) with other measures. We have separated this chapter from the norm-referenced evaluation chapter (13) for two reasons: (a) the analysis of distributions is appropriate for all types of evaluations (norm, criterion, or individual), and (b) the focus of this chapter is on the *analysis of items and tests,* while the norm-referenced evaluation chapter focuses on *interpreting student performance.*

AN OVERVIEW OF DISTRIBUTIONS

The content of the first section is delineated in Figure 4.1. Before proceeding with the specifics, it is important to note that all measures result in distributions, whether planned or accidental. A **distribution** is a quantitative or visual display of the range of scores and the frequency with which these scores were obtained. These distributions generally are deter-

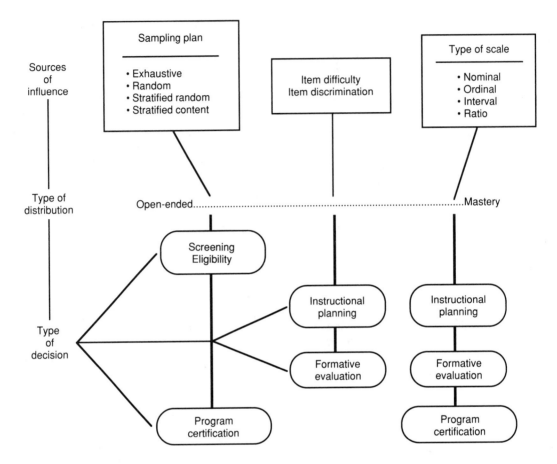

FIGURE 4.1
Analysis of distributions: Their sources of influence and the types of decision that they support

mined by the types of items in the test, the manner in which they have been sampled, the degree to which they are difficult or discriminating, and the type of scale they represent. As a result of this distribution, certain decisions can be made more or less effectively. Screening and eligibility decisions will be better made if the distributions are open-ended (survey-level); instructional planning and formative evaluation are best completed by proceeding from open-ended (survey-level) to mastery (specific-level)

distributions; program evaluation can be completed with either type of distribution.

Open-Ended or Mastery Tests

An important concept in all achievement testing is that only a finite number of items can be presented to a student at any one time. Depending upon the type of decision to be made and the kind of material being tested, it is possible to create two types of distributions. Hopkins and Antes (1978) refer to these distributions as *open-ended* and *mastery*, which differ in the sampling plan used to generate the items from a domain and in item difficulty/discrimination. The reason for noting these types of distributions is that sampling plans for including items on the test will result in one type of distribution or another.

An **open-ended** distribution implies that no boundaries exist for scaling achievement, particularly on the high end. Such a test typically employs a much broader domain for sampling items. Items are configured to be of average difficulty, with approximately 40–70% of the students passing any item. Some of the items are easy and most students can answer them correctly; some of the items are difficult and only a few students can answer them correctly.

In a **mastery** test, the sampling plan is narrower and more limited in scope. Difficulty is a function of exposure to the material from which the items have been sampled. If the test is administered prior to instruction, the items should be very difficult, with few students passing any item; however, upon administration of the test following instruction, the items should be relatively easy, and most students should pass them. Students' scores are expected to be at or near some minimal level of success. Often, the items sampled are from a fairly limited domain.

Establishing Domains

Because we are starting with the premise that we cannot exhaustively test a student in any area regardless of the breadth of the domain, we must develop a sampling plan for including items on our tests. The **sampling plan** specifies the criteria for including any given item and is based on two facets: (a) a definition of the domain, and (b) procedures for sampling items in that domain. Since domain definition is inex-

tricably related to the content to be tested, we have discussed it earlier in the chapter on measurement planning.

Domain Analysis. Open-ended and mastery distributions depend on the definition of sampling plans in relation to the age or grade of students. If the sampling plan is very broad and/or too advanced for a particular age or group of students, it is likely to result in a floor effect. With the *floor effect,* students' scores often are very low, in which case the test can be described as extremely difficult. This type of test typically represents a frustration level of functioning and is very insensitive to changes in student performance over time. Often, a large amount of time is needed to show any changes in performance. In contrast, if the domain is very narrow and/or is low in its level of knowledge for a given age or group of students, it is likely to result in a ceiling effect. A *ceiling effect* represents a maximum level that students cannot exceed. It is insensitive to the effects of instruction and represents an independent level of functioning. Unlike floor effects, ceiling effects cannot change over time. Generally, either effect represents an extreme that we should avoid, in part through a sensible plan for sampling test items.

If a domain is broadly conceived, for example, *arithmetic computation problem solving,* we probably would have an open-ended measurement, since this domain includes all operations: addition, subtraction, multiplication, division, and perhaps fractions and decimals. Furthermore, no limit has been specified as to the range. Arithmetic computation problem solving could include simple facts within each of the four operations all the way up to the use of multidigit numbers: two- and three-digit numbers added to two- and three-digit numbers or five- and six-digit numbers multiplied by five- and six-digit numbers. Indeed the domain of arithmetic computation problem solving is very broad and most likely will result in open-ended measurement.

If the domain were narrowly organized, for example around addition facts only, it would likely be a mastery test. This is true only if we are talking about an appropriate age or grade of the student. Addition facts may actually represent an open-ended measurement for first-grade students, becoming more mastery-oriented between the second and third grades, when most students will score at or near at the optimal level of success. Therefore, an important concept behind domain definition and its effect on distributions relates to the target group of examinees who will be taking the test.

Sampling plans. A sampling plan is simply a systematic procedure for determining which items to include in a measure and in what proportions, relative to the total number of items in the measure. Four strategies are helpful when determining which items to include within a test. They differ primarily in their criteria for inclusion. The review below presents the most comprehensive strategy, with no criteria, first and the least comprehensive, with several criteria, last.

Exhaustive sampling. With *exhaustive sampling,* we can employ in this plan, *all* items in the domain. Here, we specify the domain with enough clarity that it is possible to sample items with common attributes. An example would be consonant-vowel-consonant (CVC) words, possibly for a reading or spelling test. This domain is very clear: it includes all words in the English language that begin with a consonant, have a vowel in the middle, and end with a consonant; all other words are excluded. Furthermore, this domain is fairly finite and comprises approximately 125 words. Exhaustive sampling requires the most restrictive definition of a domain because it is not possible

to use it with many domains. Very few domains are small enough to be sampled in their entirety. For example, even sets of math facts within the four operations conceivably can be large if they include all arrangements of each number from 1 to 9 in each of the different positions.

Random sampling. A more limited sampling strategy is *random sampling* from a domain. Here, the domain can be broader than for exhaustive sampling. Items are pulled with no order or criteria for their selection, very much as with lotteries and/or sweepstakes. The domain can be slightly broader than that used in the exhaustive technique, but still needs to be relatively well defined, since we need to generalize from performance on the test to performance in that domain. If it is extremely broad, a random sample could be inadequate in allowing generalization from the test to performance in the larger domain. One way for countering this problem is to use successive random sampling so that multiple tests are created, administered, and scored. As we discuss later in the book, the individually referenced approach for evaluating instruction utilizes this system, in which any one test is viewed only as a sample. Multiple testing over time provides a more accurate and generalized analysis of a students' performance in a larger domain.

Stratified random sampling. In *stratified random sampling,* some specific feature or attribute is identified for blocking or controlling the sampling process. For example, spelling words may be controlled by sampling equal numbers of words with certain characteristics: for example, (a) every consonant is present in the initial position, (b) both long and short vowel sounds are included, or (c) every possible digraph with the vowel *e* is used (*ei, ea, eu, eo*). A stratified random sample is useful if one has a fairly large domain and is uncertain that a random sample will appropriately draw or include all of the features represented in that domain. It ensures more accurate generalizability from the test performance to the domain, particularly if few alternate forms of the test are available.

Stratified content sampling.   The final sampling strategy, *stratified content sampling,* involves selection on the basis of a priori content analysis. As presented in the description of levels of knowledge, this framework may not only be used to classify information and structure tasks on tests, but can also provide the essential criteria for inclusion as part of a sampling strategy. An example of stratified content sampling is presented in Table 4.1, in which a test on "findings from the effective teaching of literature" has been developed.

Item Difficulty and Discrimination

All items are more or less easy and discriminating than other items. Everybody may pass the easiest items, and/or fail the most difficult items. Neither is very discriminating. While **item difficulty** focuses on the number of students passing, **item discrimination** focuses on the capacity of the item to sort students into the appropriate group (master and nonmaster). As Thorndike, (1967) has noted, "Each item is in

a very real sense a little test all by itself" (p. 203). If the item sorts students into similar groups as does the test, the item is working well. While difficulty applies to all test items, discrimination applies mainly to criterion-referenced tests in which students are classified in a dichotomous (i.e., mastered and nonmastered) fashion.

Both difficulty and discrimination can be manipulated through the sampling plan or directly in configuring the item. When a sampling plan is broad, the chance of pulling in more difficult items is higher, since knowledge or skill is so encompassing. When the sampling plan is narrow, the likelihood of pulling in easy items is higher, since limits have been imposed upon what content to include. Overlap between the items on the test and the content of either students' immediate prior learning or general background knowledge may be considerable.

In addition, the manner in which the item is written probably has a substantial influence on its difficulty. We assume that if items are oriented toward higher intellectual operations (prediction, evaluation, or application), they are likely to be more difficult than items centered on lower intellectual operations (reiteration or summarization). It is further assumed that they are also more discriminating, in that students who master the test pass such items, and students who fail the test also fail such items.

TABLE 4.1
Blueprint for selecting items using stratified content sampling

Item Nos.	Topic	Level of Knowledge	Content	Points per Item
1,2,3	Modeling	Reiteration	Fact	1
4,5	Questioning	Summarization	Principles	4
6	Review	Illustration	Concept	4
7	Corrections	Evaluation	Principle	10
8	Reinforcement	Application	Principle	10
9	Active Learning	Summarization	Concept	2
10,11,12	Grouping	Summarization	Fact	1
Total				40

A number of strategies are available for determining an item's difficulty and discrimination. Hopkins and Antes (1978) defined difficulty as the frequency of incorrect responses associated with an item and compute it in the following manner:

$$PD = [N_w/N_t] \times 100$$

> PD = Problem difficulty for an item.
>
> N_w = Number of individuals answered incorrectly.
>
> N_t = Total number of individuals.

Discrimination, which reflects the item's capacity to sort those scoring high (i.e., meeting criterion or the upper 27%) and those scoring low (i.e., not meeting criterion or the lower 27%) on the total test, is calculated in the following manner (Hopkins & Antes, 1978):

$$D = U/N_u - L/N_L$$

> D = Discrimination index for an item.
>
> U = Number of students meeting criterion that answered item correctly.
>
> N_u = Number of students meeting criterion.
>
> L = Number of students *not* meeting criterion that answered item correctly.
>
> N_L = Number of students not meeting criterion.

For example, if 27 students completed a test, and 21 met criterion and 6 did not, the following data on each item would reflect their difficulty (*PD*) and discriminating power (*D*):

| Item Number | Number Answering | | | PD | D |
	Incorrectly	Correctly Above Criterion	Correctly Below Criterion		
5	6	18	3	.22	+ .36
6	6	21	0	.22	+1.00
7	3	18	6	.11	− .14

Most of the items are easy, with low levels of difficulty (.11–.22), but the discrimination index varies considerably. Item 5 is somewhat discriminating (18 of 21 passing the test answered it correctly and only 3 failing the criterion passed the item); Item 6 was perfectly discriminating (everyone passing the criterion answered it correctly, everyone failing the criterion answered it incorrectly); and Item 7 was not very discriminating (some of the students not meeting criterion answered it correctly and some meeting criterion answered it incorrectly).

The appropriate difficulty and discrimination are functions of the type of test and the format. For mastery tests, after instruction, we expect most or all students to answer the items correctly. Therefore, problem difficulty should be low and discrimination high. For survey-level tests that have a broad sampling domain or for mastery tests given prior to instruction, problem difficulty should be moderately high, with discrimination near zero. The format of an item, also will greatly influence the item's difficulty. For selection-response items, appropriate difficulty is the point midway between chance (incorrect) and total perfection (no incorrect). For example, with a four-item, multiple-choice test, appropriate difficulty will be midway between 75% and 0% (37.5%); for a true-false item, appropriate difficulty will be between 50% and 0% (25%). Discrimination indexes, ranging from − 1.00 to + 1.00, should be positive and very high to be appropriate following instruction. However, as Roid and Haladyna (1982) caution, this index is influenced by the range of scores on the total test; furthermore, a low index is not inherently a sign of a poor item, since instructional effects confound simple interpretations. For production responses, item difficulty and discrimination are much more difficult to ascertain. Following is a chart for analyzing item difficulty and discrimination.

TABLE 4.2
Guidelines for selecting criterion-referenced test items

Item Characteristic	Criterion	Index Value
Item-objective congruence	Matches objective being assessed	None[a]
Difficulty	Difficult for uninstructed group	0–50[b]
	Easy for instructed group	70–100[b]
Discrimination	Positively discriminates between criterion groups[b]	High positive[c]

[a]There is no index of item-objective congruence for teacher-made tests. An index of agreement among content specialists for tests developed at the district and state levels can be used (Rovinelli & Hambleton, 1977). For those applications the index values should be high positive.
[b]This index is the opposite of difficulty and reflects problem easiness (PE = No. Correct/Total × 100).
[c]The actual value will vary according to the method used to compute discrimination.
Source: Reprinted from Berk, R. A. (1984). Conducting the item analysis. In R. A. Berk (Ed.), *A guide to criterion-referenced test construction* (pp. 97–143), p. 122. Baltimore, MD: John Hopkins University Press.

Measurement Scales

At this point, tests can be thought of as "yardsticks" that can give us accurate and useful information. But one problem that plagues us is that there are several kinds of educational yardsticks available, not all of which meet our specific educational needs. These yardsticks have been calibrated to reflect achievement, status, gains, and changes. Although domain definition, sampling plans, and item difficulty and discrimination affect calibration of the yardstick to a great degree, these characteristics don't tell the whole story. We also need to consider the measurement scale upon which tests are based, which in turn influences the degree of test sensitivity, or in other words, the manner in which students' scores group together or change over time. A measurement scale is a definitional system for assigning mathematical properties to numbers.

Each kind of yardstick we use in educational testing corresponds to a type of measurement scale. The cruder forms of measurement scales we will learn about, such as *nominal* and *ordinal,* have limited mathematical properties that restrict their use. More sophisticated scales, such as *interval* and *ratio,* are necessary for precise measurement of student performance. We describe measurement scales with reference to our fictional class of fourth graders.

Nominal. The *nominal scale* is the most rudimentary level of measurement and is applied to numbers that are used to keep track of things, such as labels or categories. It does not provide quantitative information; we can conduct no mathematical operations with the measures.

As an example, assume the teacher in our fourth-grade room wants to conduct a spelling bee. Starting at the front of the room, she has the students count off, alternating between *1* and *2*. In this instance, each student's team membership is indicated by either number *1* or *2*. However, this quantification has no numeric interpretation: Team 1 has not been established to be better than Team 2. Other nominal scales in schools include grade level and coding girls as *1* and boys as *2* on computer printouts. Numbers used in nominal scales are labels only.

Ordinal. From the simplistic nominal scale, we move to the *ordinal scale*. Although it has some mathematical properties, the ordinal scale is still too limited for precise measurement. According to Nunnally (1967),

> an ordinal scale is one in which (1) a set of objects or people is ordered from "most" to "least" with respect to an attribute, (2) there is no indication of "how much" in an absolute sense any of the objects possess the attribute, and (3) there is no indication of how far apart the objects are with respect to the attribute. (p. 12)

We cannot conduct any mathematical operations with ordinal scales; for example, we cannot add or subtract numbers to arrive at a total that has any meaning. What we can do is make comparisons of greater or less.

To establish an ordinal scale in the classroom, teachers rank a group of students on a given skill area. For example, if our fourth-grade teacher wishes to set up three reading groups, s/he might rank order our 10 fourth graders as shown in Table 4.3.

As you can see, the teacher has ranked the reading skills of her fourth-grade class from 1, which is *best*, to 10, which is *worst*. On this basis, the three reading groups, *1, 2* and *3*,

TABLE 4.3
Example of ordinal scale with fourth-grade class

Student	Teacher Ranking	Assigned Reading Group
Jennifer	1	1
Andy	2	1
Megan	3	1
Nicky	4	1
Michael	5	2
Sue	6	2
Linda	7	2
Bonnie	8	3
Shawn	9	3
Johnny	10	3

have been formed. We have two types of measurement scales: the teacher ranking reflects an ordinal scale, and the assigned reading group reflects a nominal scale (although, if it is used to reflect reading status—as 1 = high, 2 = middle, and 3 = low—we can view this number as an ordinal one).

With ordinal scales, we have no idea of the degree to which students are good readers (have specific skills), or how much better readers some students are than others. For example, Jennifer may be the best reader of the 10 students, but this does not tell us the extent to which she has the skills necessary to master fourth-grade reading material. Has she mastered fourth-grade vocabulary? Can she decode new words presented to her? Can Jennifer comprehend fourth-grade passages? A second problem with the ordinal scale, as pointed out in the passage by Nunnally, is that there is no indication of how far apart students are on reading skills. For example, while Nicky is ranked fourth and Michael is ranked fifth, is Nicky so much better in reading that he qualifies for Group 1, while Michael is not eligible for the same group? How much better are Group 2 students than Group 3 students? Such answers are not readily apparent from the use of ordinal scales. To obtain this information, the measurement scale must be more sophisticated.

Schools have many measurement systems based on ordinal scales. Examples will appear in the chapter on written expression, where you will see that a major form of scoring is to rate students on dimensions of quality such as organization, clarity, and creativity. Many teacher-made tests that employ ratings of quality, (e.g., essay tests using higher intellectual operations) are based on ordinal scales. In fact, probably the most important ordinal system used in public schools today is the grading system, in which we order students on a scale of overall achievement and deportment (A, B, C, D, F).

Interval. The *interval scale* increases the precision of measurement and

> is one in which (1) the rank ordering of objects is known with respect to an attribute and (2) it is known how far apart the objects are from one another with respect to the attribute, but (3) no information is available about the absolute magnitude of the attribute for any object. (Nunnally, 1967, p. 13)

An important characteristic of this scale is that it assumes the intervals are equal, regardless of the number of persons at various points on the scale. Interval scales allow us to add and subtract numbers to arrive at a meaningful total. We can take scores from subtests of achievement measures and add them to arrive at a total score. We have all of the advantages of an ordinal scale, in which we can rank students in terms of *more or less, and* we know how much more or less students differ from each other.

An example of an interval scale from our classroom is the use of standardized, norm-referenced achievement tests. Let's examine the test scores of our 10 fourth-graders (Table 4.4).

The scores on this standardized test of reading range from 81 for Shawn to 122 for Jennifer. Since these standardized scores represent an interval scale, and we know the scores are ranked, we can assume the intervals between units are equal. However, we have no knowledge of the absolute magnitude of reading skill. For example, we know that the ranking of reading-skill level is Jennifer, Andy, Megan, Nicky, Michael, Sue, Linda, Bonnie, Johnny, and Shawn. We also know that the difference from Bonnie at 92 to Linda at 99 is the same as the distance of Megan at 114 to Andy at 121. However, we have no idea of the absolute quantity of the skill that these scores represent. Andy's score of 121 seems to be fairly good, but it does not provide us with the precise magnitude of skill level. To what extent does the 121 represent mastery of fourth-grade vocabulary?

Ratio. A *ratio scale* is based upon all of the above features of ordinal and interval scales, but has the added advantage of having a zero point, representing the absolute lack of the characteristic being measured. We know that objects measured with a ratio scale can be ordered, that the actual differences between objects can be meaningfully quantified, and that the relative difference also can be quantified. Mathematically, we can now use all four basic operations; we can add and subtract scores from each other and, more importantly, we can compare the ratios of scores by multiplying and dividing.

Several physical measurement systems exist that are true ratio scales, including temperature (when using degrees Kelvin), weight (using pounds or kilograms), sound (using decibels), and light (using angstroms). In all of these examples, an absoute zero is possible, representing the complete and total absence of the characteristic. However, we must be careful in using these scales: Temperature measured in centigrade or Fahrenheit, for example, does not contain a real zero point. With these scales, zero is only a convention, and it would be incorrect to say that 60 degrees is twice as warm as 30

TABLE 4.4
An interval scale with standardized test scores

Student Name	Test Score
Jennifer	122
Andy	121
Megan	114
Nicky	109
Michael	105
Sue	102
Linda	99
Bonnie	92
Johnny	91
Shawn	81

degrees. We can say, however, that the difference between 60 and 30 degrees is the same as between 100 and 70 degrees.

Few measures of achievement have a zero point; thus we cannot accurately assess the absolute magnitude or breadth of knowledge with a ratio scale. Most achievement scales lack a real zero point. The ratio scale is the most precise form of measurement and provides the most information. However, it is limited to very precise domain-based skills in which specific items of a certain type are defined and sampled (i.e., printing letters for first grade students). Within these domains, it is possible to obtain an absolute zero point. Broad measures of achievement, in contrast, cannot function as ratio scales because the domain generally is too broadly defined and contains no absolute zero point.

Two Types of Distributions

The discussion to this point has been limited to individual items as reflections of a domain of knowledge, in part structured by the breadth of the domain, strategies for including items, and procedures for manipulating item difficulty/discrimination. Individual items also are configured with a particular calibration (measurement scale), which influences their sensitivity to documenting achievement status or change. However, as alluded to in Table 4.2, students rarely respond to one item; they answer many questions on tests, getting some of them correct and some of them wrong. Each time a student receives a score, it must be interpreted relative either to that of others who took the test, a minimum level of acceptability, or his or her previous performance. For example, to know that Megan received a score of 50 on a reading test is quite meaningless. But if we knew how others in her class responded, we would be able to interpret her skills.

This section introduces you to two types of distributions for norm- or criterion-referenced

testing: (a) histograms and (b) frequency polygons. Both distributions express data by plotting the ranges of scores. In a histogram, the chart is a bar graph, while a frequency polygon is a closed line or distribution graph. Both graphs display successive score intervals on the x-axis, or *abscissa,* and the frequency of students or examinees on the y-axis, or *ordinate.*

Histogram. The *histogram* is a graphic display that represents scores or values using bars, in which the abscissa, or x-axis (horizontal line), is scaled with successively larger values or scores or qualitatively different categories or groups; the ordinate, or y-axis (vertical line), is scaled with the frequency of individuals having each value on the x-axis. They are particularly important for ordinal scales, since they can reflect the concepts of greater or less, but do not have to represent continuous data on the x-axis. For examples, the categories could be different years or groups of students by ethnicity. Figure 4.2 is an example of a histogram.

Frequency Polygon. A *frequency polygon* is a systematic arrangement of raw scores in which we plot the frequency of individuals receiving each score using a line, or distribution, graph. Again, the values of successive scores are scaled along the x-axis and the number of individuals receiving a given score is scaled along the y-axis. A dot is placed at each value or score for the number of individuals receiving that score. This graph is appropriate for interval data, since the x-axis usually reflects continuous data with equal intervals. An example of a frequency polygon appears in Figure 4.3.

This procedure is reasonable only if a few individuals are to be plotted or if relatively few different scores have occurred. When we want to plot the scores of a large group of students, and/or the number of unique scores is large, we should group the data into intervals. Ap-

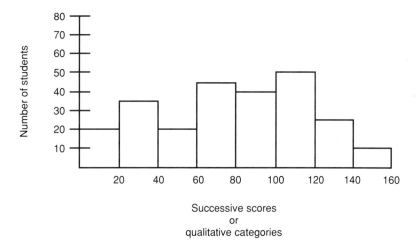

FIGURE 4.2
An example of a histogram

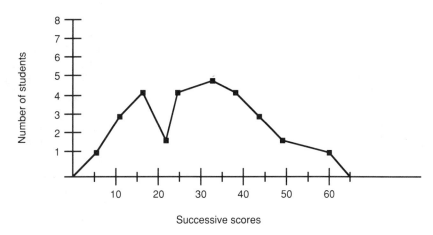

FIGURE 4.3
An example of a frequency polygon

proximately 10–20 intervals should be developed using the following procedures:

1. Calculate the range of scores (highest score minus lowest score).
2. Divide the range by 20 and again by 10.

3. Establish an interval between these two numbers; make the interval an odd number.
4. Establish the lowest interval using a number that is divisible by the interval size and lower than the lowest score.
5. Count successive intervals.

6. Tally the number scores falling within the interval.

For example, with a range of scores from 11 to 65 (54), the interval size could be 3 (between 54/20 = 2.7 and 54/10 = 5.4); the lowest interval with scores would be 9, and the highest interval would be 54: 9–12, 13–15, 16–18, . . . 52–54.

In summary, distributions can reveal a considerable amount of information about how a test is working. All we need to do now is analyze them more specifically by looking at their shapes: measures of central tendency and variability.

TECHNICAL ANALYSIS OF DISTRIBUTIONS

Distribution Indices

As stated earlier, a distribution naturally results from decisions about test construction and is central to any measurement system. The distribution should be appropriate for the type of decision to be made. Because of the domain definition, sampling plan, and item difficulty/discriminations, open-ended tests are likely to have very different distributions than mastery tests. In describing the distributions, we need first to attend to the general shape and then quantify it specifically in terms of two constructs: (a) *central tendency,* the point in the distribution that reflects some type of typical performance and, (b) *variation,* an index of performance extremes or differences.

General distribution shape. Any distribution is characterized by groupings of students along the scale. In nontechnical terms, this feature can be described as where students tend to "lump" together. As you can see, we consider two characteristics: the lump itself and where it occurs.

Two terms to describe these features are *kurtosis,* reflecting the breadth of the lump, and *skewness,* reflecting its location. In a normal distribution, the majority of students tend to gather in the middle, with fewer students scoring at the extremes (either high or low). The kurtosis is even (neither flat and broad nor narrow and restricted), and the lump appears in the middle. That is, most students score in the middle, and few students score either very high or very low. An example appears in Figure 4.4.

Kurtosis. The range of scores is reflected in the kurtosis of the curve. There are two types of kurtosis, as shown in Figure 4.5. If a small range exists, most students will be together in a narrow band, and the distribution is labeled *leptokurtic.* If a great range exists, then this band is broad and flattened, incorporating scores at both extremes, and is labeled *platykurtic.* If tests are to be used for screening students or determining eligibility, then they should be more platykurtic than leptokurtic. In essence, the device should be sensitive to extremes and not narrowly calibrated, with most students appearing similar to each other. Since we know that students differ, we must construct tests that reflect these differences.

Skewness. In addition to kurtosis, distributions are characterized by skewness, or the point on the scale where students are performing similarly. Skewness is different from kurtosis in that, rather than reflecting the range of scores, the concept reflects the location of the *majority* of scores. We consider two specific types of skewness, indicating whether the majority of students score at the positive or negative end of the distribution.

FIGURE 4.4
An example of normal
distribution

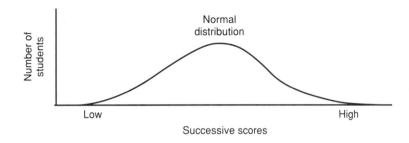

In the test with a floor effect, most students score at the low end, and only a few score at the high end; this is considered *positively skewed,* since the tail is at the high end. In contrast, a ceiling effect is represented by a distribution in which most of the students score at the high end, and only a few students score at the low end. This type of distribution has been referred to as *negatively skewed,* since the tail is at the low end. It is important to remember that the tail defines the type of skewness. Figure 4.6 shows both types of distributions.

To learn more about distributions, we must quantify student scores. Although the above indices are helpful in describing distributions, they convey no quantitative information; rather,

the descriptions are qualitative. For example, a distribution might be characterized as generally platykurtic and negatively skewed. Such a test would be fine for screening students, since it yields a distribution that is sensitive to some of the low-performing students. However, it would be worthless for evaluating instructional programs. In contrast, a distribution that is leptokurtic and positively skewed would be appropriate if it were obtained prior to instruction, but it would be disastrous if it were obtained following instruction. Can you explain why?

To move beyond a qualitative description of distributions, we need to consider measures of (a) central tendency and (b) dispersion. Together, these two indices provide information

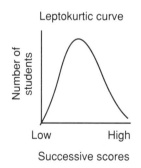

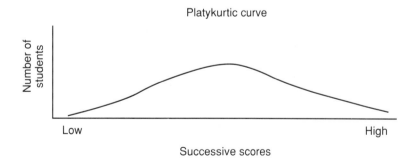

FIGURE 4.5
Two types of kurtosis: Leptokurtic and platykurtic

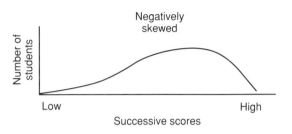

FIGURE 4.6
Positively and negatively skewed distributions

that help interpret both the distribution and an individual's score within that distribution. Importantly, if only one of these indices is reported, neither the distribution nor score within it is interpretable. For example, if a teacher were told that his or her best student had scored 95 on a test, and that the average score was 75, he or she still could not adequately interpret the score of 95. Until some measure of dispersion is also reported, the score of 95 is only vaguely interpretable.

Measures of Central Tendency. Probably the quickest and easiest way to interpret a test score, an observation, or any type of response to a specified stimulus is to compare that behavior, or group of behaviors, with performance considered typical. We usually define typical performance by examining a large group of scores representative of a normal population. This set of observations is known as the distribution of scores. For example, if we reexamine our 10 fourth-graders and how they performed on the reading test in Table 4.3, we see a distribution of scores. One way to summarize this distribution is to describe its **central tendency,** which is defined as one of the following: mode, median, or mean. These measures represent points in a distribution around which most scores tend to center. However, they are more or less important in reflecting that center, depending upon the shape of the distribution.

Mode. The *mode* is the most general measure of central tendency, represented by the score that appears most often in a distribution. An example with the TOP (Test of Performance), a fictional reading test used to illustrate a histogram in Figure 4.7. All scores occur only once, except the score of 9, which appears twice. Thus, the mode for our class would be 9.

The mode may be important in reporting data from rating scales or checklists; however, when the data represent actual scores on an interval scale, the mode is very uninformative.

Median. A more sensitive measure of central tendency is the *median.* After all scores are ranked from low to high, this value cuts the distribution in half, ignoring the actual differences between successive values. When an odd number of data points is available, the median is an actual value; when an even number of data points is available, the score is halfway between the two middle scores.

Consider the following group of scores: 5, 2, 7, 6, 4. The median, or middle score, is 5. Often when dealing with a large distribution by hand, it is easier to rank the scores and then to count up (or down) to the middle score. When working with an even number of scores, we encounter a special problem because no score can actually be the middle one. For example, if we rank the scores from Table 4.5, we have 7, 8, 9, 9, and 11 as the five lowest scores, and 12, 13, 15, 17, and 19 as the five

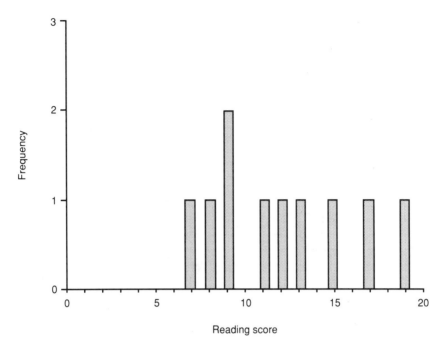

FIGURE 4.7
Histogram showing the mode of our fourth-grade class on the TOP

highest scores. We now have half of the scores at or below 11 and half the scores at or above 12. In this situation, the median would be halfway between 11 and 12, or 11.5.

TABLE 4.5
Reading scores for our fourth-grade class

Student	Raw Score
Shawn	8
Sue	13
Megan	17
Bonnie	9
Johnny	7
Linda	9
Jennifer	19
Nicky	11
Andy	15
Michael	12

The median is an excellent measure of central tendency when the distribution is skewed, with extremely high or low scores. Because this measure uses only ordinal ranks of scores, not actual values, the middle is not thrown off from such extreme values. Often, with a small group of scores, the median is a more accurate measure of central tendency than the mean, which can be overly influenced by extreme scores; the median offers more stability.

As an example, let's consider the family incomes of our 10 students. Imagine that 9 of the families have annual incomes of $20,000. Linda's mother, however, just won the Illinois state lottery, and as a result, she has an income of $1 million per year. For this group of 10 pupils, the median family income is still $20,000. Because we often find extreme scores in the classroom, the teacher developing tests for small group sizes may want to consider using the median rather than the mean.

Mean.   The *mean* is that value representing the average score in a group or distribution of scores. It is the most comprehensive and informative of all measures of central tendency because it is influenced by all scores and their actual values. It is also the most sensitive index of central tendency. If we calculated the mean family income of our students in the example above, we find the average family income is $118,000. The median provided a much different result. Which figure best represents central tendency of the 10 families? Obviously, when comparing these two figures, the median, which is not affected as much by the extreme income of Linda's family, gives us a more realistic measure of central tendency.

It is calculated by totaling the values of the observed scores and then dividing by the number of scores. For example, assume we want to find the mean of the reading subtest of the TOP, which has four stories and five multiple choice items for each story, for our fictional class. Student scores range from 0 to 20 correct. In Table 4.5, we see how our 10 pupils scored: 8, 13, 17, 9, 7, 9, 19, 11, 15, and 12 words correct. First, we total these scores and find that the sum is 120. We then divide this number by 10, the number of scores; the result is a mean score of 12. It is this index of central tendency that tells us important information about our reading test. We now know that typical performance in our class, as measured by the mean, is 12 correct items for the TOP.

Relationships Among the Mode, Median, and Mean.   Unless the distribution is extremely skewed, the mean is the best measure of central tendency. With a normal distribution, the mode, median, and mean are all located at the same value. When the distribution is extremely skewed, the mean is pulled in the direction of the skew. If it is very positively skewed, the mean is greater than the median; if it is negatively skewed, the mean is less than the median. Figures 4.8 and 4.9 show the relationship between the mode, median and mean for three types of distribution.

Measures of Variability

While measures of central tendency are helpful in giving educators an idea of typical performance for a given set of scores or group of students, they do not provide all the information necessary for interpreting pupil performance. We know that not all students will score at or close to the mean or median. Therefore, when Shawn scores 8 on the TOP, and the mean for this test is 12, we have little information about how Shawn has performed on the test in relation to peers. Is he close to the mean? Is he far away? To gain a better understanding of how Shawn scored compared to other students, we need to examine the concept of dispersion, which is expressed with measures of variability.

Let us think of **variability** as the degree to which scores in a distribution are spread out, or scattered. Measures of central tendency describe the center of the distribution, while measures of dispersion describe the variation of the distribution. Many measures are available to depict such variations; they are comparable to each other but provide different information.

In our class example, where Shawn has scored an 8, let's examine the distribution of scores of the 10 fourth-graders. Referring to Table 4.5, we see that class scores range from 7 to 19. Assume that another class of 10 fourth-graders has taken the TOP, and the resulting scores are 2, 4, 5, 7, 13, 16, 17, 18, 18, and 20. This distribution of values is plotted in Figure 4.10. Although both our class and the other class have a mean of 12, the distribution of scores for the second class is much more spread

FIGURE 4.8
Relationship between the
mode, median, and mean
for normal distribution

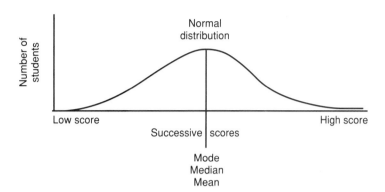

FIGURE 4.8
Relationship between the
mode, median, and mean
for normal distribution

out and variable. Shawn's score of 8 looks much better in this class. While both classes have identical measures of central tendency (the mean equals 12), the difference in variability indicates that the two classes are quite dissimilar.

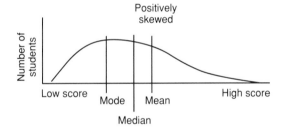

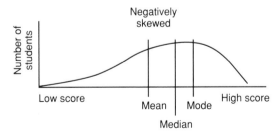

FIGURE 4.9
Relationship between the mode, median, and mean for positively and negatively skewed distributions

Two important statements can be made about variability. First, the concept allows us to describe more precisely the performance of populations, in this case, individual students. Second, it is possible to move beyond speaking of variability as *large* or *small* and to describe variability in quantitative terms.

Range. Probably the simplest notion of test-score variability is the *range*. In examining a set of test scores, teachers need only to identify the lowest and the highest scores. As a single metric, the range describes the distance between extreme scores but provides no information about the number of students at various score values. Its primary use is supplemental; it is rarely employed alone. In the example in Table 4.5, the number of correct items in Shawn's class ranged from 7 to 19. While this datum describes the outer limits of performance in the class, it does not give the teacher any indication of where most pupils are performing. Do most students perform at the lower end of the range? Do they score at the upper end? Or do the pupils tend to congregate about the median, which lies between 11 and 12? This might be useful information to supplement other measures. Since the range does not provide information about the concentration of test

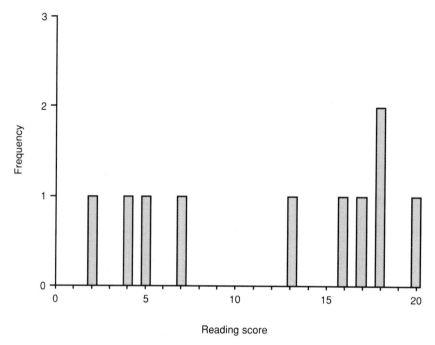

FIGURE 4.10
Distribution of TOP for another fourth-grade class

scores within the extremes, another approach is necessary.

Quartile Deviation.   The measure called *quartile deviation* depicts the amount of variation of the middle 50% of the scores, with the lower bound being the 25th percentile and the upper bound being the 75th percentile. For example, the scores plotted in Figure 4.11 (represented on the vertical axis) are from eighth-grade students given a list of words to spell that had been randomly sampled from a list of commonly misspelled words (Guiler, 1944). The plot depicts semi-interquartile deviations, with the top of the box equal to the 75th percentile, the bottom of the box equal to the 25th percentile, and the line in the middle of the box equal to the 50th percentile.

Standard Deviation.   In determining the extent to which scores are dispersed on a test, the best strategy is to average the variability of all students taking the test. To calculate average variability, we should find out how different each individual's score is from other individuals who were administered the test. Subtracting an individual's score from all other possible individuals' scores and then continuing this process until all possible combinations have been exhausted would be a very time-consuming task. It is more efficient to assess the extent to which each individual differs from the test mean. Such *deviation scores* then are used to calculate the average deviation, or standard deviation.

The *standard deviation* is the standardized difference among scores around the mean of the distribution. This measure is the most pow-

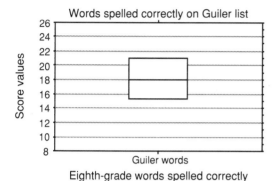

Words spelled correctly on Guiler list

Eighth-grade words spelled correctly

FIGURE 4.11
Example of quartile distributions depicting variability

erful and descriptive index of variation in a distribution and is used in the eventual calculation of other indices. To calculate this metric, we first determine the extent to which each individual in the population deviates from the test mean. If our mean is 12 items correct, as it was with the TOP test, and Johnny scores at 7, he has a deviation score of −5. Each deviation score then is squared and summed across all individuals. Since deviation scores have either positive or negative values, we square them to eliminate the canceling-out effect when later summing them. To find the average squared deviation score, we divide the sum of the squared deviation scores by the number of individuals. Our final step is to calculate the square root of the average squared deviation, which is the standard deviation. In expressing performance, the units are the same as that of the original metric, which was correct items.

In the example in Table 4.6, our fourth-grade class is used to calculate the standard deviation of the TOP. Shawn has a raw score of 8 and a deviation score of −4, which equals 16 when squared. Next on the class list is Sue, who had 13 correct items on the TOP. Her deviation score

is 1, which equals 1 when squared. When we add all of the squared deviation scores, the sum is 144. To obtain the average squared deviation, we divide by the number of observations and get 14.4. Finally, the square root of 14.4 is approximately 3.8. Based on this class's performance, we now know for the TOP that the average difference from the test mean is about 4 items.

In this example, the standard deviation (*SD*) is equal to $\sqrt{(x - X)^2/ N}$ or $\sqrt{144/10}$, with a final result of 3.8. Basically, we totaled the squared deviations, divided by the number of students (10) and then took the square root.

The Normal Curve

While the standard deviation tells us what average variability we can expect on the TOP, it has even greater potential when linked to the concept of the normal curve, referred to previously as the *bell-shaped curve* upon which most norm-referenced tests are based. The concept was popularized around the turn of the century by British mathematicians, who noted that when the scores of a large number

TABLE 4.6
Example of standard deviation (*SD*)

	Scores	Deviation Scores	Squared Deviations
Shawn	8	−4	16
Sue	13	1	1
Megan	17	5	25
Bonnie	9	−3	9
Johnny	7	−5	25
Linda	9	−3	9
Jennifer	19	7	49
Nicky	11	−1	1
Andy	15	3	9
Michael	12	0	0

of people are plotted on a given attribute, the resulting frequency distribution had certain special characteristics. The most important property of this normal curve is the ability to compare an individual's performance on an attribute to that of the entire population. This can be done effectively because populations disperse themselves about the mean with regularity.

If our entire standardization sample for the TOP consisted of our fourth-grade class, the standard deviation of the test would be 3.8. What useful information does this impart? Given the special properties of the normal curve, statisticians tell us that approximately 34% of the population scores between the test mean and one standard deviation above that test mean. Similarly, about 34% of the population can be expected to score between one standard deviation below the test mean and the test mean. Thus, 68% of a population fall within +1 or −1 standard deviation of the test mean. In addition, we also know that on the normal curve about 14% of our population scores between +1 standard deviation and +2 standard deviations. Similarly, approximately 14% of the normal population scores between −1 and −2 standard deviations. Given these parameters, we can estimate that about 2% of our total population falls below −2 standard deviations and about 2% is above +2 standard deviations. These laws of variability improve our ability to interpret pupil performance in peer-comparison situations.

If the scores are plotted and appear to be normally distributed, the proportions shown in Figure 4.12 exist.

Given that +1 and −1 standard deviation includes about 68% of our population, we can infer that on the TOP, about ⅔ of fourth graders will score between 8 and 16 correct items (e. g., 12 − 3.8 is approximately 8, and 12 + 3.8 is approximately 16). If we were to add and subtract 2 standard deviations from the mean of 12, we would know that 96% of our sample would score between 4 and 20.

Knowing this information, we can make interpretive statements about our students. Only Shawn falls below −1 standard deviation. Therefore, he is probably in the lowest 16% of the total population (2% + 14%). Bonnie, Linda, Nicky, and Michael all score between 8 and 12 and will be located between the 16% and 50% reference points in the population. Sue and Andy have scores between 13 and 16 and would be placed between the 50% and 84% points in the distribution. Finally, Megan and Jennifer are above 16 and can be considered to be above the 84% point in the total population. In chapter 15, we provide a more exact conversion between standard deviations and the percentages of the population under an area of the normal curve.

Correlation: Distribution of Relationships

At this point, we will take a detour and add one last term to your arsenal of measurement concepts. You know how tests get developed to reflect similarity and variation in student performance. We started out by defining domains and sampling items; we then added in the idea of measurement scales, a concept related to calibration. Finally, we considered distributions themselves.

The theme behind these ideas is that an item on a test cannot be considered in isolation; rather, it reflects the relationship of many different considerations: From what domain the item was sampled, how it was sampled, how it was formatted and worded to be at a certain level of difficulty, how it was calibrated, and how it generated similarities and differences among students when it was considered with

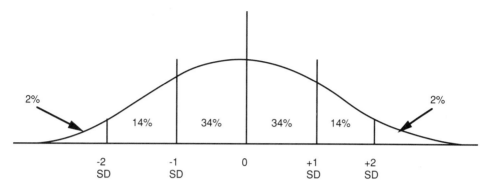

FIGURE 4.12
Proportions of the population falling within areas of the normal curve

other items. The important concept is *relationships.*

An important statistical concept all educators should know is the idea of **correlation** (literally, co-relation). In education, it often is to our benefit to know how closely two variables are related. The *correlation coefficient* was invented for this purpose, to allow us to measure the strength of association between two variables. The next two chapters cover reliability and validity, two concepts that are intricately founded on relationships. The content area chapters provide more specific information on relationships between and among different measures. Since this concept will permeate the remainder of the book, we need to understand it conceptually before applying it specifically to the areas of reliability and validity in the next two chapters.

A high relationship means that if the score is high once, it also is high again on a repeated measure; if it is low once, it is low again on a repeated measure. These repeated measures can be different forms of the same test, the same test given on different occasions, different scorers summarizing performance on the same test, or different tests or measures.

Figures 4.13, 4.14, and 4.15 demonstrate the relationships between two measures through the use of a scattergram. For these figures, we assume that the same test has been given at two times; it could have been different forms or scorers (in which case, reliability is at issue). Or, for that matter, it could have been different tests, like a paper-pencil test of achievement and teacher judgment (in which case, validity is at issue).

In Figure 4.13, the relationship between the two measures is very high: Scores at Time 1 are similar to scores at Time 2. The actual coefficient, if calculated, may be around .70 to .85.

In Figure 4.14, the relationship between the two measures is nonexistent: students with high scores at Time 1 have both low and high scores at Time 2 and vice versa. The actual coefficient if calculated, would be near zero.

In Figure 4.15, the relationship between the two measures for Time 1 and 2 is high, but in a negative, or inverse, direction: When a student scores high at Time 1, the score for Time 2 is low and vice versa. The actual coefficient, if calculated, would be $-.70$ to $-.90$.

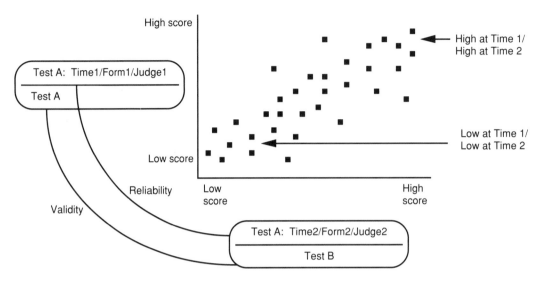

FIGURE 4.13
Example of two highly correlated measures: Same measure on two occasions (reliability) or two measures (validity)

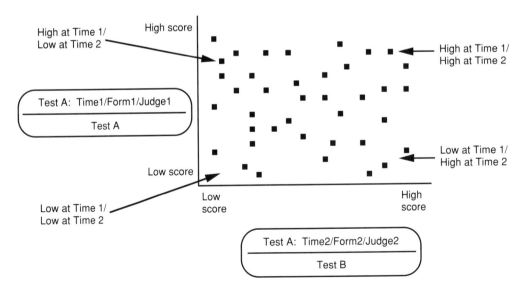

FIGURE 4.14
Comparison of two uncorrelated measures

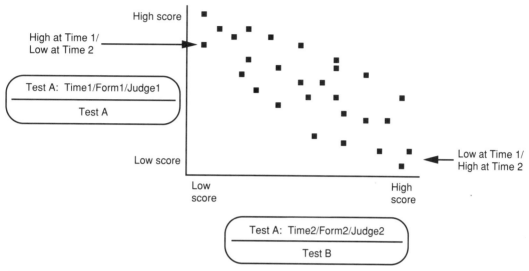

FIGURE 4.15
Example of negative correlation between two measures

CHAPTER SUMMARY

This chapter introduced numerous technical terms that centered on the idea that all tests will result in distributions. The only obligation is to determine the appropriateness of the distribution for the type of decision to be made. We can manipulate distributions through the domains that we define, by the strategy we use for sampling items, and by the difficulty or discrimination we build into an item through its wording and format. We also can calibrate items, utililizing any of four measurement scales. The more sophisticated our scale, the more likelihood we have of creating sensible distributions. Finally we can analyze those distributions, their shapes, and the manner in which students perform similarly or differently. All of these concepts let us know how our test is working. Ultimately, though, we need to consider performance on our test as but one measure within a measurement net that allows us to see how it relates to other measures.

An essential premise of this book is that quantification of performance as a function of the quality of our measures. Only when we know how our instruments work can we use the results from testing with any degree of confidence—to screen students, determine their eligibility for special programs, diagnostically plan a course of instruction for them, formatively evaluate the effects of that instruction, or summarize overall program outcomes. The next two chapters present two strategies for analyzing the adequacy of classroom-based measures of performance, using reliability and validity to quantify and verify any and all outcomes from our tests.

Following is the English translation of the Norwegian paragraph at the beginning of this chapter: Not for the life of me do I understand why you work so much; you shall die young. And then, what will you do when nobody remembers you, not even your family?

CHAPTER 5

Reliability

Have you ever wondered about the medicine you buy at the local pharmacy? Is it safe? Will it produce the same effects each time you take it? Have you ever had questions about what you eat? Are the ingredients listed on the side of the box really the same as those inside? What herbicides have been sprayed on your produce? If you are like most consumers, these types of questions probably have entered your mind. And like most consumers, you may have found some comfort in the fact that the U.S. government has a regulatory agency, the Food and Drug Administration (FDA), whose primary responsibility is to ensure that food and drug products in this country are safe and/or effective.

But do the same requirements for extensive research and documentation of outcomes for medicine and food also exist for the educational consumer? Can teachers, psychologists, and specialists, who use the hundreds of tests available in the educational market, be sure the product adequately fulfills the stated purpose of the assessment procedure they administer? The answer frequently is no. Traditionally, the only research data on test outcomes have been provided by test publishers and university research personnel. A formal government institution or regulatory agency does not yet exist to review the adequacy of the educational tests we use for assessing students. This is unfortunate because tests must be reliable if they are to be useful, and the outcomes must be predictable and consistent.

CHAPTER OBJECTIVES

Because teachers cannot be assured that published tests are reliable, they must understand test concepts and their implications and be able to make decisions about test construction and adoption based upon the predictability of scores generated. Any interpretations of performance must be qualified by considerations of test reliability.

By the end of this chapter, you should have the knowledge and skills to

- Define reliability and its relationship to measurement error.
- Apply minimum standards to tests for their review and adoption or in their construction.
- Consider the sources of error that enter into test performance, knowing also which types of reliability we can and should consider in controlling for these sources.
- Relate the major assumptions, calculation procedures, and interpretive cautions for each type of reliability: parallel form, test-retest, parallel form and test-retest, internal consistency, and interjudge or intrajudge.
- Apply reliability to three important concepts—standard error of measurement, estimated true scores, and confidence intervals—and be able to define these terms, and know how to calculate them.
- Know what happens to reliability when the difference between two tests is calculated.

KEY VOCABULARY

A considerable amount of new vocabulary appears in this chapter. Most of the terms have a colloquial synonym or meaning that will suffice for now.

This chapter addresses measurement error and procedures for understanding and controlling it. The major concept is *reliability*, which is a synonym for repeatability. The different types of reliability describe the conditions under which (student) performance should be repeated: (a) with *parallel form*, performance on two versions of the same test should be similar, (b) with *test-retest*, performance should be similar (repeatable) across time, (c) with the combined version (*test-retest and parallel form*), both of the above conditions apply, (d) with *internal consistency*, performance should be similar across different parts of the same test, and (e) with *inter-judge* or *intrajudge* reliability, performance repeats across people or across two occasions for the same person. Also in this chapter, three fairly complex terms are introduced: *standard error of measurement* (*SEM*), which is simply a metric for quantifying the amount of error around an individual score; *estimated true scores* (*ETS*), a theoretical concept that reflects what student performance would be if no measurement error existed; and *confidence intervals,* a term used to report performance as falling within a range of scores, rather than as one value.

To illustrate reliability, we will use two fictional reading tests in this chapter as examples, the Test Of Performance (TOP), which is reliable, and the Performance Overview Of Reading (POOR), which is unreliable. We will see how our fictional class of fourth graders does on both of these tests. We will answer questions such as; "How do I know if I have a reliable test like the TOP or an unreliable one like the POOR?" "If my test is not reliable, how can I correct it and make it reliable?" "How should I interpret performance with my test?"

RELIABILITY: SOURCES OF ERROR AND TYPES OF DOCUMENTATION

In this section, you will learn what reliability is, why it is important, and how it is documented and interpreted. Several sources of error will be presented, followed by four specific procedures for establishing reliability.

Definition and Meaning

The **reliability** of a test refers to how well it provides a consistent set of results across sim-ilar test situations, time periods, and examiners. "Reliability concerns the extent to which measurements are *repeatable*" (Nunnally, 1967, p. 172). Any discussion of reliability must take error into account. It is generally assumed that all measurement contains error, meaning that scores fluctuate. If a score fluctuates randomly (inconsistently) on repeated occasions, then it lacks reliability. This fluctuation or variability is partially due to error: the greater the variability, the greater the obtained or measured error. Therefore, the more variation in a measure from one occasion to another, the lower the reliability of that measure.

If we used an elastic ruler to measure a board several times in 2 minutes, and the length varied from 42 inches to 53 inches, we would have an unreliable estimate of the board's length. The true length should not vary. Therefore, something must be wrong with the ruler: It is an unreliable device and does not produce consistent lengths on repeated occasions. Suppose we measure the board's length several times in 2 minutes with a steel ruler. We might not find the same measurement because of our hastiness, but the variation in length, say, from 46 7/8 inches to 47 1/8 inches, would be considerably less than found with the elastic ruler. The second set of measures is *more reliable* than the first because it is *less variable.*

The measurement of human skills and achievement is analogous. Test results would have little meaning if they fluctuated wildly from one occasion to the next. We would not administer a test to a child if we knew that without additional instruction, he or she might earn a score 20% higher or 20% lower when retested on the same test. For an educational test to be useful, it must be reliable or consistent. Thus, if we determine that a student's reading performance is at the 50th percentile in reading achievement, we would expect this observation or measurement to be repeated if he or she were administered a similar test, were tested again the next day, or were tested by another teacher.

How much error is present or attached to a particular score must be an estimate. Reliability most often is estimated by relating two sets of scores. It is represented by a real number between .00 and +/− 1.00, reflecting the degree to which two variables (sets of scores) are related. As in our discussion of correlation in chapter 4, a high relationship means that if the score is high once, it will be high again on a repeated measure; if it is low once, it will be low again. These repeated occasions utilize different forms of the same test, the same test given on different occasions, or different scorers summarizing performance.

Standards

For educational purposes, the only type of acceptable relationship between measures of achievement is a positive number that is somewhat high. The problem is: How high should the coefficient be for making decisions? The highest value, 1.00, is never achieved, so we have to accept something lower. Is .50 high enough, or should we accept only measures that are .90 or above? Although an educational FDA does not exist, there are two processes by which educators can judge the merits of standardized tests.

First, the American Psychological Association, the American Educational Research Association, and the National Council for Measurement in Education (1985) have published guidelines that promote the design of technically adequate tests. Known as the *APA test standards,* the guidelines strongly recommend that test authors gather data documenting a test's reliability, validity, and norms (if appropriate).

A second option for educators is to consult Buros' *Mental Measurement Yearbooks.*

Founded by the late Oscar K. Buros, the Institute for Research on Tests has provided test users with technical reviews of educational and psychological tests for more than 40 years. This institution is housed at the University of Nebraska–Lincoln. In their review of reliability, validity, and norms, researchers from the Buros Institute make recommendations about the efficacy of existing tests. The *Tenth Mental Measurements Yearbook* (Conoley, Kramer, & Murphy, 1989) lists over one thousand tests and contains hundreds of test reviews and has several thousand references on the technical adequacy of the tests grouped in one convenient listing for easy use by the reader.

The preceding sources cite standards that have been established by psychometric experts. Webb (1983) reviewed the work of several experts (Cronbach, 1960; Miller, 1972; Payne, 1974; Thorndike & Hagen, 1969) and reported the ranges and their meanings that appear in Table 5.1.

Cronbach (1960) recommends that only those tests that exceed .90 should be used for educational purposes. Nunnally (1967) states that while a .80 coefficient is useful for research purposes, for specific test scores for individuals the coefficient ".90 is the minimum that should be tolerated, and a reliability of .95 should be considered a desirable standard" (p. 226).

TABLE 5.1

Ranges of coefficients and their meanings

Coefficient Size	Meaning
.80 and less	Weak
.81 to .84	Moderate
.85 to .90	Average
.91 to .93	Strong
.94 to .99	Almost perfect

Reprinted from Webb (1983). A scale for evaluating standardized reading tests, with results for Nelson-Denny, Iowa, and Stanford. *Journal of Reading, 26,* 424–429, Table 2, p. 426.

Types of Error

As noted above, reliability involves measurement error. Unfortunately, error exists in all tests or measurement procedures. Whether measuring something as simple as weight or temperature or as complex as intelligence or white blood cell count, we discover that measurement error is inescapable. Obviously, the charge of the test author is to reduce error to levels permitting educationally accurate observations. Two types of error should concern educators: *systematic* (also known as *bias*) and *random* (Nunnally, 1967). The former relates to validity; and the latter to reliability.

An example of systematic measurement error is a scale that always registers 2 pounds lighter than one's actual weight. While this might be popular in our weight-conscious society, it obviously is not a true representation. In education, the use of a test that consistently places a child one grade higher in reading than other tests would be biased and untruthful.

Random error also contributes to misinterpretation of test scores. In the example of a weight scale, random error is present when the readings fluctuate. If the magnitude of random error is large, the accuracy of measurement is seriously compromised, whereas low-magnitude random error has minimal impact on interpretation. The same issues apply to measuring student performance: If wild fluctuations exist, it is difficult to discern real performance levels.

According to APA standards, at least four sources of error exist:

(a) response variation by the subject (due to changes physiological efficiency, or in such psychological factors as motivation, effort, or mood): these may be especially important in inventories of personality; (b) variations in test content or the test situation (in "situational tests" which include interacting persons as part of the situation, this source of variation can be

relatively large); (c) variations in administration (either through variations in physical factors, such as temperature, noise, or apparatus functioning, or in psychological factors, such as variation in the technique or skill of different test administrators or raters; and (d) variations in the process of observation. In addition to these errors of observation, scoring-error variance in tests scores reflects variation in the process of scoring responses as well as mistakes in recording, transferring, or reading of scores. (p. 26)

Response Variation by Students. Students, especially those at earlier grade levels, often experience response variation. Many younger students may find it difficult to maintain constant attention, motivation, and energy when responding to items during lengthy test sessions. Because of this inconsistency, test scores will be subject to error. This source may include a number of variables.

1. Motivation of the student. Students have different histories with achievement testing; some students have done well in the past, are encouraged by their parents and teachers, and have been reinforced for high performance. Others do poorly, have not been encouraged by their parents and teachers, and have been given little reason to perform well. These factors all reflect the student's motivation. Since most achievement testing is oriented toward documentation of optimal performance, motivation is an important factor.

2. Learning, development, and education. Obviously, the purpose of achievement testing is to document skills that students have acquired. As students proceed through school, it often appears that individual differences in achievement actually become more, rather than less, accentuated over the years. For example, while most students are just learning to read and write in first grade, and

differences between them are slight, great differences exist between the highest and lowest performers by sixth grade. When great variation exists among students, the reliability of the test becomes more difficult to ascertain.

3. Test anxiety. Depending upon the contingencies that occur during the test, students may perform with anxiety. Often a small amount of anxiety may be appropriate, providing an alerting response. However, if the pressure is excessive, it is likely to impede performance. Some tests are more prone to provoke anxiousness, like entrance exams and minimum competency tests, on which significant decisions about one's future are based.

4. Experience with tests. Each year, students become more familiar with tests. As they experience different formats, they become increasingly proficient in taking tests. However, as already noted, test-taking skills actually may not improve for those students who have histories of failure; instead, this experience may be a source of anxiety that adversely affects performance.

5. Coaching. Unfortunately, many teachers spend a considerable amount of instructional time coaching students on end-of-year achievement tests. Under the guise of facilitating student familiarity with testing formats, they often operate under pressure to attain achievement levels equal to or greater than those attained the previous year. Therefore, all of the special education students may be tested on a different schedule (and not added into a school's average) and heavily coached. Generally, such coaching may be helpful in familiarizing the students with formats (See Dobbin, 1984, *How to Take a Test: Doing Your Best,* published by Educational Testing Service). But on any test that provides a broad measure of achievement and encompasses many diverse items

(e.g., most published achievement tests), specific coaching on knowledge and skills is sorely misplaced.

6. Physiological variables. Such variables as hunger, comfort, and thirst also influence performance. For testing to accurately reflect optimal levels of performance, their influence must be minimized. The actual testing situation should be carefully controlled to minimize distractions, and well-rehearsed administration directions should be given to students who are comfortably seated.

Variation in Test Content. Poorly constructed tests may contribute to inconsistent variation. Tests may be inappropriately difficult, so that students perform erratically. If a test is too hard, guessing and inconsistent responses are likely. Students may even react emotionally, perhaps crying. If a test is too easy, variation among individuals is likely to be masked, and a meaningful estimate of reliability is difficult to attain. Variation of test content within a test may create error. For example, if a math test has mixed problem types (of the various operations), students may make errors in responding to the sign; thus, the outcome does not estimate true skill. Items also can be intrinsically ambiguous if they are imprecisely worded or inadequately framed and prompt distinctions that cannot be made validly from the information available. Finally, a small sample of items can make a test inadequate or unreliable. An important concept of reliability is that it is as much a function of the number of items in the test as anything else. One procedure for improving reliability is to increase the number of items in the test. Many published tests have adequate levels of reliability for total test scores only; although the publishers suggest the use of subtests and report subtest scores, the information at this level is actually unreliable and should not be used.

Variation in Administration. A number of quasi-administrative issues may be present. Certainly, a teacher administering a test in a nonstandard fashion introduces error in the assessment process. An important goal is to standardize testing so that it is maximally effective and informative (i.e., consistent and replicable). Anyone giving a test should practice administering it and should closely follow scripted directions. An important advantage of standardized administration procedures is that they make performance outcomes more interpretable. Not only will the information be more reliable, but it will also be more accurate and understandable. It is important to recognize that the term *standardization* refers to the employment of consistent procedures for administering tests and scoring responses. Many educators think it applies only to the presence of a norm-group (often referred to as a *standardization sample*).

Variation in administration is not limited to the manner in which test directions are implemented; it can also apply to the general testing situation. It is not difficult to imagine students performing differentially when administered a test (a) in their own classroom of 25–30 students by their teacher, (b) in the lunchroom (entire grade level of 100 students) by an aide, and (c) one-to-one by a school psychologist in a small private room outside of the classroom. As these three examples illustrate, an important consideration is who gives the test. Some research suggests that examiners' familiarity with the examinee influences student performance (Fuchs & Fuchs, 1986).

Environmental variations also impact pupils' test performance, which can create error in measurement. Extraneous factors such as room temperature, noise, and frequent interruptions affect test scores. One of the authors vividly remembers testing a group of second-graders in a school lunchroom while a crew of carpenters hammered away to remodel a kitchen. It

was not surprising to find that these students' test scores were lower than those of comparable peers.

Variation in Scoring. Another source of error occurs when there are deviations in the scoring and coding process. While this is not a problem with many standardized tests whose format consists primarily of multiple-choice items that are scored by computer[s], it can be a difficulty when performance is subjectively scored, as with essay tests. Whenever judgments must be made as part of the scoring process, it is important that well-developed scoring guides be present to help anchor judgments and create consistent response sets by the scorers. In addition, the scoring process should be monitored closely. To the extent that interjudge or intrajudge agreement is lacking, there will be considerable error in test performance.

Types of Reliability

Since error can arise from these four sources, either in concert or in isolation, we must be attentive to strategies for controlling it. But at some point, we have to recognize that error is always present, even though we have done our best to control it. An additional strategy for quantifying performance appropriately, in recognition of the presence of error, is to calculate the appropriate form of reliability coefficient. Various methods for estimating the reliability of tests take into account different sources of measurement error. Five approaches for estimating reliability are parallel form, test-retest, parallel form/test-retest, internal consistency, and interjudge agreement. For each type, we will present (a) a basic definition along with an example showing when it is needed and how it is calculated, (b) the assumptions upon which it is based, and (c) some guidelines and cautions for interpreting it.

Parallel Form Reliability. Parallel form reliability is also referred to as *alternate form* or *equivalent form* reliability. It measures the equivalence of items sampled from the same domain and represents the correlation coefficient between the scores obtained on *two forms of the same test.* By having two administrations at least 1 day apart using two forms of the same test, it should be possible to ascertain comparability. This form is particularly sensitive to variation in student responses and test content.

When needed. Parallel form reliability is crucial when two or more equivalent forms of the test exist. Two forms are particularly important when students are tested in a pre-post format over a short time period, since any statements about real change must be free of a practice effect (precluding the use of only one form) and error resulting from the use of two forms. If alternate forms are equivalent for both tests, we expect equivalent results for a person who is tested with both forms. Disagreement between the two forms indicates poor reliability and calls for revision of the two forms before publication.

Definitional example. Let us assume that we have created parallel forms for the TOP (Form A and Form B) and the POOR (Form X and Form Y) for our fourth-grade classroom. In this instance, we have used the correlation coefficient between the two forms to estimate the reliability coefficient. In the example in Table 5.2, our 10 pupils were administered Form A and Form B of the TOP, as well as Form X and Form Y of the POOR. We have reported standard scores for all four tests and calculated the correlation coefficients.

As you can see in this example, Forms A and B are parallel (the outcomes repeat for both forms), while Forms X and Y are not parallel, since there is a fair amount of disagreement. For example, on the TOP, Megan scored 100 on Form A and 103 on Form B; she scored 97 on the POOR's Form X and 106 on Form Y. Similarly, Shawn scored 80 on Form A and 77 on Form B of the TOP, while on the POOR, he scored 68 on Form X and 92 on Form Y. If we calculate the parallel form reliability for the TOP and the POOR, our suspicions are verified: The reliability coefficient for the TOP is .96, which is acceptable, but the parallel form reliability for the POOR is .68, an unacceptable coefficient for Forms X and Y.

TABLE 5.2
Comparison of parallel form reliability of the TOP and POOR

	The TOP		The POOR	
	Form A	Form B	Form X	Form Y
Megan	100	103	97	106
Nicky	110	108	113	105
Shawn	80	77	68	92
Sue	97	102	103	95
Johnny	80	77	74	76
Jennifer	118	117	120	124
Linda	94	94	92	78
Michael	104	108	105	125
Bonnie	95	93	94	74
Andy	120	112	121	110

As can be seen, calculation of this form of reliability requires the following:

1. Develop (or adopt) a test with at least two forms that use (a) the same sampling plan from the same domain and (b) unique items.
2. Give each test to a group of students in successive testing situations.
3. Correlate the results of the test (let the computer crunch the numbers). Of course, this form of reliability is limited to those tests for which two forms are available.

There is a great deal of variation in the reliability coefficients for many tests. In most cases, lower coefficients exist for individual subtests, while higher coefficients are found for total scores of these tests. In general, such data indicate that educators should look closely at the published reliability information for any test they choose to administer.

Assumptions. Parallel form reliability is based on five assumptions. First, we assume that both forms measure the same trait or skill. If the different forms sampled different skills, we would have two unique tests, not parallel forms of the same test. This issue is critical when the sampling procedures do not adequately represent a domain (like a spelling test that samples too few words, in which case parallel form reliability may be difficult to obtain). Have you ever wondered why the Test of Written Spelling (Larsen & Hammill, 1986) doesn't establish this form of reliability? (See chapter 9 for the answer.)

Second, we assume that both forms have been standardized on the same population. Another way of saying this is that we can only vary one thing at a time. If we gave two different tests to two different groups, it would not be possible to ascertain whether variation in outcome was a function of the groups we tested or the forms we used.

The third assumption is that both forms of the test ask different questions or elicit different responses. To clearly establish this form of reliability as parallel, the items need to be equivalent, but not the same. We usually establish this form of reliability with two testing situations closely scheduled in time; if we used the exact same items, we would very likely create some type of practice effect.

Fourth, we assume that the means and variances for the students tested on both forms are the same; that is, when parallel form reliability is established, we need not only high correlations, which represent the ranking of a group on two forms of the same test, but also the same distributions. It is possible to have a high correlation while one form is much more difficult—with a lower mean and more variation—than the other form.

Finally, we assume that test administration and scoring are the same for both sessions. To ensure that student performance is similar (repeatable), we do not want any differences in the manner in which we gave the test or scored performance.

Cautions and interpretive guidelines. Several cautions and interpretive guidelines are necessary when we employ parallel form reliability. An advantage of parallel form reliability is that students are not subject to sensitization (or practice) effects since they have not been tested with the same items twice. However, the domain for sampling items sometimes is so broad that it is difficult to establish this form of reliability adequately. A test may have poor parallel form reliability but still have adequate internal consistency or test-retest reliability. Thus, the test may be suitable for some decisions (e.g., screening), but not others (e.g., measuring growth over a short time period).

For many purposes, this type of reliability is impractical (e.g., when the user needs one form and does not have the resources or time to develop an alternate). Since it requires two test administrations, the testing time is doubled; therefore, examinee cooperation, motivation, fatigue, and boredom present additional practical obstacles. The practical difficulties associated with developing two forms of a test and the problems of two administrations are often insurmountable. Therefore, methods for establishing reliability that require only one administration are more commonly employed, especially for teacher-made tests.

Test-Retest Reliability. This reliability is the correlation between scores on *the same test administered twice,* separated by a brief period of time. This measure reflects the stability of individual scores between testing and retesting, using the same questions or items. Since most educational skills change little over short periods, it is necessary that tests reflect this constancy. This form of reliability is particularly sensitive to variation in student responses and test administration, since nothing changes from one administration to the next. If performance is different on these two occasions, one must question how students responded or how the test was administered. The test-retest approach may also be used to determine variation of test content, particularly if doubts exist about the domain of items. Finally, when we employ subjective scoring systems, test-retest reliability helps establish consistent scoring procedures that do not drift.

When needed. Because this form of reliability serves as a ballast, it is particularly desirable and necessary when we need broad measures of achievement. On most published achievement tests, in which items are not linked closely to instructional content or curriculum,

test-retest reliability should be present and, of course, high. On more specific achievement tests, with items drawn from a narrow range of instruction or the curriculum, test-retest reliability may be neither possible nor desirable. Criterion-referenced tests, in which performance may change drastically within a week, are not expected to have test-retest reliability.

Definitional example. In Table 5.3, the test-retest reliability of the TOP and the POOR has been checked with our fourth-grade class. Each test was readministered with a 2-week interval.

As you can see, the results for Time 1 and Time 2 are much more consistent for the TOP than they are for the POOR. For example, Nicky has standard scores of 112 at Time 1 and 110 at Time 2 on the TOP. On the POOR, however, his score drops from 117 at Time 1 to a standard score of 102 at Time 2. Lack of stability on the POOR is also evident in Bonnie's performance. She scored 91 and 95 on the test-retest sessions for the TOP, but went from 81 at Time 1 to 94 at Time 2 on the POOR. Of course, there may be a slight shift in the ordering of the students, particularly in the middle of the distribution, but the general shape and order should remain substantially the same. Test-retest reliability coefficients for our two tests confirm these observations. For the TOP, test-retest analysis showed a correlation of .92 for Time 1 and Time 2. However, only a .65 test-retest reliability coefficient was found for the POOR.

Procedures for developing test-retest reliability are very straightforward:

1. Develop or adopt a test with a broad range of items.
2. Test a group of students the first time.
3. Give them the same test within approximately 2 weeks.
4. Correlate the results of the two tests.

TABLE 5.3
Comparison of test-retest reliabilities of the TOP and POOR

Student	The TOP		The POOR	
	Time 1	Time 2	Time 1	Time 2
Megan	98	102	95	114
Nicky	112	110	117	102
Shawn	86	83	72	90
Sue	98	103	105	94
Johnny	81	75	75	80
Jennifer	119	115	118	127
Linda	97	95	96	88
Michael	102	110	100	117
Bonnie	91	95	81	94
Andy	117	111	125	109

The calculation of test-retest reliability is similar to that for parallel form reliability. In its simplest form, we use the correlational analysis. Rather than correlate two equivalent forms of one test for a group of pupils, students take the same form of a test twice over a specified interval.

As in parallel form reliability, subtests typically are less reliable than total tests, and considerable variation exists among the tests on the market.

Assumptions. With this form of reliability, we assume that student performance should not fluctuate much from Time 1 to Time 2 without any intervening instruction that is specific to the test. However, scores may be influenced by the length of the retest interval. If the time between testing is too long, learning may affect changes in scores; if the time between testing is too short, then memory or a practice effect may affect changes in scores. As with parallel form reliability, we assume that the two test administrations and the scoring of responses are conducted comparably. Again, we are trying to rule out differences that are solely functions of the retest, so everything else should remain the same.

Cautions and interpretive guidelines. As mentioned earlier, test-retest reliability is more appropriate for broad band tests, which contain items that have been sampled from a large domain. If the test has sampled from a small or narrow domain, retest reliabilities may be poor because (a) the homogeneity of items has eliminated the variation among students (with minimal standard deviations, reliability will be adversely affected); (b) a practice effect has occurred, with memory accounting for different performance; and (c) learning has taken place, since the amount of material is so circumscribed and the time between testing relatively long. In all three instances, retest reliabilities will be low, indicating in a somewhat false manner that the test is at fault, when in fact the problem really arises from the use of the wrong reliability estimates.

A curious fact is that test-retest reliability usually is higher than parallel form reliability because the latter permits a new sampling of the content universe, while the sampling of test content is not allowed to vary in test-retest procedures. Since all reliability estimates are based on the concept of dispersion, any formats that enhance this outcome will appear to be better. Therefore, we need to discuss the special case of establishing reliability for criterion-referenced tests, which are based on the idea of mastery, not dispersion.

The special case of criterion-referenced reliability. Thus far, discussion has focused on reliability as the repeatability of performance. Typically, its basic premise is the idea of variance, since the five specific types of reliability depend on correlation coefficients. However, when we use criterion-referenced tests, with items often quite limited in both depth (not many of any type) and breadth (not many different item types), little variance exists among students. If we calculate any of the five types of reliability for these tests, the estimates of repeatability may be low, not because the test is unreliable, but because the manner for calculating reliability is not appropriate. Therefore, another form of reliability that has been proposed for criterion-referenced tests utilizes the *consistency of decision over two repeated administrations.* Since we estimate it from two administrations, we describe this type of reliability as a form of test-retest reliability.

Millman (1974) proposed three indices to establish the reliability of criterion-referenced tests. First, we can calculate the number and percentage of individual items that have been answered the same (whether correct or not) upon two administrations of the same test separated by at least a week. Second, we can calculate the percentage of students scoring at various percentages of discrepancy between the two administrations. Third, we can calculate the difference between observed and chance proportions of agreement in mastery decisions for each of two administrations of the same test. Tindal et al. (1985) reported on these reliability estimates for three criterion-referenced tests commonly used in public schools [Houghton Mifflin, Durr et al. (1981), Scott, Foresman; Aaron et al. (1981), and Ginn 720, Clymer et al. (1980)]. They found that traditional estimates of reliability and the corrected

proportions of examinees scoring the same across two administrations of the same test were in agreement and generally quite high.

An interesting finding was that these tests were not very reliable for making mastery decisions, with a range of from 15% to 33% of the students misclassified using total test scores. Mastery decisions based on subtest scores, although promulgated by the publishers, were even worse, since fewer items were sampled, and ranged from 15% to 46% misclassification.

Parallel Form and Test-Retest. Another form of reliability is based on parallel form and test-retest reliability, which provides the most stringent assessment of consistency. Again, procedures involve the administration of *two unique forms of a test at two times.* As with parallel form reliability, two tests are administered; as with test-retest reliability, these two administrations are separated by 1 or 2 weeks. In both parallel form and test-retest reliability, all students receive both forms. However, in the combined format, only half of the students receive either form at each time: Counterbalancing the administration controls for a potential problem with sequence of administration by form.

When needed. This form of reliability is rarely used, in part because it is so stringent, and adequate levels are difficult to achieve. Another reason for its infrequent use probably is related to the type of application for which it is most appropriate: measuring growth on a large domain over a long period of time. This type of reliability is only applicable with a published, norm-referenced achievement test as a pre-post measure of growth over a long period of time.

We may be interested in measuring growth over a long period or over a large domain; rarely are we interested in both, although we may assume that to achieve growth over a large domain, we need an extended period of time.

However, as we argue in chapters 13, 14, and 15, the best measures of growth are not likely to be pre-post testing on large domains. By using both parallel form and test-retest reliability, we have the best of both worlds. The former assures us that the growth was not specific to the items that appeared in our first (or pre) test; the latter assures us that the change made over the time interval was real and not spuriously attained.

Definitional example. If the second form of the TOP (described in Table 5.2) is administered 2 weeks later using different items and not just a few hours or days after the first, or if the POOR samples unique items from the same domain and isn't just a repeat version of the same test, we have an example of parallel form and test-retest reliability. We hope that the same outcomes will appear: On the TOP, students should be in the same relative ranking on both versions of the test; on the POOR, they will likely move around a lot. Generally, the estimates of reliability will be lower than the combined averages of the two types; for the TOP, it may be around .80 to .85; on the POOR, it might be around .50 to .60.

We perform the following procedures to determine this type of reliability:

1. Develop or adopt two forms of the same test. Each form should have unique items that have been sampled from the same domain.
2. Test students in the following manner: Give Test 1 to half of the students and Test 2 to the other half.
3. Wait for 2 weeks and switch the tests given to each group.
4. Correlate the results.

Assumptions. Because this approach is a combination of parallel form and test-retest reliability, all assumptions made earlier are necessary. From parallel form, we assume that each form measures the same skills, that both occasions measure the same population, that the items on each form are unique and not repeated, and that the means and standard deviations are the same for both forms. From test-retest, we assume that the interval between testing is neither too long, so that a learning effect could occur, nor too short, so that practice or memory effects could occur. For both types of reliability, we assume that both versions of the test have been similarly administered and scored.

Cautions and interpretive guidelines. Since this form of reliability is so stringent, a decision not to adopt a test based on a poor showing may be wrong. Therefore, we should consider further analysis of each type of reliability alone. As mentioned earlier, this form of reliability also should fit the application for which measurement is to be obtained. If the purpose is less than measuring growth on a large domain over a long time, a decision to select either component type of parallel form and test-retest reliability may be in order.

Internal Consistency Reliability. Internal Consistency Reliability, also referred to as *odd-even and split-half* reliability, is based on an analysis of items that make up a test. This form is useful if we want our test items closely related. Basically, internal consistency reliability measures the degree of *interrelationship between items on the same test* and is based upon the average correlation among items within a test.

When needed. Internal consistency is important to establish when defining domains, either because of the broad and diverse nature of the items that the domain includes or because we want to make inferences about a student's generalized performance in a domain or skill area. This form of reliability is probably the most common type in published achievement tests because of three related issues: (a) Most of these achievement tests sample items from very broad domains, thereby creating the need to consider only those items that relate to each other; (b) many of these tests establish analyses that include only those items representing middle levels of difficulty; and (c) documenting this type of reliability is the cheapest and most convenient option, since only one form is produced and the test needs to be given only once.

An example of adequate internal consistency with the TOP and poor internal consistency with the POOR appears in Table 5.4. For purposes of illustration, let us assume there are only four items in each test, although in most cases there would be more. All of our fourth-grade students are listed and their performance on each item is recorded. A plus sign (+) denotes a correct response on the item, and a minus sign (−) means an incorrect response.

As you can see, the four items of the TOP are fairly consistent. The class had 6 correct responses on Item 1, 7 correct on Item 2, 5 correct on Item 3, and 7 correct on Item 4. This kind of consistency is not evident on the POOR.

The class had 6 correct answers on Item 1 and 7 correct on Item 2. However, there was only 1 response right on Item 3, and all 10 students had Item 4 correct. This wide discrepancy in the last two items suggests that Items 3 and 4 are not consistent with Items 1 and 2. Therefore, they should be eliminated from the test.

The procedures for determining internal consistency reliability follow:

1. Develop or adopt one form of a test that contains a substantial number of items. Since the test will be split in half, each half must have an adequate number of items to provide an estimate of reliability.
2. Administer the entire test to a group of students.
3. Divide the test (and each student's performance) into two halves using odd-even items (1,3,5,7,9, etc. for one half and 2,4,6,8, etc. for the other half) or splitting the test into a first and second half. Obviously, we can use the latter procedure only with tests that mix items randomly in terms of difficulty. If items grow progressively easier or more difficult, they should be divided into odd and even groupings.

TABLE 5.4
Example of internal consistency on the TOP and the POOR

	The TOP					The POOR				
	1	2	3	4	Total	1	2	3	4	Total
Megan	+	+	−	+	3	+	+	−	+	3
Nicky	+	+	−	+	3	+	+	−	+	3
Shawn	+	−	+	−	2	+	−	−	+	2
Sue	−	+	−	+	2	−	+	−	+	2
Johnny	−	−	+	−	1	−	−	−	+	1
Jennifer	+	+	+	+	4	+	+	−	+	3
Linda	−	+	−	+	2	−	+	−	+	2
Michael	+	−	+	+	3	+	−	−	+	2
Bonnie	−	+	−	−	1	−	+	−	+	2
Andy	+	+	+	+	4	+	+	+	+	4
Total	6	7	5	7		6	7	1	10	

4. Correlate the two sets of scores. This form of reliability coefficient is based on only half the items (since the test was split); therefore the coefficient should be adjusted mathematically using a correction procedure.

Assumptions. An important assumption for this form of reliability is that we can sort the two parts to form equivalent halves of a test. Although the strategies mentioned above (sorting items on an odd-even or first- and second-half basis) may be suitable for most situations, they are inadequate if the pool of items is very heterogeneous and assymetrically formatted throughout the test. Two halves of a test with a wide range of content and diverse formats (including multiple-choice and extended-answer items) may not be equally difficult on the simple basis of odd-even or first and second half. Thus, we may need to formulate some other division.

Another assumption is that the test contains enough items to split it into halves. If the test has too few items, any further division will preclude using this form of reliability. Even with a correction for attenuation, which should be done to obtain an estimate of the reliability for the entire test had it not been split, a test with few items is unlikely to be reliable.

Cautions and interpretive guidelines. Two reasons for caution should be considered when using this type of reliability. First, it should not be used if all students do not finish the test. To ensure that the test has generated enough samples of behavior, every item should be completed. Otherwise, because of the pairwise matching of items across the two halves, missing data (for an item) creates an assymetry in the alignment of the items. If the test is timed, not all items may be completed, so this type of reliability should not be used.

The second reason for caution about internal consistency reliability is that it provides no estimate of stability over time or forms. Typically calculated with coefficient alpha (Cronbach, 1951) or Kuder-Richardson's KR-20 formula (Nunnally, 1967) for dichotomous items, an upper limit is set on the level of reliability that can be obtained. Nunnally (1967) notes that if it is too low, there are either too few items in the test or the items do not have much in common.

Inter and Intrajudge Agreement Interjudge or intrajudge agreement denotes the agreement among judges or within judges over time. This form of reliability is sensitive only to variation in scoring and is not likely to pick up any of the other sources of variation noted earlier.

When needed. Interjudge or intrajudge reliability is important when subjective factors affect test scoring. For example, direct measures of written expression often employ subjective scoring based on rating scales. For such tests, in which the magnitude of disagreement can play a prominent role in decisionmaking, this type of agreement must be kept as high as possible. It may also be important for teacher-made testing when student performance is hand-scored and the results tallied individually: Mistakes in scoring or totaling results can have a great impact. This form of reliability has little bearing on most published achievement testing, since all student protocols are machine-scored.

We also use this type of reliability to document the degree of intrajudge agreement, in which an *individual's* scoring is independently repeated at a later time. Here, the major concern is with scoring drift and the consistent application of scoring standards. For example, a group of 10th-grade students may have their writing compositions rated on a dimension of creativity (using a scale of 1 to 5); 2 weeks later, the same judge rescores the compositions to determine the degree of consistency (repeatability) from Time 1 to Time 2.

We can again employ correlation analysis to determine the reliability coefficient in this domain, whether the concern is among or within judges. In the example in Table 5.5, two judges have scored over 10 students on the TOP and the POOR. The correlation coefficient demonstrates the degree to which the judges are reliable.

As you can see, Ms. Hendrix and Mr. Nelson had much greater agreement on the TOP than on the POOR. Evidence of poor interjudge reliability is demonstrated by the 21-point disagreement for Megan and the 18-point difference for Michael. The correlation coefficient for interjudge reliability on the TOP is .94, and for the POOR it is .63. This example would also apply to the scores of one judge at two times.

The procedures for calculating interjudge or intrajudge agreement are simple:

1. Test a group of students.
2. Independently score the protocols using either two (sets of) judges or one judge at

two times. It is important that (a) scoring on both occasions is *independently* completed and (b) each score is separately tracked and recorded.
3. Correlate the results.

While published tests rarely use this form of reliability, primarily because they employ selection responses that are obviously correct or incorrect and require no judgment, curriculum-based measures (CBM) generally use production responses that cannot be machine-scored. Therefore, this form of reliability is critical. The research completed on the reliability of CBM (Tindal, Marston, & Deno, 1983; Marston & Deno, 1981) indicates very high interjudge reliability, as summarized in Table 5.6.

Assumptions. Interjudge or intrajudge reliability is based on the assumption that scoring is conducted under the same conditions on both occasions. To maximize consistency and obtain a high coefficient, scoring conditions should be optimal; that is, they should (a) be completed in an environment that is quiet, comfortable, and free of distractions, (b) utilize a review of scoring standards prior to actually scoring any protocols, and (c) employ scoring sessions of moderate length. In essence, the

TABLE 5.5
Student performance on the TOP and POOR as scored by two teachers

	The TOP		The POOR	
	Ms. Hendrix	Mr. Nelson	Ms. Hendrix	Mr. Nelson
Megan	97	100	94	115
Nicky	114	111	117	104
Shawn	85	82	71	88
Sue	99	104	106	92
Johnny	80	75	74	82
Jennifer	118	115	116	125
Linda	96	94	96	87
Michael	103	109	101	119
Bonnie	91	96	80	91
Andy	115	109	126	107

TABLE 5.6
Interjudge agreement with curriculum-based measures

	Range of Reliability Coefficients
Reading	.97–.99
Spelling	.91–.99
Written expression	.90–.98
Mathematics	.87–.99

task is to create the same response set for both sessions.

We make no assumptions about the use of guides or scoring aides, but we assume that the judges have been trained and are following the same directions. Occasionally, we use exemplars (i.e., range finders for various qualities of written-expression protocols); at other times, we use rating scales with well-defined anchors. In both cases, judges should be trained in how to use the scoring guides.

Since we test students only once, it is important that we employ standardized administration conditions; however, this facet is not critical to establishing this form of reliability—only in interpreting the results.

Cautions and interpretive guidelines. Interjudge and intrajudge reliability means that a score is not an idiosyncratic or individually defined outcome, but represents a commonly agreed-upon result. Anyone who is trained in the same manner as the judges can "see the same thing." It does not endorse or support the judgment itself, only the commonality of that judgment. For example, if written compositions are judged on a dimension of *flavor,* we can attain agreement (reliability) on the amount of *flavor* in a paper, but still disagree over the importance of this dimension in written compositions.

Any measures that employ production responses must establish interjudge or intrajudge reliability by establishing rules for scoring responses. For example, in reading, what constitutes an error or miscue? In written expression, how do we define a word? Therefore, in reporting this form of reliability, we should also report a description of the definitions and scoring procedures. Anyone using the measure must employ the same procedures to be assured of reliability.

Summary of Types of Reliability. At this point, we have addressed two issues: (a) All measurement contains error, for which various strategies can be used as controls, and (b) we need different forms of reliability to document the amount of error present. Each form of reliability has a place in the assessment process. Parallel form reliability improves a teacher's choice tests that contain alternate forms. Using tests with high test-retest reliability assures teachers that student scores are stable and can be used with confidence for program planning. Teachers who are concerned about the similarity or homogeneity of test items should consider internal consistency reliability. For subjective tests with more than one person scoring the results, interjudge or intrajudge reliability is necessary.

APPLICATION OF RELIABILITY TO SCORE INTERPRETATION

Until now, we have argued that reliability is important, but we have not quantified or used it, other than to make judgments about whether to adopt or utilize the results of a test. In this section, we move beyond the concept, its definitions, and component analysis, and apply it to individual student performance. To do this, we must first understand the concept of true scores. We can then extend reliability analysis to three sequential applications: (a) calculation of a standard error of measurement, (b) estimation of true scores, and (c) establishment of confidence intervals within which true scores are likely to appear. Now we can actually use reliability to interpret individual score performance. Reliability is meaningless in and of itself; its only relevance is the influence it has on these three psychometric indices.

Reliability and True Scores

We can quantify the reliability of a test by looking at error distributions and calculating a reliability coefficient, which is defined as the ratio of the variance of a set of true scores on a test to the variance of the corresponding observed scores. The formula for this equation is written

$$r_{YY} = \frac{S^2 \text{ True scores}}{S^2 \text{ Observed scores}}$$

The index r_{YY} represents the reliability of a test. S^2 is the variation of either **true scores** (the actual scores we would get with a perfect test) or observed scores (the scores we get from tests). If a set of obtained scores is very similar to true scores, the ratio approaches 1.0 and represents perfect reliability. When obtained scores vary significantly from true scores, the reliability coefficient approaches 0.0 and signifies no reliability. This formula and the definition are obviously heuristic, since we can never know a student's true score. As you see later, though, we can estimate it.

Table 5.7 illustrates this principle. Let us assume we know the true scores in reading for our classroom of 10 pupils, and we have their observed scores from the TOP and the POOR. In order to calculate the variance of true scores, we must subtract each student's score from the test mean and square the remainder. This is the squared deviation in Table 5.7. We then calculate total variance (S^2) by adding the squared deviations. This sum is entered into the preceding reliability formula.

As you can see, the variances of true and observed scores on the POOR are not similar when the means for both tests and the true scores are 100. For example, Linda has a true reading score of 94 but an observed score of 86 on the POOR. Andy has a true score of 114, but a score of 121 on the POOR. The result is a low reliability coefficient, because the ratio of the classroom's total true score variance to observed score variance is .496 (125/252). However, the variances of the true scores and the observed scores for the TOP are similar and assure us that this measure is quite reliable. For example, Megan has a true score of 100 in reading and a score of 102 on the TOP. Nicky has scores of 110 for both the true score and the observed score on the TOP. The ratio of true score variance to the observed score variance on the TOP is .908 (125/137.6).

Observed scores and true scores for each of our students appear in Table 5.10. If true scores were always readily available, the effects of test reliability would be easy to estimate. But all tests contain error, so we have no way of knowing a student's true score on any test. As a result, we must make estimates based on test reliabilities.

Standard Error of Measurement

Studying the amount of error on a test by examining the distribution of errors for each person on that test is useful for quantifying reliability. The calculation of the standard deviation of these error scores is known as the **standard error of measurement** and provides valuable information.

We know from the previous chapter that certain characteristics of the standard deviation and its relationship to the normal distribution tell us much about a group of scores. The analogy is as follows: Standard deviations are to groups

TABLE 5.7
Comparison of true scores with observed scores from the TOP and POOR

Pupil	True Score		The POOR		The TOP	
	True Score	Squared Deviation	Observed Score	Squared Deviation	Observed Score	Squared Deviation
Megan	100	0	106	36	102	4
Nicky	110	100	112	144	110	100
Shawn	88	144	83	289	87	169
Sue	97	9	90	100	96	16
Johnny	80	400	76	576	80	400
Jennifer	118	324	125	625	119	361
Linda	94	36	86	196	93	49
Michael	104	16	108	64	104	16
Bonnie	95	25	93	49	94	36
Andy	114	196	121	441	115	225
Average	100	125	100	252	100	137.6

of students as the standard error of measurement is to an individual student. The large, bell-shaped curve in Figure 5.1 shows the results of a test taken by 100 students. The smaller bell-shaped curve shows the results of an individual taking the same test a number of times (say 100 times). We know that students differ from each other—hence, the distribution. We can apply the same principles to both the standard deviation of groups and the standard error of measurement of individuals. For example, if the deviation in performance in Test A is 15, but 25 in Test B, we know there is much more variability in scores for Test B (whether the variability is between students and within a student over repeated testing).

We also know from reliability theory that when an individual takes a test, the scores include measurement error, causing the same score not to repeat—hence, the distribution. Both distributions are expressed in terms of deviation units.

As presented in chapter 4 with the normal curve, we know the percentage of the population that appears within standard distances from the mean. When the distance was $+/-1$ standard deviation, 68% of the population was included; when the distance extended out to $+/-2$ standard deviations, more than 95% of the population was included.

Given two tests with equal means, if Test A has a standard error of measurement equal to 5, and a if a person has an observed score of 100, we know that approximately 68% of that person's test scores on Test A will fall between 95 and 105 ($+/-1$ standard error of measurement). However, the same observed score on Test B, which has a standard error of measurement of 10, gives us a range from 90 to 110 where one would expect 68% of that student's scores to fall. Figure 5.1 displays these two concepts.

The standard error of measurement is calculated by the following formula:

$$SEM = SD \sqrt{1 - \text{Reliability}}$$

where SD signifies the standard deviation of the distribution; SEM represents the standard

FIGURE 5.1
Relationship between
standard deviation and
standard error of
measurement

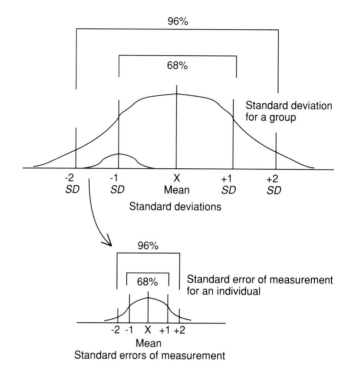

Standard errors of measurement

error of measurement (in the formula); and *SD* is the standard deviation of the test (in the formula).

It should be obvious that two indices influencing the *SEM* are standard deviation *(SD)* and test reliability (r_{yy}). As we can see in Table 5.8, the *SEM* increases with increasing standard deviations and decreasing reliabilities.

Let's use some of the reliability coefficients from previous examples to determine the standard error of measurement for the TOP and the POOR. If we apply the parallel form reliability from our previous example, we have a reliability of .96 for the TOP and .68 for the POOR. When we use these coefficients in our equation (assuming a standard deviation of 15 for both tests), we find a standard error of measurement of 3.67 for the TOP and 8.68 for the POOR. As this example shows, the

standard error of measurement increases as reliability decreases.

Figure 5.2 illustrates low and high variability. Megan was measured on Test A, the TOP, which has little random error, and Test B, the POOR, which has considerable random error. Assume that she had a true score of 100 on both tests (remember, it is only hypothetical). However, if we repeatedly test her reading skills on these tests, two very different pictures of her performance emerge. In Test A, where random error is reduced and Megan's observed scores fall within a much narrower range around the true score of a 100, reliability is better, and the examiner can be more confident that her true score is close to 100. In Test B, with a large magnitude of error, the distribution of repeated, observed test scores is varied, ranging from 50 to 150. Because many of these observed scores

TABLE 5.8
Relationship of standard deviation, reliability, and standard error of measurement

SD	r_{yy}	SEM
10	0.9	3.16
15	0.9	4.74
20	0.9	6.32
25	0.9	7.91
10	0.8	4.47
15	0.8	6.71
20	0.8	8.94
25	0.8	11.18
10	0.7	5.48
15	0.7	8.22
20	0.7	10.95
25	0.7	13.68

are poor estimates of Megan's real performance, we cannot confidently assess her reading skills.

Estimated True Scores

As Figure 5.2 shows, a true score is important for judging the worth of a test's results. The beginning of this section presented reliability as a ratio of true to observed score variance. How do we find a student's true score (since it is really a hypothetical notion and can only be estimated)? Because all tests contain some source of measurement error, we know that the obtained score from any test cannot be the best possible index of one's performance. Reliability theory tells us that if we wish to estimate one's true score, we should sample for that individual an infinite number of tests (Nunnally, 1967). Since such an effort is obviously impossible, we must settle for an **estimated true score,** attained by examining the mean and the reliability of a test. Once we determine a test's reliability, we can make a best estimate of a stu-

dent's true score by multiplying the difference between the test mean and obtained score by the reliability coefficient and adding this product to the test mean: $x' = X + (r_{yy}) (x - X)$. In this formula, x' is our estimated true score, or r_{yy} is the reliability of the test, x is the score we obtained on the test, and X is the mean.

Let's examine this concept with Shawn's scores on a test in which the mean is 50 and reliability is .90 or .70. Table 5.9 shows his estimated true score with scores of 15, 20, 25, 45, 55, 65, 70, and 75. In this table, the numbers in the column labeled x represent the different scores Shawn could have obtained on a test with a mean (X) of 50 and either a reliability of 0.9 or 0.7 (r_{yy}). In the column ETS are Estimated True Scores; to appreciate the influence of these two different levels of reliability on the ETS, the last column lists the difference between the ETS and obtained score (x).

Notice that all of Shawn's estimated true scores move toward the mean; those above it are adjusted downward, and those below are adjusted upward. Furthermore, the amount of adjustment is determined by the distance from the mean; those that are farthest from the mean

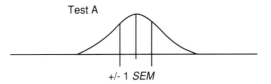

Test A

+/- 1 SEM

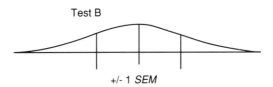

Test B

+/- 1 SEM

FIGURE 5.2
Comparison of low and high variability in a distribution of scores

TABLE 5.9

Relationship of observed score (x) with the mean (X), reliability (r_{yy}) and estimated true score

x	$X = 50$	r_{yy}	ETS	ETS $- x$
15	50	0.9	18.5	3.5
20	50	0.9	23	3
25	50	0.9	27.5	2.5
45	50	0.9	45.5	0.5
55	50	0.9	54.5	-0.5
65	50	0.9	63.5	-1.5
70	50	0.9	68	-2
75	50	0.9	72.5	-2.5
15	50	0.7	25.5	10.5
20	50	0.7	29	9
25	50	0.7	32.5	7.5
45	50	0.7	46.5	1.5
55	50	0.7	53.5	-1.5
65	50	0.7	60.5	-4.5
70	50	0.7	64	-6
75	50	0.7	67.5	-7.5

are adjusted more. According to Nunnally (1967), "Obtained scores are biased estimates of true scores. Scores above the mean are biased upward, and scores below the mean are biased downward" (p. 200). All of these adjustments are influenced by the reliability and standard deviation: As the reliability of a test decreases, the estimated true score comes closer to the test mean; and of course, estimates of reliability are in part determined by the standard deviation.

As another example, assume Johnny's observed score is 76 on both the TOP and the POOR. Given a certain reliability (.94 for the TOP and .67 for the POOR), we have estimated true scores of 77.44 on the TOP and 84.04 on the POOR. Since the POOR is a more unreliable test than the TOP, the estimated true score for the POOR is more discrepant from the observed score (EST = x).

However, as Figure 5.2 implies, we should be somewhat leery of expressing a student's score as an exact point. Because of measurement error, this value may actually be a little greater than or a little less than the value obtained.

Confidence Intervals

An important use of the reliability coefficient is the determination of **confidence intervals**. Remember that we took the standard error of measurement to describe the distribution of a student's scores when repeatedly tested. Drawing upon further knowledge about the normal distribution, we can set the limits of the probability, or confidence, about where a score lies. We know that two of three scores *from a group* fall within $+/-1$ standard deviation of the mean; or two of three scores for an individual fall within $+/-1$ standard error of measurement from the mean. When it is added and subtracted from a test's mean, we can make a probability statement about the location of an estimated true score. The only issue left is determining how probable (or confident) we want to be. If we want to be 68% confident (two out of three times), we would use 1 standard deviation (or standard error of measurement). If we want to be much more confident (i.e., 95%), we must expand the range of our distribution, to $+/-2$ standard deviations (or standard errors of measurement). By multiplying the standard error of measurement by a measure of deviation, in this case a z-score, which expresses scores as standard deviations from the mean, we can determine a range of scores within which we have a certain level of confidence that the score falls.

Confidence intervals contain both an upper and lower bound. Because they usually are expressed on the basis of estimated true scores (the symbol for which is x'), we write the formula for confidence intervals with xL' representing the lower bound or xU' representing the upper bound. The formula for confidence intervals follows:

$$xL' = X - z(SEM)$$
$$xU' = X + z(SEM)$$

Generally, we consider only two levels of confidence: (a) 68% (in which case, z is equal to 1) and (b) 95% (where z is equal to 1.96).

For example, if we want to know the range of scores within which the estimated true score falls and wish to place 95% confidence in this estimate, we multiply the standard error of measurement by 2 (actually, a z-score of 1.96 corresponds to 95% of the normal distribution) and add or subtract this product from the estimated true score. Table 5.10, which shows Shawn with an obtained score of 50, shows several confidence intervals for different standard error of measurement and levels of confidence ($z = 1$ for 68% and $z = 1.96$ for 95% confidence). The confidence level has been calculated for both a lower limit (xL') and an upper limit (xU').

Inspection of Shawn's score of 50 and the various standard errors of measurement in Table 5.10 provides some interesting situations. For example, if we use a 68% confidence range,

TABLE 5.10

68% and 95% confidence intervals for selected observed scores and standard errors of measurement

$Z = \%$ Confident	SEM	$xL' = X' - Z \times SEM$	$xU' = X' + Z \times SEM$
1	2.5	47.5	52.5
1	3	47	53
1	3.5	46.5	53.5
1	4	46	54
1	5	45	55
1	6	44	56
1	7	43	57
1	8	42	58
1.96	2.5	45.1	54.9
1.96	3	44.12	55.88
1.96	3.5	43.14	56.86
1.96	4	42.16	47.84
1.96	5	40.2	59.8
1.96	6	38.24	61.76
1.96	7	36.28	63.72
1.96	8	34.32	65.68

we see that in those cases with a small standard error of measurement (2.5), we have a very narrow range within which we can confidently expect his score to fall, 47.5–52.5. However, when the standard error of measurement is large, such as 8.0, the 68% confidence range increases to a range of from 42 to 58. Because this is a much larger interval, it signals the teacher that there is much greater error in the measurement of his performance.

If we want to increase our confidence in the scores, we might select the 95% confidence level. In this situation, our expected ranges increase dramatically. For example, when the standard error of measurement equals 2.5, the confidence interval is 45.1–54.9, a range of about 9 points. For an standard error of measurement of 8.0, the 95% confidence interval is 34.32–65.68, a range of approximately 30 points. To have a large degree of confidence in a test with low reliability, we can expect the estimated true score to vary widely, giving the obtained score very little meaning.

Summary of Standard Error of Measurement, Estimated True Score, and Confidence Interval

The relationship between estimated true scores and confidence intervals is depicted in Figure 5.3. A low obtained score moves up (closer to the mean), with the confidence interval wrapped around it; a high obtained score moves down (closer to the mean), with the confidence interval wrapped around it. The amount of movement and/or width of the interval is a function of the reliability of the measure, the standard deviation of the group, and, therefore, the standard error of measurement.

Reliability of the Difference Score

Difference scores play an important role in educational decisionmaking for two reasons. First,

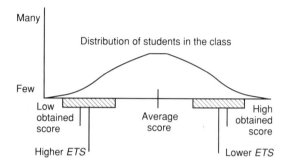

FIGURE 5.3
Relationship between estimated true scores and confidence intervals, relative to the mean of the distribution

the measurement of change or progress often depends upon the difference between how well a pupil scores on a test at Time 1 and at Time 2. Second, the diagnosis of learning disabilities traditionally has emphasized the difference score found by subtracting a child's score on an achievement test from his or her score on an intelligence test. While both of these uses are popular, there are significant problems related to the reliability of these scores. According to Thorndike and Hagen (1977), two highly reliable tests that also correlate highly with each other will have a low reliability of the difference score. This is shown in the following formula:

$$r_{\text{diff}} = \frac{\frac{1}{2}\,(\text{rel. } A + \text{rel. } B) - r_{AB}}{1 - r_{AB}}$$

where r_{diff} is the difference score reliability and r_{AB} is the intercorrelation of the two tests.

If, for example, Tests A and B have reliabilities of .90 and an intercorrelation of .80, the resulting reliability of the difference score is .50. Unfortunately, this situation is not too dissimilar from the achievement and ability tests typically used in identifying learning disabled (LD) pupils.

How is it that two reliable tests can create a difference score with unacceptable reliability?

This seeming paradox is explained in Figure 5.4, which breaks the component parts of an intelligence test and achievement measure into three categories. First, because the tests are highly correlated, significant sections of each test have something in common. A second component that is specific to each test is the characteristic that the test uniquely measures: ability for the IQ test and academic performance for the achievement measure. Finally, assuming that the error associated with the test is random, each measure has its own unique error component. When the achievement test score is subtracted from the intelligence mea-sure, as is done in the identification of learning disabilities, the common factors cancel out. All that remains are the specific factors and the error components that make up a significant portion of the difference score. It is the large magnitude of the error score in relation to the specific factors that accounts for the unaccept-ably low reliability coefficient found in the ear-lier example.

CHAPTER SUMMARY

We have discussed the importance of reliability and the need to have consistent, stable scores

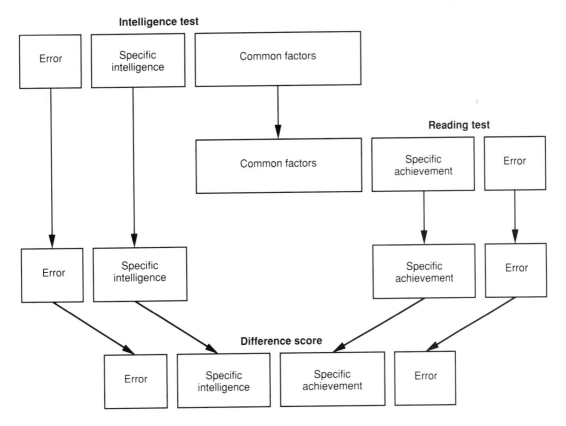

FIGURE 5.4
Illustration of the reliability of the difference score

across tests, test situations, time, and examiners. All test procedures contain some degree of error. Our job in measurement is to reduce this error to the point that we have confidence in the obtained scores as the best possible estimates of student performance. The extent to which classroom teachers use reliable tests will affect the decisions they make. As shown with our fictional fourth-grade class, use of the TOP rather than the POOR greatly enhanced teacher knowledge of actual student performance.

The first section included the sources of error in measurement and the strategies for both examining and controlling them. Specifically, five types of reliability were considered: parallel form; test-retest; parallel form and test-retest; internal consistency; and inter/intrajudge agreement. The second section applied the concept of reliability to the qualification of individual student scores, presenting three important concepts. First, information was given on how to calculate the standard error of measurement, which normally is included in test manuals but is often ignored. Tests with small standard errors of measurement are preferable to tests

with large standard errors of measurement because they minimize error in our decisions about students. Second, since all scores contain error, we have to estimate what the score would be if no error existed, establishing an estimated true score. However, since we can never be exact in our estimates, we learned that most scores should be expressed as falling within a range of values that have a known probability of occurring. That is, it is possible to create confidence intervals close to our estimated true scores, which should improve our decision making. Finally, we discussed problems with the reliability of difference scores.

These concepts are essential building blocks to good assessment. As Fred Kurlinger, an expert in measurement and statistics at the University of Oregon, is reported to have said: "Reliability is like money; it's no problem, as long as you have some." Tests without high reliability cannot be seriously considered for student evaluation. Through the remainder of this book, discussion of educational tests will rest upon this notion.

CHAPTER 6

Validity

The use of handguns in the United States has generated considerable debate. Advocates of gun control say small handguns should be outlawed and other types of guns should be registered. But members of the National Rifle Association (NRA) believe such laws would infringe on constitutional rights, stating that "guns don't kill, people do."

A similar debate occurs over testing. Many tests are inappropriate; that is, they lack reliability or validity. We could argue that such tests should not be published, but we could also say that tests are not inappropriate in themselves; rather, individuals use them inappropriately.

CHAPTER OBJECTIVES

At the end of this chapter, you should have the knowledge and skills to:

- Understand what validity is and be aware of its four basic types: content, criterion-concurrent, criterion-predictive, and construct.
- Know how to read a technical manual and interpret validity coefficients, using your interpretations about a test's validity for making a specific decision rather than relying on the publisher's statements.
- Distinguish which types of validity are important for particular decisions.
- Suggest strategies for validating a test for a number of specific decisions.

KEY VOCABULARY

The first key vocabulary word introduced in this chapter is *validity*, a synonym of which is *truthfulness*. You will find the term *content validity*, referring to the type of items that comprise a test. *Criterion-related*, which relates to an external standard, usually is used in conjunction with one of two words, *concurrent* and *pre-dictive*, which describe a point in time now or in the future, respectively. *Construct* is another word for *idea* or *concept*. All of these words deal with relationships: If two things are highly related, knowing one, I can predict the other. Validating a test is finding out what test performance is related to, now or in the future, and using the information to make a decision.

Definition of Validity

Validity refers to whether a test truthfully does what it is constructed to do. "Validity of a test is dependent upon the use of the test. Most tests are valid for something; the issue is whether a particular test is valid for the purpose to which it is put" (Leinhardt, 1983 p. 154). It is not accurate to say a test is valid; it should be valid for a purpose, such as screening, determining eligibility for specialized settings, planning instruction, formatively evaluating instruction, or summatively evaluating instructional outcomes. Typically, the process of test validation requires empirical investigations and is an unending process. Furthermore, "validity is a matter of degree rather than an all-or-none property" (Nunnally, 1967, p. 75).

The previous chapter noted that there is no educational equivalent to the Food and Drug Administration (FDA) to verify whether tests meet certain standards. Probably the closest thing to criteria would be the American Psychological Association (APA) test standards, which specify that tests not only need to be reliable, but they must be valid: They must be vindicated for some specific decision-making purpose. Generally, data supporting a test's validity should be collected by the publisher and reported in a technical manual. However, if a test is to be used for purposes other than its original design, test users probably will have to collect such data themselves to establish the validity of the test.

TYPES OF VALIDITY

According to APA standards, there are three types of validity: content, criterion-related, and construct validity. Tests need not exhibit all three criteria, but they should address the type of validity most appropriate to the type of decision for which they are used.

Content Validity

Content **validity** is the degree to which a test has an explicated domain (or universe) represented by items in the test and specific procedures describing how they were selected. Obviously, demonstration of content validity depends upon examination of those items that comprise the test. How adequately does the test sample the domain in which we wish to make inferences? Using APA standards, we want to determine "how an individual performs at present in a universe of situations that the test situation is claimed to represent" (p. 12). The concept of relationships still applies: If two domains (instruction and tests or curriculum/instruction and tests) are related, students' performance on the test adequately reflects their performance in the larger domain.

Figure 6.1 depicts three domains. A *test* is given to assay the amount of learning from *instruction* using specific *curriculum* materials. These terms connote different domains, represented by boxes that contain content items presented to students (Leinhardt, 1983).

Six statements can be made about tests and their content validity:

1. Many items appear in the curriculum but are neither taught nor tested (A).
2. Many items from instruction within the curriculum are not tested (B).
3. Some items from instruction do not appear within the curriculum and are not tested (C).

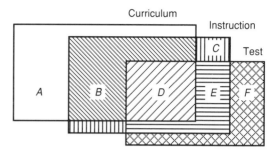

FIGURE 6.1

Three domains for assaying content validity: Curriculum, instruction, and tests

Source: Leinhardt, G. (1983). Overlap: Testing whether it is taught. In G. F. Madaud (Ed.) *The courts, validity, and minimum competency testing.* Boston: Kluwer-Nijhoff Publishing, p. 159.

4. Some items sampling both instruction and the curriculum are tested (D).
5. Some test items are drawn from instruction outside of a curriculum but are tested (E).
6. Some items that have not been introduced in the curriculum or instruction are tested (F).

Content-valid items are restricted to two areas: D and E. If the purpose of testing is to determine the effects of instruction, items appearing in F will not be content valid.

Inappropriate test use can occur when learning in a curriculum is evaluated with published norm-referenced achievement tests. It is possible to find such a test with adequate validity data; inspection of its technical manual reveals hundreds of coefficients that reflect a strong relationship between the test in question and other accepted tests. Yet a detailed description of the sampling procedures for developing items is sketchy or missing entirely. Few of these tests have been validated for making decisions about learning or growth within a curriculum because they have failed to draw a sufficient number of items in a systematic manner from any clearly defined curriculum. Therefore, they cannot be considered valid measures of specific learning attainment in that curriculum. But they may be valid for making statements about students' generalized (achievement) performance, compared to other students who are similar in age, background, and current circumstances.

Published, norm-referenced achievement tests fail to sample curricula adequately. They differentially sample many curricula used in schools. Thus, test scores do not truly represent absolute pupil skill level, because to a large extent they do not measure what children have been taught in their curricula. The conclusion of several researchers has been that content validity is often lacking with these tests.

Research Findings. Several studies of content validity in reading have been done. One of the earliest was reported by Jenkins and Pany (1978a), who analyzed five curricula along with reading subtests from five published achievement tests. They found that students learning all words in a curriculum may perform more or less poorly, depending upon which specific achievement test was used. Shapiro and Derr (1987) recently updated this study, replicating the major findings. Leinhardt (1983), in addition to explicating procedures for analyzing content validity in reading and mathematics, presented data from two projects that concluded as follows: (a) The amount of overlap between tests and either curriculum or instruction is often minimal, and (b) overlap is a powerful predictor of end-of-year test performance. Good and Salvia (1988) conducted an investigation of content validity using actual student performance on different reading achievement tests after instruction from a specific curriculum. They found significant differences in test performance that could be predicted by differences in content validity (overlap with the curriculum).

In mathematics, Freeman et al. (1983) found that the overlap between five tests and four curricula was negligible. The percentage of curriculum topics covered by tests was as low as 16% and as high as 28%; the percentage of test topics covered by curricula ranged from 22% to 85%. Together, these findings indicate that curricula present most topics included in tests, but most tests do not assess curriculum topics that have been presented. Knifong (1980) compared the computational requirements of word-story problems across five published achievement tests. Although he did not consider specific curricula, the focus was problem types, and his findings indicated great differences across tests. Petrosko's (1978) review was confined to standardized mathematics tests used in high schools, with particular attention devoted to an analysis of topics covered in the tests, as well as their strengths and weaknesses. Four topics were analyzed on 39 criteria of test quality. Many of the tests provided insufficient or unsupportive descriptions of item-selection procedures, reliability, validity, and interpretive techniques.

Ascertaining Content Validity. The solution for determining and describing the content validity of any test is to submit it to a panel of expert judges who examine its merits with respect to (a) completeness or representativeness, (b) appropriateness, (c) format, and (d) bias.

Because all tests provide a sample of behavior, we can ask how representative the test items are as samples from the larger domain. Certainly, one could not consider a test of elementary spelling skills complete if it contained only words taught at the first-grade level. Test authors can help clarify this issue by describing the *domain* from which their tests sample items and the *manner* in which they sample them. Such information, however, must be specific; a vague statement that "curricula in current use in schools were sampled for vocabulary words or computation problems" is not enough.

Item appropriateness, or the level of difficulty of test questions and the degree to which they are appropriate for examinees, can influence content validity significantly. Many curricula are spiral; content is repeatedly presented over several grade levels with increasing complexity. Therefore, the same content may be differentially appropriate, depending on how it is framed. For example, one would expect tests covering the Declaration of Independence and the Constitution to differ when one audience is a seventh-grade social studies class and another is an undergraduate group of students majoring in American history.

Content validity is in part a function of test format, or the manner in which test stimuli generate student responses. Does the test employ multiple-choice, yes-no, true-false or fill-in-the-blank items? Do the items require recognition, recall, or a more complex form of response production? Is the response format written or oral? All of these issues are important because they can influence one's ability to assess examinees' knowledge base or skill level considerably.

Content validity must attempt to ensure that all test items are as free of bias as possible. The Item Review Form in Figure 6.2 provides one approach to analyzing test items and judging their potential for biasing effects.

Can a test be worth anything if it is not content valid? Yes. Many tests need not be, or cannot be, content valid. Although content validity may be critical when assessing growth in a specific curriculum, it is not a ubiquitous feature. Most published achievement tests have serious content validity problems, but this limitation does not imply that they are worthless: They are only useless for evaluating growth in learning from a specific curriculum. Imagine that you are the director of special education

in a metropolitan area, in which individual buildings use different curricula. Would it be possible to develop a test to measure achievement in a comparable fashion?

In fact, this very issue came up in a rural education cooperative where one of the authors worked. Six districts employed four reading curricula (Scott, Foresman, Houghton Mifflin, Ginn 720, and Holt, Rhinehart). Having adopted a curriculum-based measurement approach, personnel in each of the elementary buildings developed their own measures. But when norms were compared across the districts, two buildings were significantly lower than two others. The principals were curious if the students in their buildings were really that much less skilled or whether the reading passages they had sampled were more or less difficult. Fortunately, a common measure (non-curriculum-based measures) also had been given, and when the schools were compared on that measure, no significant differences were found. It appears that either curriculum differences or the specific passages that were sampled for the norms were the cause of the lower performance (Tindal, Germann, Marston, & Deno, 1983).

Thus, it is possible to need a measure that is not curriculum-bound or content valid. Whenever statements about generalized skill or transfer of training are at issue, non-curriculum-bound measures become necessary. Or, when great differences exist between different schools, particularly in their instructional programs, and comparisons between them are needed, we can and should use non-content based measures to document performance.

Criterion-Related Validity

A second type of test validity is established by comparing performance on an accepted standard, or criterion (another test that is similar in

---

Item Review Form to Detect Bias

Reviewer: _____ Date: _____ Objective: _____

This review form has been designed to assist in the identification of test items which may reflect sex, cultural, racial, regional and/or ethnic content bias and stereotyping. Place your name, the date, and the objective number at the top of the review form.

In the spaces at the right under the heading "Test Item Number" provide the numbers of the test items you will review. When the number of test items for review exceeds ten, use a second review form.

Next, read each test item and answer the six questions below. Use " " for YES, "X" for NO, "?" for UNSURE, and "NA" for NOT APPLICABLE. When your rating is negative ("X" or "?"), indicate what you think is the problem in the test item and suggest a revision on your copy of the test item.

When you have completed your review task, staple the test items to your review form(s) and return.

1. Is the item free of *offensive* sex, cultural, racial, regional and/or ethnic content?
2. Is the item free of sex, cultural, racial, and/or ethnic stereotyping?
3. Is the item free of language which could be offensive to a segment of the examinee population?
4. Is the item free from descriptions which could be offensive to a segment of the examinee population?
5. Will the activities described in the item be equally familiar (or equally unfamiliar) to all examinees?
6. Will the words in the item have a common meaning for all examinees?

Source: Berk, R. A. (1984). Conducting the item analysis. In R. A. Berk (Ed.) *A guide to criterion-referenced test construction*, (pp. 97–143). Baltimore, MD: John Hopkins University Press. Adapted from Hambleton, 1980, p. 101.

FIGURE 6.2
Sample Item Review Form used to examine test content bias

content or focus and already has established reliability and validity). If the two measures are similar (result in similar rank ordering), we can say the test in question has adequate criterion-related validity. Remember the concept: When two things are highly related, knowing one, we can predict the other.

Concurrent. Let's examine the criterion validity of the reading test we created in chapter 4, the Test of Performance (TOP). If the TOP is in agreement with an accepted measure of reading at the fourth-grade level, it has **criterion-concurrent validity** because we are examining performance on both our test and the criterion at the same time. To illustrate, let's use the standard scores from our fourth-grade class on

the TOP (Form A) as shown in Table 5.2. In addition, we can use Form A of the Reading Comprehension subtest of the Stanford Diagnostic Reading Test (Karlsen, Madden, & Gardner, 1976) as our accepted criterion measure. The Stanford Diagnostic Reading Test (SDRT) has excellent reliability and validity, and well-constructed norms. After administering the TOP, we administer the SDRT, which has standard scaled scores ranging from 212 to 640 (a score of 434 represents the 50th percentile). Student TOP and SDRT scores are presented in Table 6.1 (along with the students' GPA which was ascertained later in the year).

If we wish to determine the extent to which the TOP has criterion-concurrent validity, we must find the correlation coefficient between

TABLE 6.1
Fourth-grade class performance on the TOP, SDRT, and GPA.

Student	Standard Score on the TOP	Scaled Score on the SDRT	GPA 4 Years Later
Megan	100	489	3.1
Nicky	110	528	3.5
Shawn	80	423	2.8
Sue	97	479	3.6
Johnny	80	379	2.5
Jennifer	118	640	3.9
Linda	94	512	3.5
Michael	104	470	2.9
Bonnie	95	500	2.8
Andy	120	588	3.6

these two measures. Figure 6.3 shows a scatterplot of this relationship. There appears to be a strong association between these two tests—high scores on one measure are associated with high scores on the other measure, and low scores on one measure are associated with low scores on the other measure. For example, Johnny, who may need some special education service, has a low score of 80 on the TOP and low scores on the SDRT, 379. Jennifer, who is the best reader in our fourth-grade class, has a high score on the TOP, 120, and a high score

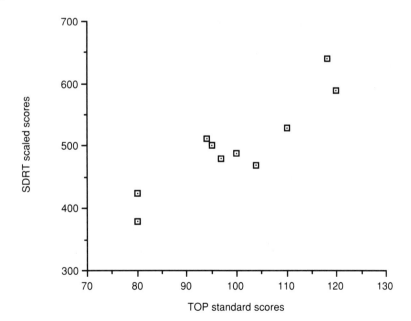

FIGURE 6.3
Scatterplot of TOP and SDRT scores of fourth-grade class

of 640 on the SDRT. If we calculate the correlation coefficient for the TOP and the SDRT we find it is .91, a very high and positive relationship, indicating the TOP is a valid measure of reading.

Predictive. If we are interested in how well the TOP predicts later performance, we need to examine its **criterion-predictive validity**. Let's assume we want to know the extent to which performance on the TOP predicts later success in school as measured by grade point average (GPA). We know the GPAs of our students 4 years later at the end of the year (Table 6.1): They range from 2.5 (Johnny) to 3.9 (Jennifer) on a 4-point scale. The scatterplot for these two variables appears in Figure 6.4. The correlation coefficient between these two variables is .76, which demonstrates the TOP has high criterion-predictive validity.

Although these examples are based on fictional data, the concept is accurate. Not only

do published achievement tests employ criterion-related validity, but it is one of the more important procedures for establishing the truthfulness of teacher-developed measures. For example, since 1979, Deno and associates (Fuchs, Marston, Mirkin, Shinn, Tindal, Wesson, and others) have investigated a number of measurement systems that teachers can develop and use in their classrooms. These systems have been called *curriculum-based measures* (Deno, 1985; Germann & Tindal, 1985, Marston & Magnusson, 1985; Shinn, 1989). As later chapters will describe, the measures sample basic skill areas in reading, writing, spelling, and mathematics. Many criterion-validity studies have been done in which these curriculum-based measures have been correlated with published achievement tests. As in the example above, a group of students is tested on both types of measures and ranked (from high to low). When the two measures reflect similar ranking, the correlation is high; when

FIGURE 6.4
Scatterplot of TOP scores
and GPA 4 years later

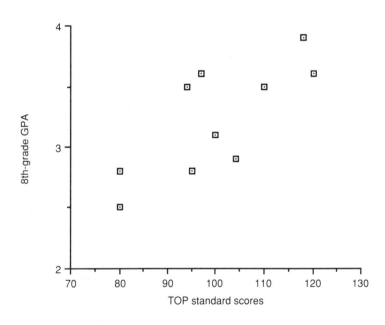

the ranking is not similar, the correlation is low. The results from this line of research (Shinn, in press) appear in Table 6.2.

If these standards are applied to the criterion-concurrent validity of curriculum-based measures, it appears that the language arts measures (reading, spelling, and writing) have above-average validity, while the math measures have average validity. In other words, knowing how well a student performs on the curriculum-based measures, I can predict how well he or she will perform now or in the future on many published achievement tests.

Construct Validity

Think about the words we use to describe students. For reasons of social convenience, we rarely use specific descriptive terms. We rarely describe a student as out of his or her seat most of the time, fidgeting with pencils and crayons when sitting, frequently playing with hair and clothes, talking incessantly, and always moving; rather, we describe him or her as *hyperactive.* Other words include *intelligent, ambitious, learning-disabled, emotionally disturbed,* and *talented and gifted.* High-inference words are not limited to student's behavioral characteristics: We also use such terms when talking of student achievement. For example, what do we mean when we say *comprehension?* Are we talking about literal and inferential interpretation, evaluation, synthesis, illustration, or application? Or how should we define

written expression? Should we focus on mechanics and punctuation like most published achievement tests do, or should we address syntax and semantics also? Should the measurement of written expression take into account the reaction of the reader? How should that be measured? As you can see, many words are used to describe achievement. They are complex in their meaning, and therefore, we may not agree on the meanings.

The essential concept of **construct validity** is to anchor the meaning of high-inference words into everyday, observable events and relationships. However, because these words are so complex and have so many meanings, there is no one way to do this; rather, a number of investigations have to be done, and the explication of the word (or construct) built in an incremental fashion. Furthermore, the findings from several investigations should converge and all come out the same for a construct to be validated.

Construct validity is critical when testing more abstract concepts that are difficult to observe. Obviously, the more concrete the idea, the easier it is to establish content and criterion validity. Theoretical constructs are more difficult to observe and therefore do not easily lend themselves to empirical validation (scientific investigation). Using APA standards, we need to "infer the degree to which the individual possesses some hypothetical trait or quality (construct) presumed to be reflected in the test performance" (American Psychological Association, 1985, p. 12). To do so, research must specify

TABLE 6.2
Criterion-concurrent validity of curriculum-based measures

Academic Area	No. of Studies	No. of Students	No. of Tests	No. of Corr.	Mdn. Corr.
Reading	13	807	24	90	.75
Spelling	4	205	3	4	.85
Writing	6	379	5	11	.66/.76
Math	4	183	3	16	.43

a set of observable events or variables that are hypothesized to relate and not relate to the theoretical construct. Given the hypotheses about how these variables interrelate, the investigator conducts a series of studies and/or experiments testing his or her hypotheses. This search for predicted patterns among observed entities has been referred to as creating a *nomological network* (Cronbach & Meehl, 1955).

Using the TOP, let's see how the nomological network operates. In Figure 6.5, the construct is reading. While there are many approaches to the measurement of reading, no one definitive method or test assesses reading. Therefore, reading is quite similar to the hypothetical constructs to which Cronbach and Meehl refer. In trying to develop construct validity for our fourth-grade reading test, the TOP, let's hypothesize that it looks like and acts like a mea-

sure of reading. Similarly, we hypothesize that well-accepted tests such as the Stanford Diagnostic Reading Test also serve as a measure of reading. However, if we just administer these two tests, we are establishing criterion-concurrent validity, not construct validity. Therefore, we need to add some other measures. In addition, we assume that teacher judgment of reading is highly associated with the assessment of the central construct of reading.

Figure 6.5 depicts this pattern of corresponding relationships schematically. Where do other academic measures fit into the nomological network? For example, are math measures related to reading? One would think there is no relationship, but there is a moderate correlation among measures of academic performance; that is, students who do well in reading also tend to do well in math (i.e., can solve

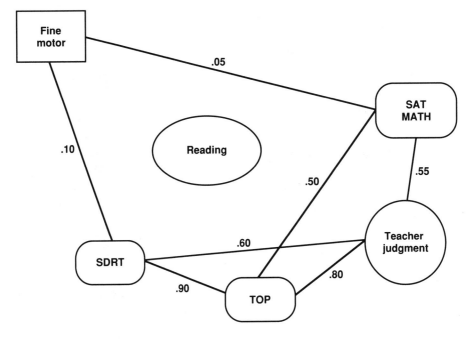

FIGURE 6.5
Example of a nomological network in reading

word-story problems). As a result, we hypothesize some relationship between our measure of math and the reading construct, which is also shown in Figure 6.5.

To complete the nomological network, we should include other educational or psychological constructs that one would not believe are related to reading. In Figure 6.5, such an entity is *fine motor* skill, which should not be closely related to the construct of reading.

The question becomes: How can we verify the nomological network empirically? One approach is to analyze the proposed patterns outlined in the illustration by actually correlating these measures. In this example, we have determined that the correlation between the TOP and the SDRT is about .90 and between the TOP and teacher judgment, approximately .80. The correlation of the TOP and SAT math is only .50. There is no correlation between the TOP and fine motor performance. By examining this pattern of interrelationships, we build a network of relationships that lend credibility to the hypothesis that the TOP has construct validity as a measure of reading. Our measure relates more strongly to other, very similar measures and weakly to less related measures.

Although construct validity may seem far from the classroom in its implications, such is not the case. In preparing to write this book, we reviewed many published achievement tests and scrutinized the technical manuals for reliability and validity. While doing so, we looked at correlations between similar and different academic areas in these tests, such as the interrelationships of reading subtests and the relationships of reading and math subtests. This type of validation is based on convergent and discriminant validity (Campbell & Fiske, 1959; Cronbach & Meehl, 1955), in which it is hypothesized that similar measures should correlate more highly with each other than with something different. Was this true?

We found almost no differences in the correlations between similar subtests and with other dissimilar subtests. In other words, subtests in reading correlated about the same with each other as they did with math subtests. Remember, if two things are highly related, knowing one, I can predict the other. Thus, if I wanted to know a student's math performance, I could measure his or her reading skill. As unlikely as this finding sounds, it is true. With published achievement tests, there is almost no divergent validity. All of the intercorrelations are in the average to above-average range, using Cronbach's interpretations.

We then looked at curriculum-based measures. We had just finished norming an entire elementary school, so we had performance scores from about 60 students each in grades 2–5 in all academic areas: reading, writing, spelling, and math. When we assessed the interrelationship between these measures, we found low to no correlation. Thus, it appears that you cannot predict a student's math performance based on spelling or reading performance.

The bottom line for the classroom teacher is that published achievement tests are global and act very much like intelligence tests; rather than *g* for generalized intelligence (Guilford, 1967), we postulate *a* for generalized achievement. High performance on one subtest is likely to predict high performance on other subtests. If I wanted to be efficient (and were allowed the leeway), I would administer only the reading subtests once in the fall or spring. And, for distributing students on a common scale, that would be sufficient; the information could be used to flag students who are low enough to warrant further attention. However, since I would need to place students into curriculum materials and instructional groups, as well as develop instructional plans, I would then proceed to administer a series of curriculum-based measures.

Size

How do we judge the size of validity coefficients (either type of criterion or construct)? Unfortunately, there is no absolute standard by which we can say a test has or does not have criterion validity. Remember, Nunnally (1967) said it is not an "all-or-none" process. Typically, experts say moderate to high coefficients are necessary to assume a test is criterion valid. We offer the following guidelines: .70 and above is high, .50 to .70 is moderate, and below .50 is low. Coefficients below .30, while they may still represent a minimal relationship, are of no use in documenting a test's validity. Cronbach (1960) suggested ranges and meanings that appear in Table 6.3.

APPROACHES FOR ASSESSING VALIDITY

As you can see, validity is a complex issue based on relationships between different measures. A number of procedures are used in establishing validity: some of them involve simple measurement and others require experimentation. Each type of validity previously defined can be established using a wide range of specific techniques.

TABLE 6.3

Acceptable standards for interpreting validity coefficients

Ranges	Interpretation
.00–.20	Little/no validity
.21–.40	Below-average validity
.41–.55	Average validity
.56–.80	Above-average validity
.80–.99	Exceptional validity

Source: Webb, II., M. W. (1983). A scale for evaluating standardized reading tests, with results for Melson-Denny, Iowa, and Stanford. *Journal of Reading, 26* (5), 414–424. Table 2, p. 426.

Approaches to Examining Validity

Table 6.4 delineates five strategies for establishing validity. In the intraobjective approach, the question focuses on the relationship among items within the same objective (or task). In the interobjective approach, the concern is with the relationship among different items within similar and different objectives or tasks. In the criterion-related approach, the unit of analysis moves beyond objectives and into relationships between measures of performance and other external standards or criteria. In the experimental approach, we manipulate an independent variable to determine if the outcome occurs as predicted. For example, if teaching were manipulated in one group (experimental) to increase comprehension and not in another group (control), an increase in the comprehension measure for only the experimental group would provide construct validity information to the measure. The final approach, multimethod/multitrait, takes the criterion strategy one step further, using multiple measures of many different constructs and looking at the relationship between different ways of measuring the same construct (should be high) and different constructs measured in the same manner (should be low).

Before moving to validity's connection with decisionmaking, we need to consider it as a function of the adequacy of any normative reference group. Obviously, this issue is less relevant for criterion- and individual-referenced interpretations. To make a valid (truthful) interpretation using a norm-referenced test, the norm group (often referred to as the *standardization sample*) upon which the interpretations of the test are based must be appropriate. When screening students and determining their eligibility in specialized programs, the test must be a norm-referenced device because it is not possible to specify deviance without the range of normal variation in a test. In addition, pro-

TABLE 6.4
Five approaches to examining validity

Approach	Description
Intraobjective	Measure of internal consistency at the objective level (e.g., KR-20) Item analyses Content specialists' ratings of item-objective congruence, bias, technical quality, and representativeness (content validity) Confirmatory factor analysis (do the items fit a hypothesized structure?) Distractor analysis (for example, do many of the high performers choose an incorrect answer choice?)
Interobjective	Confirmatory factor analysis Scalogram analysis Convergent validity studies (includes studies of relationships between test scores and other tests that measure the same objectives or measure traits that should correlate with the objectives) Divergent validity studies (includes studies of relationships between tests that purport to measure different skills or traits)
Criterion-related (continuous or dichotomous criterion variable).	Correlation between domain score estimates obtained from "actual" and the "lengthened" test (called *"domain validity"*) Correlation of test scores with instructor ratings, on-the-job criterion measures (or simulated on-the-job measures), self-ratings, or peer-ratings Comparison of examinee performance on the test before and after instruction Comparison of the score distributions or percentage of masters for (1) "masters" and "nonmasters" (as identified by means other than the test itself), or, for example, (2) "uninstructed" and "instructed" groups of examinees Correlation between test scores and the number of years of preparation Correlation between test scores and examinee performance in real or simulated situations representing the same or similar content Bias studies to determine if unexpected differences arise due to race, ethnic background, sex, etc.
Experimental	Studies to investigate sources of possible invalidity such as degree of speededness (for example, administer test with and without time limits to compare performance), clarity of directions, answer sheets, race and sex of test examiner Study of pretest and posttest performance with treatment and control groups Study of the influence of response sets and personality on test performance.
Multitrait/multimethod	Simultaneous investigation of construct validity of several objectives utilizing two or more methods for assessing each objective

Source: Reprinted with permission from Hambleton, R. K. (1984). Validating the test scores. In R. A. Berk (Ed.), *A guide to criterion-referenced test construction* (pp. 199–230). Baltimore, MD: John Hopkins University Press, p. 204.

gram certification often occurs over widely divergent instructional programs and curricula, necessitating a common measure that is norm-referenced. When using norm-referenced tests, we must consider not only the three types of validity; we must also address two specific issues about the normative group: (a) the size of the group and (b) the comparability of the normative sample.

Size of the Norm Group. Norm-referenced tests often vary considerably in the number of students included in the norm groups. For example, only 1,401 students have been normed on the Gray Oral Reading Test—Revised (Wiederholt & Bryant, 1986), while more than 600,000 students composed the normative group on the California Achievement Test (CTB/McGraw-Hill, 1985). Interestingly, many of the curriculum-based measures reported in Table 6.3 have been employed in establishing normative performance levels. In the Pine County Special Education Cooperative, approximately 200 students at each grade level (1–12) were measured in basic skill areas, to make a total normative group of 2,400 students. In Minneapolis, more than 9,000 students were assessed in these same basic skill areas. In contrast, many tests are available that do not have an adequate number of students in their normative samples. Salvia and Ysseldyke (1988) suggest that enough subjects should be tested to keep the sizes of interpolations and extrapolations relatively small; 100 subjects represents the minimum number for which a full range of percentiles can be computed and for which standard scores between ± 2 standard deviations can be computed with extrapolation.

Comparability of the Norm Group. In addition to size, the norm group should be representative of the population for which the test is to be used. Salvia and Ysseldyke (1988) warned professionals of this issue, reporting an example where it was not done. In the late 1960s, the Peabody Picture Vocabulary Test (Dunn, 1965) was used to evaluate the effectiveness of Head Start programs in inner-city New York. Unfortunately, the Peabody Picture Vocabulary Test at that time had only been normed on white, upper-middle-class children from Tennessee. Obviously, the norms did not represent the population the test was administered to, and methodological problems ensued.

D. Fuchs, Fuchs, Benowitz, and Barringer (1987) analyzed 27 tests commonly used in special education decision making, involving measures of achievement, ability, and perceptual processing. They found that few of these tests had even included special education students in their normative sample, precluding their validity for making decisions regarding handicapped students.

VALIDITY AND DECISION MAKING

A test cannot be considered technically adequate unless it is shown to be reliable and then validated for a specific use or decision. Earlier in this chapter, we made the point that in order to demonstrate that a test is valid, we must link it to a decision or the purpose for which it is to be used. Figure 6.5 presents a chart that establishes the necessary types of validity for three major educational decisions.

Screening and Eligibility Decisions

Screening decisions are useful in flagging students for more labor-intensive, elaborate, specific-level testing. To serve as valid measures, they should relate to other accepted measures, both concurrently and at some time in the future. In fact, predictive validity is crucial, since

Screening	Instructional planning	Program
Eligibility	Formative evaluation	certification

Appropriateness of norm	Content	(Appropriateness of norm)
Criterion-concurrent	Criterion-concurrent	(Content)
Criterion-predictive	Criterion-predictive	Criterion-concurrent
Construct		Criterion-predictive
		Construct

FIGURE 6.6
Validity requirements for different educational decisions

the decision made during screening is that a student may be deviant enough to warrant more assessment.

Construct validity is at the heart of all eligibility decisions. To label a student *learning disabled* or *educable mentally retarded* is to make a great leap of faith in the terms. As shorthand, these terms are worthless, but they may function administratively as indicators of need for specialized instruction. At the center of all screening/eligibility decisions is the sorting of students, using some characteristic, into groups of those with a lot and those with little. As Thurlow, Christensen, and Ysseldyke (1983) and Ysseldyke and Thurlow (1983) have reported, the construct validity for much of our referral and classification system for learning disabilities is bankrupt. We don't sort students very well on this construct.

If a screening and eligibility test generates many false positive errors (students whom the test incorrectly flags as deviant), the test may not be valid. In fact, in research conducted at the Institute for Research on Learning Disabilities, several studies reported many normal students being classified as learning disabled. The test also is invalid if it generates many false negative errors (students who were incorrectly not flagged as needing more specialized assessment).

There are a number of procedures for establishing the construct validity for a measurement system. One procedure for validating a screening test is to sort the number of students identified as needing more specific-level and elaborate assessments and compare that number with those students actually placed into specialized programs. Another strategy is to compare students in specialized environments with those in regular education environments. Any significant differences help support the construct validity of the instrument used to assign students into the two groups. The bottom line is that whenever high-inference terms are used to characterize students, it is incumbent upon those using these tests as the basis of such opinions to validate them.

Instructional Planning and Formative Evaluation

Decisions regarding instructional planning and formative evaluation represent the most commonplace, yet elusive, areas for generating validation data. Certainly, the heart of such validity revolves around the content of the test. However, both types of criterion validity add explanatory power to the decision making. For example, if we regularly monitor a group of students, using the number of words read correctly and test them at the end of an experimental instructional program on a similar oral reading-fluency task, the conclusion that the program was effective would be confounded by the frequent practice on the measure (reading aloud). To validate our measure, we might also assess the students at the end of the program in another reading task that is unrelated to our frequent measure. If we found growth on both measures, we would not only better support the conclusion (that the instructional program was effective), but also add a certain amount of criterion validity to our oral reading measures.

Program Certification

The last decision for which validity data should exist is in the final summary of overall program outcomes for program certification. You will notice that all types of validity may be relevant here. Potentially, content validity may be needed, since we are evaluating programs. Both types of criterion validity will help establish that measurement outcomes are not limited to just one measure. Construct validity is important if we are making high-inference statements about programs or students. For example, one of the authors completed a program evaluation in which the following question was asked: Do teachers need to be certified in the same handicapping conditions affecting the students they serve in order to be effective? In Minnesota, only learning disability (LD) teachers can serve students identified as having learning disabilities; only those students identified as educable mentally retarded (EMR) can be taught by teachers with that certification. In this study, LD students were randomly assigned to be taught by LD and EMR teachers; likewise, EMR students were assigned to be taught by either LD or EMR teachers. What was the finding? It didn't matter. Students with either disability could be

effectively taught by teachers with either certification (Marston, 1987a). Good teaching is good teaching. The point is that, for a program certification decision (Is this program effective?), all types of validity may be needed.

CHAPTER SUMMARY

The material presented in this chapter is the center of all assessment activities and the core of the book. If you had difficulty understanding the concepts, please go back over the material: The content in the specific skill area chapters is based on validity issues.

Most important is the need for educators to begin questioning the tests that for too long have been assumed to be adequate. We make many important decisions about students, and we cannot be ignorant of the issues. Therefore, we must consider content, criterion, and construct validity, particularly in reference to the decisions that we make. Content validity is imperative for planning and formatively evaluating instruction, but it is not that relevant for distributing students on a common scale (using published achievement tests). Yet why all the interest in trying to prove these tests are not content valid? Published achievement tests *must* be both criterion and construct valid for making screening and eligibility or summative program-evaluation decisions. But other than D. Fuchs et al. (1987), no one is performing research on the composition of the norm groups. And *no* researcher has tackled the ultimate question of whether the decisions we make based on these tests are any better than not using them or using other information. Consumers must fill in these gaps.

To help prompt a regular and consistent consideration of both reliability and validity, we have provided a matrix to use in reviewing tests. Table 6.5 provides a framework for examining the technical adequacy of a test. How would

TABLE 6.5
Determining the technical adequacy of a test: A decision-making matrix

Elements of technical adequacy	Purpose of testing					
	Screening/Eligibility			Instructional planning/ Evaluation		Program certification
	Prereferral	Screening	Identification	Program planning	Progress monitoring	Program evaluation
Reliability						
Alternate form						
Test-retest						
Internal Consistency						
Inter-rater						
Validity						
Content						
Criterion						
Construct						
Norms						
Sample size						
Representative						

the matrix work for specific tests? Let's use the Stanford Achievement Test, a norm-referenced test, as an example. If we were to complete Table 6.5 for this test, we would find the SAT has excellent reliability, validity, and norms. These data, however, exist primarily for purposes of screening and program evaluation. With respect to the other decisions, the Stanford Achievement Test has not been adequately researched. For example, it should not be used to plan instruction or formatively evaluate instructional effects. You will see that we have added both reliability and validity to reinforce the concept that you cannot have validity without such reliability. Using this matrix, should allow teachers to make systematic use of the information provided in chapters 5 and 6 and to judge the merit of any test.

CHAPTER 7

Reading Assessment

CHAPTER OBJECTIVES
KEY VOCABULARY
LITERATURE ON READING ASSESSMENT
ASSESSMENT STRATEGIES
CHAPTER SUMMARY

Few educators agree on a definition of reading, the identification of component skills for reading, or stimulus-response configurations for assessing reading. For example, what do the following tasks have in common as assessments of reading skill?

At times, we ask children to look at pictures, letters, words, sentences, text, and graphs. We also engage them in a host of different tasks. We have them discriminate between beginning, middle, and ending vowels or consonants, select words or phrases that have the same or different meanings, fill in the blanks with missing words that best complete sentences, answer questions about material that was just read, or look up information and solve prob-

Task 1 • The following exercise appears in a second-grade Scribner (Cassidy, Roettger, and Wixson, 1987) workbook (Join the Circle):

Phonics • Decoding: Relating initial and final /n/ to **n**

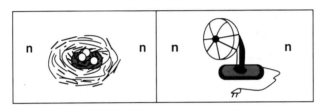

Children are asked to say the letter names and trace the letters;
• if the picture's name begins with the letter, they circle the letter in front;
• if the picture's name ends with the letter, they circle the letter after the picture.

Task 2 • In *Ginn 720* (Clymer et al., 1980), the following decoding task appears in a mastery test in Level 10 (fourth grade):

Bill's _____ made it difficult for him to volunteer in class.

<u>Shyness</u>   Stiffness   Stillness

Task 3 • In Houghton-Mifflin's (Durr et al., 1983) Banners (Level L for fifth graders) Test of Basic Reading Skills, the following item appears in Test Four: Reading Graphs:

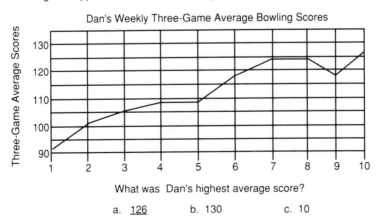

What was Dan's highest average score?

a. <u>126</u>   b. 130   c. 10

lems. There is very little that we don't do under the guise of reading assessment.

This chapter provides a model of reading assessment that cuts through this web of definitions and simplifies reading in accord with the psychometric literature that has been accumulating for nearly 50 years. Rather than directly describing specific reading assessment procedures, we present a conceptual model. In few areas are professionals and lay people more opinionated than in their conceptions of reading. Therefore, this initial material, although somewhat technical, provides the foundation for the specific assessment tactics described in the second section.

CHAPTER OBJECTIVES

When you have completed studying this chapter, you should have the knowledge and skills to

- Describe a low inference theoretical rationale of reading assessment.
- Devise and administer a curriculum-based measurement to assess both oral reading fluency and student reactions to the material.
- Interpret the results from a curriculum-based measure (CBM) to make several different educational decisions (screening and eligibility for specialized programs, or placement into reading materials, evaluating instructional outcomes, and summarizing program outcomes).
- Devise and administer an informal reading inventory to determine three levels of performance, relating to where a student (a) reads with difficulty, (b) can be taught, and (c) reads without instruction or monitoring.
- Devise and administer an objective reaction using either the cloze or maze formats.
- Develop and implement an integrated assessment in reading, using a case example as a prototype.

KEY VOCABULARY

This chapter introduces a considerable amount of technical language. The material in the first section, which reviews the psychometric literature, centers on reading as a *construct,* which means it is a word loaded with multiple meaning. Of course, a chapter on reading is not complete without reference to *decoding,* the act of translating print to sound, and *comprehension,* the term often used to mean understanding. We replace these two words with *reading* and *reacting,* reflecting a more narrow interpretation of the reading process as the presentation of connected prose to ascertain a response. We describe two major assessment procedures: (a) *curriculum-based measurement,* in which we assess production responses on a timed basis to provide data for a variety of educational decisions, and (b) *informal reading inventories,* in which we present successively difficult material to determine three levels of performance (*frustration, instruction,* and *independent*). Finally, we describe two objective measures of reading reactions: the *cloze,* in which words from a passage are deleted to determine if the student can correctly insert them, and the *maze,* in which the same task is accompanied by multiple-choice replacements for each blank, and the student selects the correct word.

LITERATURE ON READING ASSESSMENT

Few educators would argue that the purpose or goal of reading is to derive meaning from text. However, considerable controversy exists in the process of achieving that goal (the means of instruction) and the manner in which attainment of the goal is determined (assessment of the end product). Disagreement abounds in basic definitions of reading, in the components or constructs considered integral to any model of reading, and in the operationalization of assessment techniques used to quantify performance.

> Within the community of reading researchers, theorists, and practitioners there exists very little agreement concerning any single aspect of the reading process. Controversy exists—about measurement, about the relevance of subskills, about developmental and related cognitive issues, about the adequacy of research paradigms, and about instruction. (Farr & Carey, 1986 p. 28)

A Traditional, Two-Component Model of Reading

Most conceptions of reading identify two major dimensions: decoding and comprehension. A variety of test names are then used, which specify with even more detail, skills and processes presumed to underly these major dimensions. For example, Barr and Sadow (1985) propose a model quite typical of others that divides skills into two major components: (a) translation of print, or word reading, and (b) comprehension, comprising both word knowledge, and comprehension strategies. Print translation skills involve phonics, structural analysis, and syllabication, permitting a student to identify previously unknown words and recognize words instantaneously. Comprehension occurs at several levels, from individual word knowledge and vocabulary skills that provide meaning to both words and concepts to the attainment of meaning through intra- and intersentence structures. Typically, "two of them, print translation and word knowledge, represent conditions that are necessary before the third, comprehension strategies, may be employed" (p. 5).

Researchers often view these separate components as developmental, because reading evolves through several major stages, beginning with decoding and ending with comprehension (Chall, 1983). In the early stages students learn the alphabet, letter sounds, and combinations of letters (preschool to Grade 2); later they learn to decode words (Grades 2 and 3); finally they begin to understand meaning, acquire knowledge, and appreciate perspectives (Grades 4 through college). These stages are sequentially ordered: Mastery of earlier stages precedes mastery of later stages. Figure 7.1 depicts this view of reading.

These theories of reading translate into assessment strategies, reflecting the dual emphasis on decoding and comprehending. Wallace and Larsen (1978) focus on word analysis and comprehension. Zigmond, Vallecorsa, and Silverman (1983) divide reading assessment into word recognition and comprehension. Evans, Evans, and Mercer (1986) concentrate on word recognition and comprehension (understanding words and ideas). Howell and Morehead (1987) cover decoding and comprehension in two separate chapters. However, the psychometric literature has failed to support the independence of these two components of reading; rather, they are so intertwined that it is difficult to speak of one without the other.

Decoding. Most researchers and theorists in the field of reading define **decoding** and **word recognition** as the translation of print necessary for the eventual attainment of meaning. Word recognition skills focus on the relationship between the printed letters and the spoken sounds, between letter clusters and sounds, identification of syllables, and use of other word parts in identifying words. However,

> there is no validated list of skills which are vital to learning to read, nor is there any hierarchy of skills. In addition, there is much debate about the relation of so called separate skills of reading to the actual act of reading. Despite the lack of evidence for the existence of separate reading skills, the search for the apparently elusive list of reading skills continues. (Farr & Carey, 1986, p. 64)

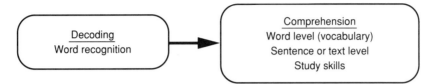

FIGURE 7.1
A traditional, two-component model of reading—decoding and comprehension

Assessment of word recognition reflects one of three basic approaches that structure reading instruction: analytical, synthetic, and strategies. In an analytical approach, children are taught generalizations from words that are already known, learning to decode words by sight before word recognition skills are taught. Assessment based on this approach utilizes sight words and word recognition based on whole words. In a synthetic approach, children are taught the relationship between sounds and letters, first in isolation and then blended together. Assessment focuses on phonetic regularities and word families. Finally, a strategies approach emphasizes the use of cue systems in the determination of meaning; word recognition is never separated from the total act of reading. Assessment is directed more immediately toward comprehension, either through vocabulary and word meaning or sentence and text-level questions (Farr & Carey, 1986).

These models of word recognition instruction also appear in many different assessment devices. For example, the IOWA test of basic skills includes a word analysis subtest reflecting an analytical approach with its subsequent emphasis on sight words. In contrast, the Wood-cock Reading Mastery Test (1987) has a nonsense-word subtest that uses a synthetics/phonics approach in which students sound and blend successive letters. And finally, the holistic model, which assumes no skill hierarchy or direct instruction, is reflected in the Reading Miscue Inventory (Goodman & Burke, 1971).

Farr and Carey's (1986) review of five popular group tests reveals that the word recognition subtests differ not only in theory but also in five other areas, including (a) the number and type of subskills tested, (b) the level at which they are tested, (c) the extension of the subskill to the reading process, (d) the format for assessing any one skill, and (e) the number of items presented to measure the skills.

Comprehension. The controversy over decoding assessment, however, is not nearly as complex as the controversy over comprehension assessment. Most educators agree on what decoding is, even if they disagree on how it should be taught and/or assessed. However, one of the primary problems that persists with comprehension is the disagreement on its definition. If people cannot agree about its basic meaning, other differences are likely to arise in how it is assessed and what the assessment data mean.

Probably the most popular conception of **comprehension** is based on the definition by Pearson and Johnson (1978) who identified three different types: (a) text-explicit, (b) text-implicit, and (c) script-implicit. Text-explicit questions address information that is embedded *directly* in the reading material. This type of comprehension often is referred to as *literal comprehension*. In text-implicit comprehension, the questions and their answers are *not* derived *directly* from any one source in the passage; rather, teachers employ multiple sources of information or logical extensions of the information to develop questions and answers. This type of comprehension is typically referred to as *inferential comprehension* in reading literature. Finally, a script-implicit relationship implies that, although information needed to answer a question is present in the text, additional *personal information* from the reader is necessary to correctly answer the question. This type of comprehension is confounded with the background knowledge of the reader.

In contrast to Pearson and Johnson's (1978) simple taxonomy, Crowell and Au (1981) define comprehension in relation to the difficulty or complexity of cognitive skills needed to correctly answer the questions. They delineate five types of questions: (a) association, which elicits recall of detail, (b) categorization, (c) seriation and sequence of events, (d) integration, or pulling together various elements of a story, and (e) extension, or prediction and extrapolation. Their typology implies degrees of difficulty, with successive increases in difficulty from (a) to (e).

The most elaborate taxonomies of comprehension may include the following variables: (a) literal comprehension, including recognition and recall of details, main ideas, sequence, comparison, cause-effect relationships, and character traits; (b) reorganization via classifying, outlining, summarizing, and synthesizing; (c) inferential comprehension of supporting detail, main ideas, sequence of events, comparisons, cause-effect relationships, character traits, predicted outcomes and figurative language; (d) evaluation, involving judgments of reality or fantasy, fact or opinion, adequacy or validity, appropriateness, worth, desirability or acceptability; and (e) appreciation of content/imagery, characters, incidents, or the author's use of language.

The term *comprehension* holds no universal meaning. Not only has the debate over its meaning been considered from a logical or conceptual view, but also from an empirical perspective, in which data from controlled studies are used to help understand the meaning of the term *comprehension*. As we point out in the chapter on validity, the focus is on construct validity, in which different instructional tactics and measures are concurrently obtained and analyzed to sort out relationships.

Two forms of validation procedures have been employed in this research: (a) clusters of skills are assessed to determine if they "hang together" and form some higher order construct, or (b) intercorrelations of tests are analyzed to determine how different test content and formats are similar to and different from each other. In the former methodology, the findings depict comprehension as a complex clustering that, although it comprises several skill-groupings (i.e., organizing, identifying, sequencing, etc.), is dominated by word knowledge or vocabulary meaning (Davis, 1944; 1968; 1971). "Thus, although certain comprehension skills can be differentiated, present types of reading comprehension tests, as distinct from word knowledge tests, largely measure one basic ability, which may well correspond to the label of reasoning in reading" (Spearritt, 1972, p. 110). In the studies that intercorrelate different tests, similar findings of complex relationships occur. For example, the Massachusetts Department of Education assessment of 14 reading objectives of 4,500 twelfth-graders, identified five domains that intercorrelate very highly with each other: (a) basic word meaning, (b) literal comprehension, (c) interpretive comprehension, (d) evaluative comprehension, and (e) location of information (Lyons, 1984). Generally, reading cannot be clearly demarcated into clear subskills as most standardized reading programs and tests assume (Farr, 1968; Farr & Roelke, 1971). Of course, if different tests or measures are highly interrelated, it will be even more difficult to sort out subscores on the same measure. Although many tests include and report subscores, these different measures on the same test are so highly interrelated that they should be reported as one total score. If publishers of curriculum and tests do provide subtests, it is imperative that they also provide evidence that the subtests measure different attributes (Drahozal & Hanna, 1978).

In summary, although most reading professionals agree that the purpose of reading is comprehension, "the essential issue that obfuscates valid reading assessment remains the same. We are still asking, 'What is reading comprehension?'" (Farr & Carey, 1986, p. 32).

A Critical-Effect View of Reading

In contrast to the traditional, two-component model of reading, we propose a one-component model in which the focus is not on identifying separate subskills of the reading process. Rather, the critical effect of reading provides the basic definition of the process: Material is read and/or reactions are communicated to others. **Reading** and **reacting** reflect behaviors in response to different stimuli. In this view, reading and reacting are not linear, with a beginning and an end, nor do developmental stages exist. The model does not define the two primary behaviors, reading and reacting, as cause and effect, but they are temporally ordered: Reading is assumed to occur first and reacting later, either immediately or over an extended time. An important assumption of this view is that the assessment process, not the reading process, is broken up to focus on different behavior. Figure 7.2 is noteworthy for its circular conception of the entire reading/reacting process. In this model, we may view reading on its own or consider it within the context of reacting to the material. This model is similar to one proposed by Valencia and Pearson (1988), in which reading is viewed as the interaction

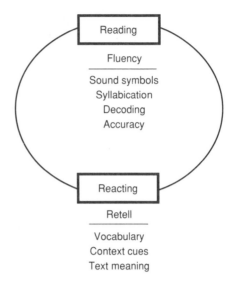

FIGURE 7.2
Unitary model of reading, focusing on the critical effect

between the reader, the text, and the context, with many different skills orchestrated together in a dynamic act.

Research Supporting the Model. Research supporting a unitary model comes from three directions: (a) basic psychological investigations of decoding and comprehension, (b) descriptive and experimental studies of fluency and comprehension conducted in classrooms, and (c) a theoretical conception. In this section, the terms *decoding, fluency,* and *comprehension* are used only because they are the terms used in the literature.

Decoding and comprehension. Generally, good comprehenders are also skilled decoders. As early as 1920, Buswell noted that poor comprehenders also had inadequate decoding skills and were found to (a) make more comprehending errors, (b) make more nonintrusion errors, (c) take more time to read the stories and answer comprehension questions (Willows, 1974), (d) perform poorly on word-scanning tasks (Katz and Wicklund, 1971), and (e) make more decoding errors that detracted from the meaning of the passage (Fairbanks, 1937) or remained uncorrected more frequently (Steiner, Weiner, & Cromer, 1971; Webber, 1970).

Good and poor readers differ primarily in their skill in decoding and organizing text (Golinkoff, 1975). Often, latency for decoding words appears to be a function of word familiarity; skilled readers are rapid decoders with unfamiliar or pseudowords (Golinkoff & Rosinski, 1976; Perfetti & Hogaboam, 1975). Accessing the meaning of the word depends upon the reader's skill in decoding it: "That is, if a word cannot be decoded readily, its meaning may not be retrieved" (Pace and Golinkoff, 1976, p. 765). Such low decoding skills have also been associated with low vocabulary skills and poor organizational skills (Cromer, 1970).

Descriptive and Experimental Studies. Instead of latency in decoding, another line of research, reading fluency, has been used to distinguish good and poor comprehenders. The outcomes from early research generally have not been consistent; sometimes a strong relationship is found, and occasionally a weak relationship is found. The relationship between reading fluency and comprehension is apparently influenced by reading materials, reader characteristics, and testing procedures (Rankin, 1970).

However, more recent research on fluency, begun with the establishment of curriculum-based measurement (S. L. Deno, 1985), is much more consistent in finding high relationships between fluency and comprehension. In identifying relevant classroom behaviors that would be useful in frequently monitoring student's learning, Deno, Mirkin, Chiang, and Lowry (1980) developed five measures of reading from curriculum material: (a) oral reading from passages (oral reading), (b) oral reading from word lists (words in isolation), (c) identifying missing words (cloze), (d) defining key words from passages (word meaning), and (e) reading key words within passages (words in context). All five measures were designed for frequent use, necessitating brief measures; as a consequence, 1-minute timed tasks were devised. The initial three validation studies, found high correlations between these measures, particularly between oral reading fluency and performance on published achievement tests. Following this initial validation research, a number of other studies have found that oral reading fluency

- Is highly related to teacher judgments of proficiency (L. S. Fuchs, Fuchs, & Deno, 1982; Marston, 1982).
- Can be used for placing students into instructional materials (Hall & Tindal, 1989; Parker, Hasbrouck, & Tindal, 1989; Wesson, Vierthaler, & Haubrich, 1989) with high criterion validity with other measures of achievement (Fuchs, Fuchs, & Deno, 1982).
- Is correlated with criterion-referenced tests in basal curricula and may be an improvement upon mastery-based decision-making (L. S. Fuchs & Fuchs, 1984; L. S. Fuchs, Fuchs, & Tindal, 1986; Tindal, Fuchs et al., 1985).
- Differentiates between students in special, compensatory, and general education programs (Deno, Marston, Shinn, & Tindal, 1983; Shinn, Tindal, & Stein, 1988; Shinn, Ysseldyke, Deno, & Tindal, 1986; Shinn & Marston, 1985).
- Serves as a valid index that is highly related to other measures of instructional outcomes of program effects (Fuchs, Deno, & Mirkin, 1984; Tindal, 1988).
- Is a powerful component of interventions, resulting in significant achievement gains when embedded in a frequent measurement system (Fuchs & Fuchs, 1986b).

- Can be used in evaluating special education program placement, using either prereferral outcomes (Marston, 1988) or end-of-year results (Tindal, Shinn, & Germann, 1987).

Most of this research on the relationship between fluency and comprehension is correlational, with the mistaken conception that there is a causal connection: Rate causes comprehension. "Interestingly, the potential of an inverse causal connection—where the comprehension affects rate—gets little if any attention" (Farr & Carey, 1986, p. 117). The preceding research cannot clarify the direction of influence; it does not show whether improvements in reading rate result in subsequent improvements in comprehension or increased skill in comprehension results in increased reading rate. We only know that students who read more fluently also perform higher on comprehension tasks.

To ferret out the direction of influence, we need experimental research that systematically treats experimental and control groups with different interventions, either focusing on rate or comprehension. However, very few such studies have been completed, few have found consistent significant effects, and none have been methodologically adequate. For example, Samuels, Dahl, and Archwamety (1974) and Fleisher, Jenkins, and Pany (1979) found no effects reflecting a relationship between speed of word recognition and comprehension. Yet, Roberts and Smith (1980), and Hansen and Lovitt (1976) found positive experimental effects, reflecting a high relationship between fluency and comprehension.

Theoretical conception. Citation of research without any underlying theory is difficult to interpret. If definitions of comprehension are elusive *and* high relationships are found between measures of fluency and comprehension (however it is defined), then we must address an explanatory reason. The general theoretical conception for viewing reading as a unitary construct is provided by LaBerge and Samuel's (1974) construct of automaticity, which views reading in terms of information-processing stages.

A major issue in the attainment of skillful reading is the achievement of fluent decoding, in which instantaneous processing of information occurs and the component skills of reading become automatic. In effect, separate processes are consolidated, so that word identification supersedes the phonic associations and blending, and phrase identification replaces individual word reading (Barr & Sadow, 1985). According to LaBerge and Samuels (1974), readers systematically transform printed stimuli into visual, chronological, and semantic codes, with a number of substages occurring at each of these three levels. Both accurate responding and automatic responding are needed, with the important distinction that attention is necessary for accuracy but not for automaticity. Assuming that decoding and comprehension are interrelated skills, a reader who devotes more attention to decoding has less available for comprehension, or vice versa. In other words, when a task can be done automatically, more attention can be devoted to intersentence meaning (Fleisher et al., 1979). As children learn to read, they devote less attention to decoding print, therefore freeing up its translation into meaning (LaBerge & Samuels, 1974).

Beginning with Buswell's (1920) research, it appears that good comprehenders read in larger units and use information more efficiently both within and between words than poor comprehenders, allowing them fewer pauses and more active text processing. Skilled comprehenders use the largest unit possible to gather meaning from the text (Gibson & Levin, 1975). The research summarized by Golinkoff (1975) depicts poor comprehenders as concerned with decoding each word and failing to utilize the interword relationships that could speed up the decoding process and permit more efficient text sampling. The good comprehender, however, appears to scan for meaning, organizing text into at least phrase-size units and sampling from other areas at the same time. (p. 646)

We can explain this relationship between decoding fluency and comprehension in either a strong or weak form. In the strong form, fast decoding is a *sufficient* condition for skilled comprehension, with a fairly direct connection between these two components. By implication, improvement on one results in improvement on another. In the weak form, fast decoding is a *necessary but not sufficient* for skilled comprehension. In this version, the link is not as direct between the two components; other conditions may need to be present for comprehension to improve (Fleisher et al., 1979). It is quite likely that the relationship is complex, and the latter explanation accounts for the mixed findings in the research.

The essential reason for reviewing the research on decoding and comprehension is to vindicate the adoption of two major assessment strategies for the classroom: curriculum-based measurement and informal reading inventories. These two strategies fit well within the research, are empirically justified, and encompass the critical behaviors needed to make decisions about students' educational programs. Both techniques incorporate reading within the assessment process, in contrast to many other strategies that focus only on reacting and assume that actual reading behavior is well developed. Both techniques are also flexible in their application to the classroom, allowing teachers to make a variety of decisions. However, because both strategies are complex in their assessment of reactions, we describe two additional techniques at the end of the section: cloze and maze. These two techniques may be useful and efficient supplements to a comprehensive assessment of reading and reacting.

ASSESSMENT STRATEGIES

In the model, the stimulus materials that engage students in the act of reading itself can come from either of two sources: (a) the curriculum from which instruction is delivered, or (b) materials within tests. Regardless of the source, reading can occur either silently or orally, and we can score the latter in terms of many different error types. Reactions to reading also can be generated from different sources: a priori interest, intellectual operations, or story maps. Regardless of the source, reactions can reflect different response types, including active retell productions, answers to questions, or fill-in-the-blank tasks (cloze or maze). Likewise, we can score reactions objectively or subjectively. Figure 7.3 depicts the model.

Although the model in Figure 7.3 identifies reading and reacting separately, the text reviews various strategies as a single process. For example, **curriculum-based measurement** typically utilizes basal materials to engage student reading. Performance is summarized as rate correct, and retell procedures are used to assay reactions if they are deemed necessary. This system is used in special education for a multitude of decisions, including screening and eligibility, planning instruction and formatively evaluating its effect, and summatively evaluating programs. In contrast, informal reading inventories occasionally employ curriculum reading materials and at other times use testing materials to engage students in reading. Performance is summarized as percent correct, and structured questions are typically used to ascertain reactions. This system is used in general education for identification of reading performance levels and placement of students into

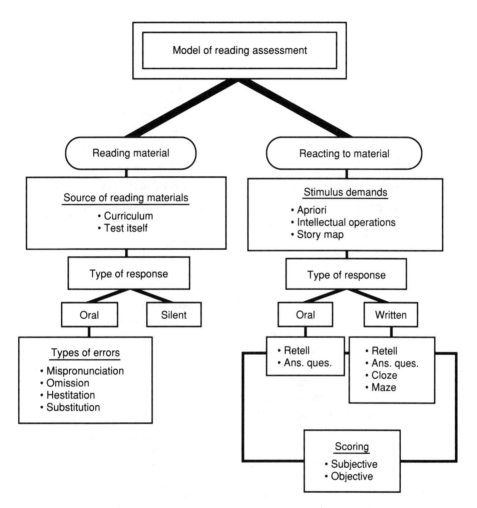

FIGURE 7.3
Model depicting two dimensions of reading assessment—reading and reacting

reading groups. The last two assessment strategies reviewed in this section, cloze and maze, incorporate reading and reacting into a single behavioral act.

Curriculum-Based Measurement: Reading Fluency

In measuring oral reading fluency (Deno & Fuchs, 1987; Deno, Mirkin, & Chiang, 1982),

students read a passage under timed conditions, and the examiner counts the number of words read correctly and incorrectly; student performance is summarized as the rate correct. Although errors are counted, they are used clinically to ascertain error patterns and generate hypotheses, since few relationships have been found between error patterns and reading performance (Parker, Hasbrouck & Tindal, 1989). An important dimension of CBM is the use of standardized administrations in which directions to the student are scripted and scoring procedures delineated, thus potentially increasing the reliability of the data.

Oral Reading Fluency. Often, both curriculum-based and curriculum-free reading passages or word lists are administered, allowing maximally sensitive comparisons of students within grades and curricula and across grades and curricula. As discussed in chapter 2, we may use different sampling strategies to select appropriate materials. In addition, a considerable amount of research (L. S. Fuchs & Fuchs, 1986a; L. S. Fuchs, Fuchs, & Deno, 1982; L. S. Fuchs, Tindal, & Deno, 1981; Tindal, 1988; Tindal & Deno, 1981) and practice (Deno, Mirkin & Wesson, 1984; Fuchs, 1986; Mirkin, Fuchs, & Deno, 1982; Wesson, Deno, & Mirkin, 1982) has been devoted to establishing appropriate measurement materials. Typically, passages from material to be taught throughout the entire year are randomly sampled (often referred to as *long-range goal material*). Each selection (passage or list) has a tester's copy (with numbers along the right side) and a student copy (with no numbers present). The numbers on the tester's copy represent a cumulative count of words for each successive line in the passage or every group of five words on the list. The length of the measurement is 1 minute.

The test is individually administered in an area free from distraction, using the following procedures:

1. Put the student copies in front of the student in the same order as yours.
2. Place your copy out of the student's view.
3. Read the directions *verbatim* for the first administration. Say to the student:

   When I say "start," begin reading at the top of this page. If you wait on a word too long, I'll tell you the word. If you come to a word you

cannot read, just say "pass" and go on to the next word. Do not attempt to read as fast as you can. This is not a speed reading test. Read at a comfortable rate. At the end of one minute, I'll say "stop."

- Don't use the word *Go* to begin, since it implies racing, particularly when stated in the presence of the stop watch.

4. Follow along on your copy, crossing off the following incorrectly read words:

- Misread words such as *house* for *horse*, *hug* for *huge*, *home* for *house*, *big* for *huge*.
- Words the student cannot read within about 3 seconds. After that period of time, tell the student the word.
- Words not read (omission); count all words in skipped lines as errors.
- Reversals of letters within words (e.g., *saw* for *was*) or pairs of words (e.g., *the red, big dog* instead of *the big, red dog*).

The following miscues are not counted as errors:

- Proper nouns that are mispronounced more than once.
- Self-corrections.
- Words added into the text by the student (additions or insertions).

5. At one minute, say "Stop," mark the last word read with a bracket (]), and quickly move to the next reading task. Place the top sheet over and to the side and tell the student you would like to continue in the same manner. Repeat this procedure until all reading tasks are completed.
6. Count the number of words read correctly and incorrectly by taking the cumulative count and subtracting the number of errors. For the basal reading passages, simply use the number to the right of the last full line read; add the number of words read in the

next (partially read) line to obtain the total number of words read. The number read correctly is found by subtracting from this total amount the number of words read incorrectly. The same strategy is used for word lists: take the cumulative count from the last group of five words, add any words read from the next group, and subtract the number of errors made.

Advantages. This reading assessment format has several advantages. Extensive research conducted in elementary schools indicates that the reliability and validity data are overwhelmingly supportive (S. L. Deno, 1985; L. S. Fuchs, Fuchs & Deno, 1982; Deno & Fuchs, 1987; Deno, Marston, Shinn, & Tindal, 1983; Shinn, 1989a). Because the administration procedures are standardized, comparable data can be collected across individuals and over time, and since it is so easy to train others to administer and implement the measure, instructional assistants and even students can take part in the assessment process (Bentz, Shinn, & Gleason, 1988). Such data can be used for multiple decision making in special education, including the three major types that we identified in chapter 2: screening and eligibility (Shinn, Tindal, & Stein, 1988), instructional planning and formative evaluation (L. S. Fuchs, 1986; Tindal, 1988), and summative program certification (Tindal, 1989). Importantly for general education classroom teachers, they can use the data to place regular students into reading groups (Parker, Hasbrouck & Tindal, 1989; Hall & Tindal, 1989).

Disadvantages. Probably the biggest disadvantage to oral reading fluency is the lack of *face validity.* This term was not introduced in chapter 6 because it is not a legitimate form of validity, but it is often considered by educators in making adoption decisions of assessment instruments. Face validity refers to the look of a test: Does the behavior sampled on the test *appear* relevant? For example, many reading curricula contain mastery tests that purport to measure student skill attainment (they look relevant) but are in fact unreliable and invalid for making such decisions (Tindal et al., 1985). Since the correlations between reading fluency and comprehension are high but not perfect, it may be important to obtain student reactions to reading, particularly if suspicions exist that the student is a "word caller." Frankly though, most students will rank themselves on both reading and reacting measures in a consistent manner, so this strategy should be reserved for use only when suspicions exist.

An important but subtle disadvantage to oral reading fluency is its dependence upon norms to operationalize or define it. The following dialogue is very common in the many training workshops that the authors and their CBM colleagues have conducted:

Teacher: I have a student who can read very well but afterward doesn't know what she read.

CBM Trainer: What do you mean by reading well?

Teacher: I don't know. I mean, she can read most of the words.

CBM Trainer: Not knowing how well the student reads is a problem, but let's assume you did know specifically how well the student read. Would you estimate her oral reading fluency as 50 words correct per minute? 60 words correct per minute?

Teacher: Yes, that seems about right.

CBM Trainer: And you said the student was in the fifth grade?

Teacher: Yes.

CBM
Trainer: Well, based on what you said, that a fifth-grade student is reading 60 words correctly per minute, I'd say that student is, in fact, very dysfluent and not reading well at all. If she were in a district with normative performance available, you would see that fifth-grade students often have a mean performance around 145 words correct and a standard deviation of 30–40. The student you described is performing over 2 standard deviations below this mean, or probably below the 5th percentile. So you really cannot say that you have a student who is fluent but can't comprehend, rather, she can neither read nor comprehend!

As this dialogue indicates, fluency is a norm-referenced notion, and it is not possible to rely upon absolute criteria to establish fluency. Therefore, to fully utilize a CBM approach, a local curriculum and local student group may need to be normed (see Shinn, 1988 for a description of normative strategies).

Silent Reading. In secondary settings, oral responses are not always appropriate, so another method, silent reading, has been used. With this method, students self-measure the time taken to read a passage (Tindal & Parker, 1989). Since students begin the written retell at different times (as soon as each is finished reading), the elapsed time is written on the board in 15-second intervals until the last student has completed his or her written retell. From the moment the teacher says "Begin reading," they write on the board the elapsed time. The following directions can be used to structure this assessment format:

Write your name and today's date on the board (in the form Month/Day/Year). When you get your Written Retell Test, please *keep the story side down on your desk.* Write your grade, school, and my name at the top of the sheet. Copy the date from the board. This is a silent-reading, written-retell test where you silently read a story, and then write down all you remember about the story. Here is a short story for you to *carefully* read, entitled _____ . As soon as you are finished reading, look up at the board, and copy the posted time into the Elapsed Time box at the bottom of the passage. Then, *without looking back at the story,* turn the page over and write everything you can remember about what you have read. When you are done writing, look up at the board and copy the posted time into the Elapsed Time box at the bottom of that side. Your writing will be judged in two ways: (a) How many facts or ideas from the story you have accurately written down; (2) the quality of your writing (spelling, capitalization/punctuation, sentence structure, and paragraph writing). You will get *partial* credit, even if your spelling, use of vocabulary, sentence structure, or memory of facts is not completely correct. You must finish both the reading and writing within 15 minutes. I'll warn you when there are only 2 minutes left. If you need more writing space you may get an extra sheet of paper, but only after the sheet in front of you now is full. Are there any questions? . . . Begin reading now.

The teacher or test proctor writes on the board the elapsed time in 15-second intervals, erasing the old time as the new elapsed time is written: :15, :30, :45, 1:00, 1:15, 1:30, 1:45, 2:00 etc. Even slower students should finish within the 15 minutes. Early finishers can quietly continue with other seatwork. When all students are finished, the passages are collected, and the task is completed.

Advantages. Probably the strongest advantage of this format is its natural relevance:

The goal of reading is silent, fluent reading. Other than that, the system has little to offer because actual reading behavior is inferred when reactions are obtained.

Disadvantages. Obviously, the reliability of such assessment practices is suspect because silent reading is impossible to measure. Again, not much can be said for or against silent reading in and of itself, since the behavior that is assessed is the reaction.

Curriculum-Based Measurement: Assessing Reactions

Although curriculum-based reading assessment has focused primarily on oral fluency, increasing attention is being devoted to eliciting student reactions. To remain consistent with brief measurements and production responses, teachers have used the retell technique, in which the student must describe either in spoken or written form the content of some material immediately after having read it (Kalmbach, 1986; S. P. Smith & Jackson, 1985). As in most production-response formats, construction of the task is less problematic than scoring the response, although certain guidelines help generate consistent results. Two types of responses are possible, an oral and a written response, which we review in the following sections. Furthermore, either type of response can be scored subjectively or objectively. In an effort to generate reliable data, the emphasis has been on objective systems, although subjective scoring procedures are often used as criteria in validation studies. We discuss only two strategies for objectively scoring oral retells. Subjective scoring involves teachers rating the retell on some dimension of importance (e.g., organization, clarity, completeness, etc.), using a rating scale with a range of from 1 (*low or poor*) to 5 (*high or well-developed*). Chapter

9 contains a detailed description of subjective scoring procedures for written expression.

Oral retell. The basic idea behind oral retell is to ascertain readers' reactions to a previously read story or passage, allowing them to frame responses in their own language. Very little preparation is needed in structuring the task itself, since minimal cueing is desired. However, scoring the responses can be very problematic, requiring either well-developed, follow-along systems or tape recordings and transcriptions. Probably the only issue in test administration is whether prompts will be given and how they will be structured. For example, many students may say only a few words and a gentle prompt, such as "Can you tell me any more?" may be useful to generate more retelling behavior. In determining whether such prompts will be used, the degree of standardization in the test administration is of paramount importance. If the prompts cannot be consistently administered (in terms of when and how they occur), they should probably not be used.

The following procedures were developed and were subsequently used in a validity study of reading (Isano, 1987), for creating an oral retell task. These procedures are particularly appropriate for narrative (fictional) rather than expository (nonfictional) passages.

1. Select a fictional text at the students' approximate instructional reading level. The text should be long enough to provide several different selections of about 250 words at a consistent difficulty level. The content should be of interest to the students who will be taking the story-retell test.
2. Select passages of approximately 200–250 words from the beginning of a chapter or where a major change of time or setting has just occurred within a chapter. Avoid passages that consist mainly of dialogue

or expository text. Retype or copy the entire passage selected for the story-retell test from the book so it is in clear, moderate-sized print for the students to read. The proctor should have one copy of the passage for each student being tested and should mark it for accuracy as the student reads from his or her own copy.

3. Map the passage by identifying the facts and details in each phrase of all sentences: the characters, events or actions, settings, time frames, reasons for the characters' actions, and any descriptive details. List these in the order in which they occur in the story under the headings shown in Figure 7.4.

4. After listing the characters, events or actions, settings, time frames, reasons for characters' actions, and any descriptive details from the passage under the appropriate headings, use dashed lines (-------) under each heading to connect the words or word phrases that are related to each other in some way. An example of a story map appears in Figure 7.5.
   Make one copy of your story map for each student you will be testing.

5. The examiner should have one copy with the student's name and the date written clearly on top.

6. Give the students the following directions:

   • I want you to read a story for me. When you are finished, I will ask you to tell me everything you can remember about the story, so please read it carefully.

7. Hand each student a copy of the typewritten passage to read and have them begin reading. It is a good idea to record these testing sessions, so the student's retelling markings can be checked later if necessary. When the student has finished reading, say:

   • Take a moment to think about what you just read. (Pause for 3–5 seconds.) Now tell me everything you remember about the story.

8. As the student retells the story, the examiner uses a highlighting pen to mark on the map protocol any fact or detail from the story mentioned by the student. The examiner makes a decision regarding the correctness of the response. The student must get the gist of the idea correct for a mark to be made by the examiner. If the student correctly connects two ideas or facts from the story, the examiner marks both of the two items *and* the connecting line between these two items. The examiner may draw connecting lines around omitted ideas or facts. If the student mentions anything that was not stated in the story, ignore these responses and make no mark on the protocol.

9. When the student indicates that he or she cannot remember anything more about the story, the examiner may give a neutral prompt such as the following:

   • Is there *anything* more you can remember?

10. This can continue until the student fails to give any more responses about the story. The examiner later can go back to the tape to check the marking of each student's story-retell protocol.

11. Score the protocol in the following manner:

   • Give 1 point for each item mentioned under each of the 6 main headings and under each of the 6 descriptor headings.
   • Give 1 point for each connecting line that was marked.
   • The sum of all the points is the student's total score for the story-retell test.
   • A student's percent correct can be calculated by giving 1 point for each item

WHO   DID WHAT   SAID/THOUGHT WHAT   WHERE   WHEN   WHY/HOW

Use the following definitions to place the components of the story under the above categories:

- *WHO:* The character(s) mentioned in each phrase/sentence, including people, animals, etc. List the characters' names under this heading, if they are given in the story, even when a pronoun is used. For example, *dog/Pepper* or *children/Violet, George, John.*

  Descriptors: The words describing the characters, such as their ages, descriptive features, characteristics, etc. For example, *had brown hair, the youngest of the three, looked very mean.*

- *DID WHAT:* The action(s) and events(s) in each phrase/sentence. Verbs and verb phrases, including direct objects and indirect objects, are included (e.g., *did not cry, pumped water,* or *gave us permission*)

  Descriptors: The words describing the action(s) or event(s), often adverbs, adjectives, or phrases such as, *first, quickly, or* all that was left.

- *SAID/THOUGHT WHAT:* The words spoken or thought by a character(s) if any. List each phrase or sentence separately.

  Descriptors: The words describing how the characters were spoke or thought, such as *quickly or nervously.*

- *WHERE:* The setting(s) of each phrase/sentence, if explicitly stated in the passage. This will include prepositional phrases that modify the verb listed under DID WHAT or SAID/THOUGHT WHAT, such as *in front of the bakery,* or *under the table.*

  Descriptors: The words or phrases describing the settings, if any.

- *WHEN:* The time frame(s) of each phrase/sentence, if explicitly stated in the passage. This can include phrases such as *in the night, at 11:30,* or *as the men approached.*

  Descriptors: The words or phrases describing the time frame(s) of each phrase/sentence, if any.

- *WHY/HOW:* The reason(s) why or how the actions or events occurred, if explicitly stated in the passage. Inferences about why or how an action or event occurred are not listed.

  Descriptors: The words or phrases describing the words listed under WHY/HOW.

FIGURE 7.4

WHO	DID WHAT	SAID/THOUGHT WHAT	WHERE	WHEN	WHY/HOW
Mary	ran		to the boat		to find her mom.
Mary		called, "Mom! Where are you?"			
Mary	looked		all around the boat	for several minutes	

FIGURE 7.5
Example scoring for student retell

mentioned under all 12 headings and for each connecting line and finding the sum of all these points to find the total possible Score.

- The student's total score is then divided by the total possible score.

This idea of using a preconstructed story map to follow a student's retelling of a story has great potential for instructional purposes. By looking at any patterns of errors, a teacher can see areas for remediation. Perhaps the student remembers a great deal from the end of the story but not the beginning. Perhaps the student recalls characters and their actions, but never any descriptors (details) or time (when) or causality (why) factors. Of course, consistent with a curriculum-based measurement (CBM) approach, such diagnostic information represents hypotheses that may guide initial plans and activities but must be evaluated through instruction and subsequent retelling assessments.

Clark (1982) developed another objective strategy that uses a retelling procedure for assessing students and scores student responses according to the number of *pausal units*. In this approach, teachers are directed to do the following:

1. Break the passage to be used for recall into pausal units by placing a slash wherever a good reader would normally pause during oral reading (at punctuation points and/or conjunctions); or break the passage into *t-units*. (See Chapter 9 for definition of t-units.)
2. List the pausal units sequentially down the left side of the paper with a blank line to the right of each pausal unit.
3. Direct the student to read the passage.
4. Ask the student to recall everything he or she can or to retell the passage in the same order in which the material was presented. When the student is done saying what he or she can (either states that or remains

silent), provide one follow-up question: "What else can you recall?"

5. Tape the student's responses while you record his or her retelling and sequentially number the order for retelling each pausal unit. For example, a student might successively recall the information in the first 3 pausal units, and then retell information in the pausal units 10, 13, and 15.
6. Score the retelling using any number of different measures, such as the number or percentage of (a) pausal units recalled, (b) pausal units weighted according to importance to the main ideas or important events, or (c) pausal units retold in sequence, scaled objectively or subjectively (Krauss, 1989).

Advantages. Assessments of student reactions that utilize a retelling of the content provide clear descriptions of the interaction between the text and the reader; the reader is allowed to impose his or her own structure and content in developing the response (Wood, 1985). Often, it is optimally sensitive to the manner in which readers restructure information in their existing knowledge base. The retelling is a story in itself, reflecting a selection process that may provide important diagnostic information about the reader. Student understanding and interpretation of the story can be assessed, including both perceptions and difficulties in their organization of the story, their personal comprehension (Moore, 1983).

Tests are constructed directly from the information in the text, which controls their content. Evaluative and interpretive prompts and/or questions can be framed consistently; their difficulty or level of inference can be easily controlled. Questions (if used) can vary according to the content *and* structure of the text. The information in the text and the format for recalling the information (test item) contain consistent vocabulary. Therefore, assessment is closely linked to and can be integrated within instruction. The behavior sampled during the assessment is highly relevant and important across a wide range of content areas. Furthermore, retellings can be used to judge the appropriateness of stories given to students.

Disadvantages. Oral retell also has some disadvantages. For example, scoring of student performance is often subjective and may not be reliable. First, the examiner must map the reading selection, and then develop the response units. Comparability across alternate passages may also be limited because the questions within and among passages may vary in difficulty. The test may be easy to give but very time-consuming to score. Development of appropriate scoring response units is both time-consuming and difficult. Differences in scoring may be a function of the person constructing the map or guide, raising problems in consistency of content and subsequent differences in test difficulty. Establishing technical adequacy beyond content validity is difficult. The range of scores may be limited, depending upon content, making it difficult to reveal growth over time. Also, this format may not be appropriate for expository passages.

Written Retell. Like oral retell procedures, the actual stimulus for assessing reader's reactions through written retell is very straightforward, requiring minimal preparation; to make sure the tester doesn't lead student responses, the test should use minimal cueing. Unlike the oral retell, this procedure can be administered to a group, with all students directed to react to the story in a variety of ways. The procedure previously described with the silent reading task is a good example for structuring the written retell response. The students should be told to read the story carefully because they will be asked to relate as much information as they can. Furthermore, they should be told how the response will be scored, thus helping structure an assessment aimed at generating optimal performance. Although the test is easy to administer, it is difficult to score; responses can be scored through subjective judgments or objective counts.

Since subjective scoring for written expression is virtually the same as subjective scoring of written retells and we discuss it in chapter 9, we present this information here with minimal detail. Subjective evaluations of written retells typically depend upon rating scales that standardize high-inference judgments on some scale of valence or value. For example, Irwin and Mitchell (1983) applied the logic of written expression assessment to comprehension assessment. Arguing that the whole of a retelling is greater than the sum of its parts, they stress the need to obtain a summative measure of performance. Using both a rating scale and a checklist derived from that rating scale, they focused on the following six variables: (a) generalization beyond the test, (b) statement of the thesis, (c) summary of the major points, (d) explication of supporting details, (e) inclusion of supplemental information, and (f) attention to coherence, completeness, and comprehensibility. The anchors in their rating scales were judgments of *high* (5), *good* (4), *adequate* (3), *some* (2), and *poor* (1), using the following descriptions:

- 5—Generalizations are made beyond the text; includes central thesis and major points, supporting details, and relevant supplemental information; exhibits coherence, completeness, and comprehensibility.
- 4—Includes central thesis, major points, supporting details, and relevant supplemental information; exhibits coherence, completeness, and comprehensibility.

3—Relates major ideas, includes supporting details and relevant supplemental information; exhibits adequate coherence, completeness, and comprehensibility.

- 2—Relates a few major ideas, supporting details, and relevant supplemental information; exhibits some coherence, completeness, and comprehensibility.
- 1—Relates no major ideas, but details only irrelevant supplemental information; low degree of coherence, completeness, and comprehensibility.

Smith and Jackson (1985) also developed an assessment system similar to that described with the silent reading task. Their system utilizes student writing of recalled material. In this technique, the student is asked to read a passage and then write about the main idea of the passage. Reading the passage follows a study-for-exam format, in which students read the material, take notes, and rehearse summarization of the material. Then they are asked to reconstruct the content of the material they have just read without the aid of the passage. Therefore, the behavior tapped in the assessment situation is similar to the behavior required to be successful in high schools and colleges. Scoring is accomplished by attending to three dimensions: (a) major generalizations, (b) correct and relevant details, and (c) coherence of expression. Surface characteristics of the writing, such as spelling, punctuation and syntax, may or may not be considered in scoring responses. Trained raters examine the protocols, and the final score is determined through an average from two raters. While high reliability coefficients have been obtained using this technique, its criterion validity has yet to be established.

It is important to be clear on what is being rated when using rating scales to judge comprehension. When a student is asked to write a retell, and the retell is rated, two dimensions are present: (a) the quality of the retell and (b) the quality of writing (use of grammatical features, syntax, spelling, legibility, etc.). Therefore, it may be important to define explicitly the rating of comprehension and actively include directions (a) *not* to consider the medium for expression (oral or written production) or (b) to consider the medium for expression as a *separate* dimension, which could be rated using different anchors than those for the comprehension component.

An objective count focuses on a discrete aspect of student's writing that requires minimal judgment. Since written retells provide a permanent product (unlike oral retells), objective counts are relatively easy to obtain. Furthermore, the emphasis with CBM is on objective systems with several options available.

A procedure developed by L. S. Fuchs, Fuchs, and Maxwell (1988) requires students to write as much as they can about a story they have just read. Then their writing is scored on the number of (a) words, (b) pausal units, and (c) content words from the passage (proper and common nouns, verbs, adverbs, adjectives). The authors found a high relationship between the number of words written and student performance on other measures (e.g., Stanford Achievement Test, cloze, and oral recall). Tindal and Parker (1989) counted the number of: (a) words written, and (b) idea units, along with a subjective evaluation (1 to 5 scale of *communicative effectiveness*), and found a strong relationship among all three.

Advantages. Written retells, whether they are subjectively or objectively scored, have several advantages: (a) They are easy to construct and administer, requiring minimal preparation; (b) students respond in their own language, minimizing the influence of testing procedures on responses; and (c) a large number of students can be assessed in groups.

Subjective evaluations have the benefits of minimal preparation or implementation time and great flexibility to focus on a wide range of critical dimensions. Also, it is usually easy to explain these dimensions to others and train them in their use. The score is considered a holistic judgment, reflecting the belief that the sum is greater than its parts. With subjective evaluations, time spent scoring student performance is minimal, although securing reliable results may be difficult.

In contrast, objective scoring of written retells provides firm, descriptive counts of specific aspects of compositions. Reliability is often relatively easy to establish, and training and implementation are straightforward. Also, because instruction can be more directly configured from the assessment data, writing may be decomposed into its many parts. However, scoring is considerably more difficult and time-consuming than with subjective evaluations.

Disadvantages. Both subjective and objective evaluations of written retells have several disadvantages. With subjective scoring, attainment of adequate reliability may be difficult, mostly because of the rating scales from which results are summarized. These scales are often anchored with values that represent highly subjective words and may represent different concepts or constructs to different people. To obtain adequate reliability, extensive training may be necessary. Even though the results appear easy to communicate, it is difficult to control the reactions of others in the interpretation of results. The actual scaling of the anchors may pose problems: If a midpoint is employed that represents a neutral reaction, it may be selected more often. Most judgments tend to center in the middle rather than the extremes, regardless of whether a neutral midpoint is used. Scales with different ranges on the continuum may be created, presenting difficulties in interpretation. Also, because the score is represented with only

one single-digit number, the link between assessment and instruction may be weak; furthermore, change on this scale may be difficult to accomplish because scales often range only from 1 (*low*) to 5 or 7 (*high*).

Written retells that use objective scoring are often questioned because of a lack of synthesis; a skill as complex as writing may not be adequately broken down into discrete components. As in reading, breaking down written compositions into identifiable components may have face-validity problems. Because the critical effect from the retell is not in the writing itself but in the effect that it has on others, responses may need to be scored subjectively. Most objective scoring systems are also time-consuming.

Summary of Curriculum-Based Measurement

The basic strategy behind curriculum-based measurement in reading assessment is to generate production responses, using a brief task that can be repeatedly administered. As the name implies, the reading materials are derived from the curriculum. We can assess both reading and reacting in one administration through oral or silent reading; reactions may be completed orally or in writing. Administration of either the oral or silent reading is easy and straightforward; but only *administration* of the retell is as easy: *Scoring* presents a number of potential problems relating to reliability and efficiency.

Usually, oral reading and retell is appropriate for elementary grades, while silent reading and written retell is more appropriate for middle and high school students. However, reading and reacting are very highly related, and it is unusual to find students who are poor readers but can structure well-developed reactions. A more efficient strategy is to at least determine a student's oral reading fluency and, if necessary, ascertain the degree to which he or she can structure a reaction. In secondary settings, oral reading fluency may be appropriate for students in specialized programs; otherwise silent reading can be followed by an oral or written retell; the teacher flags those receiving the bottom values for more intensive objective measurements.

Although the data from reading and reacting may be more difficult to obtain than the typical selection-response, criterion-referenced test that is given at the end of a unit, the data are more powerful and useful. The biggest advantage is the applicability of the data for all three types of interpretive reference: norm, criterion, and individual. It is easy to generate norms that display an entire grade level; we can identify individual, skills and apply error patterns to determine instructional programming; and, finally, we can establish long-range goals and individual monitoring systems with the data that are collected and evaluated over time. For this reason, such data are applicable for a wide range of decisions: screening and determining eligibility, planning instruction, and formatively and summatively evaluating instructional programs.

In contrast, informal reading inventories have a far more limited range of flexibility and applicability. And although they are less efficient and potentially more difficult to conduct than CBMs, informal reading inventories represent an extremely functional form of assessment and incorporate production responses on relevant classroom tasks.

Informal Reading Inventories: Assessing Reading

In contrast to a focus on rate of behavior in the measurement of reading fluency, informal reading inventories (IRIs) assess oral reading and comprehension accuracy. Johnson, Kress, and Pikulski (1987) define an **informal reading inventory** as "a detailed study of an individual's overall performance in the area of reading as well as some of the language and thinking skills that are a necessary part of the reading process" (p. 2). IRIs allow for a thorough, careful evaluation of word identification skills and strategies. They also serve the area of reading comprehension, which includes understanding written messages intended by the author and the active manipulation of the ideas represented through print. Similarly, Johns and Lunn (1983) describe the informal reading inventory as

an individually administered reading test . . . composed of a series of graded word lists and graded passages. During the pupil's oral reading of the passages, the test administrator notes reading miscues, such as mispronunciations, omissions, repetitions, and substitutions. After the oral reading, the test administrator asks the pupil comprehension questions. Silent reading passages, accompanied by comprehension checks, are also usually included. (p. 8)

Determining Student Level of Functioning. Informal reading inventories have received much support from reading experts and, at times have appeared to be the most frequently employed assessment technique and the most precise form of assessment. The major function of IRIs is to place students in instructional levels or reading groups. Four specific levels are identified, but only three are of particular importance: independent, instructional, and frustration (Johnson et al., 1987). We will mention the listening-comprehension level but not discuss it in great detail.

Independent reading level. The independent level is one at which "children can function on their own and do a virtually perfect job of responding to the printed material" (Johnson et al., p. 13). Quantitative guidelines for this level include reading with 99% accuracy of word recognition and performing with 90% accuracy on comprehension tests. Criteria for word recognition and comprehension must be met in order to determine the independent level. Table 7.1 illustrates the independent reading level.

Instructional reading level. The instructional level is one at which we can meaningfully teach children. Quantitative guidelines include performing with 95% accuracy on the oral reading task and performing with 75% accuracy on the comprehension component. When considering the instructional level, however, a range of levels rather than a specific level is more likely to be found. For example, a child may be performing at a different level in natural science than he or she is in social science or in the basal reader. Table 7.2 illustrates the instructional reading level.

Frustration reading level. This **frustration level** is defined as one at which "the child be-comes completely unable to handle reading materials" and is assumed to be frustrated (Johnson et al., 1987, p. 19). The suggested quantitative criteria for this level include oral reading with 90% or less accuracy and performing at 50% or less accuracy on the comprehension component. Table 7.3 illustrates the frustration reading level.

Listening comprehension level. The listening comprehension level is defined as the highest level at which children can satisfactorily understand materials. The quantitative summary at this level includes performing at 75% accuracy on comprehension questions asked about the materials (Johnson et al., p. 20).

Other Purposes for Informal Reading Inventories. IRIs can accomplish five purposes. First, as mentioned, they can be used to estimate reading levels for independent functioning, an increasingly important purpose given the amount of work that children complete inde-

TABLE 7.1
Criteria for independent functioning with IRIs

Independent Level
The independent level is one at which readers can function on their own and do a virtually perfect job responding to printed material.

Qualitative Indicators	Quantitative Criteria
Oral reading Fluent, rhythmical Absence of behaviors associated with reading difficult material Few deviations from print; deviations do not affect meaning	99% accuracy[a]
Comprehension (oral and silent) Answers to questions or retellings reflect full understanding of material Balanced merger of prior knowledge and text information Retellings well-organized; reflect organization of text	90% accuracy[a]

[a]Both oral reading and comprehension criteria must be met.
Source: Johnson, M. S., Kress, R. A., & Pikulski, J. J. (1987). *Informal reading inventories—2nd Edition.* Newark, DE: International Reading Association, p. 21.

TABLE 7.2
Criteria for instructional functioning with IRIs

Instructional Level	
The level at which readers will profit maximally from teacher-directed instruction in reading.	
Qualitative indicators	Quantitative Criteria
Oral reading Fluent, rhythmical; few indicators of difficulty Few deviations from print that affect meaning; deviations from meaning are self-corrected Near absence of behaviors associated with reading difficult material Oral rereading improved over oral reading at sight	95–98% accuracy[a]
Comprehension (oral and silent) Meets most language and background of experience challenges of the material, and integrates prior knowledge with text information Answers to questions and retellings reflect good understanding for and memory of the material Retellings basically reflect organization of text; no serious intrusions or distortions Shows the ability to manipulate and critically respond to ideas in the text, although minor misinterpretations may occur	75–89%[a]

[a]Both oral reading and comprehension criteria must be met.
Source: Johnson, M. S., Kress, R. A., & Pikulski, J. J. (1987). *Informal reading inventories—2nd Edition.* Newark, DE: International Reading Association, p. 22.

pendently in classrooms. These materials must be structured for success. Second, IRIs can assist in diagnosis of individual strengths and weaknesses: we view readers' observed behavior as the interaction between language and thought, and develop hypotheses for determining skills and deficits. A third use of IRIs is in determining the nature of reading problems, the sources of and reasons for reading problems in particular. A fourth purpose is to bring self-understanding of skills and deficits to readers when they read selections of different difficulties. Finally, when we compare later performance to previous performance, IRIs help evaluate progress. Although several types of IRIs are available, most are commercial, curriculum-embedded, or teacher-devised (Johnson et al.).

Construction and Administration of Informal Reading Inventories. Procedures for administering, recording, and scoring individual informal reading inventories are straightforward. The examiner selects passages that are similar to most other selections in the book. Two or three selections usually are sampled at each level: one for oral reading, one for silent reading, and one for evaluating listening comprehension. The passages are of increasing length, from preprimer through the highest level: Preprimer to primer has 50–75 words, first to second has 100 words, third to fourth has 150 words, fifth to sixth has 200 words, and seventh and above has 250 words. Often, reading specialists concentrate only on oral reading and comprehension skills at the instructional level,

TABLE 7.3
Criteria for frustration functioning with IRIs

Frustration Level	
The level at which reading materials become so difficult that children cannot successfully respond to them, even with teacher direction and guidance.	
Qualitative Indicators	**Quantitative Criteria**
Oral reading	
Slow, labored, nonfluent	90% or less
Deviations from text affect meaning	
Appearance of behaviors (e.g., finger pointing, head movement) associated with reading very difficult material	
Oral rereadings is not improved over oral reading at sight	
Comprehension (oral and silent)	
Prereading discussions suggest weak language skills and background knowledge for understanding content of selections	50% or less
Answers to questions or retellings reveal lack of sensitivity to organization of materials, poor memory for content, and misinterpretations of content selection	

Source: Johnson, M. S., Kress, R. A., & Pikulski, J. J. (1987). *Informal reading inventories—2nd Edition.* Newark, DE: International Reading Association, p. 23.

but Johnson et al. have delineated 12 steps for adminstering a complete IRI.

Step 1: Preparation for testing. Collect materials and consider the testing procedures prior to testing.

Step 2: Establishment of rapport. Before testing a student, establish rapport with him or her. Make the student comfortable, at ease, and give him or her the purpose of the test and testing procedures.

Step 3: Determination of the level at which to begin. Several strategies are available for finding the appropriate level of difficulty at which to begin testing: reviewing school records and folders, obtaining previous teachers' judgments, and administering individual word recognition tests. "A reasonable procedure for

determining where to begin administering the reading inventory is at least one level lower than that at which the child first encountered difficulty on the word recognition test" (p. 28).

Step 4: Establishment of readiness and purpose for reading. Prior to reading, prepare the student for the reading material. Give the student also a reason for reading. (i.e., "Two boys have found something no one else knows about. Read this passage to discover their secret.")

Step 5: Oral reading. Using a watch to time the reading, the examiner should ask the student to read the passage orally. While the student reads, all errors and other features of oral reading should be tracked. Figure 7.6 contains the symbols for the error-tracking system described by Johnson et al. (1987).

Recording Symbol	Behavior Noted
HM	Head movement
FP	Finger pointing
PC	Use of picture clues
↑↓	Rising or falling inflection
was	Repetition
saw⟋was	Substitution
saw⟋ was	Self-correction
was⟋	Omission
the/man	Pause (one per second)
WXW	Word by word
the⌃big man	Insertion
(was)	Examiner help given
X	Punctuation ignored

Source: Johnson, S. M., Kress, R. A., Pikulski, J. J. (1987). *Informal reading inventories-2nd Edition.* Newark, DE: International Reading Association, p. 30.

FIGURE 7.6
System for recording oral reading at sight

Usually, we count four types of errors in the oral reading component of IRIs: mispronunciations, insertions, omissions, and examiner assists. However, commercial IRIs identify many other kinds of errors.

Step 6: Assessment of comprehension with orally read materials. Immediately following administration of the oral reading, ask the student a series of questions that you have prepared ahead of time. He or she must retell the story. In this step, the student does not have access to the reading materials but must answer the questions or describe the content as well as he or she can based on the oral reading. Most of the quantitative assessments of comprehension accuracy are based on answering 5–10 questions rather than story retelling, which is very difficult to quantify and requires considerable examiner judgment for scoring student responses.

In the traditional procedure ten questions are prepared ahead of time, dealing with four types of comprehension: factual, inferential, vocabulary, and evaluation. Factual recall questions involve information that has been directly stated by the author somewhere in the selection. Inferential questions require the reader to manipulate the information from the passage and draw some type of conclusion combining information from various sources. Vocabulary questions focus on the meaning of content-laden words in the selection. Evaluation questions demand that the reader come to conclusions and make judgments about some particular point of view. The questions should be passage dependent so that they cannot be answered without reference to information in the passage.

Step 7: Preparation for silent reading. If silent reading is to be assessed, direct the student to silently read a second selection that has been sampled from approximately the same level.

Step 8: Observation of silent reading. While the student is reading the second selection, the examiner should time the reading and record the behavior of the student as illustrated in Figure 7.7.

Recording Symbol	Behavior Noted
PC	Use of picture clues
LM	Lip movement
HM	Head movement
FP	Finger pointing
V	Vocalization
(was)	Examiner help given

Source: Johnson, S. M., Kress, R. A., Pikulski, J. J. (1987). *Informal reading inventories-2nd Edition.* Newark, DE: International Reading Association, p. 34.

FIGURE 7.7
Notations used in silent reading assessment

Step 9: Assessment of comprehension of silently read materials. The same strategy used for comprehension with oral reading employ: Ask ten questions that deal with factual, inferential, vocabulary, and evaluation issues.

Step 10: Oral rereading. In this step, the examiner should establish some purpose for orally rereading a portion of the selection that previously had been read in silence. The purposes are to assess the student's skill at skimming, measure the student's ability to read for a specific purpose, and determine the difference in fluency.

Step 11: Test across successive levels. The examiner should evaluate the student's performance on both oral reading and comprehension to either increase or decrease the material's difficulty levels.

Step 12: Evaluation of listening comprehension. We determine listening comprehension by finding the highest level at which the student can understand materials that are read to him or her. Such tests are usually begun one level above the first level administered. First establish a purpose for reading, and then read a passage to the student. Assess comprehension through questioning strategies or the use of a retelling procedure. Successively higher levels are attempted until the student fails to maintain 75% accuracy.

Of course, these 12 steps represent a very thorough administration of an IRI, and we frequently use a more abbreviated format. For example, most teachers have some information about students from files, records, other teachers, and test scores when they arrive in their classrooms. Therefore, administration of a word list to locate the material with which to begin testing is inappropriate. In contrast, we often devote great attention to Steps 5 and 6,

in which students orally read and are asked comprehension questions. Finally, rather than ascertaining silent reading skills, many teachers elect to move through the various levels of performance (frustration, instructional, and independent).

Informal Reading Inventories: Assessing Reactions

Informal reading inventories, whether teacher-developed or published, generally employ questions asking for reader reactions (Steps 6 and 12). Often, we assess reactions through the use of multiple-choice tests or oral, open-ended questions that require short answers. The next section reviews three strategies for developing such questions: (a) a priori importance, (b) intellectual operations, and (c) story mapping.

A priori Importance. The easiest format, which is probably the most frequent, is to create questions with no scheme or guiding strategy. This is a priori importance. When produced by commercial informal reading inventories, questions are initially developed with item discrimination, and difficulty analyses are subsequently conducted to ascertain appropriateness; when produced by teachers, the tests involve no such analyses. The material is read and questions that are thought to be appropriate are devised, utilizing either a selection-type or a short-answer response format. The depth or breadth of the question can vary considerably, ranging from specific information presented in the material to highly inferential reactions derived from such information.

Advantages. The biggest advantage of this strategy is the great amount of flexibility embedded in assessing reactions. Questions can be very diverse, fitting the passages as desired and spanning a wide array of responses.

Most students and teachers are very familiar with question-asking assessment strategies because they have a long history of use in schools.

Disadvantages. A priori importance also has some disadvantages. With flexibility and diversity come problems in establishing comparability and appropriateness. Questions may be differentially difficult and, when answered incorrectly, may reflect test inadequacy, not student skill. However, the problem is never identified because no information has been collected on question discrimination or difficulty, particularly with teacher-made inventories. A second problem is that most tests are predicated on differentially assessing literal and comprehension skills, but no adequate empirical support has distinguished these two subtypes of comprehension. Third, the use of multiple-choice questions requires an intensive time commitment to create them; with open-ended questions, on the other hand, the time commitment is in reliably scoring them. Finally, questions often fail to control adequately for student background, even though this problem also is present in most other procedures.

Intellectual Operations. A second strategy for question development is to use the taxonomy of intellectual operations, described in chapters 2 and 3, to develop questions that relate to an appropriate intellectual operation or level of knowledge. Questions reflect two dimensions: One focuses on content (facts, concepts, and principles), and the other focuses on intellectual operations or tasks (reiteration, summarization, illustration, prediction, evaluation, and application). As we discussed in chapter 3, test construction should follow specific procedures for sampling material, determining core information, and framing the questions, the correct answers, and, if a selection response is used, the foils.

Advantages. By sampling a wide range of reactions from reiteration to application and encompassing three levels of content, we gain a full profile of student reactions. This diversity in intellectual operations may be helpful in locating low performers or identifying areas of difficulty. Question development follows both a theoretical conception and a planned strategy, thus precluding an inadvertent focus on recall of factual information. Without planning, questions are likely to focus on reiteration and summarization tasks. The intellectual-operations strategy is appropriate for a wide range of materials, including fiction and nonfiction.

Disadvantages. As we discussed in chapter 2 on measurement planning and chapter 3 on test construction, the level of knowledge implied in the questions should be consistent with the type of information or level of knowledge presented in the passage to make important decisions. The same time commitments for question-development necessary when using a priori importance is equally applicable here. The tester must either work longer on developing the questions or on scoring the responses.

Story Maps. Finally, the third strategy is to use a story map. The basic premise behind the use of story mapping is to structure assessment so that questions reflect the material. The procedures are generic, and the text determines the specific content. There are two major types of text: (a) narrative text, which can be depicted through story grammar, and (b) expository text, which is hierarchically organized around topics and concepts. In both types, however, the manner in which information is structured and oriented within a domain-specific knowledge base has important bearing on its comprehensibility. Selection and and analysis of text passages is based on capturing all dimensions:

organization, coherence, and domain of knowledge (Wixson & Peters, 1987).

For narrative text, story grammar provides the rule-system for describing the regularities appearing in the prose (Mandler, 1984). In essence, story maps are created to emphasize the interrelatedness of story components. For example, stories in Western cultures have a structure that organizes the content: A plot or theme is typically present and is executed through an episode or series of episodes; the compositions take place somewhere during a specific time frame and contain one or more characters; finally, in the unfolding narrative, the sequence consists of an initiating event, attempts at resolution, accomplishment of some end state, and the reactions of the main characters (Marshall, 1983). For narrative stories, the theme is highlighted at two levels of abstraction: the main idea and the abstract theme. Plot characteristics include setting (location and importance to theme), major characters (names, traits, and functions), problem, conflict, resolution, and major events (Wixson & Peters, 1987).

Marshall (1983) developed a generic format of questions for narrative text that we summarize below. The questions can focus on information that is explicitly or implicitly stated in the text.

Theme:
What is the major point of the story?
What is the moral of the story?
What did ____ learn at the end of the story?

Setting:
Where did ____ happen?
When did ____ happen?

Character:
Who is the main character?
What is ____ like?

Initiating events:
What is ____'s problem?
What does ____ have to try to do?

Attempts:
What did ____ do about ____?
What will ____ do now?

Resolution:
How did ____ solve the problem?
How did ____ achieve the goal?
What would you do to solve ____'s problem?

Reactions:
How did ____ feel about the problem?
Why did ____ do ____?
How did ____ feel at the end?
Why did ____ feel that way?
How would you feel about ____?

Source: Marshall, N. (1983). Using story grammar to assess reading comprehension. *The Reading Teacher, 36,* 616–618.

In expository text, we demarcate three levels of ideas (central purpose, major ideas, and supporting ideas), and two outcomes (reason and result for issues raised in the text). For concept maps, representing expository, informational text, the focus is on externalizing "the hierarchical structure of text by highlighting the important relations among superordinate, coordinate, and subordinate concepts . . ." (Wixson & Peters, p. 343).

For both narrative and expository text, questions focus on the type of processing required for the reader to respond, and they reflect the amount of text to process in answering the question: (a) intersentence processing requires attention to meaning across several sentences; (b) text processing requires attention to large sections of text; and (c) beyond-text processing requires readers to rely on background information as well as text information. All questions are formatted along both dimensions: content and process. For example, we may categorize a question for assessing comprehension of a narrative text as 'character: text '; the reader must address a description of a character in the story using information from the entire passage. Or, a question for an expository passage may focus on 'Main idea: beyond text'; the reader must consider information from both the text and other sources to derive an answer about the main idea (Wixson & Peters).

For either type of story map, we can score student performance in a variety of ways. If we use multiple-choice questions, the count may be the number of answers correct and incorrect. If we use open-ended responses, the scoring criteria may include a count of the number of items that are correctly retold or some type of rating scale that has a weight for free recall versus prompting (i.e., 2 points for mentioning without prompt, 1 point for repeat question or present prompt, and 0 for no recall, with follow-up/prompt).

Advantages.   The biggest advantage to a story map for creating questions is that there is a close relationship between the passage and the questions. Unlike the a priori strategy, in which we develop questions extemporaneously, and unlike the intellectual operations strategy, in which questions follow a set taxonomical analysis, questions developed for story maps are inherently relevant to the material from which they arise, which provides a structure that ensures a high degree of relationship that is broadly defined and applicable to many different passages and materials. This strategy takes advantage of the increasing research in reading that supports a complex view of the process as an interaction between the writer and the reader.

Disadvantages.   Although the story map questions are highly related to the text, differences among them may occur both within one passage or across different passages. This for-

mat can employ either selection-response questions (i.e., multiple-choice) or short-answer questions (oral responses), resulting in the same advantages and disadvantages of time commitments in question development and/or scoring responses as for intellectual operations and a priori importance. A final caution about this technique relates to the limited amount of research that has been conducted in this area. Most educators treat reading as consisting of two separate components, decoding and comprehension, even though the psychometric research has failed to convincingly demonstrate separate constructs. And within the area of comprehension, names have been created for all sorts of subtypes, even though little evidence supports them. It is likely that the same effect will occur in this area: New names will be given to cognitive processes, educators will reify the names, using them as explanatory fictions to justify the very constructs they purport to measure, and no one will attend to the basic research being done on their nonexistence.

Summary of Informal Reading Inventories

Reading specialists and teachers have long incorporated some version of informal reading inventories into their classroom assessment practices. The goal of such inventories is to determine performance levels (frustration, instruction, and independent); however, great discrepancies exist in the completeness with which specific procedures are implemented. Informal reading inventories include the following components: (a) determination of an entry level for assessment (usually using a word list), (b) oral reading and comprehension assessment of successive passages, (c) reading passages and asking questions to ascertain listening comprehension, and (d) final determination of or placement in a material that reflects difficulty and frustration. Although published inventories are available, we can easily adapt these procedures for use with curriculum materials. The research completed on informal reading inventories is not entirely supportive, with problems most apparent in determination of performance levels and the lack of standardization in the administration procedures, particularly in comprehension assessment. However, informal reading inventories incorporate behavior that is relevant in the classroom, and they are likely to be used.

Although seemingly comparable, curriculum-based measurement and informal reading inventories have only one similarity: Students read through materials that range in difficulty. In all other respects, they are quite different, as you can see from the summary in Table 7.4.

In summary, the two assessment procedures are very different. Although IRIs have a longer tradition historically, CBM is the more-preferred and better-vindicated procedure. It is standardized, incorporates classroom-relevant behavior, and is technically adequate; most im-

portantly, it has substantial empirical support for use in the decisions for which it is applied.

To completely describe the full range of reading assessment practices, we must consider two more techniques: the cloze and maze. Not only do they fit within our conception of reading as a unitary construct, but they also provide important supplementary information about oral reading fluency. As mentioned earlier, CBMs often suffer from a lack of face validity. Although this form of validity is not really appropriate, it is important in generating widespread adoption. Therefore, the two procedures described in the next section, particularly the maze, may be considered the best supplemental methods to using CBM reading assessment.

Cloze and Maze: Reader Reactions

The last two forms of assessment incorporate silent reading; therefore the only behavior they

TABLE 7.4

Comparison of curriculum-based measurement (CBM) and informal reading inventories (IRIs)

	CBM	IRI
Decision	Multiple: Screening—eligibility, Instructional planning, instructional Evaluation-formative and summative.	Three performance levels: Frustration, instruction, independent.
Administration	Standardized and replicable across and within administrators	Unstandardized and often noncomparable across administrators.
	Timed	Untimed
Materials	Curriculum-based	Published and curriculum-based
Behavior sampled	Oral and silent reading	Oral and silent reading
	Written retell	Answers to comprehension questions
Metric	Fluency (rate correct per minute)	Accuracy
	Error presence or absence only	Errors analyzed as specific miscues and diagnostically used
Reliability	Well documented, typically coefficients in range of .85–.95 (using alternate form, test-retest, and interjudge)	None reported
Validity	Well established	None reported

generate is in relation to reader reactions. Of all forms of assessment reviewed in this chapter, these two techniques most closely reflect the unitary act of reading and reacting. The cloze, a fill-in-the-blank procedure, has a long history of research and practice in reading assessment. In contrast, the maze, a multiple-choice, fill-in-the-blank procedure, is a more recently developed technique. However, both strategies are easily incorporated into classroom practice, using curriculum materials.

Cloze. Introduced by Taylor in 1953, the cloze technique is named after the gestalt concept of closure. The research conducted on the cloze format is extensive, spanning the last 20–30 years. McKenna and Robinson (1980) have compiled an extensive annotated bibliography of this research, organizing it into several major topical strands. They define the **cloze procedure** as "a method of systematically deleting words from a prose selection and then evaluating the success a reader has in accurately supplying the words deleted" (p. 5). The cloze test provides an interesting confluence between the background knowledge and expectations of the reader and the language and context cues provided by the writer. Generally, we consider it a measure of comprehension; a considerable amount of research has focused on its relationship with other, more traditional measures of comprehension (multiple-choice questions and instructional placements).

For example, Rankin and Culhane (1969) found a moderate relationship between performance on cloze and multiple-choice tests, ranging from .54 to .77. However, absolute performance levels were typically quite different. Scores of 19%–31% on a cloze test were comparable to scores of 50%–65% on multiple-choice (MC) tests; 35%–46% on the cloze test was comparable to scores of 60%–80% on the MC test; finally, scores ranging from 50%

to 57% on the cloze were similar to 90%–100% on the MC test (Bormuth, 1967, 1969).

Some research on instructional placement compares placements obtained by cloze and those obtained by teacher judgments. For example, Pikulski and Pikulski (1977) used the following guidelines for placement using the cloze test: for independent level, 45% or better; for instructional level, 30%–45% on the cloze; for frustration level, 30% or less on the cloze (Ransom, 1968; Jones & Pikulski, 1974). Overall, only 67% of the students were similarly placed using the cloze as compared to teacher judgment, which was considerably less than the level of 80% found by Jones and Pikulski. Finally, Rakes and McWilliams (1979) have compiled various performance levels on the cloze into a placement table, listing a wide range of scores for determining the ratio of correct responses to the number of passage deletions in determining independent, instructional, and frustration levels.

Two techniques are available for constructing a cloze task. The first and more traditional procedure involves the following steps:

1. Select a passage of approximately 250 words.
2. Leave the first and the last complete sentence intact.
3. Select every *n*th (frequently every 5th or 7th) word, beginning with the second sentence of the passage, continuing up to but not including the last sentence.
5. Copy or retype the passage to replace the selected words with a standard-length blank space and underline.
6. Direct students to read the passage orally and supply the missing word.
7. Score responses according to the number of exact or semantically correct word matches.

The second strategy involves planned selection of words for replacement rather than random selection. There are five guidelines to consider in using this strategy. First, the deleted word should relate to the content of more than one sentence, helping the reader integrate information from several sentences. Second, the deleted word should be predictable and capable of being clarified by the surrounding text. Third, deleted words should be relevant for instructional purposes, providing a focus on specific content or syntactical features. Fourth, if multiple choices are used (see the description of the maze procedures below), the alternative choices should be attractive distractors. Finally, students should be highly motivated to read and complete the cloze (Marino, 1981). All previously described steps for the cloze remain the same; only Step 3 is different (Bormuth, 1968):

Step 3. In each sentence except for the last, select important content words that fall within any or all of the following categories: nouns, adverbs, adjectives, and verbs.

The following example uses the first cloze strategy—every sixth word was deleted—but it would have been just as easy to use the second strategy and delete only content words.

Organs working together make up systems. Two of these systems are skeletal system and the muscular _____. The human skeleton is made _____ of bone and cartilage. One _____ between the two is that _____ does not contain the calcium _____ phosphorus compounds that bone contains. _____ makes cartilage more flexible than _____. There are 206 bones in _____ human skeleton. Some of these _____ are connected to each other _____ ligaments. Since ligaments stretch easily, _____ allow the bones to move _____. This forms what is called _____ movable joint.

Advantages. Using the cloze for assessment of comprehension has several advantages. The cloze has been developed over the past 20 years, and a fair amount of research has been conducted on its technical adequacy and applications (Bormuth, 1969; McKenna & Robinson, 1980). It is an acceptable indicator of comprehension partly because of its high reliability and criterion validity with conventional, multiple-choice tests (Farr & Carey, 1986). Because the deleted words are generally text-dependent, performance is generally free of background knowledge. Also, it is easy to develop alternate forms of the cloze for classroom use. Another advantage is that consistent and standardized development and administration are possible; furthermore, it can be group administered and is relatively easy to score. We can derive objective and quantifiable scores that can encompass a wide range of values, providing a distribution of item difficulty. Finally, the assessment information has a relationship with diagnostics and instruction, particularly when we employ the second construction strategy, deleting content words.

Disadvantages. The cloze technique is not without problems. Serious questions exist about exactly what the cloze measures, its uncertain relationship to syntactic competence, and the influence of context on performance. The cloze technique provides little control for either passage differences or the reader's background knowledge, necessitating multiple passages that include different content. A "passage effect" may be present, in which issues of relevance, interest, and difficulty potentially affect performance. Selection of every *n*th word may result in word deletions of little value. Passages that aren't redundant may deflate scores. Finally, scores are often low (ranging from 30% to 50% correct), precluding its use with very low-performing students (see chapter I and discussion of the mildly handicapped).

The most rational approach to this problem is never to use only a cloze test as an index of comprehension—just as one should not rely only on multiple-choice tests. It seems likely that some aspect of cloze performance taps into some part of comprehension performance, but to make decisions based on the use of cloze only is to make a less-than-informed choice. (Farr and Carey, 1986, p. 37)

Maze.   Many teachers object to the cloze technique because it is too difficult. An alternative procedure for assessing comprehension is the **maze,** which is similar to the cloze but is not as difficult (Guthrie, Seifert, Burnham, & Caplan, 1974). Criterion scores for acceptable performance are usually higher because the task is essentially recognition (selection) rather than recall (production).

Every *n*th word is replaced with multiple choice words for the student to select in completing the sentence. Typically, three to five choices, using one of the following strategies: (a) random selection of words selected for replacement or (b) specific word types—nouns, verbs, modifiers, and function words (Guthrie, 1973).

The steps for creating the maze test follow:

1. Select a passage of approximately 250 words.
2. Leave the first and last complete sentence intact.
3. Develop three to five alternate word choices for each blank.
4. List the four choices: (a) aligned with the blank, (b) below the blank, or (c) at the right margin of the passage.
5. Tell students to read the passage, select the correct word from among the four or five options, and place the answer in the appropriate blank underline.

Difficulty of the maze task is a function of the difficulty of the passage and the distractors.

For example, Figure 7.8 shows two versions of a passage entitled "One-Celled Organisms," which we have constructed from each procedure just described. The first example involves random selection of choices from a pool of deleted words, but the second passage may be the most difficult because its choices are based on samples of content words, not random selection.

In the first example, all the words listed on the right come from the pool of words that were deleted. They have not, however, been blocked by syntactical correctness, so that a student filling in the blank has two clues to the correct answer: syntax and semantics. It is possible to answer any item correctly without actually knowing the word, its meaning, or its contextual relationship within the sentence.

A more difficult form of the maze appears in the second passage. By blocking the ability to select responses through syntax or semantics, the test requires a student to know the word and its meaning to get the correct answer. When combined with a word-selection strategy that is not random (i.e., *n*th word) but samples content words (nouns, adverbs, adjectives, or verbs), this form of the maze is probably more difficult.

Generally, maze measures have been used to place students into instructional groups. For example, Guthrie et al. (1974) originally suggested the following placements based on 3–4 administrations: (a) Performance levels of 90% accuracy or above represent independent level, (b) 60%–70% accuracy could be considered instructional level, and (c) if performance falls below 60%, the material could be considered at the frustration level. Howell and Morehead (1987) consider a score of 60%–80% an acceptable level. They also say that scores of 90% indicate that material is too easy, and scores of 55% indicate that material is too difficult. Pikulski and Pikulski (1977) found that

---

One-Celled Organisms
(Random selection from word pool)

During summer, a thick, green scum covers part of a pond. This scum is so thick, __(1)__ cannot see through it. Pond __(2)__ is actually chains and chains __(3)__ plant-like cells. These cells contain __(4)__ green bits called *chloroplasts.* The __(5)__ are coil-shaped. They __(6)__ the pond scum its distinctive color, __(7)__ also help generate food.

(1) give, you, not, food, pond
(2) others, do, into, scum, turns
(3) of, give, algae, organisms, the
(4) make, little, can, cell, into
(5) energy, no, eat, chloroplasts, cell
(6) give, scum, own, cell, others
(7) pond, a, make, and, no

One-Celled Organisms
(Content-word selection)

Some __(14)__ are one-celled organisms. Often, they float by themselves in __(15)__ . Some, like __(16)__ scum, live together in chains. Others live together in large groups and have root-like __(17)__ . These help __(18)__ hold on to rocks or soil.

(14) algae, chloroplasts, ponds, scum, cells
(15) water, food, energy, soil, organisms
(16) organism, chloroplast, cell, pond, energy
(17) ends, energy, cells, soil, food, type
(18) chloroplast, them, energy, you, ponds

FIGURE 7.8
Examples of a (modified) maze task for a sample passage using different strategies for word selection

at the independent level, maze tests underestimated placement, but for both instructional and frustration levels, they drastically overestimated placement. Interestingly, if the level for instructional placement had been 60–70% as originally suggested by Guthrie et al. (1974), "the maze would have overestimated the skills of all thirty-eight students included in that group" (p. 769). However, when we combine the maze with tests of oral reading fluency from curriculum-based measures, remarkable accuracy of placement into groups is possible (Parker, Hasbrouck & Tindal, 1989).

Advantages. The maze test is very useful as one component within a comprehension-assessment package. It is easier than a cloze test, reducing frustration for low-performing students, and the range of scores is typically greater, particularly with low-performing students. The difficulty of the test can be systematically manipulated through the use of distractors that vary according to semantics and syntax. Also, the maze format is more accommodating for students with language or writing problems because they select the answer rather than produce it. It can be group-administered and therefore used with more students more frequently, and it is very easy to score and summarize performance. When combined with oral reading fluency, the maze is very accurate in predicting placement into reading groups for elementary students (Parker, Hasbrouck & Tindal, 1989) with accuracy levels of 94% and 100%. Furthermore, such a strategy is much more efficient than using an IRI, requires less time and training, and can be accomplished with known technical adequacy.

Disadvantages. The maze test, however, does have several potential problems. For instance, difficulty is a function of the passage content, deleted words, *and* multiple-choice distractors. The link between assessment and instruction is more confounded. The response is a selection-response, not a production-response, limiting error diagnostics. It is not as easy to form hypotheses regarding the etiology of problems, and therefore it is harder to vindicate explanations for student performance. Finally, construction of the test requires more time and effort.

Summary of Cloze and Maze. The two measures that combine reading and reacting into one assessment, the cloze and maze, are very objective measures, which are likely to generate reliable data. Their validity, however, may be open to question because of how they look (face validity) rather than how they work. Their technical adequacy is quite substantial, and teachers should incorporate them into their assessment practices. However, to ensure a full picture of student performance, cloze and maze tests should be accompanied by other measures that reflect more naturally occurring classroom reading behavior.

An Integrated Assessment of Reading

This example of an assessment program assumes that teachers need to make educational decisions in an accurate and efficient manner, using technically adequate data. Furthermore, it assumes that their students have varied reading skills. At the beginning of the year, most decisions focus on deployment of resources, requiring teachers to assess the full range of skills and to group students into roughly comparable skill levels. In this process, very low-performing students (receiving Chapter I or special education services) need to be included, especially for determining how different they are from their general education peers. In this first round of assessment, referred to as *survey-level assessment,* the goal is to create a measure that reflects the natural variation in the class. The teacher may then create more specific-level assessments for students with unique needs or special concerns.

Elementary Students. We must address four topics in conducting an integrated assessment for students in elementary schools: material selection, test administration, performance display and interpretation, and the decision-making framework.

Material selection. To begin the assessment process, we must select appropriate material. Assuming that the school or grade has adopted a curriculum, the teacher needs to identify the level at which average students should be proficient by the end of the year. For instance, on the basis of previous teaching experience, a teacher may identify a particular level that represents typical material in difficulty and variety for that grade level. The object is to sample several passages and administer them to all students. By comparing all students on the same measure, it is possible to generate a norm-referenced data base for screening students. Ideally, all teachers of the same grade should work together in identifying common passages for scaling all students at that grade level. An even more powerful system could be developed if teachers from all grade levels completed the same task, identifying grade-appropriate passages. In selecting this material, nine sample passages would be optimal, allowing three passages for administration at three times during the year. All passages should reflect similar difficulty (possibly based on their readability).

Once materials are selected, they can be prepared by creating a student copy retyped to eliminate picture distractions and a teacher copy (with the cumulative number of words on successive lines printed along the right margin). The results of this step, once completed, are good for the life of the basal adoption and can be organized into notebooks for safe storage and easy retrieval.

Test administration. The testing should follow the procedures presented in the curriculum-based measurement section. Students should receive standardized directions (deemphasizing any racing in their reading), and the measure may be timed for 1 minute. All passages for that time of the year (i.e., three passages for the fall) should be given to each student, and the performance should be scored for the number of words read correctly (total minus errors). With three passages, the median score is probably the easiest and most appropriate to calculate. Because the decisions at this level are screening decisions, only the reading fluency measures need to be given. Later, after identification of extremely low students or in the case of peculiar results where the student is suspected of word calling, students can receive more in-depth assessments of their reactions to the reading.

Performance display and interpretation. Once all students in the class or grade are tested on the three passages, and the median score for each student known, the teacher can complete a plot of the entire class or grade. For example, in the box plot shown in Figure 7.9, an entire fourth-grade class of 55 students in three classrooms was assessed exactly as described, with the exception that only two, not three, passages were selected in the fall. The top and bottom T represent the 90th and 10th percentiles. The box itself incorporates the middle 50% of the population, the bottom of the box equals the 25th percentile, the top of the box represents the 75th percentile, and the middle bar in the box is the 50th percentile. All circles outside the 10th and 90th percentiles are individual extreme values.

The data from this local normative sample reveal several interesting issues. First, some students read very poorly and probably need to receive specialized services (Chapter I or special education). The converse is also true: some students are extremely fluent in material in which they haven't yet been instructed (these data are from the fall quarter). The two passages, although selected according to grade-level readability, are quite different; the average for Passage A, 85 words read correctly, is significantly lower than the average for Passage B, 105 words read correctly. Therefore, an important consideration in using this system is to sample multiple passages to average artifacts from the passages themselves. Although this may seem to be a problem with this form of measurement, such passage differences seem to be inherent in most curricula; rather than ignoring it, such a measurement system at least identifies and quantifies it.

Decision-making framework. Teachers can use these data for several purposes: (a) identifying extremely low performers in need of specialized services, (b) placing students into instruc-

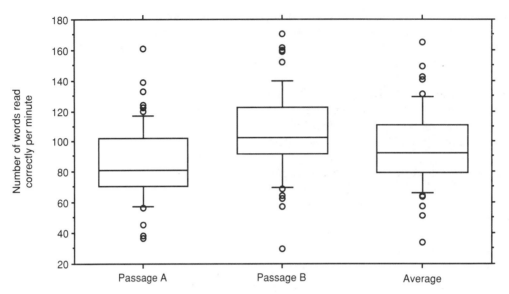

FIGURE 7.9
Box plots of oral reading fluency for a fourth-grade class

tional groups, (c) planning instructional programs, and (d) providing sampling plans for use in establishing long-range goals (for special education students). For example, Hall and Tindal (1989) used the normal curve from this type of assessment to create three reading groups (*low* = 1 standard deviation below the mean, *middle* = between −1 and +1 standard deviation around the mean, and *high* = 1 standard deviation above the mean); they were very accurate (relative to teacher judgments) in placing low and high students and somewhat accurate in placing the middle students. Similarly, Parker, Hasbrouk, and Tindal (1989) were very accurate in placing students into groups that were consistent with teacher judgment when they used both oral reading fluency and a maze task. Finally, on the basis of error-pattern analysis (as described with informal reading inventories), teachers can also use these data to plan instructional programs.

For teachers who work with low-performing and special education students, however, the real power of this assessment system is its applicability in establishing a formative evaluation system. By administering successively lower- or higher-level materials from other grades and comparing performance to the normative levels for those grades, it is possible to establish both current functioning and appropriate goal-level functioning. Rather than placing students into instructional material according to the percentage correct, as is done with informal reading inventories, we can make an empirically-based placement by placing the student in the level where they are most comparable to others. For example, if a fifth-grade student performed most closely to students in second-grade reading material, placement in this material is justified; furthermore, judgments of appropriate goals can then be established, given the time frame and available resources. Figure 7.10 presents an example of a student who was in the fifth grade but was placed instructionally in third-grade material; the eventual goal for the student was successful performance in fourth-grade material by the end of the year. Consistent with the long-range goal measurement described by Deno and Fuchs (1987) and L. S. Fuchs (1986), the formative evaluation graph in the figure represents growth in this fourth-grade material.

Secondary Students. We must also consider four topics in developing an integrated reading assessment for secondary students, but the major differences are in the first three areas: material selection, test administration, and performance display and interpretation.

Material selection. Because middle and high schools are organized around content areas, material selection centers on sampling an appropriate subject and appropriate passages within that subject. For example, a number of areas are required of all students and/or appropriate mainstream classrooms, such as social studies, English, general science, and history; other subjects such as physics, chemistry, and advanced biology are inappropriate because they are not required and represent unusually technical material. Selection of passages should be based on two considerations: appropriate difficulty and adequate length and detail coverage.

Test administration. The reading test is comprised of a silent reading task and written retell, much like that described earlier in curriculum-based measurement. The important considerations are student self-timing, and presentation of advance notice to the student on the retell scoring system (i.e., detail and organization). The teacher can also administer

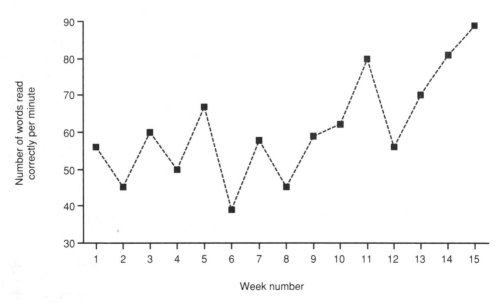

FIGURE 7.10
Performance on long-range goal material to evaluate instructional programs and outcomes

Test Type by Behavior Matrix		Curriculum-based Measurement	Informal Reading Inventories	Cloze Maze	Published Achievement Tests
Reading	Type of response	• Orally read	• Orally read	• Silent reading	• Silently read or listen
	Focus of response	• Rate correct	• Percent correct • Type of error		• Word recogntion • Decoding • Syllabication
Reacting	Type of response	• Write	• Orally answer	• Write/ select	• Select answers
	Focus of response	• Retell	• Questions	• Words	• Questions

FIGURE 7.11
Reading behaviors sampled from four major test types

more traditional reading assessment in which students are asked questions. The procedures described in chapters 2 and 3, employing six levels of intellectual operation and three types of content, would be appropriate for this tactic.

Performance display and interpretation. Both subjective (holistic evaluation of completeness/quality) and objective (number of correct word sequences as described in chapter 9) measurement systems can be employed. Because of efficiency, a two-fold system may be the most appropriate. At the screening level, only subjective ratings and objective counts of the number of words written are counted; however, for more intensive assessments and/or for those students with the lowest subjective evaluations, the number of correct word sequences is counted. Once all these components are in place, a decision-making framework is possible by addressing these three areas consistently to collect evaluative data.

Summary of Integrated Assessment. This integrated assessment uses data from each step and decision to collect further data in a consistent manner. The survey level assessment screens students and identifies more instructionally relevant behaviors to monitor in evaluating instructional programs and outcomes. The decisions are highly related to each other and logically organized to reflect teacher priorities and concerns. Importantly, all behaviors sampled are instructionally relevant.

CHAPTER SUMMARY

This chapter presents a low-inference model that focuses on the critical effect: reading and reacting as a holistic behavioral sample. This perspective avoids the problems of sorting out the influence of a reader's background by incorporating it into the assessment process. The research literature supports this perspective mostly from correlational studies. Therefore, the relationship between decoding and comprehension is probably quite complex, and certainly no cause-effect relationships are implied. Given this orientation of a unitary model and a production response, we described both curriculum-based measurement and informal reading inventories and presented specific administration procedures for each technique. These procedures were organized under a more general model that systematically identified sources of material, types of behavior, and scoring systems. Curriculum-based measurement consists of either oral or silent reading, oral or written retell, and objective or subjective scoring systems. The data support a wide range of educational decisions. Informal reading inventories consist only of oral reading, with reactions obtained through question-asking. Such data support only a limited range of decisions, primarily focusing on determining three levels

of performance: independent, instructional, and frustration. Finally, we presented two strategies that incorporate the reading and reacting processes into one assessment act: cloze and maze. For all specific assessment procedures described, a number of advantages and disadvantages were presented. In conclusion, we presented an integrated assessment that systematically generated data for a wide range of decisions. Figure 7.11 summarizes the four assessment systems discussed in this chapter, along with that for published achievement tests.

In comparing these systems, the type of behavior sampled is of paramount importance. In selecting specific assessment techniques, teachers must begin by identifying the kinds of behaviors students need to succeed in the classroom; then they must scrutinize those devices that reliably and validly assess those behaviors.

CHAPTER 8

Spelling

Our Querr Lingo

When the English Tongue we speak
Why is "break" not rimed with "freak"?
Will you tell me why it's true
We say, "sew," but likewise "few"?
And the maker of a verse
Cannot rime his "horse" with "worse"?
"Beard" sounds not the same as "heard";
"Cord" is different from "word";
"Cow" is cow but "low" is low;
"Shoe" is never rimed with "foe."
Think of "hose" and "dose" and "lose";
and Think of "goose" and yet of "choose."
Think of "comb" and "tomb" and "bomb,"
"Doll" and "roll" and "home" and "some"
And since "pay" is rimed with "say"
Why not "paid" with "said," I pray?
Think of "blood" and "food" and "good";
"Mould" is not pronounced like "could."
Wherefore "done," but "gone" and "lone"-
Is there any reason known?
To sum all, it seems to me
Sounds and letters don't agree.
—Anonymous

This poem is an excellent representation of the problems associated with the delivery of spelling instruction and the assessment of its outcomes. The English language contains rules for assigning sounds to print, but many of them are not uniformly applicable. Thus, the question is whether to teach and assess knowledge and application of spelling rules or to focus on individual words, regardless of their phonetic structure. For an appreciation of this controversy and other issues in the assessment of spelling skills, it is important to review basic facts about spelling.

CHAPTER OBJECTIVES

When you have completed this chapter, you will have the necessary knowledge and skills to

- Employ spelling terminology and describe the complex building blocks of spelling.
- Use an assessment model for sampling words and generating responses.
- Select words according to their phonic regularity, frequency of usage, or from within written compositions.
- Generate either selection or production responses.
- Score performance according to words or letters in correct sequence.
- Analyze performance for specific error types.
- Conduct an integrated spelling assessment for making decisions using norm- , criterion- , and individual-referenced guidelines.

KEY VOCABULARY

The building blocks of spelling are complex and diverse with a very encompassing terminology needed to highlight them. *Graphemes* (letters), *phonemes* (letter sounds), and *vowel/consonant* combinations interact to make some spelling patterns quite stable and others quite limited. Therefore, a *model of spelling assessment* is needed that provides a planned system for *sampling items (words)* and *generating responses*. Teaching and assessment of spelling usually follow one of two approaches. Proponents of one perspective, *word phonic-regularity base*, argue that there is enough systematicity in the English language for learning and assessing rules to improve spelling skills. Those in support of the other perspective, *word-frequency base*, feel that the English language is so irregular that learning sets of generalizable rules for spelling is not efficient. This approach focuses on learning words that appear frequently and are likely to be a part of many people's vocabulary. A combination of the two perspectives is also possible. We can sample words from within *written compositions* in which students generate their own functional words.

Once words have been sampled, the *type of response* becomes an important issue. Spelling assessment can include *selection* responses (word or sentence *editing*) or *production* responses (writing words from *dictation*). With the latter, we can score student performance in terms of *words spelled correctly* or *correct letter sequences (CLS)*. Scoring performance according to CLS provides an opportunity for analyzing *error patterns,* for which there are many systems. An example of an *integrated spelling assessment* is presented at the end of the chapter, based on a cascade of decision making. Beginning with a *norm-referenced* database, students are screened, then *criterion- and individual-referenced* approaches are used to identify individual skills and plan and modify instruction. The entire program is summarized to determine overall effectiveness.

OVERVIEW OF THE SPELLING PROCESS

The assessment of spelling is necessary to ensure that students learn to communicate in writing consistently and conventionally. But not everyone agrees on what spelling is. Wallace and Larsen (1978) call it "the ability to arrange properly letters into words that are necessary for effective written communication" (p. 363). Graham and Miller (1979) have a broader definition: They say spelling is "the ability to recognize, recall, reproduce, or obtain orally or in written form, the correct sequence of letters in words" (p. 2). The definition chosen influences not only the type of student response required to determine spelling proficiency, but also the methods to assess spelling. In the first definition, spelling is confined to a production re-

sponse in which students concatenate letters within the writing process. But many other responses also are possible, as the second definition implies. Recognizing letter sequences as well as orally generating letters of words are both important dimensions of the skill. In this chapter, the premise is made that spelling involves recognition and production. As a result, spelling measurement is broadly conceived, providing a wide range of assessment techniques involving both multiple-choice tests and actual writing tasks.

Terminology

At the broadest level of spelling is linguistics, the study of human speech and language, including phonetics, meanings of words, and grammar. More specifically, **phonetics** is the science of speech sounds as represented by graphic symbols; its application to specific sounds in spelling and reading is referred to as **phonics** (Blake & Emans, 1970).

One major source of difficulty in spelling is that the components of words are not systematic. The science of phonetics is built upon **phonemes,** similar sounds that cannot be interchanged without rearranging the meaning of a word. Phonemes are meaningless in themselves, but they provide the link between written and oral language when combined into written words by way of **graphemes,** which are alphabetical symbols or letters that represent a phoneme sound. Phonemes are expressed through the use of graphemes. A problem arises from the lack of one-to-one relationship between phonemes and graphemes. Twenty-six letters are used to generate at least 40 sounds. Feigenbaum (1958) reported at least 251 different ways to graphemically represent these 40 + English morphemes. Two types of inconsistencies exist: Some letters represent more than one sound (e.g., *c* makes both the *s* and *k* sound), while some sounds are represented by more than one letter or group of letters (e.g., the schwa sound can be represented by *i, e,* and *a*). These inconsistencies can present difficulties in both instruction and assessment.

While phonemes are the building blocks of sounds, the smallest meaningful unit in the structure of words is the **morpheme**, which can appear in two forms: (a) *free*, comprising monosyllabic words (e.g., hat, feign), and (b) *bound*—affixes combined with other morphemes. Bound morphemes change the meanings of words when attached. There are three forms: (a) *prefixes*, which appear at the beginning of words; (b) *suffixes*, which appear at the end of words; and (c) *inflectional endings*, which appear at the ends of words to form plurals, possessives, verb tenses, comparatives, and so forth.

All words are divided into syllables, which are units of sound. A *syllable* consists of a vowel and often a consonant that can be either open (ending in a vowel) or closed (ending in a consonant).

In addition to phonemes and morphemes, words consist of **vowel/consonant** combinations. The six vowels in the English language, whose sounds are made with the oral passage relatively unobstructed, can be either short or long. Short vowels carry the same sound as the medial letter in words having a consonant-vowel-consonant (CVC) structure; the sound of long vowels is the same as the letter name used in reciting the alphabet. There are 24 consonant speech sounds, formed primarily with the lips, teeth, tongue or palate; the name of the letter (grapheme) represents the sound (phoneme). The correspondence between phonemes and graphemes is greater for consonants than vowels. For example, most consonants have only one sound (e.g., *b, d, f, k*), only a few have multiple sounds (*c* and *g*), but all vowels have multiple sounds, particularly when they appear with other vowels or consonants.

Sounds created by vowels and consonants depend upon the letters surrounding them. A *diphthong* comprises two vowels that create a sound (with both vowels heard) that is different from that of each vowel sounded in isolation (i.e., *boy*). When two or more consonants occur together without losing their individual sounds, they form a *consonant blend* (i.e., *bleach, sting*). In contrast, when they occur together to form one consonant sound, they are called *consonant digraphs*. There are eight common digraphs: *th, sh, ch, ng, wh, ph, gh,* and *nd*. Vowels may also combine to form a single sound, with the following four used most often: (a) first vowel long and second silent (i.e., *team*); (b) first vowel silent and second long (i.e., *break*); (c) first vowel short and second silent (*heavy*); and (d) new sound from both vowels, unlike the short or long sounds of either separately (*multifarious*). A special vowel sound that occurs in an unaccented syllable is the *schwa* sound (signified as δ). *Woman, taken, pencil, lemon,* and *circus* are words in which the second vowel forms the schwa sound (Blake & Emans, 1970).

Entire words can be spelled using the same graphemes but different phonemes. For example, when two words are spelled the same but have different sounds, they are called *homographs* (*bow tie, curtsy and bow*). Words can also have the same phonemes and different graphemes. For example, when two words sound the same, are spelled differently, and have different meanings, they are referred to as *homonyms* (i.e., *blue, blew*).

In summary, the building blocks of spelling form an intricate combination of units of sound (phonemes), symbols (graphemes), and size and meaning (morphemes and words). The units of sound (vowels and consonants) are produced by various parts of the mouth and relate to each other depending upon specific sequences. Many inconsistencies exist at all levels, making instruction and the assessment of learning outcomes difficult to accomplish. As we discuss later, the selection of items for spelling assessments must reflect this structure if we are to make accurate diagnoses and summaries of student performance.

Issues in Spelling Skill and "Spellability"

The primary question concerning spelling proficiency is, "What makes someone a skillful speller?" Are people born with the ability to spell, or is it acquired through learning? How is skill in spelling related to the other communication systems of reading, speaking, and writing? Is spelling skill influenced by speech patterns (Groff, 1979; Kligman, Cronnell, & Verna, 1972; Tabbert, 1974), pronunciation (Dale, O'Rouke, & Bamman, 1971), handwriting (Petty, 1964), word attack skills (Blair, 1975), vocabulary knowledge (Mangieri & Baldwin, 1979), or cognitive development (Beers, 1980; Bookman, 1984; Zutell, 1980)?

An important consideration relating to spelling skill is whether the English language is consistent enough to allow generalizations to be made about words or students. The English language is described as phonetically consistent (Groff, 1968; 1982; Hanna, Hodges, & Hanna, 1971) or inconsistent (Hillerich, 1977). If a word is pronounced with certain sounds, are words with similar spelling pronounced the same? If a student can spell a word with a certain grapheme-phoneme relationship, can other words that have similar or different phonemes or graphemes be spelled the same way? To address this issue, we must look at the multifarious influences on spelling and *spellability*, the degree to which words can be spelled consistently.

Spelling can be influenced by a number of factors. The relationship between reading and spelling has obvious and direct bearing on grapheme-phoneme or spelling-sound correspon-

dences. Word frequency, or the frequency with which words appear in the written language, is an important dimension. Visual and auditory aspects that affect spelling are physical properties, visual perception, auditory perception, and phonological context. Serial position and word length appear related to spellability; errors tend to occur at the center of a word and to the right of center (at Position 5 in 7-letter words and Position 7 in 11-letter words) (Cahen, Craun, & Johnson, 1971). In fact, error analysis, which we discuss later, forms a major component of most spelling assessment systems (Howell, Kaplan, & Serapiglia, 1980).

Issues related to spelling are complex and laden with controversy. To organize the themes and provide an empirical direction for developing appropriate assessment systems, this chapter contains three sections that deal with (a) selection of words and word types, (b) student responses, and (c) how selection and response are integrated.

A MODEL OF SPELLING ASSESSMENT

Spelling involves both spoken and written components. To profit from instruction, students must have rudimentary skills in associating sounds with letters and concatenating letters into words. A complex network of prerequisite skills, involving spoken language, handwriting, and decoding, is necessary before spelling instruction and assessment can begin.

Spelling is then premised on the need to spell. A student who is uncertain how to spell a word can approximate the correct spelling or select an intrinsic or extrinsic strategy for spelling it correctly. The intrinsic approach calls for the speller to utilize information from five sources to spell the word: (a) semantics, (b) syntax, (c) morphemes, (d) phonetic spelling strategies, and (e) generate-and-test techniques. The extrinsic procedure calls for the speller to use human or written aids, such as dictionaries, books, or charts (Graham & Miller, 1979).

This chapter presents the following **model spelling assessment:** Structured tasks are presented that require students to produce words and/or arrange them according to proper patterns. These spelling tasks must be developed from an analysis of some domain and may reflect a bias in either rule-governed or frequency-based sampling plans. In the production mode, students must produce correctly spelled words that successfully communicate ideas. Selection responses are required of students who are editing writing and using extrinsic sources for correcting misspelled words.

Spelling errors signify more than the general difficulty of a word spelled incorrectly: They provide clues about the types of spelling rules

and phonetic patterns students use or know how to use. The core of our specific model of assessment focuses on procedures for (a) sampling items and (b) generating responses. Figure 8.1 illustrates the model.

Sampling Items (Words)

All spelling assessments must begin with procedures for **sampling items** or words, which includes the following two steps: (a) a domain must be established or identified that specifies where words will be derived; and (b) a system must be employed for actually selecting words from that domain (refer to chapter 4 for a description of different sampling strategies).

Because assessment eventually should relate to instruction, an immediate consideration for determining student proficiency with spell-

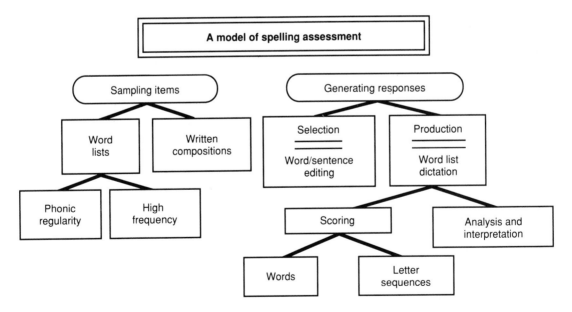

FIGURE 8.1
Model depicting two dimensions of spelling assessment: sampling items and generating responses

ing is the curriculum (Graham, 1985). For educational decisions such as screening/eligibility, instructional planning/evaluation, and program certification, student performance relates to the material that will be used. However, we cannot assume that all spelling programs are equal, since the scope and sequence of various curricula are likely to vary according to the introduction of rules for spelling and/or the manner in which high-frequency words are introduced (DiStephano & Hagerty, 1983). By analyzing curricula for their application of spelling rules or word presentation, one can (a) determine appropriate sampling plans for selecting words and word types, thus ensuring a high degree of test-curriculum overlap, and (b) develop possible explanations for the errors that students make. To maximize the assessment of skills taught in their own curricula, educators should be able to develop or identify an explicit or implicit sampling plans for spelling measures.

As depicted in the poem used to introduce the chapter, words are spelled and spoken with varying degrees of consistency. Some words, using the same letter combinations, are spoken differently; some words with different letter combinations are spoken the same. This issue, the word phonic-regularity base or degree of consistency in spelling-speaking words, is at the heart of the major controversy in spelling. If it is consistent, we can present instruction and assessment strategies using phonically regular words. But if it is inconsistent, we should make sure students can spell the high-frequency words they are most likely to use and see. In the first approach, which Lerner (1985) calls *linguistic,* the stress is on phonological, morphological, and syntactical rules, with a consistent scope and sequence that reflects a number of phonological generalizations. The second approach is based on the frequency of word usage: More frequently appearing words are introduced first, followed by those used less often.

Word Lists. Regardless of which sampling approach we employ, we select words and place them into lists for editing or dictation. These lists reflect a phonic or frequency approach.

Word phonic-regularity base. This term refers to the degree of consistency or generalizability of the grapheme-phoneme relationships. According to Hillerich (1982), spelling diagnosis is based on two assumptions: (a) The English language is regular, and (b) spelling can be analyzed in terms of errors. When an error is made, it represents a misrule that will generalize to other examples of the same rule until corrected. Howell and Kaplan (1980) defend the assumption that the English language is regular, citing the following evidence: (a) Eighty percent of all phonemes (sounds) in the spoken language are predictably written by the same graphemes, (b) consonant sounds and blends are regularly spelled 90% of the time, and (c) 75% of vowel sounds present no serious problems because vowel speech sounds are spelled regularly from 57% to 99% of the time in the vocabulary analyzed (Deverell, 1971).

Hanna, Hodges, and Rudolf (1966) completed one of the most extensive analyses of English spelling ever performed and found a surprising consistency among the 17,000 words analysed. When programmed with 203 basic rules, the computer they used could spell 50% of the words without an error, 37% with one error, 11% with two errors, and only 2.3% with three or more errors. These results have been interpreted to support the regularity of spelling and the need to teach and assess spelling in both rule applications and assessment of generalized skills.

In a research review on phonetics in spelling instruction, Groff (1968) found more studies supported phonics. He concluded, "The number of recent studies that phonics supporters can cite for their position is larger than the number that their opponents can find to the contrary" (Groff, 1979, p. 273). There are three typical objections to phonics: (a) Spelling is best learned incidently as children read and write, (b) spelling of English is not predictable enough to use rules of phonics, and (c) use of phonics rules will result in only 87% of common words to be spelled correctly. However, learning spelling in an incidental manner is not empirically supported. Research on the relationship between reading and spelling indicates that (a) good readers may or may not be good spellers, (b) more difficult words should be taught directly, with greater opportunity for practice, (c) 87% percent of common words spelled correctly is better than nothing, and (d) the relationship between spelling ability and knowledge of spelling rules is higher (.92) than between spelling ability and reading comprehension (.72). In the final analysis, research supports the use of phonics as a transitional step from random to natural spelling (Groff, 1979).

Given that researchers have found English sufficiently regular in its phoneme-grapheme correspondence, students may need to be taught certain spelling rules that allow them to generalize to untaught words. Spelling instruction *and* measurement can benefit from the use of spelling rules and sound patterns in which the *predictability* of words, not the frequency of usage, determines the grade level at which the word is taught (Groff, 1982). Table 8.1 lists important generalizations presented by Blake and Emans (1970).

Word-frequency base. Some researchers assert that the relationship between phonemes (sounds) and graphemes (written spellings) is not predictable. An obvious example is the poem at the beginning of this chapter. Or consider the many ways that the long _a_ sound is spelled in the English language (e.g., *ei* in *weight*, *ay* in *day*, and *ey* in *they*). Teaching spelling through **word frequency** means that we can use few generalizable rules because so many

exceptions exist. Instead, the focus is on teaching those words that appear frequently and are likely to be a part of many people's core writing vocabulary.

Researchers promoting the use of high-frequency spelling instruction contend that students should be pretested to distinguish words they do and do not know how to spell because the phonetic regularity of the English language is not sufficient to warrant instruction according to rules. Such assessment provides a basic "security" list composed of words that children use in their writing (Hillerich, 1977). Two assumptions support this position: (a) Words cannot be grouped according to difficulty, and (b) generalizations are weak, making it difficult to predict the spelling of an unknown word from the spelling of known words.

A study of word frequencies in written language reveals several interesting findings. Only 3 words (*a, and, the*) account for 10% of all words in print; just 8 words (*the, a, is, was, in, on, and, it*) constitute 18% of words used in writing; and 9 words (*a, and, the, of, to, in, that, it, is*) constitute 25% of the total words used (Betts, 1982). Horn (1926) and Rinsland (1945) have found that relatively few words account for most conventional usage. They report that 1,000 words account for 89% of all words used by children; 2,000 words account for 95%, and 3,000 words account for 97%. Furthermore, 4,000 words account for 98% of all words used by either adults or children. Of these 4,000, 2,000 are used commonly by both adults and children, 1,000 are used by adults alone, and 1,000 are used by children alone. Rinsland's (1945) results are similar to Horn's: Sixty percent of nontechnical writing consists of 100 words that are used repeatedly; 1,000 words account for 90% of all words written; and the 3,000 most frequently used words account for 97% of words written by children. In contrast, unabridged dictionaries typically include more than 450,000 words (Hillerich, 1977).

TABLE 8.1

Spelling generalizations for the English language

1. With one–syllable words that have a long vowel sound followed by a consonant, use silent *e*; same rule for the final syllable in polysyllabic words. Examples: *make, rake, same, rune, dome, dune.*
2. When the *i* sound comes in the beginning or middle of a word or syllable, use the letter *i*, not *y*. Examples: *collide, insult, injust.*
3. When the *i* sound comes at the end of a word, use the letter *y*. Examples: *happy, defy, heavy, rely, very.*
4. When the long *a* sound comes in the middle of the word, use *ai*. Examples: *refrain, detain, stain, refrain, hail, frail, derail.*
5. When the long *a* sound comes at the end of a word, use *ay*. Examples: *cray, delay, fray, mainstay.*
6. If *ful* is a suffix, it is spelled with one *l*. Examples: *beautiful, dutiful, graceful, awful.*
7. Before the vowels *a, o,* and *u,* the *k* sound is spelled with a *c*. Examples: *cut, care, cot, cat, come, can.*
8. Before the vowels *e* and *i,* the *k* sound is spelled with a *k*. Examples: *kitchen, kitty, kill, kennel.*
9. When the *k* sound follows a long vowel sound, use the letter *k*. Examples: *awaken, joke, flake, take.*
10. The letter *q* is always followed by the letter *u.*
11. Change *y* to *i* before adding any suffix not starting with *i* when the final *y* is preceded by a consonant; when the suffix begins with *i*, keep the *y*. Examples: *rely–reliable, defy–defiant, comply–compliant, reply–replying, comply–complying.*
12. Do not change the *y* when adding a suffix if it is preceded by a vowel. Examples: *stay–stayed, convey–conveyed, play–played.*
13. One–syllable adjectives occasionally retain the *y* before adding *–ly* or *–ness.* Examples: *dry–dryly, spry–spryly.*
14. When adding a suffix to a word ending in silent *e,* retain the silent *e.* Examples: *hate–hateful, lone–lonesome.*
15. If the suffix begins with a vowel, drop the silent *e.* Examples: *make–making, love–lovable, give–giving.*
16. If the suffix begins with *a* or *o,* reverse the above two rules for words that end in *ce* or *ge.* Examples: *change–changeable.*
17. If a word ends in a single consonant and is preceded by a single vowel, double the final consonant before adding the suffix. Examples: *hop–hopping, stop–stopping.*
18. Plurals can be formed by
    - adding *s.* Example: *cake–cakes.*
    - adding *es.* Examples: *stake–stakes.*
    - changing *y* to *i* and add *es.* Examples: *money–monies.*
    - changing *f* or *fe* to *v* and add *es.* Example: *life–lives.*
    - changing internal vowels. Examples: *tooth–teeth.*
    - doing nothing: singular and plural are the same. Example: *deer.*
    - changing the ending letters. Examples: *datum–data.*
19. *i* comes before *e* except after *c* and in words with a long *a* sound. Examples: *receive, conceive, believe, achieve.*
20. Abbreviations are followed by a period. Examples: *Mr., Mrs., Dr.*
21. Use capital letters to begin proper nouns and adjectives formed from proper nouns. Example: *Mississippi, Western United States, Oregon.*
22. Most words add *ly* without changing the base word. Examples: *heaven–heavenly, awkward–awkardly.*
23. To add *ly* to a word that ends with *y,* change the *y* to *i* and add *ly.* Examples: *happy–happily.*

The assumption in this approach is that word frequency should dictate grade placement; for example, if a word appears frequently in writing, it should be taught early. Hildreth (1955) and Horn (1969) believe the most frequently used words are short and therefore easier to learn, but these words are often exceptions to phonic rules. For example, Groff (1982) found that 159 of the 222 most persistently misspelled words were among the 1,000 words with the highest frequency in reading texts. Therefore, in a list of monosyllabic words with the same phoneme-grapheme correspondence, children would spell low-frequency words more accurately than high-frequency words. In a study that included five vowel spelling patterns of varying frequencies in 350 monosyllabic words, Groff concluded that

the findings . . . do not support the claim that the relationship of the frequency of a word's occurrence in written material is a highly useful or critical criterion for deciding at what school grade a word should be taught. Rather, words should be assigned to grade levels based on the relative predictability of their spellings. (p. 129)

Word lists can be taken from many sources: Rinsland (1972), Hillerich (1978), Fitzgerald (1951), Kucera and Francis (1967), Carroll, Richman and Davies (1971) Harris and Jacobson (1972), Thomas (1974), and Petty (1959). Lists also have been developed from the following sources: (a) primary-grade words frequently misspelled by higher-grade pupils (Guiler, 1944); (b) the 100 words most often misspelled by children in elementary grades (Leslie Johnson, 1950); (c) reexamination of the Dolch word list, organized into the 82 words that do not appear in the 220 most frequent words of the Kucera-Francis corpus, and the 82 words in the top 220 of the Kucera-Francis list that are not on the Dolch list; (d) the entire list of Dolch words summarized in terms of the

number of occurrences in the Francis-Kucera list (Dale Johnson, 1971); (e) Walker's (1979) compilation of high-frequency words for Grades 3 through 9; (f) Fry's (1980) updated list of Instant Words originally developed 20 years ago (Fry, 1957), in which the new list is based on a frequency count of 5,088,721 running words appearing in 500-word samples taken from 1,045 different books in 12 subject areas typically offered in Grades 3 through 6; (g) Sakiey, Fry, Goss, and Loigman's (1980) syllable-frequency count list of the 322 most common unweighted graphemic syllables in the English language, ranked in the order of frequency of the 5,000 most frequent words and (h) the 500 most frequently appearing words compiled by Carroll et al. (1971) and summarized according to their frequency per million, a standard frequency index, an index of dispersion, their total frequency, and their word type. The most recently developed list of words compiled according to frequency of usage is the last one, which presents a running count of 5,000,000 words in the English language.

Combined word-frequency and phonic-regularity base. A position intermediate to those of Hillerich (1977) and Groff (1982) has been taken by Graham and Miller (1979), who believe phonic instruction that employs relatively few rules with applicability across a wide range of words should be used in conjunction with a security list of 2,000 to 3,000 words, arranged from most to least frequently used words. However, the nucleus of the phonics component includes base words, prefixes, suffixes, and consonant, consonant blend, digraph, and vowel sound-symbol associations, using the following six rules:

1. Proper nouns and most adjectives formed from proper nouns begin with capitals.
2. Adding suffixes is rule-based (e.g., changing *y* to *i*, dropping silent *e*, etc.).

3. Use periods in writing abbreviations.
4. Apostrophes indicate possession.
5. The letter *q* is followed by *u* in English.
6. English words do not end in *v.*

Many factors must be taken into account to determine why students spell words incorrectly. To a considerable degree, the structure of the English language dictates the spelling difficulty of individual words, with two factors having an influence: (a) rule consistency and (b) frequency of occurence. Assuming that the English language is regular, we can employ a sampling plan for generating a subset of words, with performance on this subset accurately reflecting performance on the entire universe of all words with a corresponding structure. However, if one assumes that the English language is not regular, any subset based on phonetic regularity is worthless, because few generalizable patterns exist. In this case, we would use a sampling plan based on word frequency and then use the resulting subset of words to predict performance on common writing tasks.

Written Compositions. Even though production responses are used when students spell words from dictated word lists, they lack natural relevance. Outside of elementary classrooms, we seldom need to spell words from dictation. But if spelling is assessed within the context of written expression, an inherently valid context exists for the expression of spelling with a focus on the terminal behavior (Graham & Miller, 1979). In this form of spelling assessment, administration procedures focus on generating student writing through story starters, topic sentences, or pictures (Deno, Marston, & Mirkin, 1982). Students may create compositions, which are scored for the number of words spelled correctly.

An advantage of such an approach is that it emphasizes learning only words that present problems for students. Another advantage of

this format is that it allows assessment of spelling in either teacher- or student-developed compositions. But a major problem with analyzing spelling in this manner is that students actually misspell few words in written compositions. For example, Tindal, Germann, and Deno (1983) found that regular education students misspell only 3–4 words on a composition containing 20–70 words. The reason may be that free writing compositions consist of words they *know* how to spell. As a consequence, such a test may lack sensitivity to growth. Another disadvantage of this approach is the lack of control for the *types* of words students use in the writing; depending upon the format for generating compositions, certain words or word-types may be differentially emphasized. A topic sentence about outer space may generate words that are difficult, of low frequency, and idiosyncratic. In contrast, a topic sentence or story starter about pets may unintentionally sample frequently appearing, monosyllabic words. Additionally, free handwriting compositions are likely to be more difficult to decipher than single words on separate lines. Physical alignment, use of punctuation, and homophones can lower reliability in scoring performance.

Summary of Sampling Items. Regardless of the manner in which we select a domain, assessment should focus on determining appropriate spelling placement level based on the words students have mastered and not mastered. Probably the most important component, therefore, of any spelling program is the pretesting of students to determine known and unknown words and to locate difficult spots in the words on the unknown list.

Generating Responses

Word sampling is only one aspect in the assessment of spelling; another is the formatting of spelling tasks that require students to respond in certain ways with a **type of response**. We can use either selection or production responses. Selection responses can be scored only in terms of words spelled correctly, while the production response format used with written compositions can be scored in terms or words or letter sequences correctly spelled. The two issues within the response dimension involve (a) selection or production responses from *word lists* and (b) a *scoring strategy* with production responses that have been generated from dictated word lists or written compositions.

Selection Response: Word or Sentence Editing. The strategy involving word or sentence editing encompasses a combination of word lists and written expression, using single words or sentences. Generally, an incorrectly spelled word is underlined, and the student is directed to select the correct spelling of the word from several options. Examples appear in Figure 8.2. A variation, also presented in Figure 8.2, is to leave a blank space (representing a specific word) in a phrase. The student is directed to select the correct word from several options, only one of which is spelled correctly.

Most norm-referenced spelling tests employ one of these strategies because they are easy to administer and score, and they offer the potential for sampling many words at the same time. Furthermore, as determined by many researchers, performance on such tests is often highly correlated with production tests in which students spell from a dictated word list.

Although widely used in published tests, recognition tests are much less prevalent in the classroom. Two major criticisms have been made of such proofreading tasks: (a) They lack natural relevance, and (b) they have the potential for leading students to learn misspellings. In other words, by viewing a number of misspelled words, students actually may be learning these misspellings.

This area of research has generated a number of studies, partly because of the heavy investment in recognition responses made by publishers of standardized tests. Some researchers claim that dictation tests are the most valid format and are more difficult than recognition tests (Carpenter & Carpenter, 1978; Cartwright, 1969; Croft, 1982; Nisbet, 1939; Peters, 1967). Others have found that dictated and multiple-choice tests correlate highly with each other and with written compositions (Freyberg, 1970), although actual levels of performance on the two types of tasks may be different (Allred, 1977).

In an effort to develop measures that teachers could create and administer frequently in the classroom, researchers at the University of Minnesota's Institute for Research on Learning Disabilities found high relationships between selection and production responses. They developed curriculum-based word lists from various grade levels and administered them to elementary-aged students, who also took other standardized spelling tests that used selection and production responses. They found that (a) correlations with several different achievement tests were high, (b) correlations increased with size in domain, (c) listing the words in an order of difficulty resulted in lower correlations, (d) correlations on performance between the various lists was high, and (e) the data within both regular and learning disabled (LD) programs were comparable.

Production Response: Word-List Dictation. **Dictation,** probably the most frequently used spelling task in the classroom, consists of a teacher orally presenting words for students to spell on a blank piece of paper. The teacher often reads words from a list and/or uses them in a sentence. For example, the teacher would say the following: "Ambitious. She was an ambitious person. Ambitious."

---

*Choose the correct word to replace the underlined word
that is spelled incorrectly.*

The girl ran after the <u>kat</u>.
a. kot
b. cat
c. cot
d. kat

He saw the <u>trane</u> coming.
a. traen
b. tran
c. train
d. trane

Select the correct word for the blank space in this sentence.

Johnny _____ going to the zoo.

a. licked
b. liked
c. lieked
d. likt

FIGURE 8.2
Example of proofreading and error-recognition spelling items

Advantages of this format include (a) the small amount of advance preparation needed to prepare such tests, (b) the possibility for assessing many students concurrently, (c) its efficiency for presenting many words, (d) the potential for more complete word-selection sampling plans, and (e) the fact that high correlations have been found between such tests and written work. According to Horn (1944),

> written tests are to be preferred to oral tests since they make possible the record of each pupil on each word and hence the results are more readily utilized for instructional purposes. Recall tests are superior to and more difficult than recognition tests. The evidence indicates that the most valid and economical test is the modified sentence recall form, in which the person giving the test pronounces the word, uses it in a sentence and presents it again. The word is then written by the student. (p. 1179)

Dictation tests with written student responses also have several disadvantages, including the following: (a) Scoring may be unreliable because of illegible writing, (b) spelling correctness may be influenced by the examiner's pronunciation, and (c) writing skill is a prerequisite for the expression of spelling skills. For example, Greene and Petty (1963) have proposed the following time limits for each grade in seconds per letter, based on standard writing tasks for students' handwriting skill: Grade 2 (1.84 seconds), Grade 3 (1.4 seconds), Grade 4 (1.2 seconds), Grade 5 (1.0 seconds), Grade 6 (0.9 seconds), Grade 7 (0.8 seconds), and Grade 8 (0.7 seconds). By implication, administration of a 10-word test, in which each word contains an average of 7 letters per word, to a group of fifth-graders would require a minimum of 7 seconds writing time per word and take a total of 70 seconds for dictation alone. These parameters would have to be followed to avoid confusing spelling skill with handwriting proficiency.

In conclusion, research on the use of selection and production tasks indicates that they are highly related and reflect comparable rankings of students. The decision to employ either procedure in the assessment process is likely to be more a result of convenience than science, but teachers should decide according to the type of decision to be made. Selection responses may be convenient and efficient, serving well as screening measures; however, for making instructional planning, delivery, and evaluation decisions, production responses probably are more essential because instruction in spelling is not likely to improve proofreading and vice versa (Groff, 1979).

Scoring strategy. The second issue related to spelling responses is the manner in which we score and report performance. Two options are available: (a) the unit of analysis for scoring performance and (b) interpretation of performance, using an error-analysis strategy. Al-

though most spelling curricula and tests analyze performance in terms of correctly spelled words, a more sensitive unit is correct letter sequences, which was introduced first by White and Haring (1980). Increases across different grades often are more evident with correct letter sequences than with correctly spelled words (Tindal, Germann, & Deno, 1983), and differences between students in regular and LD programs are greater for correct letter sequences than for words spelled correctly (Deno, Marston, & Mirkin, 1982).

Words spelled correctly involves the correct spelling of an entire word. Probably the only issue with this strategy focuses on the presence of homophones (i.e., *blue* and *blew, wait* and *weight*). Dictation tasks must use the targeted words within sentences to provide appropriate clues about which word is meant.

Letters in correct sequence focuses on every pair of letters that appear correctly together. Assuming that spelling is the correct concatenation of letters in sequence, this strategy focuses on the successive pairs of letters. An example appears in Figure 8.3.

For any word spelled correctly, there will be one more caret (letter in correct sequence) than there are letters in the word. *Direct* contains six letters, so there will be seven letters in correct sequence if the word is spelled correctly.

Analysis and interpretation. Regardless of whether we use a rule-based or frequency-analysis sampling plan, and irrespective of the scoring strategy, the final analysis of spelling skill involves making instructional decisions about students. Spelling appears to be highly individualistic, in that no absolute generalizations can be made about either word types or hard spots in words; thus, assessment must focus on identifying words that are known and unknown by each student. The test-study-test

Spell: <u>Direct</u>

1. Every word must have a beginning letter, which implicitly means that no other letter appears prior to the first. That is, there is a blank space at the beginning of the word. If the word begins with a <u>D</u>, place a caret (inverted V) over the blank space and the <u>D</u>:

$$\wedge$$
_____ D

2. If the next letter to follow <u>D</u> is an <u>I</u>, the letters <u>D I</u> are in the correct sequence; place a caret so it joins the <u>D</u> and the <u>I</u>:

$$\wedge \wedge$$
_____ D I

3. If the next letter is an <u>R</u>, again the two letters <u>I R</u> are in correct sequence. Repeat Step 2 for the letters <u>I R</u>:

$$\wedge \wedge\wedge$$
_____ D I R

4. Repeat this process for each pair of letters until the entire word is scored. As in the blank space implicit in beginning each word, the word must end with the correct letter being followed by a blank space.

5. The following is the correct way to score the entire word — Direct:

$$\wedge \wedge\wedge \wedge \wedge \wedge$$
_____ D I R E C T _____

6. A misspelling of the word <u>Direct</u> as <u>Direkt</u>:

$$\wedge \wedge\wedge \wedge \qquad \wedge$$
_____ D I R E K T _____ (5 correct and 2 incorrect sequences).
$$\vee \vee$$

FIGURE 8.3
An example of the letters-in-correct-sequence method

method is better than the study-test method (Fitzsimmons & Loomer, 1982): It is designed to teach spelling efficiently, without spending time studying or reviewing words already learned. Spelling assessment should be individualized: Words that are difficult for one student are not difficult for others. Furthermore,

the most important instructional component is the opportunity for students to receive feedback on their spelling performance and correct their own spelling errors. Groff (1979) reports that 95% of learning can be explained by this component. Therefore, frequent and individualized assessment is useful in highlighting weaknesses and suggesting ways in which instruction should be altered to meet students' needs.

To structure the interpretation and/or analysis, we make the following assumptions (Ganschow, 1981):

1. Children do not make random errors; they stem from children's hypotheses about the rules governing a particular task.
2. Some errors are more productive than others.
3. A systematic collection of errors on a specific task provides diagnostic information about a child's rule system.
4. Given sufficient samples, teachers can simulate a child's rule system.
5. Error analysis is useful in understanding learning strategies.
6. Knowing a child's learning strategies for a particular task can help teachers design prescriptive approaches.

To diagnose spelling **error patterns,** a classification system is necessary for organizing word types and student responses. A review of several error diagnostic systems follows.

We can group errors into large response classes such as (a) hearing sounds in words, (b) sound-symbol correspondence, (c) irregular spellings and sequences, and (d) morphological rules (Zigmond, Vallecorsa, & Silverman, 1983). Alternatively, we can note whether errors represent (a) regular words to which consistent phoneme-grapheme rules can be applied, (b) homonyms, in which spelling is based on the context of the script, and (c) irregular words, which must be memorized (Wallace & Larsen, 1978).

In contrast, we can employ more specific error-analysis and classification systems. Probably the most popular classification system has been developed by Spache (1940). Errors are organized into 1 of 12 types.

1. Omission of a silent letter (e.g., *wether* for *weather, reman* for *remain,* fin for *fine*)
2. Omission of a sounded letter (e.g., *requst* for *request, plasure* for *pleasure, personl* for *personal, juge* for *judge*)
3. Omission of a doubled letter (e.g., *suden* for *sudden, adress* for *address, sed* for *seed*)
4. Doubling (e.g., *untill* for *until, frriend* for *friend, deegree* for *degree*)
5. Addition of a single letter (e.g., *darck* for *dark, nineth* for *ninth, refere* for *refer*)
6. Transposition or partial reversal (e.g., *was* for *saw, nickle* for *nickel, bron* for *born*)
7. Phonetic substitution for a vowel (e.g., *prisin* for *prison, injoy* for *enjoy*)
8. Phonetic substitution for a consonant (e.g., *prixon* for *prison, cecond* for *second, vakation* for *vacation*)
9. Phonetic substitution for a syllable (e.g., *purchest* for *purchased, financhel* for *financial, naborhood* for *neighborhood, stopt* for *stopped*)
10. Phonetic substitution for a word (e.g., *weary* for *very, colonial* for *colonel*)
11. Nonphonetic substitution for a vowel (e.g., *rad* for *red, reword* for *reward*)
12. Nonphonetic substitution for a consonant (e.g. *watching* for *washing, inportance* for *importance*)

Edgington (1968) has placed spelling errors into 13 categories:

1. Addition of unneeded letters.
2. Omission of needed letters.
3. Mispronunciation spelling.
4. Dialectical spelling.
5. Reversal of whole words.
6. Reversal of vowels.
7. Reversal of consonant order.
8. Reversal of vowel or consonant directionality.
9. Reversal of syllables.

10. Phonetic spelling of nonphonetic words or word-parts.
11. Incorrect association of phoneme-grapheme.
12. Neographisms bearing no association between phoneme-grapheme.
13. Combinations of error types 1 through 12 above.

We can make some generalizations about error-classification systems: (a) Serial position affects errors, which more often appear in the middle or latter parts of words, (b) vowel sounds are spelled incorrectly more frequently, (c) word endings account for 38% of all errors, (d) letter names influence the choice of vowel spellings, (e) homophones are persistent problems, (f) meaningfulness is often associated with successful spelling, and (g) spelling difficulty may be related to frequency of use.

All error systems rely on the assumptions that students' responses can be placed into one category and that knowing such information will be useful in planning instruction. It is important to remember that both considerations are hypotheses only, not stated facts.

When we subject samples of student performance to an error analysis, we should double-check the stability of the error type by presenting many opportunities for students to make the same mistakes. To assume an error is prevalent based upon the presence of one or two examples is tenuous. In addition, error-classification systems probably are valid only for individual students; we should not use them to establish word lists for groups. Analyses of the most frequently misspelled words indicate that "a word that is a demon for one child is not necessarily a demon for another" (Groff, 1982, p. 141). As discussed earlier, a composite of four lists of "demon" words with 398 words contains 286 words that are on one list only, and only 10 that are on all four lists. Therefore, careful and individualized analysis

is necessary in classifying errors in order to establish appropriate instruction.

Although diagnosis may be useful in establishing initial instructional programs, we should collect data on program effectiveness continually. The relationship between errors and remediation is less than certain and must be verified through student performance outcomes. In summary, knowledge of these issues, along with specific information on student skills and weaknesses, should enable teachers to develop effective instruction/evaluation systems in spelling.

An Example of an Integrated Spelling Assessment

This section provides an example of an **integrated spelling assessment** that is (a) based on many of the preceding issues and (b) summarized in the findings reported by Fitzsimmons and Loomer (1978). Their findings follow:

- Students should be presented their spelling words in list form rather than in sentence or paragraph form.
- Students should study words of highest frequency in children's and adult's writing.
- Students should correct their own spelling under teacher direction.
- Students do not have to learn word meanings to learn spelling.
- Students should learn spelling of whole words rather than syllables within words.
- Instruction in phonic rules is of little value given the nature of the English language.
- The test-study-test method of spelling instruction is superior to the study-test method. According to Horn (1947), use of a pretest with immediate correction accounts for 95% of all learning in spelling.

Alternate word lists of a survey-level spelling task sample words from the entire curriculum at each grade level. Dictating words from one or two forms of these word lists has three functions: (a) to screen students and help determine who should be placed in specialized instructional support settings, (b) to plan instruction and establish individualized instruction for each student, and (c) to establish a base level of performance for conducting program evaluations.

When all students in a grade level take the same test at the beginning of a school year, a norm-referenced data base is available for allocating instructional resources and assigning students to appropriate settings. Students who are considerably low (for example, more than 1 standard deviation below the mean for the grade level) may need to be assessed further for placement into special education settings and to establish individual educational plans in spelling.

Because a production response is generated, we can analyze performance to find specific error types for individual students. We can then use this information to plan more specific-level assessments to corroborate certain error patterns and to plan instructional programs immediately. As students study individual word lists throughout the year, a combination of words representing individual error types and high-frequency words should be included on the weekly spelling tests.

Given an adequate sample of words that students will study during the year, we can create alternate forms of the same test and compare performance across tests. An alternate form of the test can be administered at select times to determine if general improvement is occurring with individual students and overall improvement for an entire program.

Let's examine our fictional fourth-grade class. Its school district has a spelling curriculum at each grade level. In this instance, there are approximately 400 words to be taught in the fourth grade. Our teacher has randomly selected 20 words from this domain each week for testing. Three of those lists are presented in Table 8.2.

At the start of testing, the room should be quiet and free from distractions. All students should have a spelling response form and a pencil. Directions should be given verbatim for the first administration in each classroom; however, once students become familiar with the administration procedures, it may be possible to shorten the directions. The spelling test itself consists of pronouncing each spelling word on the list in isolation, in a sentence or phrase, and again in isolation. Presentation is best accomplished through a rolling dictation procedure, with a word presented every 10 seconds (Grades 1–5) or every 5 seconds (Grades 6–8).

TABLE 8.2

Three randomly generated 20-word lists from the fourth-grade curriculum

List 1	List 2	List 3
deal	cities	toothbrush
land	we've	chicken
those	suddenly	together
bubble	busiest	quite
meant	car	plenty
travel	finer	again
price	putting	chain
whistled	Monday	more
upon	circus	add
best	scold	follow
making	thousand	man
hard	nail	oil
classes	thirty	sack
tease	scare	show
world	August	fifteen
one	shoes	moose
during	ours	spray
screen	proud	women
weekly	aged	mean
partly	doesn't	wrong

The teacher does not acknowledge specific questions and ignores student comments (i.e., "Slow down") during dictation. Each measurement is done for 2 minutes and is group-administered.

Figure 8.4 displays two examples from our fourth-grade class. Both Shawn and Megan have been dictated the words from the third list, which has a possible total of 20 words correct and 124 correct letter sequences. Megan, who is

	Megan			Shawn		
1.	toothbrush	c	11	tothbrush	✓	9
2.	chicken	c	8	cicken	✓	6
3.	together	c	9	togethar	✓	7
4.	quiet	✓	3	qrite	✓	4
5.	plenty	c	7	plenty	c	7
6.	agane	✓	3		✓	0
7.	chain	c	6	chane	✓	3
8.	wore	c	5	whar	✓	1
9.	add	c	4	add	c	4
10.	follow	c	7	folew	✓	4
11.	man	c	4	man	c	4
12.	oil	c	4	oyel	✓	2
13.	sack	c	5	sake	✓	2
14.	show	c	5	show	c	5
15.	fifteen	c	9	fiften	✓	6
16.	mouse	✓	4	mose	✓	4
17.	spray	c	6	spray	c	6
18.	woman	c	6	wimen	✓	4
19.	mean	c	5	meen	✓	3
20.	wrong	c	6	rong	✓	4

FIGURE 8.4
Scoring of correct letter sequences with Megan and Shawn

an excellent speller, has 17 words correct (marked *c* for correct and √ for incorrect) and 116 correct letter sequences (the number of correct letter sequences for each word is recorded to the right of each word). Shawn performs poorly: Of the 20 words he attempts, he has only 5 words correct and 85 correct letter sequences.

Screening Decisions. Figures 8.5 and 8.6 represent the norms from a fourth-grade class (*n* = 62) tested in the fall using the procedures just described for our fictional class. They summarize the ranges of performance (lowest to highest) with five percentile marks highlighted: 10th, 25th, 50th, 75th, and 90th. Individual scores (represented by the circles) are displayed above and below the 90th and 10th percentiles, respectively. The box in the middle of the graph shows the range at which most students perform (i.e., the bottom is the 25th percentile, the top is the 75th percentile, and the line in the middle is the 50th percentile). Figure 8.6 summarizes performance for correct letter sequences from the same class.

Both graphs depict relatively normal distributions. For a screening decision, the skills of at least five students appear very low. Based on this information, further assessment should be conducted to determine if more specialized placement is necessary.

Instructional-Planning and Formative-Evaluation Decisions. An analysis of the students' individual protocols depicted with the scoring of correct sequences reveals some errors for both Megan and Shawn that may warrant more specific-level, follow-up assessments. For Megan, two rules governing long vowel sounds may be confused (*again* versus *agane*) and for Shawn, several misrules appear: long vowels (double vowels, silent -*e*), *r*- and *w*-controlled vowels, use of -*u* after *q*, and diphthongs. But before making any specific instructional plans, further opportunities to spell words representing these error types should be administered.

Because of the great uncertainty in making appropriate instructional planning decisions, the next step is to develop a sampling plan for selecting appropriate words to be administered on a weekly basis. For Megan, words from the entire curriculum may be appropriate because her spelling from a random sample appears quite skillful. However, for Shawn, the teacher may need to sample words that are more specific for combinations of vowel sounds in the

FIGURE 8.5
Norms from a fourth-grade class

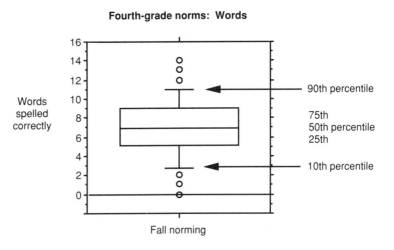

Fourth-grade norms: Words

FIGURE 8.6
Performance for correct
letter sequences

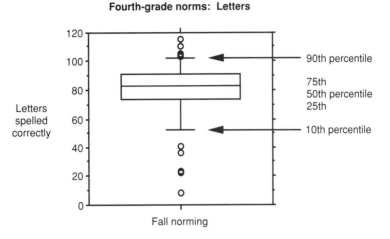

Fourth-grade norms: Letters

As you can see in these graphs, performance

middle position of words and words with *w-/r*-controlled vowels. If you remember the concepts of sampling from chapter 2, the sampling plan for Megan will be a simple random one, but for Shawn, we will use a stratified random sample. Once we have a sampling plan, we can proceed with our instruction and continuous assessment, sampling words from these domains each week (probably using a random sampling plan within each domain). Assuming we have done this throughout the fall quarter, we might generate the graph in Figure 8.7 to use in formatively evaluating instruction.

These data indicate that Shawn's spelling program is effective and he is improving over time. Notice how the change of performance is greater in the last several weeks of the quarter than it is in the first several weeks.

Program-Certification Decisions. At the end of the year, considerable data have been generated. Because it is difficult to evaluate the overall program effects from so much data, we need a way to reduce the data and summarize it more programatically (Tindal, 1989). We can count the number of students who made sufficient progress on their individual graphs, but

we would need to define what is meant by the term *sufficient progress*, which is hard to define without some controversy. A much easier strategy is simply to use the norm-referenced word list that was employed at the beginning of the year. Since these words sample randomly from all words in the curriculum that students have encountered, no bias exists in favor of any one student. We can then compare how students fared in general across the two or three time periods. We do not want to use these data to make statements about individual students because our graphs provide much better data, but we do wish to aggregate their scores and look at the general distributions. If growth has occurred, the lowest levels of performance (the 10th percentile mark) and the middle box depicting the majority of students should be higher; the 90th percentile may not actually increase much, since we are likely to have a ceiling effect. Figures 8.8 and 8.9 display a fall and winter comparison for the same fourth-grade class that was reported in Figures 8.5 and 8.6.

As you can see in these graphs, performance improves at all percentile levels: The 10th, 25th, 50th, 75th, and 90th percentiles are all higher in the winter than in the fall. The spelling program appears to be effective in improving stu-

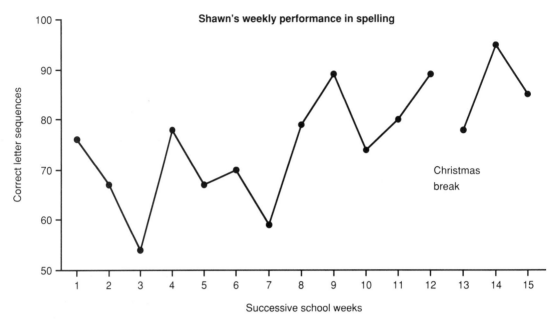

FIGURE 8.7
A graph for formatively evaluating instruction

dent skill in spelling whole words and letters in correct sequence.

SUMMARY OF
INTEGRATED ASSESSMENT

Appropriate assessment of spelling relies on sampling a variety of words and behaviors. Words may be phonetically regular, to test key rules in spelling generalizations, and/or those that appear frequently in the English language. Most importantly, though, spelling domains should reflect the individual skills and weaknesses of students.

We can use a number of sources to generate word lists that will reflect the content of instruction and/or the grade level of the curriculum, and we can employ a security list in addition to words from the curriculum. Most sampling

techniques in spelling programs are based on instruction in a core group of words for 1 week, with new words introduced in successive weeks. Students master words on a weekly basis, with little preview and no review.

The strategy suggested here involves specifying the entire domain to be learned during the year and sampling from this domain to establish alternate forms. Subsequently, words are randomly sampled with replacement each week; once selected for a weekly test, the word is thrown back into the sampling pool and has an equal chance of appearing on subsequent lists. This technique allows for preview and review of words over time. To ensure that all words are eventually sampled, it relies upon frequent testing—on a weekly basis at a minimum.

We measure performance in our assessment strategy using dictation of words from a list and production responses. Although writing within

FIGURE 8.8
Growth in number of
words spelled correctly

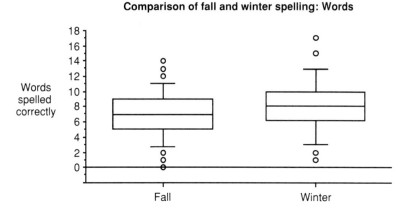

Comparison of fall and winter spelling: Words

a compositional context represents the terminal behavior for expression of correct spelling, tests employing writing samples pose problems because spelling performance is influenced by a lack of opportunity to misspell words and by poor handwriting. More opportunity to spell more diverse words results from the use of dictated word lists.

Our system indexes student performance with local norm-referenced and curriculum-based strategies *and* monitors it frequently over time, with a view of both the specific errors students make and improvement over time in gaining spelling skills. Locally developed as-

sessment materials are based on the building or district curriculum and developed by the teacher, making such tests useful in allocating students to educational services, determining student placement in the curriculum, monitoring student pacing through the curriculum, diagnosing specific spelling difficulties, and assessing instructional effectiveness. The format for assessment is multiple-referenced, allowing for a range of decisions.

Norm-referenced data focus on the amount of educational support needed, but they are not adequate for making instructional decisions. When the test is administered to a local

FIGURE 8.9
Growth in the number of
correct letter sequences

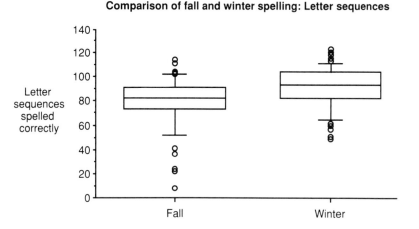

Comparison of fall and winter spelling: Letter sequences

norm-group, we can compare individual students' performances to those of other students to both allocate services and evaluate or certify programs. Screening and eligibility are local to the students in the school, so the available resources are matched more appropriately. Program evaluation decisions can involve the same basic data as initially employed in the screening decisions.

Both criterion- and individual-referenced data are available to help determine placement in a curriculum, generate hypotheses concerning specific skills upon which to base instruction, and formatively evaluate the effects of instruction over time. These teacher-made, criterion- and individual-referenced tests are more flexible than those created with the norm-oriented strategy because spelling instruction and assessment are more responsive to the needs of individual students. Frequent assessment is useful in highlighting student skill deficits and suggesting ways in which to alter instruction in order to meet student needs.

CHAPTER SUMMARY

To help in the discussion of spelling, this chapter defined terms such as *phonemes, graphemes, morphemes, vowel/consonant combinations (digraphs, blends, and diphthongs)*. We presented a model of spelling assessment and considered major dimensions of spelling: (a) how words are sampled and (b) what response is generated. The chapter described four sampling strategies. The first, based on the assumption that the English language is regular, is a sampling plan that can be used for generating subsets of words with the same phoneme-grapheme relationships. Performance on this subset reflects performance on the entire universe of all words with a corresponding structure. With the second strategy, which requires the assumption that English is not regular, any subset based on phonetic regularity is worthless because few generalizable patterns are assumed to exist. In this case, the sampling plan is based on the frequency of appearance of individual words in written discourse. This subset of words is used to predict performance. These two approaches are considered together as a third approach. A fourth sampling strategy that should not be considered seriously is sampling words from students' written compositions.

This chapter also reviewed spelling responses, including proofreading, error detection, and producing words during dictation tasks. Assuming that students produce their spelling, two types of scoring systems are possible, in which words are scored according to (a) their correctness as entire words or (b) the number of letters in correct sequence. The latter strategy can provide the basis for analyzing performance in terms of error patterns, several of which were presented. Finally, we presented an integrated example of a spelling assessment, in which several decisions were made using all three types of reference. Screening decisions were made using norm-referenced interpretations, instruction was planned using criterion-referenced interpretations, instruction was modified on the basis of an individual-referenced data base, and the entire program for all students was summarized using norm-referenced information.

CHAPTER 9

Written Expression Assessment

Y ou have been asked to serve as a judge for a local writing project in which contestants have submitted samples of their best writing. Your job is to sort through the compositions and decide which one represents the best writing sample. The final decision has boiled down to two samples from which these excerpts have been taken:

> Sample 1: "He was asked by his judges whether he would rather be thrashed thirty-six times by the whole regiment or receive a dozen lead bullets at once in his brain. Although he protested that men's wills are free and that he wanted neither one nor the other, he had to make a choice; by virtue of that gift of God which is called *liberty*, he determined to run the gauntlet thirty-six times and actually did so twice. There were two thousand men in the regiment. That made four thousand strokes which laid bare the muscles and nerves from his neck to his backside. As they were about to proceed to a third turn, Candide, utterly exhausted, begged as a favor that they would be so kind as to smash his head; he obtained this favor; they bound his eyes and he was made to kneel down. At that moment the King of the Bulgarians came by . . .". (Block, 1956, p. 113)

> Sample 2: "You can use your handbrakes to help true your wheel. Make sure the brake is centered in the frame. Watch the brake rubbers as you spin the wheel slowly. If the wheel stays the same distance from the rubbers all the way around, your wheel is perfect. If not, wait until the rim gets to a place where it is closer to one side. Stop the wheel there. If you don't have handbrakes, watch where the rim passes through the frame. Or hold a piece of chalk near the rim first on one side and then the other and spin the wheel. Where the chalk marks, the spoke nipples need turning." (Garvy, 1986, p. 56)

Choosing the best passage would be difficult. Not only have you not been given any help in the evaluation process, but you know little about these two composition excerpts. The former sample is taken from an English translation of *Candide*, written by Voltaire in 1759. The latter excerpt appears in the sixth edition of Helen Garvy's *How to Fix Your Bicycle*. Each work was written for different audiences and contains different topics; one is a philosophical treatise on the plight of humanity, and the other is a quick and pragmatic set of directions to keep a bicycle in operation. Direct comparison of the quality of these two writings would be ludicrous. In fact, any comparison begs the question: Comparison on what dimension?

In many ways, the behaviors necessary for written expression are more complex than those involved in reading, spelling, or answering math problems. For this reason, the assessment of written expression is more diverse if not problematic. Pupil responses in reading, math, and spelling tend to be discrete and objectively measured; but written expression behaviors can be difficult to evaluate because they vary in purpose and audience, and require the integration of several basic skills. These characteristics of written expression make the task of judging pupil performance a demanding one.

CHAPTER OBJECTIVES

At the end of this chapter you will have the knowledge and skills to

- Use both direct and indirect approaches to written expression assessment.
- Ensure that the necessary conditions for reliable and valid data are present.
- Use any of several administration formats to assess written expression.
- Score written compositions with a variety of subjective scoring systems.
- Score written compositions with a variety of objective scoring systems.

- Use any of several different prompts to generate writing for a specific purpose.
- Implement an integrated assessment.

KEY VOCABULARY

Vocabulary in this chapter includes the distinction between *direct* and *indirect* measurement, centering on whether a writing actually occurs or not. If students are to write, we must devise a system for *prompting* their writing, in which they are provided a context for and directions to engage in writing. Another salient distinction is the difference between a *subjective* scoring system, in which the reader must exercise judgment to determine the correctness of a response, and an *objective* scoring approach, in which overt, external criterion are employed. We present three subjective scoring systems: (a) a *holistic approach*, which is based on a general impression, (b) an *analytic scale*, which addresses separate components of compositions, and (c) a *primary-trait* system, which considers the influence of audience and purpose. We also present several objective measurement systems, including *fluency*, a measure of word counts; *syntactic maturity*, use of syntax and grammar to structure written discourse; *vocabulary*, use of specific word types; *conventions*, use of punctuation and capitalization; and finally *multiple-factor* measures, which include many of these measures. Finally, we provide an integrated assessment to show how different educational decisions can be made from the same assessment formats and data base.

OVERVIEW OF WRITTEN EXPRESSION: A DEFINITION

Written expression is a complex skill that requires fluency in many areas, including speaking, reading, spelling, handwriting, capitalization, punctuation, word usage, and grammar (Wallace & Larsen, 1978). It is no wonder, then, that the ability to communicate in written form is considered the highest achievement in language for people in all cultures (Polloway, Patton, & Cohen, 1981).

Written expression involves three diverse areas: communication, the conventional manipulation of graphic symbols, and social skills. Poteet (1980) defines *written expression* as "a visible representation of thoughts, feelings, and ideas using symbols of the writer's language system for the purpose of communication or recording" (p. 88). Odell (1981) describes *writing competence* as "the ability to discover what one wishes to say and to convey one's message through language syntax and content that are appropriate for one's audience and purpose" (p. 103).

Because written messages involve organizational skills that are often not easy to quantify, the assessment of written expression is difficult, time-consuming, and ambiguous. It is also a highly debated topic. Consequently, assessing students' writing skills is probably the most difficult area of academic diagnosis.

Some factors that we must consider in assessing written expression are the nature of written expression, audience, type of discourse, and the components of writing, which are the focus of assessment. With these issues in mind, we must then construct, administer, and score measures of written expression.

In constructing written expression tests, we need to either develop items that either generate student writing or employ writing samples to which students respond. If we want production responses in which students actually write, what prompts should we use? How can we structure a purpose for writing? If we want students to edit writing samples, what components should be considered: grammar, capitalization, punctuation, spelling, syntax, etc.? Whether production or selection responses are used, such issues of test construction must be considered first.

How are tests to be administered? Most students spend a great portion of their day writing; yet how is the assessment process different from or similar to the format students regularly use? What directions are students given? What is the physical arrangement of the assessment? Will there be time limits for the students to complete their compositions? What is the impact of reading skills in the assessment process?

When the administration procedures are in place, testers must decide how to score responses and scale writing proficiency. How will student scores be generated? If using a subjective evaluation system, they must consider how to score the protocols: holistically or with an analytic evaluation strategy. What system will they employ for scorer training and qualification of the scoring process? What selection and specification criteria have been used to develop rating criteria? Are the evaluative criteria specific and well anchored? Is the scale sensitive to change and capable of measuring individual growth? What is the range of writing skill reflected in the scoring criteria? Does the score reflect diagnostic information useful for instructional planning? What is the criterion for assessment validation?

Assessment should reflect the purpose, process, and product of written expression, and it particularly should reflect the types of decisions to be made, including eligibility and placement, planning and evaluation of instructional programs, and summarization of program effects. The assessment strategy should be delineated clearly so that administration, scoring, and reporting are structured appropriately. These components include (a) the general context of assessment, (b) stimulus demands on the student, (c) administration strategies and procedures, (d) the composing process, and (e) scoring systems for judging skill level.

We must address all of these issues to assess written expression adequately, although consideration of one is likely to influence others. For example, if assessment data indicate the need for placement into special education, a normative sample may be necessary; thus, scorers may adopt assessment strategies that emphasize easy-to-score writing features. In contrast, decisions about instructional planning necessitate more emphasis on writing content, thereby allowing more choice in adopting either a subjective, objective, or combined system for scaling proficiency.

To address the multifarious issues involved in the assessment of written expression, this chapter contains two parts. The first section covers issues in the assessment process. Because written expression is such a complex skill, considerable controversy exists not only about definitions and assumptions, but also about the types of behavior sampled and the evaluation strategies employed to scale achievement. This section includes specific applications of written expression assessment and various subjective and objective scoring systems. Within each approach we describe and illustrate several systems. The second section presents an integrated assessment, using the information from the chapter.

The Writing Process

The instructional process should direct assessment procedures, which in turn reflect the content and context of instruction. The goal of testing is to use the data to evaluate instructional programs at some level. Following is a brief description of a model of written expression, which also appears in Figure 9.1.

The purpose for writing is a critical feature of both the process and the product of written expression (Isaacson, 1985). Unless we consider the reason for writing, assessment cannot focus on critical effects. Furthermore, because

FIGURE 9.1
A model of written expression assessment

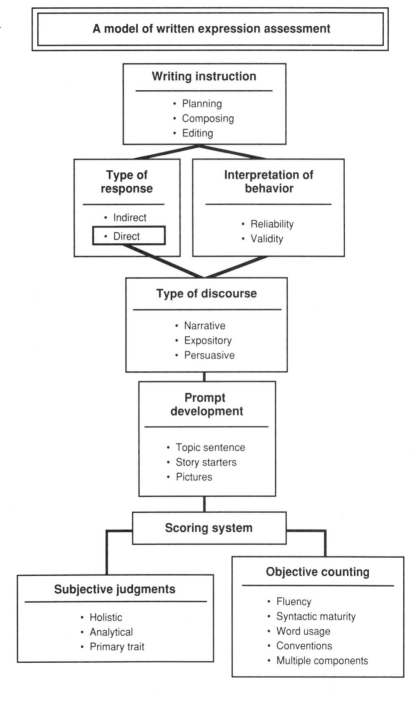

written expression is generally under the (stimulus) control of the respondent, his or her purpose has a major impact on assaying outcomes. Purpose has a major impact on the scoring and evaluation of products.

Writing involves three major behavioral activities: (a) planning, which involves idea development, content, and organization, (b) composing, which follows the conventions of language usage, and (c) editing, which deals with refining the finished product. Although most assessments (particularly published achievement tests) focus on editing, it is critical that we address the other activities with equal attention and specificity. However, little is currently known about them, let alone the procedures for including them in the assessment process. To capture these different activities, both direct and indirect measures are needed. **Direct** measures illustrate planning and composing skills, and **indirect** measures deal primarily with editing tasks. By using direct and indirect measures, the test highlights both semantic communication and mechanics. In this way, writing is broadly conceived, from planning (prewriting) to editing.

Operationalizing Written Expression Assessment

When moving from a model of written expression to an assessment of its process and product, we must consider two major issues. First, what behavior are we sampling? The behavior or response generated, whether it reflects the composing and writing process directly or infers the presence or absence of skills indirectly through conventions and transcription review, restricts the selection of an assessment procedure. Second, how can we ensure reliability and validity? Our measurements of written expression must be both stable and relevant to be useful in making educational decisions.

These two concerns have often been related to the use qualitative or quantitative indices of performance.

Direct or Indirect Measurement. Moran (1987) describes **direct measures** as assessments that present writers with a stimulus prompt and direct them to write a response expressing themselves in a particular manner. For example, describe an emotional reaction, recount an event, describe an object, explain a procedure, or defend a position. Direct assessment utilizes a specific and standardized administration format that is scored in a prescribed manner and reported according to a certain format. In contrast, **indirect measurement** requires no production response: Instead of writing, students select correct answers from a menu of options. Often such items use multiple-choice formats, and focus on sentence structure, word usage, spelling, punctuation or capitalization.

Direct and indirect testing should not be confused with objective and subjective scoring, which refer to the replicability of the scoring procedures. The term **objective** refers to the presence of overt and external criteria for scoring a response. In contrast, the term **subjective** refers to internal criteria in which there is some degree of scorer judgment in determining the quality or correctness of a response. Both types of measurement, direct and indirect, can use objective or subjective scoring systems. Direct measurement focuses on composition skills, and indirect measurement concentrates on language usage and convention. Many direct written expression measures utilize subjective criteria, a rating scale that reflects dimensions of quality. Direct measures, however, may be scored by objective means, employing well-defined external criteria for scoring a response as correct (i.e., correct word sequences, which we introduce later in the chapter). Likewise, most indirect writing measures employ an objective scoring format that avoids reference to judgment or inference of quality. However, indirect measures also may employ subjective criteria (i.e., sentence order and word usage) in which judgments are made based on internal criteria.

According to Moran (1987), analysis of direct measures of writing is advantageous because (a) the original connected text is available for analysis, (b) they incorporate a variety of both transcription and composition skills, (b) higher content validity is likely with actual writing samples, and (c) the potential exists for focusing on process assessment, which deals with how students perform rather than the result or product of their performance.

Disadvantages of direct measurement using writing samples include the following: (a) They are often time-consuming, and (b) they may generate scores with low estimates of reliability. Bias also has been ascribed to the type of prompt employed, the degree to which the prompts tap prior knowledge (Langer, 1982), the specificity of the audience for whom the writing sample is addressed (Applebee, 1981), the type of discourse generated (Lloyd-Jones, 1977), and varying cognitive demands placed upon the student (Flower & Hayes, 1981). Finally, writing samples often fail to present opportunities for evaluating specific skills because students are free to use their preference of grammatical or syntactical features.

Qualitative or Quantitative Dimensions of Writing. Most current methods used to measure written expression are either qualitative or quantitative (Charney, 1984). Qualitative measures employ some form of subjective rating of quality. The basis for rating may be the clarity in communication, use of stylistic devices, creativity in writing to a particular audience, or the display of specific types of discourse. Quantitative indices arise from objective measures, with writing decomposed into a series of countable components. Examples of quantitative

measures include a count of the number of words written, mature words, correctly spelled words, and so forth (Deno, Marston, & Mirkin, 1982; Deno, Mirkin, & Marston, 1980). Many published achievement tests include items that require students to review sentences and select from multiple choices to demonstrate proficiency with word order, punctuation, syntax, style, grammar, and spelling. When the final score is the number of items correctly answered, this type of test represents a quantitative measure.

As stated earlier, debates over qualitative and quantitative measures often focus on the use of direct or indirect measurement. Generally, most direct measures employ a qualitative measure, while indirect measures utilize quantitative measures. However, it is possible and probably necessary to eliminate this artificial dichotomy and initiate procedures for quantifying direct assessments for concurrent use with qualitative measures.

Reliability and Validity. These two issues, directness versus indirectness and qualitative versus quantitative, are at the root of controversy in defining the essential features of appropriate and technically adequate (reliable and valid) measures of written expression. According to classical measurement theory, reliability, while necessary, is not a sufficient condition for validity. That is, it is necessary at least to have reliability (consistency or replicability), but having it is no guarantee that the measure contains validity (truthfulness). For a measure to be valid, it must be reliable and highly related to other relevant measures or indices.

Many practitioners argue that indirect measures may be reliable but are not valid because they do not really measure the essence of writing. These researchers assert that although the components may be necessary, prerequisite skills for accomplishing a finished written task, they are not representative of the communicative function of writing. For example, McColly (1970) notes that such tests "are not measures of writing. For the purposes of judging writing ability, they should be ignored" (p. 149).

In contrast, other researchers have countered that the direct measures may be thought of as valid in assessing the essential communication function of writing, but they are often not reliable because they are usually scored qualitatively. Since a test must be reliable to be valid, this latter argument is difficult to reconcile. For example, Diederich (1974) describes the evaluation of 300 essays by a group of educated but untrained individuals in which "101 received every grade on the scale; 94% received a score of 7, 8 or 9 different grades; and no essay received less than 5 different grades from these 53 readers" (p. 6). The question remains whether the ratings of the different judges were valid because of such disagreement.

Determining reliability. Generally, the debate on reliability has focused on qualitative scoring systems with direct measures because few problems in replicability exist with indirect measures scored quantitatively. Many factors influence the reliability of qualitative scoring systems, including the following: (a) number of separate readings of each writing sample, (b) size of rating scale, (c) number of writing samples from each student, (d) writing topic, (e) training of evaluators, and (e) conditions under which ratings have been done. Rater background is important as well, regardless of specific training in the particular assessment (Charney, 1984; McColly, 1970). Another issue noted by Braddock, Lloyd-Jones, and Schoer (1963) is time limits, with primary-grade children needing as much as 20 to 30 minutes, intermediate-graders needing as much as 35 to 50 minutes, junior high-school students requiring 50 to 75 minutes, high-school students

requiring 70 to 90 minutes, and finally college students taking 2 hours.

Charney (1984) lists five conditions necessary for qualitative or subjective measures to be reliable and valid: (a) Training focuses on the important components of evaluation; (b) evaluators are qualified; (c) evaluators have been calibrated to specific criteria; (d) the criteria are appropriate; and (e) evaluators work quickly and with a clear focus. Probably the most important component in establishing reliability is evaluator calibration, which usually is completed in the early phases of training. It is imperative that raters review several compositions and compare findings with each other. They should discuss disagreements and make adjustments accordingly. The initial focus is on getting raters to move to the average of the group, raising standards where criteria have not been applied with sufficient rigor and developing more flexible standards if too much rigidity has been applied.

Rater agreement can be accomplished in one of two ways (Charney, 1984). The first procedure calls for criteria to be established inductively, with student compositions serving as the means for differentiating quality. Exemplary papers are chosen as *anchor papers* that represent the entire range of quality. Evaluators determine the type of discourse, the criteria for distinguishing one exemplary paper from another, the number of anchors to include, and the range of tolerance to allow in assigning papers to categories.

In the second strategy, the categories for evaluating papers are developed in advance. Many of the same decisions are necessary: to determine the aim of discourse, the range of categories, the anchors used in each category, and the tolerance for inclusion or exclusion to any given category. These criteria are then applied to student compositions independently of each other, rather than in reference to each other.

The major difference between these two *evaluative strategies* is that training proceeds concurrent with evaluation in the first and is completed a priori in the second. In both cases, training is explicit and consistent with the purpose of the assessment. Holistic ratings often employ the former strategy, calibrating the raters through exemplars found in the group of compositions, while analytical and primary-trait evaluations are based on the latter technique, employing categories that have been defined a priori.

Regardless of whether we specify the criteria and evaluation before or concurrent with evaluation, the entire process is premised on agreement with the criteria and their operationalization (Charney, 1984). The validity of the assessment is limited to the degree of agreement, despite the background and training of the evaluators. If evaluators feel that important dimensions of writing are not present or are applied inappropriately, their assessment of face validity will be adversely affected. Often, raters greatly disagree in their holistic judgments of writing, and the basis of their disagreement lies in the different values that are attached to a few traits of writing (Hirsch, 1977).

It is possible to get generally reliable judgments if the training and monitoring are sufficient. For example, Prater and Padia (1983) obtained reliability coefficients of at least .75 for three types of discourse after raters were trained. Mishler and Hogan (1982) noted that few studies have estimated interscorer reliability across various types of writing; their estimates of such reliabilities from published studies are .85, with intrascorer reliability estimated at .90.

Establishing validity. If we establish reliability at an acceptable level, we may use two types of validity: face and concurrent (Charney, 1984). Face validity means that assessment is highly relevant and sensible on a surface level. No quantitative methods are employed; the assessment is judged on whether it "seems" right. For example, a definition of written expression may focus on purpose and audience with which compositions should be consistent. Most quantitative measures do not possess face validity (Charney, 1984).

Concurrent validity calls for an intercorrelation between a measure of writing and an appropriate criterion. It is based on empirical results, not logic. Regardless of the definition of writing (a face validity issue), two measures that are highly correlated are generally regarded as measuring some of the same skills. Thus, if quantitative measures correlate highly with qualitative measures, we could use one system in place of the other.

Researchers have established the validity of quantitative measures, using qualitative measures as the criterion. A summary of studies by Spandel and Stiggins (1981) reported six sets of correlations, describing the relationship between direct and indirect measures of writing (Breland, Conlon, & Rogosa, 1976; Breland & Gaynor, 1979; Godshalk, Swineford, & Coffman, 1966; Hogan & Mishler, 1980; Huntley, Schmeiser, & Stiggins, 1979; and Moss, Cole, & Khampalikit, 1982). While most of these investigations have focused on high-school and older students, two of them included elementary students. The range of correlations was .20–.76 with most at least .60 and above. As Spandel and Stiggins note, "the results of these studies suggest that the two approaches assess at least some of the same performance factors; yet each deals with some unique aspects of writing skill" (p. 2).

ASSESSMENT PROCEDURES IN WRITTEN EXPRESSION

The three issues just covered are important whenever any type of assessment is under consideration for either development or adoption: Directness versus indirectness, qualitative versus quantitative, and determination of reliability and validity. These issues all influence the first step in the selection/development process. This chapter says little more about indirect assessments, although we cover some simple strategies for developing them in the material on language usage and mechanics. Otherwise, most indirect assessments are more easily adopted than developed. Assuming that we have chosen direct measurement, there are two areas to consider next: the topic to use in generating writing samples and the manner in which those writing samples are scored.

Prompts and Topic Selection

Prompts are directions to a writer to elicit writing (Prater & Padia, 1983). A number of different types of prompts are available, including pictures, topic sentences, story starters, incomplete sentences, and reading passages. To be consistent with most contemporary views that writing is a multiskill construct (Odell, Cooper, & Courts, 1978; Lloyd-Jones, 1977), prompts must take into account the type of writing required.

Three types of writing have been delineated: (a) expressive or narrative, which is writer-oriented because the purpose is to express feelings, attitudes, and perceptions; (b) explanatory or expository, which is subject-oriented in that the aim is to describe, explain, or present information; and (c) persuasive, which is audience-oriented, with the author taking a position on a topic and attempting to convince the audience. Narrative/descriptive writing has a purpose of presenting personal experience—recounting autobiographical information. It is closest to inner speech, can be viewed as self-expression, and is less discursive than other forms of writing. Expository writing contains a purpose, setting forth an idea that either informs or explains: it relates observations, presents analyses, and conveys information. Finally, persuasive writing is designed to convince others to adopt or endorse the writer's view (Breland, Camp, Jones, Morris, & Rock, 1987).

The type of discourse and the writing topic are critical influences on the writing act itself (Tindal & Parker, 1989). Writing in response to a persuasive mode generates different results than writing in response to a narrative or expository mode. The best explanatory model of writing takes the topic into account. But as Breland et al. note "This is unfortunate in that a good student could appear to be a good writer given one topic and a mediocre writer given an alternate topic within the same mode" (p. 47).

When we develop writing prompts, we must consider three issues: (a) the type of discourse generated, (b) student familiarity with the prompt or topic, and (c) the training and scoring needed to provide a reliable and valid assessment (Quellmalz, 1984). If a topic is too open-ended, the reliability of the scoring may decrease. Different topics generate different responses, making it impossible to rate them as if their responses were the same. Furthermore, it is assumed that some purpose or aim is inherent in the definition of writing and that different aims necessitate different types of writing, ill-defined writing tasks may be noncomparable. Finally, it may be important to hold the effects of knowledge constant and select general knowledge topics that are not content-specific (Charney, 1984).

For example, compare the three examples of holistic prompts that were developed by the National Assessment of Educational Progress for 9-year-old students. The critical point is to determine if student writing is differentially influenced by the prompt instead of reflecting stable characteristics of performance (Myers, 1980).

1. Going to school. Think about what happens when you go to school. Write a story that tells what you do from the time you leave where you live until you get to school. Be sure to include everything that you think is important.
2. Forest fire. Here is a picture of something sad that is going on in the forest. Look at the picture for a while. Do you see the forest fire? Write a story about what is happening in the picture. This is an important story because you want people to know about this sad event.
3. Astronaut. Here is a picture of an astronaut on the moon. Look at the picture for a while and think about what is happening. Now pretend that you were the astronaut, and write a story about walking on the moon (p. 7).

In summary, topic selection is an important component of writing assessment. It is important in itself and as it interacts with the manner in which compositions are scored and evaluated. For example, a holistic evaluation or general-impression manner of scoring implies that all writing is equal, and therefore the topic is less important. To address this issue, holistic ratings have been developed that are specific to various types of discourse (Cooper, 1977; Lloyd-Jones, 1977; Odell, 1981). Furthermore, as noted by Lloyd-Jones (1977), an obvious trade-off is that a dichotomy often occurs between samples that reflect specific types of discourse and topics that are interesting to students. Some students, even though they have the skill, are simply less motivated to write on certain topics and in certain discourse structures.

Subjective Scoring Systems

Scoring writing is difficult because of the lack of stimulus control in the assessment process. The correctness of the response for dimensions other than grammar or syntax cannot be determined. For example, a reading task can be controlled very easily if a passage presents skills that students are expected to demonstrate. In spelling, words dictated to students can be selected to assess specific phoneme-grapheme relationships. But teachers have little control over their students' writing, other than to specify the topic and the characteristics they desire. Thus, instructors can evaluate writing samples with their criteria in mind only with the proper scoring system. As a result, their method of scoring determines the degree to which the desired skills will be measured sensitively.

All subjective scoring systems require criteria for judging student writing samples. Cooper (1977) described subjective evaluation systems as "a guided procedure for sorting or ranking written procedures" (p. 3). This can be done by taking a sample and (a) matching it to another sample, (b) scoring it according to predefined quality, or (c) scoring it for prominence of certain features.

When matching it to other samples, anchor papers often are used to sort the range of quality from high, or exemplary, to low, or inadequate, although specific criteria also may be attached to the various values on the rating scale. Other students' writing is a natural source for creating a full range of samples with which to compare any particular composition. Papers are compared to anchor papers to determine writing quality.

Judge-established criteria, based on predefined qualities or the presence of specific features, are often necessary for scoring compositions. These scales can be holistic or analytic, and they can also be discourse-free or discourse-defined. In the holistic scoring, a judge assigns a single, general impression according to some a priori criteria rather than in comparison with other students; analytic scoring utilizes the same approach, but it deals with multiple dimensions, not just one general impression. For example, organization, clarity, and vocabulary usage may be all separately evaluated using an analytic system. Discourse-free scoring does not relate to any particular purpose or audience. On the other hand, discourse-defined scoring, which is often referred to as *primary-trait,* scores the writing according to purpose or audience. In either case, we must establish a guide to define the prominent features. If multiple features are identified, scoring is more time-consuming than with a holistic scoring system that uses anchor papers or pre-defined criteria (Prater & Padia, 1983).

Three important qualitative evaluation strategies have been established in written expression: (a) holistic scoring, initially used by the Educational Testing Service (ETS) in the National Assessment of Educational Progress (NAEP) and several large-scale assessments conducted by many states (Spandel & Stiggins, 1981); (b) analytic scale, developed by Diederich (1974); and primary-trait scoring, developed by Lloyd-Jones and later used in the NAEP evaluations. (1977; see also Odell and Cooper, 1980; Spandel, 1981).

Holistic Scoring. The **holistic scoring approach** is comprised of quick, impressionistic judgments that are not designed to identify a composition's strengths and weaknesses (Charney, 1984). Rather, raters review compositions to determine an overall impression. Although many factors such as grammar, syntax, punctuation, style, tone, and organization may enter into the reasons for rating a paper, they are not specifically isolated or identified. Holistic evaluation is premised on the assumption that writing compositions cannot be subdivided; the qualities of writing—form, content, style, sentence usage, and syntax—are so intertwined that evaluation must proceed likewise.

The first step in conducting a holistic evaluation is to develop a prompt for students. The prompts can be based on topic sentences, story starters, or pictures and should be appropriate for the type and age of students who are completing the writing. Prompts can vary considerably and do not need to be specific to the type of writing. After the writing has been generated, it can then be scored.

Rating papers holistically involves assigning a value from a rating scale, which typically ranges from 4 to 7 points. If it is important to avoid neutral ratings, which occur in the middle of an odd-numbered scale, use an even-numbered scale. The rating procedures usually begin by quickly reviewing the papers to identify "range finders," those papers that will be used to typify a particular value on the scale. It is important that no preconceived notion of the ideal paper be defined a priori; furthermore, judges should discuss their observations during the process. A paper assigned the highest value on the scale will simply be a relatively high-quality paper within a given group; it may or may not be an excellent paper in its own right (Spandel & Stiggins, 1981).

Concurrent with and following selection of the anchor papers, we must develop a summary of the characteristics, differentiating the various categories. (Myers, 1980). The commonalities of the papers placed at each value on the scale should be highlighted and summarized. For example, after scanning all papers and placing two sample papers into each category, we can make the following distinctions based on a 5-point scale:

5—A perspective is established that is very cogent, built upon several ideas and themes, which are integrated with each other and culminate in a very clear composition.

4—A well-articulated perspective is presented through several ideas and themes; however, they are tangentially related to each other and fail to be developed with clarity.

3—Several ideas are expressed; a perspective is developed, but is not clear and not carried to any conclusion.

2—Several ideas are expressed but are not related to each other; the perspective proposed is vague, inconsistent, and difficult to discern.

1—Ideas are expressed in sentences with little connection between them; few unique and cogent ideas are expressed and the perspective is left undeveloped.

After the range finders have been selected and their influential characteristics described, raters are trained to read the papers quickly, compare them to the range finders and assign a value. The evaluation should be completed quickly because increased reliability and validity are more likely with increased speed. Greater time spent in the evaluation process increases the likelihood that tangential issues and idiosyncratic criteria will enter into the judgments that are made (McColly, 1970). Judges should be told to read fast, do not think about a paper too much, and score their first impression, making certain it fits the anchor (Myers, 1980).

Ideally, the content validity of holistic ratings is higher than that of any other evaluative procedure because writing is a creative endeavor that is viewed by most people as a gestalt phenomenon. That is, a holistic evaluation provides a nonreductionistic response to writing as a whole. Therefore, the focus of training is to eliminate personal biases from entering into the judgments, although several studies have demonstrated that reader judgment often is based on characteristics of the writing sample other than a general first impression. For example, physical appearance often influences the ratings assigned to compositions (McColly, 1970). Word choice is another characteristic (Grobe, 1981; Nielsen & Piche, 1981; Nold & Freedman, 1977). Freedman (1979) found that

sentence structure and mechanics influence holistic scores; however, the content scores were most highly predictive of quality. Length of essay and spelling errors appear to influence judgments of quality as well.

> (T)he assumption that training in holistic rating leads readers to employ a consistent standard based on substantive criteria is not confirmed by the available evidence. In fact, there is evidence that holistic ratings may be reliable because, given the unnatural reading environment imposed upon the readers, the scores can only reflect agreement on salient but superficial features of writing, such as quality of the handwriting or the presence of spelling errors. (Charney, 1984, p. 78)

Because raters will be influenced differently by these various qualities of writing, the score should be based on a summation of multiple raters. Interrater reliability has been reported in the range of .60–.85. Diederich (1974) reports that reliability of .67 can be achieved with one sample. However, this value is considerably less than the .80–.90 level needed for group and individual educational decisions. Therefore, we may need two writing samples and two independent raters. With such procedures and specific, extensive training, it is possible to attain levels of reliability of .80 and above. A third reader is recommended for those cases of disagreement greater than 1 point. Estimates of the likelihood of this happening range from 20% (Myers, 1980) and 10% (Diederich, 1974) to less than 5% (Spandel & Stiggins, 1981).

The end result of the rating process is a distribution of papers that reflects a normal curve. To accomplish this, most evaluations put several grades of students together.

> (T)he fact is that in a fourth- through twelfth-grade reading, some fourth-graders always do as well as some twelfth-graders. Grade levels, the readers are told, are separated for study after the reading is over. Putting all papers into

the same reading ensures that the range of writing skill will be expressed in the distribution of the scores. (Myers, 1980, p. 42)

Advantages of holistic scoring. Holistic scoring is quick and efficient: Each paper often takes 2 minutes or less to complete. If readers are trained, sufficient levels of reliability can be attained so that scores can be taken seriously. One of the most significant advantages of holistic scoring is its flexibility in evaluating a wide range of writing styles and modes of discourse from various ages of students, including business letters, narrative compositions, expositional pieces, and persuasive writing for students in Grades 3–12. Advance preparation is negligible because the only major concern is with topic selection, a relatively easy and efficient task. A range of topics is available, including writing a letter of invitation, recording a telephone message, describing historical events, and so forth (Myers, 1980). If scored papers include compositions from several grades, accelerated or remedial instruction may be identified for individual students.

Disadvantages of holistic scoring. Many serious problems are present with holistic scoring. The most controversial issue is that the validity of this type of measurement is inherently assumed. That is, no criterion for acceptable writing is available or established in a manner independent of the use of the same format for evaluating writing. Another problem in establishing validity is that the focus is too exclusively on evaluation of products rather than processes. Such evaluations can never be truly diagnostic; they only provide summative scores. "It gives no meaningful diagnostic information beyond the comparative ranking it represents. . . . All we have is a single score, where we might wish to have a profile" (White, 1984, p. 406). In terms of using student performance to evaluate change

over time, the data generated from holistic scoring are virtually worthless. Such an evaluation format lacks sensitivity to change; improvements of 1 and 2 points are all that can be expected. If several grades are pooled in the evaluation process, specific, individualized grade-level diagnostics are not available.

Example of holistic scoring. Figures 9.2, 9.3, and 9.4 present three written compositions from our fourth grade. Each student was presented with a story starter that began, "Pretend you are at the playground and a spaceship lands nearby. What happens?" Then, students were given 30 seconds to think of a story and told to start writing. They had 3 minutes to write a composition. The story in Figure 9.2 was written by Megan, one of the better students in our fourth-grade class. Linda, whose performance is average for her class, wrote the story in Figure 9.3. The last story, shown in Figure 9.4, was written by Johnny, whose academic skills are below normal.

A 5-point scale, with 5 representing the highest score and 1 representing the lowest, was used to evaluate the three compositions from our fourth-grade class. Megan's story was assigned a score of 5 for the following reasons: She had developed a perspective with a story line and characters; she wrote in well-connected sentences that related to each other; and the writing style reflected generally correct expression, syntax, punctuation, and handwriting. Also, the use of one brief quotation enhanced the story.

Linda's composition received a rating of 3. The strength of this story was the beginning of a creative perspective, although the story line was incomplete and not well connected. The composition included some misspellings and a run-on sentence.

Johnny's story, which is difficult to read and understand, was rated 1. His story should read,

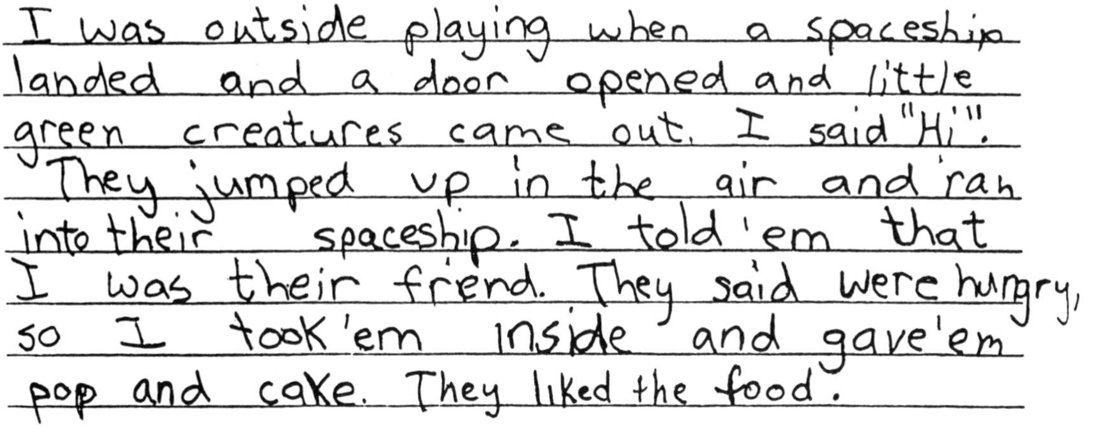

I was outside playing when a spaceship landed and a door opened and little green creatures came out. I said "Hi". They jumped up in the air and ran into their spaceship. I told 'em that I was their friend. They said were hungry, so I took 'em inside and gave 'em pop and cake. They liked the food.

FIGURE 9.2
Megan's written expression sample from the fourth-grade class

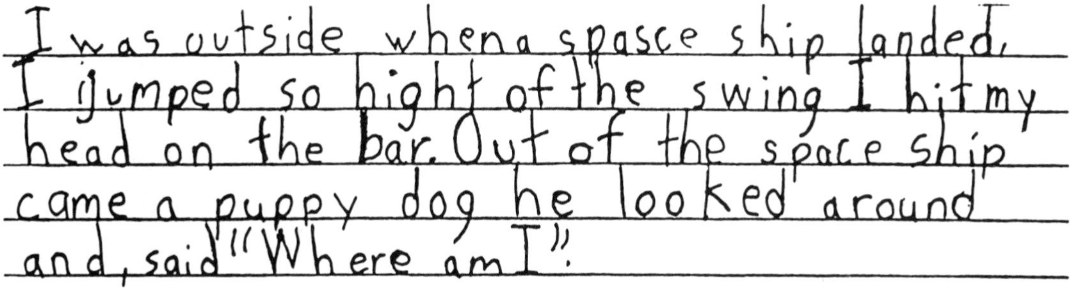

I was outside when a spasce ship landed, I jumped so hight of the swing I hit my head on the bar. Out of the space ship came a puppy dog he looked around and, said "Where am I".

FIGURE 9.3
Linda's written expression sample from the fourth-grade class

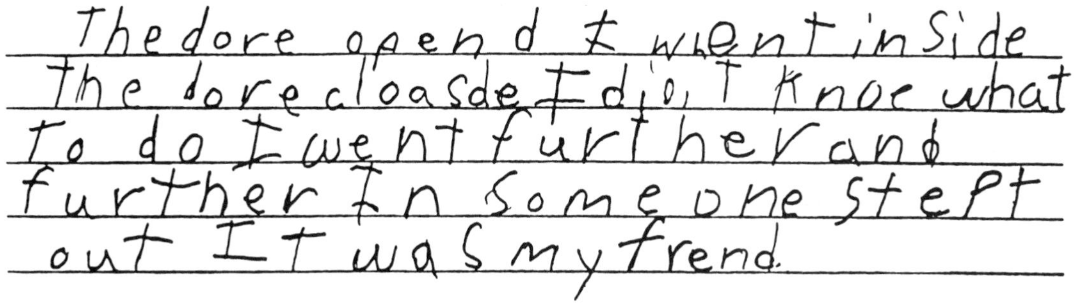

The dore opend I went inside The dore cloasde I di'n't knoe what to do I went further and further In some one stept out It was my frend.

FIGURE 9.4
Johnny's written expression sample from the fourth-grade class

"The door opened. I went inside. The door closed. I didn't know what to do. I went further and further in. Someone stepped out. It was my friend." The composition lacks any real story line, the sentences, although grammatically correct, are syntactically immature, and the writing contains many misspelled words, poor handwriting, and little punctuation.

A summary of the six steps in holistic scoring, the same steps used to score Megan's, Linda's, and Johnny's stories, follows:

1. Collect a large number of responses, using any type of suitable prompt.
2. Identify range finders that illustrate the various levels of quality.
3. Develop implicit criteria for distinguishing between papers of different values on the range-finder scale. These criteria may be listed or used in the training of the readers.
4. Train and calibrate raters, evaluating papers and giving feedback until a consensus has been established.
5. Read each paper quickly and impressionistically and assign a value on the scale.
6. Have two or three raters read each paper and combine or average their scores.

Analytical Scoring. The **analytical scoring scale** focuses on predetermined characteristics and specific, salient writing conventions. In contrast to holistic analysis, in which the range finders are selected from within the corpus of student compositions, this format relies on specific traits that have been identified a priori, with clear and operational definitions provided to help in the judgment process. "Traits must be explicit and well-defined so that all raters understand and agree upon the basis for making judgments" (Spandel & Stiggins, 1981, p. 26).

Analytical scoring comes from Diederich (1974), who completed a study at ETS in 1961 to determine "what qualities in student writing intelligent, educated people notice and emphasize when they are free to grade as they like" (p. 5). Five factors were established initially and have subsequently been used to form the prototypical analytical scale. Diederich describes the largest important cluster as "ideas expressed: their richness, soundness, clarity, development, and relevance to the topic and the writer's purpose" (p. 7). The next largest factor has the highest percentage of comments on errors in "usage, sentence structure, punctuation, and spelling" (p. 7). The third cluster is organization and analysis; the fourth general factor is "wording and phrasing—the choice and arrangement of words, including the deletion of unnecessary words" (p. 8). Finally, the fifth and least important cluster emphasizes "style, individuality, originality, interest, and sincerity—the personal qualities revealed by the writing, which we decided to call 'flavor'..." (p. 8). In summary, Diederich writes:

> It was interesting and illuminating that we found five and only five distinct schools of thought among these fifty-three distinguished readers, emphasizing ideas, mechanics, organization, wording, and flavor respectively. There is some room for argument as to the exact interpretation of these five factors, but there is no reasonable doubt that our study revealed just five different bases for the judgment of our sample of 300 papers, or that the distinctive emphases of these five ways of looking at student writing could be described fairly accurately by the labels we chose. (p. 9)

Later, Diederich notes that the five factors explained 43% of the variance in grades; the remaining 57% was unexplained because of either student or rater characteristics, both of which would be considered writing measurement error.

This evaluation scale is based on the premise that we can evaluate writing on a number of qualities that can be established a priori and yet developed upon reflection by a sophisticated reader. The most typical qualities of this evaluation procedure are Diederich's original five (ideas, organization, wording, flavor, and usage) in addition to punctuation, spelling, and handwriting. An implicit assumption of this scoring format is that these qualities are equally important in all types of discourse.

The scoring procedures are the same as for the holistic approach described in the previous section: Writing prompts are created, writing is generated, evaluation criteria are developed, raters are trained and calibrated, and scores are generated. The writing prompts can be flexible and include a wide range of topics and audiences because the evaluation criteria are not bound by them. The most important step is the establishment of both dimensions for evaluating writing and creation of anchors that reflect these dimensions. For example, writing samples may be scored on *organization,* which we must define. A scale also must be created, ranging from high levels (a score of 5) to low levels (a score of 1); however, the term *organization* must be detailed specifically, and each of the values on the scale delineated. Once a dimension or several dimensions are identified, described, and scaled, composition evaluation must be based consistently on these criteria, and no others. To protect from observer drift when we employ several dimensions concurrently, all the papers should be evaluated on only one dimension at a time. Importantly, the definitions of the scale values should be perused frequently and throughout the review process. When the papers have been completely reviewed on all characteristics, they should be summarized separately. The total score should not be reported, since the numeric system underlying the scoring is ordinal, not interval.

Advantages of analytical scoring. An analytical scoring system has several distinct advantages. It provides a specific focus on dimensions of writing that have been deemed important and therefore may be thought of as having more content validity. Flexibility exists in the characteristics identified for evaluation. With specific evaluative criteria established ahead of time, training may take less time; certainly, less trial and error is present in the development of the anchors. In this sense, reliability may actually be easier to establish. Also, we can specifically tailor the evaluation criteria to instruction, providing a stronger link between assessment and evaluation. Because it has multiple dimensions, the scale allows a more sensitive assessment of student performance, potentially reflecting strengths and weaknesses and forming a more individualistic assessment and instructional system.

Disadvantages of analytical scoring. One problem with a multifaceted scale is that a halo effect can occur: Scores from one dimension may influence the scores obtained in other dimensions. This is particularly true if raters remember their scores on other dimensions, which is likely when they evaluate only a few papers. A counter to the above argument of increased reliability has been noted by White (1984), who states that reliability may be more difficult to establish both within and across individuals when using an analytical scoring system. This scoring format assumes that writing subskills are separable, which may not be true. Although an ordinal scale is used for each of the separate components, the student's score often consists of the summation of these subscores. As we discussed in chapter 2, ordinal numbers should not be added together; therefore, when used in this manner, problems are inevitable in later analyses. An interesting problem that may occur is the lack of any papers on some scale values. For example, although criteria may be established for a 4 paper, we may find no instances of papers reflecting that level. Consequently, the distribution may not be normal and may be difficult to use in making some educational decisions. Finally, the system is much more time-consuming, possibly averaging 15 minutes per paper versus the 1 minute required for holistically evaluation.

Example of analytical scoring. Let's examine how well our fourth-graders did using this scale. To review their stories, look back at Figures 9.2, 9.3, and 9.4. In using this approach, our fourth-grade teacher divided the 5-point scale into three dimensions—wording, organization, and flavor—using the following general definitions and specific criteria:

Wording: the degree of precision in purpose and detail that the writer expresses.

5—The writer uses very unique words and phrases that are not repeated, converge on common themes, and are integrated into the sentence structure; presence of colorful words and phrases, but marked by repetition and lack of variety.

4—The writer uses a sprinkling of uncommon words or familiar words in an uncommon manner.

3—Words and phrases are quite varied but lack uniqueness; many words are repeated.

2—Words and phrases are only somewhat varied, nonrepetitive, and somewhat unique but contain little convergence across the different words/phrases.

1—Presence of many trite and common words and phrases; very vague and incoherent.

Organization: the paragraph structure and organization focuses on the use of topic sentences, supporting sentences, and concluding statements.

5—The writer uses paragraphs that are not only intact in terms of sentences within them,

but also in terms of the flow from one paragraph to the next. Structure is well developed; ideas are expressed in systematic fashion. This paper starts at a good point, has a sense of movement, gets somewhere, and then stops.

4—Paragraphs are present, topical structure and supporting detail is well developed, and concluding sentences are used.

3—Paragraphs are present and have some structure but are not well connected. The organization of this paper is standard and conventional. There is usually a one-paragraph introduction, three main points each treated in one paragraph, and a conclusion that often seems tacked on or forced.

2—Paragraphs are present but lack a topic sentence; sentences within a paragraph are marginally related to each other.

1—The writer has no paragraph structure. The main points are clearly separated from one another, and they come in a random order as though the writer had not given any thought to what he or she intended to say before starting to write.

Flavor: the use of colorful words, phrases, and literary devices, such as anaphora, analogies, metaphor, and so forth.

5—The writing sounds like a person, not a committee. The writer seems sincere and candid and is writing about something that he or she knows about, possibly from personal experience.

4—The general impression is quite fresh and interesting but drifts into jargon on occasion.

3—The writer usually tries to appear wiser or better than she or he really is. There is a tendency to write in lofty terms and broad generalities. Sometimes, it is correct, but colorless, without personal feeling or imagination.

2—The manner of expression is only slightly more controlled than a rating of 1, but stills appears stilted or common.

1—The writer reveals his or her position well enough but in a highly conventional manner, with very common language.

Megan's ratings were 3 for wording, 4 for organization, and 3 for flavor. In her comments, the teacher stated that Megan's strengths were mechanics, penmanship, and punctuation. While the story met the requirements of the story starter, its wording and flavor did not meet this teacher's highest expectations. Specifically, Megan lost points for her excessive use of *and* in the first sentence.

Linda's story was scored as follows: 2 for wording, 3 for organization, and 3 for flavor. Our fourth-grade teacher liked the paper's flavor, the use of the quotation, and the novelty of bumping her head. However, Linda's lack of punctuation and wording skills detracted from the communication of her story and resulted in a rating of 2.

Johnny's story received very low ratings: 1 for wording, 1 for organization, and 1 for flavor. His inability to spell, write complete sentences, and punctuate detracted significantly. Where Johnny had punctuated correctly, the sentences are only three or four words long. Few unusual words appear, and the flavor of the paper is not unique.

Primary-Trait Scoring. **Primary-trait** scoring, like analytical scoring, focuses on a specific characteristic of writing. However, rather than identifying several components or conventions of writing, the central tenet is that writing is designed for a specific audience and is characterized by a particular purpose. "Primary-trait

analysis is rhetorically and situationally specific" (Spandel & Stiggins, 1981, p. 27). This format for evaluation is premised on the questions: What is the rhetorical context and intended purpose of the writing? As mentioned earlier in the discussion of topics, several purposes are possible, including expressing, informing, and persuading. To the degree that these differing purposes generate a range of writing samples, we assume that evaluation criteria must also be different for each type of discourse.

The writing samples themselves are analyzed in terms of the rhetorical strategies employed. In contrast to holistic scoring procedures, which compare papers to others within the same distribution, or analytic scoring procedures, which evaluate compositions on important components of writing, this format deals with the degree of consistency in the purpose of writing. Therefore, readers must be familiar with the trait underlying the writing exercise and with the various anchors and definitions for each of the categories on the scale.

The first and most important step in creating a primary-trait scoring system is to define and operationalize the trait. Although three traits have been identified earlier (expressing, informing, and persuading), a more diverse range can be considered. For example, the trait may be creativity, depth of detail, expressive range, and so forth. The identified trait needs to be described sufficiently so that anchors can be created. For example, if the important trait were imaginative creativity, we might define it as "introduction of unique and novel ideas, juxtaposition of unusual objects and events, or sequencing unexpected and surprising activities." Once the dimension is defined, it must be operationalized through a rating scale that reflects high and low levels. These and the remaining steps are most similar to those employed in establishing an analytic scale: applying the criteria to each paper separately.

Advantages of primary-trait scoring. With primary-trait scoring, the composition is viewed in relation to both discourse type and audience; therefore, it must appear consistent with the social context in which communication was conducted. Like the analytical scoring system, primary-trait scoring allows written compositions to be analyzed for specific features rather than global and summative evaluations. Therefore, more specific and diagnostic information is available, which in turn gives more specific feedback to teachers, students, and parents. Because such criteria are defined more specifically and prior to the actual evaluation process, it is likely that the scoring will be more reliable. Furthermore, training is likely to be shorter, more efficient, and less vulnerable to drift over time. Given a similar trait on other compositions, comparisons of performance may be more appropriately completed; all other subjective evaluations may be only loosely compared, since topics and purposes are so different. Because the trait is audience- or purpose-specific, it allows for a more focused evaluation than is possible with holistic scoring; yet writing is not broken into multiple components as in analytical scoring. Primary-trait scoring produces a score that is uncontaminated.

Disadvantages of primary-trait scoring. One of the biggest disadvantages of primary-trait scoring is the anchors used in judging papers. Since we typically devise them ahead of time, they may not include some essential features that become prominent in the paper's content. As a consequence, score distributions may not be normal because a priori criteria are isolated and not formed from existing papers by way of range finders. Also, evaluation time may increase, because the evaluation is more specific. Of course, like all subjective systems, the score itself is limited (has a minimal scale), may not be sensitive to change, and is somewhat unlinked to specific instructional programs.

Example of primary-trait scoring. The primary trait for which our students' writing was evaluated involved *creative characters*, defined as a story with an unexpected cast of characters depicted through both descriptions and actions. Criteria were then assigned to each of the values on a 5-point scale, and the compositions were assigned scores:

5—The story line has unusual characters who look *and* act very differently from any known character.

4—The story line has unusual characters who look unique *or* engage in somewhat unusual behavior.

3—The story line has typical characters who look somewhat different from that which is expected *and* who engage in unusual behavior.

2—The story line has typical characters who look somewhat unusual *or* are engaged in unusual behaviors.

1—The story line contains characters who look *and* act in a typical and expected manner.

Megan received a score of 5 because she described a unique character (green creatures) and related an action that is unusual when greeting others (jumping up); however, the remainder of her story described some very typical events. Linda received a score of 2 since she described a typical character (a puppy dog) who engaged in unique behavior (speaking). Finally, a 1 was given to Johnny because he depicted typical characters (friends) and no unusual behavior.

Summary of Three Assessment Methods. These three assessment methods have individual strengths and weaknesses. The holistic evaluation procedures typically are vague in diagnosing writing problems and suggesting how they can be improved. Although the analytic scale initially may appear more precise in this capacity, it also may be somewhat problematic in diagnosis and formative evaluation. The qualities with which the writing samples are evaluated are broad terms, subject to multifarious interpretation (Odell & Cooper, 1980). Furthermore, the separate dimensions probably interact significantly as a function of the topic, the writer, and the judge. The strongest and most amenable approaches to diagnosis, formative evaluation, and instructional development are either analytical or primary-trait scoring. These formats are both consistent with current discourse theory and precise enough to provide direction in the improvement of writing skills. Furthermore, they allow comparability of compositions over time.

However, all subjective evaluations suffer the major problem of sensitivity. Because rating scales are used to quantify performance, a limited range of scores is possible. For this reason, all subjective evaluations should be conducted in conjunction with an objective system, allowing both a sensitive scale with potential for change and an anchored scale for ascertaining the critical effect.

Objective Scoring Systems

While subjective scoring systems are based on judgments of quality through rating scales, with the final score inferentially determined, objective systems are based on actual counts of specific characteristics. The most frequently used objective scoring systems include fluency, syntactic maturity, vocabulary, content, and conventions. A sixth format incorporates more than one of the above and is referred to as a *multiple-factor measure* (Isaacson, 1985).

Fluency. Fluency can be defined as "the degree to which the student becomes more proficient at writing down words and sentences into compositions of gradually increasing length" (Isaacson, 1985, p. 409). As in our definition of fluency in the reading chapter, this term is normatively based. Given a sample of students, fluency can range from just a few words at the low end to many words at the high end. Basically, fluency is the rate of word production per minute.

This measure has been researched at great length with some interesting outcomes. First, the reliability of this measure has been shown to be quite high (Marston & Deno, 1981). The validity of this measure has been studied also. Deno, Marston, and Mirkin (1982) found it to be highly correlated with performance on both norm-referenced achievement tests and teacher judgments of quality at the elementary grade levels. Using the Test of Written Language (Hammill & Larsen, 1983) and Developmental Sentence Scoring (Lee & Canter, 1971) as criteria, validity coefficients ranged from .62 to .84. In addition, the total number of words written has differentiated regular education, Chapter I, and special education students (Shinn & Marston, 1985). Furthermore, Marston, Fuchs, and Deno (1985) demonstrated that *total words written* was sensitive to student growth in written expression across 10- and 16-week periods. Deno, Mirkin, and Marston (1980), examined the typical performance of students in Grades 3, 4, 5, and 6. Table 9.1 presents the mean number of words written on a three-minute story starter and the standard deviations for both regular and special education stu-

TABLE 9.1
Average number of words written by students in Grades 3–6

Grade	Sample Size	Mean Number of Words	Standard Deviation
3	20	26.1	20.1
4	46	47.6	20.2
5	33	49.9	22.2
6	31	54.1	22.5

dens combined. Performance ranges from an average of about 26 words for third graders to 54 words for sixth graders. When the two groups of students are separated, great differences were found in their rates of production.

Syntactic Maturity. **Syntactic maturity** is defined as "the degree to which a student uses expanded, more complex sentences" (Isaacson, 1985, p. 410). Two methods for assessing syntactic maturity include (a) counting the number of sentences that fall into several different categories (fragment, simple, compound, or complex), and (b) calculating the average T-unit length (Hunt, 1965; 1977).

To count the number of sentences that are fragmented, simple, compound, and complex, we must apply the following definitions:

- Fragmented sentence: A grammatically incorrect sentence characterized by any number of problems such as no subject, verb, or object, subject-verb disagreement, or other syntactical problems. For example: *Sevrina at noon well fit.*
- Simple sentence: Has only one subject, verb, and possibly an object with no dependent clauses. For example: *Sally went home early.*
- Compound sentence: Has one subject, verb, and possibly an object and utilizes a conjunction to create an independent clause. For

example: *Jim had dinner, and then he went to the movie.*
- Complex sentence: Has multiple main subject and verb, with subordinating conjunctions that introduce dependent clauses. For example: *Bill and Sam, although they had not eaten in three days, kept hiking, in hopes they would reach town before dark.*

Generally, as students move from early writing proficiency to skilled writing proficiency, the sentence structure increases in both complexity and diversity.

T-units are phrases that can stand alone in a grammatically correct fashion. "A T-unit may be thought of as an independent clause plus whatever subordinate clauses or phrases accompany it" (Spandel & Stiggins, 1981, p. 31). A sentence written correctly may contain one or more T-units, while there are none in an incorrectly written sentence, since the stipulation is made that the phrases and clauses must be grammatically correct. The measure is simply a total count of the number of words written divided by the number of T-units present, giving the ratio of average T-unit length.

The following sentence contains one T-unit and 29 words, thus the average T-unit length is 29/1 or 29: "While I was in Pittsburgh, a town known for its delightful, rehabilitated downtown, I happened upon an old friend, who was just completing his final year at Carnegie Mellon." This writing sample is more sophisticated than the following: "I was in Pittsburgh. It has a delightful, rehabilitated downtown. While there, I met an old friend. He was just finishing his final year at Carnegie Mellon." This last sample has 27 words and includes four T-units, with the average T-unit length equal to 9. As Hunt (1977) reported, a general increase in the average T-unit length occurs throughout the school years. The averages for several grades follow: Grade 4 (5.4), Grade 6 (6.8), Grade 8

(9.8), Grade 10 (10.4), Grade 12 (11.3), average adult (11.9), and superior adult (14.8).

Vocabulary. **Vocabulary** scoring focuses on the uniqueness or maturity of words that are used in a composition. This may be accomplished by subjectively or objectively counting the number of unusual words. In the subjective method, the number of words that seem unique or mature are counted; in the objective system, three options are available. First, the scorer might count the number of *large words* contained in a written sample using the definition provided by Deno, Mirkin, and Marston (1980): 7 or more letters, excluding words with *ing* and *ed* endings. In their examination of written compositions of 86 students in Grades 3 through 6, they found correlations that ranged from .47 to .60 between the number of large words and criterion measures (Test of Written Language, Developmental Sentence Scoring, and Stanford Language subtest). While these correlations are significant, their moderate nature indicates insufficient evidence of validity.

In a second approach, all the words in the student's writing that appear on a chosen list of most frequently used words are eliminated, leaving only the number of unique or infrequent words. The remaining words are referred to as mature words. Deno, Mirkin, and Marston (1980) found validity coefficients that ranged from .72 to .74, suggesting that they may be a more valid measure of vocabulary than large words. Table 9.2 presents the typical performance of students in Grades 3 through 6 on the Mature Word Index, combining students in regular and special education. These data show the mean score for mature words ranges from 6.1 at the third grade to 12.3 at the sixth grade. The performance of general education students was far greater than the performance of special education students.

Alternatively, we can assess a student's vocabulary level by calculating a *type-token ratio*,

TABLE 9.2

Average number of mature words written by students in Grades 3–6

Grade	Sample Size	Mean Number of Mature Words	Standard Deviation
3	20	6.1	5.3
4	46	10.4	6.7
5	33	11.2	6.2
6	31	12.3	6.4

defined as the proportion of unrepeated words in a composition (Cartwright, 1969). Given a count of the total number of words written, the number of words that were repeated is subtracted (e.g., *he* repeated once indicates that 2 is subtracted from the total number of words). The number of unrepeated words is then divided by the total number of words to arrive at a percentage of original words.

Conventions. The category of **conventions** includes any factor—primarily mechanical—that makes a composition grammatically correct and presentable to others. A number of different conventions can be used to assess conventions: word usage (subject-verb or noun-pronoun agreement), margins (left, right, name, date, skipping lines, centering titles, and indentations), punctuation (capitals, periods, question marks, commas, quotation marks, etc.) and handwriting (touching lines, legibility, and correct formation). Some variables, like handwriting, may require the use of rating scales to be applied (Isaacson, 1985). The errors in writing conventions are counted and subtracted from the total number of conventions employed.

Another specific measure of conventions is the number of words spelled correctly, using spelling as a convention of appropriate and effective written communication. To use this system, scoring needs to take into account the sentence in which the word appears and the meaning of the word. For example, if a student wrote, "The men road home on horses," one word, *road,* would be scored as incorrectly spelled because of the meaning of the word in the sentence. Generally, the number of correctly spelled words is just less than the number of words written. Few people use words they cannot spell; instead, they choose alternate words rather than risking spelling errors (Tindal, Germann, & Deno, 1983).

Deno, Marston and Mirkin (1980), for example, analyzed the number of words spelled correctly and the number of correct letter sequences in written compositions. Both measures correlated highly with pupil performance on criterion measures of written expression, ranging from .76 to .86. The typical performance of students in Grades 3–6 for words spelled correctly appears in Table 9.3. On a 3-minute story starter, the average number of words spelled correctly is 22.9 for third-graders and increases to 49.1 for sixth-graders. There is a similar improvement across grade levels for correct letter sequences. In Table 9.3, the mean number of correct letter sequences is 99.5 at the third grade and improves to 227.9 at the sixth grade. Again, for both spelling measures, when the group of students is separated, and regular education students are compared to special education students, they far exceed them in level of words and letters spelled correctly.

Multiple-Factor Measures. More than one of the preceding factors may be used to form a composite index, which is referred to as a **multiple-factor measure.** The best example of a multiple-factor measure is the number of *correct word sequences* (CWS), defined as two adjacent, correctly spelled words that are acceptable within the context of the phrase to a native English speaker (Videen, Deno, & Marston, 1982, p. 11). In addition, words beginning and ending a sentence correctly are credited with one correct word sequence. When periods or commas are missing, the sequence is incorrect. For any given correct sentence there will be one more correct word sequence than the number of words in the sentence. For example, assume two students write the sentence, "The boy is in the tree."

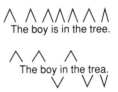

In the first example, the six-word sentence is totally correct, and there are seven correct word sequences. However, in the second example, credit is given only for the first two sequences and the combination of *in-the* because the verb *is* has been dropped, and the word *tree* is misspelled. The total number of correct word sequences for the second example is three.

Videen, Deno, and Marston (1982) researched the correct word sequences method of scoring writing samples and found a high relationship between CWS and "total number of words (fluency), words spelled correctly, holistic composition ratings, and word scores weighted according to developmental level" (Isaacson, 1985, p. 417). Furthermore, developmental changes over Grades 3–5 are apparent as Table 9.4 shows.

In looking at the compositions presented in Figures 9.2, 9.3, and 9.4, we find the following objectively scored information: Megan wrote a total of 59 words, Linda wrote 37 words, and Johnny wrote 28 words. In Megan's story, all of the sentences except for the first were written

TABLE 9.3

Average number of words spelled correctly and letters in correct sequence in a written composition by students in Grades 3–6

Grade	Sample Size	Mean Number of Words Spelled Correctly	Standard Deviation	Sample Size	Mean Number of Letters in Correct Sequence	Standard Deviation
3	20	22.9	19.8	15	99.5	90.3
4	46	41.6	20.5	32	198.1	93.1
5	33	45.3	23.5	25	242.0	101.9
6	31	49.1	24.9	25	227.9	87.9

correctly. The teacher counts this first sentence as three T-units: "I was outside playing when a spaceship landed and a door opened" and "little green creatures came out." The total number of T-units is eight with a mean T-unit length of 8.4 words. Linda's story is actually more complex. Her first two sentences each qualify as separate T-units, with the second sentence actually being a T-unit that is 14 words long. The third sentence may be broken into two T-units: "Out of the spaceship came a puppy dog" and "he looked around and said, 'Where am I?'" Linda's total number of T-units is 4, and the mean T-unit length is 9.3, longer than Megan's. Although Johnny doesn't punctuate, his composition can actually be broken into seven discrete T-units. Since there are 28 words in this writing sample, the average length

TABLE 9.4

Average number of correct word sequences in a written composition by students in Grades 3–6

Grade	Sample Size	Mean Number of Correct Word Sequences	Standard Deviation
3	9	27.3	13.9
4	20	41.3	24.7
5	11	48.2	26.2
6	10	58.8	27.2

is 4.0 words. If we examine the normative data provided in the previous paragraph, we can see that both Megan and Linda are above the fourth-grade mean of 5.4, while Johnny scores below this average.

Megan's story has 4 large words, 16 mature words, and a type-token ratio of 53%. Her mature word index is well above average for her grade level. Linda's composition with 3 large words, 12 mature words, and a type-token ratio of 62% appears to be typical, although her type-token ratio exceeds Megan's. Johnny also has 3 large words, only 7 mature words, and a type-token ratio of 43%.

In an effort to look at the use of conventions, our fourth-grade teacher reviewed the three stories and counted the number of instances where punctuation, including capitals, periods, question marks, commas, quotation marks were correct and incorrect. Megan, for example, correctly used punctuation in 20 places without an error. Her writing included capitalization of "I," quotations, the apostrophe in "em," and several periods. Linda used punctuation correctly in 9 instances, with 4 errors. Johnny's only correct use of punctuation involved capitalizing "I." He had a total of 5 correct punctuation instances and 7 mistakes.

Johnny spelled 19 of the 28 words in his story (Figure 9.4) correctly, with 117 correct letter sequences. When the teacher analyzed the composition for correct word sequences she found 15 CWS. Linda's story, (Figure 9.3) had 33 of 37 words spelled correctly and 164 correct letter sequences. The number of correct word sequences was 38. Finally, in Figure 9.2, Megan spelled 56 of 59 words correctly and had 286 correct letter sequences and 63 correct word sequences.

Comparing Subjective and Objective Evaluations

In reviewing the subjective and objective scoring systems we have described, it would be instructive to make direct comparisons of these approaches, as shown in Table 9.5. In general,

there appears to be a high degree of congruence among scoring methods within these two approaches and across the subjective and objective systems. Our fourth-grade teacher found that all three subjective systems—holistic, analytic, and primary trait—would rank Megan, Linda, and Johnny from best to worst. The objective scoring systems, with the exception of mean T-unit length and type-token ratio, also ranked our students Megan, Linda, and Johnny. For those systems where there was disagreement, the scores were fairly close. Megan's story had a mean T-unit length of 8.4, whereas Linda's had 9.3. On the type-token ratio, the difference did not appear as great: Linda had 62% and Megan had 53%. In her final comments,

TABLE 9.5
A comparison of subjective and objective scoring systems on three, fourth-grade writing samples

Measure of Written Expression	Megan	Linda	Johnny
Subjective scoring			
Holistic (1–5)	5	3	1
Analytical (1–5)			
Wording	3	2	1
Organization	4	3	1
Flavor	3	3	1
Primary-Trait (1–5)	5	3	1
Objective scoring			
Fluency			
Total words	59	37	28
Syntactical maturity			
T-Units	7	4	7
Mean T-Unit length	8.4	9.3	4.0
Vocabulary			
Large words	4	3	3
Mature words	16	12	7
Type-token ratio	53%	62%	43%
Conventions			
Correct punctuation	9	2	0
Incorrect punctuation	2	4	7
Correctly spelled words	56	33	19
Correct letter sequences	286	164	117
Multiple-factor measures			
Correct word sequence	63	38	15

the fourth-grade teacher suggested that longer writing samples might equalize the performance of these two students. However, all other objective measures, including fluency, vocabulary (mature words and large words), conventions, and multiple-factor favored Megan's composition as superior to Linda's. Certainly, with reference to the normative data collected on the objective measures, Megan typically scored above average, Linda was usually close to the mean, and Johnny always fell below the typical scores.

An Example of Integrated Written Expression Assessment

The examples were meant to describe the scoring procedures, but it is important to remember that the data should be collected to make specific educational decisions. We described three general decisions that all educators must make: (a) screening and eligibility decisions, (b) instructional planning and evaluation decisions, and (c) summative program certification decisions.

When students begin school in the fall or enter a new classroom, teachers must organize and place them into various groups. These decisions result in students receiving their primary instruction from assistants, worksheets, teachers, or peers. Often the amount of time and money available to make these initial decisions is scarce, so they must be made quickly and efficiently. Our perspective is to adapt assessment to the purpose and program for which students are to receive instruction. In the fall, teachers may want to determine the performance levels of all students in writing. Therefore, some coordination is necessary with other teachers in the scheduling and administration of measures.

In the following example of an integrated written expression assessment, we identify two major components. First, we establish the procedures for conducting the assessment, following a standardized format. Second, we develop scoring systems to provide an efficient and sensitive outcome for making wide-range educational decisions.

Procedures. First and foremost, this written expression assessment required a standardized measure of writing. Although both teachers had their students engage in writing activities in the classroom, the formats were so different that no comparisons could be made between them. One teacher had students write in a journal every day, relating some personal reaction to an event at school, while the other teacher gave students the opportunity to write some of the spelling words within a compositional context, providing prompts and help in incorporating the words into sentences and stories. Therefore, the following procedures were agreed upon, and the two teachers group-administered a writing measure on the same day.

> Today I want you to write a story. I am going to read a sentence to you first, and then I want you to compose a short story about what happens. You will have 1 minute to think about the story you will write, and then you will have 3 minutes to write it. If you do not know how to spell a word, spell it the best you can. When I say "go" begin writing. Please do not copy the words at the top of the page, but start your story right from there.

Each student was given a lined sheet of paper, and when the teacher said "Begin writing," the students started constructing stories. At the end of 3 minutes, the students were told to stop writing, and all stories were collected. Later in the day, the two teachers and two parent volunteers worked to establish the important scoring rules.

Scoring. All compositions were scored subjectively and then objectively. The primary reason for this order was that the objective assessments were likely to result in compositions with many marks, which could either distract or influence the subjective judgments. Because the writing was extremely brief, specific analytic and primary-trait evaluation strategies were ruled out; the compositions were subjectively and holistically evaluated, using range finders established from the papers themselves. A scale was established with 5 intervals, and after sorting through all compositions from the 65 students, the scorers selected 10 papers as representative of values on the scale (1 - *lowest* to 5 - *highest*). Four copies of the same randomly selected compositions were then made, a score was assigned to them, and scorers compared their results. With the exception of a slight disagreement on three papers in the middle of the scale, which were eventually reassigned, the scores seemed to be in agreement. The remaining papers were then assigned a score by each person. The final score for each student was the average of the middle two scores assigned from the judges, with the absolute highest and lowest judges' scores thrown out. The teachers were most interested in the students with the lowest value (1) on the scale.

The compositions were then scored for the number of words written. A few of the papers with extremely bad handwriting were scored by all four judges to ascertain agreement. The remainder of the 60 papers were divided and scored by only one person. All scores from this objective scoring were graphed using a box plot like that displayed in Figure 9.5 and the lowest students were identified. Actually, the data displayed in Figure 9.5 is from approximately 65 fourth-grade students with writing samples collected exactly as described and scored according to all three measures: words written, words spelled correctly, and words in correct sequence.

All students below the 25th percentile (the bottom of the box) were identified, and their subjective judgments were considered. Most of these students had been judged low on the holistic comparison with their peers. A few students who had been judged low were not in this group, and a few students with middle-range scores on the subjective judgments were also in this group. A new group of students was identified upon which to conduct a more elaborate scoring system: correct word sequences. This group was comprised of those students with both low subjective evaluations and low word counts and those students with low subjective evaluations but not low word counts; students who had received middle or high subjective evaluations were excluded from any further analyses.

This second round of evaluation scored correct word sequences using syntax, spelling, punctuation, and capitalization. Four copies of three compositions were made, and the judges scored them independently and compared their results. Disagreements were talked out, and a final score was established for them; the remaining seven compositions were then distributed among the four judges. The scores established for these students were used to determine who was writing few words in correct sequence and establish for them a baseline level with which to compare future levels. A total of four students were identified with very low performance levels on this subsequent measure. Throughout the year, all students were assessed weekly on a written expression task like that given in the beginning of the year. Although all compositions were collected and scanned, not all compositions were scored with elaborations like the original system. However, the four students initially identified with low subjective evaluations, low word production, and few words in correct sequence were systematically monitored, using correct word sequences. Indeed, their performance steadily

FIGURE 9.5
Example of a box plot of
written expression for 65
fourth-grade students

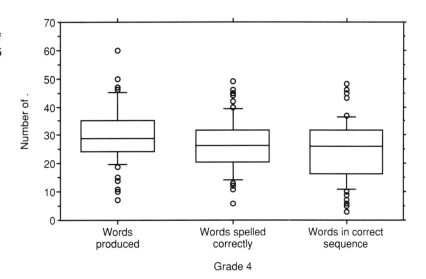

improved with the delivery of systematic instruction and supplemental practice, as indicated by the graph in Figure 9.6.

Several important issues underly this integrated assessment. First, teachers need to consider the cost of the assessment in relation to the gain in information. At a survey level, they may not need to assess all students in great depth. Second, both subjective and objective evaluations should be used, providing a mea-

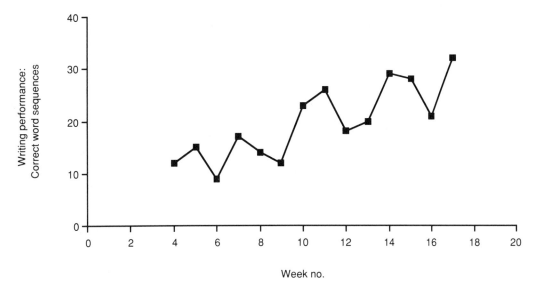

FIGURE 9.6
Exemplary graph of a student's improvement in writing words in
correct sequence

surement net in which contradictions and exceptions can be identified and resolved both logically and empirically. Third, decision making is integrated at several levels, with norm-referenced data used to initiate collection of more specific-level, criterion-referenced data, which is also used to extend evaluation into more individual-referenced evaluations. This system allows assessment to begin and end with classroom-relevant tasks, yet it is efficient enough to actually complete.

CHAPTER SUMMARY

Written expression is a complex skill that is difficult to assess and may be even more difficult to teach. Common sense indicates that it is intricately intertwined with other areas in language arts: spelling, reading, and speaking. Until the past 20 years, most assessments were informal and indirect. However, with the recent surge of interest in testing, new formats have been developed. As a consequence, teachers must be aware of many different issues. They must know, for example, about the controversy between direct and indirect measures and the advantages and disadvantages of each type. Direct assessment in which students actually write, is virtually always preferred to indirect assessments, in which, students do not write, but respond to syntactical and grammatical cues. However, direct assessments must be done with reliability and validity, often a difficult-to-accomplish objective.

Once we resolve these general issues, the actual task of constructing assessment formats begins. We must devise procedures to generate writing to score compositions. Both issues, the type of stimulus used to generate writing and the nature of the writing that is generated, are obviously highly related to each other. The stimuli used to generate writing affect the manner in which it is scored and interpreted. Emphasizing direct assessment, we presented three strategies for prompting writing: story starters, topic sentences, and pictures. We also identified three types of writing: (a) narrative, which focuses on the writer's perspective, (b) expository, which focuses on the subject matter, and (c) persuasive, which focuses on the audience. Once compositions have been generated, we can use two broad scoring strategies: subjective and objective. Because writing is usually designed to have an impact on the reader, subjective judgments are a major element in any evaluation; however, they should be made in a systematic manner. We described three specific techniques, along with their advantages and disadvantages, and provided an example. Holistic evaluation draws from general impressions, analytical evaluation is multifaceted, and primary-trait evaluation focuses on the type of discourse and audience.

All subjective evaluations are limited, however, in their utility for making many educational decisions. Therefore, we also described objective scoring systems. These measures are likely to be more sensitive to the effects of instruction and growth than the subjective measures. Several specific, objectively defined and scored indices were presented, including (a) number of words, (b) syntactical maturity, (c) vocabulary words, (d) conventions, and (e) combinations of these indices. Both the descriptions of the subjective and objective scoring systems included examples from a classroom. However, only the last case, organized as part of the integrated assessment, described the impact of the evaluation method on data for decision making.

CHAPTER 10

Math Assessment

I magine that you lack basic mathematical proficiency. You are able to count, print numbers, and understand something about adding and subtracting, but you cannot handle everyday events such as doubling a recipe, balancing a checkbook, or other simple acts predicated on the manipulation of numbers within lawful relationships. Consider the following conversation with a 6-year-old.

Q: If I bought a pack of gum for 5 cents and macaroni for $1, how much did I spend?

A: $1.05.

Q: If I gave the clerk $5, how much money would I get back?

A: 5 cents.

Q: If Portland is 115 miles from Eugene and Grants Pass is 135 miles from Eugene, which city is farthest from Eugene?

A: Grants Pass.

Q: If I drove 60 miles per hour to each city, which trip would take less time?

A: Grants Pass.

Q: If I had 15 crayons and wanted to give them to five friends, so each had the same number of crayons, how many would each friend receive?

A: I don't know. If you had three friends, each one would get five crayons. (She then drew five people, gave each one two, added them up to get 10, and then gave them one more to get up to 15). Three.

Q: Which is longer, 50 minutes or 3 feet?

A: 3 feet.

This child clearly had some math skills, and may even have been quite proficient given her age. But many math concepts were missing. In particular, units of measurement were not meaningful concepts to her, and relationships among these units were even more abstract.

The child probably will learn much about math and become proficient enough over the years to engage in an independent life. Throughout her schooling, she will be presented with lawful relationships based on mathematical concepts and principles. This chapter begins with a review of these concepts and principles before covering more specific issues of assessment.

The American public has been barraged with reports on students' basic skills. Performance reportedly is lower now than it was 5 or 10 years ago: today's students are supposedly less capable problem solvers than those of the Sputnik era, and schools are perceived as less demanding in attaining adequate levels of achievement. Concurrent with declining scores on standardized achievement tests and college entrance exams, there is heightened awareness of the need for remedial and compensatory programs. As a result, debates have evolved about which skills should be taught, how to teach them, and the procedures for evaluating their attainment (Cheek & Castle, 1981).

The need for greater efforts in teaching higher-level mathematical concepts is reflected in a report by the National Assessment of Educational Progress (NAEP), which gathered information on the educational achievement of 9-, 13-, and 17-year-old students across the country in 1972–73, 1977–78, 1981–82, and 1987–88.

It appears that American schools have been reasonably successful in teaching students to perform routine computational and measurement skills, and to answer questions assessing superficial knowledge about numbers and geometry. It is encouraging to note positive change on items assessing knowledge and skills not only in numerical computation, but also in geometry and measurement. On the other hand, it appears from the low percentage of success on some items that schools have thus far taught only a small percentage of students how to analyze mathematical problems or apply mathematics to nonroutine situations. (National Assessment of Educational Progress, 1983, p. 2)

NAEP's results indicate that schools are doing a good job in teaching mathematical topics such as figure recognition and fairly low-level cognitive tasks such as routine computation. Yet recent changes in educational policy emphasize the importance of mathematical problem solving: (a) Test developers need to include items that reflect higher-level objectives and emphasize the comprehension of mathematical concepts and the application of knowledge and skills to solve mathematical problems in both routine and nonroutine situations, and (b) procedures for solving problems must incorporate modern technologies, such as calculators and computers, and emphasize underlying concepts and skills in geometry and measurement.

CHAPTER OBJECTIVES

The purpose of this chapter is to help you develop a knowledge and skill base so you can teach and/or assess various levels of mathematics effectively. By the end of this chapter, you will

- Know that mathematics is systematically composed of specific content domains.
- Apply these content domains in a generally hierarchical fashion to understand instruction, curriculum, and assessment.
- Apply a model of mathematics assessment that directs decision making.
- Incorporate a wide range of test item types that address levels of abstraction, intellectual operations, and response formats.

- Focus assessment on the two critical learning products: sentence solving and problem solving.
- Skillfully apply different scoring systems to best reflect student performance and learning.
- Analytically apply different patterns of errors to establish potentially appropriate instructional programs.
- Establish an integrated assessment system tying educational decisions together.

KEY VOCABULARY

Some of the terminology presented in this chapter is new because it is specific to mathematics, and some should be familiar by now. The first new term is *content taxonomy*, which reflects our interest in systematically sampling test items from various domains. In mathematics, seven domains are available; selection among them depends upon the purpose of instruction or assessment. The field is premised upon *sets*, which are aggregations of similar and different objects or concepts. Mathematics uses a variety of *symbols,* or graphic representations, most often including *numbers and notations*. Four basic *operations*—addition, subtraction, multiplication, and division—are used, and their relationship to each other is defined according to specific *properties*. *Algorithms*, which are rules for executing procedures, are used in all mathematical problem solving. All of these content domains converge in applications of *sentence solving*, which is confined to a mathematical context, and *problem solving*, which incorporates a social context. These last two applications represent the products of learning, which we can assay through *selection* or *production* responses, the latter of which are generated by students in the sentence and problem solving processes. The seven domains can be considered at three *levels of abstraction* (as facts, concepts, or principles) and in relation to six *intellectual operations* (reiteration, summarization, illustration, prediction, evaluation, and application). With production responses, we must address two issues: (a) *scoring* the response and (b) *analyzing errors*. Either answers or digits within problems and answers can be scored to obtain the most efficient and sensitive metric for scaling performance; a variety of analytical systems is available to ascertain faulty algorithms. Finally, an *integrated assessment* provides an example of the systematic decision making process and several interpretive strategies.

DEFINITIONS OF SKILLS TO ASSESS IN MATHEMATICS

To understand the implications of the NAEP results and other research findings, we must establish definitions of mathematical knowledge and skill and create assessment domains. For example, the NAEP assessments (1983) contain items developed by panels of educators, scholars, and parents to measure students' attitudes toward mathematics and their abilities in various content areas: numbers and numeration; variables and relationships, geometry (size, shape, and position); measurement; probability and statistics; graphs and tables; and technology, which includes the use of calculators and computers. Additionally, four levels of the cognitive process (Bloom, et al., 1956) are addressed: knowledge, skills, understanding, and application.

A general definition of mathematics has been developed by a wide range of educators who included elementary, middle, and high-school teachers and academicians. It contains 12 basic skills (Denmark & Kepner, 1980):

1. Elementary computation (skills normally introduced in Grades 1–6)
2. Advanced Computation (skills normally introduced in Grades 5–8)
3. Applications (use of mathematics in problem solving)
4. Estimation (giving "ball park" answers)
5. Measurement (using English and metric systems, perimeters, areas, volume)
6. Algebra (applying formulas, solving equations, simplifying expressions)
7. Understanding (describing rationale and logic for solutions/procedures)
8. Geometry (construct shapes, prove theorems)
9. Probability and statistics (interpret charts and graphs, make predictions)
10. New math (apply set language, read/write non-base-10 numerals)
11. Calculator use (to solve computation problems)
12. Mathematics appreciation (incorporate math into a larger social context)

We could use these domains to structure our perspective on assessment, except that certain problems are embedded within them: What is elementary versus advanced? How integrated are measurement and geometry? How are computational skills considered within problem solving? Therefore, this chapter defines another domain definition on the basis of the content taxonomy described in the following section, which is based on three assumptions:

1. Mathematical principles and conventions are lawful and generally hierarchical; some content must be learned before other content. For example, our basic number system is ordered from elementary numbers (counting) to very abstract and complex numbers (real); learning about more complex numbers is based on mastery of more elementary numbers.

2. Mathematical operations apply in two dimensions: (a) horizontal—the same operations and algorithms apply to different contents and in different contexts and (b) vertical—the same operations and algorithms apply to different number types. These dimensions influence the complexity of any mathematical sentence or problem.
3. Mathematical learning is developmentally linked: The applicability of content is limited by the ages for which instruction and assessment are structured.

We predicate item development and analysis upon these three assumptions. Given absolute lawfulness, clear domains, and age-appropriateness, we can scrutinize all items to ensure measurement of learning is reliable and valid.

Content Taxonomy

This chapter divides mathematics into seven domains on the basis of a **content taxonomy** adapted from Glennon and Wilson (1972). Six of the domains function by manipulation of four number types. All seven domains and four number types are presented in Figure 10.1.

At its most basic level, mathematics is premised upon the first domain, **sets,** which are objects within and across groups that possess commonalities. Three subdomains of sets focus on (a) fundamental concepts and notations, (b) operations available for application to these concepts, and (c) properties and laws that govern these operations. For example, the concept of comparing two sets using one-to-one correspondence (a) may involve their union (b), which defines objects belonging to either or both sets (c).

The other six domains are based upon manipulation of number **(symbol)** types, which are defined in an increasingly comprehensive manner. At the lowest level is counting, which is limited to whole positive numbers. The next

most encompassing number type is integers, which we can express with positive or negative values. The third level utilizes rational numbers, which we can express as fractions or decimals. These are a subset of real numbers, those with infinite decimals that repeat (rational numbers) or do not repeat (irrational numbers). As Figure 10.1 shows, each type is a subset of the next.

Generally, students learn these number types at several levels. First, they must learn number concepts and notation systems, including the basic meanings of numbers as one-to-one correspondences and how to express or manipulate them. Number concepts and notational systems also are premised on place value and/or position (i.e., binary expression of numbers). Then students learn the operations of addition, subtraction, multiplication, and division in reference to this **number and notation system,** which are governed by specific properties. For example, multiplication of counting numbers is associative: If a, b, and c are counting numbers, then $(a \times b) \times c = a \times (b \times c)$. However, multiplication distributes over addition: If a, b, and c are counting numbers, then $a \times (b + c) = (a \times b) + (a \times c)$ and $(a + b) \times c = (a \times c) + (b \times c)$.

Number concepts and notation systems, operations, and properties define principles and **algorithms** (rule-governed procedures), in which symbols and numbers are interrelated in a lawful manner via specific operations and properties. Algorithms express lawful relationships within a variety of contexts: the basic operations, algebra, geometry, trigonometry, and calculus.

The last two levels in the taxonomy define the social applications within which the learning products are expressed. **Sentence solving** expresses mathematical symbols in a problem form, which may be as simple as basic computation skills (e.g., $1 + 3 = \underline{\quad}$) or as complex as using algorithms to solve novel problems

FIGURE 10.1
Mathematics content tax-
onomy: Seven domains
and four number types

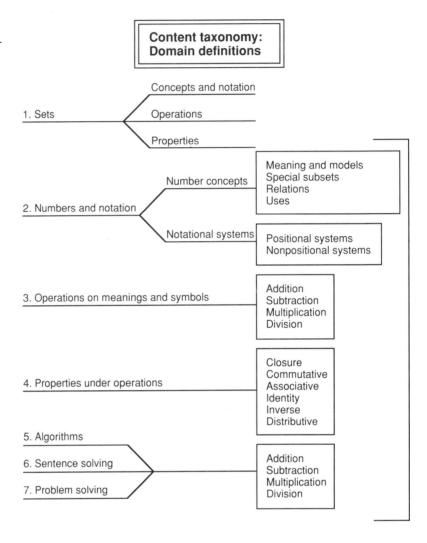

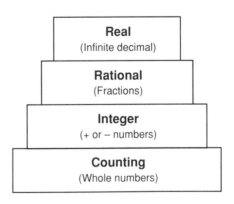

(e.g., Given that the area of a circle equals 9π, what is the area of a square that surrounds and encompasses the circle). **Problem solving** gives a social context to a problem that must be translated into a sentence solution (e.g., If a bag of chicken pellets can feed 18 chickens for 54 days, how much longer will it last if only 12 chickens need to be fed?).

This taxonomy is *generally hierarchical* (Glennon & Wilson, 1972), which means that students need familiarity and minimal proficiency with earlier content areas before they can become similarly proficient in later content areas. However, the exact level of proficiency is not clear, so an absolute mastery sequence may be inappropriate. Understanding, knowledge, and skill must begin with set content, which establishes the base from which the other six content areas are derived. Students must then learn different number types: Counting numbers are learned before integers, understanding of integers and skill in their use must precede work with rational numbers, and real numbers. These subsequent areas (Domains 2–7) are thus sequential, with knowledge, understanding, and skill needed in the following order: number/notation system, operations, properties, algorithms, sentence solving, and problem solving. For example, it is unlikely that students could solve the preceding problem about the area of the square without knowledge of real numbers (π), or that they could solve the story problem about chickens without knowledge of rational numbers. Furthermore, the problem involving the area of a square requires the application of an algorithm, while the story problem requires setting up the problem and then applying an algorithm. Both necessitate knowledge of certain operations and the properties that govern them.

Mathematics is also hierarchical in that operations involving many symbols, properties, and algorithms apply equally across the different number types. Figure 10.2 reveals a sequential "spiral": many topics are taught at several grade levels but with differing degrees of complexity. For example, as early as first grade, students are introduced to fractions, which typically are limited to pictures that have been sectioned off to form geometric figures (e.g., halves, thirds, or quarters). Consideration of fractions is continually developed until about sixth grade, when the concept of rational numbers is introduced. At this time, such treatment becomes complex and detailed, and includes all operations ($+$, $-$, $\times$, $\div$).

MODEL OF ASSESSMENT

To utilize the seven-domain taxonomy, we need a model of assessment to define the manner in which students demonstrate knowledge and skills on specific tasks. The next steps in creating a mathematics measure are to (a) specify *which* items will be included and *how* they will appear (i.e., the response they will generate), (b) determine the scoring system to be applied, assuming students generate production responses, and (c) consider how to interpret responses, using a variety of analytic systems.

The next three sections present strategies for creating domains and formatting items. The first section presents various levels of abstraction and intellectual operation, using the taxonomy of content shown in Figure 10.1. Given a certain content, level of abstraction, and intellectual operation, we can then configure either selection or production responses. The choice between these two responses depends primarily upon the need for diagnostic and process information, which require production responses. Selection responses provide no diagnostic information about *how* or *why* students solve problems in any particular manner. Therefore, we give primary consideration to production responses, in keeping with our focus on direct assessment and critical effects.

Grade 1
>   Numbers to 10
>   Addition and subtraction facts to 6
>   Addition and subtraction facts to 8
>   Addition and subtraction facts to 10
>   Place value to 100
>   Time and money
>   Addition and subtraction facts to 12
>   Geometry and fractions
>   Addition/subtraction of 2-digit numbers
>   Measurement
>   Addition/subtraction facts to 18

Grade 2
>   Addition and subtraction facts to 10
>   Place value to 100
>   Addition and subtraction facts to 14
>   Addition and subtraction facts to 18
>   Place value to 1,000
>   Time and money
>   Addition of 2-digit numbers
>   Subtraction of 2-digit numbers
>   Geometry and fractions
>   Measurement
>   Addition/subtraction of 3-digit numbers
>   Multiplication

Grade 3
>   Addition and subtraction facts
>   Numeration and place value
>   Addition
>   Subtraction
>   Time and money
>   Multiplication facts
>   Division facts
>   Measurement
>   Multiplication facts
>   Division
>   Fractions and decimals
>   Geometry

Grade 4
>   Addition and subtraction facts
>   Numeration
>   Addition and subtraction
>   Multiplication and division facts
>   Graphing
>   Multiplying by 1-digit numbers
>   Dividing by 1-digit numbers
>   Measurement
>   Fractions and mixed numbers
>   Multiplying by 2-digit numbers
>   Dividing by 2-digit numbers
>   Decimals
>   Geometry

Grade 5
>   Numeration
>   Addition and subtraction
>   Multiplication
>   Dividing by 1-digit numbers
>   Dividing by 2-digit numbers
>   Graphing
>   Number theory and fractions
>   Addition and subtraction of fractions
>   Multiplication and division of fractions
>   Measurement
>   Addition and subtraction of decimals
>   Multiplication and division of decimals
>   Geometry
>   Ratio and percent

Grade 6
>   Numeration
>   Addition and subtraction
>   Multiplication
>   Division
>   Graphing
>   Number theory and fractions
>   Addition and subtraction of fractions
>   Multiplication and division of fractions
>   Addition and subtraction of decimals
>   Multiplication and division of decimals
>   Measurement
>   Geometry
>   Ratio and percent
>   Integers

Grade 7
>   Addition /subtraction of whole numbers
>   Multiplication/division of whole numbers
>   Equations
>   Addition and subtraction of decimals
>   Multiplication and division of decimals
>   Number theory
>   Addition and subtraction of fractions
>   Multiplication and division of fractions
>   Ratio and proportion
>   Percent
>   Measurement
>   Geometry
>   Perimeter, area, and volume
>   Probability and statistics
>   Integers

Grade 8
>   Whole numbers and operations
>   Decimals
>   Number theory
>   Fractions
>   Solving equations
>   Geometry
>   Ratio
>   Percent
>   Measurement
>   Perimeter, area, and volume
>   Integers
>   Rational numbers
>   Probability and statistics
>   Real numbers and the coordinate plane
>   Right triangles, similarity, trigonometry

FIGURE 10.2
Scope-sequence for Harcourt Brace Jovanovich (Abbott & Wells, 1985)

The second section applies different scoring systems to sentence and problem solving. The third section presents error-analysis techniques for both sentence and problem solving. Figure 10.3 summarizes the model.

LEVEL OF ABSTRACTION AND INTELLECTUAL OPERATION

Chapters 2 and 3 presented a taxonomy with three types of content format (facts, concepts, and principles, redefined in this chapter as lev-

els of abstractions to avoid confusion with the seven domains, which are to be viewed as content domains in Figure 10.1) and six intellectual operations: reiteration, summarization, illustration, prediction, evaluation, and application (Roid & Haladyna, 1982). To review, all intellectual operations are not appropriate for each level of abstraction. Facts are applicable only to reiteration and summarization; concepts are applicable to these two operations and also to illustration and prediction; and principles can be assessed with respect to all six intellectual operations.

FIGURE 10.3
Model depicting dimensions of mathematics assessment

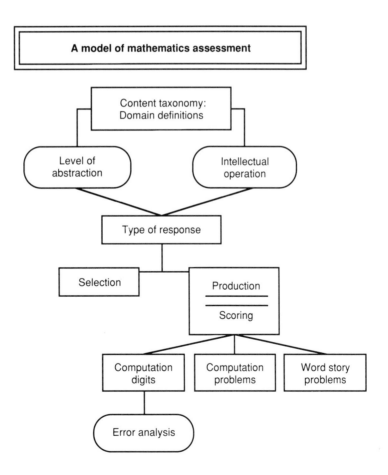

Furthermore, not all levels of abstraction are applicable to the various content domains. Other than the two most basic content areas, sets and number/numeration, principles dominate this matrix. As Figure 10.4 shows, mathematics is primarily concerned with relationships, and lawful ones at that. Indeed, most instruction and assessment focus on the last two content dimensions, *sentence* and *problem solving*. All other instruction and assessment are generally expressed in the application of mathematical principles for solving either single (sentence) problems or complex problems couched in a social context.

Facts

Fundamentally, mathematics is premised upon basic facts:

- "A set is a collection of objects of any sort" (Kelley & Richert, 1970, p. 4).
- "Each counting number has precisely one decimal name" (Kelley & Richert, 1970, p. 33).
- "An operation is a function whose domain is a set of ordered pairs" (Kelley & Richert, 1970, p. 258).

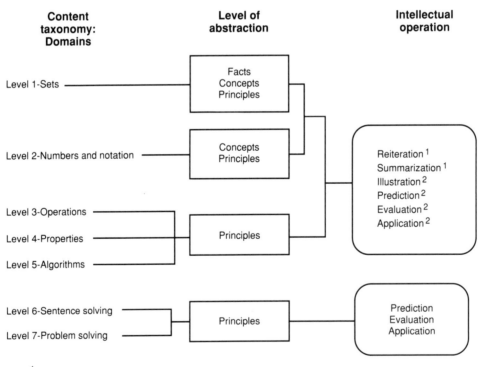

FIGURE 10.4
Matrix of content, level of abstraction, and intellectual operation for mathematics item development

Facts can be applied only to the first two levels of the content taxonomy (sets and number/notation systems) that appears in Figure 10.1; the remaining domain levels are limited to principles only. Mathematics actually has few facts as we have defined them, since it fundamentally involves the "study or development of relationships, regularities, structures, or organizational schemata . . ." (Reid & Hresko, 1981a, p. 292). An association between names, events, and places should not be confused with *basic math facts*, which reflect a principle of an operation applied to counting numbers; they represent statements based upon principles of counting and a base-10 numeric system. Because we consider basic math facts as principles, they are not covered here.

Concepts

Mathematics also is composed of concepts, which are any grouping of objects that share an attribute or characteristic. In fact, set theory is premised upon concepts, since it provides the basic logic concerning how objects are the same or different (belong to a common or separate set). For example, the number types defined above (counting, integer, rational, and real numbers) reflect the concept *proper subsets*. Both sets and concepts are closely related and are defined with the same operations (e.g., union, intersection, disjunction, and difference). Because of its integral relationship with sets, this level of abstraction is very important with regard to sets. Note also that we apply concepts primarily within the first two levels of content shown in Figure 10.1.

Principles

Principles, or lawful relationships among objects or events, are the most important content area in mathematics. They can be as fundamental as the following:

- "If a product of two counting numbers is divisible by a prime, then at least one of the two numbers is divisible by the prime" (Kelley & Richert, 1970, p. 131).
- "If r, s, t, and u are rational numbers, such that $r > s$ and $t > u$, then $r + t > s + u$" (Kelley & Richert, 1970, p. 201).

Principles can be commonplace as well:

- $2 + 7 = 9$
- $10\% \times \$500 = \$50$

Principles can be assessed in all seven content domains, but they are important only in the last two. Additionally, a specific kind of principle, *procedures*, is used within these two content domains. Procedures involve a sequence of activities to solve problems, gather information, or achieve a goal (adapted from Roid & Haladyna, 1982). Mathematical procedures may be executed in fixed or branching formats (Anderson & Liu, 1980). In a fixed format, all activities follow a specified order (e.g. $5 \times (2 + 3) = (5 \times 2) + (5 \times 3) = 10 + 15 = 25$); in a branching format, prior activities determine later ones (e.g., most two-step word story problems).

We can place most mathematics problems in one of two categories of intellectual operations: prediction or application. Prediction is the reverse of application. It involves using known information and, making a prediction based on an algorithm. Application requires taking the outcome and establishing the initial conditions necessary for that outcome. Evaluation items can be used but occur rarely in mathematics assessment. They involve selection or generation of the criteria necessary for attaining a solution.

Prediction is more common than application; such problems provide all information—only the answer is missing. An example of a sentence problem using prediction follows:

$$12 + 17 = \underline{\hphantom{XXX}}$$

Here is an example of the same problem expressed as an application item:

$$12 + \underline{\hphantom{XXX}} = 29$$

In many math texts, this particular problem is known as a *missing addends* problem type. Interestingly, it is a more difficult problem than $12 + 17 = \underline{\hphantom{XXX}}$. In the 1977 NAEP Mathematics Tests, 76% of the 9-year olds correctly answered the former problem type (prediction), while only 63% of these same 9-year-olds correctly answered the second problem type (application). The format for expressing mathematics problems makes an important difference in the problem difficulty, and hence in the interpretations that we can make from the assessment.

Before we give specific examples of the intellectual operations for the various content areas, it is important to note that all assessment items require either a selection or production response (see Figure 10.2). The examples below alternate between these two formats, although later in the chapter, we emphasize production responses exclusively in considering different scoring systems and conducting specific error analyses.

Level 1—Sets

Facts. At the most basic level of the content taxonomy in Figure 10.1 are sets, which provide the basic level for discussing mathematics. Consider the following.

- A 1–1 (one-to-one) correspondence between two sets is a precise pairing of the members of the first set with the members of the second set.

To assess students' knowledge of this fact, they could be asked to reiterate the statement, repeating it exactly, or to summarize it, using a selection or response format.

Concepts. We could also have students learn concepts about sets. For example, we could test whether students understand the following concept, requiring a selection or production response.

- To be a subset, all members of one set also must be members of another set.
- A set can be a proper subset of another set, provided that every member is also a member of this other set and that at least one member of this other set is not a member of the first set.

Furthermore, we could ask students to engage in any of the six intellectual operations on this concept: reiteration, summarization, illustration, prediction, evaluation, or application. Reiteration of this example would call for students to select or produce the statements exactly as they appear; summarization calls for paraphrasing the statements, illustration items involve the use of a previously unseen example. An example follows:

- Illustrate a proper subset given two sets of birds: (a) ducks (pintails, mallards, and canvasbacks) and (b) waterfowl (swans, shearwaters, and ducks).

For prediction items, students employ a rule to predict changes, as in the following. An example:

- If we add eiders to the original set of ducks, would we still be able to create a proper subset?

An evaluation item would require students to use the criteria for defining a proper subset and make a judgment. For example:

- We have two sets of trees. Set 1 is composed of conifers with flat needles: balsam fir, eastern hemlock, and American yew. Set 2 is conifers with four-sided needles: red spruce, black spruce, and Norway spruce. Determine whether either set is a proper subset of Set 3: cone-bearing, needle-leaved plants with evergreen leaves throughout the year.

     Set 1 is a proper subset of Set 3   T   F
     Set 2 is a proper subset of Set 3   T   F

An application item requires students to describe or apply the original conditions needed for an outcome to occur. For example:

- I have classified the following wildflowers into 2 sets. What characteristics should I apply to assign them as a proper subset of Set 3: daisy family?

     Set 1: Goldenrods: tall, sweet, late, early, bog
     Set 2: Sunflowers: ox-eye, western, hairy, showy, woodland
     Set 3: _____ , _____ , _____ , _____

Principles. Students could be required to learn principles underlying the notation system for sets and to use either selection or production responses to demonstrate their understanding. For example, the following principle might form the basis for both instruction and assessment:

- If two sets have the same number of members, then they must match; conversely, if two sets match, they must have the same number of members.

We can use all six intellectual operations to measure understanding of this principle. Reiteration and summarization are self-explanatory by this point. Following are examples of the remaining intellectual operations that pres-

ent a basic sentence stem is presented. We can frame each example as a selection or production problem.

- Divide your class into two sets, boys and girls, and count the number of students in each set. (Illustration)
- If Jimmy were given 3 quarters and sent to the store to buy candy bars costing $.25 each, would he have two matching sets? (Prediction)
- There are two groups of students: John, Mary, and Susan in Group 1 and Bill, Sam, and Karen in Group 2. Do these two groups represent matching finite sets? (Evaluation)
- Mrs. Hambone grouped students based on the number of pencils they have. Jim received 5, Bill received 3, Jane received 7, Jerry received 3, and Katie received 5. Group the students into matching sets based on the number of pencils they have received. (Application)

Level 2—Number or Notation Systems

At Level 2 of the content taxonomy, facts and concepts are applicable. For example, mathematics makes use of many numbers and symbols, each of which conveys meaning, and of many facts that use these numbers and symbols. Principles or if-then relationships, although possible, are not appropriate with this domain, because they imply operations, the next domain level of the taxonomy. The best example of principles within number and notation systems are basic math facts.

Facts
- The counting number 5 represents a specific number of objects.
- Exponentiation is expressed with a base number and an exponent, signified by a superscript expressing the number of times the

base number is multiplied by itself: $10^5 =$ 10 × 10 × 10 × 10 × 10 = 100,000
- There are an infinite number of prime numbers.

We can assess all of these facts by having students reiterate or summarize information, using a selection or production response.

- Count the number of stars below and write the number on the blank to the right:

  ⋆ ⋆ ⋆ ⋆ ⋆ _____
- Write, in numbers, the following amount: 10 to the fifth: _____
- Circle all prime numbers appearing in the sequence below:

  3   12   13   23   45

Concepts. Many basic facts of our number and notation system may also be considered concepts, which we can assess using reiteration, summarization, illustration, or prediction evaluation or application. Concepts of numbers and or polygons are described in the following examples:

- There are four types of numbers: counting (positive whole numbers), integer (positive or negative whole numbers), rational (positive or negative fractional numbers), and real (fractional numbers with either repeating or nonrepeating decimals).
- A polygon is a closed figure in a plane comprised of line segments that meet at their endpoints.

We could teach students these concepts and then assess their learning by asking them to reiterate verbatim the information from the lesson, summarize this information, illustrate the concept, predict something based on the information, evaluate and make judgments, or establish conditions given certain outcomes. The

first two tasks are obvious; examples of illustration and prediction items follow.

- Match each number type listed on the left with an example listed on the right by drawing a line connecting them: (Illustration)

Number Type	Example
Integer	12.3
Counting	3
Rational	3.141596 . . . (π)
Real	−13

- Circle the irregular polygon. (Illustration)

- Place the next consecutive prime numbers in the blanks below. (Prediction)

  1   3   5   7   __   __   __

Evaluation and application tasks are also possible, though infrequently used, with number and notation systems. Evaluation items would simply present different numbers and notations and require a judgment using some criteria (which may also be required in the item). For example, the following problem is an evaluation item for odd and even counting numbers:

- Circle all the following odd numbers that are greater than 4.

  1   7   3   2   9

- Are the following expressions the same or different? Circle all those that are the same.

  $\frac{64}{100}$ .64   .064   6400

These items require the examinee to make a judgment about number or notation conventions. The focus is on odd numbers (a concept) and greater or less than (a principle) in the first problem and notation systems in the second problem.

An application item for number or notation systems would include the following:

- If a box with five parts has 60 percent of its parts shaded, what is the proportion of boxes that need to be shaded? Shade in the number of boxes below.

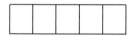

- If we wanted to solve the following problem, which operation would we use?

$$\frac{2}{3} \quad \square \quad 6 = 4$$

Both problems have an outcome and require the examinee to set the conditions needed to attain it; They also focus on number or notation systems (and implicitly use principles in their level of abstraction).

Level 3—Operations

Four operations are available for manipulation within the mathematical symbol system: addition, subtraction, multiplication, and division. At the base of the mathematical system, a set of finite facts is used as building blocks upon which to establish more complex problems. With a base-10 number system, the basic math facts include every number from 0 to 9 used in one of four mathematical operations. With addition, these facts extend from $0 + 0 = 0$ to $9 + 9 = 18$; in subtraction, the range is similar: from $0 - 0 = 0$ to $18 - 9 = 9$. In multiplication and division, the problems extend to include 81 as the largest number (9×9).

But we need not be confined to operations on whole or counting numbers. We can ma-

nipulate all numbers described in Figure 10.1 with these four operations; furthermore, we can manipulate many specialized symbols and notations (i.e., π, letters representing specific units like height, depth, width, and arbitrary units).

Following are several examples of operations expressed as principles, the only applicable intellectual operation for this content domain.

- If m is an integer, $m + -m = 0$, or the sum of a number and its opposite is zero.
- If p and q are counting numbers, and $p \geq q$, $p - q$ is the solution to _____ $+ q = p$.
- If r and s are two nonzero rational numbers, the reciprocal of their product is the product of their reciprocals: $(r \times s)^{-1} = r^{-1} \times s^{-1}$.

We can use all six intellectual operations to assess understanding of the principles of mathematical operations. Examples of illustration, prediction, evaluation, and application follow.

- For two nonzero rational numbers, give an example of what is meant by this statement: The reciprocal of their product is the product of their reciprocals. (Illustration)
- Calculate the sum of $-5 + 5$. (Prediction)
- Is the following statement true? If $7 - 5 > m - 1$, $m < 2$. (Evaluation)
- $236 -$ _____ $= 166$ (application)

Level 4—Properties

All operations are governed by specific **properties**, such as association, commutation, and distribution. These properties dictate how numbers are manipulated with the specific operations. For example, with all operations applied to two numbers, the associative property dictates that the order in which numbers are applied to an operation is unimportant (i.e., $1 + 2 = 2 + 1$). But when the operations are applied to more than two numbers, the order in which the numbers are grouped is important for some operations, as shown in the following examples. Principles are the only level of abstraction that apply to properties.

- The associative property applies to all numbers and all addition and multiplication operations: $1 + 3 = 3 + 1$; $1 \times 3 = 3 \times 1$. This same property does not apply to subtraction or division: $1 - 3 \neq 3 - 1$; $3 \div 5 \neq 5 \div 3$.
- Multiplication of integers distributes over addition and subtraction: $p \times (q - r) = (p \times q) - (p \times r)$ and $(p - q) \times r = (p \times r) - (q \times r)$.

Addition or subtraction of integers does not distribute over multiplication:

- $5 + (3 \times 2) \neq (5 + 3) \times 2$

Only illustration prediction, evaluation, and application can be used to assay understanding of mathematical properties. We can ask students to predict, evaluate, or apply answers in solving these problem types:

- Give an example of the associative property in addition (illustration).
- $(2 + 5) \times 3 = $ _____ (Prediction)
- Is $(5 - 1) \times 3 = 5 - (1 \times 3)$? (Evaluation)
- (_____ $+ 10) \times 3 = 39$ (Application)

Level 5—Algorithms

Algorithms are procedures or rules for deriving solutions, so only illustration prediction, evaluation, and application are appropriate in this level. For example, we could use the following algorithm to form a problem about parallel lines:

- The algorithm for parallel lines dictates that when they are intersected by a transversal, alternate interior and corresponding angles

are equal and interior angles on the same side of the transversal are supplementary.

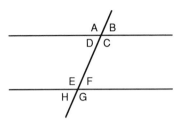

D = F, C = E
A = E, B = F, C = G, D = H
C + F = 180 degrees
D + E = 180 degrees

The problem could be as follows:

- Illustrate the relationship between angles with two non-parallel lines.
- If Angle B is 60°, how many degrees is Angle H? _____ (Prediction)

A commonly known algorithm is the Pythagorean theorem:

- The square of the length of the hypotenuse is equal to the sum of the squares of the lengths of the legs.

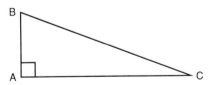

A possible problem follows:

- If $AB = 10$, $AC = 15$, then $BC = $ _____
  (a) 18.02　(b) 325　(c) 115　(d) 225
  (Prediction)

Using the formula $(BC)^2 = (AB)^2 + (AC)^2$, the length of the hypotenuse is simply the square root of $(BC)^2$.

Algorithms are based upon and incorporate principles—specifically, prediction or application of principles. As previously noted, when the problem is written with the solution unknown, it is a *prediction* operation; when the solution is known and one of the steps must be completed, it becomes an *application* operation. An example of a prediction problem follows:

- $\dfrac{5}{6} \div \dfrac{7}{8} =$ _____   (a) $\dfrac{40}{42}$ (b) $\dfrac{35}{48}$

  (c) $\dfrac{12}{14}$ (d) $\dfrac{35}{40}$

The algorithm for division of two unlike fractions states that one of the fractions should be inverted and multiplied by the other fraction ($\frac{1}{2} \div \frac{3}{4} = \frac{1}{2} \times \frac{4}{3}$). Although the previous problem used a prediction format, we could format this problem type as an application item, as follows:

- $\dfrac{7}{9} \div$ _____ $= \dfrac{32}{38}$ (a) $\dfrac{11}{12}$ (b) $\dfrac{14}{18}$

  (c) $\dfrac{4}{5}$ (d) $\dfrac{8}{11}$

The algorithm for division of real numbers states that decimals in the divisor should be moved to the right until the number can be expressed as an integer; the decimal in the dividend must be moved to the right an equal number of places.

- $3.6 \div .12 = 360.0 \div 12$ T   F

As before, problems can be formatted as application or prediction items. An example of a prediction problem follows:

- $3.6 \div .12 =$ _____
  (a) 3.0   (b) .30   (c) 300.0   (d) 30.0

Level 6—Sentence Solving

The **sentence-solving** content domain involves deriving a solution to a numerically expressed problem by way of principles. Sentences can be diverse in format and content; their only limitation is an emphasis on numerical rather than compositional content. Intellectual operations for this level include prediction and application.

- $3 + 4 =$ _____   (a) 7   (b) 1
  (c) 5   (d) 17

  (Prediction)
- $3 +$ _____ $= 7$ (a) 4   (b) 1
  (c) 5   (d) 17

  (Application)

All computation problems are classified as examples of mathematical sentences; they follow syntactical rules (e.g., an operation is always identified) and they may be built into any level of complexity. The actual format may, however, be expressed in a variety of ways, using numbers stacked in vertical columns or horizontally in a sentence. The following expressions, which employ prediction formats, represent sentence problems with a wide range of difficulty:

- $\begin{array}{r} 42 \\ 23 \\ +\ 18 \\ \hline \end{array}$ $\begin{array}{r} 11 \\ \times\ 91 \\ \hline \end{array}$ $\begin{array}{r} 35 \\ -\ 17 \\ \hline \end{array}$ $14\overline{)280}$

- $567 + 907 =$ _____
  $405 - 203 =$ _____
  $23 \times 10 =$ _____

We can express the operation and/or numbers in words or in notation and employ selection or production responses.

- What is the sum of 24 and 64?
  (a) 88   (b) 78   (c) 40   (d) 84

- Find the absolute difference between 120 and 85:   (a) 45   (b) 35   (c) 205   (d) 15
- Write the numerals for seventeen and five and add them together: _____

Other examples of sentence solving using prediction items follow:

- $(3x + 4y)(12x + 3y) =$ _____
- Another way to describe $2x - 1$ dimes is:
  (a) $20x - 10$ (b) $10x$ (c) $19x$ (d) $x/5 - 1$
- $5^4 =$ _____
  (a) 25   (b) 625   (c) 125   (d) 20
- If a cube is 3 in. $\times$ 4 in. $\times$ 5 in., what is its volume? _____
  (a) 27   (b) 12   (c) 60   (d) 35

An example of an application item is:

- If the volume of a cube is 60 inches, and two sides are 3 and 4 inches, what is the length of the third side?
  (a) 3   (b) 6   (c) 5   (d) 4

Level 7—Problem Solving

In **problem solving**, we express mathematical problems within the context of a social situation, in which information needed to solve the problem must be identified first and then utilized. Only principles can be applied at this level, and the operations of prediction, evaluation, and application are possible. The contexts within which we express the problems may include information unnecessary to solve the problem; furthermore, the number of operations required to solve any problem may be one or several.

- Bill had 5 apples and Jim had 3 apples. How many apples did they have altogether? (Mono-operational problem)
- In a 2-day period, Jim earned $125 as a waiter, 15% of which was from tips. How much did Jim earn in wages alone for these 2 days? (Dual-operational problem)

Students should engage in at least four steps to solve story problems successfully: (a) read the problem accurately, (b) identify the relevant information—determine the operation needed and establish the unit for expressing the answer, (c) set up the problem with the correct numbers, and (d) complete the calculation and check the answer for appropriateness. To answer items requiring problem solving correctly, respondents must apply the following skills:

1. Reading skills, with which they must comprehend or understand the verbal statement.
2. Process skills, with which they identify the mathematical operations and quantities needed to solve the problem.
3. Computational skills, with which they must carry out a computation accurately.

Both simple, one-step problems and non-routine problems that require more than an application of a single arithmetic operation are necessary to completely assess skill in problem solving. Many students have difficulties with nonroutine problems because they fail to consider all the information in the problem.

Summary of Intellectual Operations and Content Domains

The seven content domains, considered in relation to symbol type, level of abstraction, and intellectual operation, provide a comprehensive perspective for structuring the assessment process, which can incorporate any of several dimensions. However, the assessment process should take advantage of the hierarchical nature of mathematics. To execute sentence and problem solutions, students must be skilled in the application of the previous five content domains. For example, test items focusing on properties (Level 4) may be less desirable than computation sentences that are solved using prediction, evaluation, or application of these properties (Level 6).

In fact, we can test students' understanding of the first five content levels with these two domains. For example, instead of asking about the property of zero for addition (when you add zero to any number, the sum equals the number), actual problems such as $0 + 7 = \underline{\quad}$ (Prediction) can be used to test knowledge and skill with this property. With proficiency in skill or knowledge in any of the first five levels comes success in sentence or problem solving. As a consequence, most mathematical assessments should focus on these latter two levels of the domain taxonomy.

SCORING SYSTEMS FOR PRODUCTION ANSWERS

For all seven content domains, but particularly for sentence solving and problem solving, we can give students problems that require them to produce answers. Because mathematics is so obviously correct or incorrect (no answers are more or less correct), assessments can incorporate production responses easily, which is in stark contrast to most scoring systems for written expression and most essay tests on knowledge. Since mathematics is lawful, production responses are not as difficult to score as in other academic areas, which often must rely upon subjective scoring systems or elaborate objective scoring systems that suffer from credibility problems (face validity). Therefore, the remainder of this chapter focuses almost exclusively on production responses within the last two content domains (sentence solving and problem solving). Computation problems are emphasized.

We present two systems for evaluating student performance on computation problems: (a) counting the number of problems com-

pleted correctly and (b) counting the number of digits in the correct place value. The entire answer is scored for its correctness, or parts of the answer and the steps needed in the process of executing the answer is scored for their correctness respectively. Both types are applicable for sentence and problem solving. The difference is one of efficiency and sensitivity (the potential for reflecting differences between students or change over time). The former strategy is far more efficient, but much less sensitive; the latter is less efficient, but more sensitive. Although most scoring systems count entire problems as correct or incorrect, counting the number of digits in the correct place value may be more sensitive to changes in student performance. In this section, all four basic operations, fractions, and decimals are analyzed for both problems and digits correct.

Computation: Problems Computed Correctly

To count problems completed correctly, we compare student answers with those on the answer keys. Students' work need not be shown, and no intermediate steps are considered. Each problem is given a value of 1, regardless of the number of steps, the use of multiple operations, or problem difficulty. The following four items might appear on a problem sheet, with each one given a value of 1.

Problem 1	Problem 2
5 + 6 ――― 11	35 + 67 ――― 102

Problem 3	Problem 4
15 x 21 ――― 15 30 ――― 315	24 r 8 23⟌560 46 ――― 100 92 ――― 8

Notice that Problem 1 involves little computation since it is a math fact; Problem 2 includes carrying; Problem 3 has intermediate steps, two with multiplication math facts and another with addition; and Problem 4, like Problem 3, has intermediate steps as well as three operations (division, multiplication, and subtraction). Nevertheless, when scoring student performance for the number of problems correct and incorrect, such differences between problems are ignored.

Differences in complexity also occur with selection-response problems. Problem 1 below requires no carrying and it is mono-operational. Problem 2 requires multiplication and addition skills. The difficulty of the two problems is not considered if they are scored as problems calculated correctly.

```
┌──────────────┐
│  Problem 1   │
└──────────────┘
            A. 4943
    403     B. 4934
    120     C. 4374
 + 3211     D. 3374
 ──────     E. None of these
```

```
┌──────────────┐
│  Problem 2   │
└──────────────┘
            A. 1005
            B. 1550
     42     C. 1050
   x 25     C. 1510
   ────     E. None of these
```

Computation: Digits Correctly Computed

To compensate for degrees of difficulty in problems, we can score digits in correct place for all intermediate steps and for answers themselves. Scoring computation problems by way of the number of digits correct and incorrect provides a more expansive and presumably more sensitive scale to reflect student proficiency.

The general rule for scoring problems according to digit placement is to compare students' work with answer keys digit by digit for all steps after the equal sign. For example, the 1's column is analyzed, then the 10's column, 100's column, and so forth. If the digits are the same as those in the answer key, students receive 1 digit correct for each matched pair; if the digits are different, students receive 1 digit incorrect.

Three types of errors are identified with this scoring system. The most common error is substitution, in which the digit in a student's answer is not the same as that in the answer key. Another error type is the omission of numbers or steps in a problem. Third, an error of insertion can occur if the student inaccurately places a digit within the steps or in the answer. Such problems include more digits than are possible in the answer. The last two error types often result in further errors. A domino effect begins with an error of omission or insertion, so that subsequent digits in other place values are wrong. Therefore, the digits-correct method incorporates all three error types. Following are examples of digits correct and incorrect, organized by operation.

Addition. Scoring for addition focuses only on the answer and none of the intermediate steps when the problem involves carrying. In the two examples below, 3-digit and 2-digit problems have been computed incorrectly and scored according to the number of digits correct. The answer has only 1 correct digit in the first problem, primarily because of the addition of an extra digit from incorrectly carrying; in the second problem, no digits are in the correct place because of the number-value reversal.

```
    42
    23
 +  18
   713 ◄──── 1 digit correct
```

```
    14
 +  57
    17 ◄──── 0 digits correct
```

Subtraction. Scoring subtraction problems for the number of digits correct also focuses on the answer only, not on any intermediate steps. Following are two problems: one that does not require borrowing to solve the problem successfully and another that does require borrowing. In both, the correct answer has 2 digits; only 1 digit is correct in the incorrectly solved problem.

```
    58
 -  23
   305 ◄──── 1 digit correct
```

```
    51
 -  35
    26 ◄──── 1 digit correct
```

Multiplication. The following example depicts 2 digits multiplied by 2 digits without carrying. The correct answer has a total of 8 digits, with 4 digits counted from the two intermediate steps and 4 digits from the answer itself. The student has finished the first step with 2 digits correct and the second step with 1 digit correct. In the answer, only 2 digits are completed correctly (1's column and 1,000's column).

Correct
```
      11
   X  91
      11
      99
    1001
```

Incorrect
```
      11
   X  91
      11 ◄──── 2 digits correct
      19 ◄──── 1 digit correct
    1911 ◄──── 2 digits correct
```

The most difficult scoring problem to resolve in multiplication occurs when either the multiplicand or multiplier end in zero. Often in such problems, zeros are used as placeholders, which influences the number of possible digits. An example is presented below (2 digits times 2 digits).

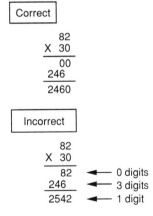

Correct
```
      82
   X  30
      00
     246
    2460
```

Incorrect
```
      82
   X  30
      82 ◄──── 0 digits
     246 ◄──── 3 digits
    2542 ◄──── 1 digit
```

Division. As in multiplication, all steps for division are scored for the correctness of digits in each place value. In the example below, 11 digits correct are possible. Nine of those digits come from the five intermediate steps needed to solve the problem: (a) 2 times 12 equals 24, (b) 35 minus 24 equals 11, (c) bring down 1 to make 111, (d) 9 times 12 equals 108, and (e) subtract 108 from 111 for a remainder of 3. In the incorrect problem below, the student has: (a) incorrectly completed Step 1 (2 times 12), losing 2 of the 3 digits awarded for that step, (b) incorrectly completed Step 2 by subtracting 36 from 35, losing 1 of 2 digits, (c) correctly brought down the 1, which allows at least 2 digits to be correct of the 3 digits available, (d) incorrectly multiplied the divisor by 1, which has resulted in the loss of 4 digits possible, and (e) incorrectly subtracted 12 from 11 to arrive at a remainder of 1, resulting in 1 less correct digit. The student has completed 2 digits correct out of the 11 digits possible.

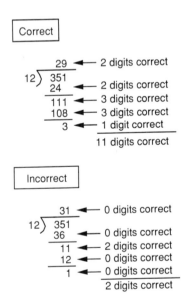

Summary of Scoring Rules. To score problems for number of digits correct and incorrect, we need to make decisions about the presence of zero in any of the steps and the remainder, if one is found. Should zeros as placeholders in multiplication problems be counted in the intermediate steps? If the remainder is zero in a division problem, should a 0 be placed at the bottom of the last step? What about work not shown—should it be scored incorrect when not present?

Multiplication and division problems present some difficulty in scoring. In part, this is because we score intermediate steps in such problems. In these intermediate steps, zeros are used as placeholders in the most detailed and absolute completion of the problem; therefore, extra digits are possible. But as students become more proficient, they learn quicker strategies for solving problems that do not rely on zeros. In fact, with extremely easy multiplication and division problems involving math facts, the answer can be written with no work shown. For example:

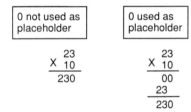

One procedure that awards proficient students the maximum possible points, yet retains scoring procedures that are sensitive for low-performing students, is to use the following rule: When a student's answer is completely correct and no work is shown, the student should receive all points for the problem; when the student's answer is not completely correct and the work is not shown, the answer should be scored accordingly (comparing it to the answer key), and all other digits (not shown) should be considered incorrect. Extending this rule to the problem with implied zeros used as placeholders means that we would count them in the scoring of the answer key (both versions of 23 × 10 are considered as 8-digit problems). If the student's intermediate steps do not include the zeros but are correct, the problem is scored as correct, as if the placeholders had been employed. If the intermediate step is incorrect and implied zeros are not shown, the problem is scored as incorrect. The logic in this strategy is that when the work is not shown, the student obviously has made a mistake, although it is not possible to determine where it occurred.

Fractions. Two rules can be applied when scoring fractions according to digits correct: (a) Fractions are used for addition, subtraction, multiplication, and division, necessitating analysis of the numerator and the denominator, and (b) fractions must be reduced to the lowest common denominator and expressed as a fraction or complex number.

Students can solve fraction problems in a variety of ways, only some of which are awarded points consistent with an answer key. For example, the following problem can be solved with at least two strategies, as shown. The first strategy involves a 13-digit solution and the bottom one has a 5-digit solution.

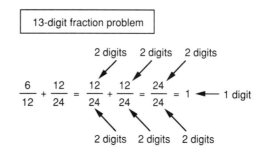

The choices available to solve fraction problems can create difficulty when scoring by digits correct. This can be resolved only by scoring (a) the answer key according to the most specific and extensive procedure, with all possible intervening steps included, or (b) the student's work as the percentage of digits computed correctly. One way to control for equitability of student work is to include directions for the administration of the assessment that inform students of the scoring procedures. In particular, students should be directed to show all of their work and reduce the answer to reflect all successive reductions if they are uncertain of the final answer.

In the preceding problem, the most specific solution involves 13 digits. Answers that are completely correct are awarded all 13 digits whether the work is shown or not, and irrespective of the steps employed in solving the problem.

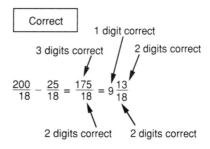

If students solve the problem differently, they receive credit for their solution to the furthest point that it is consistent with the answer key or expresses an equivalent form. In the following problem, the student has made a mistake; however, the steps employed in the solution were consistent with the answer key. Of the 10 digits possible, this student scored 8 correct.

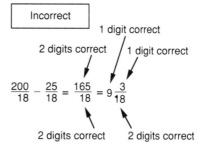

Decimals. Decimals are receiving more emphasis in today's elementary school math programs than in the past. Such coverage is appropriate not only because of the increased use of calculators and metric measurement but because of a reexamination of the scope and sequence of common fractions. Many students have difficulty understanding the place values in decimal problems. Another problem is difficulty in establishing the meaning for many decimal concepts and skills without first establishing their relationship with fractions (Carpenter et al., 1981). For both of these reasons, scoring decimal problems as digits in correct place may be very important. The scoring strategies are the same as those described earlier for addition, subtraction, multiplication, and division.

Scoring Systems for Problem Solving

Scoring systems for problem solving are similar to those described for computation problems: (a) the entire problem is scored as correct or incorrect, or (b) the steps required to solve the problem and the digits in the computational steps are scored for their correctness.

The scoring of problems computed correctly is quite obvious—the entire answer, the final numeric outcome, and its expression all must be correct for the problem to be awarded any points.

> A gardener charges $2.50 per square meter of sod. How much does the gardener charge for 900 square meters of sod?

The preceding problem would be valued the same (one item correct if the student answered $2,250.00) as the following.

> A picnic at the beach was attended by 40 people, 13 of whom brought volleyballs. At another party in the park, 60 people attended, and 19 brought volleyballs. Was there a larger proportion of people at the beach or the park in attendance with volleyballs?

This problem is more complicated than the previous one, not only because rational numbers are used, but because this is a proportion problem. Compare the two problems just mentioned with the next one.

> One side of a triangular garden has a length of 3.7 meters; a second side is twice this length, and the third side is 2 meters less than this second side. How much greater or less in area is this garden than one in which the three sides are 5.0, 2.3 and 3.7 meters?

This last problem is clearly the most complicated of the three. It requires knowledge of simple addition and subtraction to determine length, algorithms for calculating areas of triangles, and subtraction to calculate differences between areas. Although it requires more steps, its value is the same as for the previous two, if they are scored as *problems* correct or incorrect.

PROBLEM SOLVING: STEPS AND COMPUTATION COMPLETED CORRECTLY

Instead of scoring a problem only in terms of the answer, we can break it down into component parts and score them separately. As a result, even if a student does not solve an entire problem correctly, he or she can receive credit for some of the work. Points can be awarded at each step in the problem-solving process: The student (a) reads the problem correctly, (b) identifies the relevant information, (c) converts it into a computation problem, and (d) calculates the answer. In addition to the possibility of 4 points per problem, several more points are possible if digits correct are scored.

This system requires individual administration because the first two steps require oral responses. Only the last two steps can be scored as a group-administered task. We can score each step or all digits in each step as correct or incorrect, and award an extra point for identifying the proper unit for expressing the answer.

Following are several examples of problem solving that are scored by steps and computation completed correctly.

A lap around the Indy 500 race track is approximately 4,400 yards. How many laps are needed to travel 330,000 yards?

Step 1 (1 point for entire step, or 17 points for all correctly placed digits in answer):

$$
\begin{array}{r}
75 \quad \leftarrow 2 \text{ digits} \\
4{,}400 \overline{)\ 330000} \\
30800 \quad \leftarrow 5 \text{ digits} \\
22000 \quad \leftarrow 5 \text{ digits} \\
\underline{22000} \quad \leftarrow 5 \text{ digits}
\end{array}
$$

Step 2 (1 point for correct identification of unit): 75 laps

The total number of points of this problem is 18 if 1 point is awarded for each of the number of digits in correct place and 1 point for correct identification of the unit of the answer; if only steps are counted, the problem has 2 points.

Kevin bought a compass for $1.05, a ruler for .$45, three notebooks for $2.75, and eight pencils for $.80. How much change did he get back from a $10 bill?

Step 1 (2 points for entire answer of each step, or 6 points for all correctly placed digits in each answer):

$$
\begin{array}{r}
1.05 \\
.45 \\
2.75 \\
+\ .80 \\
\hline
5.05
\end{array}
\qquad
\begin{array}{r}
10.00 \\
-\ 5.05 \\
\hline
4.95
\end{array}
$$

Step 2 (1 point for correct identification of unit): $4.95

The first step of this problem can be worth 1 point for each answer, or all digits in the answers (intermediate as well as final answers) can be counted to increase the score to 6 points.

One final example should suffice for scoring problem solving with both steps and correct computation of digits:

Jim picked 11 quarts of strawberries on Friday and another 16 pints on Saturday. He divided the total amount equally among three friends and himself. How many quarts did each person receive?

Step 1 (4 points for each answer or 15 points for all correctly placed digits in each answer):

$$
\begin{array}{r}
11 \\
\times\ 2 \\
\hline
22
\end{array}
\qquad
\begin{array}{r}
22 \\
+\ 16 \\
\hline
38
\end{array}
\qquad
\begin{array}{r}
19 \\
2\overline{)38} \\
\underline{2} \\
18 \\
\underline{18}
\end{array}
\qquad
\begin{array}{r}
4 \\
4\overline{)19} \\
\underline{16} \\
3
\end{array}
$$

Step 2 (1 point for correct identification of unit): Each person receives 4.75 quarts of strawberries.

More points are possible for this problem than for the previous two. Scoring for answers only, it is worth 5 points. With the digits computed in the answers for all intermediate operations and the appropriate units for expressing the answer, the problem totals 16 points.

In summary, scoring problem-solving items in a specific manner requires more planning and care, but allows greater sensitivity. With some students, this allows more appropriate instructional decisions. Whether sentence- or problem-solving items are the focus of testing, more precise scoring of not just the answer but the work that is embedded within the answer directs attention to *how* students completed their work. This more precise focus can then be expanded into an error analysis, in which we begin the search for possible explanations.

Assuming that we have employed production responses, we can obtain considerable diagnostic information from analyzing student performance. Three possible reasons for a problem being completed incorrectly are: (a) The problem was not read correctly, (b) although read correctly, the problem was misunderstood and the wrong process applied to solve it, and (c) although the problem was read correctly and the appropriate operation applied, a calculation error occurred.

Error analysis is the most popular target of research and writing in the field of mathematics. Because mathematics employs rules without exceptions, the analysis of student errors has been considered an inside view of faulty algorithms. This is an important area in the assessment process and is described in the next section.

ERROR-ANALYSIS PROCEDURES FOR COMPUTATION PROBLEMS

Item types can be considered representative of a larger domain containing alternate forms of the same type. Therefore, error analysis provides information on sampling strategies for item selection and can help us develop generalizations about specific student skills. In addition to tests, we can assay worksheets and assignments for error types. When students complete their assignments, they often leave a record of the manner in which they have solved problems, including calculations, drawings, graphs, depictions, and symbols. An analysis of these permanent products may be very helpful in explaining incorrect performance. One disadvantage of worksheets and assignments, however, is the uncontrolled nature of problem diversity and difficulty. Sampling within different problem types and across various operations is often unsystematic and unrepresentative of the larger domain from the instruction or the curriculum.

General Issues in Error Analysis

Cox (1975) has distinguished among three types of computational errors. *Systematic* errors are computation errors that occur in at least three out of five problems for a specific algorithmic computation. *Random* errors occur in at least three out of five problems but contain no discernible patterns. *Careless* errors occur in one or two out of five problems.

We must also consider test formats, noting that vertical problems and horizontal problems are differentially difficult. For example, the third National Assessment of Educational Progress (1983) determined that when 13-year-olds were given an addition problem in vertical form, 66% of them could solve it correctly. When the same problem type was presented in horizontal form, only 42% of the students solved it correctly. Furthermore, the position of the unknown has also been identified as an important factor. For example, unknown quantities in the medial position ($4 + \_\_\_\_ = 10$) generally pose less difficulty than problems in which the unknown is in the primary position ($\_\_\_\_ \div 4 = 10$). However, difficulty may be very individual.

Diagnostics may include not only an error analysis but also (a) interviews with children to determine how they describe the process of solving problems, (b) the use of manipulative materials and observations as the students perform solutions, and (c) the depiction of problems as pictures by students.

While organizing errors into patterns is important, we must determine potential reasons *why* the errors occur. Two reasons may be that students lack understanding of (a) basic place-value concepts of carrying or regrouping or (b) the basic algorithm itself (Berman & Friederwitzer, 1981). In either case, reasons for such performance may include a lack of experience in the use of manipulatives or their association with vocabulary and/or symbols. Children often lack an understanding of place-value concepts and the base-10 concept (Cox 1975).

Addition and Subtraction

Berman and Friederwitzer (1981) placed addition and subtraction errors into seven groups in an effort to develop specific remediation techniques. They felt that children make mistakes because they (a) don't understand regrouping and treat each column as a separate problem, (b) mix up the 1's and 10's in their carrying, writing the 10's and carrying the 1's, (c) forget to carry the 10's (in addition problems) or regroup the 10's (in subtraction problems), (d) forget to carry the 100's (in addition problems) or regroup the 100's (in subtraction problems), (e) forget to change both the 10's and the 100's, (f) and regroup 100's and 1's, but forget to regroup the 10's, and finally, (g) regroup when it isn't required.

Most errors in addition and subtraction involve problems with carrying and borrowing. Following are several examples of error patterns as proposed by Ashlock (1986).

Adding and recording the 1's, then 10's, and so forth.

Correct	Incorrect
67	67
+ 78	+ 78
145	1315

Adding from left to right, with carrying to the digits on the right.

Correct	Incorrect
245	1
+ 932	245
1177	+ 932
	187

Adding all numbers without consideration of place value.

Correct	Incorrect
35	35
+ 3	+ 3
38	11

Adding a number twice.

Correct	Incorrect
1	1
45	45
+ 6	+ 6
51	111

Subtracting successive places without borrowing.

Correct	Incorrect
45	45
− 26	− 26
19	29

Unnecessary regrouping.

Correct	Incorrect
78	$^{6}\cancel{7}^{1}8$
− 35	− 35
43	33

Incorrect subtraction of zeros.

Correct	Incorrect
315	315
− 205	− 205
110	100

Incorrect regrouping.

Correct	Incorrect
6 11 1	5 1 1
7 2 3	7 2 3
− 3 4 5	− 3 4 5
3 7 8	2 8 8

Multiplication and Division

Most multiplication and division problems in-volve addition, subtraction, and placeholders, including zeros. An analysis of 3,294 multipli-cation examples generated by 121 students from six classes in six schools (Kilian, Cahill, Ryan, Sutherland, & Taccetta, 1980) revealed only three major error types: (a) calculation er-rors, (b) procedural errors, and (c) errors that could not be classified. Of the procedural er-rors, the following four types were delineated.

1. Digit not used (not reported).
2. Carrying mistakes (24%).
3. Mistakes involving zeros (11%).
4. Columns misplaced (not reported).

Almost 97% of these errors were calculation (41%) or procedural (56%) errors. More spe-cific analyses of the calculation errors indicated that addition errors, miscalculation of 5×8, and miscalculation of 6×9. Following are examples of error types proposed by Ashlock (1986).

Carrying in all steps of multiplication problems.

Correct	Incorrect
^{2}34	^{2}34
x 25	x 25
170	170
68	88
850	1050

Forgetting to carry within multiplication.

Correct	Incorrect
6	6
^{1} 68	^{1} 68
x 28	x 28
544	484
136	126
1904	1744

Adding carried number before multiplying.

Correct	Incorrect
1	1
^{4} 15	^{4} 15
x 93	x 93
45	65
135	455
1396	4655

Ignoring place values in the dividend.

Correct	Incorrect
31 r 4	31
20) 624	20) 624

Recording the answer from left to right.

Correct	Incorrect
71 r 4	17 r 4
8) 572	8) 572
56	56
12	12
8	8
4	4

Forgetting to retain zero as a placeholder.

Correct	Incorrect

$$8\overline{)927} \quad \begin{array}{r} 103 \\ 9 \\ \hline 2 \\ 0 \\ \hline 27 \\ 27 \end{array}$$

$$8\overline{)927} \quad \begin{array}{r} 13 \\ 9 \\ \hline 27 \\ 27 \end{array}$$

Alignment of work and the use of zeros.

Correct	Incorrect

$$8\overline{)2456} \quad \begin{array}{r} 307 \\ 24 \\ \hline 5 \\ 0 \\ \hline 56 \\ 56 \end{array}$$

$$8\overline{)2456} \quad \begin{array}{r} 370 \\ 2400 \\ \hline 56 \\ 56 \end{array}$$

Fractions

Many error patterns can materialize in the computation of fraction problems. Errors can involve incorrect division, reduction of the problem, and faulty algorithms for applying basic operations (addition, subtraction, multiplication, and division). Following are several patterns proposed by Ashlock (1986).

Incorrect cancellation procedures with numerals that are the same in the numerator and denominator.

Correct	Incorrect

$$\frac{15}{45} = \frac{1}{3} \qquad \frac{15}{45} = \frac{1}{4}$$

Continuing reduction to the lowest denominator.

Correct	Incorrect

$$\frac{6}{12} = \frac{1}{2} \qquad \frac{6}{12} = \frac{3}{6}$$

Dividing the larger by the smaller number and ignoring the remainder.

Correct	Incorrect

$$\frac{2}{8} = \frac{1}{4} \qquad \frac{2}{8} = \frac{2}{4}$$

Adding the numerators and denominators to obtain the sum.

Correct

$$\frac{7}{9} + \frac{3}{6} = \frac{23}{18} = 1\frac{5}{18}$$

Incorrect

$$\frac{7}{9} + \frac{3}{6} = \frac{21}{15} = 1\frac{6}{15}$$

Forgetting to add whole numbers.

Correct

$$12\frac{3}{4} + 3\frac{1}{2} = 16\frac{1}{4}$$

Incorrect

$$12\frac{3}{4} + 3\frac{1}{2} = \frac{5}{4} = 1\frac{1}{4}$$

Forgetting to adjust the numerator after determining the correct denominator.

Correct

$$\frac{8}{15} + \frac{2}{5} = \frac{8}{15} + \frac{6}{15} = \frac{14}{15}$$

Incorrect

$$\frac{8}{15} + \frac{2}{5} = \frac{8}{15} + \frac{2}{15} = \frac{10}{15} = \frac{2}{3}$$

Subtracting smaller denominator from larger denominator.

Correct

$$3\frac{1}{2} - 2\frac{1}{4} = 1\frac{1}{4}$$

Incorrect

$$3\frac{1}{2} - 2\frac{1}{4} = 1\frac{1}{2}$$

Incorrect conversion of mixed numbers to fractions.

Correct

$$5\frac{5}{8} = \frac{45}{8}$$

$$-\ 3\frac{1}{4} = -\frac{26}{8}$$
$$\overline{\qquad\qquad}$$
$$\frac{19}{8} = 2\frac{3}{8}$$

Incorrect

$$5\frac{5}{8} = 5\frac{45}{8}$$

$$-\ 3\frac{1}{4} = -\ 3\frac{13}{8}$$
$$\overline{\qquad\qquad}$$
$$2\frac{32}{8} = 6$$

Error Analysis for Computation Sentences

Students who incorrectly solve sentences often assume that if the unknown number was on one side of the equation—not on the same side as the symbol for the operation—the operation itself was followed. In contrast, if the unknown appeared on the other side of the equation— on the same side as the symbol for the operation—the inverse of the operation was required (viewing addition and subtraction, multiplication and division as inverses of each other) (Sadowski & McIlveen (1984). For example, students know that $14 - 6 =$ _____ is a subtraction problem, but would think $14 -$ _____ $= 8$ is an addition problem.

Predominance of Error Types

In addition to identification of what types of errors are made, research has focused on the prevalance of errors. Guiler (1946) investigated the nature and prevalence of errors in decimal computation problems that persist at the termination of the program of formal instruction in arithmetic and found some interesting consistencies. It is uncertain if the following error types are present in today's youth, but the taxonomy is still quite useful.

1. Weakness in various phases of work with decimals: difficulty in adding and subtracting decimal numbers, changing fractions to decimals, changing mixed numbers to decimals, and dividing decimal numbers.
2. Placement of the decimal portion in the division of decimal numbers.
3. Changing fractions to decimals and changing mixed numbers to decimals.
4. Faulty computation in addition and subtraction of decimal numbers, specifically in number combinations.

5. Placing the decimal point too far to the right, both in multiplication and division of decimal numbers.

Building from the earlier work of Roberts (1968) and expanding on two specific error types (random response and defective algorithm), Engelhardt (1977) classified student errors into the following patterns:

1. Basic fact error, in which a mistake was made in recalling basic number facts.
2. Defective algorithm, in which a systematic but incorrect procedure was used.
3. Grouping error, in which attention was not given to the positional nature of the number system.
4. Inappropriate inversions, in which a reversal occured in some critical dimension of the operational procedures.
5. Incorrect operations, in which the wrong operation was used.
6. Incomplete algorithm, in which the basic steps were correct, but not completed or complete (a step was missing).
7. Identity errors, in which 0 was misread for 1.
8. Zero errors: those in which problems with zero are solved as if the zero was not there or was treated as a 1.

Basic error facts were made most frequently (38%), followed by grouping errors (22%), inappropriate inversions (21%), defective algorithms (18%), incomplete algorithms (7%), zero errors (6%), incorrect operations (4%), and identity errors (1%). Clearly the first four types account for most of the errors made (96%). Furthermore, "the error type which most dramatically distinguishes highly competent performance is the defective algorithm error type" (Englehardt, 1977, p. 153). However, the most common error in all quartiles was from incorrect recall of basic facts.

In summary, analysis of student computational skills is the most researched area in mathematics. Generally, error analysis is a major component of this research. At times, the purpose is to develop normative taxonomies and to describe the general patterns for groups of students with certain problem types (Brueckner, 1928; Easterday, 1980; Guiler, 1946; Kilian et al., 1980; Englehardt, 1977). At other times, the goal is to explain learning, how it occurs, and identify factors of influence (Ashlock, 1986; Radatz, 1979; Roberts, 1968; Shaw & Pelosi, 1983). However, most attention in assessing math computation skills is devoted to the development of prescriptive instructional programs (Beattie & Algozzine, 1982; Baroody, 1984; Berman & Friederwitzer, 1981; Cox, 1975; Dodd, Jones, & Lamb, 1975; Engelhardt, 1982; Pincus et al., 1975; Sadowski & McIlveen, 1984; West, 1971). These articles and reports describe specific error-analysis systems, make diagnostic statements, and propose suggestions regarding suitable instructional programs.

The problem with such attention to computation problems is that little research has been completed in the assessment of problem-solving skills. Yet the goal for math instruction in our schools should be to ensure that students have the requisite skills to solve problems in the natural world. For example, everyday experiences present individuals with the need to calculate such things as price differentials, interest rates, cumulative expenditures, and area or volume estimates, all of which are couched within a context that must be first established and then calculated. Therefore, although all problem solving eventually reduces to computation, the manner in which problems are translated *and* solved is more near the goal of instruction than simple rote computation using the four operations.

Error Analysis of Problem Solving

As soon as we see the importance of problem solving, we can then appreciate the impact of component skills. For example, Forsyth and Ansley (1982) found the influence of computation skills was minimal in solving story problems. A study by Caldwell and Goldin (1979) compared the relative difficulties for elementary school children of four types of word problems (abstract factual, abstract hypothetical, concrete factual, and concrete hypothetical). Two stages in solving verbal problems in mathematics were included: translation and computation. The authors assumed that the kind of situation described by the problem statement could affect the difficulty of translating it into mathematical expressions and consequently affect the overall difficulty of the problem. They found that instruction was successful at improving problem solving mainly by improving computational skills; the children who already had those skills differed from grade to grade.

While problem solving may be more representative of situations presented in the social world outside school walls, it is necessary to focus assessment on specific skills. As Carpenter, et al. (1980) suggested, students' ability to solve simple, one-step verbal problems seems to reflect their basic understanding of the operation involved in the problem. Failure to learn the basic concepts underlying an operation results in both poor computational skills and an inability to apply a given operation in problem-solving situations.

Given the dominance of computation skills in both the research literature and as a requisite for problem-solving skills, it is important to analyze other factors that influence student performance to improve learning. Generally, problem solving is comprised of several interrelated skills, all of which must be used successfully to complete problems correctly.

Students must (a) read words and sentences to understand the problem, (b) isolate critical information needed to solve the problem, (c) arrange this information to reflect a correct computational sequence having a proper unit of expression, and (d) complete the calculation correctly to arrive at an answer. Take the following example:

> A Subaru 4WD wagon can carry 5 people. A full-size Pontiac station wagon can carry 9 people. How many people can be carried by 15 Subarus and 22 Pontiac wagons from Seattle to San Francisco? (273)

To successfully complete this problem, students must read it correctly and identify relevant information. For example, the fact that the cars are Subarus or Pontiacs is irrelevant except for the need to appropriately match each type with a number. The trip itself is completely irrelevant. The information must be sequenced appropriately: Calculate 5×15, calculate 9×22, and add the two products together. The student could calculate 9×22 first (applies the law of associativity), but the product of 5×9 or 5×22 and so forth, would not be correct. In a related manner, the unit of analysis must be correctly identified (people, not cars, in this example). Finally, the computation problems must be accurately completed to ensure a complete and correct solution to the problem. These four components all present the opportunity for errors.

Language and Readability.   Many researchers feel that children's difficulties with word problems have to do with the fact that reading is involved, but its importance may be less than traditionally assumed. Knifong and Holtan (1977) found that poor reading ability accounted for only 10% of the incorrect problems. Each child in their study successfully read the passage aloud in which he or she had erred. When asked to explain the setting and what the problem was asking them to find, they were correct, but when asked how the problem would be worked, they were unsuccessful. Reading was not the problem; rather, students needed to learn how to isolate relevant information, sequence it into a problem sentence, and apply their computational skills to solve it. Instruction on reading skills (which is valuable in its own right) to correct word problem difficulties is unlikely to be effective in improving problem-solving skill.

These authors also found that 52% of all incorrect problems was due to clerical or computational mistakes (Knifong & Holtan, 1977). Therefore, although reading should not be ignored entirely, math instruction and assessment need not focus primarily upon it.

Informational Content. To solve story problems successfully, students must identify relevant and critical information and ignore irrelevant or unessential information. Many young children experience difficulties in solving problems because they consider irrelevant aspects of the problem, which are generally referred to as *noise* or *distractors*. It is assumed that children who attend to distractors are less likely to attain solutions than those who ignore them.

Spatial-numerical aspects, which introduce unneeded numbers into the problem, appear to be the strongest distractors (Bana & Nelson, 1978). For example, in the following story problem, the number of cups of flour is irrelevant to the solution, but some students might try to solve the problem using that information.

> A recipe calls for 6 cups of water per cup of flour, in addition to a number of other ingredients, to make 10 servings. How many cups of water are necessary to make 30 servings?

Sequence of Information. Story problems can be mono- or multioperational. A mono-

operational problem requires only one step for its solution. The information is identified, the correct operation is established, and the correct answer is calculated. The following two problems allow this approach.

> A restaurant plans to serve 72 people for a retirement banquet. They have tables that can seat 9 people. How many tables should be set?

> It takes 160 hours to paint a three-bedroom ranch house. The owner wants to have the house painted in a standard 40-hour week. How many painters should the owner hire?

Multioperational problems require several operations to determine answers, partly because information that is presented in one sequence must be rearranged to solve the problem. The problems below require three operations and an accurate arrangement of steps.

> A farmer harvested 50 bushels of corn per acre last year and 65 bushels per acre this year. In both years, he had planted corn in 100 acres. How many more bushels can he harvest this year over last year's total? (1,500)

> A bank has offered to loan money at 6% interest annually. If a customer borrows $10,000, how much must be paid in principal and interest to pay off the loan in one year? ($10,600)

Operation/Calculation Required to Solve Problems. The last critical step necessary for solving story problems is their computational completion. Obviously, students must successfully complete addition, subtraction, multiplication, and/or division operations to solve a problem. As reviewed in the preceding section on error analysis and performance scoring for digits correct, a number of possible problems exist.

Error Analysis Summary. Although error analysis may be helpful in establishing instructional programs and developing curricular materials for remediation of faulty algorithms, it is insufficient for establishing effective programs. Consistent with the perspective described in the first chapter, the strategies we emphasize for assessing math skills are evaluation-oriented. In this approach, diagnostic information is collected prior to instruction, but the major emphasis of assessment is on the concurrent evaluation of programs during implementation.

Other Factors of Influence

In summary, problem-solving items provide a great deal of opportunity for students to make mistakes. Certainly, the four areas described above should be considered as a first-level analysis of student difficulties. It is likely that the last two or three steps provide the essential information for developing hypotheses about student's faulty algorithms. Analysis of student performance in problem solving, however, need not be limited to error analysis: Other factors may influence performance. The critical question to address before interpreting any protocol is whether the assessment provides valid data that indicate actual levels of student proficiency and how we can use these data to improve performance.

Variables that have been shown to influence problem difficulty include the following:

1. Context familiarity (Brownell & Stretch, 1931).
2. Number of words (Jerman & Rees, 1972).
3. Sentence length (Jerman & Mirman, 1974).
4. Readability (Linville, 1969; Thompson, 1967).
5. Vocabulary and verbal cues (Jerman & Rees, 1972; Steffe, 1967).
6. Magnitudes of the numbers (Suppes, Loftus, & Jerman, 1972).
7. Number and types of operations or steps (Searle, Lorton, & Suppes, 1974; Shepard,

1974; Suppes, Loftus, & Jerman, 1972; Whitlock, 1974).
8. Sequence of operations (Bergland-Gray & Young, 1940).

Even broader varieties of influence may be at play. The National Longitudinal Study of math abilities suggests that (a) different patterns of math achievement are associated with the use of different texts, (b) math achievement is a multivariate phenomenon involving multiple skill areas, (c) students are more likely to learn what they have been taught, with groups performing best in the areas stressed in their particular textbooks, (d) great variability in pupil achievement exists when we consider teacher effectiveness, (e) attitudes of both sexes deteriorate during secondary school years, with the decline greater for girls, and (f) teacher characteristics do not account for a significant percentage of variance: It is too low to be of value in practical school decisions (p. 271).

In a major review of assessment variables that influence estimates of skill proficiency, Hembree (1987) completed a metanalysis of the effects of influential noncontent variables. From 120 research studies reported in two journals (*Journal for Research in Mathematics Education,* 1970–1985 and *The Arithmetic Teacher,* 1954–1970), he calculated effect sizes for many variables within two major considerations: ambient and treatment conditions. The former included test administration conditions, size of the test group, incentives, test limits, context, test format conditions, style of writing, location of work space, location of answers, style of test, multiple-choice options, item arrangement, and word problem format. The latter included test-preparedness, knowledge of results, written comments, notification of an impending test, cognitive level, and frequency of testing. He found that the following conditions enhanced test performance: personal manner of test administration, praise delivered at the start of administration, work space located adjacent to the test problems, items arranged from easy to difficult, pictures accompanying the word problems, proper ordering of the data in word problems, training in taking tests, and knowledge of results given item by item during the test. Students also were found to have improved performance if they knew their progress and tests were unannounced and frequent.

Given these findings, Hembree suggested the following guidelines:

1. Prior to testing, try to equate the test-preparedness levels of the test group. A pretest discussion can acquaint testees with the style of the test, item arrangement, directions for marking answer sheets, instructions with regard to guessing, and other information that might raise the level of test-wiseness.
2. Provide numerous pictures for studying and testing the solution of word problems. The students may thus be encouraged to solve word problems holistically, using in concert the verbal and visual styles of mental processing. Students should also be taught to create and use their own drawings in solving word problems.
3. Pay heed to the powerful effects of frequent testing.

The degree to which students have been actually taught is an extremely important consideration in determining whether they learn. We cannot create content valid tests if instruction does not occur or is unrelated to items on the test. For example, Alford (1986) investigated the alignment of textbook and test content and found that *all* textbooks emphasized computation more than did any test. The match between texts and tests at a given grade was never very strong and varied for different test-text pairs; a large proportion of the material in textbooks was not covered on standardized tests. Obviously, teachers should be aware of the differences between what they are expected to teach and what textbooks advise.

Two other studies have corroborated the low degree of overlap between problem types in the curriculum and those in tests. Knifong (1980) investigated how well the word problem sections of popular achievement tests sampled problems. For the following tests, little comparable coverage was found in the curriculum of different computational problem types or digital complexity: California Achievement Tests (CAT), Comprehensive Tests of Basic Skills (CTBS), Iowa Test of Basic Skills (ITBS), Metropolitan Achievement Test (MAT), and Stanford Achievement Test (SAT). Many of these tests included a large proportion of certain problem types or none at all. For example, children who can compute money values would have a better chance on the ITBS and the MAT 1977 test than the SAT or CAT. Children who are weak in the mechanics of computation should find the MAT 1977 much easier than the ITBS: more than one-third of the problems on the MAT do not require computation.

In a more detailed analysis involving not only test analyses but also curriculum analysis and test-curriculum alignment, Freeman et al. (1983) found considerable variations. Four conclusions from their work follow: (a) texts emphasized computation more than tests; (b) few topics were commonly emphasized in both curricula and tests; (c) the match between tests and texts was differentially distributed, with some texts more evenly aligned with some tests; and (d) tests included far fewer topics than were covered in the texts.

> Only 22 specific content areas satisfied one or both definitions for core topics. Of these 22 topics, only 6 were emphasized in all textbooks and tests analyzed. Three topics were emphasized in all books but in no tests. Three other topics were covered in all tests, but received limited attention (i.e., did not meet the criterion

for emphasis) in the books. The other 10 topics were emphasized in all four books, but they appeared in only some tests (p. 504).

These authors found that the core curriculum, those topics appearing in both the tests and texts, included computational skills involving addition, subtraction, and multiplication, and conceptual understanding, including geometric terms, place value concepts, and fractions as represented by pictures. The range of the differential sampling of item types in both the curriculum and the tests was 28% at the lowest (the match between Addison-Wesley and MAT) to 47% (Holt and Houghton-Mifflin texts with CTBS-II). Furthermore, "at least three of the topics covered by 20 or more items in all four books were not covered by a single item on any of the five tests" (p. 508). In contrast, many item-types were tested but not taught: Never were more than 50% of the items on any test ever presented in more than a cursory fashion by the texts. In summary, they state that "When there are mismatches between content taught and content tested, standardized tests underestimate student achievement." (p. 511).

AN EXAMPLE OF AN INTEGRATED ASSESSMENT

To illustrate the information in this chapter, we present the following example. Donny has been in our fourth-grade classroom for a short time because his family recently moved into the district from another town in the state. Although his parents report no problems in his overall ability and in his achievement in schools attended previously, the teacher is having difficulty keeping him within the classroom instruction. To determine if Donny needs extra help, the teacher decides to assess his math skills. The two main areas of concern for her are computation problems and one- and two-step word story problems. She is less concerned about measurement and geometry, since Donny's problems in computation and problem solving are potentially quite serious. She uses the following procedures to develop her assessment.

Materials

The teacher's curriculum follows a fairly typical spiral introduction of successive skills throughout the grades, presenting different number types and operations from grade to grade, with review sprinkled in along the way. She notices that every five units end with a review unit and two tests: a practice test and a progress-check test. Since the year is almost one-third over, she wants to determine how he compares to others in the classroom and whether Donny is proficient in the current skill. That is, she wants both a norm-referenced and a criterion-referenced measure of his performance, respectively. The former allow some judgments to be made about using more specialized placements outside the room, either now or near the end of the year, when the same norm-referenced measure can be readministered, and the latter will help place him in the math program more effectively. Therefore, the teacher decides to develop two different types of measures. To ensure stable results, she also makes alternate forms of the same measures and gives them to the entire class at the beginning and the end of the week.

The domain for selecting the problems on the test includes computation problems with all four operations (addition, subtraction, multiplication, and division) using 2- and 3-digit numbers; these problem types occur throughout the book. All sections from the curriculum have story problems, which are quite similar in the operations that are concurrently presented; they are mostly one- and two-step problems. This information is used to structure the sampling plan in Figure 10.5 for the survey-level, norm-referenced test.

Three story problems are sampled: two are one-step problems using multiplication and division, and one is a two-step problem using addition and subtraction. This sampling plan is used to construct the test that follows.

Administration and Scoring

All measures are administered with the following directions for students:

> When you get the page of problems, it should be kept face down until I tell you to turn it over. The page has 33 problems on it. Most problems are computation problems in addition, subtraction, multiplication, and division. Be careful to look closely at the sign, since they follow no pattern. The problems use whole numbers, fractions, and decimals. When I say "Start", turn the page over and begin answering the problems. Start on the first problem of the first row and work across the row; when you come to the end of the row, go down to the next row and begin answering problems from left to right. Don't work on the story problems until you are completely done with the computation problems. If you cannot an-

swer a problem, place an X across the box and go on to the next problem. You will be given a maximum of 15 minutes for this test; I will be writing the test-taking time on the board and will warn you at 13 minutes. When you complete the entire sheet, write the time that is on the board in the lower right corner of your sheet and turn it over. Are there any questions? O.K. Begin.

The teacher then proceeds to proctor the test, starting the timer with the word "Begin" and writing down the elapsed time on the board in 15-second intervals. When 13 minutes have elapsed, the teacher states the time. Two minutes later, she says, "Stop. Pencils down and eyes up here."

On the computation measure, for both the survey-level, norm-referenced measure and the specific-level, criterion-referenced measure, she scores performance in terms of digits computed correctly in the answer only (digits in the steps are not counted). The word story problems are scored for the number of digits computed correctly in any step or answer plus 1 point for expressing the answer in the correct unit. This part of the measure generates 15 points across the three problems.

Operation	Integers	Rational	Real
1. Addition	2-digit	1-digit	2-digit
2. Addition	3-digit	1- & 2-digit	3-digit
3. Subtraction	2-digit	1-digit	2-digit
4. Subtraction	3-digit	1- & 2-digit	3-digit
5. Multiplication	Facts	Reduce frac.	Convert decimal to fraction
6. Multiplication	2-digit	1-digit	2-digit
7. Multiplication	3-digit	1- & 2-digit	3-digit
8. Division	fact	convert to decimal	Convert % to decimal
9. Division	1- & 2-digit	1-digit	2-digit
10. Division	2- & 3-digit	1- & 2-digit	3-digit

FIGURE 10.5
Sampling plan for math computation problems

The data generated on the survey-level, norm-referenced test with computation problems is summarized using a box plot, as shown in Figure 10.6. As predicted, Donny is in the lowest 10th percentile of the class distribution. His performance on the word story problem was even worse; he is the absolute lowest in the class, with only 2 points.

Based on Donny's performance on these measures, the teacher decides that (a) work with rational and real numbers is inappropriate because it is too difficult, and (b) more addition and subtraction problems with integers probably are unnecessary because he answered most of these problem types correctly. In Figure 10.5, the problems appearing in rows 1–6 under the integers column, are either correct or inconsistently incorrect (no error pattern was obvious, and the few errors Donny made seemed to be careless). However, his performance with rational and real numbers on all operations was consistently incorrect. The few basic facts were accurate, but all other problems were completed incorrectly. His performance on the story problems was very poor, with two consistent errors occurring, whether the problems involved one or two steps: The problem was incorrectly setup and the calculations were incorrect for the two problems employing multiplication and division. Based on this information, the teacher creates a specific-level measure to place Donny in the curriculum and to plan supplemental instructional help within the classroom, using problems employing integers and sampled from rows 7–10. Her plans are to improve his skills in multiplication and division first, then systematically introduce decimals and fractions with addition and subtraction. Next year, she hopes, he will be skilled enough to work multiplication and division problems with rational and real numbers.

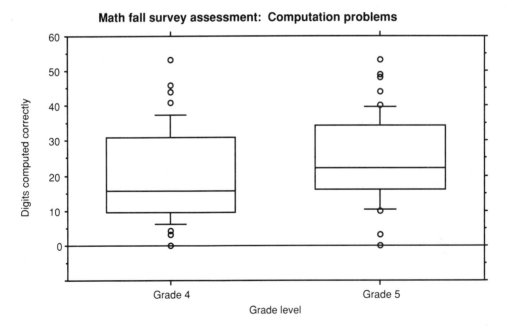

FIGURE 10.6
Math survey assessment of computation problems

The teacher decided that Donny needed to become proficient in computation problems before emphasizing word story problems. Her instructional plan, therefore, reflects this emphasis: She primarily taught computation skills (multiplication and division with integers) and modeled the steps necessary for completing word story problems; however, she spent considerably less time on them. Her graph of Donny's performance improvement, shown in Figure 10.7, also reflected this emphasis; it plots the number of digits computed correctly as a line graph. When introduced, the number of correct points on three word story problems will be displayed as a bar graph on the same measurement days (only three one- and two-step story problems will be presented each time).

Summary of Issues in the Integrated Assessment

Several issues related to this example deserve highlighting. First and most important, the as-

sessment proceeded from a general screening, norm-referenced survey of many skills to a more systematic sampling plan using problem types appropriate for the individual student. All decisions were based implicitly on the taxonomy and the generally hierarchical organization. Rather than sample problems employing a wide range of algorithms (measurement of area and volume, angles and polygons, graphs and coordinates, and probability and statistics, all of which are driven by very specific algorithms), the teacher decided on a minimal measure with different number types and all basic operations. It is unlikely that success in these other areas can occur without skill in basic operations on all number types.

Items were chosen by stratified random selection, with one problem of each type sampled from the domains specified in Figure 10.7. Compare this sampling plan to the one for spelling, which used a simple random sample. The test itself was formatted with the problems randomly displayed on the sheet, rather than

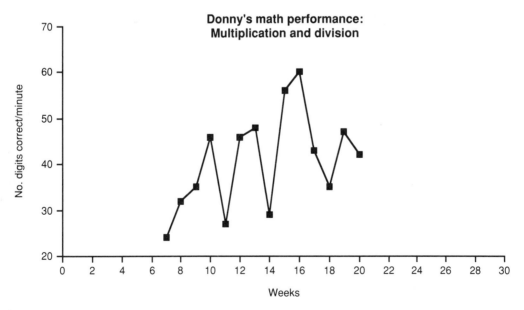

FIGURE 10.7
Example graph for evaluating instructional programs and outcomes

organized with easier problems first and more difficult problems later. Several reasons support such a practice: (a) students don't necessarily end the test on failure, (b) problem difficulty is an individually defined characteristic, (c) more variance is created when students have the opportunity to solve longer-step problems earlier, particularly with a timed test, and (d) such random ordering builds attention into the test, a critical feature of any math problem-solving task.

As we argued earlier, assessment should emphasize the critical effect and help tie educational decisions together. The test utilized production responses, which allowed an error analysis and the generation of an instructional plan. However, we must be cautious in such interpretations: At this point we know more about how the student performed than we know about how we should perform. Therefore, the initial instructional program is tentative and we should develop a system for frequent measurement to track the students' learning. Finally, with a norm-referenced measure that is appropriate for a range of different students and allows for easy construction of an alternate form, we can evaluate the program with a repeat administration at the end of the year.

CHAPTER SUMMARY

The chapter began with two concerns: (a) how troubled school systems appear to be when it comes to mathematics and (b) how broad the field of mathematics is when it includes lawful manipulation of symbols, using specific operations and properties. We presented a taxonomy that was broadly defined to incorporate all possible domains from which math items could be sampled. Seven specific content domains included: sets, number and notation systems, operations, properties, algorithms, problem sentences, and problem solving. The final two content domains represent the products of learning and served as the basis for expanding this content taxonomy in two directions: levels of abstraction (including facts, concepts, and principles) and intellectual operations (reiteration, summarization, illustration, prediction, evaluation, and application). We translated this content into problem types to assess student learning. In translating content into actual tests, two major considerations were the format of the response and the techniques for scoring and analyzing performance. In keeping with the critical-effect focus of assessment, we emphasized production responses, particularly given the lawfulness of mathematics (allowing easy and objective scoring systems). Examples of both computation and word story problems were presented, with two scoring systems: (a) one considering the answer as a single unit, and (b) one considering the steps used to generate the answer, in addition to the answer itself. Finally, we examined interpretations of performance from three vantage points: error analysis for computation problems and for word story problems, and consideration of other (noncontent) influential factors. The entire focus of this information is to guide the creation of more specific and individualized assessments or to structure instruction and its outcomes. A comprehensive example was presented to bring the information in the chapter together.

CHAPTER 11

Assessment in Preschool and Kindergarten

Erma Bombeck, in her syndicated newspaper column on the challenges of modern family life, wrote that one day she received a note from her son's kindergarten teacher telling her that her son was "immature." When she asked the teacher what that meant, the teacher said, "It means he is very childish." Bombeck responded that if this teacher "were a 5-year-old boy dressed in a pair of short pants with a duck on the pocket and carrying a note in his fist all day with B-O-Y-S written on it so he could match it up with the right restroom, she'd be called immature, too" (Bombeck, 1989).

Bombeck's point, of course, is that young children are *supposed* to be immature. Children who are 3, 4, and 5 years old are not just small versions of adults. They are in a unique and important stage of their development. When children in this age group are enrolled in preschool and kindergarten classes, they must, at various times and for various reasons, be tested. The assessment of these young children must be treated as a subject apart from a general overview of classroom tests. Testing preschool children crosses many domains at once and often includes measurement of physical, social, and emotional development. The level of maturity of the children themselves also influences the design and use of the tests. A test for a 3-year-old with limited verbal and fine-motor skills and a short attention span is, by necessity, a very different test from one designed for a 9- or 12-year-old. Young children have limited repertoires for responding. Preschool and kindergarten children are growing and developing much faster than older children. Children between 3 and 5 years old undergo dramatic changes in all domains from one year to the next. For these reasons both the content and the form of tests for preschool and kindergarten

children are distinctly different from those of other tests.

CHAPTER OBJECTIVES

When you have finished this chapter you will have the knowledge and skills to

- Identify current issues in the area of preschool and kindergarten assessment.
- Understand the purposes for testing preschool and kindergarten children.
- Identify the four major types of tests for young children.
- Identify four types of non-test assessment.
- Use the information learned in the chapter to make an appropriate selection of assessment procedures for testing children in preschool and kindergarten.

KEY VOCABULARY

The purpose of this chapter is to examine one specific application of assessment: testing children in preschool and kindergarten. Much of the vocabulary is generic assessment terminology and has been introduced in earlier chapters. Terms include *reliability, validity, domains, predictive validity, norm-referenced, criterion-referenced, multiple-referenced, observations, interviews, screening, eligibility, diagnostics/ planning, formative evaluation,* and *program evaluation.*

Some terminology specific to the testing of young children is introduced in this chapter. *Developmental stages* (or *milestones*), the performance levels in various domains expected of children at different ages, are used as reference points in some preschool screening tests. *Visual discrimination* (ability to discriminate between visual stimuli such as different shapes or letters) and *auditory discrimination* (ability to discriminate between auditory stimuli such

---

This chapter was written by Jan Hasbrouck of the University of Oregon.

as sounds in words or rhymes) are skills frequently assessed in tests of young children.

Early childhood, as used in this chapter, includes children aged 3–5 years who are enrolled in preschool or kindergarten programs. The major types of tests administered to children of these ages include *developmental screening* tests, designed to identify children who may need special attention or special services, *readiness* tests, which help teachers decide the skill and knowledge levels of students as they enter a program, and *achievement* tests, used to assess students' academic growth. *Informal testing* refers to procedures without rigid administration or scoring and interpretation rules; it includes *observations, anecdotal records* (descriptions of events recorded as they occur), *teacher rating scales and skills checklists* (guided observation instruments with embedded weighting scales for scoring), and *parent questionnaires and interviews.*

This chapter also briefly describes five different types of early childhood educational programs:

1. *Basic skills approach* emphasizing early fundamental skills and knowledge, such as social skills, spoken language, motor skills, problem solving, and so forth.
2. *Psychological constructs approach* stressing motivation, self-concept, cognition, creativity, and so forth.
3. *Preacademic approach* providing training in regular school skills, including reading, writing, math, science, and social studies.
4. *Remedial* or *diagnostic-prescriptive approach* identifying children's skill deficits and providing instruction specifically to correct those deficits.
5. *Developmental approach* focusing on learning through play experiences and instruction from all developmental domains including communication, socialization, affective, and intellectual development.

The selection and use of appropriate assessment procedures for use with young children is based on both the types of decisions a teacher needs to make and the type of educational program involved. Figure 11.1 presents a model for the assessment of young children.

ISSUES IN PRESCHOOL AND KINDERGARTEN ASSESSMENT

Although there is general agreement that implementation of some kind of systematic assessment of children is vital to the success of any early childhood education program (Abbott & Crane, 1977; Day, 1983; Spodeck, 1982, Teale, 1988), ideas about what form that assessment should take vary greatly.

Children with special needs should be identified as early as possible so that we can provide them with necessary support services. Yet many educators are concerned about labeling and possibly misclassifying these children. Many tests have limited reliability and validity and are administered and interpreted by unqualified examiners. Such tests do not provide teachers with relevant instructional information. These issues are the major concerns of experts in the assessment of young children.

Early Identification of Children with Special Needs

Testing young children to identify special needs has increased since the early 1970s, a natural result of the surge of interest in early childhood education (Gallerani, O'Regan, & Reinherz, 1982), legislation authorizing federal appropriations for the development of compensatory early education programs such as Head Start and Follow Through (Abbott & Crane, 1977), and the implementation of Public Law 94–142 which included "child find" provisions and

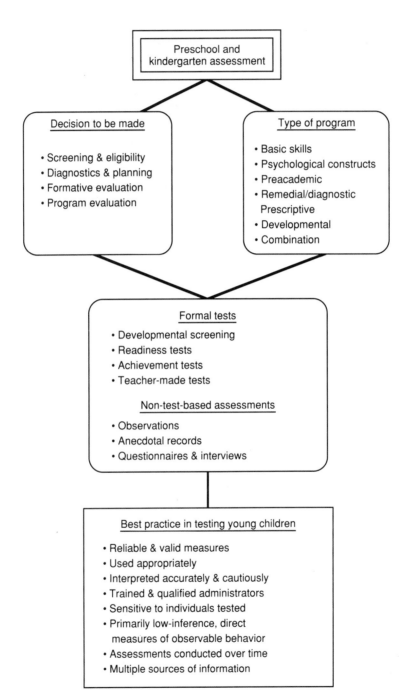

FIGURE 11.1

Using tests with preschool and kindergarten children

mandated a broad range of special educational and related services for the handicapped in schools (Paget & Cox, 1987). Early detection of learning problems and placement of children into special programs are popular topics, and educators involved take opposing philosophical stands on the issues (Reynolds, 1979).

One side argues that early instructional intervention is a valuable asset in remediation and can prevent learning and behavior problems from appearing in later school years. The best time to improve the chances of low-performing and handicapped children for future school success is from birth through early childhood (Linder, 1983), especially when intervention programs are specifically matched to the deficits of individual children. Early intervention can significantly alter the abilities and developmental potential of many children who are at risk during their early years (Meisels & Anastasiow, 1982; Reinherz & Griffin, 1977; Schweinhart & Weikart, 1986). In some cases, total or near total remediation of these problems can occur prior to entry into first grade (Reynolds, 1979). Helping children obtain early intervention services can contribute to the eventual reduction of the number of children who experience school failure and who need special services in later years (Meisels, 1985). Schools have found it less costly and usually more effective to *prevent* academic, developmental, and behavioral problems than to *remediate* them (Harrington & Jennings, 1986).

The opposing side of this argument maintains that, even if the opportunity to help children with special needs is available, the potential for misidentifying students as handicapped or at risk is too great and the consequences too serious to take the risk. It is often difficult to accurately determine which children are the most vulnerable and in greatest need of intervention (Stringer, 1973). Cognitive domains sampled at young ages are only moderately related to the cognitive skills demanded later

by reading and other academic tasks (Shepard & Smith, 1986). In Minnesota, the Early Childhood Assessment Project began offering free health and developmental screening to all $3\frac{1}{2}$–5-year-olds in the state in 1977. Since then the project has tested over 45,000 children using a variety of screening instruments. Thurlow, O'Sullivan, and Ysseldyke (1986) report tremendous variability in the percentages of children identified in the various school districts involved in this project. Some found problems in *all* children screened, while others did not find problems in *any* child. Referral rates for further testing ranged from 0 to 86%. Labeling and classifying young children as handicapped often results in their being viewed in a socially negative light (Bricker, 1978). Placements of children into alternative programs rarely address the possible effects on the child's self-esteem or on the parents' perceptions (Gredler, 1978).

Assessing young children is necessary to provide teachers and parents with information. When we identify children with special problems, labeling is often mandated. Therefore, we need to generate high-quality data from technically adequate tests appropriately administered to provide instructionally relevant information for teachers.

Technical Adequacy of Tests

Many tests used with preschool children lack reliability, validity, and practicality (Abbott & Crane, 1977; Bagnato & Neisworth, 1981; Levin, Henderson, Levin, & Hoffer, 1975, Meisels, 1989, Shepard & Smith, 1988, Wolf & Kessler, 1987). Reliability and validity suffer in part from the limited behavioral repertoire of young children and the uneven development that occurs in relatively short periods of time. Ultimately interpretation problems arise, whether we compare performance to developmental stages or norms of other preschoolers.

Tests of developmental milestones, although widely used in the assessment of young children, are suspect because children are highly individualistic in their progression through the developmental stages (McLoughlin & Lewis, 1986). Dependence on developmental assessment can be limiting because we can only measure developmental deficits when children have missed a major milestone (Lewis & Brooks-Gunn, 1982). This can delay the identification of at-risk students. Young children experience developmental bursts and inconsistencies that defy normative comparison and "none of the available tests is accurate enough to screen children into special programs without a 50% error rate" (Shepard & Smith, 1986, p. 80). Thus, we must interpret the results of these types of tests cautiously. Many early childhood tests vary in what they measure in similarly named areas (Bailey & Wolery, 1984), which makes interpretation of test results difficult at best.

Up-to-date norms on general preschool development are often not available. Many tests are based on norms developed over forty years ago from a narrow sampling of children (Barnes, 1982). Tests are also insensitive to the expression of young children's abilities across socioeconomic or cultural lines (Day, 1983). Readiness tests identify a disproportionate number of poor and minority students as unready (Shepard & Smith, 1988).

We are not likely to solve these problems until more and better research is conducted on the relevant and essential behaviors that young children need to succeed in their current educational environment and to be prepared for future educational experiences. Typically, the development of assessment instruments for young children has not been based on research findings (Lewis & Brookes-Gunn, 1982). However, if such research is conducted, it must focus on behaviors, not on highly inferential constructs that are reflected in test norms.

Teachers must be skilled in administering tests and interpreting the results. They must make such critical decisions as selecting appropriate tests, judging their quality, and correctly interpreting students' scores. Yet early childhood teacher-training programs do not generally include courses in assessment techniques (Abbott & Crane, 1977; Southworth, Burr, & Cox, 1980).

Taking tests always involves a certain level of anxiety and stress, perhaps especially in young children, who are generally not good test takers. The National Association for the Education of Young Children (NAEYC) in its position statement on the testing of young children (1988b) states that too often tests are children's first experience with school. Tests are frequently administered to young children in large groups, in unfamiliar environments, by strange people, perhaps during the first few days at a new school or under other stressful conditions. Children are asked to perform unfamiliar tasks for which the reason is often not explained. These problems add to the general concerns about testing young children.

There are ways to address concerns about the lack of technical adequacy in tests of preschool and kindergarten age children: We can design tests specifically to address the short attention spans of young children, which assess observable behaviors through appropriate response requirements, and which trained personnel administer in minimally stressful environments. However, the information obtained through these assessments is also of critical importance.

Matching Assessment to Programs

Many tests provide little instructionally useful information for teachers. Although some tests might be helpful in locating children with learning and/or developmental problems, there is often no connection between assessment and teaching. Young children are often tested to provide the teacher with information about what they know and do not know. However, teachers seldom use test results to adapt instruction to individual needs and, regardless of test results, often teach the same content to all children in the same manner (Durkin, 1987). Traditional practices in early childhood assessment—which emphasize the exclusive use of global, norm-referenced, intellectual measures—are inappropriate because they lack precision in evaluation and are ineffective in creating a direct link between diagnosis/assessment and intervention/teaching (Bagnato & Neisworth, 1981).

The link between testing and teaching is at the center of the underlying controversy in testing preschoolers. A fundamental difference of opinion exists among professionals concerning the correct way to teach young children (Barnett, 1984; McLoughlin & Lewis, 1990, National Association for the Education of Young Children, 1988a), with corresponding disagreements regarding the correct way to test them. Five types of instructional programs have been identified for use with preschool children along with types of assessments most suited to each program:

1. *Basic skills approach:* Teaching emphasizes fundamental skills and knowledge including socialization, spoken language, attention, fine and gross motor skills, self-help, problem solving, and retention. Assessment focuses on determining a child's skill attainment within each instructional area.
2. *Psychological constructs approach:* Emphasizes the development of psychological processes, including motivation, self-concept, locus of control, cognition, achievement motivation, and creativity. Assessment focuses on determining each child's level of development on a particular trait.

3. *Preacademic approach:* This approach prepares children for the academic content of the regular school; it provides training in language, reading, numbers, arts, and science as a downward extension of public school curricula. Assessment furnishes information about a child's standing in each academic area.
4. *Remedial, or diagnostic-prescriptive, approach:* This model provides the strongest link between assessment and curriculum and is most often used with children identified as having special academic needs. Assessment focuses on identifying students' skill strengths and weaknesses and measuring progress toward improved skills (Salvia & Ysseldyke, 1988).
5. *Developmental tasks approach:* The traditional nursery school program for the whole child involves instruction and experiences from all basic developmental domains including communication (speech and language), socialization and self-care, fine and gross motor competence, and affective and intellectual development. Assessment includes observation for attainment of skills from a task analysis of the skill being assessed. (Bagnato & Neisworth, 1981).

Many early childhood programs are combinations of these approaches. Eclectic or holistic programs, which combine features of several different program types, are the most common (Barnett,1984). Preschool programs that combine comprehensive skill analysis with a developmental approach have been called *developmental prescriptive* (Anastasiow & Mansergh, 1975); they support curriculum planning based on comprehensive skill assessment and developmental sequencing. Other combinations of basic program types are possible. These combination programs correspondingly require the use of a variety of tests and assessment procedures to provide the information teachers need for effective decision making.

TYPES OF TESTS FOR YOUNG CHILDREN

Teachers should select tests on the basis of the decisions to be made and the general philosophical intent of the instructional program. When this doesn't happen, and the assessment is conducted without any clear educational decision, or it does not match the program goals or methodologies, testing can be useless and even detrimental.

The primary reason for assessing young children is to make *individual* decisions about their instructional programs, either current or future (Bagnato & Neisworth, 1981). The type of decision to be made dictates the kinds of skills that will be assessed and the types of measures selected. Examples of decisions facing educators include the following:

1. Which children need assistance?
2. What skills does this child have? What skills does she or he lack?
3. What program is best suited for him or her? What instructional plan should be followed for this child?
4. Is this child making progress in the program?
5. Is the overall program effective for all students served?

These decisions follow the categories identified in an earlier chapter: screening and determining eligibility (1), diagnostics/planning (2), formative evaluation (3 & 4), program evaluation (5).

Assessment of 3–5-year-olds typically reflects the synthesis of developmental information from several measures and sources and across many domains. This emphasis on multiple-referencing is essential in early childhood testing because of the lack of reliable instruments for young children undergoing rapid behavioral and developmental change (Paget, 1987).

While older children's performance can be assessed in fairly discrete categories, such as academic skills or fine motor skills, assessing children aged 3–5 requires a broad sampling of many different types of behaviors in several domains. Testing across domains allows teachers to obtain a more accurate picture of the young child's abilities. The four domains usually considered when assessing preschool children follow:

1. Physical-motor (neurological status, general health, gross and fine motor skills).
2. Speech-hearing-language (auditory and visual acuity, language and communication skills, articulation patterns).
3. Academic-intellectual (concept formation and other cognitive functions, such as memory, problem solving, and creativity; general aptitude and specific learning abilities; school readiness).
4. Social-emotional (affective development; self-help and adaptive skills; social skills).

Because young children develop rapidly and often cannot concentrate on focused tasks for more than brief periods of time, testing becomes very specialized. Direct measures of children's specific observable behaviors are needed with which we can conduct assessments over time to gather a number of samples of behavior. These assessments should occur, as much as possible, in the children's natural environments, where they have greater opportunity to engage in a wider range of functional behaviors. We can use such information to supplement specific tests which can be classified within three general categories: (a) developmental screening tests, (b) school readiness tests, and (c) general achievement tests.

Developmental Screening Tests

Developmental screening in early childhood can be defined as "a brief assessment procedure designed to identify children who, because of the risk of a possible learning problem or handicapping condition, should proceed to a more intensive level of diagnostic assessment" (Meisels, 1985, p.1). These tests are norm-referenced: They compare the child to his or her peers. Developmental screenings can determine quickly and efficiently whether a child should undergo further assessment and evaluation. Screening can serve as the first step in an evaluation and intervention process intended to help children achieve their maximum potential.

Skills Assessed. Developmental screening tests are clear examples of the multidimensionality of preschool tests because they often assess many areas: (a) visual-motor/ adaptive skills, including controlling fine motor movements, coordinating eye-hand movement, memorizing visual sequences, drawing two-dimensional visual forms, and reproducing three-dimensional visual structures; (b) language and cognition skills, including language comprehension, verbal expression and articulation, reasoning, counting, remembering, and repeating auditory sequences; (c) gross motor/ body awareness, including balance, large motor coordination, and imitation of body positions from visual cues; and (d) social/emotional development, usually assessed through observation and parent interview. Children's performance in each area is compared to a standard called a **developmental milestone**, the average expected age at which children typically demonstrate certain abilities. Commonly accepted developmental milestones include sitting without assistance at 6 months, taking steps without support at 1 year, stating first name at 2 years, dressing without supervision at 3 years,

and drawing a figure of a person with main body parts at 4 years.

The interpretation of results from developmental screening tests must be carefully considered, since children normally attain developmental milestones at widely varying times and accurate identification of a missed or delayed milestone can only happen well after a child has definitely passed the expected developmental period. We can validly assess the developmental capabilities of young children if we select measures that are developmentally based, survey functional skills across multiple developmental domains derived from multiple sources, and contain tasks that match what is taught in the curriculum (Bagnato & Neisworth, 1981). We can use observations of children being taught to supplement screening test scores and provide important details relevant to placement, instructional, and evaluative decisions (see the section on *Informal Assessment Techniques* following).

Practice. Guidelines for selecting a screening instrument and procedures to be used have been suggested by a number of researchers (Barnes, 1982; Bloom, Madaus, & Hastings, 1981; Meisels, 1985; Levin, Henderson, Levin, & Hoffer, 1975; Salvia & Ysseldyke, 1988; Zeitlin, 1976). Screening tests should do the following:

1. Sample the domain of developmental tasks, rather than the domain of specific, academic readiness accomplishments
2. Focus on children's performance in a wide range of areas of development
3. Include normative data (including the date of the norms) along with the reliability and validity of the instrument
4. Contain items appropriate to the age range of the child being assessed
5. Be inexpensive and cost effective

6. Be capable of being administered quickly, lasting less than a half-hour, and be paced to hold the attention of the child (Zeitlin, 1976)

7. Use nonthreatening procedures and include opportunities for the child's movement

8. Contain items that are as culture-free as possible (Hegarty & Lucas, 1978); identify children on the basis of school-related factors rather than cultural, ethnic, or other factors unrelated to school success (Kunzelmann & Koenig, 1981)

9. Be conducted individually

10. Minimally score responses as *pass*, *no pass*, or *questionable*

11. Be easily administered and scored by both trained certified faculty and noncertified support staff

12. Identify at-risk children with predictive accuracy while maintaining a noncategorical approach (identifying potentially high-risk children regardless of the reason for the potential learning problem).

Advantages. Early testing can identify those children for whom certain educational programs may be inappropriate. We may then alter the child's environment to provide what will be essentially readiness activities that help to ensure future school success (Reynolds, 1979). When assessment generates information specific to a child's deficits and strengths, we can pinpoint instructional targets within a program curriculum. A well-conducted developmental screening can be the first step in accessing a continuum of opportunities important in development (Paget & Cox, 1987).

Disadvantages. Problems arise when prediction is misconstrued as the primary purpose for developmental assessment. Single scores from developmental screening tests do not provide an accurate basis for predicting later developmental functions and do not offer information specific enough for use in planning intervention strategies (Lewis & Brooks-Gunn,1982; Zeitlin, 1976). Assessment using developmental scales should emphasize current functioning only, which is all these instruments reliably measure. If children are labeled as *low-skilled* or *handicapped*, development of a positive self-image may not occur and continued placement in special programs may result regardless of future development (i.e., the label becomes a self-fulfilling prophecy).

Readiness Tests

The term **readiness** is generally used to mean ready for successful initial entry into school, both academically and socially. The primary difference between readiness tests and developmental screeners is that developmental tests focus on children's *ability* to acquire skills, while readiness tests focus on *acquired* skills and knowledge (Meisels, 1985). Readiness tests are typically administered before school entry or during kindergarten and are used to predict initial school success and identify those in need of delayed school entry or remedial and compensatory educational programs (Salvia & Ysseldyke, 1988). They also help to determine appropriate program placement and instructional program design.

Readiness tests can be criterion-referenced, norm-referenced, and individual-referenced. Norms are sometimes established to compare the performance of children on these tests (norm-referenced). The tests often include items that reflect the content of instructional programs and are used to determine what a child knows or what he or she may still need to be taught (criterion-referenced). Finally, we can administer readiness tests more than once to individual children to measure their progress in acquiring skills, thus providing individually-referenced information.

Skills Assessed. Areas of skills and knowledge which have been identified as being related to children's future success in school include (a) understanding general concepts important to school success, such as location, direction, quantity, and time; (b) processing information within three learning modalities—language-auditory (such as identification of sounds of letters in words), visual-perceptual motor (such as recognition of similarities and differences in letters, numbers, and shapes), and body awareness and control; (c) verbal reasoning and comprehension (including understanding and expressing language, following directions); (d) social and adaptive skills (such as maintaining task-relevant behavior, cooperating with peers and adults, self-help skills such as toileting); and (e) fine and gross motor activity (including drawing and copying geometric shapes, letters, and numbers, age-appropriate body control) (Gallerani, O'Regan, & Reinherz, 1982). These are typical of many of the areas assessed in readiness tests used in preschools and kindergartens.

Practice. The recommended practices for readiness testing parallel those for developmental testing. Readiness tests should do the following:

1. Sample the domain of specific, academic readiness accomplishments
2. Focus on children's performance in a wide range of skills and knowledge areas
3. Include normative data (including the date of the norms) along with the reliability and validity of the instrument
4. Include test items appropriate to the age range of the child being assessed
5. Be inexpensive and cost effective

6. Proceed quickly and be paced to hold the attention of the child
7. Use nonthreatening procedures and include opportunities for the child's movement
8. Utilize items that are as culture-free as possible
9. Be administered individually
10. Be minimally scored using *pass*, *no pass*, or *questionable*
11. Be easily administered and scored by trained certified and noncertified personnel
12. Give teachers information about children's skill strength and deficits
13. Provide interpretive guidelines.

Advantages. Well-designed and accurately administered readiness tests can be used to guide both placement and curriculum planning decisions. Results can help teachers determine whether or not a child will have a successful kindergarten or first-grade experience. Readiness tests can help teachers make decisions about placement into instructional groups and, at the item level, can guide teachers' decisions about instruction. For example, if several children are tested and all have deficits in counting to 10 or identifying all colors, the teacher can use this information to group them and plan instruction in these areas.

Disadvantages. As with all tests used with young children, readiness tests must be used and interpreted with caution. Shepard and Smith (1986), in a comprehensive review of research on school readiness assessment, state that "it is not possible to make highly accurate assessments of school readiness" (p. 84). Most publishers of tests being used to determine students' readiness for school are careful about the claims they make for their tests, and few maintain that they will accurately predict which students will succeed and which will fail to make progress in school. Readiness tests do not have sufficient reliability or validity to support special placement decisions such as the decision to enter a student in a preprimary or junior first grade. Often these readiness tests identify a disproportionately high number of poor and minority children as unready for school. This concept of being not ready to learn implies that school is a fixed and rigid entity and that these students are unready for the specific curriculum the school is prepared to teach (Shepard & Smith, 1988).

Achievement Tests

Achievement tests are the most common form of evaluation in primary school assessment (Abbott & Crane, 1977) and are frequently used with kindergarten and first-grade students (Southworth, Burr, & Cox, 1980), those at the upper end of early childhood programs. These group-administered tests are not designed to provide teachers with specific information to use in individualizing instruction or improving learning. Instead, as norm-referenced assessments, they supply comparative information about students' overall achievement. In contrast, teachers often use readiness tests directly for planning and evaluating instruction.

Skills Assessed. Typical achievement tests assess the range of basic academic skills, including language arts (reading vocabulary and comprehension, spelling, language mechanics and expression) and mathematics (computation and concepts). Some also assess knowledge in science and social studies. These skills and knowledge are necessary for successful academic achievement in the immediate future. They include following directions, understanding the language of instruction, knowing colors and shapes, and prereading and number skills (such as knowledge of letter names and sounds, numeral identification, and counting

skills). Standardized achievement tests are appropriate for use only in primary-grade classrooms with curricula emphasizing academic skills.

Practice. The National Association for the Education of Young Children (1988b) proposed seven guidelines to be followed when young children are formally tested:

1. All standardized tests used in early childhood programs must be reliable and valid according to the technical standards of test development (American Psychological Association (APA), National Commission on Measurement in Education, (NCME), American Educational Research Association (APA).
2. Decisions that have a major impact on children, such as enrollment, retention, or assignment to remedial or special classes, should be based on multiple sources of information, never on a single test score. Appropriate sources of information may include systematic observations, work samples, anecdotes from family members, and other appropriate test scores.
3. Use standardized tests only for the purpose for which they are intended and for which supporting data exist.
4. Interpret test results accurately and cautiously.
5. Select standardized tests on the basis of how well the tests match locally developed theory, philosophy, and objectives of the specific group. If no existing test matches the curriculum in use, it is better not to use a standardized test.
6. Testing of young children must be conducted by individuals who are knowledgeable about and sensitive to the developmental needs of young children and who are qualified to administer tests, including trained certified and noncertified staff.

7. Testing of young children must be sensitive to individual diversity.

Advantages. Achievement tests are often constructed with careful consideration of technical adequacy. The results of these group-administered tests can provide teachers with important information for determining a student's overall achievement relative to an appropriate norm group. These tests are often easy to obtain and relatively easy to administer and score.

Disadvantages. The administration of standardized achievement tests to young children has increased in recent years, and many schools routinely administer these tests for admittance to kindergarten or promotion to first grade. For example, the state of Georgia now requires 5-year-olds to pass a standardized achievement test before they can be promoted to the first grade (Seligmann & Murr, 1988).

Yet achievement tests can be overused and the results misinterpreted. They seldom include items that measure achievement in problem-solving skills, affective development, and creativity skills that are emphasized in many discovery-oriented and developmental programs. Since achievement tests do not take into account the process by which a child arrives at an answer, a child may be penalized for creative thinking, a consequence of assessment that focuses on the product rather than the process.

Teacher-Made Tests

Many teachers of young children construct their own tests to screen students for program placement and/or instructional planning. The information that teachers use and need most for teaching does not come from standardized tests but from tests they make themselves and from structured performance samples. Locally-made tests have the advantage of increased relevance and utility (Stiggins, 1985).

A concern with teacher-developed assessments, however, is their technical adequacy. In a survey of 150 different teacher-made screening instruments or procedures, only 16 were even minimally appropriate for screening decisions (Meisels, 1985). If a teacher wants to develop a test for assessing preschool students, it should follow relevant test-construction procedures and tactics and should be technically adequate (reliable and valid). Instruments that do not undergo an acceptable test development phase may lead to the misidentification and misplacement of children (Meisels, 1985). If high technical standards are not met, we must use test results with caution and use them clinically, not for making classroom decisions.

Local norms for teacher-made tests should be developed even if national norms are available (Meisels, 1985). Teachers can gain important information from comparing students' performance with that of their local peers.

Scores from a locally developed test administered to a group of students before they enter kindergarten could be compared to scores from relevant performance indicators administered in the middle of the year and again at the end. These results would help establish the predictive validity of the test for use as a screener with future students. For example, if the students with the lowest scores on the readiness tests continue to perform poorly on checklists, ratings, and teacher-made tests, the readiness test would reflect predictive validity.

An example of a teacher-made criterion-referenced screening test designed to be used as a pre- and posttest with kindergarten students is included at the end of this book. This test covers several domains and is primarily performance-based. It assesses skills typical of those required in many kindergarten activities (e.g., identifying and writing first and last names, identifying and copying shapes, identifying colors, counting, writing numerals from dictation, identifying and copying letters.) It also assesses motor and self-help skills (e.g., students' ability to zip, lace, button, skip, balance, walk backwards.) and social/interpersonal skills. Test results provide the teacher with information about what students know and what skills they have upon entering kindergarten, and they support end-of-year decisions regarding students' placement in the fall.

Non-Test-Based Assessments

An important trend in early childhood assessment involves the increasing use of informal techniques for the multidimensional measurement necessary to reliably assess young children. Teachers frequently use measures other than tests to gather information about their students. These **informal testing** measures include direct observations of children in both free play and structured environments, anecdotal records, teacher ratings and skills checklists, and parent questionnaires and interviews (Abbott & Crane, 1977).

Observations. Naturalistic observations form the cornerstone of non-test-based preschool assessment (Paget, 1987). Observations are often considered more useful than standardized measurement in early childhood settings because they can be used unobtrusively and yield information that more formal testing instruments cannot obtain. They also provide valuable supplemental information in such areas as application of knowledge, use of reasoning skills (synthesis or analysis), problem solving; development of positive self-concept, interpersonal communication, and social skills (Abbott & Crane, 1977).

Structured observation of young children differs from casual watching. The trained observer takes detailed field notes, which are later thoroughly examined, coded, quantified, and analyzed (Sylva, Roy & Painter, 1980). In a preschool or kindergarten, observations can be made during successive periods of 1 minute each. In the sample form (Figure 11.2), each numbered row stands for a one minute observation period. The observer attempts to write down exactly what the target child is doing and saying, without selective interpretation. The general setting is recorded in the "Observation Field Notes" section under "Setting/behaviors." Entries might include *sitting at table, playing in sandbox, riding tricycles, group story time,* and so forth. The column labeled "Language" is for recording verbal interactions. The "Analysis" columns labeled "Activity" and "Grouping" are used to code the various types of actions in which the target child and others engage in (e.g., adult-directed activities, manual play, art, music, formal games, and pretend.) and in what combinations —single child, pair (TC and other), small group (3–5), large group (6-10). These codes can later be analyzed for patterns of behaviors that may alert the teacher to a particular problem. For example, the isolated target child who frequently plays alone in pretend activities may need some encouragement to begin socializing with peers.

Although this format may be cumbersome at first, abbreviations make note taking easier. Sylva, Painter, and Roy (1980) suggest using *TC* for the target child (the child being observed), *C* for any other child, *A* for any adult and → to show an interaction.

These abbreviations are particularly helpful when observing verbal interactions.

TC/All   (Group singing)
(Target child and all other children singing together)

TC   (Sings to self)
(Target child singing)

Observer:　　　　Target Child:　　　　Sex:　　Age:　　Date/Time:

• Observation field notes •		• Analysis •	
Setting/behaviors	Language	Activity	Grouping
1. All at piano, sitting on floor	TC/all singing	Music/ rhythms	Large group
2. TC moves to play area	TC sings to self	Cruising between activities	Single child
3. TC joins C playing with puzzle	TC ➛ C I have that puzzle	Social interaction	Pair

FIGURE 11.2
Sample observation-recording form

Source: Adapted from Sylva, Painter, & Roy (1980). *Childwatching at Playgroup and Nursery School*. London. Grant McIntyre Co.

TC　(Walks to C playing with puzzle)
(Target child walks to join another child playing with a puzzle.)

TC→C　I have that puzzle.
(Target child says to other child, "I have that puzzle.")

C→TC　It's too hard. I can't do it.
(Child says to target child, "It's too hard. I can't do it.")

A→TC　Can you help C. work this puzzle?
(Adult joins children. Says to target child, "Can you help C. work this puzzle?")

TC→A　O.K.
(Target child says to adult, "O.K.")

TC→C　(Conversation)
(Target child and other child engage in conversation; observer not able to hear words spoken)

A full-page version of the form shown in Figure 11.2 is shown on page 454.

Anecdotal Records. Anecdotal records are descriptions of events directly observed by the teacher and then immediately recorded and are an important source of information about children. Incidents that the teacher believes to be meaningful to the overall development of the child are recorded during regular classroom activities in less than the time required by more structured observations. To increase accuracy and objectivity, the teacher records anecdotes immediately following the events. Interpretation of the event must be clearly distinguished from the factual description.

Compiling a series of anecdotes over time can assist teachers in forming a picture of a child's development and achievement. For example, a series of anecdotal notes made over a period of weeks may reveal a pattern of aggressive reaction when other children attempt to play with a child ("e.g., Angela playing with dolls. Hit J. when she reached for a doll; Angela using blocks. Kicked over tower built by John nearby; Angela pushes Jessica out of line for the slide"). A teacher who observes an emerging negative pattern of behavior can intervene with a systematic program. Future anecdotal notes can help the teacher decide if the intervention has been successful. Patterns of positive growth can also be noted, and teachers will find summaries of anecdotal notes useful when communicating with parents.

Teacher Rating Scales and Skills Checklists. To obtain information about a child with the contextual validity of structured observations but from a broader perspective and using a more flexible format, many preschool and kindergarten teachers use rating scales and checklists. A sample seven-part behavioral checklist/rating scale that teachers could use (and adapt) when observing children appears in Figure. 11.3.

This list reflects collective judgments from a diverse group of practitioners about important

---

To use as a behavioral checklist, note when and how often behaviors occur on successive days or at different times during a single day.

To use as a rating scale, rate each behavior on the following 5-point scale:

1	2	3	4	5
Never occurs	Rarely occurs	Sometimes occurs	Occurs regularly	Occurs frequently

Task involvement
Focuses on a task
Resolves a problem
Completes a task
Leaves a task
Is inattentive
Wanders about the room

Cooperation
Seeks participation with a child or adult
Is involved with a child or adult
Joins an activity with a child or adult
Takes turns

Autonomy
Selects an activity
Asks permission
Works independently
Chooses to join a group activity
Chooses not to join a group activity
Rejects requests to join an activity

Verbal interaction
Talks with a child or adult
Requests information from others
Responds to a child or an adult
Speaks to self

Materials use
Uses materials in an activity
Combines materials from different areas
Abuses or misuses materials

Maintenance
Takes responsibility for picking up
Volunteers to help in a maintenance activity
Helps an adult prepare an activity
Waits for a teacher to prepare an activity

Consideration
Observes the activity of others without disruption
Respects the physical space of others
Shares materials with others
Helps or offers sympathy to a child in distress
Disturbs the activity of others
Threatens or strikes another child

Source: Adapted from Day (1983). *Early Childhood Education: A Human Ecological Approach.* Glenview, IL: Scott, Foresman.

FIGURE 11.3
Sample behavioral checklist/rating scale

developmental behaviors of young children (Day, 1983). Teachers can use checklists for estimating or recording children's behaviors a number of times on successive days or at different times during a single day. Rating scales are more appropriate as summary statements of behavior over time. For such instruments to be reliable, each behavior should be clearly defined by those using the checklist, so that the the ratings or observations can be made consistently and interpreted accurately.

Parent Questionnaires and Interviews. Obtaining information about young children's developmental histories from their parents is a common practice of preschool teachers. Parents can be interviewed, formally or informally, or asked to fill out a questionnaire related to their child's physical, emotional, and social backgrounds.

Children who have failed in school because of academic, social, and emotional problems often exhibit signs of forthcoming problems that have been noted by teachers and parents (Reinherz & Griffin, 1977). This information might have arisen in interviews between teachers and parents and used to design appropriate instructional and remedial programs for these children.

However, developmental histories of children obtained through lengthy interviews may be less useful to kindergarten teachers than more current information (Gallerani, O'Regan, & Reinherz, 1982). Furthermore, the association between family history and second-grade reading performance may be weak, with little connection between end-of-second-grade achievement and various measures of environmental stimulation (DeHirsh, Jansky, & Langford, 1966). Therefore interviews and rating scales should be included as part of an assessment battery only if the information obtained is directly relevant to the decisions being made. Lengthy interviews may be eliminated from screening procedures with little ill effect.

Depending upon the decision to be made, both formal and informal tests can provide a wide range of information with the necessary multiple references. In addition to developmental screening tests, readiness tests, achievement tests and the informal assessment procedures, teachers often construct their own tests to provide themselves with information unobtainable from other sources.

SELECTING APPROPRIATE ASSESSMENT PROCEDURES

Although the previous section identified three types of early childhood assessment, the actual divisions between them are often unclear. Experts on the assessment of young children use different terminology for similar types of tests. For example, a published test may include the word *readiness* in its title, but will be used by a school district as part of their *screening* process. Some consider readiness tests as a form of achievement testing while others put them into distinctly different categories (Abbott & Crane, 1977). In fact, "developmental" tests can be used to assess the "readiness" of children to enter first grade.

When selecting instruments to assess children's readiness, to screen children for possible future diagnostic testing, or to determine how children compare to others on achievement, the two most important factors to consider are the type of decision to be made and the type of program being considered. The test must then meet the criteria for best practice in early childhood assessment and be

1. Technically adequate (reliable and valid)
2. Used appropriately, for only the purpose for which it is intended
3. Interpreted accurately and cautiously
4. Administered by trained and qualified individuals

5. Sensitive to the special needs of young children and their individual diversity
6. Low-inference, using direct measures of observable behaviors
7. Conducted over time
8. Based upon multiple sources of information.

Early childhood is characterized by a limited behavioral repertoire predominantly sensori-motor in nature. Early developmental skills are quantitatively and qualitatively different from later skills. Young children are highly distractable, and demonstrate transient responsiveness. Therefore we must consider multiple factors when assessing young children and use adaptive testing procedures (Bagnato & Neisworth, 1981). Single scores, which hypothetically reflect the overall functioning of a child, are not accurate predictors of later functioning (Lewis & Brooks-Gunn, 1982).

CHAPTER SUMMARY

In this chapter you learned that we must conduct the assessment of children in preschool and kindergarten with careful attention to the special requirements of young children. There are several concerns about how young children are currently being tested, including controversies regarding the early identification of children with special needs, the generally poor technical adequacy of tests used with young children, the inadequate procedures used to administer and interpret test results, and the need for a direct link between assessment procedures and different types of early childhood programs.

We discussed several purposes for testing preschool and kindergarten children, all of them based on the need for teachers to make decisions: Which children need assistance? What skills does this child have and which does she or he lack? What kind of program is best suited

for this child? What instructional plan should be followed? Is the child making progress in the program? Is the overall program effective for all students served? These decisions can be placed in the categories of screening and eligibility, diagnostics/planning, formative evaluation and program evaluation.

We outlined three major types of tests frequently used for assessing young children and described the advantages and disadvantages of each. The suggested appropriate uses of developmental screening tests are to determine whether a child is in need of further assessment, and to help decide if the child needs special assistance to achieve at his or her maximum potential. Readiness tests are relevant in helping teachers to make decisions about program entry and placement and about program design. Achievement tests are useful when teachers need to compare the performance of their students to that of their peers. We discussed teacher-made tests and provided an example of a locally-developed kindergarten readiness test.

To supplement the information that can be obtained from these types of tests, four types of non-test-based assessments can be useful: observations, anecdotal records, rating scales and skills checklists, and parent questionnaires and interviews.

Finally, we described how to make appropriate selections of assessment procedures for testing children in preschool and kindergarten. Selection of a test should be based upon the type of decision being made and the type of program being considered or evaluated. The assessment procedure must be judged according to the criteria for best practice for testing young children. Whenever possible, teachers should use a variety of measures to make decisions about young children in preschool and kindergarten.

CHAPTER 12

Assessment of Communicative Interaction in the Classroom

The irony with language is that most children begin their schooling with intact language systems and that it is not systematically taught in our schools. Yet, if there is an academic area that sets the occasion for prejudice and intolerance, it is langauge: How people communicate verbally. Consider the young girl who uses the following phrase at recess: "It don't matter if the bell goes off." Or the young boy who says: "We was walking down the street and would have went into the store, but got tired of the game." In both examples, the message is clear enough; the conventions used in communicating that message, however, are incorrect. Or consider the problems associated with children who pronounce s as th or young adults who stutter. The problems arise in our interpretations of these behaviors. Are they simply "bad habits of usage"? Or, do they signify more serious problems? The complexity of language stems from its dual focus on the form and content.

Assessment of communicative competence within classroom settings can be a difficult area to approach for several reasons. Aspects of communicative competence are an integral part of most traditional classroom activities (e.g., listening, speaking, reading, writing, asking and answering questions, and responding to requests and directives). Students need to communicate appropriately to accomplish a wide range of functions within classroom settings. Teachers must consider a variety of features, ranging from the form of communicative responses (e.g., voicing, articulation, syntax) to the meaning/content and function of the communication (e.g., the semantic and pragmatic appropriateness). In addition, the majority of teachers in regular education classrooms often have no specialized background in assessing communicative behavior, other than the traditional oral and written behaviors taught in language arts curricula. Therefore, it is difficult to know when students may need referral for more specific and intensive communication assessment and possible intervention, or to know how to interpret results of standardized language or communication tests that are encountered in the course of interdisciplinary staffings or individual education plans (IEPs). The impetus for this chapter comes from the integral importance of communicative competence in the classroom and the growing need for teachers and paraprofessionals to have valid and useful methods for screening or identifying students who may have significant commmunication difficulties (Damico & Oller, 1985).

CHAPTER OBJECTIVES

This chapter should enable you to do the following:

- Provide a brief overview of important aspects of communicative competence within the classroom.
- Describe the typical sequence of development for various aspects of communicative competence (e.g., articulation, grammar/syntax, semantics, social rules).

This chapter was written by Robert O'Neill, University of Oregon, and Christine A. Marvin, University of Nebraska–Lincoln.

Support for Robert O'Neill during the preparation of this chapter was provided in part by the Rehabilitation Research and Training Center on Community-Referenced Behavior Management, funded by the National Institute on Disability and Rehabilitation Research at the University of Oregon (Cooperative Agreement #G0087C0234), and by Grant #G008430057 from the Special Education Programs Office, U.S. Department of Education (Hill M. Walker, Principal Investigator). The positions expressed herein do not necessarily reflect the opinions or policies of the supporting agencies, and no official endorsement should be inferred.

Correspondence concerning this chapter can be addressed to either Robert O'Neill, Specialized Training Program, College of Education, University of Oregon, Eugene, OR 97403; or Christine Marvin, Department of Special Education and Communication Disorders, Barkley Memorial Center, University of Nebraska, Lincoln, Nebraska 68583-0732.

- Give an overview of predominant methods of assessment that are in use in this area.
- Be familiar with several popular tests of speech and language.
- Delineate an interactive model for looking at the communicative behaviors of both student and teacher in the classroom.
- Present and discuss some procedures and instruments for conducting simplified, basic assessment/screening within typical teacher/classroom situations.

KEY VOCABULARY

The major areas of definition and measurement of language and communication covered in this chapter are presented in Figure 12–1. A number of specific terms are presented throughout the chapter that focus on language concepts. For example, an important distinction is made between *comprehension,* or receptive understanding of verbal messages, and *expression,* the actual transmission of verbal messages. In language assessment, *form* and *content* have been considered the primary areas of assessment and intervention; the former focuses on the structure of verbal behavior (*sounds, units of speech,* and *fluency*) and the latter focuses on the meaning of the message (*syntax* and *semantics*). The study of the social context within which language inherently occurs, known as the area of *pragmatics,* has received increasing attention in recent years. Most language assessment is based on *developmental* progressions, in which proficiency increases with age and practice. One of the more controversial areas in language assessment is the manner in which language is *evoked* or solicited: either in controlled settings using *imitative* responses or in natural settings using *spontaneous* speech. While many *standardized instruments* are available using preestablished administration and scoring procedures, a new

group of strategies is becoming increasingly popular, in which behavior is rated or checked for prominent features within *communicative interactions* in the classroom, including student interactions with teachers and curriculum.

BASIC ASPECTS OF COMMUNICATIVE BEHAVIOR IN THE CLASSROOM

The interactive communication that typically occurs in most or all classroom activities includes both **comprehension** and **expression** (Bloom & Lahey, 1978). Students must comprehend and respond appropriately to verbal directions, questions, and requests from teachers and peers (e.g., "Open your books to page twelve," "Mary, please come and work Problem 3 on the board," "What is the capital of Alaska?"). Comprehension of written communication is also very important for reading textbooks, following directions, and completing assignments. Students' expressive communication becomes important with classroom assignments such as book reports, written exams, class presentations, oral responses to teachers' questions, small-group discussions, and cooperative learning ventures with peers. Many teachers in regular educational settings are concerned with determining whether or not students' expressive performances are appropriate for their age and grade level. Such concern may focus on one or more aspects of form, content, and the use of expressive communicative responses (Bloom & Lahey, 1978).

Form. Three different aspects of **form** may contribute to and be problematic for a student's verbal production. One aspect related to communicative form is *phonology,* which refers to the way in which individual speech sounds are articulated. Phonological errors might involve omitting certain sounds in words, saying a *w*

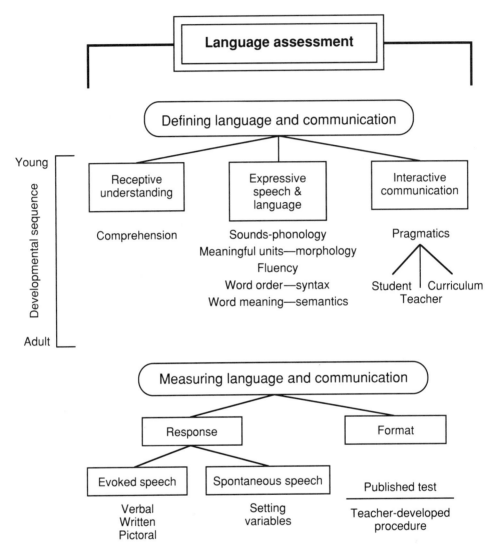

FIGURE 12.1
Model of language assessment

sound instead of an *r*, or dropping unaccented syllables in multisyllabic words. In addition, individual sounds can alter the meanings of words. Phonology problems may also entail intonation and stress patterns in certain words or parts of words within sentences. For example, the same sentence might either be a statement ("He's going to the store") or a question ("He's going to the store?"), depending on whether it is said with a falling or rising intonation.

Morphology refers to the presence or absence of the small units of speech that can alter the meanings of words but do not stand alone as words themselves. These units, or *morphemes*, include endings of words such as *s* to indicate plurals or possession, *-ing* or *-ed* to indicate different verb tenses, or any of several prefixes. Students may demonstrate subtle, but significant difficulties in this area as they develop their proficiency with the English language.

Another aspect of communicative form is **syntax,** or the arrangement or order of words in a statement. Syntax, or sentence structure, is obviously very important in that different sequences of words can convey different meanings and messages. Note the similarity of words and differences in meaning in the following two sentences: (a) John hit the truck; (b) The truck hit John.

A final aspect of communicative form that is closely related to the features mentioned thus far is **fluency,** or the smooth, connected flow of a communicative response. A universal definition of fluency problems has been somewhat controversial over the years, particularly with regard to younger children. This feature is often most noticeable when it is absent and stuttering or other dysfluencies occur. Generally, episodes of dysfluency at any age include one or more of the following: (a) repetitions of parts of words or whole words, (b) abnormal audible or silent prolongations of sounds, and (c) interjections of extraneous sounds or syllables into an utterance (Hutchinson, 1983). The severity of fluency problems for an individual depends upon the frequency and intensity of these three types of behaviors. We all display some level of dysfluency in our everyday conversations; young children ages 2–6 years display higher incidences of dysfluency for short periods of time in the preschool years. The most severe form of dysfluency, stuttering, is reserved for broken speech patterns that persist over time and include excessive frequency and tension.

Content. Along with form parameters, teachers may be concerned about the **content** of a student's communicative responses. Language content, often considered under the domain known as **semantics,** refers to the meanings or referents of individual words within a communicative response (e.g., a statement or sentence), as well as the overall message conveyed by the relationship of the words within the response. Obviously, the content or message depends upon both the components (e.g., words) of the response and their order, or syntax. Thus, a student may have a large vocabulary but have difficulties in ordering the words in a sentence; conversely, a student's responses may demonstrate proper syntax but employ limited or inappropriate vocabulary.

Function. The study of **pragmatics,** or variables related to the use and functions of communication in context, has received increasing attention over the last decade (Hart, 1981; McLean & Snyder-McLean, 1984; Prutting & Kirchner, 1987). While debate has ocurred over the definition of pragmatics, it has generally focused on various verbal and nonverbal interactive aspects of communication, such as appropriate introduction and maintenance of topics, turn-taking, use of repetition, cohesion, or relatedness across time, requests for revision or clarification, vocal quality and intensity, physical proximity, facial expression, and story grammar and appreciation for expository discourse. While obviously intertwined with the form and content of communicative responses, pragmatics focuses more on the function or effects that a response may have on the interactive partner and the variables that affect or modify such functional effects (Prutting & Kirchner, 1987). Thus, a teacher may observe that a student's vocabulary and syntax are at an appropriate level, but he or she consistently interrupts others and "steps on" what others are saying. Or a student's vocal quality may be such that it calls attention to him or her in a

TABLE 12.1
Summary of aspects of communicative behavior

Phonology:	Concerns the way individual speech sounds are articulated; also intonation and stress patterns of words and parts of words in sentences
Morphology:	Concerns the presence or absence of small units of speech which can alter the meaning of words (e.g., *-s, -ing, -ed*)
Syntax:	Concerns the arrangement or order of words in a statement (i.e., sentence structure)
Fluency:	Concerns smooth, connected flow of a communicative response (i.e., absence of repetitions, prolongations, or interjections)
Semantics:	Concerns meanings or referents of individual words in a communicative response, and overall message conveyed by the response
Pragmatics:	Concerns variables related to interactive use and the function of communication in context; emphasis on function or effects that a response may have on an interactive partner, and vice versa

negative way or distorts the clarity of the response.

Table 12.1 summarizes the above aspects of communication. These features of communication are probably familiar to most teachers, from formal coursework in language arts, language development, and/or their own observations of students communicating within classroom settings. In considering these communicative features, both separately and interactively, an assessment-related question comes to mind: When are one or more of these features considered problematic for a particular student? To begin answering this question, the next section presents some normative data on the sequence of communication development within populations of children without communication difficulties.

SEQUENCES OF DEVELOPMENT OF COMMUNICATION FEATURES

This section begins with a caveat. The information that is presented and discussed relevant to normal sequences of development *should not* be misconstrued as absolute rules or ex-

pectations. In developing **developmental** taxonomies of any type, it is always important to remember that children of similar ages exhibit widely varying levels of behavioral performance. While behavioral characteristics may consistently follow a particular *sequence* across given children, the rate or age at which children will display particular characteristics can be very different (Prutting, 1979). The purpose of this section is to provide some *general* guidelines and background information for teachers. This information can then be used to set the stage for later discussion in the chapter, and may be useful in helping determine when a particular student is having greater-than-normal difficulty and is in need of more intensive assessment and/or training opportunities.

Development of Communication

Phonology (Articulation). This area addresses how individual speech sounds are articulated. Figure 12.2 shows average age estimates for consonant production (Sanders, 1972). These data are still recognized as a reliable reference for articulation norms for American children. The bar for each sound begins

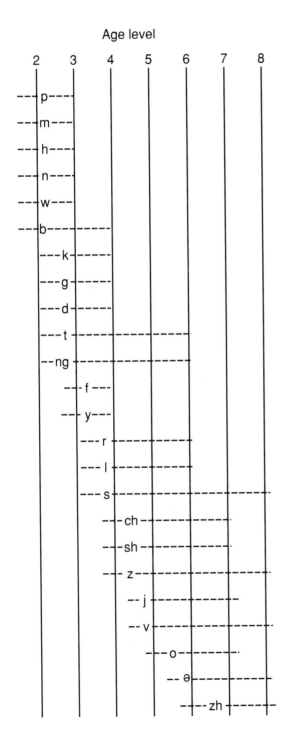

Age level

at the median age at which children typically articulate the sound correctly and ends at the point where 90% of all children typically produce the sound correctly. These data nicely illustrate the variability children display. For example, children may begin correctly producing an *r* sound anywhere between the ages of 3 and 6 years, although approximately 10% of children may not do so until even later ages. However, the majority of students correctly produce these sounds by age 8.

Morphology. This area concerns parts of speech that serve to modify the meanings of words, but are not words in themselves. Table 12.2 presents four major morphological classes (plurals, tenses, progressives, and comparatives) and the approximate ages at which they are consistently displayed (Gruenewald & Pollak, 1984). As with the phonological sounds, children can consistently and correctly use morphological forms by approximately the age of 12. However, many more sophisticated and less often used morphological rules are still just emerging in children ages 9–19 years (Nippold, 1988). The social and academic demands placed on these older students often require the use of communicative patterns not necessary in the younger years.

Syntax (Structure) and Semantics. Beyond simple, one-word referential labeling behavior, the semantics or meaning of communicative

FIGURE 12.2

Inventory of phonology

Average age estimates and upper age limits of customary consonant production are shown. The solid bar corresponding to each sound starts at the median age of customary articulation and stops at the age level at which 90% of all children are customarily producing the sound.

Source: E. R. Sanders, "When Are Speech Sounds Learned?" *Journal of Speech and Hearing Disorders* 37 (1972): 55–63.

TABLE 12.2
Approximate developmental progression for morphological classes

By age 4	Plural—uses -s and -z but not consistently
	Tenses—Uses progressive (-ing); simple past (-t and -d) not consistent
	Progressives—My/mine emerging; uses nouns with final -s; his, her
	Comparatives—Not used
By age 5	Plurals—Uses -s and -z more consistently; -es, -ez not consistent
	Tenses—Simple past, future tense, and present progressive more consistent; have and have not not used
	Possessives—Use of -s, my, mine, and more consistent
	Comparatives—Not used
By age 6	Plurals—Uses -es and -ez more consistently; irregular form emerges
	Possessives—Uses correctly with greater consistency.
	Comparatives—Regular
By age 7 and 8	Plurals—Improves use of irregular form
	Tenses—Have and had developed
	Comparatives—Uses irregular correctly

Source: L. J. Gruenewald and S. A. Pollak, *Language Interaction in Teaching and Learning.* (Baltimore: University Park Press, 1984), p. 69.

responses becomes highly interdependent with response syntax or structure: The message conveyed depends upon the order of the words. Gruenewald and Pollak (1984) describe three major sentence structures:

1. *Simple* sentences, composed of a subject, verb, and object (e.g., "The girl kicked the ball," "The man bought rice.")
2. *Compound* sentences, composed of two simple sentences connected by a conjunction (e.g., "The girl kicked the ball and the girl won the game.")
3. *Complex* sentences, composed of one or more independent clauses and one or more dependent clauses joined by a subordinate conjunction (e.g., "The large ball rolled away when the box fell over.").

Although children of ages 4–5 can use all three types of sentences (Brown, 1973), it is important for teachers to have some idea of the developmental changes that occur in such structures during the elementary school years. Table 12.3 presents an approximate develop-

mental progression for sentence structures during the elementary years. In addition, the table provides information about the average approximate number of words per communication unit (Loban, 1976), an index of the typical length or number of words contained in communicative responses.

Table 12.4 presents a progression for the initial development of a variety of important syntactic/semantic components, such as the use of adjectives, pronouns, prepositions, conjunctions, and questions. Children regularly use many of these forms and components by the time they are 6–7 years of age.

To provide further detail on one aspect of such syntactic/semantic development, Table 12.5 presents the progression for the development of *wh-* questions in terms of the (a) forms involved, (b) types of concepts involved, and (c) structure of the required responses.

Tables 12.2–12.5 provide basic information on typical developmental sequences of the phonological and syntactic forms and semantic functions exhibited in children's language. It is

TABLE 12.3
Approximate developmental progression for major sentence structures

Ages 5 and 6	Children consistently use pronouns and verbs in the present and past tenses. Complex sentences appear frequently. Conditionality (*You eat your dinner, you have banana.*) and causality (*Don't sit on 'at radiator—very hot.*) expressed by *why, because,* and *if* are implicit in the children's language. The average number of words per communication unit will be about 6.8.[a]
Ages 6 and 7	Further progress in complex sentences, especially those with adjectival clauses. Conditional dependent clauses, such as those beginning with *if* appear. The average number of words per oral communication unit will be about 7.5 with a variation between 6.6 and 8.1[a]
Ages 7 and 8	Children can now use relative pronouns as objects in subordinate adjectival clauses (*I have a cat which I feed every day*). Subordinate clauses beginning with *when, if,* and *because* appear frequently. The gerund phrase as an object of verb appears (*I like washing myself*). The average number of words per communication unit in oral language will be about 7.6.[a]
Ages 8, 9 and 10	Children begin to relate particular concepts to general ideas, using such connectors as *meanwhile, unless, even if*. About 50% of the children begin to use the subordinating connector *although* correctly. They begin to use the present participle active: *Sitting up in bed, I looked around*. The perfect participle appears: *Having read Tom Sawyer, I returned it to the library*. The gerund as the object of a preposition appears: *By seeing the movie, I didn't have to read the book*. The average number of words per communication unit in oral language will be 9 with a variation from 7.5 to 9.3.[a]
Ages 10, 11 and 12	At this age, children form hypotheses and envision their consequences. This involves using complex sentences with subordinate clauses introduced by connectives like *provided that, nevertheless, in spite of*, and *unless*. Auxiliary verbs such as *might, could,* and *should* will appear more frequently than at earlier stages of language development. They have difficulties in distinguishing and using the past, past perfect, and present perfect tenses of the verb, and almost none of them use the expanded forms of the past perfect or the future perfect. The stage of thinking *if this, then (probably) that* is emerging, usually applied to temporal things rather than to nontemporal ideas and relations. *If the cost of higher education escalates, then (probably) enrollment will falter.* The average number of words per spoken communication unit will be about 9.5, with a variation from 8 to 10.5.[a] The average number per written unit in the study was 9 with a range from 6.2 to 10.2, depending upon the child's verbal proficiency.

Source: L. J. Gruenewald and S. A. Pollak, *Language Interaction in Teaching and Learning.* (Baltimore: University Park Press, 1984), p. 71.

[a]A communication unit may be defined as a group of words that cannot be further divided without a loss of their essential meaning (Loban, 1976, p. 105). In Loban's research, this communication unit generally appeared to be comprised of an independent clause with its modifiers.

TABLE 12.4
Approximate developmental progression for syntactic/semantic components

---

By age 4
Adjectives—Adjectives (*simple*) used
Adverbs—Adverbs of location (*there, here*) used
Pronouns—*I* and *me* inconsistent; *it*
Conjunctions—*And* used consistently to coordinate; *because* emerging; *if* and *so* not used
Negation—*Not, no, can't*, and *don't* used
Questions—Upward intonation at end of sentences; *what, what do* used
Prepositions—*In, on, with, of, for, to, up*, and *at* used

By age 5
Adjectives—Errors in agreement between adjective and noun
Adverbs—Adverbs of time and manner in addition to location
Pronouns—Consistently used; reflexive pronoun emerging
Conjunctions—*Because* used more consistently; *if* and *so* emerging
Questions—*Why* questions inconsistent; inversion of subject and auxiliary
Prepositions—*After, before, until, down, through, over, under*, and *near* used

By ages 6–7
Conjunctions—*But, after, before* (temporal), *if*, and *so* more consistently used; *because* and *therefore* used as *then* with no causal relationship
Pronouns—Reflexive pronoun used
Prepositions—Correctly used
Questions—*How* emerging

Source: L. J. Gruenewald and S. A. Pollak, *Language Interaction in Teaching and Learning*. (Baltimore: University Park Press, 1984), p. 73.

important to keep in mind that this information is a very broadly defined overview of a very complex domain, and provides only basic guidelines and rough expectations.

Occurrence of Dysfluencies. The imprecise definition of true stuttering or dysfluency, especially in younger children, has made it difficult to come up with reliable and valid information about incidence and prevalence rates, particularly across developmental periods. Research evidence also indicates that a large percentage of children who show significant dysfluencies at a particular time eventually recover spontaneously (Hutchinson, 1983). Therefore, many workers in this area take an individualistic focus on a child's particular speech features at a given time, rather than identifying progressive aspects (Wingate, 1976).

Pragmatics

It is considerably more difficult to identify and discuss normative patterns and sequences of development in the interactive use of communicative responses in context. Problems abound in defining, observing, and measuring broader pragmatic aspects of communication, which are often dependent upon other features of communication form and semantic function. Research has been conducted on several aspects of pragmatic abilities, often focusing on differences between the performance of chil-

TABLE 12.5
Approximate developmental progression for *wh-* questions

Question Form	Concept Presented	Structure of Response
What + be	Identify	Noun
What + do	Action	Verb
Where	Space	Adverb/prepositional phrase
What kind (color, shape, size)	Classification	Adjective to description
Who	People	Noun, pronoun
Whose	Possessive	Possessive
Why	Cause/effect	Because phrase
How	Manner/method	Adverb/adjective
Many/few	Number	
Much/little	Quantity	
Often/soon	Time	
Far/near	Distance	
Long/short	Linear measure of time	
Heavy/light	Weight	
Big/small	Size	
When	Time	Adverb/prepositional phrase/tense
Which	Selection/multiple choice	

Source: L. J. Gruenewald and S. A. Pollak, *Language Interaction in Teaching and Learning.* (Baltimore: University Park Press, 1984), p. 74.

dren with and without diagnosed communicative disorders. For example, areas of research includes children's responses to requests for revision (Brinton, Fujuki, Winkler, & Loeb, 1986), incorporation of "new" and "old" information (Skarakis & Greenfield, 1982), speech modifications based on the presence of different listeners (Shatz & Gelman, 1973), and responses to "indirect directives" (Shatz, Shulman, & Bernstein, 1982).

Roth and Spekman (1984a and 1984b) presented a conceptual model for assessing pragmatic abilities, focusing on communicative intentions, presuppositions involved in the communicative context, and the organization of discourse (e.g., turn-taking, topic maintenance). Prutting and Kirchner (1987) provided results from a pragmatic assessment protocol for children and adults with and without various

communicative disorders. Although this assessment covered a broad range of verbal and nonverbal pragmatic parameters, the children were all approximately 7–10 years old, precluding a focus on developmental aspects. They do state, however, that the assessment should only be used for children 5 years of age or older, as most or all of the abilities they were assessing are present, to at least some degree, in children of that age.

In summary, a variety of communication features can be important for classroom functioning at particular stages of development. Teachers must have some capacity with regard to determining whether or not a student's communicative ability is problematic. The next sections review the assessment formats typically employed with features of communication and several popular tests that teachers may encounter in their interactions with communication specialists.

TYPICAL FORMATS AND METHODS FOR COMMUNICATION ASSESSMENT

Assessment of children's communicative expression and comprehension typically employs several different formats (see Meitus & Weinberg, 1983, and Miller, 1981, for reviews). These formats range from structured, standardized techniques to less structured, spontaneous approaches. The more structured, **standardized instruments** or tests are typically norm-referenced; that is, they allow comparison of a given student's performance against that of other children of similar age and characteristics. These formats often require the student to **imitate** the examiner's model, answer specific questions with single words or sentences, and/or read written material silently or aloud. Less structured approaches, such as **spontaneous speech** samples, provide a more functional look at a student's communication patterns. They can be used to gather information that can be compared to normative standards, or can be criterion-referenced, to compare the student's communication patterns in specific areas to certain established levels of performance. We discuss both of these methods for assessing communicative competence in the following sections.

Assessment of Communication Productions

Evoked Imitation Assessments. Some measures of expressive communication rely on using evoked imitation to obtain samples of a child's speech production. That is, children are asked to repeat what the examiner says, either immediately or after a delay, and their re-

sponses are recorded and analyzed. Children may be asked to repeat single consonant sounds, single words, or whole sentences.

Evoked imitation procedures are primarily used in the assessment of phonological/ articulatory processes and more general assessment of a student's syntactic responses. For example, a child may be asked to repeat lists of words that sample a variety of consonant sounds or to repeat sentences of varying levels of syntactic complexity. We can analyze a child's responses in a variety of ways, focusing on the percentage of words articulated correctly, or sentences repeated verbatim. More detailed analysis can determine if there are consistent patterns in the types of errors that occur. Obviously, the use of imitative procedures for single words and/or sentences depends on the student's ability to understand and respond to the task requirements.

Evoked Responses to Picture Stimuli. Another approach to evoking productive communication responses is to present a picture stimulus (e.g., a drawing or photograph) and ask "What is it?", or "Tell me what's happening in the picture." Such a procedure can be used to help assess phonological production, the presence of dysfluencies, or the semantic/syntactic structure of communicative responses, using single-word responses or more complex phrase and sentence structures.

The type of picture stimuli and the wording of the prompts significantly influence the length and complexity of responses elicited from the students. Asking a question such as "What is this?" generally elicits single words or a short descriptive phrase. Asking a student to tell a story about the picture provides an opportunity to speak in longer statements tied together with repetitive use of *and then* or *and*. Presenting a known storybook picture frequently elicits predictable words and story lines associated with the story. However, these statements may be memorized by the student and may not reflect his or her true syntactic/semantic ability. For other suggestions regarding the collection of speech samples refer to Miller (1981) and Lund and Duchan (1988).

Reading Words/Sentences/Paragraphs. For students who can read, it may be possible to ask them to read written material aloud (e.g., words, sentences, paragraphs) to obtain samples of communicative responses. Some communicative assessments, particularly for older school-age children, include various measures of reading comprehension as well as production. Oral reading samples can be audiotaped for later scoring and analysis of phonology/articulation, disfluencies, sentence structure, and/or vocabulary choice.

Spontaneous Speech Samples. Along with the more structured assessments described above, audio- or videotapes also can be made of students speaking in more naturalistic situations (e.g. classroom, playgrounds, etc.). Students may be asked to tell a story or describe an event, or engage in spontaneous conversation or a play interaction with another person for a brief period of time (15–30 minutes). Such samples typically need to be transcribed, or put into written form. Virtually all of the communication characteristics that have been mentioned above can be assessed, including articulation, disfluency, syntax, and pragmatic aspects of interactive communication. The more open-ended the examiner's question or prompt, the more opportunity is present for the student to elaborate and expose his/her true expressive abilities or difficulties.

Assessment of Comprehension

One major class of techniques to assess communicative comprehension employs picture stimuli. Vocabulary is often assessed by pre-senting a set of pictures to a child who is then told, "Point to ___." Complex pictures allow assessment of more elaborate semantic and syntactic structures (e.g., "Point to the big ball on the chair," versus "Point to the little ball on the floor."). Alternatively, a child may be asked to listen to or read a phrase or sentence, and then perform the action described or answer the question. Students at more advanced levels may be asked to judge the grammatical correctness of spoken or written phrases or sentences.

Issues Concerning Assessment Methods

Influence of Administration/Data Collection Procedures. The use of the preceding methods has been predominant in communication assessment for the last two decades (Emerick & Hatten, 1979). However, within the last 10 years, a variety of concerns have been raised that call into question the utility of some of these measurement formats (Lund & Duchan, 1988). The central controversial issue is whether structured assessments conducted in atypical settings are representative of typical spontaneous performance.

For example, research has called into question the relationship between results obtained from structured evoked imitation tasks and results from spontaneous language samples. Children often produce syntactic structures during imitation tasks differently (either better or worse) than during a spontaneous language sample (Bloom, 1974; Dailey & Boxx, 1979; McDade, Simpson, & Lamb, 1982; Prutting & Connolly, 1976; Prutting, Gallagher, & Mulac, 1975). Thus, performance on an imitation task may not provide a good picture of a student's true ability.

Researchers have also examined the influence of various setting variables on the spontaneous language samples of children. Longhurst and File (1977) compared four conditions for gathering speech samples from 3–5-year-old children enrolled in a Head Start program. Some conditions involved pictures or objects for children to talk about, while one less-structured condition involved the child and experimenter in conversation about more personal topics (e.g., home, family, and school). The children displayed the most grammatically well-developed sentences during the less-structured condition, when they were engaged in conversation.

Scott and Taylor (1978) compared language samples gathered from normally developing children (2–5 years of age) during unstructured clinician-child interaction in a clinical setting and during unstructured mother-child interaction in a home setting. The variety of syntactic forms and structures produced in the two settings was similar; however, children produced significantly longer utterances in the home setting and many qualitative differences were evident. During clinical samples, children primarily talked about ongoing or imminent activities; during home samples, there was substantially greater use of past tense verb forms, complex utterances, and questions.

Obviously, such context or setting variables need to be considered in interpreting the presence or absence of particular syntactic structures. Results such as these have led writers and researchers in the field to encourage caution concerning the influence of assessment conditions upon performance outcomes. Many have recommended a focus on assessment within meaningful contexts to increase the probability of obtaining representative samples of communicative behavior (Lund & Duchan, 1988; Roth & Spekman, 1984b). Obtaining information from a variety of contexts may also be important; for example, children should be observed interacting with a variety of communicative partners (peers, adults, teacher) and in many representative settings. For preschool-aged children, such functional assessment might include observing during snack time, free play, or show-and-tell; other situations would be appropriate for older school-aged children, such as group activities and projects, class presentations, lunchtime, or recess (Roth & Spekman, 1984b).

These conceptual and technical concerns are extremely important in screening and identification decisions made by typical classroom teachers. In the lower elementary grades, many teachers have extensive opportunities to observe students' communicative interactions under varying conditions and situations. Thus, they can serve as an ideal resource for information relevant to screening. However, they must also be sensitive to both the strategies for collecting data and interpretation of those data.

Other Psychometric Issues. Along with the influence of general administration and data-collection variables, there has also been concern with psychometric properties of many of the available standardized tests. For example, Sommers, Erdige, and Peterson (1978) reviewed several studies that investigated the relationships among various tests that purported to assess different aspects of communicative competence. Typically, a battery of expressive and receptive tests were administered to a group of children and their interrelationships analyzed. The authors concluded that many standardized measures lack construct and content validity (see chapter 5). There were very often moderate to high correlations between subscale and total test scores from different instruments. Many subscales and subtests appeared to be measuring the same, rather than different, skills. Different tests were not very effective in validly measuring different, specific skills or aspects of communicative performance. Such tests are not necessarily useless; however, clinicians and other professionals need to be cautious in making assumptions or planning intervention strategies based on very specific results from such tests and their subscales.

Obviously, there are important issues to be considered in evaluating the results of *all* types of standardized communication assessment. The following section reviews some of the standardized communication assessment instruments that teachers are likely to encounter when reviewing files, or participating in interdisciplinary staffings. These instruments have not been chosen for any particular positive or negative qualities, but rather because they are in relatively widespread use by speech/language pathologists and related professionals.

DESCRIPTIONS OF STANDARDIZED COMMUNICATION ASSESSMENTS

Literally dozens of instruments have been developed for assessing different aspects of communicative competence in children and adults

with and without communication problems. Table 12.6 presents a list of often-used specific and more general language tests, along with the types of tasks they employ, the age ranges for which normative data are available, and the dimension of language ability upon which they focus. As previously mentioned, not all of the measures that have been developed have undergone thorough analysis and establishment of their psychometric properties (test-retest reliability, construct and content validity, appropriate normative data collection, etc.). However, many more recently developed tests have begun to improve in these areas.

For each test, we present the format, type of scoring and interpretation, and some psychometric characteristics. The review includes some of the more popular standardized instruments in use by speech/language pathologists who work in educational settings. Rather than exhaustively evaluating the construction and use of these tests, we provide basic information to familiarize teachers with the types of tasks and scores that the tests generate.

TABLE 12.6

List of language tests, the types of tasks involved, the age ranges for which they have normative data, and the communication features they assess

Norm-Referenced Measure	Type of Task(s)	Normative Ages	Dimension(s) Examined
Test for Auditory Comprehension of Language (Carrow, 1973)	Comprehension	3–6	Semantics, syntax
Peabody Picture Vocabulary Test (Dunn, 1965/1980)	Comprehension	2:6–18:0	Semantics
Full Range Picture Vocabulary Test (Ammons and Ammons, 1948)	Comprehension	2:0–35:0	Semantics
Boehm Test of Basic Concepts (Boehm, 1969)	Comprehension	Grade Levels K–2nd	Semantics
Miller-Yoder Test of Grammatical Comprehension (Miller and Yoder, 1972)	Comprehension	5:6–21:5[a]	Syntax

TABLE 12.6 (continued)

Norm-Referenced Measure	Type of Task(s)	Normative Ages	Dimension(s) Examined
Assessment of Children's Language Comprehension (Foster, Giddan, and Stark, 1973)	Comprehension	3:0–6:5	Syntax
Northwestern Syntax Screening Test (Lee, 1971)	Comprehension, production (delayed imitation)	3:0–7:11	Syntax
ITPA Verbal Expression Subtest (Kirk, McCarthy, and Kirk, 1968)		2:7–10:1	Semantics
Stephens Oral Language Screening Test (Stephens, 1977)	Elicited imitation	4:4–7:0	Semantics, syntax
Carrow Elicited Language Inventory (Carrow, 1974)	Elicited imitation	3:0–7:11	Syntax
Developmental Sentence Scoring (Lee, 1974)	Production	2:0–6:11	Syntax
Michigan Picture Language Inventory (Wolski and Lerea, 1962)	Comprehension, production	4:0–6:0	Semantics, syntax
Sequenced Inventory of Communication Development (Hedrick, Prather, and Tobin, 1975)	Comprehension, production	0:4–4:0	Semantics, syntax
Test of Language Development (Newcomer and Hammill, 1977)	Comprehension, production, elicited imitation	4:0–8:11	Semantics, syntax
Test of Adolescent Language (Hammill et al., 1980)	Comprehension production	Grade Levels 7–12	Semantics, syntax

Source: Meitus and Weinberg, 1983.

[a]Experimental data based on mentally retarded subjects.

Articulation/Phonology

Goldman-Fristoe Test of Articulation. The Goldman-Fristoe (1986) test includes three subtests: in the Sounds-in-Words subtest, the child must produce one-word labels for pictures; in the second subtest (Sounds-in-Sentences), the child must tell a story about a set of pictures; and in the third (Stimulability Subtest) the child has multiple opportunities to imitate correctly specific sounds that were marked as errors during the first subtest. For each subtest, the examiner scores whether particular sounds were correct or incorrect for single words or in certain key words in sentences. Separate notations indicate position (e.g., initial, medial, and final position in words) and particular types of errors (e.g., omissions, substitutions, distortions).

The test manual provides percentile rank norms for the number of errors for both the Sounds-in-Words subtest (for males and females ages 2–15), and for the Stimulability subtest (for males and females ages 6–16 +). The authors recommend that these percentile ranks be used in communicating results to other professionals. The judgment as to whether or not a student has a mild, moderate, or severe problem "is an arbitrary judgment which must be made by the user of the test" (Goldman & Fristoe, 1986, p. 14).

The test manual reports one-week test-retest reliability percentages in the .80–.99 range for specific type and position of incorrect sounds. It also presents percentages for inter- and intrarater reliability, which were in a similar range. No validity data are presented (e.g., comparisons to other similar tests), although the authors report data comparing performance on the first two subtests, which reflects measurement of different skills.

Fisher-Logemann Test of Articulation Competence. The Fisher and Logemann test (1971) is another test of articulation with two subtests: one that asks children to label 35 pictures with single words and another that asks them to read 15 sentences. The examiner records the number and type of errors for specific sounds on a form that classifies sounds by their distinctive features. The results are analyzed in terms of error patterns in the place of articulation (e.g., lips, tongue, palate), the manner of formation (e.g., plosion, friction, stops), and the voicing of sounds (e.g., *b* vs. *p*). Thus, the test provides relatively specific information about problem sounds for a particular child and

may not be readily useful by persons without specific training in the area of phonetics.

One rather large drawback of this test is that the authors generally describe the manner in which the test was developed and pilot-tested (by 30 speech pathologists in Chicago), but do not provide any data on reliability or validity (at least there were none in the manuals we read). They heavily emphasize the fact that the test is based on established principles of phonological and phonemic development, but the supporting data are simply not present.

Goldman-Fristoe-Woodcock Test of Auditory Discrimination. The Goldman, Fristoe, and Woodcock (1970) test assesses a person's ability to receptively discriminate different phonological sounds. The test presents 30 words via audiotape, preferably using headphones. For each word presented, the person is to point to the appropriate picture out of a set of 4. The list of words is presented twice, once without background noise (Quiet Test) and once with a certain level of background noise (Noise Test), to assess the person's optimal and functional discrimination skills.

The examiner records the person's response for each word and analyzes the results by calculating the number of errors, using either percentile ranks or standard scores. It is possible to analyze more specific types of error patterns, but the authors caution that this should only be done for research or exploratory clinical purposes, as these subcategories have relatively poor reliability.

The test was normed on 745 persons, aged 3–84. Significant differences were found with advancing age, as anticipated. Two week test-retest reliabilities (on a small sample of 17 subjects) were .87 for the Quiet Test, and .81 for the Noise Test. The authors claim reasonable construct validity, in that persons show changes in performance with age, as would be expected, and a limited analysis has shown that the test has relatively low correlations with other measures.

Semantics

Peabody Picture Vocabulary Test-Revised (PPVT). The Peabody Picture Vocabulary Test (Dunn & Dunn, 1981) focuses on receptive vocabulary (there are two parallel, equivalent forms) and is very popular and widely used in educational settings, given its relative simplicity. The examiner presents four pictures and asks the subject to point to the correct picture when given the verbal label. The examiner records responses as correct or incorrect and records which picture was chosen on error trials. The test can be used with persons aged 2½–40 years. Basal and ceiling levels are determined, thereby eliminating the necessity to administer the entire 130 items of the test.

The test has been standardized on over 4,000 individuals across the country, so the examiner can convert an individual's raw scores to percentile ranks or standard scores. Adequate reliability and validity have been established through test-retest, internal split-half reliability, comparisons with other measures, and so forth. Although the test is often used as a measure of verbal intelligence, the limited nature of the testing format should inspire *great* caution in anyone who wishes to use IQ scores based on the PPVT results. It would probably be better for teachers (or others) to focus on percentile scores and age and grade equivalent scores.

The Word Test. A wider variety of semantically oriented abilities are assessed by The Word Test (Jorgensen, Barrett, Huisingh, & Zachman, 1981), which focuses on six major areas: (a) associations—the student chooses the 1 word from a group of 4 that does not belong, and explains why; (b) synonyms—students provide a one-word synonym for a stimulus word; (c) semantic absurdities—students ex-

plain why a sentence is absurd; (d) antonyms—students provide a one-word antonym for a stimulus word; (e) definitions—students explain the meanings of words; and (f) multiple definitions—students supply two meanings for a stimulus word. Recording and scoring methods vary for the different tasks. The subtests sample a variety of expressive as well as receptive semantic abilities.

Raw scores are generated for the different test areas and the total test, and the examiner can convert them into age equivalents, percentiles, or standard scores. The test was standardized on a sample of 476 children, ages 7–12, that contained nearly equal numbers of males and females and was representative of minority groups. The test reports split-half reliability, but not test-retest. The major validity data are changes in test performance with groups of increasing age, and correlations among items and the total score and among the different subtasks. The great advantage of this test is its ability to tap various expressive vocabulary skills. In contrast, the PPVT mentioned earlier is limited to assessing only receptive knowledge of words.

General Communicative Abilities

Test of Language Development (TOLD—Primary and Intermediate). The TOLD (Newcomer & Hammill, 1982; Hammill & Newcomer, 1982) is available in two versions, the Primary Level for ages 4–9 and the Intermediate Level, for ages 8½–13. Each version includes a variety of subtests that sample expressive and receptive abilities related to phonology, morphology, syntax, and semantics in different ways. For example, the eight subtests of the TOLD—Primary involve pointing to pictures after being given a verbal label, giving oral definitions, selecting the correct picture corresponding to a stimulus sentence, sentence imitation, sentence completion, judgement of sound similarity of word pairs, picture labeling, and sentence reading to sample particular sounds. The five subtests of the TOLD—Intermediate version involve combining simple sentences to form complex sentences, determining the truth of simple sentences, ordering random words into a sentence, explaining why three given words are alike or are parts of a class, and identifying grammatically incorrect sentences.

A variety of scoring methods are used for the different subtests. Both tests yield raw scores, percentiles, standard scores for the subtests, and quotients, which are scores based on different composites of the subtests (e.g., a Spoken Language Quotient, a Listening Quotient, and so forth). The TOLD–Primary also yields a language age score. The TOLD—Primary was standardized on 1,836 children in 19 states and one Canadian province; the TOLD—Intermediate was normed on 871 children in 13 states. Both tests report acceptable levels of internal consistency and test-retest reliability. Relatively extensive analyses are presented for content, criterion-related, and construct validity (e.g., relations to other measures, subtest correlations, relations to expert judgment)—more extensive than those of most other tests in this area. The authors and their colleagues (Hammill, Brown, Larsen, & Wiederholt, 1980) have also developed the Test of Adolescent Language (TOAL), for use with students in Grades 7–12, which involves more complex assessment of these various language skills and includes assessment of these skills in reading and writing tasks as well.

Clinical Evaluation of Language Function-Revised (CELF-R). The CELF (Semel, Wiig, & Secord, 1988) was developed to assess expressive and receptive abilities related to phonology, semantics, syntax, and memory. Eleven subtests include activities, such as pointing to the correct picture given a stimulus sentence, fol-

lowing complex instructions, recalling information from spoken paragraphs, imitating sentences, and so forth. A variety of scoring and recording procedures are used for these subtests.

Detailed analyses of types of error patterns and their implications are conducted. The authors present age-level criteria for the different subtests (ages 0–5 to 16–11), which indicate when further evaluation is appropriate. Although the test is designed for administration in its entirety, a teacher can give individual subtests to explore possible areas of difficulty requiring further testing by a communication expert. The test was standardized on 2,426 children, ages 5–16, across the United States; the sample is representative of gender and minority-group participants. The test manual presents some valid data (e.g., internal consistency, correlations with other measures), along with reliability data presenting high retest correlations and predictive power in identifying communicatively impaired students.

Pragmatics

Several different observational checklists and informal guides are available to assess the complexity of conversational or narrative discourse in students, two important dimensions of pragmatic behavior. Standardized instruments, however, are rare. The difficulty of defining behaviors across settings, partners, and cultures, and the relatively recent development of this area in the study of communicative disorders may contribute to the limited number of thorough instruments.

One instrument that has begun to receive more attention in public schools is a test by Simon (1985) entitled Evaluating Communicative Competence (ECC): A Functional Pragmatic Procedure. The ECC is a criterion-referenced tool designed to probe students' language in Grades 4–12 (age 9 or older). The ECC evaluates the integration of thinking, listening, and speaking skills as they relate to the student's success in school academics. Administration of the ECC takes from 45 minutes to 1 hour, and probes speech quality, syntax, and communicative style. The auditory processing section probes responses to *wh*-questions, detection of absurdities, auditory integration, memory and recall, and auditory comprehension. Other sections focus on sentence composition and topic maintenance. The functional language section probes explanation of absurdities in paragraphs, similarities and differences, simple to more complex description of familiar objects, situational analysis, description, and use of questions. The ECC also looks at story-telling behavior, in terms of sequence, imagination, and organization.

Summary

The preceding descriptions should give the reader a general idea of the types of communication tests commonly used today, how they are conducted, and the information they yield. Readers who are interested in using a particular instrument or come in contact with others who frequently use a test to make significant decisions, should carefully consider reliability and validity data. This will help avoid problems from using tests for purposes for which they are not designed, and making decisions (e.g., diagnosis, classroom placement) that are incorrect or inappropriate.

To some extent, we have written about somewhat typical or standard features of communication and their assessment. Such an approach has both positive aspects and problems, some of which we have discussed. The next section presents a broader perspective on communication in classroom settings, that moves beyond a narrow focus on the linguistic features of communication behavior to consider the communicative interactions observed between teacher and student in the classroom.

A THREE-COMPONENT INTERACTIVE MODEL FOR CONCEPTUALIZING COMMUNICATIVE BEHAVIOR IN CLASSROOM SETTINGS

Many of the assessment approaches and instruments previously described focus primarily on the communicative behavior of the student alone. Most structured tests emphasize assessing specific expressive and receptive abilities of the student under particular conditions, some of which may not be very typical or natural. In assessing communication problems, such an approach appears to place most or all of the emphasis on the student and his or her capabilities, ignoring the influence of the communicative setting and partner.

In recent years an alternative approach has appeared, due to various conceptual developments in the special education and communicative behavior fields related to pragmatics, and the broader social-interactive characteristics of communication (Gallagher & Prutting, 1983; Hart, 1981). The new approach considers a larger variety of variables as influences on the student's communicative performance in classroom settings. In addition to the student's own communicative repertoire, such an approach considers at least two other major components of classroom interactions: teacher characteristics and curriculum characteristics. Figure 12.3 diagrams these components, which we discuss in the following sections. Such a three-part model is based upon the work of Gruenewald and Pollak (1984).

Components of Communicative Interactions in the Classroom

Student-based Communication Characteristics. The component that has received the most attention in the past is student-based communication characteristics. Of major interest here

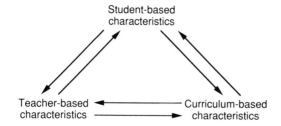

Student-based
characteristics

Teacher-based   Curriculum-based
characteristics   characteristics

FIGURE 12.3

Diagram of major interactive components of
classroom communication

Source: Adapted from Gruenewald and Pollak (1984).

are the basic expressive and receptive repertoires of the student, in terms of phonology,
semantics, and syntax. Of course, along with
the form or topography of a person's repertoire,
we are also interested in pragmatic aspects, or
the way that the forms are used in social-com-
municative interactions to achieve particular
functions.

Teacher-based Communication Characteristics.
The form, content, and manner of presentation
of the teacher's communicative responses during classroom interactions are all major aspects
of the second component. From an interactive
perspective, the teacher's communicative responses obviously make a large difference in the
way in which students respond. The teacher's
style of asking questions, giving instructions, and
lecturing, significantly influence students' ability
to respond to the communicative content (the
message) appropriately. For example, the length
of an utterance, the rate of speaking, or the use
of semantically difficult words can all result in
difficulties in students' responses.

Curriculum-based Language Characteristics.
The third major component involves the content and form of specific curricular materials
and tasks. The level or complexity of language
used in books and instructions, and the format

of worksheets, problems, or directions written
on the board are all considered in this area.
Knowledge of a curriculum's complexity allows
a teacher to understand the occasional communication inaccuracies in the student's responses to the material. As with teacher-based
communication, the content and form of curricular materials must be at an appropriate level
for students to respond correctly and efficiently.

Assessment Considerations

In assessing whether or not a particular student
has a problem with communicative interactions in the classroom, an interactive perspective requires that we consider all three
components. The diagram in Figure 12.3 illustrates the interdependence of these three areas.
The minimum level of interaction would involve at least two of these areas (i.e., teacher
and student, student and task/materials); however, typically all three aspects are involved, in
that a teacher and student are often communicating about a specific relevant task or curricular materials.

This conceptual approach has both advantages and disadvantages. It is well suited to an
individualized approach to assessing and influencing student performance. Using diagnosti-
cally-oriented standardized tests may only
provide limited information about specific characteristics of a student's difficulties and the context in which they occur. More broadly based
assessment may help to identify the points or
areas where one or more of these components
interact in creating problems in student performance. A communication problem, either receptive or expressive, may be related to the
student's repertoire, the form and manner in
which the teacher presents material, the characteristics of the material itself, or some interaction of these three variables. As previously
mentioned, the classroom teacher may be in
an ideal position to provide information about

these areas, due to the opportunity for ongoing observation under a wide variety of situations and demands.

A disadvantage of this approach is that assessing multiple variables in different situations is often more difficult or time-consuming than sitting down with a student and administering a particular specific test. This extra effort must be balanced against the types of information that may be gained. In the next section we present and discuss different methods and protocols that may be useful for teachers in typical classrooms.

SOME SCREENING/ASSESSMENT METHODS FOR USE IN THE CLASSROOM

Conducting broad-based screening and assessment activities in the classroom is often difficult and time-consuming because of shortages of instructional personnel and time. Thus, there is a critical need for instruments and methods that teachers can use in a relatively quick and easy manner in typical ongoing classroom situations, and that still yield useful information.

In this section we present some specific observational and rating instruments that may be useful for conducting general and basic screening or assessment of student communication in the classroom. The four specific instruments or protocols are best used to make screening decisions to identify students who may need more intensive assessment/intervention and which aspects of their communication should be the focus of such activity. They may *not* provide specific, detailed information about a student's performance in particular areas. Generally, they have not undergone extensive psychometric development or analysis, although reliability and validity research is beginning. They are not specific diagnostic tests, but they

may be useful to teachers in typical classrooms who want strategies for conducting basic screening activities.

We assume that appropriate hearing or audiology screening and assessments have been conducted. Hopefully, periodic hearing screenings are an ongoing part of most students' school careers, at least in the elementary grades. Any time a student presents communication difficulties, appropriate audiometric evaluation should be conducted by a qualified professional to either eliminate or confirm the possible contribution of hearing problems to the communicative concerns.

Student Language Use Inventory

The form in Figure 12.4 is a part of an overall system for assessing and remediating classroom language problems. The Student Language Use Inventory (Gruenewald & Pollak, 1984) contains a list of questions that teachers can consider for assessing a variety of student receptive and expressive communication patterns in a variety of classroom tasks and situations. Most of the items on the inventory involve judgments or ratings made after conducting observations in different situations. A teacher can use the form to guide his/or her observations during various class activities over a 3–5-day period.

The inventory includes different aspects of form, content, and use, as well as receptive communicative abilities. For example, Question 2 in the first section asks about the typical length of the student's communicative responses. Question 4 in the first section, and all of the questions in the third section, are relevant to the content or message of responses. As discussed previously, such content is related to the function of a communicative response. Several of the questions (Section 3) are relevant to the types of functions or outcomes the student can accomplish in communicative inter-

I. Giving information

1. Student gives information to others_____ often _____ only when asked _____ sometimes on his own _____ usually on his own.
2. When talking and explaining things student uses _____ complete sentences _____ short phrases _____ single words.
3. Student gives information _____ in classroom discussion _____ one-to-one conversation _____ play or free time with other students.
4. The kind of information or talking the student usually does is to
   _____ talk/describe what he's doing
   _____ talk/describe what someone else is doing
   _____ name or describe things
   _____ tell what he is going to do
   _____ tell what he did or has done
   _____ tell about something (an event) that happened
   _____ explain why/why not he did something
   _____ tell what he needs or wants
   _____ tell how to do something
5. When student gives information or explains something, people _____ usually understand _____ sometimes understand _____ have difficulty understanding.

II. Getting information

1. Student gets most of his or her information (learns best) through: _____ listening _____ seeing _____ reading _____ doing it himself _____ a combination of all of these.
2. If student doesn't know something, _____ he or she usually asks _____ sometimes asks _____ rarely asks.

III. Self-expression

1. Student uses language to ask permission.
2. Student uses language to refuse to do something.
3. Student uses language to criticize something/someone.
4. Student uses language to praise something/someone.
5. Student uses language to say what he believes.
6. Student uses language to explain how he feels.
7. Student uses language to say what he wants to do.

IV. Learning new things

1. When learning something new, student practices it aloud.
2. Student practices it silently to himself.
3. Student practices it with a friend.

Source: L. J. Gruenewald and S. A. Pollak, *Language Interaction in Teaching and Learning.* (Baltimore: University Park Press, 1984), p. 71.

FIGURE 12.4

Student Language Use Inventory

Source: L. J. Gruenewald and S. A. Pollak, *Language Interaction in Teaching and Learning.* (Baltimore: University Park Press, 1984), p. 75.

actions. Question 5, in Section 1, also asks how well the student is understood by others with whom he or she interacts. Some questions (Section 2) are relevant to the student's strategies for understanding information and asking for clarification or further information when necessary (receptive language).

This inventory is primarily useful for prompting a teacher to attend to and think about relatively broad aspects of a student's language use. In terms of use, it is probably best if teachers read it over beforehand, so that they can reflect on some of the areas during interactions or observations. Then the teacher can reconsider the different questions, focusing on specific areas that appear problematic for the student and targeting them for further observation or assessment. For example, a teacher may focus on how the student seeks help or further information (or does not do so) in situations involving difficult or unknown information, tasks, or skills. The teacher can then determine which of the components of classroom communication (student/teacher/curriculum) might be problematic in given situations, and whether or not further specific and intensive assessment and intervention are warranted.

Observational Profile of Classroom Communication

The Observational Profile of Classroom Communication (Sanger, 1988) was developed primarily to identify students who exhibit difficulties in taking in and processing auditory information during classroom instruction. A copy of the profile appears in appendix A. The 33 questions on the profile are relatively specific in five areas: (a) particular stimulus characteristics of information that seem to give the student trouble (e.g., rapid or multistep instructions); (b) related environmental characteristics that may be problematic (e.g., multiple speakers, back-

ground noise); (c) types of responses given by the student; (d) particular learning strategies used by the student; and, (e) occurrence of various types of problem behavior (e.g., out-of-seat, irritability, or hostility). These areas correspond nicely to the three major communication components of student, teacher, and curriculum discussed above.

To date, teachers have used the profile to observe students for approximately a 2-week period. Then, for each item the teacher marks yes or no, or indicates agreement or disagreement with the statement or question. Sanger, Keith, and Maher (1987) used the criterion that if students had problems on more than half of the profile questions, they failed the profile, and were considered in need of specialized attention. The profile can serve multiple purposes. First, it can serve as a guide for teachers about particular areas which they may want to consider during training and instruction. Second, if a student appears to have difficulty with a large number of the items, then the teacher may want to seek input from a speech/language pathologist or communication consultant, who can assist in conducting more specific assessments and help with planning and implementing a training program.

The profile has not been standardized but has undergone some preliminary analyses of its inter- and intrarater reliability (Sanger, personal communication, 1989). *Intrarater*, or test-retest, reliability was assessed with a group of classroom teachers. The Pearson correlation coefficient for this group was high ($r = .91$). *Interrater* reliability was assessed by comparing ratings of a group of classroom teachers and a group of resource room teachers; this comparison produced a quite low correlation ($r = .29$). The authors of the scale feel that this low correlation is primarily due to the different environments and contextual influences that may have been present in the different classroom settings.

Sanger, Keith, and Maher (1987) have collected and reported data relevant to aspects of the profile's validity. The authors of the profile provided a brief in-service session on problems of auditory processing to 50 teachers, who then referred 46 children they considered to have such problems. A battery of tests was administered to the children, and the teachers were asked to fill out the Communication Profile. Of the 46 children, 87% had error scores on 50% or more of the profile items. There were statistically significant differences between the group of referred children and a normal control group. These results support the use of teacher referrals, based on the use of the profile, as a means for identifying students in need of further evaluation. Obviously, further work is necessary to establish the reliability and validity of the profile. But it appears promising at this point and potentially useful for classroom teachers, when used in the manner described.

Spotting Language Problems

Spotting Language Problems (SLP) (Damico & Oller, 1985) is a tool for helping teachers and other professionals identify students that have communication problems that may result in learning difficulties. The authors stress that it should be considered only as a screening tool and as the basis for referrals for more specialized work. It *should not be used* as the basis for placement decisions. The SLP procedures are applicable to students from age 5 to high-school level. A copy of the SLP rating sheet, instructions for completing it, and interpretation criteria appear in Figure 12.5. The person rating the student makes judgments about seven basic aspects of a student's communication during situations where the student has ample opportunity and motivation for interactive communication. These aspects are more fully described and discussed in Damico and Oller (1985).

The authors recommend the following steps for use of this instrument:

1. Read the SLP manual (available from Los Amigos Research Associates, 7035 Galewood, San Diego, Calif. 92120).
2. Become familiar with the seven SLP criteria and the examples of each.
3. Practice applying the procedure at least five times before actual use.
4. Conduct observations during spontaneous and natural communication (i.e., do not observe during artificial or contrived situations).
5. Fill out an SLP rating sheet *after*, and not during, each observation session.
6. After an appropriate number of observations, conduct an analysis of the rating scores and make a decision as to whether or not a referral is appropriate.

The authors recommend a minimum of *four* observation sessions for a student before considering referral, preferably on different days and at different times. The goal of each session should be to observe *at least* 2 minutes of active communication on the part of the student. However, to obtain this much information, it may be necessary to observe for longer periods of time (e.g., 5–10 minutes). Potential situations for such observations might include recess, free-time in the classroom, and group activities or projects. The rating sheet is completed *after* the observation is done, to help ensure that the ratings are based on the observer's overall impression of the communicative behaviors exhibited by the student.

The authors state that if a rating of 5 is given for any scale, or if a rating of 4 is recorded for any single scale for two sessions or more, the student should be considered for further assessment. If the mean, or average, rating for any scale is above 3.0, the student should also be considered for further diagnosis. If the mean rating for a scale is between 2.5 and 3.0, then at least three additional assessment/observation sessions should be conducted before a decision is made.

Initial reliability and validity studies have been conducted on the SLP procedures. Test-retest reliability was assessed on two groups of 20 children (a normal group and children diagnosed with language disorders), over an 8–11 day period. Overall test-retest coefficients were .87 and .93 for the groups respectively, while coefficients for the seven

---

Spotting Language Problems

Rating Sheet

Client's Name _____   Session #/Language ____/_____

Examiner _____   Day-Month-Year/Grade ____-____-____/_____

Teacher _____   Location _____

DIRECTIONS: Circle the number on each of the scales below which best describes the child's communicative behavior. Record scores immediately after (not during) the observational session. See *Spotting Language Problems (Experimental Edition): A Manual for the Use of Pragmatic Criteria in Language Screening*, 1985, pp. 4–6 for specific examples of the problematic behaviors addressed by each of the seven scales below. For each of the seven scales, the numerical values have the following interpretations with reference to the child being observed:

1 = NEVER exhibits the difficulty in question
2 = the difficulty is sometimes observed, but not often
3 = occurs often enough to be noticed and is sometimes distracting
4 = occurs frequently, sometimes interfering with communication
5 = ALWAYS occurs and interferes noticeably with communication

---

1. *Linguistic Nonfluency*—speaker's production is disrupted by repetitions, un-   1 2 3 4 5
   usual pauses, and other hesitation phenomena.

2. *Revisions*—makes many false starts, interrupts her/himself and starts over.   1 2 3 4 5

3. *Delays before Responding*—pauses for 2 seconds or more before responding   1 2 3 4 5
   to a question or other verbal stimulus.

4. *Use of Nonspecific Vocabulary*—uses pronouns, or other terms such as *this,*   1 2 3 4 5
   there, and *stuff* when the listener has no way of knowing what the child is
   referring to.

5. *Inappropriate Responses*—child's utterances do not seem to follow naturally   1 2 3 4 5
   what has been said or asked previously by someone else.

6. *Poor Topic Maintenance*—child changes topics so suddenly that the listener   1 2 3 4 5
   is apt to get lost.

7. *Need for Repetition*—repetition is often required before the child will under-   1 2 3 4 5
   stand a question or comment that is not apparently difficult.

Comments: _____

The Summary Matrix and Its Interpretation

Summary Matrix for Sessions and Scales

Scales Sessions	1	2	3	4	5	6	7	Scale Means
1. Linguistic Nonfluency	____	____	____	____	____	____	____	____
2. Revisions	____	____	____	____	____	____	____	____
3. Delays before Responding	____	____	____	____	____	____	____	____
4. Nonspecific Vocabulary	____	____	____	____	____	____	____	____
5. Inappropriate Responses	____	____	____	____	____	____	____	____
6. Poor Topic Maintenance	____	____	____	____	____	____	____	____
7. Need for Repetition	____	____	____	____	____	____	____	____
Session Means	____	____	____	____	____	____	____	

Grand Mean ____

Action recommended _____

INTERPRETATION: If a five (5) is recorded on any of the scales, or if a four (4) is recorded on any single scale for two sessions or more, the observer should notify the school's referral agent so that the child may undergo more detailed diagnosis. If the mean rating for any single scale (read down the column at the extreme right of the Summary Matrix) is above 3.0, the child should also be referred for diagnosis. If the mean rating for any scale is between 2.5 and 3.0, it is recommended that the child be rated again on the *SLP* scales in a minimum of three additional sessions before a decision is reached. After the additional ratings are obtained, the usual bases for referral apply. If a five (5) appears on any scale in any of the sessions, or if two or more fours (4) appear on any single scale, the appropriate decision is to refer the child for diagnosis.

Ratings in the three to five (3–5) range on Scales 1–7 indicate significant problems in *Oral Dialogic* (speech production and comprehension) which are likely to show up under further diagnostic testing; high ratings on Scales 1–5, and 7 indicate a high potential for problems in *Academic/Cognitive* undertakings in general (i.e., learning and school achievement); high ratings on Scales 1, 2, 4, and 6 indicate problems chiefly in *Oral Monologic* (speech production); and high ratings on Scales 3, 5, and 7 may indicate difficulties in *Hearing.*

Source: Damico and Oller (1985).

FIGURE 12.5
Rating sheet for Spotting Language Problems (SLP) procedures

separate scales ranged from .75 to .88. Interobserver reliability was assessed by having three different persons rate a group of 10 children over a 3-day period. Pearson product-moment correlations among the observers' scores were .95, .94, and .98.

To establish validity, observations were conducted of two groups of 30 children, a normal group and a group of children enrolled in language therapy; each child was observed five times. The scores for the two groups were highly significantly different ($p < .0001$). The authors argue that content validity is established by the fact that the seven categories used in the SLP have been demonstrated to be important in a variety of research studies. Further studies of the reliability and validity of the SLP procedures are currently underway (Damico, personal communication, 1988).

The SLP procedures appear to have several advantages: (a) they are relatively straightforward to learn and apply; (b) they have the beginnings of some reasonable empirical support and, (c) they appear to offer useful information on communication problems of students and whether or not they are in need of appropriate referrals. While the procedures are still somewhat in the experimental stage, they appear to have significant immediate potential utility for classroom teachers.

Pragmatic Protocol

The area of pragmatics, or the various interactive aspects of communication, has received increased attention in recent years. Prutting and Kirchner (1987) have created the Pragmatic Protocol, a descriptive protocol for the assessment and rating of pragmatic aspects of communication. A copy of the protocol appears in Figure 12.6.

Pragmatic Protocol				
Name: _____		Date: _____		
Communicative Setting Observed _____		Communicative Partner's Relationship _____		
Communicative act	*Appropriate*	*Inappropriate*	*No opportunity to observe*	*Examples and comments*
Verbal aspects A. Speech acts 1. Speech act pair analysis 2. Variety of speech acts B. Topic 3. Selection 4. Introduction 5. Maintenance 6. Change C. Turn taking 7. Initiation 8. Response				

Communicative act	Appropriate	Inappropriate	No opportunity to observe	Examples and comments
9. Repair/revision				
10. Pause time				
11. Interruption/ overlap				
12. Feedback to speakers				
13. Adjacency				
14. Contingency				
15. Quantity/ conciseness				
D. Lexical selection/use across speech acts				
16. Specificity/ accuracy				
17. Cohesion				
E. Stylistic variations				
18. The varying of communicative style				
Paralinguistic aspects				
F. Intelligibility and prosodics				
19. Intelligibility				
20. Vocal intensity				
21. Vocal quality				
22. Prosody				
23. Fluency				
Nonverbal aspects				
G. Kinesics and proxemics				
24. Physical proximity				
25. Physical contacts				
26. Body posture				
27. Foot/leg and hand/ arm movements				
28. Gestures				
29. Facial expression				
30. Eye gaze				

Source: Prutting and Kirchner (1987).

FIGURE 12.6
Rating sheet for Pragmatic Protocol

The protocol focuses on verbal, nonverbal, and paralinguistic aspects of communication. While some of these behaviors are relatively self-explanatory (e.g., interruption, pause time), others are somewhat more specialized; thus, the definitions for the communicative parameters involved in the Pragmatic Protocol are presented in Appendix C.

The protocol is for use with children aged 5 or older. Prutting and Kirchner (1987) recommend that the rater observe the target person during spontaneous, unstructured conversation with a communicative partner to ensure that the observed communicative behaviors of the student are truly representative of their typical communication patterns in natural settings and situations. The authors recommend an observation period of 15 minutes, after which the rater should complete the protocol. The rater is to mark each of the 30 parameters as being *Appropriate, Inappropriate,* or *No Opportunity to Observe.* Parameters are marked *Appropriate* if "they are judged to facilitate the communicative interaction or are neutral." (Prutting and Kirchner, 1987, p. 108). Parameters are marked *Inappropriate* if "they are judged to detract from the communicative exchange and penalize the individual." (Prutting & Kirchner, 1987, p. 108). If there is insufficient information or opportunity to mark a parameter, then it is scored *No Opportunity.* The authors recommend that further observations be conducted until it is possible to make a judgment.

The judgments should take into account the sociolinguistic backgrounds of the participants (e.g., the parameters are primarily for English-speaking children from monolingual homes). The authors caution that it is important to consider the influence that different partners may have on an interaction. They also note that persons may have clinical problems that do not penalize or disrupt interaction. For example, special consideration may occur for an adult with aphasia, a communicative disorder involving receptive and/or expressive language disabilities, which usually involves developmental or traumatic injury or damage to the brain. Although such a person could have difficulty with word-finding problems (i.e., coming up with the right word at the right time), they may employ a compensatory strategy of using interjections to "hold their place" in the conversation, and thus not disrupt the turn-taking interaction. As another example, a behavior may occur only once but may result in disrupting the interaction or penalizing the speaker (e.g., with regard to physical proximity/body posture, a student may abruptly proceed to lie down on the floor while talking with a partner). Thus, the authors state that "A parameter is marked inappropriate not because it is different but because the difference makes a difference in the interaction" (Prutting & Kirchner, 1987, p. 109).

Prutting and Kirchner (1987) reported the results of several studies employing the protocol with a variety of groups of normal children and adults and persons with diagnoses of various communication disorders (e.g., children with language and articulation problems and adults who had suffered cerebrovascular accidents). A significant amount of time (8–10 hours) was needed to obtain satisfactory levels of interobserver agreement between raters and the primary investigators. Agreement percentages for judgments of both appropriateness and inappropriateness were in the 90–100% range. No test-retest reliability data were reported.

Primary support for the validity of the protocol comes from the fact that different patterns of appropriate and inappropriate parameters were scored for the different diagnostic groups. For example, children and adults in the normal group received very few inappropriate judgments in any area, as would be expected. In contrast, children in the articulation group received inappropriate judgments primarily related to intelligibility, vocal quality, and fluency.

Children in the language-disordered group received inappropriate ratings on a variety of communication aspects, such as specificity, cohesion, and repair/revision. The authors feel that the usefulness of the protocol is in providing a profile of the specific pattern of parameters that may be problematic for a particular person; they point out that even persons with the same diagnostic label may have different sets of characteristics that create communicative difficulties. Teachers can target these profiles or behavior clusters for further assessment and/or remediation efforts.

The protocol requires further investigation and assessment of its reliability and validity. While it has obvious relevance and potential utility in classroom settings, it may require some time, effort, and familiarity with some relatively specialized material for its use and interpretation. Thus, it may be more difficult for classroom personnel to implement, unlike some of the other instruments and procedures discussed earlier. However, the protocol does cover a larger range of specific communicative characteristics and parameters in more detail. Thus, the extra effort and time necessary may be worthwhile. It may also be possible for a teacher to work in conjunction with a speech/language pathologist to implement and interpret the protocol.

Related Assessment Issues

The instruments and procedures we have described in this section primarily focus on the assessment of receptive and expressive spoken communication abilities in classroom activities and settings. While this concern is very important, interactions among the other components (teachers and curriculum), are important as well. For example, the teacher's language during interactions may have a crucial effect. While the preceding assessment approaches tap into the area of students' receptive abilities and

disabilities, teacher language characteristics deserve more attention (Gruenewald & Pollak, 1984). A teacher who identifies apparent problems in a student's comprehension of instructions, for example, may want to assess the effects of changes in such instructions. The teacher might vary the rate of delivery or adjust the level of complexity of instructions (e.g., multiple-step vs. single-step). The screening approaches may help to target such areas, and then additional manipulations can determine some of the potential influential variables.

A third component previously discussed was the characteristics of the curriculum materials. None of the preceeding screening methods specifically focus on assessing the comprehension of worksheet formats, written problems, or test passages in books. As with spoken instructions, a teacher may be able to vary some characteristics of such materials to determine what influence they have on student responses. Adaptations in the wording of written instructions or review questions, reordering of written directives, or reorganizing graphic material may help reduce the communicative difficulty the student displays with particular curricular material.

It is possible to go to an even more complex level and look at the interactive effects of aspects of both spoken and written instructions and formats. Assessing the interactive influence of language and communication variables in such classroom teaching and learning activities has received increasing attention in recent years, and can be explored by reviewing the work of Gruenewald and Pollak (1984), Marvin (1989), Simon (1985), and Wiig and Semel (1984).

CHAPTER SUMMARY

This chapter provides a brief overview of the development and assessment of several aspects of classroom communicative behavior and presents some procedures that should be useful for teachers assessing such behavior in classroom settings. The procedures require varying amounts of time and effort and yield different amounts and types of information. Readers should be able to use and/or adapt some of the methods in actual classroom settings. We have provided guidelines for making referrals and seeking outside input. In this regard, it is probably always wise to seek additional information and outside help, at least on an informal basis, when there are concerns about a particular student. We encourage readers to be aware of the relationships between the ideas and concepts discussed in this chapter and the concepts and methods presented in the other chapters, which concern more specific content areas relevant to classroom skills (e.g., reading, writing, mathematics). Communicative interactions form the basis for much, if not all, of the teaching/learning activity that occurs in classroom settings. The information in this chapter should help to facilitate such activities for both teachers and students.

CHAPTER 13

Norm-referenced Evaluation

Each week Garrison Keillor, the famous radio show host of *Prairie Home Companion*, described a day in the life of people living in Lake Wobegon, a small town that time forgot in northern Minnesota. Keillor ended each evening by saying, "And that's the news from Lake Wobegon, where the men are all strong, the women are all beautiful, and all the children are above average."

How did all the offspring of these hard-working Scandinavian and German immigrants get above average? Can you have a group with everyone in it performing above average? No. Of course someone has to be below average to make an average. The concept of average is inherently dependent upon a norm-referenced view of the world. Average implies groups— groups of people who have something in common, and it implies comparing individuals within groups to each other. To make these comparisons, the performance of individuals in each group has to be summarized; otherwise, each person must be compared with every other person. This chapter provides an explanation of norm-referenced evaluation procedures that can be used to summarize the performance of groups, enabling us to make interpretations.

CHAPTER OBJECTIVES

The purpose of this chapter is to describe several aspects of norm-referenced evaluations: how they originated, the primary purposes for which we use them, the different types of norm-referenced scores, and their applications in published, norm-referenced tests.

By the end of this chapter the reader will have the knowledge and skills to

- Understand the origins and development of norm-referenced testing.
- Delineate the major purposes and types of decisions that we can make from norm-referenced evaluations.
- Identify several types of norm-referenced indices and know when to use them and how to calculate them.
- Apply a norm-referenced approach in classrooms, using the assessment examples from the content chapters.
- Evaluate published, norm-referenced tests.

KEY VOCABULARY

In this chapter, you will learn the difference between *norm-referenced* and *criterion-referenced* tests. The major decisions made from norm-referenced data include *screening/eligibility*, the process of finding students who are significantly lower than their peers and placing them in specialized programs, and *program certification*, the documentation of overall program outcomes. The types of scores you will read about include the following: *raw scores*, usually the number of items correct on a given test; *rank ordering*, an ordinal scale used to sequence students from highest to lowest; *percentiles*, a score that communicates the percentage of peers who perform below a student's score; *deciles*, *quartiles* and *stanines*, which simply group students into percentile bands; *grade-* and *age-equivalent* scores, which employ grade and age as reference groups; and *standard scores*, three of which include *z-scores*, a measure based on deviation units; *T-scores*, in which variation is based on a mean of 50 and a standard deviation of 10; and *standard scaled scores*, in which variation has a mean of 100 and a standard deviation of 15.

HISTORY OF NORM-REFERENCED TESTS

The first formal attempts at developing tests are attributed to the Chinese. As early as 2200 B.C., they implemented an extensive system of civil service examinations that lasted almost

3,000 years (Dubois, 1966). Anastasi (1968) points out that the ancient Greeks established testing as part of the Socratic method of teaching and that during the Middle Ages, European universities developed formal examinations for graduation. The late 1800s saw the growth of psychological measurement, led by English biologist Sir Francis Galton, and experimentation with sensitivity to visual, auditory, and other sensory phenomena. The work by James McKeen Cattel, who coined the term *mental tests* in 1890, signaled a change in emphasis in psychological testing from measurement of sensory faculties to measurement of intellectual functioning. At the turn of the century Binet and his co-workers were given the responsibility by the French government for developing tests that would help improve the education of subnormal children in Paris. While Binet's initial interests were on linking testing to educational intervention, American psychologists began attending to differences in psychological traits and constructs. One result of this emphasis upon measuring "individual differences" was the Binet-Simon Scale, which measured judgment, comprehension, and reasoning (Anastasi, 1968). Terman, who was responsible for development of the Stanford-Binet Intelligence Test (1916) Stanford Achievement Test, and Otis Test (formerly Army Alpha), improved upon this approach by developing lengthier formal tests that provided scores and intelligence quotients to compare test takers.

Standardized norm-referenced testing continued to evolve from the 1930s to the 1950s when testing became a commonplace component of education and psychology. As interest in norm-referenced testing grew, many new tests became popular, including the Wechsler-Bellevue Intelligence Scale, which later become the Wechsler Intelligence Scale—Revised or WISC—R, the Scholastic Aptitude Test (SAT), and Graduate Record Examination (GRE). In addition, intense national interest in testing and as-

sessment was reflected in three areas: the emergence of (a) professional organizations dealing with assessment (National Council on Measurement in Education), (b) large private testing organizations (Educational Testing Service), and (c) professional journals (Educational and Psychological Measurement) (Lien, 1980).

THE PURPOSE OF NORM-REFERENCED TESTING: TYPES OF DECISIONS

Test development around the turn of the century emphasized the measurement of individual differences. This emphasis was a result of the need to screen large numbers of army recruits into various military assignments during World Wars I and II. Psychologists used the formal testing techniques of Binet to measure the individual differences of these recruits on psychological constructs such as memory and comprehension and also on specialized vocational aptitudes. During this period, tests became norm-referenced: the performance of the test taker was interpreted in relation to a specified normative group. This idea was soon adopted in education; the same type of information gave educators an idea of a student's relative standing with respect to others in that grade or age range.

The primary purpose of the **norm-referenced** approach is to compare individuals in order to document their similarities and differences. In fact, nearly all decisions regarding placement in special education programs focus on the extent to which a student's academic work or behavior is discrepant from that of his or her peers. Additionally, however, norm-referenced tests have been used to evaluate experimental programs, a focus more often reflected in university and college research programs than in instructional programs delivered in public schools.

We must make three major decisions when using norm-referenced evaluations. First, the tester must consider the type of educational decision that needs to be made, involving either screening and eligibility or program certification. If a different type of decision is needed, then norm-referenced evaluations are not appropriate. Second, we must summarize student performance through one of many outcome metrics. The particular metric adopted should communicate information in the most simple and effective manner. Finally, we must display student performance as it relates to the norm group. Figure 13.1 depicts the three decisions that are necessary when using norm-referenced evaluations.

Screening and Eligibility

As in their early uses to screen military recruits, norm-referenced tests and the data they generate are used to screen large numbers of students. In fact, the vast majority of available published tests are norm-referenced. When we use them to compare students and to determine specific knowledge or skill levels, norm-referenced tests support decisions about the allocation of resources. Taggert, Sum, and Berlin (1987) state that out of

the 20 million 19- to 23-year olds at the beginning of this decade, nearly half of the poor, half of the minorities, and two-fifths of those suffering from one or more social pathologies were

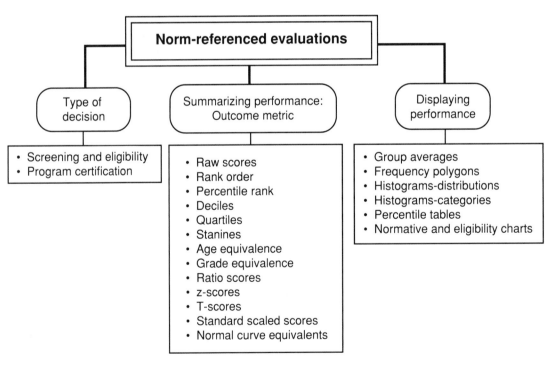

FIGURE 13.1
Decisions for completing a norm-referenced evaluation

concentrated in the bottom fifth of the basic skills distribution as measured by the Armed Forces Qualification Test. (p. 4)

Schools are faced with a critical situation. Who should receive specialized services? Schools cannot individualize instruction for everyone, so every teacher in every classroom must make decisions as to who should be grouped together and which curriculum materials should be used. To make such decisions, they usually use norm-referenced tests.

For **screening** students and making decisions about **eligibility** in specialized programs, norm-referenced testing is very appropriate. The screening process involves measuring a large group of students and determining who is significantly low and warrants more intensive and focused assessment. Determining eligibility is simply an extension of this process: More measurements are administered to students to corroborate significant departures from normative standards and establish performance levels that are aligned with specific criteria for placement into a program. Because such tests have a broad sampling plan, taking items from a wide range of content and representing a middle range of difficulty, such tests usually generate stable scores. They often include a wide range of items, varying in difficulty and content. Everyone scores something correct, and no one scores 100% correct. Furthermore, everyone takes the same test and, therefore, can be compared on the same scale.

Although norm-referenced tests may be useful in allocating services to students, they are virtually useless in helping to plan the content or format of that service. The diagnostic information obtained from such tests is generally limited because most norm-referenced tests are group-administered and employ selection responses. Without the capacity to observe *how* students perform, it is less possible

to form a plan of instruction from the results. We can make some general and vague estimates of the approximate level of functioning to help select further assessment material that is instructionally relevant, but the next set of decisions, instructional planning and formative evaluation, cannot be made with norm-referenced data. However, we can use norm-referenced tests again to evaluate overall outcomes after delivering an instructional program to a group of students.

Program Evaluation

A **program** can be defined as "a planned and multi-component intervention taking place over an extended period of time and delivered by one or more professionals with a goal of improving student performance" (Tindal, 1989, p. 203). This definition highlights four key issues. First, a program is broadly defined and may include a wide range of instructional and social interventions. Second, programs at this level take time to implement, ranging from several weeks to several months or years. Third, a program is delivered to many individuals of varying backgrounds and skill levels. Finally, a program is often implemented by more than one individual.

All of these considerations require some systematicity in the data-collection process because so many differences already exist. To be useful at a broad level, any measurement device must encompass a range of items that are appropriate to a range of students over an extended period of time. All items will not be appropriate for all students at all times, but enough will be applicable to generate meaningful scores. Furthermore, the same device must be used over the entire time period for which the program is being evaluated. Norm-referenced tests are well suited to this purpose because they broadly sample content and difficulty. Fluctuation of performance rarely occurs over a short period of time (a few months), allowing the tests to be used at the beginning (fall) and the end (spring) of the school year.

Evaluation of many instructional programs provided by Follow-Through (Rhine, 1981) was accomplished with the Metropolitan Achievement Test and the Wide Range Achievement Test, which were employed to provide uniform measures that served as evaluation anchors amongst considerable variation in instructional interventions, teachers, and students. In the massive Follow-Through study, 13 university-based educational interventions were evaluated for their impact on improving low Socio-economic status (SES) children's achievement. Many students in the primary grades who came from different regions of the country and had been instructed in dozens of different curricula had to be tested over several years. The findings of the study indicated that Direct Instruction from the University of Oregon and Applied Behavior Analysis from the University of Kansas were the most effective programs.

INTEGRATING THE DECISION-MAKING PROCESS

Screening and eligibility and program evaluation decisions are not usually related. The same tests or data used to make screening and eligibility decisions are not used to make program evaluation decisions. Furthermore, neither decision is closely aligned with instructional planning. At the end of the chapter, however, we describe a strategy for more closely integrating all decisions using norm-referenced tests and data is described. This approach, which moves from survey-level (broad sampling of behavior) to specific-level assessment (specific sampling

of skills and knowledge), is an appropriate and efficient technique.

When integrating the decision-making process, we base the system on using teacher-made tests, which require production responses (similar to the curriculum-based measurements) and follow standardized administration and scoring formats. Instruments that require production responses and follow standardized formats serve three purposes: (a) screening and eligibility, (b) diagnostics and instructional planning, and (c) program summation. Although norm-referenced instruments generally are useful only for screening and eligibility *or* program summation, it is possible to extend the range of decision making to include diagnostics and instructional planning and to link all three decisions together.

The decision-making process, however, does not proceed easily from making a test to making a decision. Rather, several steps are present between these end points. We must consider many issues about the structure of the test in the process of making a decision, including what behavior is sampled, to what degree it is adequately sampled, how test items are formatted, how difficult they are, and so forth. When these issues are addressed satisfactorily, one final issue centers on how performance should be summarized. A range of options is available, but not all are equally desirable or appropriate. For example, Tindal, Shinn, and Germann (1987) evaluated the program effectiveness of resource rooms for special education students and found the results depended on which type of score or metric was used. If raw or grade-equivalent scores were used, the program appeared to be effective, and special education students improved significantly during the year. However, if the program was summarized using z-scores, the program was not effective, and students in special education showed little improvement.

TYPES OF OUTCOME METRICS

Many types of outcome metrics are available for evaluating programs, including the following scores, which we define in this chapter: raw scores, rank orderings, percentiles, deciles, quartiles, stanines, normal curve equivalents, age equivalents, grade equivalents, and three types of standard scores. For each score or metric, we describe: (a) its calculation, (b) when to use it, and (c) the advantages and disadvantages in using it. Finally we have graphically compared them in Figure 13.3 near the end of the chapter.

Raw Scores

The number of items the student has answered correctly or incorrectly on a given test is referred to as the **raw score.**

Calculation. There are two strategies for calculating raw scores. In the first strategy, we calculate the raw score by counting the number of correct test items. In the second, we divide the number of correct items by the total number of test items to obtain the percentage correct.

When to Use. Such scores typically are not emphasized in norm-referenced tests because they provide no basis for comparison to a peer group. However, the raw score is the starting point for all norm-referenced scores. Raw scores are only appropriate when comparisons to other students or other (nonalternate form) tests are not needed. Therefore, the only way that a raw score can be used is in reference to criterion- or individual-referenced evaluations, not norm-referenced ones.

For example, if a student takes a geography test and his or her performance is summarized as a raw score, the student's score (e.g., 75) is not readily interpretable. But we can interpret the score through criterion-referenced evaluation. If *mastery* on the test is a score of 50 or above, a raw score of 75 has some meaning. It shows that the student is well above the mastery level. The chapter on criterion-referenced evaluation, chapter 14, shows how raw scores and standards of mastery are used to make judgments. The student's score of 75 can also be interpreted through individual-referenced evaluation. If the student scored 50 at the beginning of the unit and 75 at the end of the unit, then the raw score shows that some learning has taken place.

Using criterion- and individual-referenced evaluations can make raw scores more meaningful. Raw scores also can provide a better basis for interpretation when they are summarized as percentages, since we then also include not only the number of items correct, but the total number of items on the test. Summarizing a raw score as 90% correct is more informative than stating that a student had 75 items correct.

Advantages and Disadvantages. One advantage of raw scores is that we can express them in two ways—the number or percentage correct. They also can be used to measure mastery or student improvement, two important classroom decisions. The basic disadvantage of raw scores is their limited interpretability. It is not possible to use them to compare performance across time, students, tests, or content.

Rank Ordering. The easiest way to compare students with each other is to rank them from highest to lowest; this metric is called **rank ordering.** Each score in a distribution is ordered from the highest to the lowest, and we assign an ordinal number or rank that expresses each student's position in the group. Generally, we use raw scores to rank students, although most of the other scores described in this chapter can also serve as the basis for ranking.

Calculation. When ordering students, a rank of 1 is the highest. Ranks for tied scores usually are averaged, and each score is given the average rank. The lowest rank receives a rank equal to the number of students in the group.

An example of rank order appears in Table 13.1, which presents 30 students, their scores and their ranks. In this example, where scores range from 12 to 56, Student 9 is given a rank of 1.00 for having the highest score. Students 12 and 23 both received a score of 45 items correct. Because they are tied for the fourth highest score, the rankings of 4.0 and 5.0 are averaged, and each student is assigned a ranking of 4.5. Student 27, who received the next highest score (42), is assigned a ranking of 6.0 because the counting begins at the next available rank prior to the averaging process.

When to Use. We can use rank ordering when the raw score is not important in its own right and when the absolute score is not as important as relative standing. Many resources in education are limited, and often only the individuals who most need special services can be served. For example, the federal government funds personnel preparation projects on the basis of rank ordering. After having assigned points to each project based on several evaluation criteria, the projects are ranked and only a certain number on the list are funded. Scholarships are often awarded to students through a rank ordering. A classroom-focused example of rank ordering involves the identification of behavior-problem students, using the criteria defined by Walker and Rankin (1983). They have found that teachers are quite accurate in identifying students who are acting out but are less apt to identify withdrawn or passively noncompliant students. Using their identification system, teachers rank and rate

students, and those near the top, who are perceived as having problems, are further assessed using more elaborate observation. The initial ranking allows school personnel to focus immediately on those who may need services the most.

Rank ordering allows interpretation of relative standing, which is often the crux of the problem. This metric should be used when it is important to see how a student behaves or performs relative to a group. Therefore, rank ordering may be appropriate when making decisions with limited resources or when specific target subgroups need to be identified. Rank ordering is not appropriate (a) when the absolute score is more important than the relative score, (b) if rankings are bunched (many scores appear on a few specific values on the scale), and (c) when the scale is very limited and restricted, which will cause the rankings to bunch at a few scores.

Advantages and Disadvantages. The main advantage of rank ordering is the ease with which it can be completed. A glance at the range of highest to lowest performer provides useful information about the distribution and clearly depicts those at the very top and bottom. Unlike raw scores, they convey more information because a norm group is considered. The problem with rank ordering is that real interpretations are difficult to make. To say that a student is high or low says nothing about his/her actual skill in terms of mastery or learning. A subtle disadvantage of ranking is that its applicability is limited to those performers at the extremes; many individuals in the middle of the distribution are left out of the analysis and interpretation. Finally, interpretations of rank ordering is always a function of the number of students who are ranked. For example, the 5th student from the top in a group of 10 is in a different standing than if the group included 100 students.

TABLE 13.1
Rank order of 30 students
on the basis of perfor-
mance scores

Unranked		Ranked		
Student No.	Score	Student No.	Score	Rank
1	23	9	56	1.00
2	21	14	51	2.00
3	34	18	47	3.00
4	25	12	45	4.50
5	21	23	45	4.50
6	19	27	42	6.00
7	35	19	41	7.00
8	12	26	40	8.00
9	56	13	37	9.50
10	34	25	37	9.50
11	29	7	35	11.50
12	45	30	35	11.50
13	37	3	34	14.50
14	51	10	34	14.50
15	16	20	34	14.50
16	12	22	34	14.50
17	19	11	29	17.50
18	47	29	29	17.50
19	41	4	25	19.00
20	34	1	23	20.00
21	22	21	22	21.00
22	34	2	21	22.50
23	45	5	21	22.50
24	20	24	20	24.00
25	37	6	19	25.50
26	40	17	19	25.50
27	42	28	18	27.00
28	18	15	16	28.00
29	29	8	12	29.50
30	35	16	12	29.50

Percentiles

While the raw score is useful in communicating how many items the student has answered correctly, it does not tell how well the student has done in relation to other students. For example, one student, Sue, may have had 13 correct items out of 20 for 65% correct. But how well does this compare to other students at Sue's grade level? If the test was easy, then 13 correct may not be very good. On the other hand, if this test was difficult, a score of 13 might be very high in relation to peers. Further, the rank order of a student tells us if Sue performs better or worse than Bonnie, but it doesn't consistently communicate Sue's relative standing. For example, a rank ordering of 12 would be excellent in a group of 100 students but poor in a group of 15.

One way to find out how well Sue is doing in relation to a known group students at her grade level is to transform the raw score into a percentile or percentile rank. The term **percentile** refers to the percentage of individuals in a fixed standardization sample with equal or lower scores. The percentile rank represents the area of the normal curve, expressed as a percentage, that scores below a certain value (see Table 13.8 at the end of this chapter). For example, if Sue's raw score of 13 translates to a percentile of 39, then 39% of her peers scored at or below 13 and 61% performed above 13. Similarly, if Sue's raw score of 13 has a percentile ranking of 85, then 85% of the population upon which the test is based, scored at or below 13, while 15% of the standardization sample scored above 13.

Percentiles range from 1 to 99 and never include 0 or 100. The 50th percentile is equal to the median (half the students score above and half below). For increased accuracy, percentiles may be reported in decimals, so some tests may range from .1 to 99.9. Although percentiles communicate meaning by reference to a hypothetical group of 100 students, their actual interpretation must always be in reference to the group upon which the test was based.

Calculation. Percentile ranks are very easy to calculate; there are only six steps, which are listed below and illustrated in Table 13.2.

1. Rank order all scores from high to low.
2. For each score value, count the number of students that obtained it (frequency).
3. Convert the *number* of students at each score value to the *percentage* of students at each score value by dividing the former by the total number of students in the group (percent at score).
4. Multiply the percentage of students at each score value by .5 (.5 × percent at score).
5. Determine the percentage below each score value by subtracting percent at score from

100% for the first score, and all remaining values for percent at score from subsequent values of this step (percent below).
6. Add the values from these last two steps (.5 percent at score + percent below) to get the percentile rank.

When to Use. Percentiles and percentile ranks are most appropriate when we need to base relative performance on a consistent standard (hypothetical group of 100 students). It is not appropriate, however, when we want to examine changes in performance or differences in performance among students over time. We must interpret percentiles with some caution because the scaling is ordinal, in which scores reflect values of greater or less, not equal interval, in which arithmetic differences between scores can be meaningfully calculated. For example, it is reasonable to say that "John is at the 40th percentile and is better than Jane, who is at the 25th percentile, and Bill is at the 85th percentile while Sally is at the 70th percentile." In this case, John scored higher than Jane. However, it cannot be said that "John's score is 15 percentile points better than Jane's which is the same as the 15 percentile difference between Bill and Sally. The differences in raw scores between successive percentile ranks is smaller in the middle of the distribution than at the extremes as Figure 13.3 shows. Students in the middle of the distribution have an easier time changing percentiles than students with extremely low or high scores.

The group must include a sufficient number of students (generally 100 students are needed) to convert raw scores into percentiles. Furthermore, percentiles may not be appropriate when the distribution of scores is very nonnormal (skewed at the high or low end). In such cases, percentiles may be oversensitive where the scores bunch and undersensitive where the scores are few (at the tail). Since

TABLE 13.2
Calculating percentile ranks

Raw Score	Frequency at Score	Percent at Score	.5 × Percent at Score	Percent Below	Percentile Rank
56	1	3.33	1.665	96.67	98
51	1	3.33	1.665	93.34	95
47	1	3.33	1.665	90.01	92
45	2	6.66	3.33	83.35	87
45	—	—	—	—	—
42	1	3.33	1.665	80.02	82
41	1	3.33	1.665	76.69	78
40	1	3.33	1.665	73.36	75
37	2	6.66	3.33	66.7	70
37	—	—	—	—	—
35	2	6.66	3.33	60.04	63
35	—	—	—	—	—
34	4	13.32	6.66	46.72	53
34	—	—	—	—	—
34	—	—	—	—	—
34	—	—	—	—	—
29	2	6.66	3.33	40.06	43
29	—	—	—	—	—
25	1	3.33	1.665	36.73	38
23	1	3.33	1.665	33.4	35
22	1	3.33	1.665	30.07	32
21	2	6.66	3.33	23.41	27
21	—	—	—	—	—
20	1	3.33	1.665	20.08	22
19	2	6.66	3.33	13.42	17
19	—	—	—	—	—
18	1	3.33	1.665	10.09	12
16	1	3.33	1.665	6.76	8
12	2	6.66	3.33	0.1	3

most people interpret percentiles relative to a normal curve, such skewed distributions would have to be given their own interpretive standard. The chart in Table 13.8 at the end of the chapter converts percentiles to z-scores (a standard score based on the normal curve). This chart should not be used if the distribution is non-normal.

We should consider the reference group when interpreting a percentile score, which is derived from comparison with a hypothetical group of 100 students and not the actual composition of the group who took the test. For example, if a student from the fourth grade scored at the 15th percentile on an eighth-grade math test, the student's performance might appear to be poor initially. However, considering the reference group, eighth graders, the fourth grader's score is quite good. Similarly, if a fourth-grade student scored at the 95th percentile on a readiness test for kindergarten pupils, the student's performance is not impressive.

Advantages and Disadvantages. Percentiles and percentile ranks are probably the most appropriate summary metric for a norm-referenced evaluation. They are very easy to interpret, and they communicate relative standing with precision and consistency. Many non-educators understand their meaning or can be taught to understand it with little difficulty. About the only disadvantage is that they are subject to incorrect manipulation or interpretation because they are ordinal, not interval. Many teachers are interested in measuring growth in learning, but they should not use percentiles for such purposes; their use should be limited to comparing a student's performance to others. Because educators often assume percentiles are equal interval, they usually overemphasize differences near the 50th percentile and under-emphasize differences at the upper and lower ends of the distribution. The difference from the 1st to 10th percentile is not the same as the difference from 41st to 50th percentile. In fact, a student may move from the 41st percentile to the 50th percentile on a short test by correctly answering only a few more test items (see Table 13.3).

Deciles and Quartiles

We can group percentile scores into ranges to provide more general indices of ranking. When bands of percentiles are reported in widths of 10 percentile ranks, the score is known as a **decile.** Another variation of the percentile is the **quartile,** in which the width of these bands of percentiles is 25.

TABLE 13.3
Sample of percentile ranks on CBM spelling norms

90th–99th		40th–50th		1st–10th	
RS	PR	RS	PR	RS	PR
213	99	73	50	28	10
204	99	72	49	27	9
195	99	71	48	26	9
162	98	70	47	24	8
156	97	69	46	23	7
153	96	68	45	22	6
151	96	67	44	20	6
150	95	66	43	19	5
148	94	65	43	18	4
143	94	63	42	16	4
138	92	62	40	15	3
135	91			14	3
130	90			13	2
				11	1
				9	<1

RS = Raw Score
PR = Percentile Rank

TABLE 13.4
The interrelationship among percentile ranges, deciles, and quartiles

Percentile Range	Decile	Quartile
.1– 9.9	1	
10.0–19.0	2	
.1–24.9		1
20.0–29.9	3	
30.0–39.9	4	
40.0–49.9	5	
25.0–49.9		2
50.0–59.9	6	
60.0–69.9	7	
50.0–74.9		3
70.0–79.9	8	
80.0–89.9	9	
90.0–99.9	10	
75.0–99.9		4

Calculation. The only step involved in calculating deciles is to divide the range of percentiles into groups of 10. For example, the 1st decile ranges from .1 to 9.9, the 4th decile ranges from 30 to 39.9, and so forth. For quartiles, we divide the range of percentiles into four groups. The first quartile ranges from .1 to 24.9, while the last quartile includes percentiles ranging from 75 to 99.9. Table 13.4 illustrates how percentile ranges, deciles, and quartiles are interrelated.

When to Use. Both deciles and quartiles can be used when we regard percentiles as too precise and want only a rough range on this scale. More detail is provided with deciles than quartiles. All other considerations described with percentiles apply here. Either metric can be used if (a) the group includes at least 100, (b) the distribution is relatively normal, and (c) comparing a student's performance to others is the objective. Because of their crude nature, deciles and quartiles may be useful only for general screening decisions or group reporting. For

making important decisions (i.e., placing individual students into specialized programs), they are not sufficiently precise.

Advantages and Disadvantages. The major advantage of the decile and quartile scores is their ease of interpretation. Where a student falls on a given distribution is not difficult to explain to parents or other educators. Because the scale is reduced from that of percentiles, deciles and quartiles work best as global indices to show if the student is at the top, in the middle, or at the bottom. Their use as global indices can also be considered as a disadvantage because less precision communicates less information.

Stanines

The word *stanine* comes from the phrase *standard nine* and reflects a distribution that has been demarcated into 9 different sections, each with a certain percentage of the population in it. The 5th stanine is usually the middle one with 4 other stanines above and below it; the 1st and the 9th theoretically have no lower or upper bounds.

Calculation. Two procedures are employed in converting a score to a stanine. The first involves determining the percentile rank, then using the following conversion system:

Percentile ranks (X_{PR}) that are:	Receive a stanine of:
$X_{PR} < 4$	1
$4 < X_{PR} \leq 11$	2
$11 < X_{PR} \leq 23$	3
$23 < X_{PR} \leq 40$	4
$40 < X_{PR} \leq 60$	5
$60 < X_{PR} \leq 77$	6
$77 < X_{PR} \leq 89$	7
$89 < X_{PR} \leq 96$	8
$X_{PR} > 96$	9

The second way to calculate a stanine is by using the following formula in which the symbol z represents the standard score:

$$\text{Stanine} = 2(z) + 5$$

All values are subsequently rounded to the nearest whole number. For example, if a student has a z or standard score of -1.3, he or she would be in the 2nd stanine.

When to Use.   Like deciles and quartiles, stanines are appropriate when a broad gauge of achievement is needed but are useless for reflecting precise information. Since the range of scores or percentile ranks is so great within any stanine, a considerable loss of information is evident. As a general rank of students, the stanine works fine. For example, a teacher may want to divide students into three groups: The lowest is comprised of students in stanines 1–3, the middle group is comprised of students in stanines 4–6, and the highest represents students in the top three stanines (7–9). This type of precision lends itself well to the use of stanines. Otherwise, percentile ranks or standard scores are more informative.

Advantages and Disadvantages.   Stanines are easy to understand as a general index and may be more sensitive to the shape of the distribution than deciles or quartiles. That is, the percentage of the population included within any stanine reflects the position on the curve: Near the middle, the percentages of population within the stanine are greater than the percentages of population at the ends. Therefore, stanines do not distort the shape or proportions, which happens with the use of percentiles (including deciles or quartiles). A major disadvantage of stanines is their unfamiliarity: Many educators and certainly many noneducators have not heard of them, which requires some explanation.

Grade- and Age-Equivalent Scores

Grade- and age-equivalent scores express the student's performance developmentally in terms of a corresponding age or grade level. Usually, age scores are reported in years and months. Thus, if Jennifer, who is 10 years and 3 months old, has an age score of 12–5, her performance theoretically is the same as that of a child who is 12 years and 5 months old. Grade scores are reported in grade levels to the nearest tenth, which correspond to academic months. Similarly, if Jennifer, a fourth-grader, has a grade equivalent score of 6.1, she is performing at the sixth-grade, first month level.

Calculation.   Frequently data are collected only once or twice during the school year when tests are normed. For example, assume the norms for Test B are developed and standardization data are collected on the first day of school for Grades 1–6. A large number of students are tested at each grade level. To calculate grade-equivalent scores, we plot correct items, or pupil raw scores, on a graph in the manner shown in Figure 13.2. We then draw a "line of best fit" through the data to help us determine typical performance at each grade level. To simplify the illustration, only four raw scores per grade level are plotted in Figure 13.2.

In Figure 13.2, we use a statistical formula to determine the line of best fit for the normative data. It is this line of best fit that we use to estimate grade- and age-equivalent scores for every grade and age level. To do so, we choose a grade level of interest, examine its value on the X-axis, and determine the corresponding Y value that intersects with the line of best fit. An easier solution is to use the derived equation; in this case it is $Y = 3.23 + 2.67 \times$ grade. Thus, average correct items or raw score performance for Grade 1.0 is $3.23 + 2.67 \times (1.0)$, which equals 5.9. Average performance for Grade 2.0 is $3.23 + 2.67 \times$

FIGURE 13.2
Extrapolation and interpolation of grade-equivalent scores

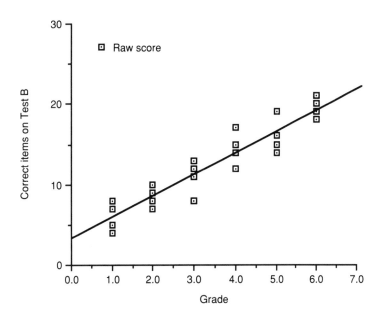

(2.0), or approximately 8.6. This process is used then for Grade 3.0, 4.0, 5.0, and 6.0.

The question now becomes, "How are the grade-equivalent scores for 1.1, 1.2, 1.3, . . . , 6.7, 6.8, and 6.9 determined?" Even though data at $\frac{1}{10}$-of-a-year intervals has not been collected, as shown in Figure 13.2, we can use the formula to estimate typical performance at these points along the line of best fit. Thus, if it is important to know what typical performance is for Grade 1.5, this value is substituted for X in the equation. Y (typical raw score at Grade 1.5) equals 3.23 + 2.67 × (1.5) or about 7.2 correct items. To calculate the typical raw score for Grade 5.4, add 3.23 and 2.67 × (5.4) to get approximately 17.7 correct items.

The process of estimating grade- or age-equivalent scores within the ranges in which data has been collected is called *interpolation*. Frequently, test producers estimate grade- and age-equivalent scores outside the range of grades or ages in which normative data is collected. This is called *extrapolation* and occurs when the line of best fit is extended beyond

the original grade levels on which the test was standardized. For example, to estimate the performance on Test B at the beginning of kindergarten (equivalent to 0.0 grade level) use the equation 3.23 + 2.67 × (0.0), which equals about 3.2 items correct. To extend the line of best fit or to extrapolate to seventh grade add 3.27 and 2.67 × (7.0) to get about 22.0 correct items.

While the results of extrapolation and interpolation appear very precise, their problem is the major assumption of consistency within and beyond grade levels. As stated earlier, the belief that all learning for all students occurs in a consistent fashion across the year is an unproven assumption.

When to Use. Over the years, so much has been written on the reasons why grade-equivalent scores should not be used that more admonishment probably is not needed. Simply put, two major professional groups involved in establishment of measurement standards and practices, the American Psychological

Association (APA) and the National Council on Measurement in Education (NCME) have recommended against their use in making any educational decisions.

Advantages and Disadvantages. At first glance, age and grade equivalents seem to have the obvious advantage of ease of communication and interpretation. Most people understand the concept of grade or age and would relate these scores easily to developmental concepts. However, four critical disadvantages outweigh this simplistic advantage. First, both scores, especially grade scores, are based upon the assumption that learning occurs consistently across the year, which has not been proven. Second, we cannot say with accuracy that a fourth-grader with a grade score of 6.1 performs like all sixth-graders in their first month. Third, age- and grade-equivalent scores are not measured in equal interval units; therefore they cannot be added or subtracted to examine improvement. Fourth, age- and grade-equivalent scores are often derived by extrapolating and interpolating from normative data.

Ratio Scores

A popular type of derived score, especially in the past with intelligence tests, is the ratio score, in which the pupil is assigned an age score that corresponds to the measured trait.

Calculation. For intelligence tests, ratio scores have been referred to as *mental age* (*MA*), which is then divided by the student's chronological age (*CA*) to ascertain the extent to which the child's cognitive abilities are above or below that expected of a same-aged student. To eliminate decimals or fractions, the quotient of this ratio is multiplied by 100. The quotient of these two terms (*MA* $\div$ *CA*) multiplied by 100 is known as the intelligence quotient (IQ). Students whose mental age equals their chrono-

logical age would score 100 (1.0 $\times$ 100 = 100). A student who has a mental age less than his or her chronological age would score below 100, and a student with a mental age greater than his or her chronological age would have an IQ above 100.

When to Use. Ratio scores are no longer used in most intelligence tests. Although teachers shouldn't use ratio scores, they should be able to interpret them when they are included in students' records.

Advantages and Disadvantages. Ratio IQ scores contain significant problems. An important issue is that they are not equal interval units and cannot be added or subtracted. Wechsler (1974) points out three major difficulties with ratio IQ scores. First, we misuse the concept of mental age when we imply that students at differing age levels with the same mental age have identical intelligence levels. Second, the concept of mental age is lost when a 5-year-old child with an *MA* of 6 is compared to a 10-year-old child with an *MA* of 12. Both have intelligence quotients of 120, but the 10-year-old child is advanced by 2 years, and the 5-year-old child is ahead by only 1 year. Third, the mental-age concept cannot be usefully employed at adult stages.

Similar to intelligence quotients are the many *developmental quotients* derived from popular tests of development. These ratio scores are just as inadequate as the ratio IQ and should be avoided.

Standard Scores

Standard scores represent a linear transformation of raw scores into standard deviation units. Rather than expressing a student's absolute score on a test, a standard score reflects the student's standing relative to others in the distribution on the basis of variation. This approach translates raw scores into a set of equal interval scores that will always have a consistent mean and standard deviation. Three popular standardized scores are the z-score, the T-score, and the standard score.

The z-score. The **z-score** transformation changes raw scores into deviation units, where the group or test mean is equal to 0.0 and the standard deviation is 1.0. Essentially, the z-score is a measure of the number of standard deviation units away from the test mean. Two important interpretive indices in z-scores are the sign (positive and negative values) and the size of the score. A negative sign means that the score is below the mean and a positive sign means the score is above the mean. Regarding size, the greater the score, the more it is below or above the mean.

The measure is expressed in standard deviation units and therefore can be interpreted with reference to the percentage of area under the normal curve. For example, a score of $+1$ means that the student is 1 standard deviation above the group mean and is performing better than 84% of the population; a score of -1 reflects performance at 1 standard deviation below the mean and is better than only 16% of the population. The chart in Table 13.8 at the end of the chapter provides conversions of z-scores into percentages of the population appearing under the normal curve (percentile ranks) in 5-percentile increments.

The formula for calculating z-scores is

$$\frac{x - X}{SD}$$

where x is the student's score, X is the mean of the distribution, and SD is the standard deviation of the distribution.

The first step in calculating z-scores is to determine the mean of the original set of raw scores (X), which is then subtracted from each score in the set ($x - X$). Second, each differ-ence attained then is divided by the standard deviation of the original group of scores ($x - X$) $\div$ SD. Z-scores resulting from this raw score conversion retain the same shape of the distribution. With a fairly normal distribution of scores in the standardization sample, the z-score has those characteristics of the standard deviation that make it a relatively easy-to-interpret, norm-referenced score.

T-score. Despite the easy-to-explain relationship with the normal distribution, the z-score can still be difficult to communicate. For example, many people get confused about the small magnitude of the scores and the negative or zero values (the normal range of most of the population is from -3 to $+3$; 68% of the population scores within the range -1 to $+1$). The T-score was designed to eliminate this confusion and retain the advantages of a consistent mean and standard deviation. The T-score transformation takes raw scores and changes them to equal interval units, where the mean is 50 and the standard deviation is 10.

The formula for calculating the T-score is

$$T = 10z + 50$$

where z is the z-score, 10 is the planned size of the standard deviation, and 50 is the planned mean.

That is, once a raw score is converted to a z-score, the teacher multiplies each score by 10 and then adds 50. Virtually all T-scores are positive since it would take a z-score of less than -5.0 to convert to a T-score less than zero. The chances of a z-score less than -5.0 are approximately 1 in 100,000.

Standard Scaled Scores. For many test publishers, the T-score remained confusing, so standard scaled scores were created. With **standard scaled scores** (SS), raw scores are transformed to a scale where the mean is 100 and the standard deviation is 15. The standard scaled score has become popular on recent tests of intelligence and achievement.

The formula for standard scaled scores is

$$SS = 15z + 100$$

where z is the z-score, 15 is the planned size of the standard deviation, and 100 is the planned mean. Like the T-score, its derivation is based on the z-score. We derive it by determining the z-score, multiplying it by the 15 and adding that product to 100. Thus, a standard score of 70 would mean the raw score was 2 standard deviations below the test mean (given a standard deviation of 15). A standard score of 120 is a raw score that is 1.33 standard deviations above the test mean.

In Table 13.5 the relationships among raw scores, z-scores, T-scores, and standard scaled scores is compared in relation to scores from a fourth-grade reading class. Assume the initial set of raw scores comes from the fourth-grade classroom TOP example. On that test, the raw score mean was 12 correct items with a standard deviation of 3.8. In Table 13.5, the z-score, T-score, and standard score values for each raw score in the class have been calculated. For example, Jennifer's 19, the highest in the class,

yielded a z-score of 1.84, a T-score of 68, and a standard scaled score of 128. The lowest score, Johnny's 7, was transformed to a z-score of -1.32, a T-score of 37, and a standard scaled score of 80.

When to Use. Standard scores are appropriate in three situations. First, we should use them to summarize student performance on a range of different measures, because they place all measures on a common scale, reflecting the natural variance in the population that took the test. We assume that comparability exists on this dimension because if the population taking the tests is considerably different, it might not make sense to compare scores. Second, if we want to perform arithmetic operations on the measures (e.g., the pretest performance is to be subtracted from the posttest performance), then we must use standard scores. Finally, if we want to identify a student's real position in the distribution, then we must use standard scores. Any of the previously described scores (raw scores, rank order, and percentile ranks) are inadequate for precisely placing the student in the distribution. In contrast, standard scores place students in the distribution relative to the

TABLE 13.5

Comparison of raw scores, z-scores, T-scores, and standard scaled scores

Student Name	Raw Score	z-Score	T-Score	Standard Score
Shawn	8	-1.05	40	84
Sue	13	.26	53	104
Megan	17	1.32	63	120
Bonnie	9	$-.79$	42	88
Johnny	7	-1.32	37	80
Linda	9	$-.79$	42	88
Jennifer	19	1.84	68	128
Nicky	11	$-.26$	47	96
Andy	15	.79	58	112
Michael	12	.00	50	100

Note: All decimal values for T-scores and standard scaled scores are rounded to the nearest whole number.

mean, while taking into account the normal variation present among different students (the standard deviation).

Advantages and Disadvantages. All forms of standard scores (z-scores, T-scores, or standard scaled scores) have four advantages. First, all three types of standard scores use equal interval units. As a result, they may be added, subtracted, and arithmetically transformed. Second, they can show at a glance how far a student is from the mean and his or her position on a normal distribution. For example, a student who has a standard scaled score of 115 is 1 standard deviation above the mean, which places him or her at about the 84th percentile. Third, when scores from different tests (taken by similar or comparable groups of examinees) are compared to each other, standard scores are scale-free and, therefore, can be directly compared. Fourth, when we want to examine absolute changes in relative performance, we can calculate them by subtracting the pre- from the posttest score.

If a student's raw score is 25 on a 30-item math test, 27 on a 30-item reading test, and 18 on a 20-item written expression test, no direct comparisons can be made between these scores. The low score in written expression may be a result of fewer items on the test. More importantly, the three tests may be differentially difficult (one may be hard and the other two may be easy). Using standard scores, we can take both problems into consideration. If the student's performance was expressed as a standard score, it might include the following: In math the score was -1.5, in reading it was $-.5$, and in written expression it was $+.5$. The scores are now directly comparable: The student is performing within a normal limit in written expression and reading, but is low in math.

In determining growth, standard scores can reflect improvements in relative standing, which cannot be adequately done with raw scores.

As in the previous example, the two tests may not have the same number of items in them or may be differentially difficult, precluding any direct comparisons. Converting their scores makes their scales directly comparable, and by taking into account the size of variation (standard deviation), we account for difficulty. A student who performed in the fall of the year with a standard score of $-.5$ and in the spring of the year with a standard score of 0 has made a substantial gain. In the fall, the student was performing at the 34 percentile, while in the spring, the student was at the 50th percentile.

In summary, the advantage of standard scores is twofold: (a) The metric is not bound by the raw score scale, allowing it to be compared to other standard scores with the same reference group, and (b) they take into account both the mean and standard deviation of the distribution, thus representing a very comprehensive metric that incorporates item/test difficulty.

Normal Curve Equivalents

The *normal curve equivalent* (*NCE*) is an example of a normalized standard score, which converts scores into a scale interpretable as percentiles based on equal intervals.

Calculation. The basic formula for calculating normal curve equivalents is $21.06(z) + 50$. The resulting number is rounded to the nearest whole value, ranging from 1 to 99, with a mean of 50.

When to Use. Often, it is important to normalize a set of scores prior to further statistical manipulation (i.e., since percentiles are not equal interval, they would need to be normalized before completing further calculations). The important reason for calculating normal curve equivalents is to enable further interpretations that are based on the normal curve and allow additional statistical manipulation of scores. For example, if we want to know improvement from fall to spring is needed, and percentile ranks have been reported, we should convert them to z-scores and then normal curve equivalents prior to calculating growth; then we can interpret performance relative to a hypothetical group of 100 students.

Advantages and Disadvantages. Normal curve equivalents allow us to describe performance with the interpretability of percentile ranks and the power of standard scores, which allows more sophisticated analyses. Normal curve equivalents are easy to calculate and interpret. Their main disadvantage is the lack of frequent use among educators.

SUMMARY OF OUTCOME METRICS

To help you to understand the relationships between the different metrics for summarizing performance in a norm-referenced approach, Figure 13.3 depicts several of the outcome metrics on the same graph.

Very little research has been conducted on the types of scores to use for specific decisions. As you can see in Figure 13.3, the same outcome metric can be easily changed to a different one by converting it to another scale. The three most important metrics are percentile ranks, stanines, and any of the different standard scores. Raw scores are the least useful from a norm-referenced view because they provide no information for interpretation. Percentiles are very informative and easily interpreted but may pose problems later when we want to make comparisons over time or show differences in performance among individuals. Stanines are helpful in summarizing groups of scores using a global index. Although standard scores are the most informative and can be used in making a wide range of comparisons,

they are also quite difficult for noneducators to interpret. Because z-scores are reported in such an unusual scale (-3 to $+3$), they are often converted to T-scores, which have a mean of 50 and a standard deviation of 10 or standard scaled scores, which have a mean of 100 and a standard deviation of 15. Although they are the most rigorous of all metrics, they may also be the most insensitive to change over time, as Tindal, Shinn, & Germann (1987) suggest. These authors found that special education students showed little change over 1 year when their scores were expressed as standard scores. One hypothesis for this phenomenon is that, for change to appear, it must be greater than the ambient noise reflected in the standard score (i.e., standard deviation).

NORM-REFERENCED EVALUATIONS USING CURRICULUM-BASED MEASUREMENT

Although most norm-referenced assessments utilize published achievement tests, it is possible to construct teacher-made tasks that accomplish the same purpose. If we use systematic sampling to create items with a middle or wide range of difficulty and use standardized administration and scoring procedures when giving and analyzing the test, then it is possible to generate norm-referenced data and distribute students on a normal curve. The prototype for this system comes from curriculum-based measurement (CBM) at the Institute for Research on Learning Disabilities at the University of Minnesota. Although the initial research began by focusing on classroom tasks that special education teachers could use to evaluate and improve instruction for students with mild learning problems, a considerable amount of interest and research turned toward CBM application in general education. Beginning with the development of a normative data

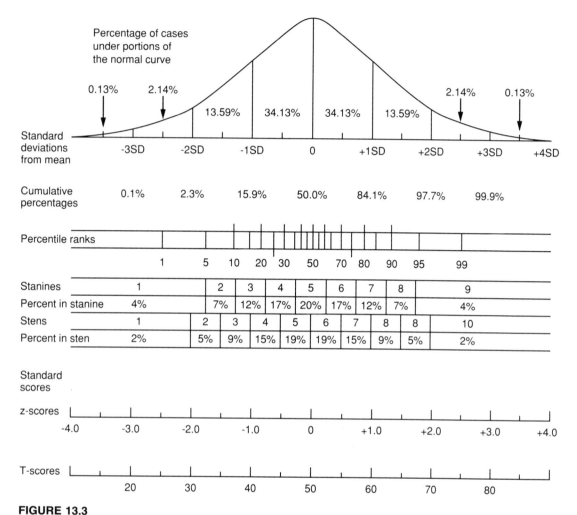

FIGURE 13.3

Comparison of different score types on the same distribution

Source: Lyman, H. B. (1986). *Test scores and what they mean—4th Edition.* Englewood Cliffs, NJ: Prentice-Hall, pp. 82–83. Adapted from *The Psychological Corporation Test Service Bulletin,* no. 48 (1964). Used with permission.

base in Pine County, the first district in the country to employ CBM systematically across the range of educational decisions, a number of districts have begun developing CBM norms. As you have seen in chapters 7–10, the content area chapters, much of the normative development is predicated on identifying critical behaviors needed for success in the classroom and creating administration and scoring procedures. We describe only the normative data summaries here because we covered most of this information in earlier chapters.

Districts applying CBM tasks within a norm-referenced evaluation have generally been interested in using the data to screen students and determine eligibility for specialized programs. Few districts have completed any program certifications or evaluations. For screening purposes, the general education population must be sampled with enough depth to generate stable data, ranging from 15 to 25% of the population (Tindal, Germann, & Deno, 1983). Typically, students are randomly selected from all teachers' classrooms and all buildings in the district. Several different strategies are employed for selecting appropriate material, ranging from that which is used in the modal group at each grade to that used by the lowest group in general education. Using standardized administration and scoring procedures, several hundred students are tested within a 1- to 2-week period. Generally, the normative data base is reestablished three times each year during fall, winter, and spring. The data are analyzed and displayed in five different ways as follows: group averages, frequency polygons, histograms, tables of percentile ranks, and eligibility cut-off graphs.

Group Averages

The Minneapolis Public Schools base normative data on a sample of approximately 7800 elementary students, with average performance measured in the fall, winter and spring. Average gains on these measures during the academic year appear in Table 13.6 (Marston & Magnusson, 1988).

By listing averages across the fall, winter, and spring, it is possible to check on the general growth over the year. As Table 13.6 illustrates, all CBM performance levels increase, regardless of subject matter or grade level.

TABLE 13.6
Average fall, winter, and spring performance of general education students in reading, spelling, math, and written expression

Measure	Grade	Fall	Winter	Spring
Words read correctly	1	19	52	71
Correct letter sequences		9	25	42
Correct digits		5	17	25
Words read correctly	2	51	73	82
Correct letter sequences		33	56	66
Correct digits		23	27	33
Correct words written		8	17	25
Words read correctly	3	88	107	115
Correct letter sequences		60	81	82
Correct digits		14	21	25
Correct words written		19	28	31
Words read correctly	4	106	115	118
Correct letter sequences		77	89	94
Correct digits		24	29	34
Correct words written		29	36	39
Words read correctly	5	118	129	134
Correct letter sequences		91	101	101
Correct digits		31	47	55
Correct words written		37	45	44
Words read correctly	6	115	120	131
Correct letter sequences		100	116	111
Correct digits		58	73	84
Correct words written		45	48	51

Frequency Polygons

The problem with listing group averages in a table is that the shape of the distribution is not visible. The distribution may be skewed or have a narrow or broad range (kurtosis), yet the averages don't reflect this information. Therefore, an important first step when using all CBM normative measures is to display the entire distribution for a grade level. Figure 13.4 shows a frequency polygon for fifth-graders, using a pool of multiplication problems confined to two digits. The data were collected in the spring with a short probe that was 2 minutes long.

Histograms

Another technique for displaying student performance distributions with normative data is to use histograms (bar charts). Figure 13.5 displays fifth-grade norms from an elementary school that assessed all students in oral reading fluency at the beginning of the year.

We can also create histograms for categorical groups like separate grades (or by student classification or sex of student, etc.), where each bar represents an average. Figure 13.6 presents data from three different reading measures given to students in Grades 1 to 6 in Pine County during the 1981–82 school year: (a) common word list, (b) a grade-level word list, and (c) grade-level reading passages.

Percentile Tables

For actual screening and eligibility decision making, however, histograms are difficult to use. For such decisions, which require specific

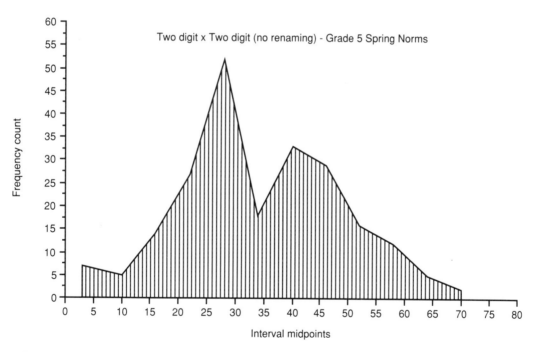

FIGURE 13.4
Frequency polygon for fifth-graders: Multiplication fluency in the spring

FIGURE 13.5
Histogram for fifth-graders' oral reading fluency in the fall

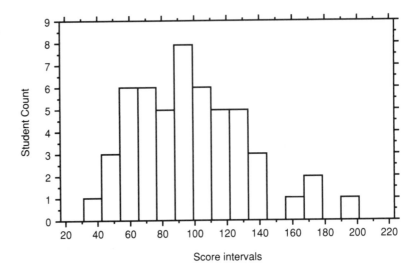

scores, the following two norm-referenced data displays present the data in a very specific manner. Table 13.3 shows percentile ranks in reading that have been calculated on data generated in several third-grade classrooms in an educational consortium. When special education teachers assess referred students, they convert the scores to percentile ranks to see how low the students are ranked.

Screening and Eligibility Charts

Although the data in Table 13.7 are very precise and useful in marking a student's performance

FIGURE 13.6
Exemplary histogram of oral reading fluency on three measures

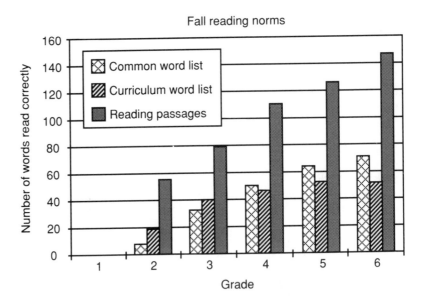

TABLE 13.7

Characteristics of norm-referenced evaluation

	Norm-Referenced Evaluation
Principal use	Survey testing.
Major emphasis	Measure individual differences in achievement.
Interpretation of results	Compare performance to that of other comparable individuals.
Content coverage	Covers a broad area of achievement.
Nature of test plan	Tables of specifications commonly are used.
Item-selection procedures	Items are selected that provide maximum discrimination among individuals. Item difficulty is the most important consideration. Easy and difficult items are eliminated from the test.
Performance standards	Level of performance is determined by relative position in some known group (i.e. ranks 5 in a group of 20).

Source: Adapted from Gronlund, N.E. (1988). *How to construct achievement tests.* Englewood Cliffs, NJ: Prentice-Hall. Table 1.1, p. 12.

relative to a norm group, they are not very helpful in supporting eligibility decisions. Figure 13.7 shows a graph with normative performance standards set at two levels: (a) the median level achieved by students in general education (thick line) and (b) one-half of this level (thin line). In this district, teachers were directed to use the one-half level when determining eligibility for specialized programming. The data plots for students referred for special education appear on this graph. If they fell below the thin line, they were eligible for placement in special education.

LIMITATIONS OF NORM-REFERENCED EVALUATIONS

Norm-referenced data such as percentiles, grade equivalents, and standard scores show how students are doing in relation to each other, but they are poor indicators of changes or learned skills. Norm-referenced scores are psycho-metric indices and are important for comparing students because they focus on measurement of individual differences (Carver, 1974). But they do not communicate students' specific skills in reading, math, oral language, and so forth. For example, a percentile rank of 64 on a norm-referenced reading test for a fourth-grade student does not show if the child has mastered fourth-grade vocabulary, reads fluently in fourth-grade material, or comprehends grade-level stories. Nor does this score describe how much better the student's reading is at the end of the year than it was at the beginning of the year.

Norm-referenced tests have many limitations (Marston & Magnusson, 1988). First, teachers often find the popular standardized tests instructionally irrelevant. In a study by Thurlow and Ysseldyke (1982), only 10%–30% of the teachers surveyed thought the Wide Range Achievement Test, the Wechsler Intelligence Scale for Children—Revised, and the Woodcock Reading Mastery Test were useful for instructional planning.

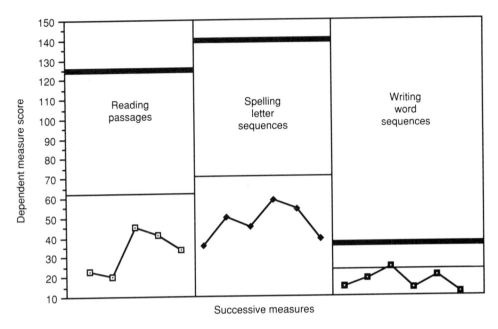

FIGURE 13.7
Normative and eligibility levels for placement in specialized programs

Another problem with norm-referenced tests is that they do not adequately measure skills taught in the curricula. Criticism has been leveled at their content validity, identification of domains for testing, and/or strategies for sampling items within domains. Jenkins and Pany (1978a) analyzed five curricula along with reading subtests from five published achievement tests and found that the performance of students who had learned all of the words in a curriculum differed depending upon the achievement test that was used. Shapiro and Derr (1987) replicated the study's major findings. Leinhardt (1983) found that the amount of overlap between tests and curriculum or instruction often is minimal, and overlap is a powerful predictor of end-of-year test performance. Good and Salvia (1988) analyzed performance on different reading achievement tests

after students had been taught from a specific curriculum. They found significant differences in test performance that could be predicted by differences in content validity (overlap with the curriculum). In mathematics, Freeman et al. (1983) found negligible overlap between five tests and four curricula. The percentage of curriculum topics covered by tests was as low as 16% and as high as 28%; the percentage of test topics covered by curricula ranged from 22% to 85%. These findings indicate that curricula present most test topics, but most tests do not assess many curriculum topics.

Knifong (1980) compared the computational requirements of word story problems across five published achievement tests and found great differences across them, while Petrozko (1978) found that many math tests provide insufficient or unsupportive descriptions

TABLE 13.8

Conversion of z-scores to percentiles

z-score	Percentiles area under curve	z-score	Percentiles area under curve	z-score	Percentiles area under curve	z-score	Percentiles area under curve
−3.00	.0013	−1.20	.1151	−1.45	.0735	0.35	.6368
−2.95	.0016	−1.15	.1251	−1.40	.0808	0.40	.6554
−2.90	.0019	−1.10	.1357	−1.35	.0885	0.45	.6736
−2.85	0022	−1.05	.1469	−1.30	.0968	0.50	.6915
−2.80	.0026	−1.00	.1587	−1.25	.1056	0.55	.7088
−2.75	.0030	−0.95	.1711	0.60	.7257	1.85	.9678
−2.70	.0035	−0.90	.1841	0.65	.7422	1.90	.9713
−2.65	.0040	−0.85	.1977	0.70	.7580	1.95	.9744
−2.60	.0047	−0.80	.2119	0.75	.7734	2.00	.9772
−2.55	.0054	−0.75	.2266	0.80	.7881	2.05	.9798
−2.50	.0062	−0.70	.2420	0.85	.8023	2.10	.9821
−2.45	.0071	−0.65	.2578	0.90	.8159	2.15	.9842
−2.40	.0082	−0.60	.2743	0.95	.8289	2.20	.9861
−2.35	.0095	−0.55	.2912	1.00	.8413	2.25	.9878
−2.30	.0107	−0.50	.3085	1.05	.8531	2.30	.9893
−2.25	.0122	−0.45	.3264	1.10	.8643	2.35	.9906
−2.20	.0139	−0.40	.3446	1.15	.8749	2.40	.9918
−2.15	.0158	−0.35	.3632	1.20	.8849	2.45	.9929
−2.10	.0179	−0.30	.3821	1.25	.8944	2.50	.9938
−2.05	.0202	−0.25	.4013	1.30	.9032	2.55	.9946
−2.00	.0228	−0.20	.4207	1.35	.9115	2.60	.9953
−1.95	.0256	−0.15	.4404	1.40	.9192	2.65	.9960
−1.90	.0287	−0.10	.4602	1.45	.9265	2.70	.9965
−1.85	.0322	−0.05	.4801	1.50	.9332	2.75	.9970
−1.80	.0359	0.00	.5000	1.55	.9394	2.80	.9974
−1.75	.0401	0.05	.5199	1.60	.9452	2.85	.9978
−1.70	.0446	0.10	.5398	1.65	.9505	2.90	.9981
−1.65	.0495	0.15	.5596	1.70	.9554	2.95	.9984
−1.60	.0548	0.20	.5793	1.75	.9599	3.00	.9987
−1.55	.0606	0.25	.5987	1.80	.9641		
−1.50	.0668	0.30	.6179				

of item selection procedures, reliability, validity, and interpretive techniques.

Norm-referenced tests also can be inadequate because they are not sensitive enough to measure pupil progress on a short-term basis. Marston, Fuchs, and Deno (1985) analyzed the growth of elementary students on standardized, norm-referenced tests of reading and language over 10- and 16-week periods and found little evidence of pupil improvement during this period.

As Carver (1974) states, "Because the psychometric dimension has been focused on traditionally, many standardized tests are used to measure gain or growth without being developed or evaluated from an *edumetric* standpoint. The danger of this approach is that the psychometrically developed tests may not be sensitive to gain when in fact there is gain" (p. 518).

CHAPTER SUMMARY

Norm-referenced evaluations provide useful information for two major educational decisions: (a) screening and eligibility and (b) program certification. They arose from the study of individual differences and have a long history of use in schools. In these two decision-making areas, it is difficult to think of using any other reference like criterion- or individual-referenced evaluations. Essentially, a norm-referenced evaluation addresses the degree to which individuals are similar or different, which is the heart of screening and eligibility. Because it addresses broad outcomes across many different individuals, program certification generally incorporates norm-referenced measures.

To take advantage of a norm-referenced measure, performance must be summarized in a manner that allows comparisons through outcome metrics. Beginning with raw scores, which are absolute and not comparative, we described a wide variety of transformed metrics. All norm-referenced measures rank students next to each other on the basis of two general strategies. One strategy is based on rank and reflects an ordinal scale: rank order, percentiles, deciles, quartiles and grade and age equivalence. The most versatile is percentile ranks. Grade and age equivalence are two out-

come metrics that should not be used. The other strategy is based on deviation from the mean and reflects interval scales, with three different forms of standard scores: z-scores, T-scores, and standard scale scores. These three metrics present the same information; they differ only in the numbers used to scale performance (i.e., z-scores are negative numbers between -3 and $+3$ while T-scores are positive numbers between 20 and 80). Therefore, it doesn't matter which outcome metric is used, but T-scores may be the best for staying away from negative numbers.

Not only can we summarize student performance differently using norm-referenced measures, but we can also display them through histograms or frequency polygons, graphs that are designed to communicate a student's relative standing or incorporate the use of a decision guide into a student's relative standing.

Presently, the different decisions in schools are made from many different types of data. However, it is possible with CBM to integrate basic skill tasks and use them in all three decision-making arenas. Although the sampling plans are different, an inherent relationship between performances on various measures is built into the decision-making process. Thus, we can use a norm-referenced measure to screen students, then administer a more skill-specific, criterion-referenced measure, developed from the outcomes on the norm-referenced measure, and finally establish a long-range goal for evaluating individual growth, based on the skills that are projected to be taught. Table 13.7 illustrates the characteristics of norm-referenced evaluation.

CHAPTER 14

Criterion-referenced Evaluation

Standards exist for almost everything these days, including food, building products, and health care. Application of standards for human performance is prevalent in many areas, including business, science, medicine, marketing, and government. Certifications are available in the working world for people who are accountants, nurses, pilots, truck drivers, teachers, beauticians, and veterinarians. These occupations have guidelines that represent minimum standards of performance for certification in order to practice the profession.

The world is predicated on the use of standards, which raises critical questions: What are standards, how are they developed, and what are the consequences of using standards to make decisions? In education, standards cannot be used to dichotomize performance levels without precise specifications of a criterion or domain of knowledge and/or skill. Any decision that is made using established standards to judge performance as qualified or competent reflects criterion-referenced evaluation.

CHAPTER OBJECTIVES

This chapter addresses criterion-referenced evaluation, which judges students according to performance standards. By the end of this chapter the reader will have the knowledge and skills to

- Distinguish between norm-referenced and criterion-referenced tests.
- Describe the definition and purpose of criterion-referenced evaluations.
- Set standards for criterion-referenced evaluations, using judgment of test items.
- Set standards for criterion-referenced evaluations, using judgment of test takers.

KEY VOCABULARY

Chapter 14 focuses on *criterion-referenced evaluations*, in which assessment is based on precisely defined skills and knowledge. Interpretation of performance often is stated in terms of *standards*, a level of performance that implies minimal success. Often such standards are translated into *mastery* versus *nonmastery*, which in turn is based on *cutoff scores*, the level of performance above which there is mastery and below which there is nonmastery. Standard setting can be based on (a) *judgment of test items*, (b) *judgment of individual test takers*, or (c) *analysis of applicable reference groups*. All standard-setting procedures utilize *judges*, experts in the field of study for which the assessment device is being constructed or implemented. These judges either predict what *borderline information* is necessary to succeed or how *borderline students* will perform. Ultimately, all decisions that dichotomize students into mastery or nonmastery may result in error. Students can be incorrectly judged as *mastered* (a *false positive* or *Type I error*) or *non-mastered* (a *false negative* or *Type II error*).

CRITERION-REFERENCED EVALUATIONS: DEFINITIONS AND PURPOSE

Criterion-referenced evaluations focus on specific knowledge and skills of students. Rather than compare the student to a peer group, as in norm-referenced evaluation, pupil performance is evaluated with reference to a criterion body of knowledge or skill. Probably the most important difference between norm-referenced tests and criterion-referenced tests is the manner in which tests are developed and scores are interpreted. In Table 14.1, norm- and criterion-referenced evaluations are compared on seven dimensions (Gronlund, 1988).

TABLE 14.1

A comparison of criterion-referenced and norm-referenced evaluations

	Criterion-Referenced Evaluation	Norm-Referenced Evaluation
Principal use	Specific level or mastery testing.	Survey testing.
Major emphasis	Describes tasks students can perform successfully.	Measures individual differences in achievement.
Interpretation of results	Compares performance to clearly specified achievement levels that are dichotomous.	Compares performance to that of other comparable individuals.
Content coverage	Focuses on a limited set of learning tasks within a unit and within a curriculum.	Covers a broad area of achievement.
Nature of test plan	Detailed tables of specifications are used to plan specific item sampling.	Tables of specifications are commonly used.
Item selection procedures	Includes all items needed to adequately describe performance. No attempt is made to alter item difficulty or to eliminate easy items to increase score variability. Item discrimination is the most important consideration.	Items are selected that provide maximum discrimination among individuals. Item difficulty is the most important consideration. Easy and difficult items are eliminated from the test.
Performance standards	Level of performance is commonly determined by absolute standards (i.e. demonstrates mastery by defining 90 percent of the technical terms).	Level of performance is determined by determined by relative position in some known group (i.e. ranks 5 in a group of 20).

Source: Adapted from Gronlund, N. (1988). *How to construct achievement tests.* Table 1.1, p. 12. Englewood Cliffs, N. J.: Prentice-Hall, Inc.

In summary, a norm-referenced evaluation documents learning in general terms, whereas a criterion-referenced evaluation delineates learning of specific skills and knowledge. Three characteristics of criterion-referenced evaluation follow:

- Test items are developed from specific performance objectives directly linked to an instructional domain.
- The score is based on an absolute, not a relative standard.
- The test measures mastery by using specific standards.

In a criterion-referenced evaluation, the focus of assessment is on what the student actually can or cannot do on specific skills and knowledge tasks. Frequently, performance is interpreted in terms of mastery (Glaser, 1963). Two components must be addressed when constructing criterion-referenced tests: (a) which specific tasks should be included and (b) how performance should be judged as mastered or not mastered (Glaser & Nitko, 1971). Chapters 2–6 presented information on test construction following a fairly traditional approach, in which test planning was followed by developing item pools, selecting test items, administering tests, and ensuring their reliability and validity. Technically, criterion-referenced testing implies a well-defined domain. In practice, most criterion-referenced tests also utilize established standards of acceptable performance, which was not addressed in earlier chapters. The three critical questions that relate to standards are the following: (a) How are standards established, (b) what is mastery or nonmastery, (c) and what are the implications of making such judgments?

This chapter reviews standards only in terms of their bearing on achievement assessment. Even this scope is quite broad, since so many educational standards exist. For example, although most technical training programs use standards to award certification, such programs are not considered in this chapter. And although many different training programs use different terminology (*mastery and nonmastery, minimally competent and incompetent, successful and unsuccessful, certified and noncertified*), such terms are treated synonymously. Whether standards are developed or adopted, they are ultimately based on judgments. We must know the procedures used to establish these judgments in order to use any standard appropriately. Figure 14.1 depicts the decisions involved in setting standards with criterion-referenced evaluations.

SETTING STANDARDS

Although many teachers and researchers may disagree with the procedures for setting **standards,** few argue about the definition of the concept.

> Standards connote excellence. They are used to separate the good from the bad, to sort goats from sheep. As with any other psychological construct that cannot be embodied exactly by concrete test scores, performance standards pose special problems for measurement experts. (Shepard, 1984, p. 169)

Criterion-referenced evaluations require a cutoff point to distinguish mastered from nonmastered or successful from unsuccessful students. The validity of this cutoff point is as critical as the validity of the test content. Standard setting "is the Achilles heel of criterion-referenced testing . . . The most elaborate domain specifications in the world cannot compensate for invalid standards" (Shepard, 1984, p. 169).

In the late 1970s there was considerable debate over standard-setting methods. The debate was best exemplified by an exchange between Glass (1978) and Popham (1978). Glass stated that standard setting rests on arbitrary premises and is so fundamentally flawed that test scores have to be interpreted by other means (primarily norm-referenced interpretations). Countering this view, Popham (1978) argued that *arbitrary* has two meanings, only one of which denotes capriciousness. The other allows for decisions to be made with careful deliberation. Eventually, Glass was the victor, and the concession was made that standards are arbitrary. "Just because excellence can be distinguished from incompetence at the extremes does not mean that excellence and incompetence can be unambiguously separated at the cutoff" (Shepard, 1984, p. 170–171). The cutoff point imposes a false dichotomy on a continuum of efficiency; if traits actually were dichotomous, standard setting would not be so difficult.

Standards can be either absolute or relative. With absolute standards interpretation does not depend on the performance of all other test takers, and no comparisons are made between individuals. With relative standards comparisons are made between individuals. Nevertheless, any standard requires some judgments, which must be (a) meaningful to the people who make them, (b) made by qualified people, and (c) sensitive to the purpose of the test. A variety of procedures, most of which are based on judgments, is available for setting standards.

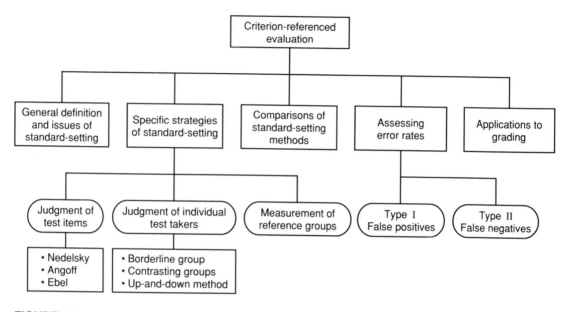

FIGURE 14.1
Decisions involved in setting standards with criterion-referenced evaluations

Livingston and Zieky (1982), review three general methods based on judgments of (a) test content, (b) individual test takers, and (c) groups of test takers. The greatest attention, however, has been on **judgment of test content,** in which the standard setters analyze test items to determine how many should be passed to reflect minimal proficiency (Livingston, 1980). Five basic steps are employed:

1. Selecting judges. **Judges** should be experts in the knowledge or skills measured by the test; they should be representative of other experts in that field. Enough judges should be selected so that one or two do not sway the process, yet there should not be so many that the procedures become cumbersome.

2. Defining borderline knowledge and skills. Judges should collectively define **borderline knowledge** and skills. In defining borderline knowledge, they must first understand what the test measures and how the test scores

will be used. Then they should describe someone who represents the borderline between acceptable and unacceptable skill. Consensus on this definition must be reached. If strong differences in opinion arise, some compromise should be attained before proceeding to the next step.

3. Training of the judges in a particular judgment process. Once the judges agree on the definition of a borderline or minimally acceptable level of performance, they should write it down with examples so people can use it as an anchor for making judgments. Training then focuses on exposing the judges to the range of exemplars that are within, above, or below the borderline definition.

4. Collecting judgments. After adequate training (in which disagreements are resolved), judgments can then be collected independently to avoid creating artificial agreement.

5. Aggregating judgments to determine a passing score. The last step depends on

which specific method is used for determining the cutoff. Although training in the judgment process is crucial, it will not eliminate subjective differences of opinion for any of the three systems: test content, individual test takers, or groups of test takers.

Judgment of Test Content

Nedelsky (1954), Angoff (1971), and Ebel (1972), each developed standard-setting procedures for judging test content. All three procedures are based on "the concept of the borderline test taker. This test taker is the one whose knowledge and skills are on the borderline between the upper group and the lower group" (Livingston & Zieky, 1982, p. 15). Judges decide on how the borderline test taker would respond to each of the questions. Such procedures can be employed either before or after the test is administered, since the focus of judgment is on the test questions; therefore, knowledge of the test content is crucial, but knowledge of student performance is not crucial and may actually bias the judgment process.

Nedelsky's Method. In 1954, Nedelsky proposed a method for making judgments on multiple-choice test items. "The judges' task is to look at the question and identify the wrong answers that a borderline test taker would be able to recognize as wrong, that is, as not the best of the answers presented." (Livingston & Zieky, 1982, p. 17). Judges can make their decisions individually or collectively; however, it is likely that more valid judgments occur if judges share opinions and information with each other after training is completed and then make independent judgments.

Procedures. The method employs the following steps:

1. Individually, judges should make a preliminary set of judgments for each of the questions, eliminating wrong answers that the borderline test taker would be able to eliminate.

2. Hold a brief discussion on each question in which the judges go through each of the distractors or foils to determine whether it would be eliminated by the borderline test taker. When judges disagree, they should explain why they thought the distractor would or would not be eliminated. At this point, agreement may not be necessary, but each point of view must be heard. Encourage the judges to change their responses based on the information they hear in this discussion. This method tends to result in fairly low cutoff scores, so it may be appropriate to provide the judges with the correct answer, potentially raising the cutoff scores.

Determining the cutoff or passing score, a relatively easy task, is based on the idea that if we first eliminate the answers the borderline test taker would know are wrong, then a random probability exists of determining the correct answer from the remaining choices. Use the following three steps in selecting a **cutoff score**:

1. Count the number of choices that have not been eliminated.
2. This number is placed in the denominator and 1 in the numerator; this fraction is converted into a decimal.
3. These values are averaged by summing them and then dividing by the number of items.

At this point, we collect a cutoff score from each judge and then aggregate the scores across judges by using either the mean, the median, or a trimmed mean. The mean allows for a composite across judges and may be useful if all the judges are somewhat close to each other. However, if one or two judges are extremely high or low, the mean may be swayed up or down. Therefore, if considerable variation exists across the judges, the median may be more appropriate to select as the cutoff score because it is not as sensitive to extreme scores. Finally, a trimmed mean may be appropriate. With a *trimmed mean*, the highest and lowest scores are thrown out, and the average of the remaining scores is calculated in the same way. The amount of trimming is a function of how many judges' decisions can be thrown out.

Assume that the following item appeared on a test given to students taking an assessment course:

The primary purpose of a norm-referenced test is to

    a. provide diagnostic information on math skills.
    b. distribute students' scores on some characteristic.
    c. predict performance in the language arts.
    d. measure factors that contribute to performance.

As most tests are constructed, some of the distractors are more tricky than others. For example, (c) is a giveaway, and even a borderline test taker would probably not select that option. Option (d), which is somewhat vague, may also be avoided by the borderline test taker. That leaves only two options that may be selected by someone with minimal skill in assessment: (a) and (b). In fact, it is likely that something was said in the book or in class about norm-referenced testing and distributing scores and diagnosing skills. Therefore, when using the Nedelsky method for determining standards, all items that would be eliminated by a borderline test taker would be thrown out. This leaves two options, with a .50 probability of a correct guess. Each item is analyzed in the same manner with a probability assigned to it.

For example, assume the following distribution of probabilities was found for a 10-item test, in which each item had one right answer out of five possible responses:

Item 1	.50
Item 2	.25
Item 3	.75
Item 4	.25
Item 5	.50
Item 6	.25
Item 7	.75
Item 8	1.00
Item 9	.50
Item 10	.75

The test contains some items that are difficult: Only 25% of the examinees are expected to answer Items 2, 4, and 6 correctly by guessing. It also has items that are easy: 100% of the examinees are expected to correctly answer Item 8 by guessing. To establish the passing score using Nedelsky's system, we compute the average probability by summing all probabilities (5.5) and dividing by the number of observations (10), resulting in the average (.55).

Other judges may obtain different results, making it necessary to calculate the scores across judges. Each item should receive an index (probability of passing the item by guessing alone), and the average probability across the test should be calculated, providing an index that serves as the passing score. We interpret the passing score as follows: On this test, any students scoring at or below this level are guessing at the items after eliminating the obviously incorrect options.

The Nedelsky procedure has three serious conceptual and technical flaws. First, it assumes examinees who don't know the answer would guess at random. Second, it assumes that distractors that haven't been eliminated are equally attractive. And third, it does not permit probabilities between 1 and .5. This procedure is likely to result in standards that are systematically lower than those of other judgmental methods (Shepard, 1980).

Classroom applications. The Nedelsky strategy is appropriate for evaluating the overlap of a multiple-choice test with the content of instruction and in determining the absolute minimum level of performance for passing. Teachers often are given a mastery test within their curriculum and asked to administer it at the end of the instructional unit. Rather than blindly adopting the test and its suggested criteria for passing (usually around 75%–85%), teachers should analyze each of the items to ascertain whether that content was indeed taught (either directly or tangentially). For those items that were taught directly or heavily emphasized, teachers may need to adjust the perceived difficulty downward (nearly everyone will get it correct by eliminating incorrect options). In contrast, for items that were not taught directly or represent generalizations from the material that was taught, the item difficulty may need to be adjusted upward. Adjusting each item in relation to what was actually taught may make the adjusted mastery score more functional in sorting students into the nonmastery group.

This procedure is also appropriate when teachers want to sort students at the very low end, rather than the high end. Since Nedelsky's technique establishes a fairly low performance standard, it is not useful in determining which students should receive grades of *A* or *B*; rather, it is better used in determining who will get a *P* (passing), *N* (not passing), or a grade of *D*. It objectively demarcates the level of performance that sorts out test-taking skills from knowledge.

Angoff's Method. The method proposed by Angoff in 1971 is similar to the Nedelsky method, but can be applied to tests that are not multiple-choice.

> In Angoff's method, the passing score is computed from the expected scores for the individual questions, as in Nedelsky's method. However, it does not require the judge to consider each possible wrong answer separately. Instead the judge considers each question as a whole and makes a judgment on the probability that a borderline test taker will answer the question correctly. (Livingston & Zieky, 1982, p. 24)

Procedures. To apply this method, a judge reads the items on the test and assigns each one a probability that a minimally competent person would answer them correctly. The judge expresses what should be true; however this judgment often involves imagining a large number of minimally competent individuals and then stating what proportion of the group would get the item correct. This method, like all methods for judging test content, is established by summing the probabilities that had been assigned to each test item.

To help judges anchor their decisions, they are asked to (a) predict how many in a group of borderline test takers would answer the question correctly or (b) consider an imagined borderline test taker and estimate the probability that he or she would answer correctly. The probability must be between .00 and 1.00. For multiple-choice questions this probability should be at least as great as the probability of guessing the correct answer. As in the Nedelsky procedure, preliminary judgments are followed by a brief discussion in which each judge states his or her probability and, when disagreement exists, provides some explanation for the decision. Determination of the passing score is completed in the same way as with Nedelsky's method. Basically, each item has a probability associated with it; the probabilities are averaged across the different test items and aggregated across the different judges by using the mean, the median, or a trimmed mean.

For example, judges might differ in their estimates of whether a borderline test taker would pass the following three items from a spelling test. The first item was given a low value (i.e., only 15% of the borderline students would pass the item), and the second item was given a much higher value (i.e. 75% of these students would get it correctly, given that a correct response can occur 50% of the time by chance alone). The last item was given a low value (15%) because it asks for an inferential example rather than a direct summarization of information.

> What is the most common (frequently appearing) word in the English language? _____
>
> Mark the following statement as either true by circling the *T* or false by circling the *F*: Performance on proofreading tasks often is highly related to performance on production tasks. *T F*
>
> In a sentence or two, explain the reason for scoring performance on a spelling test using correct letter sequences rather than words spelled correctly.

As shown in the examples, the type of the item can vary, utilizing either selection or production responses; any type of selection format is possible, including matching, classification, or multiple-choice. As in Nedelsky's procedure, each item is given a probability that the borderline test taker will pass it. The probabilities again are averaged across all of the judges for each item and then across the judges to obtain a passing score. Interpretations of the passing score are exactly the same as those from Nedelsky: They represent the probability that a borderline test taker can pass the test.

Classroom applications. Teachers should analyze the mastery tests and make them serve their purposes. Angoff's procedure can be useful in adapting a mastery score from a published, curriculum-embedded test to fit the instruction that occurred with that material. Some test items might be easy, having been stressed during instruction, while other test items might be difficult because they either were not stressed or represent generalizations. By analyzing each item, the teacher ensures that the mastery test fits instruction more closely.

The advantage of this procedure is that it can be applied to both selection and production response items. It is also faster to complete than Nedelsky's because only the item is being judged, not all components within the item. Finally, the cutoff value is not likely to be as low as Nedelsky's, making it more inapplicable for use in sorting students at the high end.

Ebel's Method. The procedure proposed by Ebel (1972) requires judges to sort items into a two-dimensional matrix (difficulty and relevance) and then assigns a probability of a borderline test taker answering it correctly.

Procedures. Judgment of difficulty has three levels: easy, medium, and hard. Relevance has four levels: essential, important, acceptable, and questionable. By classifying each item according to both dimensions, a 12-cell classification table is created. Once questions are placed into this matrix, judges estimate the probability of a borderline test taker getting the items correct in any of the cells. This probability should be high on the upper-left quadrant, where difficulty is low and relevance is essential. In contrast, probabilities may be low in the lower-right part of the matrix, where difficulty is high and relevance is questionable. For instance, if 10 questions are in a cell, the judge may decide that 6 of the 10 would be answered correctly.

In the fourth step, each judge states his or her percentage (of items) for each category and discusses any differences in open forum, possibly for changing the judgments.

The cutoff is the sum of expected scores for all cells, which is determined by taking the probability for each cell and multiplying it by the number of questions in the cell. This resulting score is averaged across all of the questions and finally across all of the judges to obtain the score needed to pass the test.

For example, assume that the matrix in Figure 14.2 is the result of analyzing a test and classifying all the items according to the two dimensions, difficulty and relevance. The total number of items for each level of difficulty and relevance is displayed on the right and bottom margins. Each cell displays the number and percentage of items of that combination of difficulty and relevance; at the lower right corner of each cell is the number of borderline or minimally qualified students who are predicted to pass the items in the cell.

As Figure 14.2 illustrates, most of the items are essential or important and are evenly distributed on difficulty. A borderline test taker is predicted to have a score of 32, which was obtained by adding all scores in the lower right corner of each cell. In the easy and essential cell, a borderline student should pass all the items; in the cell just to the right, medium difficulty and essential relevance, only 8 of the 10 items should be successfully answered.

Classroom applications. This technique can also be used to ensure that the mastery decision adequately reflects the content of instruction. Teachers can analyze each item, place it into the matrix, and then assign values for passing, all of which is done in relation to how they taught the material. If an item was heavily emphasized, it may be easier and more relevant; items that were not the direct focus of instruction may be more difficult or less relevant. The mastery score can then be adjusted to fit instruction more appropriately.

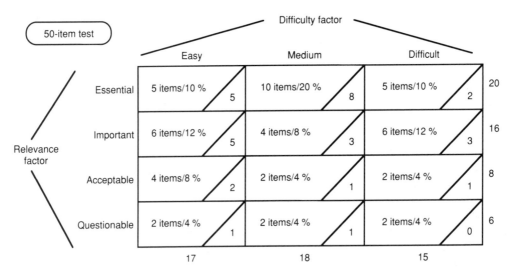

FIGURE 14.2
Decision matrix for Ebel's method

Ebel's procedure has several advantages over Nedelsky's and Angoff's. First, the scale for making these judgments is presented ahead of time, rather than relying on an idiosyncratic scale of 0 to 1 or 100. Second, the items are evaluated in terms of two dimensions (difficulty and relevance), not just one (difficulty). Third, casting the difficulty dimension into 3 units and the relevance dimension into 4 units makes the scale easy to create and interpret. Fourth, Ebel's system can be used with selection or production responses.

Judgment of Individual Test Takers

In the Nedelsky, Angoff, and Ebel procedures, judgments of test items are always made; in the three systems described next, judgments are made of individual students or test takers that involve collecting data on their performance. Importantly, though, all test data are collected after the judgment has been rendered. Both pieces of information (the judgment and the outcome) are essential and should be collected in an appropriate fashion. Judgments should reflect recommendations of qualified individuals, focus on the measures used to test the individuals, and be established appropriately. Also, the individual's performance should be accurate and current.

Borderline-Group Method. In the borderline group method, judges identify individuals who are borderline in their knowledge of the subject matter.

Procedures. The following five steps should be used in applying this system to define mastery scores:

1. Select appropriate judges.
2. Define *adequate*, *inadequate*, and *borderline* levels of the skills and knowledge tested.
3. Identify the borderline test takers.

4. Obtain the scores of the borderline test takers.
5. Set the cutoff score at the median of this group.

Classroom applications. The best use of this procedure is in corroborating results of mastery tests and/or mastery levels. Minimum standards for many curriculum-embedded tests have been established without any empirical support, possibly promoting serious problems (Tindal, Fuchs, Fuchs, Shinn, Deno & Germann, 1985). Therefore, teachers need to question seriously the levels that are suggested and adjust them upward or downward to better minimize errors in judgment. The borderline-group method for determining mastery is very appropriate for this purpose.

Teachers collect a plethora of performance information in the classroom every day, much of which they use informally to make judgments about students. For example, students complete work sheets, answer questions, and turn in assignments daily. By using other classroom information on student performance, teachers can sort students into three groups: (a) students who have the skills, (b) students who don't have the skills, and (c) students whom teachers are unable to identify as either skilled or unskilled. The middle group presents the problem.

Because a multitude of selection tests are given, and standardized administration procedures are often lacking, teachers should be leery of passing students solely on the basis of mastery tests. Student performance on other tasks can be useful in corroborating the results of mastery tests. By sorting students into three groups based on classroom functioning and comparing their performance on the mastery tests, teachers may find the mastery test is not functioning adequately. Many borderline students may pass the test, seriously weakening its applicability in making decisions. In this case, the mastery cutoff should be adjusted upward to fit the mean of this group. The mastery decision is supported when most of the borderline students fail the test, since other classroom indicators are consistent with this finding; possibly, the cutoff score needs to be adjusted downward to fit the mean of this group.

The advantage of this system is its attention to the gray area between mastery and non-mastery. As presented later in this chapter, the major concern is rarely with those students who are definitely successful or unsuccessful; rather it is with those students near the cutoff. Such attention to this group shows that the problem is not easily solved and that teachers still need to make decisions, occasionally in the presence of less-than-adequate data.

Contrasting Groups. Rather than sorting students into a group that represents the fringe between mastery and nonmastery (the borderline group), the contrasting-group method sorts them directly as mastered or not mastered; no borderline group is used. Any total test score level is then taken and analyzed to determine whether the majority of the students performing at that level are masters or nonmasters. A threshold is typically found, moving to score values where the percentage of not mastered or not qualified is greater than the percentage of mastered or qualified. A number of different values may be selected, such as the value where these two groups are divided 75–25 or 50–50.

Procedures. To set passing scores using the contrasting-group method, five steps should be followed:

1. Select appropriate judges.
2. Define *adequate* and *inadequate* levels of knowledge/skills.
3. Select a random sample of the test takers from all scores in the distribution.
4. Ask the question of those with a particular score: "Are the majority of them qualified or unqualified?"
5. Obtain the judgments and the scores (judges should not know test-takers' scores).
6. Divide the group into *qualified* and *unqualified* at each score level and compute the percentage of those falling in each group at each score.
7. Smooth the data.
8. Choose the passing score (i.e., the score where percent qualified is 75% or 50%). Which type of error is more problematic: stating a student has mastered when in fact they haven't, (Type I errors, or false positives) and stating a student has not mastered when in fact they have (Type II errors or false negatives).

The problem in setting a score for mastery is that some lower intervals actually have a greater percentage of masters than higher intervals. Therefore, Livingston and Zieky (1982) recommend using a smoothing technique that uses the average percentage for each group of three intervals. Smoothing the data is a procedure for establishing a generally increasing percentage of students who are masters (going up the scale) or nonmasters (going down the scale) at each score level.

For example, Table 14.2 shows the percentage of masters for each score interval. The column on the far right represents the average of percentages for three successive scoring intervals. Notice that we cannot obtain an average for the highest or lowest intervals, since no scores occur above or below. This system transforms raw score percentages of masters to reflect an increasing rate for successive score intervals. In this example, the mastery score could be set at 41–45, since an average of 63% of the students at that interval were masters.

Another strategy to establish a generally increasing percentage of masters at increasing

TABLE 14.2
Example of mastery established by contrasting groups with smoothing

Score Interval	Percentage Masters	Three Score Avg.
46–50	75	
41–45	50	63
36–40	65	45
31–35	20	40
26–30	35	22
21–25	10	

score intervals is to draw a line that represents the trend of best fit. Figure 14.3 shows a line drawn to reflect the generally increasing trend of more masters at each successively higher score interval; a score of 75% as a mastery score would be reached at a score of 45 or 46; or any point along this line could be selected as the cutoff.

Classroom applications. The contrasting group method is applicable in exactly the same situation as the borderline group method: to corroborate the results of a mastery test. Rather than sorting students into three groups, how-

ever, we identify only two, mastered and non-mastered, on the basis of other classroom information (assignments, worksheets, etc.). By selecting a score value and determining the number or percentage of qualified versus unqualified students, we can establish a sensitive cutoff score. The optimal score is one in which most unqualified students fail and most qualified students pass. If the mastery test is passing many students deemed unqualified, the cutoff score needs to be adjusted.

The advantage of the contrasting-group method is its sensitivity to individual score levels. By systematically comparing the proportion of mastered to nonmastered at each score level, a cutoff can be attained that is maximally sensitive to either type of mis-statement. The disadvantage of this method is the extra time required to accomplish this outcome.

Up-and-Down Method. The final method for determining a cutoff score separating masters from nonmasters is to sort a group of students into two groups as in the contrasting-group method. Rather than judging and testing all of them, we analyze only those in the middle area

FIGURE 14.3
Analyzing masters scores across successively higher score intervals

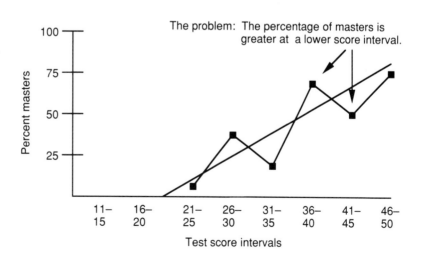

of concern. Essentially, the scores of individuals in the borderline group are successively plotted and are likely to reflect a zig-zag pattern. The score for mastery is the line that reflects no slope or change and is in the middle of the distribution.

Procedures. The specific steps for the up-and-down method include the following:

1. Select appropriate judges.
2. Select a test taker with a score near the proper passing score. Get a judgment on this test taker's skills.
3. If the first test taker was judged qualified, choose another with a lower score. If this person is judged qualified, choose a test taker with a lower score. Continue selecting test takers from around that region and judge whether they are qualified or not qualified.
4. The resulting judgments of qualified or un-qualified will move up and down in that score region.
5. Eliminate the first and last test takers who were used to find the borderline region; take the average score from the range of scores in which this judgment is up-and-down. Figure 14.4 depicts the up-and-down method; a score of 19 appears appropriate as the cutoff score.

Classroom applications. This procedure resembles the contrasting-group method but looks at individuals rather than proportions or groups. Instead of asking what proportion of individuals at a score level are masters and nonmasters, we establish the cutoff first, and then analyze a borderline student's score to determine the side on which it falls. This strategy allows analysis of cutoff scores in reference to the most difficult group—those who clearly have or have not mastered. Other classroom performance can be used to validate a score and adjust it upward or downward.

In corroborating mastery cutoffs, the up-and-down method may be as powerful and slightly more efficient than the other methods because we only analyze questionable students. The advantage to this procedure is the time and focus. Limiting attention to near failures, consumes less time, and addresses the critical group.

Measurement of Reference Groups

The final method can be used only when we have identified a group of test takers with known proficiency levels. In many occupational trades, this strategy might be used to adjust scores for certification. It is difficult to use, however, in the establishment of cutoff scores because the

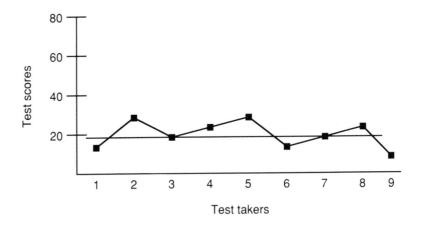

FIGURE 14.4
Determining the cutoff for mastery

criterion group, or **reference group**, is not yet identified.

Procedures. The following four steps should be used in reference-group evaluation:

1. Identify the reference group.
2. Define *adequate* and *inadequate* levels of knowledge and skills.
3. Collect the judgments of the people in the reference group who have an adequate level of the knowledge and skills tested.
4. Choose the passing score.

Classroom Applications. A variation of this system was used to investigate the adequacy of a series of mastery tests in commonly used basal reading programs (Tindal, Fuchs, Fuchs, Shinn, Deno, & Germann, 1985). Students who had passed a mastery test earlier in the year and those who hadn't yet received instruction in that level were tested, and their performance was compared. A disconcerting finding was that many students who hadn't been taught the material from which they were tested performed equally as well as those who previously had mastered the material. Using the cutoff scores given by the publishers, many students would have been misclassified.

The best application of this procedure in the classroom is with instructional material that is hierarchically ordered. Student's must have mastery in preskills before advancing to later content. Mathematics, music, and content area sciences (where vocabulary mastery is critical) are three areas where this system may be appropriate.

If students are assessed prior to training and again following training, their mastery on both programs can be compared. A perfect fit would occur if

- Only students who passed the pre-training program also passed the later program.

- All students who failed the pre-training program also failed the later program.

Of course, this outcome is unlikely, and some students would cross over (i.e., pass the pretraining and fail the later training). Essentially, the reference group consists of those who pass the later program, and any cutoff scores in the pretraining program can be set at the level students had attained.

COMPARISONS OF STANDARD-SETTING METHODS

Berk (1986) compared these various methods along several dimensions. Technical adequacy was the most important aspect and included the following issues:

1. Generation of appropriate classification information.
2. Sensitivity of the procedure to examinee performance.
3. Sensitivity of the procedure to instruction.
4. Statistical soundness of the procedure.
5. Degree to which the procedure identifies a true standard.
6. Presence of decision validity evidence.

Several practical issues were also considered, including the following:

7. Ease of implementation.
8. Ease of computation.
9. Ease of interpretation by the general public.
10. Credibility to the general public.

Finally, the methods were rated overall. In Table 14.3, a double negative sign represents serious and significant disadvantage, a single minus represents a disadvantage, a single plus represents an advantage, and a double plus represents a significant advantage.

TABLE 14.3
Technical adequacy and practicability ratings of 23 standard-setting methods

Type of Method	Technical Adequacy (TA)						Practicability (P)				Overall Rating	Mean TA Rating	Mean P Rating
	1[a]	2	3	4	5	6	7	8	9	10			
Judgment													
Adjusted/modified Angoff	+ +[b]	−	-	+	+	−	+ +	-	+ +	+ +	+	-	+ / + +
Angoff	+ +	−	-	+ +	+ +	−	+	+ +	+ +	+ +	+	+	+ +
Angoff-Nedelsky combination	+ +	−	-	-	+	−	−	-	-	+	-	-	-
Difficulty-importance estimate	+ +	−	-	-	-	-	-	+	+	+	-	-	+
Difficulty-relevance Ebel	+ +	−	-	-	+ +	−	-	+	-	-	-	-	-
Difficulty-taxonomy Ebel	+ +	+	-	-	-	−	-	+	-	-	-	-	-
Item specifications	+ +	−	-	-	−	−	+	+	+	+	-	-	+
Modified M-C Angoff	+ +	−	-	-	-	−	+ +	+ +	+ +	+ +	+	-	+ +
Nedelsky	+ +	−	-	-	+ +	−	−	-	-	+	-	-	-
Relevance-taxonomy Ebel	+ +	−	−	-	-	−	-	+	-	-	-	-	-
Two-choice Angoff	+ +	−	-	-	-	−	+ +	+	+	+	- +	-	+
Judgmental-empirical													
Absolute-relative compromise I	+ +	+	+	+ +	+	−	-	−	-	-	- +	+	-
Absolute-relative compromise II	+ +	+	+	+ +	+	−	−	−	-	-	- +	+	-/−
Angoff-contrasting groups plus composite	+ +	+ +	+	+	+	+ +	−	−	+	+	+	+ / + +	-
Informed judgment	+ +	+	+	+ +	+ +	−	+	+ +	+ +	+ +	+ / + +	+	+ +
Iterative Angoff	+ +	+	+	+	+ +	−	−	+ +	+	+ +	+	+	+
Iterative two-choice Angoff	+ +	+	+	+	+	−	−	-	+	+ +	+	+	- +
Modified Angoff-empirical	+ +	+	-	-	−	−	+	+	+ +	+ +	+	-	+ / + +
Empirical-judgmental													
Borderline group	+ +	+ +	+	+	-	−	+	+	+	-	+	+	+
Contrasting group	+ +	+ +	+ +	+	+	+ +	-	+	+	-	+	+ / + +	- +
Criterion groups	+ +	+ +	+ +	+	-	+ +	-	+	+	-	+	+ / + +	- +
Educational consequences	+ +	+ +	+ +	−	−	−	+	+	-		- +	- +	- +
Norm-referenced criterion	+ +	+ +	-	-	-	-	+	+	-	-	- +	- +	- +

Source: Berk, R. A. (1986). A consumer's guide to setting performance standards on criterion-referenced tests. *Review of Educational Research. 56* (1), 137–172, Table IV, p. 154–155.

Note. Ratings are based on author's evaluation.

[a]1 = yields appropriate classification information; 2 = sensitive to examinee performance; 3 = sensitive to instruction or training; 4 = statistically sound; 5 = identifies true standard; 6 = yields decision validity evidence; 7 = easy to implement; 8 = easy to compute; 9 = easy to interpret to lay people; 10 = credible to lay people.

[b] − = marked disadvantage; - = disadvantage; + = advantage; + + = marked advantage.

ASSESSING ERROR RATES

All standard setting-methods result in a dichotomous decision that separates examinees into successful (masters) and unsuccessful (nonmasters) groups. Two ways for incorrectly labeling students exist. First, it is possible to be incorrect in labeling a student mastered, which is known as a **false positive**, or **Type I**, error. A student also may be incorrectly labeled a nonmaster, which is known as a **false negative**, or **Type II**, error.

These two error types rarely are equally serious. For example, it is a serious problem to incorrectly award certification to a pilot. A false positive in this case is potentially far more tragic than a false negative, in which a person would be denied certification to fly even though he or she had mastered the material and training. The severity of making false positive decisions is serious in many other areas, including medicine and nuclear technology.

On some occasions, a false negative may be quite serious. For example, denying a student a high school diploma may seriously jeopardize his or her ability to enter the work force. False negatives are particularly serious when performance levels are close to cutoff scores. Another example of a serious Type II error occurs when students are not progressing through the curriculum because their performance on a mastery test is below the cutoff. Conceivably, if a student actually had the knowledge and skills, more problems may accompany such retention, with concomitant waning of interest and motivation.

Therefore, when reviewing mastery decisions, we should be aware that all measurement contains error and that dichotomous decisions may be wrong. Cutoff scores can be stabilized by ensuring that an adequate number of items are included on the test and by considering the proximity of the student's score to the cutoff score. Furthermore, rather than thinking of a student's status as definitively master or nonmaster, it is better to consider such status in terms of probabilities.

Table 14.4 shows the minimum probabilities of making a correct decision for various test lengths. The top row (π_o =) indicates the cutoff score; c represents the distance above and below that performance level where it is difficult to distinguish masters from nonmasters (labeled the *indifference zone*), the number of items on the test is listed down the left column, and the numbers in the body of the table reflect the minimum score and probability of a student's score.

Table 14.4 helps answer the following two questions:

1. What is the fewest number of items and what performance level should be expected for a cutoff level (i.e., 80% $= \pi_o = .80$) and a margin of error of .1 on either side of the cutoff score ($c = .1$)?
2. What is the probability of making a correct decision with that number of items and that cutoff score?

For example, if Test X had a cutoff level of 85% ($\pi_o = .85$), then in order to correctly label masters as those performing in the region above .95 and nonmasters as those performing below .85, it would be important to look under the column, $c = .1$, the last column on the right. Because all students performing within that region (from .85 to .95) may be incorrectly labeled as masters and nonmasters, it might be necessary to collect other information to corroborate decisions for these students. However, no one below the lower level (.85) should be labeled as mastered, and no one above .95 should be labeled as nonmastered. This certainty can be manipulated by increasing the length of the test. Therefore, the task is to develop or adopt a test with a specified length to provide both a cutoff level of performance and

TABLE 14.4
Cutoff scores and the minimum probability of a correct decision for values of π_o not in the indifference zone

Test Items	$\pi_o = .70$		$\pi_o = .75$		$\pi_o = .80$		$\pi_o = .85$	
	$c = .05$	$c = .10$	$c = .05$	$c = .10$	$c = .05$	$c = .10$	$c = .05$	$c = .10$
8	6/.5722	6/.6846	7/.5033	7/.6572	7/.6329	7/.7447	7/.4967	7/.6329
9	7/.6007	7/.7382	7/.5372	7/.6627	8/.5995	8/.7748	8/.5683	8/.6997
10	8/.5256	8/.6778	8/.6172	8/.7384	9/.5443	9/.7361	9/.6242	9/.7560
11	8/.5744	8/.7037	9/.6174	9/.7788	9/.5448	10/.6974	10/.6779	10/.8029
12	9/.6488	9/.7747	10/.5583	10/.7358	10/.6093	10/.7472	11/.6590	11/.8416
13	10/.5843	10/.7473	10/.5794	11/.7296	11/.6674	11/.7975	12/.6213	12/.8646
14	12/.5733	10/.7207	11/.6488	11/.7795	12/.6479	12/.8392	13/.5846	13/.8470
15	11/.6481	11/.7827	12/.6482	12/.8227	13/.6042	13/.8159	13/.6020	14/.8290
16	12/.6302	12/.7982	13/.5981	13/.7899	13/.5950	14/.7892	14/.6482	15/.8108
17	12/.5803	13/.7582	13/.6113	13/.7652	14/.6470	14/.7981	15/.6904	15/.8363
18	13/.6450	13/.7912	14/.6673	14/.8114	15/.6943	15/.8354	16/.7287	16/.8647
19	14/.6678	14/.8369	15/.6733	15/.8500	16/.6841	16/.8668	17/.7054	17/.8887
20	14/.6172	15/.8042	16/.6296	16/.8298	17/.6477	17/.8670	18/.6769	18/.9087

Source: Hambleton, R. K. (1984). Determining test length. In R.A. Berk (Ed.), *A guide to criterion-referenced test construction* (pp. 144–168). Baltimore, MD: John Hopkins University Press, p. 156. Adapted from Wilcox, 1976, p. 362.

a known probability of making a correct decision in the extreme regions (not between .85 and .95, which represents the indifference zone). If a test of 8 items is adopted, a 63% certainty exists of classifying students out of the indifference zone with a cutoff score of 7 items; if the test length is increased to 15 items, an 83% certainty exists of such classifications by demanding performance levels of 14 correct. Finally, with a 20-item test, almost 91% certainty of a correct classification exists if students are required to answer 18 of them correctly.

As presented in the chapter on reliability (chapter 5), all measures have error, and scores should be considered as having an unknown probability of occurring within a band that stretches above and below the actual (or obtained) score. Using the information in Table 14.4, we can establish a confidence interval around a score. Importantly, the confidence interval is embedded in the use of an indifference zone and a probability of making a correct decision. Around any mastery decision, we establish a cutoff score that potentially is more inaccurate immediately above and below it than at the extremes. Therefore, the band is established at two levels (.05 and .10), each with an upper and lower level. This band is used to say the following: "I know I may be wrong within that indifference zone, but I really need to minimize being wrong outside that region." Finally, the outcome is expressed as a probability of being wrong; although the decision is dichotomous, the probability is continuous, and nothing is absolutely certain.

EXTENDING STANDARD SETTING TO GRADING

The most common form of mastery decision made in schools is in grading students on report cards. Although the grading system has five levels (A, B, C, D, and F), a true dichotomy exists at the low end: the difference between D and F. A grade of D represents a passing grade with minimum competence, and an F represents failure, showing the student lacks minimum competence. In graduate schools, grading follows the same continuum; however, the difference between passing and failing has been adjusted upward, reflected by a grade of B (acceptable) and C (unacceptable). An adaptation of standard setting can be applied to grading because it is such a common activity in schools.

CHAPTER SUMMARY

One of the most important decisions that educators make is determining what to teach students. Decisions are often based on informal notions of what students already know and what they need to know. This chapter presented several guidelines for answering the first question using criterion-referenced evaluations. By clearly specifying knowledge and skill domains and assessing student performance and proficiency, teachers can make informed decisions. Standards are implicit components of these decisions. Although criterion-referenced evaluations can be completed without explicit standards, it is rarely done. The controversy focuses less on the domain for sampling specific knowledge and skills and more on the establishment of the standards.

When Florida first mandated minimum competency testing in high schools, problems arose over the cutoff used to award certificates of attendance or diplomas because many thought the scores were arbitrarily established.

Educational Testing Service is developing many tests for certifying teachers in various content areas using a National Teacher Examination. How have the cutoff scores been determined for these certification tests? What is the effect of raising or lowering the cutoff scores? In both examples, the controversy is over the standards.

The information in this chapter should be useful for teachers in (a) making them aware of the frailty of standard setting and (b) providing them with rational examples of how standards are set for large-scale projects (statewide assessments, national tests, etc.). Standards themselves are not necessarily problematic, but they are subjective and open to criticism. By delineating the procedures used to establish standards and understanding their limitations, however, it is possible to use them more appropriately. Given the need to sort students into two groups, a limited range of options are available. Teachers can analyze test items and make judgments about borderline performers; they can focus directly on the test takers and evaluate different cutoff scores based on the performance of mastered, borderline, or nonmastered students. Finally, teachers can employ a reference group with known performance levels to ascertain the effects of using certain standards. These strategies differ in cost, effort, and outcome. The one that provides the best information at the least expense should be the strategy that is used.

Setting the standards, however, is less of an issue than understanding the types of errors that students will make. Whenever a dichotomous decision is made, it is possible to be wrong in one of two ways: a false positive (Type I) or a false negative (Type II). Being wrong is less of a problem when choosing what to instruct from the next unit; it is quite serious when awarding diplomas. Therefore, standard setting should incorporate estimates of error, which are likely to have more impact for those who are not at the extremes. Error is not fixed but can be manipulated. For example, in determining whether a student should proceed into the next level of the curriculum, a Type II error may be more serious: Teachers should give the student the benefit of the doubt in order to avoid a false negative. This statement may be less true of special education students. In contrast, awarding teachers degrees or certificates on the basis of test results may require that Type I errors be minimized. Giving teachers who are minimally knowledgeable a teaching credential may pose more of a problem than withholding certificates in questionable cases.

CHAPTER 15

Individual-referenced Evaluation

You are about to tee off in a tournament with 30 of the the best amateur golfers in the state. The course is difficult, with a par 74, and it's been 5 years since you've played on it. But with a final score of 78, you place second.

From a norm-referenced view, you did quite well. However, if you were competing with professional golfers, your performance might not have looked as good. When you compare yourself to others, your standing is a function of that group.

How about interpreting your performance from a criterion-referenced point of view? The two issues from this perspective are the course itself (or criterion for sampling behavior) and par (the standard for mastery). Given the difficulty of the course, you did well by scoring 78. Of course, this level of performance is not quite mastery (par).

Consider an individual-referenced evaluation, in which you compare your performance on this course with that obtained on other courses over the 5 years since you began playing. If you analyze your rate of progress, you find that this game wasn't one of your better ones. If you had an average performance for each year of 64, 67, 63, 68, and 73, then a score of 78 isn't that proficient.

CHAPTER OBJECTIVES

In this chapter, you will learn about individual-referenced assessment and its primary components. By the end of the chapter the reader will have the knowledge and skills to

- Describe the four primary components of individual-referenced assessment.
- Use the direct and repeated measurement approach to evaluate instructional effectiveness.

- Establish a goal- or treatment-oriented approach to instructional evaluation.
- Use aimline-based decision rules to determine when to change programs.
- Summarize performance to document changes in level, slope, variability, and overlap and use this information to determine when programs should be changed.

KEY VOCABULARY

New vocabulary in this chapter centers on *individual-referenced assessment,* in which we evaluate student performance by comparing it to previous levels. This process includes four components: (a) *direct measurement,* in which behavior is sampled directly from relevant classroom tasks, (b) *repeated measurement,* in which testing occurs frequently, (c) *time-series graphic displays,* in which data are collected over time and graphically plotted, and (d) *data utilization and decision rules,* in which guidelines are used to determine when and what type of instructional changes to make, if any. Instructional interventions are evaluated using *goal-oriented* or *treatment-oriented* systems. With the goal-oriented approach, we compare performance with expected levels that are depicted by *aimlines* tracking expected rates of progress. The treatment-oriented approach compares different treatments successively to ascertain the most effective one. Five indices of student performance are analyzed systematically: *median,* the middle score of a distribution; *level of performance,* which consists of immediate changes across program introductions; *slope of performance,* which incorporates general trends of performance over time; *variability of performance,* the bounce across data values; and *overlap,* similar data values that reflect no changes in performance. Figure 15.1 presents a model of individual-referenced evaluation.

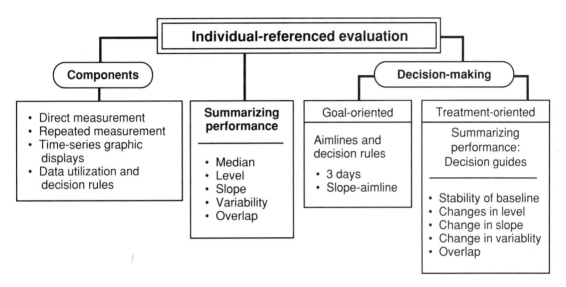

FIGURE 15.1
Model of individual-referenced evaluation

CHARACTERISTICS OF INDIVIDUAL-REFERENCED EVALUATION

Individual-referenced tests call for measurement of student performance over time and comparison of successive values to previous values. Information is gathered frequently so that changes can be made while programs are still in effect. Emphasis is placed on instructional diagnosis and the evaluation of highly salient instructional variables that are within the teacher's control (Howell, Kaplan, & O'Connell, 1979). For example, instead of assessing for a specific learning disability (requiring a norm-referenced approach) or determining whether a student has achieved minimum competency on a well-defined domain (a criterion-referenced approach), a teacher can plan, deliver, and evaluate instruction to determine what works.

Individual-referenced evaluation begins with the premise that it is impossible to determine whether academic problems result from students or instructional programs. For example, although interest in learning styles is very fashionable these days, little experimental evidence has accrued supporting them as an important dimension of learning. Tests cannot be used to identify students' modality, learning styles, or information processing to help structure appropriate instruction (Good, 1989).

Because we cannot assess student characteristics adequately apart from environmental factors, we should examine instruction and its effects. Traditional procedures in diagnosis fail to indicate (a) the extent to which problems are a result of poor instruction and (b) the remedies that should be provided. Furthermore, they fail to implicate variables that teachers can manipulate in specific and concrete ways. "In other words, we must diagnose instruction. The diagnosis must perforce be of instruction, not of the learner" (Englemann, Granzin, & Severson, 1979, p. 357).

Assessment determines inadequate aspects of instruction, why they are inadequate, and how they should be revised.

Several systems incorporate the instruction-evaluation process into an experimental method, using the basic methodology of applied behavior analysis. Foremost are Precision Teaching (Lindsley, 1964, 1971), Exceptional Teaching (White & Haring, 1980), and Data Based Program Modification (Deno & Mirkin, 1977). The salient characteristics of these systems include four main components: (a) direct measurement, (b) repeated measurement, (c) time-series graphic displays, and (d) data utilization guides to help make instructional decisions.

Direct Measurement

The systems previously mentioned are based on the concept that "what is taught is what should be measured" (Martin, 1980, p. 4). A strong emphasis is given to **direct measurement**: measurement strategies that focus directly upon behaviors of interest in the classroom. "Direct, continuous, naturalistic observation of behavior provides many of the advantages one seeks in evaluation . . . which include precision, efficiency, immediate feedback and authenticity" (Bersoff, 1973, p. 898). These measurement systems are generally low-inference, primarily referring to basic skills and overt behaviors. Only through their correlation with higher-order thinking skills do they become important in a broader arena of knowledge. Teachers implement such systems directly in the classroom or in other relevant settings in which they expect the behavior to occur.

Repeated Measurement

Another important component of individual-referenced evaluation is frequent or **repeated**

measurement with an emphasis on program planning, adjustment, and evaluation (Jenkins, Deno, & Mirkin, 1979). While norm-referenced tests can be administered only once or twice a year, individual-referenced tests can be administered daily or several times per week. In the educational lifetime of a student with 13 years of schooling (kindergarten through 12th grade), norm-referenced evaluation can occur only 26 times, while individual-referenced evaluation can be performed almost 500 times (13 grades × 38 weeks). Such frequent measurement produces not only more data, but potentially more reliable data. Frequent measurement of achievement and social behaviors allows us to describe skills accurately at their current level and determine functional relationships between the level of behavior and instruction.

Time-Series Graphic Displays

The familiar maxim that a "picture is worth a thousand words" applies to individual-referenced evaluation. The third component of individual-referenced evaluation is a **time-series graphic display** of performance that provides a more interpretable description of behavior than a numerical report. Such displays are simply line graphs that depict changes in performance over time. Graphs of data are useful for four reasons: (a) They reduce large amounts of data and information, (b) they simplify communication of results, (c) they emphasize important characteristics of performance, and (d) they set the stage for using data more proficiently and consistently. Many graphic displays are available, all of which follow basic conventions described by Tindal (1988), Chambers, Cleveland, Kleiner, and Tukey (1983), Cleveland (1985), and Parsonson and Baer (1978). Probably the most common format, however, is the line chart, which connects successive data points (see Figure 15.2).

FIGURE 15.2

Example of a line chart depicting time-series data

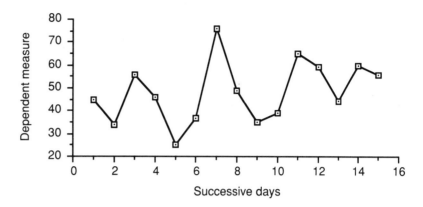

Data Utilization and Decision Rules

This fourth component of individual-referenced evaluation relates to the analysis of performance over time and the use of decision rules to summarize and evaluate change. Some educators argue that time-series data are adequate to assess pupil progress and guide instructional decisions, while others advocate decision rules for utilizing student data (White & Haring, 1980). But collecting continuous progress or performance information does not ensure that a teacher will react to that information, or that if a reaction does occur, it will be correct (White, 1977). When investigations using direct and continuous assessment fail to achieve consistent results, many argue that inadequate utilization of the data to make changes in the program has occurred (Frumess, 1973; Tindal, 1988; White, 1974).

To overcome the problem of nonutilization or inconsistent utilization of data, several investigations have been aimed at defining data decision rules (Bohannon, 1975; Martin, 1980; Mirkin, Deno, Tindal, & Kuehnle, 1982; Mirkin & Deno, 1979). **Data utilization and decision rules** are designed to assist teachers in deciding when to change programs. Therefore, they represent an attempt to improve the basis for making decisions by taking the guesswork out of deciding when to change and providing consistency to an otherwise unspecified approach to decision making. These rules are based on both student progress and the aim of the program. With a consistent rule, teacher judgment becomes more systematic and consistent; at the very least, the amount of time spent reviewing the data and making decisions is drastically reduced.

The decision-making process is instructionally diagnostic because it tells the teacher the effects of what is taught and *when* to make a change. Deno (1986) likened it to making an educated hypothesis about a child and then testing the hypothesis. Consider a third-grade child who has not developed reading fluency in first-grade materials and has difficulty sounding out phonetically regular one- and two-syllable words. What types of words should be included in instruction? Perhaps only phonetically regular words should be taught, or possibly just letter sounds and blends. This particular child might benefit from a structured phonetic approach such as Direct Instruction, but can we be sure? We could check by moving the student from his or her basal reading program to Distar and then begin to monitor change in reading performance frequently. This information is important not only in determining the effects of instruction and providing a basis for deciding when to modify a program, but also in deciding how or what to change.

Summary of Individual-Referenced Evaluation Characteristics

While many studies have demonstrated the benefits of direct and continuous assessment practices (Breuning, 1978; Mirkin, Deno, Tindal, & Kuehnle, 1982; Deno, Chiang, Tindal & Blackburn, 1979; Frumess, 1973; Haring & Krug, 1975; Haring & Lovitt, 1969), few researchers have isolated the responsible variables. It is not certain whether improved performance is a result of procedures such as curriculum-based measurement that provide repeated practice in a controlled-stimulus situation, or from the information generated from the measurement procedures, such as graphs. Finally, when more accurate student performance data are made available to the teacher, systematic decision making may be responsible for improvement. Although the source of student improvement may be difficult to isolate, individual-referenced evaluations all incorporate three aspects: direct and frequent measurement with performance displayed on graphs that are used to guide decision making.

Considerable evidence exists to support the effectiveness of direct measurement, collected repeatedly, displayed graphically, and used to make changes in programs. Deno and his associates at the University of Minnesota validated several short-duration, direct measures of academic skills in reading (Deno, Mirkin & Chiang, 1982), written expression (Deno, Marston, & Mirkin, 1982) and spelling (Deno, Mirkin, Lowry & Kuehnle, 1980). When these measures are collected frequently, they sensitively reflect change over time. Significant improvements are possible within 10–16 weeks (Marston, Fuchs, & Deno, 1985). Charting can lead to increased student performance (Brand-

stetter & Merz, 1978; Deno, Chiang, Tindal, & Blackburn, 1979; Jenkins, Mayhall, Peschka, & Townsend, 1974). Fuchs, Deno, and Mirkin (1984) demonstrated that when direct and repeated measurement data are graphically analyzed as a function of the instructional intervention, significant improvement in performance occurs. Table 15.1 summarizes the essential features of individual-referenced evaluation relative to norm- and criterion-referenced strategies.

SUMMARIZING STUDENT PERFORMANCE

We consider five characteristics of graphed data in describing and summarizing student performance: (a) median performance, (b) level of performance, (c) slope of performance, (d) variability of performance, and (e) overlap.

Median

As described in chapter 4, the **median** is a measure of central tendency, reflecting the middle score falling at the 50th percentile, that is, 50% of the scores fall above and 50% fall below. The median addresses the question: What is the typical score for that period?

There are three steps to finding the median: (a) Rank order the scores, (b) count the total number of scores, and (c) divide the total number of scores so one score is in the middle. If there is an odd number of scores, the score in the middle is the median; if there is an even number of scores, the median is interpolated by computing the average of the two middle scores. For example, 6 is the median of the following nine scores: 8, 7, 7, 6, 6, 5, 5, 4, 4. With an even number of scores such as 0, 1, 2, 3, 5, 5, 7, and 8, the median score must be interpolated by taking the average of the two middle scores (3 and 5), which is 4.

TABLE 15.1

A comparison of individual-referenced, norm-referenced, and criterion-referenced evaluation

	Individual-Referenced Evaluation	Criterion-Referenced Evaluation	Norm-Referenced Evaluation
Principal use	Monitoring long-range goals (LRG) for individual educational plans (IEPs).	Specific-level or mastery testing.	Survey testing.
Major emphasis	Document growth over time on generalized skills.	Describe tasks students can perform successfully.	Measure individual differences in achievement.
Interpretation of results	Compare actual rate of progress to an expected rate or to rates obtained under successive specific treatment conditions.	Compare performance to clearly specified achievement levels that are dichotomous.	Compare performance to that of other individuals (comparable)
Content coverage	Items sampled from within curriculum but across individual instructional units.	Focuses on limited set of learning tasks within a unit and within a curriculum.	Covers broad area of achievement across curricula.
Nature of test plan	General domain specifications are established for both item type and sampling strategy.	Detailed table of specifications is used to plan specific item sampling.	Tables of specifications are loosely used.
Item-selection procedures	Item selection is function of type of decision to be made. To screen students, confer eligibility, or evaluate programs, items are sampled from broad domains and reflect varying difficulty. For monitoring LRGs, items are sampled from material that is and will be taught.	Includes all items needed to adequately describe performance. No attempt is made to alter item difficulty or to eliminate easy items to increase score variability. Item discrimination is the most important consideration.	Items are selected that provide maximum discrimination among individuals. Item difficulty is the most important consideration. Easy and difficult items are eliminated from the test.
Performance standards	Rate of change is calculated and compared to expected rates or rates obtained under different (previous) programs.	Level of performance is commonly determined by absolute standards (i.e., demonstrates mastery by defining 90% of technical terms).	Level of performance is determined by relative position in some known group (i.e., ranks 5th in group of 20).

Source: Adapted from Gronlund, N. E. (1988). *How to construct achievement tests*. Englewood Cliffs, NJ: Prentice-Hall. Table 1.1, p. 12.

For graphed data, we find the median by counting the lowest to middle data points. If there are 15 data points, the 8th one up is the median, represented by the score of 46 in Figure 15.3. Typically, the median is indicated by a score in a teardrop above the data for that phase. When the goal is to increase performance, the median level of behavior should increase when effective program changes are made.

Level of Performance

Level of performance is calculated to answer the question: What changes occur immediately after a program modification? Does the new intervention produce an immediate step (up or down) in behavior? Changes in level provide the most conclusive evidence that an intervention had an effect; they represent a clear discontinuity in the data at exactly the time the intervention was introduced. The data in Figure 15.4 show a clear shift in level of performance; the vertical line represents a change in intervention. The second intervention creates significant change in the student.

Slope of Performance

The easiest way to analyze time-series data is to look at the graph and judge the general direction in which student performance is changing. Does it increase, decrease, or stay the same? Trend or **slope of performance** answers the question: What is this rate of change? A slope line helps us to see what is happening to performance over a period of time rather than day by day. It will show if a student's performance is increasing, decreasing, or staying the same, *and* how fast performance is changing over time. The steeper the slope, the greater the rate of change. Slope of performance can be calculated and plotted precisely with a computer or adequately with a ruler and pencil using the split-middle technique developed by White (1972). His seven-step approach to calculating the slope of improvement using typical CBM data follows.

Step 1. Draw a vertical line in the middle of the graph so that half of the data points are on the left side and half are on the right side. For an even number of data points, half are on the

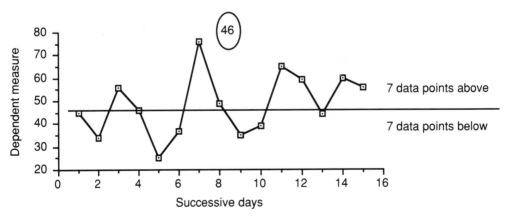

FIGURE 15.3
The median for an odd number of scores (15)

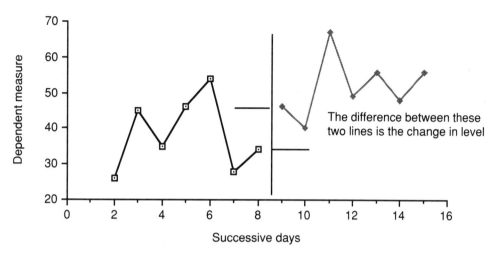

FIGURE 15.4
Upward change in level of performance

left and half are on the right of this line. For an odd number of data points, the line goes through the middle data point, as shown in Figure 15.5. Label this line number 2.

Step 2. Draw a vertical line in the first (left) half, up to line 2, so that half of the data points fall to the left and half fall to the right. Label this line number 1, as shown in Figure 15.6.

Step 3. Draw a vertical line in the second (right) half after line 2, so that half of the data points fall to the left and half fall to the right. Label this line number 3, as shown in Figure 15.7.

Step 4. Find the median of the first half (all data points up to Line 2). Draw a horizontal line at this level so that it intersects Line 1, as shown in Figure 15.8.

Step 5. Find the median of the second half (all data points after Line 2). Draw a horizontal line at this level so that it intersects with Line 3, as shown in Figure 15.9.

Step 6. Draw a line connecting these two intersections, as shown in Figure 15.10. This is a slope, or trend, line. It indicates how rapidly the student is improving over time. The steeper the slope, the faster the student is improving, indicating a more successful intervention.

Step 7. The slope line may need to be adjusted upward or downward so that half of the data points are on or above the line and half are on or below the line. As shown in Figure 15.11, the adjusted line should remain parallel to the original line, so that it will not affect the slope or trend of performance.

Once the slope line is created, it can be compared from phase to phase. The procedure to quantify the value of each slope line by calculating its actual value is simple and straightforward. First, find the slope line endpoint on the left and determine its value on the vertical axis. This is 37 units in Figure 15.11. Second, find the slope line endpoint on the right and determine its value on the vertical axis (60 in the example). Third, find the difference or in-

FIGURE 15.5
Dividing the time series
in half

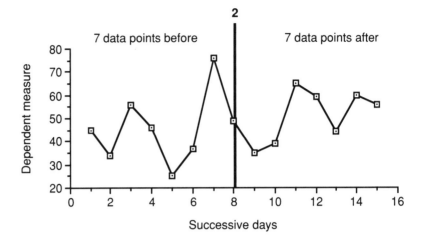

FIGURE 15.6
Dividing the first half of the
time series in half

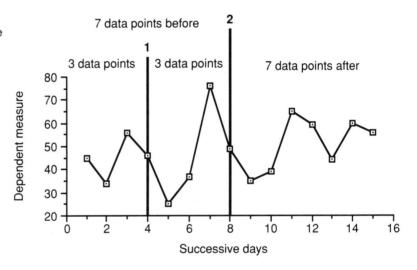

FIGURE 15.7
Dividing the second half of
the time series in half

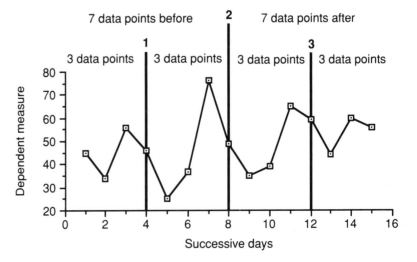

FIGURE 15.8
Finding the median of the
first half of the time series

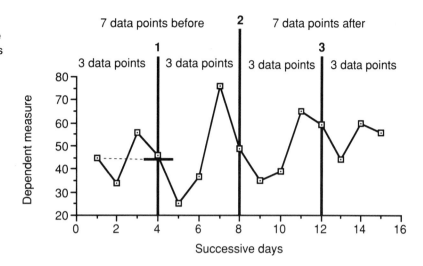

FIGURE 15.9
Finding the median of the
second half of the time
series

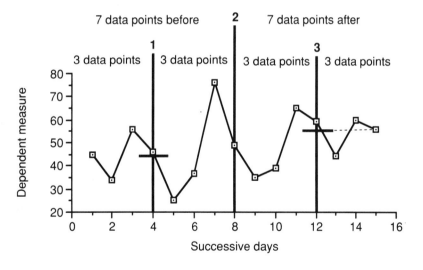

crease in this line, which is 23 units. Fourth, determine the length of time, as measured on the horizontal axis that these two values represent. For our example, let's assume 4 weeks have elapsed between these two values. Fifth, divide the difference of 23 units by 4 weeks: The slope of this line is increasing at a rate of 5.75 units per week. This value is close to that obtained with a complex mathematical formula for the same data, as shown in Figure 15.12.

FIGURE 15.10
Drawing the slope or trend of performance

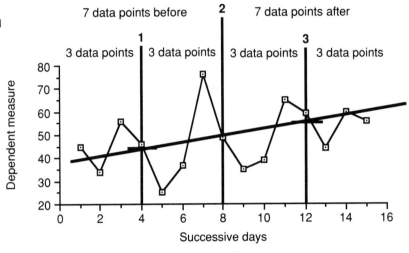

FIGURE 15.11
Adjusting the slope line to split the data values on both sides of it

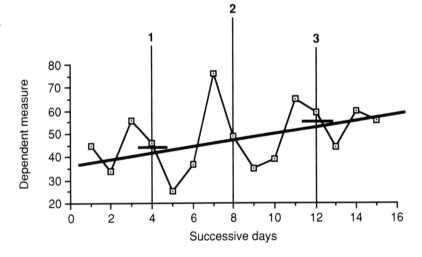

Variability of Performance

Variability of performance, or up-and-down movement, addresses the stability or consistency present in behavior from day to day. When considerable variability is present, it is difficult to predict student performance and determine effective aspects of an instructional program. Small variations in performance indicate more consistent and predictable responses, allowing

FIGURE 15.12
Mathematically derived
slope line

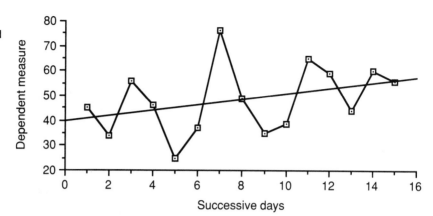

a better and more sensitive evaluation of the program.

We can use two methods to determine variability. The first is visual. We scan the data array and make a judgment about the degree of variability, ranging from high to low. This procedure is quick, but not very accurate or generalizable. Second, we can compute it by measuring the total bounce around the slope line. Few data points will fall on the slope line; they tend to bounce around it, with some falling above it and others falling below. One way to quantify variability is to measure the distance between the data points and the slope line. This approach is from Pennypacker, Koneig, and Lindsley (1972) and uses a frequency envelope around the split-middle slope line. As Figure 15.13 shows, the procedures begin with calculating a slope line.

Step 1. Draw a line parallel to the slope line, passing through the frequency dot farthest *above* the slope line, as shown in Figure 15.14.

FIGURE 15.13
Variability calculated
around the slope or trend
line

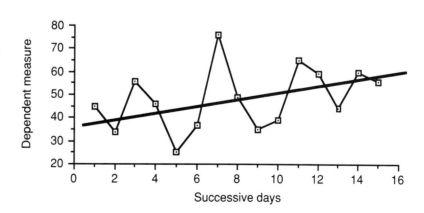

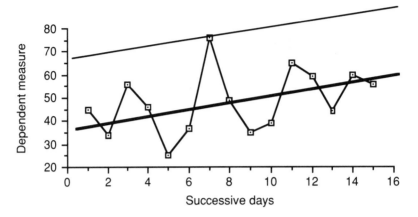

FIGURE 15.14
Variability of performance above the slope or trend line

The distance along any day line separating the slope line from this upper line is a measure of the *up-bounce.*

Step 2. Draw a line parallel to the slope line passing through the frequency dot farthest *below* the slope line, as shown in Figure 15.15. The vertical distance along any day line sepa- rating this lower line from the slope line is a measure of the *down-bounce.*

The total vertical distance in units of mea- surement along any day line between upper and lower lines is a measure of the *total bounce around the slope line.* The upper and lower lines parallel to the slope line define an *enve- lope* that encloses all of the charted frequen- cies. In Figure 15.16, the width of the envelope

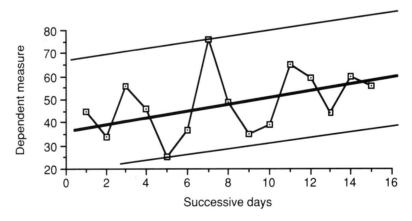

FIGURE 15.15
Variability of performance below the slope or trend line

FIGURE 15.16
Quantifying the amount of variability

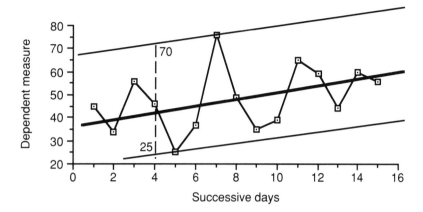

is about 45 units on Day 4 (from 25 on the lower line to 70 on the upper line).

This envelope is useful because it can be projected, like a slope line, allowing for a prediction of the *range* of future frequencies.

Overlapping Data Points

Overlap between scores of adjacent phases is another important aspect of summarizing time-series data. For programs designed to improve performance (i.e., most instructional programs), we can calculate the degree of overlap between data points prior to and following an intervention by drawing two horizontal lines across the graph: one through the highest data point of baseline (current procedure) and the other through the lowest data point following the intervention. This is shown in Figure 15.17, where two programs are separated with a vertical line. For programs designed to decrease or eliminate behaviors (i.e., having a focus on excessive behaviors), we select the lowest value prior to program implementation or change and the highest value following the program introduction or change.

In Figure 15.17, all data values between 40 and 54 overlap across the two phases. **Overlap** focuses on the best performance levels prior to program implementation or change and the worst levels following it. If a program is aimed at accelerating behavior, the best performance before the program is a high value. If the aim is to reduce behavior, the best performance before its introduction or change is a low value. Correspondingly, after the introduction or change, the worst value is low for an acceleration program and high for a deceleration program.

No firm criteria define adequate or excessive amounts of overlap. Nevertheless, treatment effects are inversely related to overlap: the more overlap, the less treatment effect. An even more refined analysis of overlap can be conducted within phases: Overlap occurring in initial sessions within a phase is of less concern than overlap from the midpoint on or throughout the entire session.

DATA UTILIZATION AND DECISION RULES

Two approaches are possible for determining whether an instructional strategy is effective and when or if it should be changed. They differ in purpose, as well as in the decisions that result. The first procedure is **goal-oriented** decision making, in which (a) emphasis is on attaining

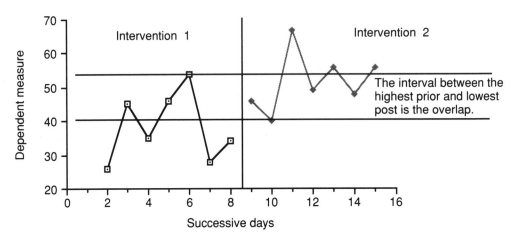

FIGURE 15.17
Data overlap across two interventions for an acceleration program

a goal, and (b) program modifications occur only when attainment of that goal is in doubt. *Aimlines* are used to pace progress toward the goal and to help determine when discrepancies occur between performance and expected levels. They are different from slope lines, which reflect *actual* rates of student change; rather, aimlines reflect *expected* rates of student change. If discrepancies become great, the instructional program is changed; when actual and expected levels are close, programs are maintained.

The second approach is **treatment-oriented** decision making, which emphasizes an experimental analysis of behavior. Rather than attaining a goal, this approach calls for determining experimentally the instructional program most responsible for improvements in student performance. However, rather than judging effectiveness on whim or belief, teachers manipulate instruction systematically and observe concurrent changes in performance. An assumption central to this approach is that it is impossible to determine ahead of time which instructional strategies will be effective. Rather, teaching is viewed as hypothesis test-

ing, and the principles of the experimental paradigm are used to determine effective strategies. Program modifications are based on visual analysis of graphed data that compare performance under different conditions.

Goal-Oriented Decision Making

Aimlines, which are lines of expected progress needed to attain a level of performance (goal) within a specified period of time, form the basis for goal-oriented decision making. A consistent rule that appears across many studies of this approach is to make program changes when performance falls below the aimline (for accelerating behaviors) or above the aimline (for decelerating behaviors) for 3 consecutive days. Aimlines are used to keep behavior paced toward the target over a certain period of time, taking into account current performance (Liberty, 1975).

Five studies have used aimlines and decision rules to experimentally verify their effectiveness (Bohannon, 1975; Deno, Chiang, Tindal, & Blackburn, 1979; Martin, 1980; Mirkin & Deno, 1979; Mirkin, Deno, Tindal, &

Kuehnle, 1980). All five studies determined that aimlines and decision rules for making changes in instructional programs are viable evaluation alternatives with empirical support. They help teachers project the level of performance needed to reach an objective within a specified time. If student performance is not improving in line consistently with the expected aim, programs need to be changed. Using aimlines and decision rules takes much of the guesswork out of data analysis.

Procedures. We establish the endpoints of the aimline for goal-oriented decision making in three steps. First, we determine entry-level performance in the following manner: (a) Measure the student for 3–5 days and plot his or her performance on the graph, and (b) determine the median of the last 3 days and mark it with an *X* on the middle day. Second, determine expected, or goal-level, performance and the date for such attainment. The goal may involve performance at a level commensurate with the student's peers, or simply a decrease in the

discrepancy between the student's current performance and his or her age-grade appropriate level. The goal is marked with an *X* on the graph on the day it is to be attained. Third, draw an aimline connecting the initial performance level with the expected level to be attained. Figure 15.18 shows these three steps.

The objective of the decision-making system is for the student to meet the prespecified goal by a certain date. The aimline begins at the level at which the student is performing before the strategy is employed and ends at the level marked by the X. Throughout the delivery of instruction, the student's *actual* performance can be compared with his or her *expected* performance (aimline). Programs are changed according to a set of circumscribed decision rules:

1. If a student's performance is *below* the aimline on 3 consecutive days, draw a new aimline on the graph. First, locate the median performance level obtained on those 3 days, then mark this point as an *X* on the middle day below the aimline. Next, draw a line

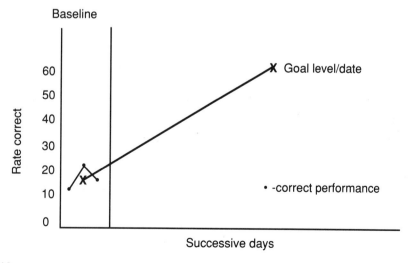

FIGURE 15.18
Establishing goal-oriented decision rules

parallel to the original aimline, extending from the X to the date of the annual goal. Use this procedure every time the student's performance is below the aimline for 3 days in a row. If a student performs above aimline for 2 days and at or below aimline on the third day or vice versa, no new aimline is needed.

2. In addition to drawing a new aimline, implement a *different teaching strategy*. Draw a vertical line on the graph that symbolizes a change in the program.

3. If the student's performance is above the aimline after 3 days, it may be appropriate to raise the aimline. Using the last 3 days of data above the aimline, mark the median with an X on the middle day above the aimline. Draw a line parallel to and above the original aimline. Extend it to the attainment date used in establishing the original goal.

Also, draw a vertical line on the graph to signify an instructional change if one has been implemented. Such changes may be limited to an increase in the goal if actual instructional strategies are working well. As Figure 15.19 shows, adjusting aimlines and changing teaching strategies when student performance is consistently above or below what is expected for 3 days should continue for the duration of the instruction.

As the figure shows, the student's performance improved dramatically after the instructional change. Therefore, a new aimline is not needed, and instruction should continue unchanged.

A variation of the 3-day rule is to compare the slope of *actual* improvement for the most recent 7–10-day period to the slope of *ex-*

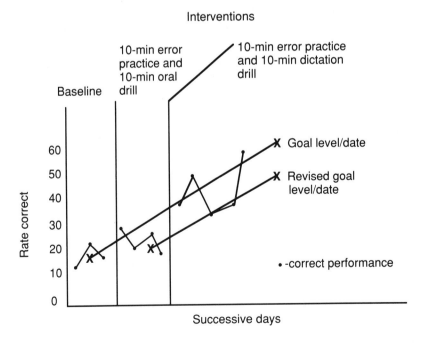

FIGURE 15.19
Goal-oriented evaluation of instruction

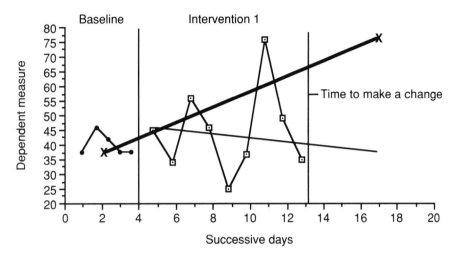

FIGURE 15.20
Decision rule comparing slope to aimline

pected improvement, which is reflected by the aimline (Fuchs, 1986; Mirkin, Deno, Fuchs, Wesson, Tindal, Marston, & Kuehnle, 1981). When expected improvement exceeds actual improvement, both goals and programs should be changed. Figure 15.20 shows this variation of the decision rule.

A Reading Example. Figure 15.21 illustrates an aimline and goal-oriented decision rules in

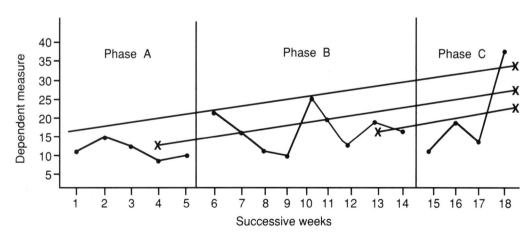

FIGURE 15.21
A goal-oriented decision-making example with Johnny

reading for one of our fourth-graders, Johnny. Performance is measured on a grade-level passage. Each week, Johnny read a randomly selected passage to his teacher from his fourth-grade reader. At the end of 1 minute, the teacher counted the number of words read correctly and graphed the information. During Phase A, Johnny's performance ranged from 10 to 16 words read correctly. His half-year goal at 18 weeks was 40 words correct.

During Phase A instruction, Johnny was taught in the low reading group. The length of reading instruction was approximately 30 minutes and included silent reading of stories, answering comprehension questions in the group, and independent seatwork with workbook activities. Phase A data indicated Johnny was falling behind his aimline. The effect of an instructional change in Phase B was negligible. Although Johnny showed no immediate changes in performance, he eventually began performing adequately. Later, the teacher decided that three reading groups did not cover the diverse needs of her students, so she expanded to a fourth group that included Johnny. During this phase, Johnny's words read correctly varied and eventually decreased to a level below the aimline. Therefore, the teacher made two major changes in Phase C: (a) addition of motivational contingencies and (b) use of choral reading with peers. A point system was implemented in the fourth reading group with some impact. The words Johnny read correctly increased immediately but then stabilized well below the projected goal of the program. Daily seatwork, previously set at 15 minutes, was reduced to 5 minutes, and 10 minutes of choral reading aloud was added. Johnny's fluency began to improve, particularly as the instructional program was implemented over time. Near the end of the program, after 16 data points, Johnny was performing near his goal level. Because the goal was attained only once, more opportunities might be needed to ascertain whether such goal performance is really stable.

Treatment-Oriented Decision Making

When the delivery of instruction is organized with treatment-oriented decision making, an experimental analysis is used. Over time, the teacher implements a number of instructional strategies and determines their relative impact. Each strategy is viewed as a hypothesis to be tested. No prespecified goal is sought, other than to increase student performance at the fastest rate possible. The maximum rate of student performance is unknown. Therefore, even though a program may appear successful, changes are made at least every 15 days that data are taken (called data days). Teachers assume that they can create an effective program only by continually implementing many strategies and comparing their effect on performance.

Although treatment-oriented decision making has no formal rules for determining when to change programs, there are some guidelines. Similarly, the effects of any given strategy are judged with a well-developed analysis. Student performance must be determined by analyzing changes in level, slope, variability, and overlap. A series of guidelines help to structure judgments and provide a valid basis for determining whether an intervention was effective or not.

Four analyses are used in judging the effectiveness of an intervention. Generally, they emphasize changes between adjacent phases, defined as a period of time in which the same intervention is used. Some time after 5 days, which is the minimum number for evaluating an intervention, but no longer than 15 days, the maximum number of days for allowing any one program to run, teachers analyze data and develop a program change. A vertical line, reflecting a new phase, is drawn on the graph and a new intervention introduced. The purpose is to compare the data before the intervention to that following the intervention, using the four analyses.

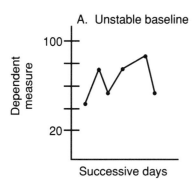

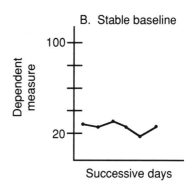

FIGURE 15.22
Stability in baseline

To initiate a treatment-oriented approach to instructional evaluation, we must establish baseline performance to represent a student's current level of functioning and provide a reference for comparing the effects of instruction. During baseline, the teacher measures the student's performance but provides no formal instruction. It is important to obtain a stable baseline because any drift in the direction of improvement makes it difficult to substantiate claims that instruction (when it was introduced) caused performance to increase. Unstable baselines have inconsistent performance, as in Graph A of Figure 15.22, and make it difficult to ascertain typical performance. Those with little variation, as in Graph B of Figure 15.22, provide a better basis for attributing change to the effects of instruction. Baseline should consist of at least 5 data points, or enough to show that behavior has become stable. Following baseline, a series of instructional strategies (phases) are systematically introduced, each indicated by a vertical line on the graph.

Changes in Level Between Phases. There is no more persuasive effect supporting the impact of an intervention than a change in level between phases. When performance shifts at the same time an intervention is introduced, there is strong evidence that the change in the program caused the change in behavior. Typically, the greater and more abrupt the changes in level, the more powerful the evidence supporting the program. But few programs produce such abrupt shifts, and the lack of a dramatic change in level is not evidence of the program's ineffectiveness. Behavior can change in level between adjacent phases in only two directions: up or down.

Figure 15.23 shows a large shift upward at the point of intervention, indicating success. If the data shift in level only, and no further change occurs in slope or variability, it is likely that the program has had a high initial impact, but the effect has dissipated. Again, there may be a ceiling effect indicating student mastery of the material.

In Figure 15.24, the shift is from high to low. Because this is contrary to the purpose of academic skill programs, an immediate program change is warranted.

Changes in Slope Between Adjacent Phases. Many data patterns are possible with changes in slope between adjacent phases. All provide strong evidence that the instructional intervention has had some effect, which we can inter-

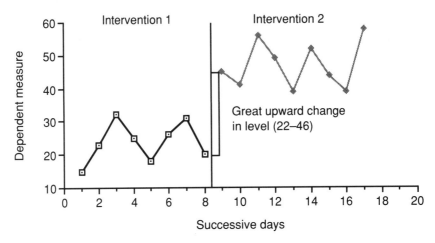

FIGURE 15.23
Upward change in level between interventions

pret directly from the steepness of the slope. In Figure 15.25, the change in slope is dramatic on the day following the change in instruction, indicating a successful strategy.

Another change in slope is shown in Figure 15.26. Here, performance reverses itself: Increasing performance is followed by a decrease. Any changes in instruction that cause academic achievement performance to decrease must be interpreted as unsuccessful and should be altered immediately.

In Figure 15.27 the same data pattern appears, but the effect is modest, with only a slightly different slope following the introduction. It is likely that performance would improve without instruction, but at a fairly slow rate. The

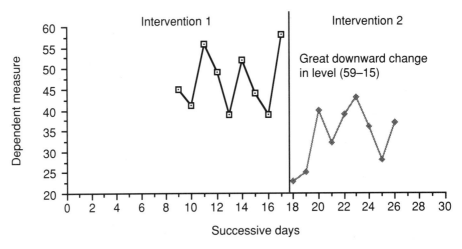

FIGURE 15.24
Downward change in level between interventions

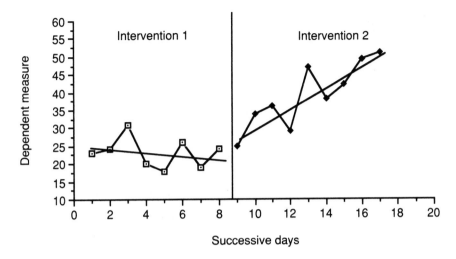

FIGURE 15.25
Change in slope: Increase

effect of instruction appears to be a slight increase in the rate of improvement; however, a very significant increase in level is apparent.

Variability Between Phases. Many patterns are possible in which performance exhibits variability either prior to or following the introduction of intervention. In all cases, if the change in performance is concurrent with the change in the program, the intervention is directly im-

plicated as a source of the behavior change. The most optimal outcome for changes in variability would be decreases, reflecting more predictable performance, as shown in Figure 15.28.

A variable baseline followed by a stable phase indicates a successful intervention and appropriate control of behavior, as shown in Figure 15.28. The implication is that the instructional program has been powerful enough to override occasional interfering baseline variables, or that

FIGURE 15.26
Change in slope: Decrease

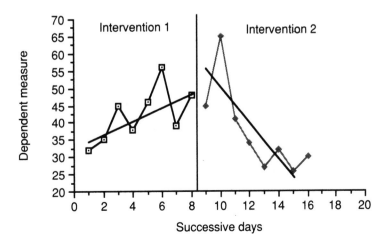

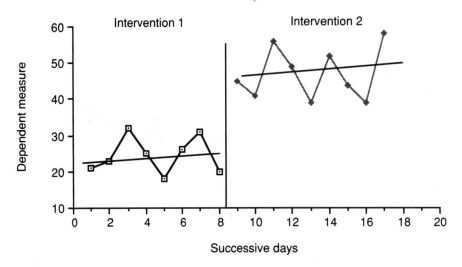

FIGURE 15.27
No change in slope

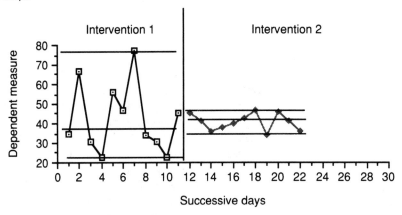

FIGURE 15.28
Variability followed by stability

FIGURE 15.29
Stability followed
by variability

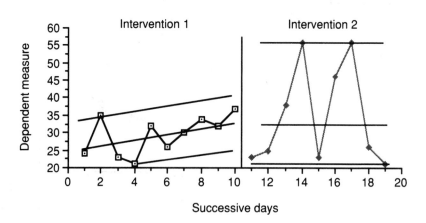

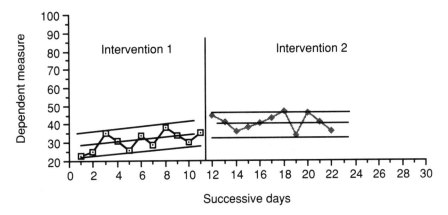

FIGURE 15.30
Low variability for both interventions

those effective baseline variables have been incorporated into the instructional program.

Figure 15.29 shows that variability has increased following a change in the program. Such dramatic changes indicate problems with the procedures that have been introduced or the simultaneous introduction of unwanted factors along with those that were planned.

In Figure 15.30, performance is stable both prior to and following an instructional intervention.

In Figure 15.31, performance is variable both prior to and following an instructional intervention, indicating little apparent effect resulting from the intervention. Such data patterns make it difficult to discern effects, especially weak ones, so it is important to determine the source of variability.

Overlap. Overlap has been calculated across successive phases in Figure 15.32: baseline to the first intervention and the first intervention

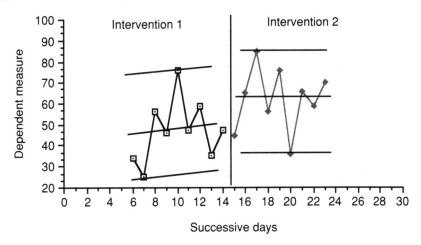

FIGURE 15.31
High variability for both interventions

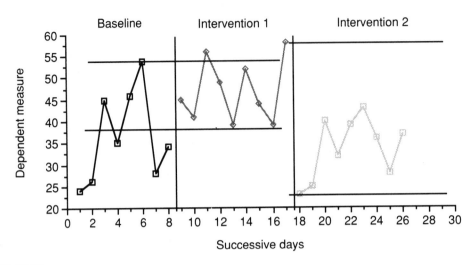

FIGURE 15.32
Analyzing overlap across interventions

to a second one. Assuming that the goal of the program is to increase performance rather than decrease behavior, the data in the figure are disconcerting. Across both successive phases, overlap is great. Only two values in Intervention 1 exceed levels previously attained in the baseline; all values attained during the subsequent intervention are included within levels already attained in Intervention 2. Intervention 1 is somewhat effective in improving performance, while Intervention 2 is ineffective in improving performance over that already attained.

Summary of Treatment-Oriented Data Utilization. Four outcomes are possible in treatment-oriented decision making when comparing performance across different interventions or phases: (a) performance may change in the level immediately following the introduction of a new intervention, (b) slope may increase, decrease, or stay the same, (c) variability may increase, decrease, or stay the same, and (d) overlap may be great or little.

Although these analyses are presented separately, they should be used together in an actual analysis of student performance. That is, when analyzing the impact of an intervention, it is important to look simultaneously at direction, level, median, slope, variability, and overlap. All of these indices may converge into a consistent interpretation and indicate that an intervention had an effect. In other situations, the data array may be inconsistent, so the presence of an effect will be hard to determine.

An experimental analysis requires the use of all these analyses to judge the effectiveness of an intervention. A program should run for 5 days, and the criteria should be applied for the next 10. That is, a program change should never be made with less than 5 days of data, and a change must be made at some time over the next 10 data days. The purpose is to continually test whether a more successful intervention can be found.

A Reading Example. Figure 15.33 presents an example of the reading performance of one

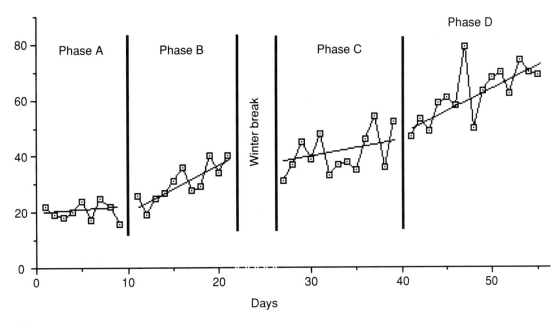

FIGURE 15.33
A four-phase, treatment-oriented decision-making example

of our fourth-graders, Linda, over an academic year. Linda was measured twice weekly in her fourth-grade reader. Her 1-minute timings indicate that she read approximately 20–25 words correctly at the beginning of the year. During Phase A, she had daily, 30-minute sessions in reading instruction. At this time, she read passages in her basal reader and completed the worksheets accompanying each unit. After 9 readings, her data were charted and a slope line of about .5 word increase per week was computed. Given that elementary-age students typically increase anywhere from 1 to 3 words per week (Deno, Mirkin, & Wesson, 1984), our teacher interpreted this slope as low and made a significant change in Linda's instructional programming.

In Phase B, the teacher decreased the time spent on worksheets and made an effort to increase academic engaged time in reading. To-

tal reading instruction was increased from 30 to 35 minutes daily. With the extra time, Linda was drilled with flash cards that included vocabulary words from her basal reader. She also practiced reading aloud into a tape recorder. Her rate of improvement was more than 3.0 correct words per week.

The significant amount of improvement in Phase B indicated to the teacher that a major change in Phase C was not necessary. After the winter break, the only change in programming involved the addition of a new student to Linda's group. The added pupil's presence coincided with a decrement in Linda's improvement, as shown by the slope line in Phase C. As a result, during Phase D instruction, the teacher supplemented Linda's reading instruction with peer tutoring. Megan, the best reader in the class, worked with Linda for 10 minutes daily. During that time, Linda selected any story she wanted to read. The tutor listened and made corrections when necessary. Phase D data suggest this intervention was extremely beneficial when compared to the treatment in Phase C. As a result of the treatment-oriented decision rules, Linda's fluency increased from approximately 20 words correct to almost 70 words correct by the end of the school year.

CHAPTER SUMMARY

The procedures described in this chapter provide a method by which classroom teachers can monitor student progress directly and repeatedly. Direct measurement focuses on the basic skills needed to succeed. Repeated measurement is advantageous because it allows teachers to make frequent determinations of how well students progress during the school year, as opposed to waiting for an entire year to review standardized test results. Time-series graphic displays of data help communicate learning information in an efficient manner. Decision rules and data utilization guidelines help orient program evaluation in a systematic and cost-efficient manner.

Two procedures are available for individual-referenced evaluation. For those interested in maximum structure requiring little analysis, the goal-oriented approach may be appropriate. Once current performance is measured and a goal is established, the decision rules focus on the discrepancy between actual and expected rates of improvement. Of course, if the goal is suspect, this system may become problematic; therefore, a strategy is built in for readjusting the goal. A more labor-intensive system is available with the treatment-oriented approach. Rather than focusing on attainment of a goal, this approach systematically evaluates instructional variables that work. The two major components of this approach are summarizing and interpreting performance. Performance summary indices to consider are median, level, slope, variability, and overlap. Because all of these indices interact with each other to form a unique data pattern, interpretive guidelines rather than decision rules are used to make evaluative statements. Regardless of the orientation, the focus of evaluation in individual-referenced evaluation is on change over time, using the student's previous performance to mark improvements.

APPENDIX A

Evaluation Tests

SPELLING TESTS

Test	Test Retest	Internal Consistency	Alternate Form	Inter-Judge
California Achievement Test (Form E)	.87	.84–.87	.72–.82	
California Test of Basic Skills (Forms U and V)		.80–.92		
Diagnostic Achievement Battery	.96	.66–.90		
Iowa Test of Basic Skills		.79–.85		
Stanford Achievement Test	.72–.87	.88–.94	.82–.89	
Woodcock Johnson Psychoeducational Battery		.81–.92		
Diagnostic Spelling Potential Test		.81–.97		
Kaufmann Test of Educational Achievement	.95–.96	.89–.95		
Peabody Individual Achievement Test	.42–.78			
SRA Survey of Basic Skills (Forms P and Q)	.72–.83	.83–.90	.75–.85	
Test of Written Spelling	.86–.99	.86–.98		
Wide Range Achievement Test	.89–.97	.88–.97		

WRITTEN EXPRESSION TESTS

Test	Test Retest	Internal Consistency	Alternate Form	Inter-Judge
Test of Written Language	.47–.90	.80–.94		.76–.98
Picture Story Language Test		.38–.84		.34–.99
3-Rs Test		.84–.92	.81–.87	
California Achievement Test (Form E)	.69–.90	.86–.93	.78–.87	
Circus/Sequential Test of Educational Progress		.65–.90	.81–.94	
California Test of Basic Skills (Forms U and V)		.84–.90		
Diagnostic Achievement Battery	.83–.95	.62–.91		
Iowa Test of Basic Skills		.73–.89		
Stanford Achievement Test	.86–.89	.88–.94	.76–.84	
Woodcock Johnson Psychoeducational Battery		.86–.90		

READING TESTS

Test	Test Retest	Internal Consistency	Alternate Form	Inter-Judge
3-Rs Test		.77–.93	.78–.89	
California Achievement Test (Form E)	.73–.93	.59–.95	.73–.87	
Circus/Sequential Test of Educational Progress		.71–.93	.81–.94	
California Test of Basic Skills (Forms U and V)		.65–.90		
Diagnostic Achievement Battery	.93–.99	.62–.98		
Iowa Test of Basic Skills		.68–.93		
Stanford Achievement Test	.44–.82	.81–.95	.83–.87	
Woodcock Johnson Psychoeducational Battery		.73–.97		
Kaufmann Test of Educational Achievement	.90–.95	.80–.97		
Peabody Individual Achievement Test	.61–.94			
SRA Survey of Basic Skills (Forms P and Q)		.72–.93		
Wide Range Achievement Test	.90–.96	.86–.98		
Test of Academic Progress	.70–.90	.91–.94		
Kaufmann K-ABC	.93–.98	.86–.97		
Test of Early Reading Ability	.82–.94	.87–.96		
Gray Oral Reading Test		.83–.98	.81–.83	
Nelson Reading Skills Test		.77–.95	.60–.92	
Nelson-Denny Reading Test			.62–.95	
Gates-McKillop-Horowitz Reading Diagnostic Tests	.94			.91–.94
Woodcock Reading Mastery Test		.34–.99		
Stanford Diagnostic Reading Test		.76 +	.66–.78	

MATH TESTS

Test	Test Retest	Internal Consistency	Alternate Form	Inter-Judge
3-Rs Test		.80–.93		
California Achievement Test (Form E)	.76–.85	.68–.94	.73–.87	
Circus/Sequential Test of Educational Progress		.84–.94	.70–.92	
California Test of Basic Skills (Forms U and V)		.67–.92		
Diagnostic Achievement Battery	.80–.95	.65–.97		
Stanford Achievement Test	.63–.83	.84–.92	.82–.91	
Woodcock Johnson Psychoeducational Battery		.67–.94		
Kaufmann Test of Educational Achievement	.83–.94	.87–.93		
Peabody Individual Achievement Test	.52–.84			
SRA Survey of Basic Skills (Forms P and Q)	.53–.85		.71–.87	
Wide Range Achievement Test	.79–.94	.78–.97		
Multilevel Academic Skills Inventory	.81–.86	.87–.97		
Test of Mathematical Ability	.71–.94	.57–.97		
Sequential Assessment of Mathematical Inventories	.78–.89	.72–.96		
KeyMath		.64–.96		
Test of Academic Progress	.70–.90	.76–.89		
Stanford Diagnostic Mathematics Tests		.71–.93		
Kaufmann K-ABC	.87–.91	.85–.89		

Observational Profile of Classroom Communication

Project Director: Dixie D. Sanger, Ph.D.
Barkley Memorial Center (1986)
University of Nebraska—Lincoln*

The purpose of this nonstandardized observational profile is to assist teachers in observing functional communication variables within the speaker, listener, content, and context. It examines ongoing communication in a classroom setting utilizing a procedure developed from the SPERS model (Lasky 1983, 1985). The questionnaire asks about the signal and presentation, the environment, the response of the child, and the learning strategies used in the classroom.

INSTRUCTIONS: THE TEACHER WILL OBSERVE THE CHILD FOR TWO WEEKS AND REPORT WHETHER THE FOLLOWING VARIABLES SEEM TO AFFECT THE STUDENT'S LEARNING.

SCORING: CHECK YES IF THE STATEMENT APPEARS TO BE TRUE IN ENOUGH INSTANCES TO AFFECT THE CHILD'S LEARNING AND NO IF IT DOES NOT.

Name: Name of Observer:

Birthdate: CA: Inclusive Dates of Observation:

Grade Level: History of Hearing Loss:

Reason for Referral:

Background Information:

*References: Lasky (1983, 1985), Lasky & Cox (1983), Nelson (1985)

	Yes	No
Signal and Presentation		
1. The child displays difficulty using stress patterns to interpret the speaker's intent.	_____	_____
2. The child is often confused by complex and embedded information.	_____	_____
3. The child has difficulty following multistage instructions.	_____	_____
4. The child misunderstands what is said, especially if the signal is presented at a fast rate.	_____	_____
5. The child displays more difficulty understanding the teacher when she moves around the room than when she is stationary.	_____	_____
6. The child frequently requires redundancy of auditory information.	_____	_____
7. The child appears to have trouble picking up new information and may require several repetitions in order to understand the material.	_____	_____
8. The child has difficulty understanding information presented at a normal level.	_____	_____
9. The child has more difficulty attending to information which is academically challenging.	_____	_____
10. The child often requires additional cues to understand information presented in class.	_____	_____

Is this true in contexts other than class?

11. The child frequently requires visual cues in addition to auditory information.	_____	_____

Comments:

Environment		
12. The child displays more difficulty learning when two or more speakers participate in the conversation.	_____	_____
13. Child appears inattentive or distracted, especially when significant background noise is present.	_____	_____
14. The child's learning seems to be affected by where he or she is seated in relation to the teacher.	_____	_____

Explain:

15. The child learns better in one-to-one situations than small group or classroom situations.	_____	_____
16. The child tends to have difficulty learning in an environment with several visual distractions.	_____	_____

Comments:

	Yes	No
Response		
17. The child often gives inappropriate or unrelated responses to questions or commands.	_____	_____
18. The child produces intermittent and inconsistent responses.	_____	_____
19. The child has difficulty recalling auditory information.	_____	_____
Can the child recall auditory information if given special cues (e.g., a choice of words, association cues)?		
20. The child displays difficulty recalling sequences of information such as telling a story or talking about an event.	_____	_____
21. The child displays difficulty formulating or generating expressive language.	_____	_____
22. The child displays language problems (evidenced in the usage of inappropriate "wh" questions, pronouns, word order, possessiveness, etc.).	_____	_____
Explain:		
23. The child displays problems with articulation (phonology) consisting of substitutions, distortions, or omissions of sounds in words (especially when producing words which are similar auditorily).	_____	_____
Explain:		
24. Does the child often give inappropriate or delayed responses?	_____	_____
Explain:		
25. Does the child have difficulty in providing complex explanations to questions:	_____	_____
Explain:		

Comments:

	Agree	Dis-Agree
Strategies		
26. The child does not tend to paraphrase information when having difficulty understanding information.	_____	_____
27. The child rarely rehearses information as a strategy for remembering it.	_____	_____
28. The child infrequently asks questions when uncertain of information.	_____	_____
29. The child is generally unaware of errors in processing information and does not attempt to get clarification of information.	_____	_____

Comments:

Behaviors:	Yes	No
30. The child displays some behaviorial problems (i.e., out-of-seat behavior, short attention span, day-dreaming).	———	———
31. The child appears unmotivated to learn (i.e., the child isn't persistent in trying to understand information he is having difficulty with; he quits easily).	———	———
32. The child shows irritability and hostility toward others, especially if he or she is having difficulty learning.	———	———
33. The child becomes frustrated when trying to learn auditory information.	———	———

Comments:

General Impressions:

APPENDIX C

Definitions for Parameters Assessed on the Pragmatic Protocol

VERBAL ASPECTS

Speech act pair analysis   The ability to take both speaker and listener role appropriate to the context. Types: Directive/compliance—personal need, imperatives, permissions, directives, question directives, and hints. Query/response—request for confirmation, neutral requests for repetition, requests for specific constituent repetition. Request/response—direct requests, inferred requests, requests for clarification, acknowledgment of request for action. Comment/acknowledgment—description of ongoing activities; of immediate subsequent activity; of state or condition of objects or person; naming; acknowledgments that are positive, negative, expletive, or indicative.

Examples: Appropriate behaviors: Initiates directives, queries, and comments; responds to directives by complying; responds to queries; responds appropriately to requests; and acknowledges comments made by the speaker. Appropriate behavior can be verbal or nonverbal as in the case of taking appropriate action to a directive or request. Inappropriate behaviors: Does not initiate directives, queries, and comments; does not respond to directives, requests, or queries by the speaker; and does not use acknowledgments made by the speaker either nonverbally or verbally.

References: (Austin, 1962; Gallagher, 1977; Garvey, 1975; Mitchell-Kernan & Kernan, 1977; Searle, 1969).

Variety of speech acts   The variety of speech acts or what one can do with language such as comment, assert, request, promise, and so forth.

Examples: Appropriate behaviors: The partner shows both appropriate use of and diversity in the number of different speech acts he can accomplish. Inappropriate behaviors: The partner shows inappropriate use or a reduced range of different speech acts he or she can use (e.g., a particular child whose productive repertoire is restricted to requests for objects with no other observed speech act types).

References: (Austin, 1962; Mitchell-Kernan & Kernan, 1977; Searle, 1969).

Topic
a. Selection   The selection of a topic appropriate to the multidimensional aspects of context.
b. Introduction   Introduction of a new topic in the discourse.
c. Maintenance   Coherent maintenance of topic across the discourse.
d. Change   Change of topic in the discourse.

Examples: Appropriate behaviors: The speaker/listener is able to make relevant contributions to a topic, is able to make smooth changes in topic at appropriate times in the discourse, is able to select appropriate topics for discussion given the context and participants, and is able to end discussion of a topic at an appropriate place in the discourse. Inappropriate behaviors: The introduction of too many topics within a specified time limit, the inability to initiate new topics for discussion, the inability to select appropriate topics for discussion given the context and participants, and the inability to make relevant contributions to a topic. Inability to maintain topic may frequently co-occur with high frequency of new topic introductions.

References: (Bloom, Rocissano, & Hood, 1976; Brinton & Fujuki, 1984; Ervin-Tripp, 1979; Keenan, 1977; Keenan & Schieffelin, 1976).

Turn taking   Smooth interchanges between speaker/listener.
a. Initiation   Initiation of speech acts.
b. Response   Responding as a listener to speech acts.
c. Repair/revision   The ability to repair a conversation when a breakdown occurs, and the ability to ask for a repair when misunderstanding or ambiguity has occurred.
d. Pause time   Pause time that is too short or too long between words, in response to a question, or between sentences.
e. Interruption/overlap Interruptions between speaker and listener; overlap refers to two people talking at once.
f. Feedback to listener Verbal behavior to give the listener such as *yeah* and *really*; nonverbal behavior such as head nods to show positive reactions and side to side to express negative effects or disbelief.
g. Adjacency   Utterances that occur immediately after the partner's utterance.
h. Contingency   Utterances that share the same topic with a preceding utterance and that add information to the prior communicative act.
i. Quantity/conciseness The contribution should be as informative as required but not too informative.

Examples: In all of the above categories, appropriate and inappropriate behavior is judged in relationship to both speaker and listener in the dyad. Appropriate behaviors: Initiating conversation and responding to comments made by the speaker, asking for clarification when a portion of the message is misunderstood and revising one's own message to facilitate understanding, avoiding interrupting or talking before the other partner is finished, giving feedback to the speaker as a way of moving the conversation forward, appropriate length of pauses in the conversation to support timing relationships in the conversation, and making comments relevant and informative. Inappropriate behaviors: Little initiation in the conversation forcing one partner to take the burden of moving the conversation forward, no response of inappropriate responses to requests for clarification by the partner, no attempt to ask for repair, long pauses that interrupt timing relationships in the conversation, pause time that is too short and results in overlap or interruptions, little or no feedback to the speaker, and inability to produce comments that are relevant and informative.

References: (Bloom et al., 1976; Brinton, Fujuki, Loeb, & Winkler, 1986; Duncan & Fiske, 1977; Ervin-Tripp, 1977; Ervin-Tripp, 1979; Gallagher, 1977; Grice, 1975; Keenan, 1977; Keenan & Klein, 1975; Keenan & Schieffelin, 1976; Sacks, Schegloff, & Jefferson, 1978).

Lexical selection/use
    Specificity/Accuracy   Lexical items of best fit considering the text.

Examples: Appropriate behaviors: The ability to be specific and make appropriate lexical choices to clearly convey information in the discourse. Inappropriate behaviors: Overuse of unspecified referents that results in ambiguity of the message. Also includes inappropriate choice of lexical items that do not facilitate understanding.

References: (Prutting & Kirchner, 1983).

Specifying relationships between and across speech acts
    Cohesion   The recognizable unity or connectedness of text. Types: Reference—semantic relation whereby the information needed for interpretation of some item is found elsewhere in the text. Substitution—cohesive bond is established by the use of substitute item of the same grammatical class. Ellipsis—substitution by zero and refers to sentences or clauses whose structure is such as to presuppose the missing information. Conjunction—logical relation between clauses. Lexical cohesion—achieved through vocabulary selection.

Examples: Appropriate behaviors: Relatedness and unity in the discourse. One is able to follow the conversation, and the ideas are expressed in a logical and sequential way. Inappropriate behaviors: A conversation is disjointed, and utterances do not appear to be related in a logical and sequential fashion. One is unable to follow the line of thinking expressed by the speaker, frequently resulting in misinterpretation and ambiguity.

References: (Halliday & Hassan, 1976; Keenan & Klein, 1975; Lahey & Launer, 1986).

Stylistic variances   Adaptations used by the speaker under various dyadic conditions (e.g., polite forms, different syntax, changes in vocal quality).

Examples: Appropriate behaviors: The ability to adjust speech style to the listener. Inappropriate behaviors: Mismatch between style and status of listener or no difference when required.

References: (Sachs & Devin, 1976; Shotz & Gelman, 1973).

PARALINGUISTIC ASPECTS

Intelligibility	The extent to which the message is understood.
Vocal intensity	The loudness or softness of the message.
Vocal quality	The resonance and/or laryngeal characteristics of the vocal tract.
Prosody	The intonation and stress patterns of the message; variations of loudness, pitch, and duration.
Fluency	The smoothness, consistency, and rate of the message.

Examples: Appropriate behaviors: Speech that is clear, not too loud or too soft; appropriate in quality; and shows appropriate use of intonation, stress, and pitch to support the communicative/ linguistic intention of the message. Inappropriate behaviors: Speech that is so unclear as to result in frequent misinterpretations of the message; speech that is too loud or too soft; a quality of speech that is inappropriate to age or sex of speaker and interferes with communication; and the lack of prosodic variation that supports affect and the linguistic aspects of the message.

References: (Duncan & Fiske, 1977; Scherer & Ekman, 1982).

NONVERBAL ASPECTS

Physical proximity	The distance that the speaker and listener sit or stand from one another.
Physical contacts	The number of times and placement of contacts between speaker and listener.
Body posture	Forward lean is when the speaker or listener moves away from a 90-degree angle toward the other person; recline is slouching down from waist and moving away from the partner; side to side is when a person moves to the right or left.
Foot/leg and hand/arm movements	Any movement of the foot/leg or hand/arm (touching self or moving an object or touching part of the body, clothing, or self).
Gestures	Any movements that support, complement, or replace verbal behavior.
Facial expression	A positive expression as in the corners of the mouth turned upward; a negative expression is a downward turn; a neutral expression is the face in resting position.
Eye gaze	One looks directly at the other's face; mutual gaze is when both members of the dyad look at the other.

Examples: Appropriate behaviors: Use of nonverbal aspects of communication that demonstrate level of affiliation between partners, aid in regulating discourse turns, and may supplement or support linguistic aspects of the message. Inappropriate behaviors: Use of nonverbal aspects that interfere with interpersonal/social aspects of communication; behaviors that detract from the content of the message rather than support and regulate discourse.

References: (Craig & Gallagher, 1982; Duncan & Fiske, 1977; Feldman, 1982; Hoffer & St. Clair, 1981; Scherer & Ekman, 1982; Von Raffler-Engel, 1980).

Source: Prutting and Kirchner, 1987.

Kindergarten Assessment

Kindergarten Assessment:
Directions for Administration

INTRODUCTION

This Kindergarten Assessment is a pilot instrument. It was constructed in part to respond to a need expressed by some kindergarten, first grade and Chapter 1 teachers who felt that it would be helpful to have a single screening instrument for making grouping decisions and instructional decisions about their students.

During interviews with some of these teachers, it was learned that each one was using some kind of screening instrument, all of which assessed very similar skills but were each unique. When it was proposed that a single instrument could be developed to test students' skills in a similar fashion to the way they were already being tested, these teachers responded very positively about the resulting consistency which would allow for better communication between teachers and others (administrators, specialists, parents, even students themselves).

MATERIALS FOR TESTING

1. One copy of the *Kindergarten Assessment: Teacher Copy* for each child to be tested.
2. One copy of the *Kindergarten Assessment: Student Copy* for each child to be tested.
3. One set of *Assessment Materials* pages 1–4; these should be put into plastic covers or laminated for ease of use. (Enough copies of Assessment Materials page 1A should be made to provide a circle for each student to cut in Item 12.)
4. A pencil for the student to use to write.
5. One stopwatch.
6. A list of each child's birthday, address, and phone number to check for accuracy of responses on Items 3–5.
7. A pair of scissors for the student to use for Item 12.
8. One each: red, yellow, blue, brown, black, orange, purple, pink, and green crayon for Item 14.
9. One can and 20 pennies for counting in Item 16.
10. Objects to zip, tie, lace, button, and buckle; ball to catch; and a jump rope for Motor/Self-help Skills.
11. Optional: copies of Assessment Materials pages 5–7 to use as a form for behavioral observations of students.

MARKING PROCEDURES

For each item on the test, the examiner will mark students' responses according to the written directions. In most cases you will either be directed to circle correct responses or X all incorrect responses. If students give no response or state that they don't know the answer to a question, mark No Response or NR. If the task was not administered to a student, mark Not Administered, or NA. NOTE THAT ALL ITEMS NEED NOT BE ADMINISTERED TO ALL CHILDREN. Teachers are encouraged to use their judgment about the appropriateness of items for their individual students.

ADMINISTRATION PROCEDURES

To compare students' performances after they all have been tested, it is important that standard procedures be followed when administering this screener. *Familiarize yourself with the test before giving it for the first time.*

Take a few moments before beginning the test to explain to each of the students what will be taking place. Avoid using the word "test" but encourage them to do their best. Then administer each appropriate task to the student, marking responses as above. The test can be broken into separate administrations if a student appears to be tiring. It is a good idea to make comments beside each item for future reference, especially observations made of students' behavior or skills during testing including any language or speech impairments, difficulty in attending to the task at hand, apparent vision problems, etc.

When a student's assessment is complete, attach the Student Copy to the back of the Teacher Copy for that student as a permanent record of all aspects of the assessment.

Please note that although this assessment does not involve any physical or health screening, this should be considered a part of any complete early childhood assessment.

INTERPRETATION OF TEST RESULTS

The Kindergarten Assessment instrument was developed using teacher input and a review of existing screening tests, relevant research and literature on the assessment of young children. The items on the test are divided into six sections:

1. Knowledge of self
2. General knowledge
3. Beginning number skills
4. Beginning literacy skills
5. Motor/Self-help skills
6. Social/Interpersonal skills

After the piloting of this test, it is possible that it may be normed so that a comparison of students' scores could be made. At this point however, the results will only yield criterion-referenced information: what skills/knowledge does a student have. Results of this assessment, in addition to other formal and informal assessments conducted in the classroom, can then be used by the teacher to make both placement and instructional decisions about individual children.

Kindergarten Assessment: Teacher Copy

Student: _____   Date: _____

Teacher: _____   School: _____

KNOWLEDGE OF SELF: ITEMS 1-8

1) WHAT IS YOUR **FIRST NAME?**   Correct   Incorrect   No response (NR)   Not Administered (NA)

   (If students correctly say first name, have them WRITE it on the Student Copy, Page 1)

   + Note hand preference: Right   Left

2) WHAT IS YOUR **LAST NAME?**   Correct   Incorrect   No response (NR)   Not Administered (NA)

   (If students correctly say last name, have them WRITE it on the Student Copy, Page 1)

3) WHAT IS YOUR **ADDRESS?**   ALL Correct   Part Correct   Incorrect   NR   NA

4) WHAT IS YOUR **PHONE NUMBER?**   ALL Correct   Part Correct   Incorrect   NR   NA

5) WHAT IS YOUR **BIRTHDAY?**   ALL Correct   Part Correct   Incorrect   NR   NA

6) HOW **OLD** ARE YOU?   ALL Correct   Part Correct   Incorrect   NR   NA

7) SHOW ME YOUR **RIGHT** HAND.   Correct   Incorrect   NR   NA

8) SHOW ME YOUR **LEFT** HAND.   Correct   Incorrect   NR   NA

GENERAL KNOWLEDGE: ITEMS 9-14

9) SAY THE **DAYS OF THE WEEK** (X incorrect responses):

   Sunday   Monday   Tuesday   Wednesday   Thursday   Friday   Saturday
   All Correct   With help   Without help   NR   NA

10) SAY THE **MONTHS OF THE YEAR** (X incorrect responses):

   January February March April May June July August September October November December

   All Correct   With help   Without help   NR   NA

Use Assessment Materials, Page 1 "SHAPES" for Items 9 & 11

11) WHAT **SHAPE** IS THIS?   point to each shape   (X those named incorrectly):

   square   rectangle   triangle   circle   diamond   oval   All Correct   NR   NA

12) USE YOUR SCISSORS AND **CUT** OUT THE CIRCLE

    <u>HOLD:</u> OK Needs Practice   <u>CUTTING:</u> NR Needs Practice   OK   Skill Mastered   NA

13) **COPY EACH SHAPE AS I POINT TO IT** (students copy shapes on their copy, Page 1). NR NA

Use crayons.

14) SHOW ME THE _____ CRAYON (X those incorrect or omitted):

red   yellow   blue   brown   black   orange   purple   pink   green   All Correct   NR   NA

BEGINNING NUMBER SKILLS: ITEMS 15-18

15) HOW FAR CAN YOU **COUNT?** (Last number said in correct sequence; up to 100 ____

                                                      NR   NA

Use 20 pennies and a can.

16) **COUNT THESE PENNIES AS YOU PUT THEM INTO THE CAN.**

                                     (Last number said correctly____   ) NR   NA

Use Student Copy, Page 2.

17) WRITE THE **NUMBER** I SAY TO YOU ON THE LINE. (X those written incorrectly or omitted):

    9   7   3   6   2   10   1   5   4   8   All Correct   NR   NA

        NOTE: If the student wrote all numbers from Item 17 above correctly <u>**SKIP**</u>
                  number dictation: Item 18; go on to Item 19

Use Assessment Materials, Page 2

18) WHAT IS THIS **NUMBER?** (X all numbers named incorrectly or omitted)

    9   7   3   6   2   10   1   5   4   8   All Correct   NR   NA

BEGINNING LITERACY SKILLS: ITEMS 19-25

19) SAY THE **ALPHABET (ABC's)** (X all letters named incorrectly, omitted or out of sequence):

A B   C D   E F G   H   I   J   K   L   M   N   O   P   Q   R   S   T   U   V   W   X   Y

        All Correct   NR   NA

Use Assessment Materials, **Page 2** for Items 20 & 21

20) WHAT **LETTER** IS THIS?   (X all letters named incorrectly or omitted)

d   j   s   w   g   o   f   l   y   a   m   q   h   c

n   b   i   t   z   x   v   k   e   p   r   u

All Correct   NR   NA

➡   ***ITEM 21 IS TIMED***

21) WHAT **SOUND** IS THIS?   (X all sounds named incorrectly or omitted)

d   j   s   w   g   o   f   l   y   a   m   q   h   c

n   b   i   t   z   x   v   k   e   p   r   u

All Correct   NR   NA   TIME:_____

Use Assessment Materials, Page 3

22) WHAT **LETTER** IS THIS?   (X all letters named incorrectly or omitted)

D   J   S   W   G   O   F   L   Y   A   M   Q   H

C   N   B   I   T   Z   X   V   K   E   P   R   U

All Correct   NR   NA

Use Student Copy, Page 2.

23) **COPY THESE LETTERS IN THE BOXES.**   NR   NA

Use Assessment Materials, Page 4

24) CAN YOU **READ / SOUND OUT** THIS WORD? (X all words read incorrectly or omitted)

f i n   r u b   m o p   w e t   s a d   dog

All Correct   With help   Without help   NR   NA

Use Student Copy, Page 2.

25) CAN YOU **WRITE** THIS WORD? (Dictate each word)

fin   rug   mop   wet   sad   dog   NR   NA

MOTOR/SELF-HELP SKILLS

Student can:	NR	Needs practice	OK	Skill mastered	NA
Zip					
Tire					
Lace					
Button					
Buckle					
Hop					
Skip					
Gallop					
Balance					
Walk backwards					
Jump rope					
Catch ball					

COMMENTS:

SOCIAL/ INTERPERSONAL SKILLS

(See Behavior Checklist for Kindergarten Students in ASSESSMENT MATERIALS, Pages 5-7 for additional information and suggestions. The skills listed below are taken from the Springfield Public Schools Progress Report; Kindergarten).

	Usually	Sometimes	Rarely	Never
ADJUSTS EASILY TO NEW AND DIFFERENT SITUATIONS				
SHOW SIGNS OF CONFIDENCE				
SHOWS SELF-CONTROL				
PARTICIPATES COOPERATIVELY IN SMALL GROUP AND LARGE GROUP ACTIVITIES				
UNDERSTANDS AND ABIDES BY SCHOOL RULES				
LISTENS WHILE OTHERS TALK				
SOLVES PROBLEMS INDEPENDENTLY AND WITH A GROUP				
SHOWS INITIATIVE IN FINDING MATERIALS OR CHOOSING ACTIVITIES				
PARTICIPATES IN A VARIETY OF ACTIVITIES				
SHOWS PERSISTENCE ON TASK				
USES MATERIALS APPROPRIATELY				
ASSUMES RESPONSIBILITY FOR CARE OF MATERIALS AND ROOM				
ATTEMPTS NEW THINGS WILLINGLY				
UNDERSTANDS AND FOLLOWS DIRECTIONS				
ASSUMES RESPONSIBILITY FOR OWN BEHAVIOR				
PARTICIPATES COOPERATIVELY IN LIBRARY				
CONTRIBUTES TO GROUP PLANNING AND CONVERSATION				
SPEAKS WITH EASE TO OTHERS IN CONVERSATION				

COMMENTS:

Kindergarten Assessment: Student Copy

Item 1: First name

_____

Item 2: Last name

_____

Item 13: Copying Shapes

Item 17: Number Writing from dictation

_____ _____ _____ _____ _____

_____ _____ _____ _____ _____

Item 23: Letter Copying

a	t	f	y	n	p

d	b	r	u	s	g

NOTE: When assessment is completed, attach this Student Copy to the back of the Teacher Copy for a complete record of the results.

Item 25: Writing Words

_____

_____

_____

_____

NOTE: When assessment is completed, attach this Student Copy to the back of the Teacher Copy for a complete record of the results.

Shapes

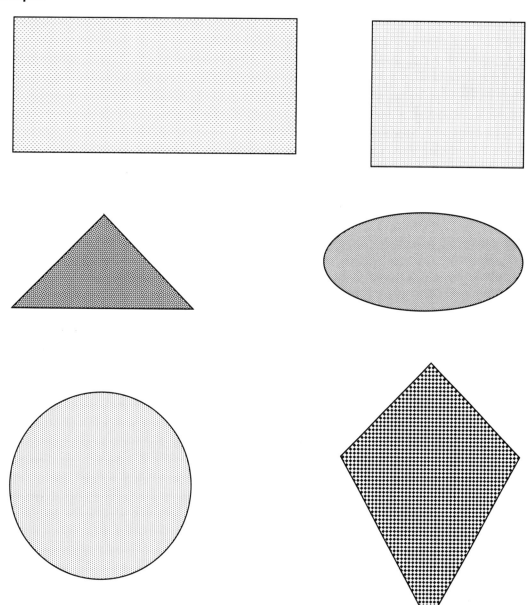

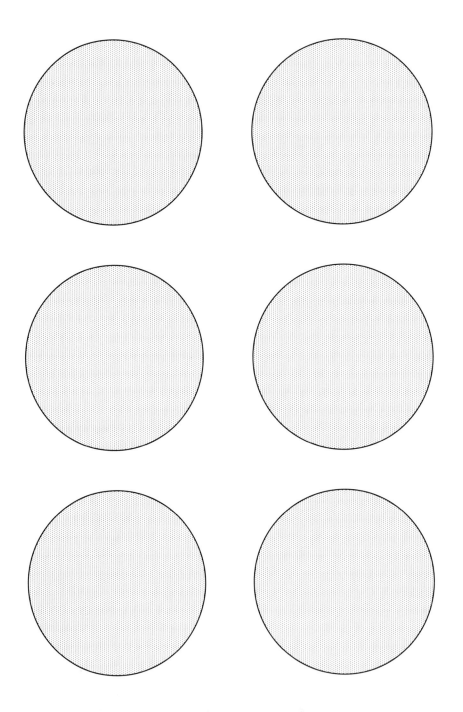

Item 18: Number Recognition

9   7   3   6   2   10

1   5   4   8

Items 20 & 21: Letter / Sounds Recognition (Lower Case)

d   j   s   w   g

o   f   l   y   a

m   q   h   c   n

b   i   t   z   x

v   k   e   p   r

u

Items 22: Letter Recognition (Upper Case)

D	J	S	W	G
O	F	L	Y	A
M	Q	H	C	N
B	I	T	Z	X
V	K	E	P	R

U

Items 24: Reading / Sounding Out

fin

rug

mop

wet

sad

dog

BEHAVIOR CHECKLIST FOR KINDERGARTEN STUDENTS

This behavior checklist was developed by David Day from research conducted in day care programs considered to be of high quality. It is not meant to be an "exhaustive account of children's behavior" (Day, p. 274), but it reflects the results of research, judgments about the developmental behavior of young children, and goals of early education accepted by a diverse group of practitioners.

This checklist can be used as an observation instrument to guide a teacher or trained observer in a classroom setting on a daily or more infrequent basis. Use the list of behaviors to guide observation of behaviors which are demonstrated by students CONSISTENTLY, SOMETIMES, RARELY, or NEVER. Ancedotal recordings of observations and comments can be made, recorded, and later summarized.

(1) TASK INVOLVEMENT: Student becomes absorbed in activities, completes games and tasks, attends appropriately to what s/he is doing.

Focuses on a task

Resolves problems appropriately

Completes tasks

COMMENTS:

(2) COOPERATION: Student engages in cooperative activities with adults and other children.

Seeks participation with a child or adult

Accepts a request to join an activity with a child or adult

Joins in group activities

Takes turns

Shares toys, materials, equipment with others

COMMENTS:

Adapted from Day, D. E. (1983). *Early childhood education: A human ecological approach.* Glenview, IL: Scott, Foresman, and Co.

(3) AUTONOMY: Student makes choices about what s/he will do.

Selects activities

Asks permission as necessary

Works independently

COMMENTS:

(4) VERBAL INTERACTION: Student initiates and participates in appropriate conversation with other children and adults.

Talks with a child or adult

Requests information from a child or adult

Responds to a child or an adult

COMMENTS:

(5) MATERIALS USE: Student uses material and equipment effectively and appropriately.

Uses materials in activities appropriately and carefully

Uses materials in activities creatively

COMMENTS:

(6) MAINTENANCE: Student helps to organize activities of the program, assisting with arranging equipment, distributing materials, and cleaning up when necessary.

Takes responsibility for picking up

Volunteers to assist a child or teacher in a maintenance activity

Helps prepare an activity

COMMENTS:

(7) CONSIDERATION: Student is considerate of other children and their activities.

Observes the activity of others without disruption

Respects the physical space of others

Helps or offers sympathy to a child in distress

COMMENTS:

PLAY OBSERVATION FORM

Observer:_____ Target Child:_____ Sex:_____ Age:_____ Date/Time:_____

OBSERVATION CODES

TC: TARGET CHILD   C: OTHER CHILD   A: ADULT: ——▶ : SPEAKS TO

• OBSERVATION FIELD NOTES •		• ANALYSIS •	
SETTING/ACTIVITIES/ BEHAVIORS	LANGUAGE/ VERBAL BEHAVIORS	ACTIVITY CODE	GROUPING CODE
1.			
2.			
3.			
4.			
5.			
6.			
7.			

ACTIVITY CODES:

(LMM): LARGE MUSCLE MOVEMENT (LSC): LARGE SCALE CONSTRUCTION (SSC): SMALL SCALE CONSTRUCTION (ART): PAINTING, DRAWING, CUTTING, ETC. (MAN): MANUAL PLAY WITH CLAY,SAND,WATER,SORTING (ADM): ADULT DIRECTED ART/MANUAL ACTIVITIES (SM): STRUCTURED MATERIALS (3R'S): READING, WRITING, COUNTING (EX): EXAMINATION (PS): PROBLEM-SOLVING (PRE): PRETEND (SVT): SCALE-VERSION TOYS (IG): INFORMAL GAMES (FG): FORMAL GAMES (MUS): MUSIC/RHYTHMS, SINGING & DANCING (SINP): SOCIAL INTERACTION, NON-PLAY (PALGA): PASSIVE ADULT-LED ACTIVITIES (DB): DISTRESS BEHAVIORS (P-NP): PASSIVE, NON-PURPOSEFUL ACTIVITIES (A-NP): ACTIVE NON-PURPOSEFUL ACTIVITIES (CR): CRUISE BETWEEN ACTIVITIES (PM): PURPOSEFUL MOVEMENT (W): WAITING (WA): WATCHING (DA): DOMESTIC ACTIVITIES

Adapted from Sylva, K., Roy, C., and Painter, M., *Childwatching at playgroup and nursery school* (London: Grant McIntyre, 1980).

REFERENCES

Aaron, I.E., Jackson, D., Riggs, C., Smith, R.G., Tierney, R.J. (1981). *Scott, Foresman Reading.* Glenview, IL: Scott, Foresman, and Company.

Abbott, J.S., & Wells, D.W. (1985). *Mathematics Today.* Orlando: Harcourt Brace Jovanovich.

Abbott, M.S., & Crane, J.S. (1977). Assessment of young children. *Journal of School Psychology, 15*(2), 118–128.

Airasian, P.W., & Madaus, G.F. (1983). Linking testing and instruction: Policy issues. *Journal of Educational Measurement, 20,* 103–118.

Alford, L.E. (1986). Alignment of textbook and test content. *The Arithmetic Teacher, 34*(3), 35.

Allen D., & Ager, J. (1965). A factor analytic study of the ability to spell. *Educational and Psychological Measurement, 25*(1), 153–161.

Allred, R. (1977). *Spelling: The application of research findings.* Washington, DC: National Education Association.

Allred, R. (1984). Comparison of proofreading-type standardized spelling test and written spelling test scores. *Journal of Educational Research, 77*(5), 298–303.

American Psychological Association, American Educational Research Association, and National Council on Measurement in Education (1985). *Standards for educational and psychological tests.* Washington, DC: American Psychological Association.

American Psychological Association (1985). *Standards for educational and psychological testing.* Washington, DC: American Psychological Association.

Anastasi, A. (1968) *Psychological testing.* New York: Macmillan.

Anastasiow, N.J., & Mansergh, G.P. (1975). Teaching skills in early childhood programs. *Exceptional Children, 41,* 309–317.

Anderson, L.W., & Lieu, J.M. (1980). *The applicability of three systematic approaches to item writing to the assessment of different types of instructional objectives.* Paper presented at the meeting of the American Educational Research Association, Boston.

Angoff, W.H. (1971). Scales, norms and equivalent scores. In R.L. Thorndike (Ed.), *Educational Measurement* (pp. 514–515). Washington, DC: American Council on Education.

Applebee, A.N. (1981). *Writing in the secondary school.* (Research Report No. 21). Urbana, IL: National Council of Teachers of English.

Arter, J.A., & Jenkins, J.R. (1979). Differential diagnosis—prescriptive teaching: A critical appraisal. *Review of Educational Research, 49,* 517–555.

Ashcroft, S.C. (1967). Blind and partially seeing children. In L.M. Duan (Ed.), *Exceptional Children in the Schools.* New York: Holt, Rinehart & Winston.

Ashlock, R.B. (1990). *Error Patterns in Computation: A semi-programmed approach.* (5th Ed.) Columbus, OH: Merrill.

Bagnato, S.J. & Neisworth, J.T. (1981). *Linking developmental assessment and curricula: Prescriptions for early intervention.* Rockville, MD: Aspens Systems.

Bailey, D.B., & Wolery, M. (1984). *Teaching infants and preschoolers with handicaps*. Columbus, OH: Charles E. Merrill.

Bana, J., & Nelson, D. (1978). Distractors in non-verbal mathematical problems. *Journal for Research in Mathematics Education, 9* 55–61.

Barnes, K.E. (1982). *Preschool screening: The measurement and prediction of children at-risk*. Springfield, IL: Charles C Thomas.

Barnett, D.W. (1984). An organizational approach to preschool services: Psychological screening, assessment, and intervention. In C.A. Maher, R.J. Illback, J.E. Zins, (Eds.), *Organizational psychology in the schools: A handbook for professionals* (pp. 53–82). Springfield, IL: Charles C Thomas.

Baron, J.B. (1981). *Will the "real" proficiency standard please stand up?* Paper presented at the Annual Meeting of the New England Educational Research Organization. Lenox, MA

Baroody, A.J. (1984). Children's difficulties in subtraction: Some causes and cures. *The Arithmetic Teacher, 32,* 14–19.

Barr, R., & Sadow, M. (1985). *Reading diagnosis for teachers*. New York: Longman.

Barrett, W. (1984). An organizational approach to preschool services: Psychological screening, assessment, and intervention. In C.A. Maher, R.J. Illback, & J.E. Zins, *Organizational psychology in the schools: A handbook for professionals* (pp. 53–82). Springfield, IL: Charles C Thomas.

Beattie, J., & Algozzine, B. (1982). Testing for teaching. *Arithmetic Teacher, 3b,* 47–51.

Beers, J.W. (1980). Developmental strategies of spelling competence in primary school children. In J.W. Beers and E.H. Henderson (Eds.), *Developmental and Cognitive Aspects of Learning to Spell*. Newark, DE: International Reading Association 3–209.

Bennett, R.E. (1982a). Cautions for the use of informal measures in the educational assessment of exceptional children. *Journal of Learning Disabilities, 15*(6), 337–339.

Bennett, R.E. (1982b). The use of grade and age equivalent scores in educational assessment. *Diagnostique, 7*(3), 139–146.

Bentz, J., Shinn, M.S., & Gleason, M.M. (1988). Training regular education pupils to monitor reading with curriculum-based procedures. *School Psychology Review*.

Berglund-Gray, G., & Young, R. (1940). The effects of process sequence on the interpretation of two-step problems in arithmetic. *Journal of Educational Research, 34,* 21–29.

Berk, R.A. (1984). Conducting the item analysis. In R.A. Berk (Ed.). *A guide to criterion-referenced test construction*. Baltimore, MD: John Hopkins University Press.

Berk, R.A. (1986). A consumer's guide to setting performance standards on criterion-referenced tests. *Review of Educational Research, 56*(1), 137–172.

Berman, B., & Friederwitzer, F.J. (1981). A diagnostic-prescriptive approach to remediation of regrouping errors. *The Elementary School Journal, 82*(2), 109–115.

Bersoff, D.N. (1973). Silk purses into sow's ears: The decline of psychological testing and a suggestion for its redemption. *American Psychologist, 28,* 892–899.

Betts, E.A. (1976). Spelling and phonics. *Spelling Progress Bulletin, 16*(2).

Blair, T.R. (1975). Spelling, word attack skills. *The Reading Teacher, 28*(6), 604–605, 607.

Blake, H.E., & Emans, R. (1970). Some spelling facts. *Elementary English, 47*(2), 37–44.

Block, H.M. (1956). *Candide and other writings*. New York: Modern Library.

Bloom, B.S., Engelhart, M.D., Furst, E.J., Hill, W.H., & Krathwohl, D.R. (1956). *Taxonomy of educational objectives. Handbook: The cognitive domain*. New York: David McKay Co.

Bloom, B.S., Madaus, G.F., & Hastings, J.T. (1981). *Evaluation to improve learning*. New York: McGraw-Hill.

Bloom. L. (1974). Talking, thinking, and understanding. In R.L. Schiefelbusch, & L.L. Lloyd (Eds.), *Language perspectives: Acquisition, retardation, and intervention* (pp. 285–311). Baltimore: University Park Press.

Bloom, L., & Lahey, M. (1978). *Language development and language disorders*. New York: John Wiley & Sons.

Boehm, A.E. (1986a). *Boehm Test of Basic Concepts: Preschool Version*. San Antonio: The Psychological Corporation.

Boehm, A.E. (1986b). *Boehm Test of Basic Concepts—Revised.* San Antonio: The Psychological Corporation.

Bohannon, R. (1975). *Direct and daily measurement procedures in the identification and treatment of reading behaviors of children in special education.* Unpublished doctoral dissertation, University of Washington.

Bombeck, E. (1989, June 7). *5-year-old burnout starts with parents.* Eugene, OR: The Register Guard, pp. 5D.

Bookman, M.O. (1984). Spelling as a cognitive-developmental linguistic process. *Academic Therapy, 20*(1), 21–31.

Bormuth, J. (1967). Comparable cloze and multiple-choice test scores. *Journal of Reading, 10* (February) 291–299.

Bormuth, J.R. (1968). Cloze test readability: Criterion-reference scores. *Journal of Educational Measurement, 5,* 189–196.

Bormuth, J.R. (1969). Factor validity of cloze tests as measures of reading comprehension. *Reading Research Quarterly, 4,* 358–365.

Bormuth, J.R. (1969). Factor validity of cloze tests as measures of reading comprehension. *Reading Research Quarterly, 4,* 358–365.

Braddock, R., Lloyd-Jones, R., & Schoer, L. (1963). *Research in written composition.* Champaign, IL: National Council of Teachers of English.

Brandstetter, G., & Merz, C. (1978). Charting scores in precision teaching for skill acquisition. *Exceptional Teaching, 45*(1), 42–48.

Breland, H.M., Camp, R., Jones, R.J., Morris, M.M., & Rock, D.A. (1987). *Assessing writing skill* (Research Monograph No. 11). New York: College Entrance Examination Board.

Breland, H.M., Conlon, G.C., & Rogosa, D. (1976). *A preliminary study of the Test of Standard Written English.* Princeton, NJ: Educational Testing Service.

Breland, H.M., & Gaynor, J.L. (1979). A comparison of direct and indirect assessments of writing skill. *Journal of Educational Measurement, 16*(2), 119–128.

Breuning, S. (1978). Precision teaching in the high school classroom: A necessary step toward maximizing teacher effectiveness and student performance. *American Educational Review, 15*(1), 125–140.

Bricker, D. (1978). A rationale for the integration of handicapped and nonhandicapped preschool children. In M. Guralnick (Ed.), *Early intervention and the integration of handicapped and nonhandicapped children* (pp. 3–26). Baltimore: University Park.

Brigance, A.H. (1977). *Brigance Diagnostic Inventory of Basic Skills.* North Billerica, MA: Curriculum Associates.

Brigance, A.H. (1978). *Brigance Diagnostic Inventory of Early Development.* North Billerica, MA: Curriculum Associates.

Brigance, A.H. (1984). *Brigance K & 1 screen.* North Billerica, MA: Curriculum Associates.

Brinton, B., Fujiki, M., Winkler, E., & Loeb, D. (1986). Responses to requests for clarification in impaired children. *Journal of Speech and Hearing Disorders, 51,* 370–377.

Brophy, J.E., & Good, T.L. (1986). Teacher behavior and student achievement. In M.C. Wittrock (Ed.) *Handbook of research on teaching-3rd edition* (pp. 328–375). New York: Macmillan.

Brown, J., Magnusson, D., Shinn, M., & Marston, D. (1984). *An evaluation of the effectiveness of special education instruction for mildly handicapped students, grades 1–6, using curriculum-based measurement procedures* (A report to the Minnesota State Department of Education). Minneapolis: Minneapolis Public Schools, Special Education Department.

Brown, R. (1973). *A first language: The early stages.* Cambridge: Harvard University Press.

Brownell, W., & Stretch, L. (1931). The effect of unfamiliar settings on problem-solving. *Duke University Research Studies in Education,* (1), 10–19.

Brueckner, L.J. (1928). Analysis of difficulties in decimals. *Elementary School Journal, 29,* 32–41.

Brueckner, L.J. (1930). *Diagnostic and remedial teaching in arithmetic.* Philadelphia: John C. Winston.

Brueckner, L.J., & Elwell, M. (1932). Reliability of diagnosis of error in multiplication of fractions. *Journal of Educational Research, 26,* 175–185.

Buros, O.K. (1978). *The seventh mental measurements yearbook.* Highland Park, NJ: Gryphon Press.

Burry, J., Catterall, J., Choppin, B., & Dorr-Bremme, D. (1982). *Testing in the nation's schools and districts: How much? What kinds? To what ends? At what costs?* (Report No. 194). Los Angeles: University of California—Los Angeles Graduate School, Center for the Study of Evaluation.

Burry, J., Herman, J., & Baker, E.L. (1984). *A practical approach to local test development* (Report No. 6). Los Angeles: University of California—Los Angeles Graduate School, Center for the Study of Evaluation.

Buswell, G.T. (1920). An experimental study of the eye-voice span in reading. *Supplementary Educational Monographs, 17,* 1–11.

Cahen, L., Craun, M., & Johnson, S. (1971). Spelling difficulty—A survey of the research. *Review of Educational Research, 41*(4), 281–301.

Caldwell, J.H., & Goldin, G.A. (1979). Variables affecting word problem difficulty in elementary school mathematics. *Journal for Research in Mathematics Education, 10,* 323–336.

Campbell, D., & Fiske, D. (1959). Convergent and discriminant validation by the multitrait-multimethod matrix. *Psychological Bulletin, 56,* 81–105.

Carey, L.M. (1988). *Measuring and evaluating school learning.* Boston: Allyn & Bacon.

Carpenter, D., & Carpenter, S. (1978). The concurrent validity of the Larsen-Hammill Test of Written Spelling in relation to the California Achievement Test. *Educational and Psychological Measurement, 38,* 1201–1205.

Carpenter, T., Corbitt, M., Kepner, H., Lindquist, M., & Reys, R. (1980). Solving verbal problems. *Arithmetic Teacher, 28,* 8–12.

Carpenter, T.P., Corbitt, M.K., Kepner, H.S., Jr., Lindquist, M.M., & Reys, R.E. (1981). Decimals: Results and implications from national assessment. *The Arithmetic Teacher, 28,* 34–37.

Carpenter, T.P., Corbitt, M.K., Kepner, H.S., Jr., Lindquist, M.M., & Reys, R.E. (1982). Student performance in algebra: Results from the national assessment. *Social Science and Mathematics, 82*(6), 514–531.

Carroll, J., Richman, B., & Davies, P. (1971). *The American heritage word frequency book.* Boston: Houghton Mifflin Co.

Cartwright, G.P. (1969). Written expression and spelling. In R.M. Smith (Ed.), *Teacher diagnosis of educational difficulties* (pp. 95–117). Columbus, OH: Charles Merrill.

Carver, R.P. (1974). Two dimensions of tests: Psychometric and edumetric. *American Psychologist, 29,* 512–518.

Cassidy, J., Roettger, D., & Wixson, K.K. (1987). *Scribner reading series.* New York: Scribner Educational Publishers.

Chall, J.S. (1983). Literacy: Trends and explanations. *Educational Researcher, 12,* 3–8.

Chambers, J.M., Cleveland, W.S., Kleiner, B., & Tukey, P.A. (1983). *Graphical methods for data analysis.* Pacific Grove, CA: Wadsworth.

Charney, D. (1984). The validity of using holistic scoring to evaluate writing: A critical overview. *Research in the Teaching of English, 18*(1), 65–81.

Cheek, H.N., & Castle, K. (1981). The effects of back to basics on mathematics education. *Contemporary Educational Psychology, 6,* 263–277.

Childcraft Educational Corporation. (1983). *Developmental indicators for the assessment of learning* (Rev. ed.). Edison, NJ: Childcraft Educational Corp.

Clark, C.H. (1982). Assessing free recall. *The Reading Teacher, 35,* 434–39.

Cleveland, W.S. (1985). *The elements of graphing data.* Pacific Grove, CA: Wadsworth.

Clymer, T. and others (1980). *Ginn 720: Rainbow edition.* Lexington, MA: Ginn & Co.

Conoley, J.C., Kramer, J.J., & Murphy, L.L. (1989). *The tenth mental measurements yearbook.* Lincoln, NE: University of Lincoln Nebraska Press.

Cooper, C.R. (1977). Holistic evaluation of writing. In C.R. Cooper, & L. Odell (Eds.), *Evaluating writing* (pp. 3–31). Buffalo, NY: National Council of Teachers of English.

Cox, J., & Wiebe, J.H. (1984). Measuring reading vocabulary and concepts in mathematics in the primary grades. *Reading Teacher, 37*(4), 402–410.

Cox, L.S. (1975). Diagnosing and remediating systematic errors in addition and subtraction computations. *The Arithmetic Teacher, 22,* 151–157.

Croft, A.C. (1982). Do spelling tests measure the ability to spell? *Educational and Psychological measurement, 42,* 715–723.

Cromer, W. (1970). The difference model: A new explanation for some reading difficulties. *Journal of Educational Psychology, 61,* 471–483.

Cronbach, L.J. (1951). Coefficient alpha and the internal structure of tests. *Psychometrika, 16,* 297–334.

Cronbach, L.J. (1960). *Essentials of psychological testing.* New York: Harper & Row.

Cronbach, L.J., Gleser, G.C., Nanda, H., & Rajaratram, N. (1972). *The dependability of behavioral measurements: Theory of generalizability for scores and profiles.* New York: John Wiley & Sons.

Cronbach, L.J., & Meehl, P.E. (1955). Construct validity in psychological tests. *Psychological Bulletin, 52,* 281–302.

Cronnell, B., & Humes, A. (1980). Elementary spelling: What's really taught. *The Elementary School Journal, 81*(1), 59–64.

Crowell, D.C., & Au, K.H. (1981). A scale of questions to guide comprehension instruction. *The Reading Teacher, 34,* 389–393.

Crowell, D.C., Hu-pei Au, K., & Blake, K.M. (1983). Comprehension questions: Differences among standardized tests. *Journal of Reading, 26*(4), 314–319.

CTB/McGraw-Hill. (1985). *California achievement tests (forms E and F): Test coordinator's handbook.* Monterey, CA: CTB/McGraw-Hill.

Dailey, K., & Boxx, J.R. (1979). A comparison of three imitative tests of expressive language and a spontaneous language sample. *Language, Speech, and Hearing Services in Schools, 10,* 6–13.

Dale, E., O'Rourke, J., & Bamman, H. (1971). Pronunciation and spelling. *Techniques of Teaching Vocabulary,* 164–191.

Dale, E., O'Rourke, J., & Bamman, H. (1971). Pronunciation and Spelling. *Techniques of Teaching Vocabulary,* (pp. 163–194), Field Educational Publications.

Damico, J.S., & Oller, J.W. (1985). *Spotting language problems* (Experimental ed.). San Diego: Los Amigos Research Associates.

Dancer, D.D., Braukmann, C.J., Shumaker, J.B., Kirigin, K.A., Willner, A.G., & Wolf, M.M. (1978). The training and validation of behavior observation and description skills. *Behavior Modification, 2,* 113–134.

Davis, F.B. (1944). Fundamental factors of comprehension in reading. *Psychometrika, 9*(3), 185–197.

Davis, F.B. (1968). Research in comprehension in reading. *Reading Research Quarterly, 3*(4), 499–545.

Davis. F.B. (1971). *Psychometric research on comprehension in reading.* Unpublished doctoral dissertation, Rutgers University, Graduate School of Education.

Dawson, M.M. (1987). Beyond ability grouping: A review of the effectiveness of ability grouping and its alternatives. *School Psychology Review, 16*(3), 348–369.

Day, D. (1983). *Early childhood education: A human ecological approach.* Glenview, IL: Scott, Foresman.

De Hirsch, K., Jansky, J.J., & Langford, W.S. (1966). *Predicting reading failure: A preliminary study.* New York: Harper & Row.

Denmark, T., & Kepner, H.S., Jr. (1980). Basic skills in mathematics: A survey. *Journal for Research in Mathematics Education,* (March), 104–123.

Deno, E. (1978). *Educating children with emotional, learning, and behavior problems.* Minneapolis: University of Minnesota, Leadership Training Institute.

Deno, S.L. (1985). Curriculum-based measurement: The emerging alternative. *Exceptional Children, 52*(3), 219–232.

Deno, S L. (1986). Formative evaluation of individual student programs: A new role for school psychologists. *School Psychology Review, 15*(3), 358–374.

Deno, S.L. (1989). Curriculum-based measurement and special education services: A fundamental and direct relationship. In M. Shinn (Ed.), *Curriculum-based measurement* (School Psychology Practitioner's Series). New York: The Guilford Press.

Deno, S.L., & Fuchs, L.S. (1987). Developing curriculum-based measurement systems for data based special education problem solving. *Focus on Exceptional Children, 19*(8), 1–15.

Deno, S.L., Chiang, B., Tindal, G., & Blackburn, M. (1979). *Experimental analysis of program com-*

ponent: An approach to research in CSCDs. (Research Report No. 12). Minneapolis, MN: University of Minnesota Institute for Research on Learning Disabilities.

Deno, S.L., Fuchs, L.S., & Fuchs, D. (1982). Reliability and validity of curriculum-based informal reading inventories. *Reading Research Quarterly, 18,* 16–26.

Deno, S.L., Marston, D., & Mirkin, P.K. (1982). Valid measurement procedures for continuous evaluation of written expression. *Exceptional Children, 48*(4), 368–371.

Deno, S.L., Marston, D., & Mirkin, P.K. (1984). Curriculum-based measurement: An alternative to traditional screening, referral, and identification. *Journal of Special Education, 18*(2), 109–117.

Deno, S.L., Marston, D., Mirkin, P.K., Lowry, L., Sindelar, P., & Jenkins, J. (1982). *The use of standard tasks to measure achievement in reading, spelling, and written expression: A normative and developmental study* (Research Report 87). Minneapolis, University of Minnesota, Institute for Research on Learning Disabilities.

Deno, S.L., Marston, D., Shinn, M.R., & Tindal, G. (1983). Oral reading fluency: A simple datum for scaling reading disability. *Topics in Learning and Learning Disabilities, 2*(4), 53–59.

Deno, S.L., Marston, D., & Tindal, G. (1985/86). Direct and frequent curriculum-based measurement: An alternative for educational decision making. *Special Services in the Schools, 2*(2/3), 5–27.

Deno, S.L., & Mirkin, P.K. (1977). *Data-based program modification.* Reston, VA: Council for Exceptional Children.

Deno, S.L., Mirkin, P., & Chiang, B. (1982). Identifying valid measures of reading. *Exceptional Children, 49*(1), 36–45.

Deno, S.L., Mirkin, P.K., Chiang, B., & Lowry, L. (1980). *Relationships among simple measures of reading and performance on standardized achievement tests* (Research Report No. 20). Minneapolis: University of Minnesota, Institute of Research on Learning Disabilities.

Deno, S.L., Mirkin, P.K., Lowry, L., & Kuehnle, K. (1980). *Relationships among simple measures of spelling and performance on standardized*

achievement tests (Research Report No. 21). Minneapolis: University of Minnesota, Institute for Research on Learning Disabilities.

Deno, S.L., Marston, D., & Mirkin, P.K. (1980). *Relationships among simple measures of written expression and performance on standardized achievement tests* (Research Report No. 22). Minneapolis: University of Minnesota, Institute for Research on Learning Disabilities.

Deno, S., Mirkin, P.K., & Shinn, M. (1979). *Behavioral perspectives on the assessment of learning disabled children* (Monograph No. 12). Minneapolis: University of Minnesota, Institute for Research on Learning Disabilities.

Deno, S.L., Mirkin, P.K., & Wesson, C. (1984). How to write effective data-based IEPs. *Teaching Exceptional Children, 16,* 99–104.

Deno, S.L., Wesson, C., Skiba, R., Sevcik, B., & King, R. (1984). The effects of technically adequate instructional data on achievement. *Remedial and Special Education, 5*(5), 17–22.

Deverell, A.F. (1971). The learnable features of English orthography. In B.B. Bateman (Ed.), *Learning Disorders* (Vol. 4, pp. 129–160). Seattle: Special Child Publications.

Diana v. State Board of Education, C. A. No. C–70–37 (N.D. Cal., July 1970) (consent decree).

Diederich, P. (1974). *Measuring growth in English.* Urbana, IL: National Council of Teachers of English.

DiStefano, P., & Hagerty, P. (1983). An analysis of high-frequency words found in commercial spelling series and misspelled in students' writing. *Journal of Educational Research, 76*(3), 181–185.

Dobbin, J.E. (1984). *How to take a test: Doing your best.* Princeton, N.J.: Educational Testing Service.

Dodd, C.A., Jones, G.A., & Lamb, C.E. (1975). Diagnosis and remediation of pupil errors: An exploratory study. *School Science and Mathematics, 71,* 488–493.

Dorr-Bremme, D.W. (1984). *Linking testing with instructional decision making: Some models and guidelines from research* (Report No. 209). Los Angeles: University of California—Los Angeles Graduate School, Center for the Study of Evaluation.

Dorr-Bremme, D.W., Burry, J., Catterall, J., Cabello, B., & Daniels, L. (1983). *The costs of testing in Amer-*

ican public schools (Report No. 198). Los Angeles: University of California—Los Angeles Graduate School, Center for the Study of Evaluation.

Drahozal, E.C., & Hanna, G. S. (1978). Reading comprehension subscores: Pretty bottles of ordinary wine. *Journal of Reading, 21*(5), 416–420.

Dubois, P.H. (1966). A test-dominated society: China 1115 B.C.–1905 A.D. In A. Anastasi (Ed.), *Testing problems in perspective*. Washington, DC: American Council on Education.

Dunn, L.M. (1965). *Peabody picture vocabulary test.* Circle Pine, MN: American Guidance Service.

Dunn, L.M., & Dunn, L. (1981). *Manual for the Peabody picture vocabulary test—Revised.* Circle Pines, MN: American Guidance Service.

Durkin, D. (1987). Testing in kindergarten. *The Reading Teacher, 40*(8), 766–770.

Durr, W.K., and others. (1981). *Houghton Mifflin Reading Program.* Boston, MA: Houghton Mifflin.

Easterday, K. (1980). Student error patterns in studying square root. *School Science and Mathematics, 80,* 141–147.

Ebel, R.L. (1972). *Essentials of educational measurement.* Englewood Cliffs, NJ: Prentice-Hall, pp. 492–494.

Ebel, R.L. (1978). The case for minimum competency testing. *Phi Delta Kappan, 59,* 546–549.

Ebel, R.L. (1980). *Practical problems in educational measurement.* Lexington, MA: D.C. Heath.

Ebel, R.L. (1982). Proposed solutions to two problems of test construction. *Journal of Educational Measurement, 19,* 267–278.

Ebel, R.L., & Frisbie, D.A. (1986). *Essentials of educational measurement.* Englewood Cliffs, NJ: Prentice-Hall.

Educational Testing Service. (1979). *CIRCUS manual and technical report.* Menlo Park, CA: Educational Testing Service.

Edwards, D. (1970). *The measurement of personality traits by scales and inventories.* New York: Holt, Rinehart & Winston.

Elliott, S.N., & Piersel, W.C. (1982). Direct assessment of reading skills: An approach which links assessment to intervention. *School Psychology Review, 11,* 267–280.

Emerick, L., & Hatten, J. (1979). *Diagnosis and evaluation in speech pathology* (2nd ed.). Englewood Cliffs, NJ: Prentice-Hall.

Engelhardt, J.M. (1977). Analysis of childrens' computational errors: A qualitative approach. *British Journal of Educational Psychology, 47,* 149–154.

Engelhardt, J.M. (1982). Using computational errors in diagnostic teaching. *Arithmetic Teacher,* (April), 16–19.

Engelmann, S., Granzin, A., & Severson, H. (1979). Diagnosing instruction. *The Journal of Special Education, 13,* 355–365.

Epps, S., & Tindal, G. (in press). The effectiveness of differential programming in serving mildly handicapped students: Placement options and instructional programming. In M.C. Wang, M.C. Reynolds, & H.J. Walberg (Eds.), *Handbook of special education: Research and practice.* London: Oxford Publishers.

Evans, S., Evans, W., & Mercer, C. (1986). *Assessment for instruction.* Boston: Allyn & Bacon.

Evertson, C.M., & Green, J.L. (1984). Observation as inquiry and method. In M.C. Wittrock (Ed.). *Handbook of research on teaching-3rd edition,* (pp. 162–213). New York: Macmillan Publishing Company.

Fairbanks, G. (1937). The relation between eye-movements and voice in the oral reading of good and poor silent readers. *Psychological Monographs, 48*(215), 78–107.

Farr, R.C. (1968). The convergent and discriminant validity of several reading tests. In G.B. Schick & M.M. May (Eds.). *Multidisciplinary aspects of college adult reading. Yearbook of the National Reading Conference, 17,* 181–191.

Farr, R.C., & Carey, R.F. (1986). *Reading: What can be measured?* (2nd Ed.). Newark, DE: International Reading Association.

Farr, R.C., Prescott, G.A., Balow, I.H., & Hogan, T.P. (1978). *Metropolitan achievement tests: Reading instructional battery.* New York: Psychology Corporation.

Farr, R., & Roelke, P. (1971). Measuring subskills of reading: Intercorrelations between standardized reading tests, teachers' ratings, and reading specialists' ratings. *Journal of Educational Measurement, 8*(1), 27–32.

Feigenbaum, L.H. (1958). For a bigger and better alphabet. *H Points, 40,* 34–36.

Fisher, C., & Berliner, D. (1985). *Perspectives on instructional time.* New York: Longman.

Fisher, H.B., & Logemann, J.A. (1971). *Therapist's manual for the Fisher-Logemann test of articulation competence.* Boston: Houghton Mifflin.

Fitzgerald, J.A. (1951). *A basic life spelling vocabulary.* Milwaukee, WI: Bruce Publishing Company.

Fitzsimmons, R.J., & Loomer, B.M. (1982). Excerpts from Spelling: Learning and instruction—research and practice. In W.B. Barbe, A.S. Francis, & L.A. Braun (Eds.) *Spelling: Basic skills for effective communication* (pp. 61–79). Columbus, OH: Zaner-Bloser, Inc.

Fleisher, L.S., Jenkins, J.R., & Pany, D. (1979). Effects on poor readers' comprehension of training in rapid decoding. *Reading Research Quarterly, 15,* 30–48.

Floden, R., Porter, A., Schmidt, W., & Freeman, D. (1980). Don't they all measure the same thing? In E. Baker, & E. Quellnalz (Eds.), *Educational testing and evaluation.* Beverly Hills: Sage.

Flower, L., & Hayes, J.R. (1981). A cognitive process theory of writing. *College Composition and Communication, 32*(4), 365–387.

Flower, L., & Hayes, J.R. (in press). Process-based evaluation of writing: Changing the performance not the product. To appear in Douglas Buttruff (Ed.), *The psychology of composition.* Conway, AK: L & S Books.

Forsyth, R.A., & Ansley, T.N. (1982). The importance of computational skill for answering items in a mathematics problem-solving test: Implications for construct validity. *Educational and Psychological Measurement, 42,* 257–263.

Forsyth, R.A., & Spratt, K.F. (1980). Measuring problem-solving ability with multiple choice items: The effect of item format on selected item and test characteristics. *Journal of Educational Measurement, 17*(1), 31–43.

Frankenburg, W.F., Dodds, J., Fandal, A., Kazuk, E., & Cohrs, M. (1978). *Denver developmental screening test.* Denver: LADOCA Publishing Foundation.

Freedman, S. (1979). How characteristics of student essays influence teachers' evaluations. *Journal of Educational Psychology, 71,* 328–338.

Freeman, D., Kuhs, T., Knappen, L., & Porter, A. (1982). A closer look at standardized tests. *The Arithmetic Teacher, 29,* 50–54.

Freeman, D.J., Kuhs, T.M., Porter, A.C., Floden, R.E., Schmidt, W.H., & Schwille, J.R. (1983). Do textbooks and tests define a national curriculum in elementary school mathematics? *The Elementary School Journal, 83*(5), 501–513.

Freyberg, P.S. (1970). The concurrent validity of two types of spelling tests. *British Journal of Ed. Psychology, 40,* 68–70.

Frumess, S. (1973). *A comparison of management groups involving the use of the standard behavior chart and setting performance aims.* Unpublished doctoral dissertation, University of Houston.

Fry, E. (1957). Developing a word list for remedial reading. *Elementary English, 36,* 455–458.

Fry, E. (1980). The new instant word list. *The Reading Teacher, 34*(3), 284–289.

Fuchs, D. (1989). Using curriculum-based measurement to evaluate pre-referral interventions. In M. Shinn (Ed.), *Curriculum-based measurement* (School Psychology Practitioner's Series). New York: Guilford.

Fuchs, D., Featherstone, N., Garwick, D.R., & Fuchs, L.S. (1981). *The importance of situational factors and task demands to handicapped children's test performance* (Research Report No. 54). Minneapolis: University of Minnesota, Institute for Research on Learning Disabilities.

Fuchs, D., & Fuchs, L.S. (1986). Test procedure bias: A meta-analysis of examiner familiarity effects. *Review of Educational Research, 56,* 243–262.

Fuchs, D., Fuchs, L.S., Power M.H., & Dailey, A.M. (1985). *Bias in the assessment of handicapped children. American Educational Research Journal, 22,* 185–198.

Fuchs, D., Fuchs, L.S., Benowitz, S., & Barringer, K. (1987). Norm-referenced tests: Are they valid for use with handicapped students? *Exceptional Children, 54,* 263–271.

Fuchs, D., Fuchs, L.S., Power, M.H., & Dailey, A.M. (1985). Bias in the assessment of handicapped children. *American Educational Research Journal, 22,* 185–198.

Fuchs, L.S. (1986). Monitoring progress of mildly handicapped pupils: Review of current practice and research. *Remedial and Special Education, 7,* 5–12.

Fuchs, L.S., Deno, S.L., & Mirkin, P.K. (1984). The effects of frequent curriculum-based measurement and evaluation on pedagogy, student achievement, and student awareness of learning. *American Educational Research Journal, 21*(2), 449–460.

Fuchs, L.S., & Fuchs, D. (1984). Criterion-referenced assessment without measurement: How accurate for special education? *Remedial and Special Education, 5*(4), 29–32.

Fuchs, L.S., & Fuchs, D. (1986a). Curriculum-based assessment of progress toward long- and short-term goals. *Journal of Special Education, 20,* 69–82.

Fuchs, L.S., & Fuchs, D. (1986b). Effects of systematic formative evaluation: A meta-analysis. *Exceptional Children, 53,* 199–208.

Fuchs, L.S., & Fuchs, D. (1986c). The relation between methods of graphing student performance data and achievement: A meta-analysis. *Journal of Special Education Technology, 8*(3), 5–13.

Fuchs, L.S., Fuchs, D., & Deno, S.L. (1982). Reliability and validity of curriculum-based informal reading inventories. *Reading Research Quarterly, 18*(1), 6–26.

Fuchs, L.S., Fuchs, D., & Deno, S.L. (1985). The importance of goal ambitiousness and goal mastery to student achievement. *Exceptional Children, 52,* 63–71.

Fuchs, L.S., Fuchs, D., & Hamlett, C. (1989). Effects of instrumental use of curriculum-based measurement to enhance instructional programs. *Remedial and Special Education, 10*(2), 43–52.

Fuchs, L.S., Fuchs, D., & Maxwell, L. (1988). The validity of informal reading comprehension measures. *Remedial and Special Education, 9*(2), 20–28.

Fuchs, L.S., Fuchs, D., & Tindal, G. (1986). Effects of mastery learning procedures on student achievement. *Journal of Educational Research, 79*(5), 286–291.

Fuchs, L.S., Tindal, G., & Deno, S. (1981). *Effects of varying item domain and sample duration on technical characteristics of daily measure in reading* (Research Report No. 48). Minneapolis: University of Minnesota, Institute for Research on Learning Disabilities.

Fuchs, L.S., Tindal, G., & Fuchs, D. (1986). Effects of mastery learning procedures on student achievement. *Journal of Educational Research, 79*(5), 286–291.

Galagan, J. (1985). Psychoeducational testing: Turn out the lights, the party's over. *Exceptional Children, 52*(3), 288–298.

Gallagher, T.M., & Darnton, B.A. (1978). Conversational aspects of the speech of language-disordered children: Revision behaviors. *Journal of Speech and Hearing Research, 21,* 118–135.

Gallagher, T.M., & Prutting, C.A. (1983). *Pragmatic assessment and intervention issues in language.* San Diego: College-Hill Press.

Gallerani, D., O'Regan, M., & Reinherz, H. (1982). Prekindergarten screening: How well does it predict readiness for first grade? *Psychology in the Schools, 19*(2), 175–182.

Ganschow, L. (1981). Discovering children's learning strategies for spelling through error patterns analysis. *The Reading Teacher, 34*(6), 676–680.

Garvy, H. (1986). *How to fix your bicycle–6th edition.* Santa Cruz, CA: Shire Press.

Gast, D.L., & Tawney, J.W. (1984). The visual analysis of graphic data. In J.W. Tawney & D.L. Gast, *Single-subject research in special education* (pp. 142–186). Columbus, OH: Merrill.

Gates, A.I., & McKillop, A.S. (1962). *Gates-McKillop reading diagnostic tests.* New York: Teachers College Press.

Gerber, M., & Semmel, M. (1984). Teachers as imperfect tests: Reconceptualizing the referral process. *Educational Psychologist, 19*(3), 137–148.

Germann, G., & Tindal, G. (1985). Applications of direct and repeated measurement using curriculum-based assessment. *Exceptional Children, 51*(2), 110–121.

Gibson, E., & Levin, H. (1975). *The psychology of reading.* Cambridge: The MIT Press.

Gickling, E.E., & Thompson, V.P. (1985). A personal view of curriculum-based assessment. *Exceptional Children, 52,* 205–218.

Glaser, R. (1963). Instructional technology and the measurement of learning outcomes: Some questions. *American Psychologist, 18,* 519–521.

Glaser, R., & Nitko, A.J. (1971). Measurement in learning and instruction. In R.L. Thorndike (Ed.),

Educational measurement (pp. 625–670). Washington, DC: American Council on Education.

Glass, G.V. (1978). Standards and criteria. *Journal of Educational Measurement, 15*(4), 237–261.

Glennon, V.J., & Wilson, J.W. (1972). Diagnostic-prescriptive teaching. In National Council of Teachers of Mathematics, *The slow learner in mathematics: The 35th yearbook*. Reston, VA: NCTM.

Godshalk, F.I., Swineford, F., & Coffman, W.E. (1966). *The measurement of writing ability*. New York: College Entrance Examination Board.

Goldman, R., & Fristoe, M. (1986). *Examiner's manual for the Goldman-Fristoe test of articulation*. Circle Pines, MN: American Guidance Service.

Goldman, R., Fristoe, M., & Woodcock, R.W. (1970). *Test of auditory discrimination*. Circle Pines, MN: American Guidance Service.

Goldstein, H., Arkell, C., Ashcroft, S.C., Hurley, O.L., & Lilly, S.M. (1975). Schools. In N. Hobbs (Ed.), *Issues in the classification of children*. San Francisco: Jossey-Bass.

Golinkoff, R.M. (1975). A comparison of reading comprehension processes in good and poor comprehenders. *Reading Research Quarterly, 4*, 623–659.

Golinkoff, R.M., & Rosinski, R.R. (1976). Decoding, semantic processing, and reading comprehension skill. *Child Development, 47*, 252–258.

Good III, R.H., & Salvia J. (1988). Curriculum bias in published, norm-referenced reading tests: Demonstrable effects. *School Psychology Review, 17*(1), 51–60.

Good III, R.H. (1989). Implications of K-ABC simultaneous/sequential processing. In G. Tindal, K. Essick, C. Skeen, N. George, & M. George (Eds.). *The Oregon Conference '89 monograph*. Eugene, OR: University of Oregon Publications.

Goodman, Y., & Burke, C.L. (1971). *Reading miscue inventory-manual*. New York: Macmillan.

Goodstein, H.A. (1982). *The impact of implementing a more rigorous standard for determining the reliability of proficiency tests*. Paper presented at the Annual Meeting of the American Educational Research Association. New York, New York.

Gordon, R. (1969). *Interviewing: Strategy, techniques, and tactics*. Homewood, IL: The Dorsey Press.

Goslin, D.A. (1969). *Guidelines for the collection, maintenance and dissemination of pupil records*. Troy, NY: Russell Sage Foundation.

Graden, J.L., Casey, A., & Christenson, S. (1985). Implementing a prereferral intervention system: Part I. The model. *Exceptional Children, 51*, 377–384.

Graden, J.L., Zins, J.E., Curtis, M.J., & Cobb, C.T. (1988). The need for alternatives in educational services. In J.L. Graden, J.E. Zins, & M.J. Curtis (Eds.), *Alternative educational delivery systems: Enhancing instructional options for all students* (pp. 3–16). Washington, D.C.: National Association of School Psychologists.

Graham, S. (1985). Evaluating spelling programs and techniques. *Teaching Exceptional Children*, (Summer), 299–303.

Graham, S., & Miller, L. (1979). Spelling research and practice: A unified approach. *Focus on Exceptional Children, 12*(2), 1–16.

Gredler, G. (1984). A look at some important factors for assessing readiness in school. *Journal of Learning Disabilities, 11*, 284–290.

Greene, H.A., & Petty, W.T. (1963). *Developing skills in the elementary schools (2nd edition)*. Boston: Allyn & Bacon.

Greenwood, C.R., Delquadri, J., & Hall, R.V. (1978). *Code for instructional structure and student academic response: CISSAR*. Kansas City, KS: University of Kansas, Juniper Gardens Children's Project, Bureau of Child Research.

Greenwood, C.R., Delquadri, J.C., & Hall, R.V. (1984). Opportunity to respond and student academic performance. In W.L. Heward, T.E. Heron, J. Trap Porter, & D.S. Hill (Eds.), *Focus on behavior analysis in education* (pp. 58–88). Columbus, OH: Charles Merrill.

Grobe, C. (1981). Syntactic maturity, mechanics, and vocabulary as predictors of quality ratings. *Research in the Teaching of English, 15*(1), 75–86.

Groff, P. (1968). Research on spelling and phonetics. *Education, 89*, 132–135.

Groff, P. (1979). Phonics for spelling? *Elementary School Journal, 79*(5), 269–275.

Groff, P. (1982). Word frequency and spelling difficulty. *Elementary School Journal 83*(2), 125–130.

Gronlund, N. (1968). *Constructing achievement tests.* Englewood Cliffs, NJ: Prentice-Hall.

Gronlund, N.E. (1985). *Measurement and evaluation in teaching.* New York: Macmillan.

Gronlund, N.E. (1988). *How to construct achievement tests.* Englewood Cliffs, NJ: Prentice-Hall.

Gruenewald, L.J., & Pollak, S.A. (1984). *Language interaction in teaching and learning.* Baltimore: University Park Press.

Guiler, W.S. (1944). Primary grade words frequently misspelled by higher-grade pupils. *The Elementary School Journal, 44,* 295–300.

Guiler, W.S. (1946). Difficulties in decimals encountered in ninth-grade pupils. *Elementary School Journal, 46,* 384–393.

Guilford, J.P. (1965). *Fundamental statistics in psychology and education.* New York: McGraw-Hill.

Guilford, J.P. (1967). *The nature of human intelligence.* New York: McGraw-Hill.

Guthrie, J.T. (1973). Reading comprehension and syntactic responses in good and poor readers. *Journal of Educational Psychology, 65,* 294–299.

Guthrie, J., Seifert, M., Burnham, N., & Caplan, R. (1974). The maze technique to assess monitor reading comprehension. *The Reading Teacher, 28*(2), 161–168.

Hagan, R.D. (1982). Factors influencing arithmetic performance on the Tennessee state-mandated eighth-grade basic skills test. *School Science and Mathematics, 82*(6), 490–505.

Haines, J., Ames, L.B., & Gillespie, C. (1980). *Gesell preschool test.* Flemington, NJ: Programs for Education.

Hall, B.W. (1985). Survey of the technical characteristics of published achievement tests. *Educational Measurement: Issues and Practices,* 6–14.

Hall, T., & Tindal, G. (1989). Using curriculum-based measures to group students in reading. In G. Tindal, K. Essick, C. Skeen, N. George, & M. George (Eds.), *The Oregon Conference '89: Monograph.* Eugene, OR: University of Oregon, College of Education.

Hambelton, R.K. (1978). On the use of cut-off scores with criterion-referenced tests in instructional settings. *Journal of Educational Measurement, 15*(4), 277–290.

Hambleton, R.K. (1980). Test score validity and standard-setting methods. In R.A. Berk (Ed.), *Criterion-referenced measurement: The state of the art* (pp. 80–123). Baltimore: Johns Hopkins University Press.

Hambleton, R.K. (1980). *Review methods for criterion-referenced test items.* Paper presented at annual meeting of American Educational Research Association, Boston.

Hambleton, R.K. (1984). Validating the test scores. In R.A. Berk (Ed.), *A guide to criterion-referenced test construction.* Baltimore, MD: Johns Hopkins University Press.

Hambleton, R.K., & Eignor, D.R. (1978). *Competency test development, validation, and standard-setting.* Paper presented at the Minimum Competency Testing Conference of the American Education Research Association. Washington, DC.

Hambleton, R.K., Powell, S., & Eignor, D.R. (1979). Issues and methods for standard setting. In R.K. Hambleton, & D.R. Eignor, *A practitioner's guide to criterion-referenced test development, validation, and test score usage* (Report No. 70). Amherst: University of Massachusetts, School of Education, Laboratory of Psychometric and Evaluative Research.

Hammill, D.D., Brown, V.L., Larsen, S.C., & Wiederholt, J.L. (1980). *Test of adolescent language.* Austin, TX: Pro-Ed.

Hammill, D., & Larsen, S. (1983). *Test of written language.* Austin, TX: Pro-Ed.

Hammill, D.D., & Newcomer, P.L. (1982). *Test of language development—Intermediate.* Austin, TX: Pro-Ed.

Hanna, P.R., Hanna, J.S., Hodges, R.E., & Rudorf, E.H. (1966). *Phonemegrapheme correspondence as cues to spelling improvement.* Washington, D.C.: Department of Health, Education, and Welfare.

Hanna, P.R., Hodges, R.E., & Hanna, J.S. (1971). *Spelling: Structure and strategies.* Boston: Houghton Mifflin.

Hansen, C.L., & Lovitt, T.C. (1976). The relationship between question type and mode of reading on the ability to comprehend. *The Journal of Special Education, 10,* 53–60.

Hardy, R.A. (1984). Measuring instructional validity: A report of an instructional validity study for the Alabama high school graduation examination.

Journal of Educational Measurement, 21(3), 291–301.

Haring, N., & Krug, D. (1975). Placement in regular programs: Procedures and results. *Exceptional Children, 41*(6), 413–417.

Haring, N., & Lovitt, T. (1969). *The application of functional analysis of behavior by teachers in a natural school setting.* Seattle: University of Washington, Experimental Education Unit.

Harrington, R.G., & Jennings, V. (1986). A comparison of three short forms of the McCarthy scales of children's abilities. *Contemporary Educational Psychology, 11,* 109–116.

Harris, A.J., & Jacobson, M.D. (1972). *Basic elementary reading vocabularies.* New York: The Macmillan Company.

Hart, B. (1981). Pragmatics: How language is used. *Analysis and Intervention in Developmental Disabilities, 1,* 299–313.

Hegarty, S., & Lucas, D. (1978). *Able to learn? The pursuit of culture-fair assessment.* Windsor, Berkshire, UK: NFER.

Heironymus, A.N., Lindquist, E.F., & Hoover, H.D. (1978). *Iowa tests of basic skills.* Lombard, IL: Riverside.

Heller, K.A., Holtzman, W.A., & Messick, S. (1982). *Placing children in special education: A strategy for equity.* Washington, D.C.: National Academy Press.

Hembree, R. (1987). Effects of noncontent variables on mathematics test performance. *Journal for Research in Mathematics Education, 18*(3), 197–214.

Herndon, E. (1980). *NIE's study of minimum competency testing: A process for the clarification of issues.* Paper presented at the Annual Conference on Large-Scale Assessment, National Assessment of Educational Progress.

Hildreth, G. (1955). *Teaching spelling.* New York: Henry Holt.

Hillerich, R.L. (1977). Let's teach spelling—Not phonetic misspelling. *Language Arts, 54*(3), 301–307.

Hillerich, R. (1978). *A writing vocabulary of elementary children.* Springfield, IL: Charles C. Thomas.

Hillerich, R.L. (1982). Spelling: What can be diagnosed? *Elementary School Journal, 83*(2), 138–148.

Hirsch, E.D. (1977). *The philosophy of composition.* Chicago: University of Chicago Press.

Hirstein, J.J. (1981). The second national assessment in mathematics: Area and volume. *Mathematics Teacher,* (December), 704–708.

Hively, W., Maxwell, G., Rabehl, G., Sension, D., & Lundin, S. (1973). *Domain-referenced curriculum evaluation: A technical handbook and a case study from the MINNEMAST project.* Los Angeles: University of California—Los Angeles, Center for the Study of Evaluation.

Hobbs, N. (1975a). *The futures of children.* San Francisco: Jossey-Bass.

Hobbs, N. (1975b). *Issues in the classification of children (Vols 1 and 2).* San Francisco: Jossey-Bass.

Hogan, T.P., & Mishler, C. (1980). Relationships between essay tests and objective tests of language skills for elementary school students. *Journal of Educational Measurement, 17*(3), 219–227.

Hopkins, C., & Antes, R. (1978). *Classroom measurement and evaluation.* Itasca, IL: F.E. Peacock.

Horn, E. (1926). *A basic vocabulary of 10,000 words most commonly used in writing.* College of Education, University of Iowa, Iowa City, IA.

Horn, E. (1944). Research in spelling. *The Elementary English Review, 21.*

Horn, T. (1947). The effect of the corrected test on learning to spell. *Elementary School Journal, 47,* 277–285.

Horn, T. (1969). Spelling. In R.L. Ebel (Ed.), *Encyclopedia of educational research* (4th ed.), (pp. 1282–1299) New York: MacMillan.

Howell, K.W. (1986). Direct assessment of academic performance. *School Psychology Review, 15*(3), 324–335.

Howell, K.W., & Kaplan, J.S. (1980). *Diagnosing basic skills: A handbook for deciding what to teach.* Columbus, OH: Merrill.

Howell, K., Kaplan, J., & Serapiglia, T. (1980). *Diagnosing basic skills: A handbook for deciding what to teach.* Columbus, OH: Bell & Howell.

Howell, K.W., Kaplan, J.S., & O'Connell, C.Y. (1979). *Evaluating exceptional children: A task analysis approach.* Columbus, OH: Merrill.

Howell, K.W., Kaplan, J.S., & Serapiglia, T. (1980). Spelling: Diagnosing basic skills (pp. 322–337). Columbus, OH: Charles Merrill.

Howell, K.W., & Morehead, M.K. (1987). *Curriculum-based evaluation for special and remedial education*. Columbus, OH: Merrill.

Hunt, K.L. (1965). *Grammatical structures written at three grade levels*. (NCTE Research Report No. 3). Urbana, IL: National Council for Teachers of English.

Hunt, K. (1977). Early blooming and late blooming syntactic structures. In C. Cooper and L. Odell (Eds.), *Evaluating writing* (pp. 91–104). Washington, DC: National Council of Teachers of English.

Huntley, R.M., Schmeiser, C.B., & Stiggins, R.J. (1979). *The assessment of rhetorical proficiency: The role of objective tests and writing samples*. Paper presented at the annual meeting of the National Council on Measurement in Education.

Hutchinson, J.M. (1983). Diagnosis of fluency disorders. In I.J. Meitus, & B. Weinberg (Eds.), *Diagnosis in speech-language pathology* (pp. 183–217). Baltimore: University Park Press.

Irwin, P., & Mitchell, J. (1983). A procedure for assessing the richness of retellings. *Journal of Reading*, (February), 391–396.

Isaacson, S. (1985). Assessing written language skills. In C.S. Simon (Ed.), *Communication skills and classroom success: Assessment methodologies for language-learning disabled students* (pp. 403–424). San Diego: College-Hill Press.

Isano, R. (1987). *Validating an informal measure on reading comprehension*. Unpublished master's thesis, Eugene, OR: University of Oregon.

Jaeger, R.M. (1976). *Measurement consequences of selected standard-setting models*. Paper presented at the annual meeting of the National Council on Measurement in Education, San Francisco.

Jaeger, R.M. (1978). *A proposal for setting a standard on the North Carolina High School Competency Test*. Paper presented at the spring meeting of the North Carolina Association for Research in Education, Chapel Hill.

Jenkins, J.R., Deno, S.L., & Mirkin, P.K. (1979). Measuring pupil progress toward the least restrictive environment. *Learning Disability Quarterly, 2*, 81–92.

Jenkins. J., Mayall, W., Peschka, C., & Townsend, V. (1974). Using direct and daily measures to increase learning. *Journal of Learning Disabilities, 7*(9), 605–608.

Jenkins, J.R., & Pany, D. (1978a). Curriculum biases in reading achievement tests. *Journal of Reading Behavior, 10*(4), 345–357.

Jenkins, J., & Pany, D. (1978b). Standardized achievement tests: How useful for special education? *Exceptional Children, 44*, 448–453.

Jerman, M., & Mirman, S. (1974). Linguistic and computational variables in problem solving in elementary mathematics. *Educational Studies in Mathematics, 5*, 317–362.

Jerman, M., & Rees, R. (1972). Predicting the relative difficulty of verbal arithmetic problems. *Educational Studies in Mathematics, 4*, 306–323.

Johns, J., Garton, S., Schoenfelder, P., & Skriba, P. (1977). *Assessing reading behavior: Informal reading inventories: An annotated bibliography*. Newark, DE: International Reading Association.

Johns, J.L., & Lunn, M.K. (1983). The informal reading inventory: 1910–1980. *Reading World*, (October), 8–17.

Johnson, D.D. (1971). The Dolch list reexamined. *The Reading Teacher, 24*(5), 449–457.

Johnson, L.W. (1950). One hundred words most often misspelled by children in the elementary grades. *The Journal of Educational Research, 44*, 154–155.

Johnson, M., Kress, R., & Pikulski, J. (1987). *Informal reading inventories*. 2nd edition. Newark, DE: International Reading Association.

Jones, M.B., & Pikulski, E.C. (1974). Cloze for the classroom. *Journal of Reading, 17*, 432–438.

Jorgensen, C., Barrett, M., Huisingh, R., & Zachman, L. (1981). *Examiner's manual for the word test*. Chicago, IL: Lingui-Systems.

Kalmbach, J.R. (1986a). Evaluating informal methods for the assessment of retellings. *Journal of Reading*, (November), 119–127.

Kalmbach, J.R. (1986b). Getting at the point of retellings. *Journal of Reading*, (January), 326–333.

Kamii, C. (1971). Evaluation of learning in preschool education: Socio-emotional, perceptual-motor, cognitive development. In B.S. Bloom, J.T. Hastings, & G.F. Madaus (Eds.), *Handbook on formative and summative evaluation of student learning* (pp. 281–344). New York: McGraw-Hill.

Kamii, C., & Elliott, D.L. (1971). Evaluation of evaluations. *Educational Leadership, 28,* 827–831.

Karlsen, B., Madden, R., & Gardner, E.F. (1976). *Stanford diagnostic reading test.* New York: Harcourt Brace Jovanovich.

Katz, L., & Wicklund, D.A. (1971). Word scanning rate for good and poor readers. *Journal of Educational Psychology, 62,* 138–140.

Kaufman, A.L., & Kaufman, N.L. (1983). *Kaufman assessment battery for children.* Circle Pines, MN: American Guidance Service.

Kaufmann, J.M. (1989). *Characteristics of behavior disorders of children and youth.* (4th Ed.). Columbus, OH: Merrill.

Kelley, J.L., & Richert, D. (1970). *Elementary mathematics for teachers.* San Francisco: Holden-Day.

Kerr, M.M., & Nelson, C.M. (1989). *Strategies for managing behavior problems in the classroom.* 2nd ed. Columbus, OH: Merrill.

Kilian, L., Cahill, E., Ryan, C., Sutherland, D., & Taccetta, D. (1980). Errors that are common in multiplication. *The Arithmetic Teacher, 27,* 22–25.

Kirklan, M.C. (1987). The effects of tests on students and schools. *Review of Educational Research, 41*(4), 303–350.

Klein, M. (1981). *Logical error analysis and construction of tests to diagnose students "bugs" in addition and subtraction of fractions* (CERL-RR-81-6). Urbana, IL: University of Illinois, Computer-Based Education Research Lab.

Kligman, D.S., Cronnell, B.A., & Verna, G.B. (1972). Black English pronunciation and spelling performance. *Elementary English, 49*(8), 1247–1253.

Knifong, J.D. (1980). Computational requirements of standardized word problem tests. *Journal for Research in Mathematics Education, 11*(1), 3–9.

Knifong, J.D., & Holtan, B.D. (1976). An analysis of children's written solutions to word problems. *Journal for Research in Mathematics Education, 7*(2), 106–112.

Knifong, J.D., & Holtan, B.D. (1977). A search for reading difficulties among erred word problems. *Journal for Research in Mathematics Education, 8,* 227–231.

Krauss, J. (1989). *An investigation of criterion and construct validity of a reading comprehension measure.* Unpublished Masters thesis, University of Oregon, Eugene, OR.

Kucera, H., & Francis, W.N. (1967). *Computational analysis of present-day American English.* Providence: Brown University Press.

Kunzelmann, H.P., & Koenig, C.H. (1981). *Manual for REFER & learning screening.* Columbus, OH: Merrill.

Kurlinski, E. (1986). *Teachers' perceptions of issues in the instruction of low achieving students.* Unpublished Master's thesis. Eugene, OR: University of Oregon.

LaBerge, D., & Samuels, S.J. (1974). Toward a theory of automatic information processing in reading. *Cognitive Psychology, 6,* 293–323.

Langer, J.A. (1982). Facilitating text processing: The elaboration of prior knowledge. In J.A. Langer, & M.T. Smith-Burke (Eds.), *Reader meets author: Bridging the gap* (pp. 149–162). Newark, DE: International Reading Association.

Larry P. v Riles, 343 F. Supp. 1306 (N.D.Cal. 1972) (preliminary injunction), aff'd 502 F. 2d 963 (9th cir. 1974); 495. Supp. 926 (N.D. Cal. 1979) (decision on merits) aff'd (9th cir. no. 80–427, Jan. 23, 1984). Order modifying judgment, C–71–2270 RFP, September 25, 1986.

Larsen, S., & Hammill, L. (1986). *Test of written spelling-2.* Austin, TX: Pro-Ed.

Lazar-Morrison, C., Polin, L., Moy, R., & Burry, J. (1980). *A review of the literature on test use.* (Center for the Study of Evaluation Report No. 144). Los Angeles: University of California Center for the Study of Evaluation.

Lee, L., & Canter, S. (1971). Developmental sentence scoring: A clinical procedure for estimating syntactic development in children's spontaneous speech. *Journal of Speech and Hearing Disorders, 36,* 315–340.

Leinhardt, G. (1983). Overlap: Testing whether it is taught. In G.F. Madaus (Ed.). *The courts, validity, and minimum competency testing,* (pp. 153–170). Boston: Kluwer-Nijhoff Publishing, Inc.

Leinhardt, G., & Seewald, A. (1981). Overlap: What's tested, what's taught? *Educational Measurement, 18,* 85–96.

Lerner, J.W. (1985). *Learning disabilities: Theories, diagnosis, teaching strategies (4th edition).* Boston: Houghton-Mifflin.

Levin, G.R., Henderson, B., Levin, A.M., & Hoffer, G.L. (1975). Measuring knowledge of basic concepts by disadvantaged preschoolers. *Psychology in the Schools, 12*(2), 132–139.

Lewis, & Brooks-Gunn (1982). Developmental models and assessment issues. In N.J. Anastasiow, W.K. Frankenburg, & A.W. Fandal (Eds.), *Identifying the developmentally delayed child* (pp. 32–34). Baltimore: University Park Press.

Liberty, K.A. (1975). *Data decision rules.* Unpublished doctoral dissertation, University of Washington, Child Development and Mental Retardation Center, Experimental Education Unit.

Lien, A.J. (1980). *Measurement and evaluation of learning* (4th Ed.). Dubuque, IA: Wm. C. Brown.

Lilly, M.S. (1970). Special education: A tempest in a teapot. *Exceptional Children, 37,* 43–49.

Lilly, M.S. (1979). *Children with exceptional needs: A survey of special education.* New York: Holt, Rinehart & Winston.

Lindeman, R.H., & Merenda, P.F. (1979). *Educational Measurement* (2nd ed.). Glenview, IL: Scott, Foresman.

Linder, T.W. (1983). *Early childhood special education: Program development and administration.* Baltimore: Paul Brookes.

Lindquist, M., Carpenter, T., Silver, E., & Mathews, W. (1983). The third national mathematical assessment: Results and implications for elementary and middle school. *Arithmetic Teacher, 31*(4), 14–20.

Lindsley, O. (1964). Direct measurement and prosthesis of retarded behavior. *Journal of Education, 147,* 62.

Lindsley, O.R. (1971). Precision teaching in perspective: An interview with Ogden R. Lindsley. *Teaching Exceptional Children, 3*(3), 114–119.

Linn, R.L. (1983). Testing and instruction: Links and distinctions. *Journal of Educational Measurement, 20,* 179–189.

Linville, W. (1969). *The effects of syntax and vocabulary upon the difficulty of verbal arithmetic problems with fourth grade students.* Unpublished doctoral dissertation, Indiana University.

Livingston, S.A. (1980). Comments on criterion-referenced testing. *Applied Psychological Measurement, 4*(4), 575–581.

Livingston, S.A., & Zieky, M.J. (1982). *Passing scores: A manual for setting standards of performance on educational and occupational tests.* Princeton, NJ: Educational Testing Service.

Lloyd-Jones, R. (1977). Primary trait scoring, In C.R. Cooper, & L. Odell (Eds.), *Evaluating writing* (pp. 33–66). Princeton, NJ: National Council of Teachers of English.

Loban, W. (1976). *Language development: Kindergarten through grade twelve* (No. 18). Urbana, IL: National Council of Teachers of English.

Longhurst, T.M., & File, J.J. (1977). A comparison of developmental sentence scores from Head Start children collected in four conditions. *Language, Speech, and Hearing Services in Schools, 8,* 54–64.

Lovitt, T. (1967). Assessment of children with learning disabilities. *Exceptional Children, 34,* 233–239.

Lovitt, T. (1976). Thomas C. Lovitt. In J.M. Kauffman, & D.P. Hallahan (Eds.), *Teaching children with learning disabilities: Personal perspectives.* Columbus, OH: Merrill.

Lovitt, T., & Hansen, C. (1976). The use of contingent skipping and drilling to improve oral reading and comprehension. *Journal of Learning Disabilities, 9*(8), 481–487.

Lund, N., & Duchan, J. (1988). *Assessing children's language in naturalistic contexts.* Englewood Cliffs, NJ: Prentice-Hall.

Lyman, H.B. (1986). *Test scores and what they mean-4th edition.* Englewood Cliffs: Prentice-Hall.

Lyons, K. (1984). Criterion-referenced reading comprehension tests: New forms with old ghosts. *Journal of Reading, 27,* 293–298.

Madaus, G., Airasian, P., Hambleton, R., Consalvo, R., & Orlandi, L. (1982). Development and application of criteria for screening commercial, standardized tests. *Educational Evaluation and Policy Analysis, 4*(3), 401–415.

Madden, R., Gardner, E.F., & Collins, C.S. (1982). *Stanford early school achievement test.* San Antonio, TX: The Psychological Corporation.

Madden, R., Gardner, E.R., Rudman, H.C., Karlsen, B., & Merwin, J.C. (1973). *Stanford achievement test.* New York: Harcourt Brace Jovanovich.

Mandler, J. (1984). *Stories, scripts, and scenes: Aspects of schema theory.* Hillsdale, NJ: Lawrence Erlbaum Associates.

Mandler, J.M., & Johnson, N.S. (1977). Remembrance of things parsed: Story structure and recall. *Cognitive Psychology, 9,* 111–157.

Mangieri, J., & Baldwin, R. (1979). Meaning as a factor in spelling difficulty. *Journal of Educational Research, 72*(5), 285–287.

Marino, J.L. (1981). Cloze passages: Guidelines for selection. *Journal of Reading, 24*(6), 479–483.

Marshall, N. (1983). Using story grammar to assess reading comprehension. *Reading Teacher, 36*(7), 616–620.

Marston, D. (1982). *The technical adequacy of direct, repeated measurement of academic skills in low achieving elementary students.* Unpublished doctoral dissertation, University of Minnesota.

Marston, D. (1987a). Does categorical teacher certification benefit the mildly handicapped child? *Exceptional Children, 53*(5), 423–431.

Marston, D. (1987b). The effectiveness of special education. In Minneapolis Public Schools, *Monographs: Curriculum-based measurement training institute* (November).

Marston, D. (1988). Measuring academic progress on IEPs: A comparison of graphing approaches. *Exceptional Children, 55*(1), 38–44.

Marston, D. (1988). The effectiveness of special education: A time series analysis of reading performance in regular and special education. *The Journal of Special Education, 21,* 13–26.

Marston, D. (1989). A curriculum based measurement approach to assessing academic performance: What is it and why do it? In M. Shinn (Ed.), *Curriculum-based measurement: Assessing special children.* New York: Guilford Publications.

Marston, D., & Deno, S.L. (1981). *The reliability of simple, direct measures of written expression* (Research Report No. 50). Minneapolis: University of Minnesota, Institute for Research on Learning Disabilities.

Marston, D., & Deno, S.L. (1982a). *Implementation of direct and repeated measurement in the school setting* (Research Report No. 106). Minneapolis: University of Minnesota, Institute for Research on Learning Disabilities.

Marston, D., & Deno, S.L. (1982b). *Measuring academic progress of students with learning difficulties: A comparison of the semi-logarithmic chart and equal interval graph paper* (Research Report No. 101). Minneapolis: University of Minnesota, Institute for Research on Learning Disabilities.

Marston, D., Fuchs, L., & Deno, S.L. (1985). Measuring pupil progress: A comparison of standardized achievement tests and curriculum-based measures. *Diagnostique, 11,* 77–90.

Marston, D., & Magnusson, D. (1985). Implementing curriculum-based measurement in special and regular education settings. *Exceptional Children, 52,* 266–276.

Marston, D., & Magnusson, D. (1988). Curriculum-based measurement: District level implementation. In J.Z.J. Graden, & M. Curtis (Eds.), *Alternative educational delivery systems: Enhancing instructional options for all students.* Washington, DC: National Association of School Psychologists.

Marston, D., Mirkin, P., & Deno, S. (1984). Curriculum-based measurement: An alternative to traditional screening, referral, and identification of learning disabled students. *Journal of Special Education, 18,* 109–118.

Marston, D., Tindal, G., & Deno, S. (1984). Eligibility for learning disability services: A direct and repeated measurement approach. *Exceptional Children, 50*(6), 554–555.

Martin, C.A. (1989). Language and learning. In D.D. Smith (Ed.), *Teaching students with learning and behavior problems.* New York: Prentice Hall.

Martin, M.A. (1980). *A comparison of variations in data utilization procedures on the reading performance of mildly handicapped students.* Unpublished doctoral dissertation, University of Washington.

Mathews, W., Carpenter, T., Lindquist, M., & Silver, E. (1984). The third national assessment: Minorities and mathematics. *Journal for Research in Mathematics Education, 15*(2), 165–171.

McColly, W. (1970). What does educational research say about the judging of writing ability? *Journal of Educational Research, 64,* 147–156.

McDade, H.L., Simpson, M.A., & Lamb, D.E. (1982). The use of elicited imitation as a measure of expressive grammar: A question of validity. *Journal of Speech and Hearing Disorders, 47,* 19–24.

McKenna, M.C., & Robinson, R.D. (1980). *An introduction to the cloze procedure: An annotated bibliography.* Newark, DE: International Reading Association.

McLean, J., & Snyder-McLean, L.K. (1984). Recent developments in pragmatics. In D.J. Muller (Eds.), *Remediating children's language* (pp. 55–82). San Diego: College-Hill Press.

McLoughlin, J.A., & Lewis, R.B. (1990). *Assessing special students* (3rd ed.). Columbus, OH: Merrill.

Medley, D.M., Coker, H., & Soar, R.S. (1984). *Measurement-based evaluation of teacher performance: An empirical approach.* New York: Longman.

Mehrens, W.A. (1981). *Setting standards for minimum competency tests.* Revision of a speech presented at the Michigan School Testing Conference. Ann Arbor, Michigan.

Mehrens, W.A., & Phillips, S.E. (1986). Detecting impacts of curricular differences in achievement test data. *Journal of Educational Measurement, 23*(3), 185–196.

Meisels, S.J. (1985). *Developmental screening in early childhood: A guide.* Washington, DC: The National Association for the Education of Young Children.

Meisels, S.J. (1989). High-stakes testing. *Educational Leadership, 46*(7), 16–22.

Meisels, S.J., & Anastasiow, N.J. (1982). The risks of predictions: Relationships among etiology, handicapping conditions, and developmental outcomes. In S.G. Moore, & C.R. Cooper (Eds.), *The young child: Reviews of research, 3* (pp. 225–232). Washington, DC: National Association for the Education of Young Children.

Meitus, I.J., & Weinberg, B. (1983). *Diagnosis in speech-language pathology.* Baltimore: University Park Press.

Miller, D.M. (1972). *Interpreting test scores.* New York: John Wiley & Sons.

Miller, H.G., & Williams, R.G. (1973). Constructing higher level multiple choice questions covering factual content. *Educational Technology, 13*(5), 39–42.

Miller, H.G., Williams, R.G., & Haladyna, T.M. (1978). *Beyond facts: Objective ways to measure thinking.* Englewood Cliffs, NJ: Educational Technology.

Miller, J.F. (1981). *Assessing language production in children.* Baltimore: University Park Press.

Millman, J. (1974). Criterion-referenced measurement. In W.J. Popham (Ed.), *Evaluation in Education:* Current applications (pp. 311–347). Berkeley: McCutchan.

Millman, J. (1979). Reliability and validity of criterion-referenced test scores. In R.E. Traub (Ed.), *New directions for testing and measurement: Methodological developments.* San Francisco, CA: Jossey-Bass.

Mills v. D.C. Board of Education, 348 F. Supp. 866 (D.D.C. 1972).

Mirkin, P.K., & Deno, S.L. (1979). *Formative evaluation in the classroom: An approach to improving instruction* (Research Report No. 10). Minneapolis: University of Minnesota, Institute for Research on Learning Disabilities.

Mirkin, P.K., Deno, S.L., Fuchs, L.S., Wesson, C., Tindal, G., Marston, D., & Kuehnle, K. (1981). *Procedures to develop and monitor progress on IEP goals.* Minneapolis, MN: University of Minnesota Institute for Research on Learning Disabilities.

Mirkin, P.K., Deno, S., Tindal, G., & Kuehnle, K. (1980). *Formative evaluation: Continued development of data utilization systems* (Research Report No. 23). Minneapolis: University of Minnesota, Institute for Research on Learning Disabilities.

Mirkin, P.K., Deno, S.L., Tindal, G., & Kuehnle, P. (1982). Frequency of measurement and data utilization as factors in standardized behavioral assessment of academic skills. *Journal of Behavioral Assessment, 4,* 362–370.

Mirkin, P., Fuchs, L.S., & Deno, S. (1982). *Considerations for designing a continuous evaluation system: An integrative review* (Monograph No. 20). Minneapolis: University of Minnesota, Institute for Research on Learning Disabilities.

Mishler, C., & Hogan, T. (1982). Holistic scoring of essays. *Diagnostique, 8,* 4–16.

Mitchell, P. (1985). *The ninth mental measurements yearbook.* Highland Park, NJ: Gryphon Press.

Moore, D.W. (1983). A case for naturalistic assessment of reading comprehension. *Language Arts, 60,* 957–969.

Moran, M.R. (1987). Options for written language assessment. *Focus on Exceptional Children, 19*(5), 1–12.

Moss, P.A., Cole, N.S., & Khampalikit, C. (1982). A comparison of procedures to assess written language skills at grades 4, 7, and 10. *Journal of Educational Measurement, 19*(1), 37–47.

Muma, J.R. (1984). Semel and Wiig's CELF: Construct validity. *Journal of Speech and Hearing Disorders, 49,* 101–104.

Myers, M. (1980). *A procedure for writing and assessment and holistic scoring.* Urbana, IL: National Council of Teachers of English and Educational Resources Information Center.

Myklebust, H.R. (1965). *Development and disorders of written language, volume one: Picture Story Language Test.* New York: Grune and Stratton.

Naslund, R.A., Thorpe, L.P., & Lefever, D.W. (1978). *SRA achievement series: Reading, mathematics, and language arts.* Chicago: Science Research Associates.

National Assessment of Educational Progress (1983). *The third national mathematics assessment: Results, trends, and issues.* 13-MA-01 Denver: Educational Commission of the States.

National Association for the Education of Young Children. (1988a). NAEYC position statement on developmentally appropriate practice in the primary grades serving 5- through 8-years olds. *Young Children, 43,* 64–84.

National Association for the Education of Young Children. (1988b). NAEYC position statement on standardized testing of young children 3 through 8 years of age. *Young Children, 43,* 42–47.

Nedelsky, L. (1954). Absolute grading standards for objective tests. *Educational and Psychological Measurement, 14*(1), 3–19.

Newcomer, P.L., & Hammill, D.D. (1982). *Test of language development—Primary.* Austin, TX: Pro-Ed.

Nielson, L., & Piche, G. (1981). The influence of headed nominal complexity and lexical choice on teachers' evaluation of writing. *Research in the Teaching of English, 15,* 65–74.

Nippold, M. (1988). *Late language development: Ages nine through nineteen.* San Diego: College-Hill Press.

Nisbet, S.D. (1939). Non-dictated spelling tests. *British Journal of Educational Psychology, 9,* 29–44.

Nitko, A.J. (1980). Distinguishing the many varieties of criterion-referenced tests. *Review of Educational Research, 50,* 461–485.

Nitko, A.J. (1983). *Educational tests and measurement.* New York: Harcourt Brace Jovanovich.

Nitko, A.J. (1984). Defining "criterion-referenced test". In R.A. Berk (Ed.), *A guide to criterion-referenced test construction* (pp. 8–28). Baltimore: Johns Hopkins University Press.

Nold, E., & Freedman, S. (1977). An analysis of readers' responses to essays. *Research in the Teaching of English, 11,* 164–174.

Northwest Regional Educational Lab (1987). *Bibliography of tests for early childhood: Chapter 1 evaluation.* Portland, OR: Northwest Regional Educational Lab.

Nunnally, J. (1967). *Psychometric theory.* New York: McGraw-Hill.

Oakes, J. (1985). *Keeping track: How schools structure inequality.* New Haven, Ct: Yale University Press.

Odell, L. (1981). Defining and assessing competence in writing. In C. Cooper (Ed.), *The nature and measurement of competency in English.* Urbana, IL: National Council of Teachers of English.

Odell, L., & Cooper, C. (1980). Procedures for evaluating writing: Assumptions and needed research. *College English, 42,* 35–43.

Odell, L., Cooper, C., & Courts, C. (1978). Discourse theory: Implications for research in composing. In C.R. Cooper, & L. Odell (Eds.), *Research on composing: Points of departure.* Urbana, IL: National Council of Teachers of English.

Pace, A.J., & Golinkoff, R.M. (1976). Relationship between word difficulty and access of single word meaning by skilled and less skilled readers. *Journal of Educational Psychology, 68*(6), 760–767.

Paget, K.D. (1987). Preschool assessment. In C.R. Reynolds & L. Mann (Eds.), *Encyclopedia of special education* (pp. 1237–1239). New York: John Wiley & Sons.

Paget, K.D., & Cox, J.M. (1987). Preschool screening. In C.R. Reynolds & L. Mann (Eds.), *Encyclopedia of special education,* (pp. 1239–1241). New York: John Wiley & Sons.

Parker, R., Hasbrouck, J., & Tindal, G. (1989). *Combining informal teacher judgment and objective test scores to make cross-classroom reading group placements* (Research Report No. 4). Eugene, OR: University of Oregon Resource Consultant Training Program.

Parker, R., Hasbrouck, J., & Tindal, G. (1989). *The utility of Pflaum's oral reading miscue categories* (Research Report No. 5). Eugene, OR: University of Oregon Resource Consultant Training Program.

Parker, R., Tindal, G., & Hasbrouck, J. (1989). *Initial validation of two classroom materials-based measures of reading comprehension.* Manuscript submitted for publication.

Parsonson, B.S., & Baer, D.M. (1978). The analysis and presentation of graphic data. In T. Kratochwill (Ed.), *Single subject research: Strategies for evaluating change.* New York: Academic Press.

Payne, D.A. (1974). *The assessment of learning: Cognitive and affective.* Lexington, MA: D.C. Heath.

Pearson, P.D., & Johnson, D. (1978). *Teaching reading comprehension.* New York: Holt, Rinehart & Winston.

Pennypacker, H.S., Koenig, C.H., & Lindsley, O.R. (1972). *Handbook of the standard behavior chart.* Kansas City, KS: Precision Media.

Perfetti, C.A., & Hogaboam, T. (1975). Relationship between single word decoding and reading comprehension skill. *Journal of Educational Psychology, 67*(4), 461–469.

Peters, M.L. (1967). *Spelling: Caught or taught.* London: Routledge and Kegan Paul.

Petrosko, J.M. (1978). The quality of standardized high school mathematics tests. *Journal for Research in Mathematics Education, 9*(2), 137–148.

Petty, W. (1959). *Improving your spelling program.* San Francisco: Howard Chandler Pub. Co.

Petty, W.T. (1964). Handwriting and spelling: Their current status in the language arts curriculum. *Elementary English, 8*(41), 53–60.

Pikulski, J.J., & Pikulski, E.C. (1977). Cloze, maze, and teacher judgement. *The Reading Teacher,* (April), 766–770.

Pincus, M., Cooman, M., Glasser, H., Levy, L., Morgenstern, F., & Shapiro, H. (1975). If you don't know how children think, how can you help them? *The Arithmetic Teacher, 22,* 580–585.

Poggio, J.P. (1982). *An evaluation of contrasting-groups methods for setting standards.* Paper presented at the Annual Meeting of the American Educational Research Association. New York, New York.

Polloway, E., Patton, J., & Cohen, S. (1981). Written language for mildly handicapped students. *Focus on Exceptional Children, 14*(3), 1–16.

Popham, W.J. (1978). As always, provocative. *Journal of Educational Measurement, 15*(4), 297–300.

Popham, W.J. (1984). Specifying the domain of content or behaviors. In R.A. Berk (Ed.), *A guide to criterion-referenced test construction* (pp. 29–48). Baltimore: Johns Hopkins University Press.

Poteet, J. (1980). Informal assessment of written expression. *Learning Disabilities Quarterly, 3,* 88–98.

Prater, D., & Padia, W. (1983). Developing parallel holistic and analytic scoring guides for assessing elementary writing samples. *Journal of Research and Development in Education, 17*(1), 20–24.

Prescott, G.A., Balow, I.H., Hogan, T.P., & Farr, R.C. (1978). *Metropolitan achievement tests: Survey battery.* New York: Psychological Corporation.

Prutting, C.A. (1979). Process: The action of moving forward progressively from one point to another on the way to completion. *Journal of Speech and Hearing Disorders, 44,* 3–30.

Prutting, C.A. (1983). Applied pragmatics. In T.M. Gallagher, & C.A. Prutting (Eds.), *Pragmatic assessment and intervention issues in language* (pp. 29–64). San Diego: College-Hill Press.

Prutting, C.A., & Connolly, J.E. (1976). Imitation: A closer look. *Journal of Speech and Hearing Disorders, 41,* 412–422.

Prutting, C.A., Gallagher, T.M., & Mulac, A. (1975). The expressive portion of the NSST compared to a spontaneous language sample. *Journal of Speech and Hearing Disorders, 40,* 40–48.

Prutting, C.A., & Kirchner, D.M. (1987). A clinical appraisal of the pragmatic aspects of language. *Journal of Speech and Hearing Disorders, 52,* 105–119.

The Psychological Corporation (1985). *Metropolitan achievement tests: Preprimer.* San Antonio, TX: The Psychological Corporation.

Quellmalz, E. (1984). Toward successful large-scale writing assessment: Where are we now? Where do we go from here? *Educational Measurement: Issues and Practice, 3*(1), 29–32.

Radatz, H. (1979). Error analysis in mathematics education. *Journal for Research in Mathematics Education, 10,* 163–173.

Rakes, T.A., & McWilliams, L.J. (1979). A cloze placement table. *Reading Improvement, 16,* 317–319.

Rankin, C.F., & Culhane, J.W. (1969). Comparable cloze and multiple-choice comprehension test scores. *Journal of Reading, 13,* 193–198.

Rankin, E.F., (1965). The cloze procedure—A survey of research. In E.S. Thurston & L.E. Hafner (Eds.), *The philosophical and sociological bases of reading.* Fourteenth Yearbook of the National Reading Conference, Milwaukee: National Reading Conference.

Rankin, Jr., E.F. (1970). The relationship between reading rate and comprehension. In R. Farr (Ed.). *Measurement and evaluation of reading,* (pp. 279–300). New York: Harcourt, Brace, and World.

Ransom, P. (1968). Determining reading levels of elementary school children by cloze testing. In J. Allen Figurel (Ed.), *Forging ahead in reading. Proceedings of the International Reading Association, 12, Part I.* Newark, DE: International Reading Association.

Reid, D.K., & Hresko, W.P. (1981). Language intervention with the learning disabled. *Topics in Learning and Learning Disabilities, 1*(2), viii–ix.

Reid, D.K., Hresko, W.P., & Hammill, D.D. (1981). *Test of early reading ability (TERA).* Austin, TX: Pro-Ed.

Reinherz, H., & Griffin, C.L. (1977). Identifying children at risk: a first step to prevention. *Health Education, 8*(4), 14–16.

Reschly, D. (1979). Nonbiased assessment. In G. Phye & D. Reschly (Eds.), *School psychology: Perspectives and issues,* (pp. 215–253). New York: Academic Press.

Reschly, D., Kicklighter, R., & McKee, P. (1988a). Recent placement litigation 1. Regular education grouping: Comparison of Marshall (1984, 1985) and Hobson (1967, 1969). *School Psychology Review, 17*(1), 9–21.

Reschly, D., Kicklighter, R., & McKee, P. (1988b). Recent placement litigation 2. Minority EMR overrepresentation: Comparison of Larry P. (1979, 1984, 1986) with Marshall (1984, 1985) and

S-1 (1986). *School Psychology Review, 17*(1), 22–38.

Reschly, D., Kicklighter, R., & McKee, P. (1988c). Recent placement litigation: 3. Analysis of differences in Larry P., Marshall, and S-1 and implications for future practices. *School Psychology Review, 17*(1), 39–50.

Reynolds, C.R. (1979). Should we screen preschoolers? *Contemporary Educational Psychology, 4,* 175–181.

Reynolds, C.R., & Willson, V.L. (1984). Standardized grade equivalents: Really! No. Well, sort of, but they are more confusing than helpful. *Journal of Learning Disabilities, 17*(6), 326–327.

Reynolds, M.C. (1982). The rights of children: A challenge to school psychologists. In T.R. Kratochwill (Ed.), *Advances in School Psychology* (Vol. 2). Hillsdale, NJ: Erlbaum.

Reynolds, M.C., & Birch, J. (1977). *Teaching exceptional children in all America's schools.* Reston, VA: Council for Exceptional Children.

Rhine, W.R. (1981). *Making schools more effective: New directions from Follow Through.* New York: Academic Press.

Rinsland, H.D. (1972). *A basic vocabulary of elementary school children.* New York: The Macmillan Company.

Rinsland, H.D. (1945). *A basic vocabulary of elementary school children.* New York: The Macmillan Company.

Roberts, G.H. (1968). The failure strategies of third-grade arithmetic pupils. *The Arithmetic Teacher, 15,* 442–446.

Roberts, M., & Smith, D.D. (1980). The relationship among correct and error oral reading rates and comprehension. *Learning Disability Quarterly, 3,* 54–64.

Roid, G.H., & Haladyna, T.M. (1982). *A technology for test-item writing.* New York: Academic Press.

Roscoe, D. (1979). Preschool screening in Hawaii. *Educational Perspectives, 18*(4), 3–7.

Ross, M.B., & Salvia, J.A. (1975). Attractiveness as a biasing factor in teacher judgements. *American Journal of Mental Deficiency, 80,* 96–98.

Roth, F.P., & Spekman, N.J. (1984a). Assessing the pragmatic abilities of children: 1. Organizational framework and assessment parameters. *Journal of Speech and Hearing Disorders, 49,* 2–11.

Roth, F.P., & Spekman, N.J. (1984b). Assessing the pragmatic abilities of children: 2. Guidelines, considerations, and specific evaluation procedures. *Journal of Speech and Hearing Disorders, 49,* 12–17.

Rovinelli, R.J., & Hambleton, R.K. (1977). On the use of content specialists in the assessment of criterion-referenced test item validity. *Dutch Journal for Educational Research, 2,* 49–60.

Sadowski, B.R., & McIlveen, D.H. (1984). Diagnosis and remediation of sentence-solving error patterns. *The Arithmetic Teacher, 31,* 42–45.

Sakiey, E., Fry, E., Goss, A., & Loigman, B. (1980). A syllable frequency count. *Visible Language, 14*(2), 137–150.

Salmon-Cox, L. (1981). Teachers and standardized achievement tests: What's really happening? *Phi Delta Kappan, 62,* 631–634.

Salvia, J.A., Algozzine, R., & Sheare, J. (1977). Attractiveness and school achievement. *Journal of School Psychology, 15,* 60–67.

Salvia, J.A., & Ysseldyke, J.E. (1988). *Assessment in special and remedial education* (4th ed.). Boston: Houghton Mifflin.

Samuels, S.J., Dahl, P., & Archwamety, T. (1974). Effect of hypothesis/test training on reading skill. *Journal of Educational Psychology, 66,* 835–844.

Sanders, E.R. (1972). When are speech sounds learned? *Journal of Speech and Hearing Disorders, 37,* 55–63.

Sanger, D.D. (1988). Observational profile of classroom communication. *The Clinical Connection, 2,* 11–13.

Sanger, D.D., Keith, R.W., & Maher, B.A. (1987). An assessment technique for children with auditory processing problems. *Journal of Communication Disorders, 20,* 265–279.

Schenk, S.J., & Welch, F.C. (1980). *The role of the IEP in the minimum competency movement.* Paper presented at the Annual South Carolina Educational Research Meeting. Charleston, South Carolina.

Schmidt, W.H. (1982). *Validity as a variable: Can the same certification test be valid for all students?* (IRT-OP-53). East Lansing, MI: Michigan State University, Institute for Research on Teaching, College of Education.

Schmidt, W.H. (1983). Content biases in achievement tests. *Journal of Educational Measurement, 20*(2), 165–178.

Schweinhart, L.J., & Weikart, D.P. (1986). Early childhood development programs: A public investment opportunity. *Educational Leadership, 44,* 4–12.

Scott, C.M., & Taylor, A.E. (1978). A comparison of home and clinic gathered language samples. *Journal of Speech and Hearing Disorders, 43,* 482–495.

Scribner (1987). *Reading Program.* New York: Scribner Publishers.

Searle, B., Lorton, P., & Suppes, P. (1974). Structural variables affecting CAI performance on arithmetic word problems of disadvantaged and deaf students. *Educational Studies in Mathematics, 5,* 371–384.

Seligmann, J., & Murr, A. (1988, April 25). Making the (first) grade: Georgia puts kindergarten skills to the test. *Newsweek,* p. 48.

Semel, E.M., & Wiig, E.H. (1980). *Diagnostic battery examiner's manual for clinical evaluation of language functions.* Columbus, OH: Merrill.

Semel, E.M., Wiig, E.H., & Secord, W. (1988). *Clinical evaluation of language fundamentals-Revised.* San Antonio, TX: Psychological Corp.

Shapiro, E.S., & Lentz, F.E. (1985). Assessing academic behavior: A behavioral approach. *School Psychology Review, 14,* 325–338.

Shapiro, E.S., & Derr, T.F. (1987). An examination of overlap between reading curricula and standardized achievement tests. *The Journal of Special Education, 21*(2), 59–67.

Shatz, M., & Gelman, R. (1973). The development of communication skills: Modifications in the speech of young children as a function of the listener. *SRCD Monographs, 5,* 1–37.

Shatz, M., Shulman, M., & Bernstein, D. (1982). The response of language disordered children to indirect directives in varying contexts. *Journal of Applied Psycholinguistics, 1,* 295–306.

Shaw, R.A., & Pelosi, P.A. (1983). In search of computational errors. *The Arithmetic Teacher, 30,* 50–51.

Shepard, W.I. (1974). *The effect of arithmetical operators on the difficulty levels of verbal problems.* Unpublished doctoral dissertation, George Peabody College for Teachers, Nashville, TN.

Shepard, L. (1976). Setting standards and living with them. *Florida Journal of Educational Research, 18,* 23–32.

Shepard, L.A. (1980). Standard setting issues and methods. *Applied Psychological Measurement, 4*(4), 447–467.

Shepard, L.A. (1984). Setting performance standards. In R.A. Berk (Ed.), *A guide to criterion-referenced test construction* (pp. 169–198). Baltimore: Johns Hopkins University Press.

Shepard, L.A. (1983). Standards for placement and certification. In S.B. Anderson, & J.S. Helmick (Eds.), *On educational testing* (pp. 61–90). San Francisco: Jossey-Bass.

Shepard, L.A. (1989). Why we need better assessments. *Educational Leadership,* (April), 4–9.

Shepard, L.A., & Smith, M.L. (1986). Synthesis of research on school readiness and kindergarten retention. *Educational Leadership, 44*(3), 78–86.

Shepard, L.A., & Smith, M.L. (1988). Escalating academic demand in kindergarten: Counterproductive policies. *The Elementary School Journal, 89*(2), 135–145.

Sherard, W.I. (1974). *The effect of arithmetical operations on the difficulty levels of verbal problems.* Unpublished doctoral dissertation, *George Peabody College* for Teachers, Nashville, TN.

Shinn, M.R. (1986). Does anyone care what happens after the refer-test-place sequence: The systematic evaluation of special education program effectiveness. *School Psychology Review, 15,* 49–58.

Shinn, M.R. (1988). Development of curriculum-based local norms for use in special education decision making. *School Psychology Review, 17*(1), 61–80.

Shinn, M.R. (1989a). *Curriculum-based measurement: Assessing special children.* New York: The Guilford Press.

Shinn, M.R. (1989b). Identifying and defining academic problems: CBM screening and eligibility procedures. In M. Shinn (Ed.), *Curriculum-based measurement* (School Psychology Practitioner's Series). New York: The Guilford Press.

Shinn, M.R., & Marston, D. (1985). Differentiating mildly handicapped, low-achieving and regular education students: A curriculum-based approach. *Remedial and Special Education, 6,* 31–45.

Shinn, M.R. Tindal, G., & Spira, D. (1987). Special education as an index of teacher tolerance: Are teachers imperfect tests? *Exceptional Children, 54,* 32–40.

Shinn, M.R., Tindal, G., Spira, D., & Marston, D. (1987). Practice of learning disabilities as social policy. *Learning Disabilities Quarterly, 10*(1), 17–28.

Shinn, M.R., Tindal, G., & Stein, S. (1988). Curriculum-based assessment and the identification of mildly handicapped students: A research review. *Professional School Psychology, 3*(1), 69–85.

Shinn, M.R., Ysseldyke, J., Deno, S., & Tindal, G. (1986). A comparison of differences between students labeled learning disabled and low achieving on measures of classroom performance. *Journal of Learning Disabilities, 19,* 545–552.

Sigmon, G. (1981). *Use of judgmental procedures by groups of raters to set minimum competency standards.* Paper presented at the Annual Meeting of the National Council on Measurement in Education. Los Angeles, California.

Simon, A., & Boyer, E.G. (1967). *Mirrors for behavior: An anthology of observation instruments.* San Francisco: Research for Better Schools.

Simon, C. (1985). *Communication skills and classroom success: Therapy methodologies for language-learning disabled students.* San Diego: College-Hill Press.

Sindelar, P., Smith, M., Harriman, N., Hale, R., & Wilson, R. (1986). Teacher effectiveness in special education programs. *The Journal of Special Education, 20*(2), 195–207.

Skarakis, E., & Greenfield, P.M. (1982). The role of new and old information in the verbal expression of language-disordered children. *Journal of Speech and Hearing Research, 25,* 462–467.

Smith, C.R. (1980). Assessment alternatives: Nonstandardized procedures. *Psychology Review, 9,* 46–57.

Smith, S.P., & Jackson, J.H. (1985). Assessing reading/learning skills with written retellings. *Journal of Reading, 28*(7), 622–631.

Sobsey, D., & Ludlow, B. (1984). Guidelines for setting instructional criteria. *Education & Treatment of Children, 7*(2), 157–165.

Sommers, R.K., Erdige, S., & Peterson, M.K. (1978). How valid are children's language tests? *Journal of Special Education, 12,* 393–407.

Southworth, L.E., Burr, R.L., Cox, A.E. (1980). *Screening and evaluating the young child: A handbook of instruments to use from infancy to six years.* Springfield, IL: C.C. Thomas.

Spache, G.D. (1940). Characteristic errors of good and poor spellers. *Journal of Educational Research, 34,* 182–189.

Spandel, V. (1981). *Using writing assessment in the classroom: A teacher's handbook.* Portland, OR: Northwest Regional Educational Laboratory.

Spandel, V., & Stiggins R.J. (1981). Direct measures of writing skill: Issues and applications (rev. ed., pp. 1–11). Portland, OR: Clearinghouse for Applied Performance Testing (CAPT) of the Northwest Regional Educational Laboratory.

Spearritt, D. (1972). Identification of subskills of reading comprehension by maximum likelihood factor analysis. *Reading Research Quarterly, 8*(1), 92–111.

Spekman, N.J., & Roth, F.P. (1984). Clinical evaluation of language functions (CELF) diagnostic battery: An analysis and critique. *Journal of Speech and Hearing Disorders, 9,* 97–100.

Spodeck, B. (1982). *Handbook of research in early childhood education.* New York: The Free Press.

Spodeck, B., & Walberg, H.J. (1977). *Early childhood education: Issues and insights.* Berkeley: McCutchan.

Steffe, L. (1967). *The effects of two variables on the problem-solving abilities of first-grade children: Teaching report No. 21.* Madison, WI: University of Wisconsin, Wisconsin Research and Development Center for Cognitive Learning.

Steiner, R., Weiner, M., & Cromer, W. (1971). Comprehension training and identification for poor and good readers. *Journal of Educational Psychology, 62,* 506–513.

Stetz, F., & Beck, M. (1979). *Comments from the classroom: Teachers' and students' opinions of achievement tests.* Paper presented at the Annual Meeting of the American Educational Research Association, San Francisco.

Stiggins, R.J. (1985). Improving assessment where it means the most: In the classroom. *Educational Leadership, 43,* 69–74.

Stiggins, R.J., Conklin, N.F., & Bridgeford, N.J. (1986). Classroom assessment: A key to effective education. *Educational Measurement: Issues and Practices,* (Summer), 5–17.

Stringer, L.A. (1973). Children at risk. *Elementary School Journal, 73*(7), 364–373.

Suppes, P., Loftus, E., & Jerman, M. (1972). Problem solving on a computer-based teletype. *Educational Studies in Mathematics, 4,* 306–323.

Suydam, M.N. (1982). Update on research on problem solving: Implications for classroom teaching. *Arithmetic Teacher, 29*(6), 56–60.

Swanson, H.L., & Watson, B.I. (1982). *Educational and psychological assessment of exceptional children.* St. Louis, MO: The C.V. Mosby Company.

Sylva, K., Roy, C., & Painter, M. (1980). *Childwatching at playgroup and nursery school.* London: Grant McIntyre.

Tabbert, R. (1974). Dialect difference and the teaching of reading and spelling. *Elementary English, 51*(8), 1097–1099.

Taggert, R., Sum, A., & Berlin, G. (1987). Basic skills: The sine qua non. *Youth and Society, 19*(1), 3–19.

Taylor, W.L. (1953). Cloze procedure: A new tool for measuring readability. *Journalism Quarterly, 30,* 414–438.

Teale, W.H. (1988). Developmentally appropriate assessment of reading and writing in the early childhood classroom. *The Elementary School Journal, 89*(2), 173–183.

Terman, L.M. (1910). *The measurement of intelligence.* Boston: Houghton-Mifflin.

Terman, L., & Merrill, M. (1973). *Stanford-Binet intelligence scale* (1972 norms ed.). Boston: Houghton-Mifflin.

Thompson, E. (1967). *Readability and accessory remarks: Factors in problem solving in arithmetic.* Unpublished doctoral dissertation, Stanford University.

Thorndike, R.L. (1967). The analysis and selection of test items. In D.N. Jackson, & S. Messick (Eds.), *Problems in human assessment.* New York: McGraw-Hill.

Thorndike, R.L., & Hagen, E. (1977). *Measurement and evaluation in psychology and education.* New York: John Wiley & Sons.

Thurlow, M.L., Christenson, S., & Ysseldyke, J.E. (1983). *Referral research: An integrative summary of findings.* (Research Report No. 141). Minneapolis, MN: University of Minnesota Institute for Research on Learning Disabilities.

Thurlow, M.L., Graden, J., Greener, J.W., & Ysseldyke, J.E. (1982). *Academic responding time for LD and non-LD students.* (Research Report No. 72). Minneapolis, MN: University of Minnesota Institute for Research on Learning Disabilities.

Thurlow, M., Graden, J., Greener, J., & Ysseldyke, J. (1982). *Academic responding time for LD and non-LD students* (Monograph No. 72). Minneapolis: University of Minnesota.

Thurlow, M.L., O'Sullivan, P.J., & Ysseldyke, J.E. (1986). Early screening for special education: How accurate? *Educational Leadership, 44*(3), 93–95.

Thurlow, M.L., & Ysseldyke, J.E. (1982). Instructional planning: Information collected by school psychologists vs. information considered useful by teachers. *Journal of School Psychology, 20*(1), 3–10.

Tindal, G. (1985). Investigating the effectiveness of special education: An analysis of methodology. *Journal of Learning Disabilities, 18*(2), 101–112.

Tindal, G. (1987). Graphing performance. *Teaching Exceptional Children, 20*(1), 44–46.

Tindal, G. (1988). Curriculum-based assessment. In J. Graden, J. Zins, & M. Curtis (Eds.), *Alternative educational delivery systems: Enhancing instructional options for all students.* Washington, DC: National Association of School Psychologists.

Tindal, G. (1989). Evaluating the effectiveness of educational programs at the systems level using curriculum-based measurement. In M. Shinn (Ed.), *Curriculum-based measurement.* New York: The Guilford Press.

Tindal, G., & Deno, D. (1981). *Daily measurement of reading: Effects of varying the size of the item pool* (Research Report No. 55). Minneapolis: University of Minnesota, Institute for Research on Learning Disabilities.

Tindal, G., Fuchs, L.S., Fuchs, D., Shinn, M., Deno, S.L., & Germann, G. (1985). Empirical validation of criterion-referenced tests. *Journal of Educational Research, 78,* 203–209.

Tindal, G., & Germann, G. (1985). Models of direct measurement in the determination of eligibility, monitoring of student progress, and evaluation of program effects. *B.C. Journal of Special Education, 9*(4), 365–382.

Tindal, G., Germann, G., & Deno, S.L. (1983). *Descriptive research on the Pine County Norms: A compilation of findings* (Research Report No. 132). Minneapolis: University of Minnesota, Institute for Research on Learning Disabilities.

Tindal, G., Germann, G., Marston, D., & Deno, S.L. (1983). *The effectiveness of special education: A direct measurement approach* (Research Report No. 123). Minneapolis: University of Minnesota, Institute for Research on Learning Disabilities.

Tindal, G., Marston, D., & Deno, S.L. (1983). *The reliability of direct and repeated measurement.* (Research Report No. 109). Minneapolis, MN: University of Minnesota Institute for Research on Learning Disabilities.

Tindal, G., & Marston, D. (1986). Approaches to assessment. In J. Torgeson, & B. Wong (Eds.), *Psychological and educational perspectives on learning disabilities* (pp. 55–84). Boston: Academic Press.

Tindal, G., & Parker, R. (1987). Direct observation in special educational classrooms: Concurrent use of two instruments and their validation. *Journal of Special Education, 21*(2), 43–58.

Tindal, G., & Parker, R. (1989). Development of written retell as a curriculum-based measure in secondary programs. *School Psychology Review.*

Tindal, G., Shinn, M., & Germann, G. (1987). The effects of different metrics on the interpretation of change in program evaluation. *Remedial and Special Education, 8*(5), 19–28.

Tobin, A. (1982). Scope and sequence for a problem-solving curriculum. *Arithmetic Teacher, 29*(6), 62–65.

Tucker, J.A. (1985). Curriculum-based assessment: An introduction. *Exceptional Children, 52,* 199–204.

Tuinman, J.J. (1971). Asking reading dependent questions. *Journal of Reading, 14,* 289–292.

Tyler, R.W., & White, S.H. (1979). *Testing, teaching, and learning.* Washington, D.C.: U.S. Department of Health, Education, and Welfare National Institute of Education.

Valencia, S.W., & Person, P.D. (1988). Principles for classroom comprehension assessment. *Remedial and Special Education, 9,* 26–35.

Videen, J., Deno, S.L., & Marston, D. (1982). *Correct word sequences: A valid indicator of proficiency in written expression* (Research Report No. 84). Minneapolis: University of Minnesota, Institute for Research on Learning Disabilities.

Walker, C.M. (1979). High frequency word list for grades 3 through 9. *The Reading Teacher, 32*(7), 803–812.

Walker, H.M., & Rankin, R. (1983). Assessing the behavioral expectations and demands of less restrictive settings. *School Psychology Review, 12,* 274–284.

Wallace, G., & Larsen, S. (1978). *Educational assessment of learning problems: Testing for teaching.* Boston: Allyn & Bacon.

Webb II, M.W. (1983). A scale for evaluating standardized reading tests, with results for Nelson-Denny, Iowa, and Stanford. *Journal of Reading, 26,* 424–429.

Webber, R.M. (1968). A study of oral reading errors: A survey of the literature. *Reading Research Quarterly, 4,* 96–119.

Weber, R.M. (1970). First graders use of grammatical context in reading. In H. Levin & J. Williams, (Eds.) *Basic studies in reading,* (pp. 147–163). NY: Basic Books.

Wechsler, D. (1974). *Manual for the Wechsler intelligence scale for children—Revised.* New York: Psychological Corporation.

Weiss, B.J., Evertts, E.L., Steuer, L., Sprout, J., & Hunt, L.C. (1980). *Holt Basic Reading.* New York: Holt, Rinehart, and Winston, Publishers.

Wenzel, E. (1977). *Research summary: Basic skills in handwriting and spelling.*

Wesson, C., Deno, S., & Mirkin, P. (1982). *Research on developing and monitoring progress on IEP goals: Current findings and implications for practice* (Research Report No. 18). Minneapolis: University of Minnesota, Institute for Research on Learning Disabilities.

Wesson, C., Vierthaler, J., & Haubrich, P. (1989). The discriminative validity of curriculum-based measures for establishing reading groups. *The Reading Teacher, 42,* 466–469.

West, T.A. (1971). Diagnosing pupil errors: Looking for patterns. *The Arithmetic Teacher, 18,* 467–469.

White, E.M. (1984). Holisticism. *College Composition and Communication, 35*(4), 400–409.

White, O.R. (1972). *A manual for the calculation and use of the median slope—A technique of progress estimation and prediction in the single case.* Unpublished doctoral dissertation, University of Oregon, Working paper No. 16, Regional Resource Center for Handicapped Children.

White, O.R. (1977). Behaviorism in special education: An arena for debate. In R.D. Kneedler, & S.G. Tarver (Eds.), *Changing perspectives in special education.* Columbus, OH: Merrill.

White, O.R., & Haring, N.G. (1980). *Exceptional teaching* (2nd Ed.). Columbus, OH: Merrill.

White, R.T. (1974). The validation of a learning hierarchy. *American Educational Research Journal, 11,* 121–136.

Whitlock, P. (1974). *An investigation of selected factors that affect ability to solve verbal mathematical problems at the primary level.* Unpublished doctoral dissertation, Fordham University.

Wiederholt, J.L., & Bryant, B.R. (1986). *Gray oral reading test-revised.* Austin, TX: Pro-Ed.

Wiederholt, J.L., & Bryant, B.R. (1987). *Assessing the reading abilities and instructional needs of students.* Austin, TX: Pro-Ed.

Wiig, E., & Semel, E. (1984). *Language assessment and intervention for the learning disabled* (2nd Ed.). Columbus, OH: Merrill.

Wilcox, R.R. (1976). A note on the length and passing score of a mastery test. *Journal of Educational Statistics, 1,* 359–364.

Will, M.C. (1986). Educating students with learning problems—A shared responsibility. *Exceptional Children, 52,* 411–416.

Williams, R.G. (1977). A behavioral typology of educational objectives for the cognitive domain. *Educational Technology, 17*(6), 39–46.

Williams, R.G., & Haladyna, T.M. (1982). Logical operations for generating questions (LOGIQ): A typology for higher level test items. In G.H. Roid, & T.M. Haladyna, *A technology for test-item writing* (pp. 161–186). New York: Academic Press.

Willows, D.M. (1974). Reading between the lines: Selective attention in good and poor readers. *Child Development, 45,* 408–415.

Witt, J.C., & Elliott, S.N. (1985). Acceptability of classroom intervention strategies. In T.R. Kratochwill (Ed.), *Advances in school psychology-Volume IV* Hillsdale, NJ: Lawrence Erlbaum.

Wingate, M. (1976). *Stuttering: Theory and treatment.* New York: Irvington Press.

Wixson, K., & Peters, C. (1987). Comprehension assessment: Implementing an interactive view of reading. *Educational Psychologist, 22*(3 & 4), 333–356.

Wolery, M., Bailey, D.B., & Sugai, G.M. (1988). *Effective teaching: Principles and procedures of applied behavioral analysis with exceptional children.* Boston: Allyn & Bacon.

Wolery, M., Bailey, Jr., D.B., & Sugai, G. (1988). *Effective teaching: Principles and procedures of applied behavior analysis with exceptional students.* Boston: Allyn and Bacon.

Wolf, J.M., & Kessler, A.L. (1987). *Entrance to kindergarten: What is the best age?* Arlington, VA: Educational Research Service.

Wood, K.D. (1985). Free associational assessment: An alternative to traditional testing. *Journal of Reading, 29*(2), 106–111.

Woodcock, R.W. (1987). *Woodcock reading mastery tests—Revised.* Circle Pines, MN: American Guidance Service.

Yalow, E.S., & Popham, W.J. (1983). Content validity at the crossroads. *Educational Researcher,* (October), 10–14.

Ysseldyke, J. E., Algozzine, B., & Mitchell, J. (1982). Special education team decision-making: An analysis of current practice. *Personnel and Guidance Journal, 60,* 308–313.

Ysseldyke, J.E., Algozzine, B., Regan, R., & McGue, M. (1979). *The influence of test scores and naturally occurring pupil characteristics on psychoeducational decision-making with children.* (Research Report No. 17). Minneapolis, MN: University of Minnesota Institute for Research on Learning Disabilities.

Ysseldyke, J.E., Algozzine, B., Regan, R., & Potter, M. (1980). Technical adequacy of tests used by professionals in simulated decision-making. *Psychology in the Schools, 17,* 202–209.

Ysseldyke, J.E., Algozzine, B., Shinn, M.R., & McGue, M. (1982). Similarities and differences between low achieving and students labeled learning disabled. *Journal of Special Education, 16,* 73–85.

Ysseldyke, J.E., & Christenson, S.L. (1988). Linking assessment to instruction. In J.L. Graden, J.E. Zins, & M.J. Curtis (Eds.), *Alternative educational delivery systems: Enhancing instructional options for all students* (pp. 91–107). Washington, D.C.: National Association of School Psychologists.

Ysseldyke, J.E., & Thurlow, M.L. (1983). *Identification/classification research: An integrative summary of findings.* (Research Report No. 142). Minneapolis, MN: University of Minnesota Institute for Research on Learning Disabilities.

Ysseldyke, J., Thurlow, M., Graden, J., Wesson, C., Algozzine, B., & Deno, S.L. (1983). Generalizations from five years of research on assessment and decision making. *Exceptional Education Quarterly, 4,* 75–94.

Zeitlin, S. (1976). *Kindergarten screening: Early identification of potential high risk learners.* Springfield, IL: Charles C. Thomas.

Zigmond, N., Vallecorsa, A., & Silverman, R. (1983). *Assessment for instructional planning in special education.* Englewood Cliffs, NJ: Prentice-Hall.

Ziomek, R.L., & Szymczuk, M. (1983). *A comparison of approaches for setting proficiency standards via Monte Carlo simulations.* Des Moines, IA: Iowa Department of Evaluation and Research.

Zutell, J. (1980). *Developmental and cognitive aspects of learning to spell.* Newark, DE: International Reading Association.

Zutell, J. (1982). Children's spelling strategies and their cognitive development.

AUTHOR INDEX

SUBJECT INDEX